2000
YEARS
OF
PRAYER

2000

YEARS OF PRAYER

COMPILED BY
MICHAEL COUNSELL

MOREHOUSE PUBLISHING

Originally published in English by
The Canterbury Press Norwich of
St. Mary's Work's, St. Mary's Plain,
Norwich, Norfolk NR3 3BH U.K.

Morehouse Publishing
P.O. Box 1321
Harrisburg, PA 17105

Morehouse Publishing is a division of The Morehouse Group.

Printed in the United States of America
02   03   04   05   06   07   6   5   4   3   2   1

Cover design by Trude Brummer
Cover image: Detail showing Male Figure Praying from 14th Century Stained Glass from Palais Rohan, CORBIS: Elio Ciol

Library of Congress Cataloging-in-Publication Data

2000 years of prayer / compiled by Michael Counsell.
      p.   cm.
   ISBN 0-8192-1921-5
    1. Prayers. I. Counsell, Michael, 1935–   . II. Title: Two thousand years of prayer.
BV245.A15 1999
242'.8–dc21   99-33794
                                       CIP

Contents

Preface

I set out to compile a personal selection of prayers, and found that I had written the history of the world as it has been heard by God. Well, that needs to be restricted to the Christian world of the last two millennia, though I do not deny that God can hear and answer prayers by worshippers of other faiths. And there will naturally be a majority of prayers written in English, despite my indebtedness to many who have translated prayers from other languages.

It is an over-simplification to describe prayer as 'talking to God'. Yet just as a child needs time to learn how to talk, so the art of prayer is something which can take many years to learn. That is why the disciples asked Jesus, 'Lord, teach us to pray.' In fact it takes more than one lifetime, so that if each generation is not going to have to start again from scratch, we need to learn from previous generations what they have discovered about prayer, how to avoid difficulties in prayer, how to come close to God.

Jesus promised that, after his ascension, the Holy Spirit would lead us into all truth. That sounds like an ongoing process. In the 2,000 years since then Christians have been learning from the Holy Spirit how to pray better, and if we are not to repeat the mistakes of earlier generations, we need to read the prayers of earlier generations, and their teaching about prayer. We stand closer to God when we stand on other people's shoulders.

This book is a personal selection of 2,000 years of prayer. 'Ironic,' I said to one of my friends, 'that it should be compiled by someone as bad at praying as I am.' 'Have you ever met anyone who thought they were any good at it?' was the reply. So perhaps for that very reason it will be helpful to anyone who wants to learn to pray better. It casts its net widely, believing that the unchanging gospel is differently expressed through many different cultures in different ages, and our prayer life is in danger of narrowness and distortion if we do not learn from Christians who differ from us. Private prayer is at its deepest when we express our sincere personal feelings in our own words. Yet our words are enriched by the ideas and vocabulary which we have heard in the prayers of others. For most Christians, also, there are times when the right words will not come at our bidding. When we are lost for words, or wish to continue a practice of disciplined prayer even when our fickle emotions do not feel like it, to read written prayers silently or aloud may bring back a lost ability to be spontaneous in prayer.

Saint Teresa of Avila is said to have been unable for a long time to think of the right words to pray, so she wrote her requests down and read them out to God, always finishing with 'Please Lord, help me to pray spontaneously and naturally.' One day her coach went off the road and, as she clambered out of a ditch full of muddy water, she complained aloud, 'Lord, it's no wonder you've so few friends – you treat the ones you have so badly!' She realized then that her prayer had been answered.

There was simply not room to include prayers by all the Christians I would have liked to quote. There is no such thing as a perfect arrangement, but I hope this compromise between a chronological and a grouped approach will help those who wish to browse prayerfully, or who wish to study the prayers of a particular period. It is impossible that anybody should 'agree with' every prayer in a collection like this. It would not be too difficult to guess where I come from, theologically as well as geographi-cally. I can only say that I have been most challenged to develop and grow in prayer where I have been struck by the 'truth' of a prayer from a totally different culture from my own.

God is honoured when we offer him of our best, and that includes the best language. I am surely not alone in finding that I am most inspired when prayers say something memorable and say it in memorable words. Writing a good prayer requires the same gifts and skill with words as writing a poem; in fact many of the prayers in this collection are poems. When I have chosen a prayer which was originally written in English I have usually left it in the original words. Where it is translated I have, when it did not involve a breach of copyright, revised the translation to the best of my ability to make it helpful to English speakers in the twenty-first century.

It is absurd to attempt to summarize the prayer life of each of the world's greatest Christians in a short paragraph and a brief quotation. My hope is that readers will be as excited as I am by the length and breadth and depth of the Christian prayer tradition, and will seek out some of the writers in their local library to read more, and where the books are still in print, build up a library of spiritual reading of their own.

Compiling this book has also been for me a confirmation of the 'human argument' for the existence of God: if all these people have founded lives of love and goodness, forgiving and being forgiven, on their experience of contact with God in prayer, how could I presume to say that they were deluded?

I have not read extensively in all of the authors whom I quote. Many of the prayers I found serendipitously during my own reading, but I should also like to express my gratitude to the editors of other anthologies from which I have borrowed prayers, including *A Chain of Prayer across the Ages* by Selina Fox, *The Oxford Book of Prayer* by George Appleton, *The Fount Book of Prayer* by Robert Van de Weyer, *The Book of a Thousand Prayers* by Angela Ashwin, and *The SPCK Book of Christian Prayers*. For the historical notes I have consulted among others *The Oxford Dictionary of the Christian Church*, *Chambers' Biographical Dictionary* and *A Dictionary of Christian Spirituality* by Gordon S. Wakefield. It is certain that nobody will accept all of the historical assessments I have made, but if anyone can draw my attention to factual errors I shall be grateful. I have tried to seek the permission of copyright holders for material I have quoted, but I apologize if any copyright has been infringed and I will hope to rectify it in future editions.

Michael Counsell
Honor Oak, London, 1998

The Background

From the burial customs and cave paintings of the earliest humans it is clear that we have always felt a need to make contact with a power beyond ourselves. There has been a growth and a deepening of Christian prayer over the past two millennia as, under the inspiration of the Holy Spirit, we have learnt from each other and from the Scriptures. It is all based on the teaching and example of Jesus in the Gospels. But Jesus was a Jew, and his life of prayer had firm foundations in the tradition of splendid Temple worship and in the Hebrew scriptural record of individuals who wrestled in intimate prayer with God.

An important part of prayer for Jesus was to join in prayer with others in the Temple and the synagogues (John 7:8–10; Luke 4:16). He commended the humble tax-collector for his penitent prayer in the Temple (Luke 18:13). He told his disciples, however, not to pray ostentatiously but to find a place where they could pray alone:

And whenever you pray, do not be like the hypocrites; for they love to stand and pray in the synagogues and at the street corners, so that they may be seen by others. Truly I tell you, they have received their reward. But whenever you pray, go into your room and shut the door and pray to your Father who is in secret; and your Father who sees in secret will reward you. When you are praying, do not heap up empty phrases as the Gentiles do; for they think that they will be heard because of their many words. Do not be like them, for your Father knows what you need before you ask him.

Matthew 6:5–8

Jesus himself found solitude praying among the hills, sometimes for a whole night (Mark 6:46; Luke 6:12). We can model our private prayer on his by looking at the words that he used in his prayers:

At that time Jesus said, 'I thank you, Father, Lord of heaven and earth, because you have hidden these things from the wise and the intelligent and have revealed them to infants; yes, Father, for such was your gracious will. All things have been handed over to me by my Father; and no one knows the Son except the Father, and no one knows the Father except the Son and anyone to whom the Son chooses to reveal him.'

Matthew 11:25; cf. Luke 10:21

Now my soul is troubled. And what should I say – "Father, save me from this hour"? No, it is for this reason that I have come to this hour. Father, glorify your name.'

John 12:27

So they took away the stone. And Jesus looked upward and said, 'Father, I thank you for having heard me. I knew that you always hear me, but I have said this for the sake of the crowd standing here, so that they may believe that you sent me.'

John 11:41

After Jesus had spoken these words, he looked up to heaven and said, 'Father, the hour has come; glorify your Son so that the Son may glorify you, since you have given him authority over all people, to give eternal life to all whom you have given him. And this is eternal life, that they may know you, the only true God, and Jesus Christ whom you have sent. I glorified you on earth by finishing the work that you gave me to do. So now, Father, glorify me in your own presence with the glory that I had in your presence before the world existed.

'I have made your name known to those whom you gave me from the world. They were yours, and you gave them to me, and they have kept your word. Now they know that everything you have given me is from you; for the words that you gave to me I have given to them, and they have received them and know in truth that I came from you; and they have believed that you sent me. I am asking on their behalf; I am not asking on behalf of the world, but on behalf of those whom you gave me, because they are yours. All mine are yours, and yours are mine; and I have been glorified in them. And now I am no longer in the world, but they are in the world, and I am coming to you. Holy Father, protect them in your name that you have given me, so that they may be one, as we are one. While I was with them, I protected them in your name that you have given me. I guarded them, and not one of them was lost except the one destined to be lost, so that the scripture might be fulfilled. But now I am coming to you, and I speak these things in the world so that they may have my joy made complete in themselves. I have given them your word, and the world has hated them because they do not belong to the world, just as I do not belong to the world. I am not asking you to take them out of the world, but I ask you to protect them from the evil one. They do not belong to the world, just as I do not belong to the world. Sanctify them in the truth; your word is truth. As you have sent me into the world, so I have sent them into the world. And for their sakes I sanctify myself, so that they also may be sanctified in truth.

'I ask not only on behalf of these, but also on behalf of those who will believe in me through their word, that they may all be one. As you, Father, are in me and I am in you, may they also be in us, so that the world may believe that you have sent me. The glory that you have given me I have given them, so that they may be one, as we are one, I in them and you in me, that they may become completely one, so that the world may know that you have sent me and have loved them even as you have loved me. Father, I desire that those also, whom you have given me, may be with me where I am, to see my glory, which you have given me because you loved me before the foundation of the world.

'Righteous Father, the world does not know you, but I know you; and these know that you have sent me. I made your name known to them, and I will make it known, so that the love with which you have loved me may be in them, and I in them.'

John 17

And going a little farther, he threw himself on the ground and prayed, 'My Father, if it is possible, let this cup pass from me; yet not what I want but what you want.' Then he came to the disciples and found them sleeping; and he said to Peter, 'So, could you not stay awake with me one hour? Stay awake and pray that you may not come into the time of trial; the spirit indeed is willing, but the flesh is weak.' Again he went away for the second time and prayed, 'My Father, if this cannot pass unless I drink it, your will be done.'

Matthew 26:39; cf. Mark 14:36; Luke 22:40

His disciples asked Jesus, 'Teach us to pray,' and he responded with the Lord's Prayer, probably in different forms on many occasions, because it

*takes the form of a series of chapter headings into which we can weave
all our praises and requests:*

P ray then in this way:
   Our Father in heaven,
hallowed be your name.
Your kingdom come.
Your will be done, on earth as it is in heaven.
Give us this day our daily bread.
And forgive us our debts, as we also have forgiven our debtors.
And do not bring us to the time of trial,
but rescue us from the evil one.

Matthew 6:9

W hen you pray, say:
   Father, hallowed be your name.
Your kingdom come.
Give us each day our daily bread.
And forgive us our sins, for we ourselves forgive everyone indebted
      to us.
And do not bring us to the time of trial.

Luke 11:2

*Jesus taught his disciples to be persistent in prayer in Luke 11:5–8 (the
friend at midnight) and Luke 18:3–8 (the importunate widow); to be
prepared by prayer for whatever might occur in Mark 11:18 and Luke 21:36;
22:40; and to be confident that it will be answered in Luke 11:9–13 (ask,
seek, knock).*

*In the Acts of the Apostles we read that the first Christians continued
in regular prayer together: Acts 1:24 (choosing Judas' replacement); 2:46
(praising God in the Temple and in praise for the release of Peter and
John):*

W hen they heard it, they raised their voices together to God and
   said, 'Sovereign Lord, who made the heaven and the earth, the sea,
and everything in them, it is you who said by the Holy Spirit through our
ancestor David, your servant: "Why did the Gentiles rage, and the peoples
imagine vain things? The kings of the earth took their stand, and the rulers
have gathered together against the Lord and against his Messiah." For in
this city, in fact, both Herod and Pontius Pilate, with the Gentiles and the
peoples of Israel, gathered together against your holy servant Jesus, whom

you anointed, to do whatever your hand and your plan had predestined to take place. And now, Lord, look at their threats, and grant to your servants to speak your word with all boldness, while you stretch out your hand to heal, and signs and wonders are performed through the name of your holy servant Jesus.' When they had prayed, the place in which they were gathered together was shaken; and they were all filled with the Holy Spirit and spoke the word of God with boldness.

Acts 4:24–31

While they were stoning Stephen, he prayed, 'Lord Jesus, receive my spirit.' Then he knelt down and cried out in a loud voice, 'Lord, do not hold this sin against them.' When he had said this, he died.

Acts 7:59

Prayers are also found in Acts 9:10 (Ananias is called to heal Saul); 9:40 (Peter prays and Tabitha returns to life); 12:5, 12 (the church prays for Peter); 13:2–3 (Christians pray for Barnabas and Saul); 10:11 (Peter's vision of unclean beasts); 16:25 (Paul and Silas pray in prison).

The letters of St Paul all begin and end with prayer. Paul tells those who read his letters to pray:

Pray in the Spirit at all times in every prayer and supplication. To that end keep alert and always persevere in supplication for all the saints. Pray also for me, so that when I speak, a message may be given to me to make known with boldness the mystery of the gospel, for which I am an ambassador in chains. Pray that I may declare it boldly, as I must speak.

Ephesians 6:18

Rejoice always, pray without ceasing, give thanks in all circumstances; for this is the will of God in Christ Jesus for you. Do not quench the Spirit.

1 Thessalonians 5:16–19

Finally, brothers and sisters, pray for us, so that the word of the Lord may spread rapidly and be glorified everywhere, just as it is among you, and that we may be rescued from wicked and evil people; for not all have faith.

2 Thessalonians 3:1

Paul welcomes the gift of ecstatic utterance, but warns that Christians must not make divisions among themselves based on spiritual gifts:

And God has appointed in the church first apostles, second prophets, third teachers; then deeds of power, then gifts of healing, forms of assistance, forms of leadership, various kinds of tongues ... Do all speak in tongues? Do all interpret? But strive for the greater gifts ... If I speak in the tongues of mortals and of angels, but do not have love, I am a noisy gong or a clanging cymbal ... I thank God that I speak in tongues more than all of you; nevertheless, in church I would rather speak five words with my mind, in order to instruct others also, than ten thousand words in a tongue.

1 Corinthians 12:27–31; 13:1; 14:18–19

He also suggests that there are times when prayer goes beyond words, when the Spirit groans within us:

Likewise the Spirit helps us in our weakness; for we do not know how to pray as we ought, but that very Spirit intercedes with sighs too deep for words. And God, who searches the heart, knows what is the mind of the Spirit, because the Spirit intercedes for the saints according to the will of God.

Romans 8:26–27

The last book of the Bible is filled with descriptions of the worship of heaven, in which the prayers of those on earth play a part:

Another angel with a golden censer came and stood at the altar; he was given a great quantity of incense to offer with the prayers of all the saints on the golden altar that is before the throne. And the smoke of the incense, with the prayers of the saints, rose before God from the hand of the angel.

Revelation 8:3–4

There are many other references to prayer in Scripture, but it is time to see how Christians down the ages have developed the art of prayer out of the precepts of the Bible.

The First Four Christian Centuries

We can watch the development of the life of prayer in the writings of the Christians between the New Testament and the end of persecution by the Emperor Constantine, usually called the Early Christian Fathers. Although they were no more sinless and perfect than Christians at any other period, they were free of the temptations that come with power, and they continued the task which St Paul had begun of applying the Hebrew religion of Jesus to the Greek-speaking Roman Empire.

Clement of Rome (*c.* 100)

At the end of the first Christian century the Bishop of Rome wrote a letter to the church in Corinth, where some of the leaders had been deposed as a result of a dispute. He refers to the leaders as overseers (episkopoi, usually translated as 'bishops') or elders (presbyteroi), and they are assisted by servants (diakonoi or 'deacons'). One of their duties is to 'offer the gifts' of bread and wine at the Eucharist.

God, the origin of creation, open our eyes to know you and place our hope in you, the highest and the holiest. You put down the insolence of the proud, and scatter the plotting of the nations; you lift up the humble and lay low the mighty; you make some rich and make others poor, kill some and bring others to life; the God of the spiritual and the material worlds; you see everything that happens; you are the helper of those who are in trouble and the Saviour of those in despair; creator and overseer of every spirit; you cause nations to grow, and you have chosen from all the world those who love you through Jesus Christ, your beloved Son, through whom you taught us, made us holy and honoured us. Lord and Master, help us and rescue all those who are in trouble; have mercy on the lowly; lift up those who have fallen; reveal yourself to the needy; heal the ungodly; convert those of your people who have gone astray; feed the hungry; release those of our number who are in prison; give power to the weak; encourage the faint-hearted. Let all the nations know that you are God alone, and Jesus Christ is your Son, and we are your people and the sheep of your pasture.

1 Clement 59

You, Lord God, made the eternal fabric of the world appear, and you created the earth. You are always trustworthy, you judge fairly, excellent and marvellous in your power; wise in creating and careful to make firm what you have made, blessing us with the visible creation and dependable for those who trust in you, merciful and compassionate. Forgive us our sins and our shortcomings, our breaking of your laws and our lack of righteousness. We are your servants; do not blame us for all that we have done wrong, but make us clean with your truth, and guide our steps to walk in holiness and righteousness and singleness of heart, that we may do those good things which will please you and win the favour of our rulers. Lord, make your face to shine upon us in peace, for our good, that we may be sheltered by your mighty hand and set free from the consequences of sin by the power of your arm. Protect us against those who unjustly hate us. Give peace and harmony to us and to all who dwell on earth, while we obey your almighty and most excellent name, and while we obey our earthly rulers and governors, as you did to our ancestors, when they prayed to you in faith and truth with holiness.

1 Clement 60

The Second Letter of Clement to the Corinthians (second century)

Less likely to be by St Clement, but obviously a very early Christian sermon, is the so-called Second Letter of Clement to the Corinthians:

To the invisible and only God, the true Father, who sent to us the Saviour and immortal Prince, through whom he revealed to us the truth and the life of heaven, to him be glory for ever and ever. Amen.

Ignatius of Antioch (*c.* 30–107)

Soon after the beginning of the second century Ignatius, Bishop of Antioch, was arrested and taken to Rome to be thrown to the lions. In the letters

which he wrote to different churches during his journey we see the calm,
prayerful way in which the early Christians accepted martyrdom.

I am writing letters to all the churches, to assure them that I am dying for God of my own free will – that is, if you don't interfere. Please, please don't make a misguided attempt to do me a kindness. Let me be fodder for the wild beasts – that's how I can come to God. I am God's wheat, and the teeth of the beasts are grinding me to flour, to be made into a pure loaf for Christ. Please encourage the animals to become my tomb; don't let them leave any scraps of my body behind. That way, when I have fallen asleep I shall be a nuisance to nobody. Then I shall be a real disciple of Jesus Christ, when the world can no longer see my body. Pray to Christ for me, that in this way I may become a sacrifice to God.

Letter to the Romans 4[1]

The Didache (first or second century)

Soon after (or even, according to some scholars, during) the time when the New Testament was written, there appeared another document known as The Didache *or* The Teaching of the Twelve Apostles. *It contains one of the most beautiful prayers for Christian unity at the breaking of bread.*

As the grain from which the bread we break was made
were once scattered over the fields,
and then gathered together and made one,
so may your Church be gathered from all over the earth
into your kingdom.

From The Didache 9

You created everything, sovereign Lord,
for your glory.
You gave to everyone food and drink
that they might enjoy it and thank you for it.
Now to us you have given the blessing
of spiritual nourishment to prepare us for eternal life,
through Jesus your Son and your servant.

From The Didache 10

The Letter of Barnabas (first century)

Another early work about whose author little is known is the so-called Letter of Barnabas.

And may God, who rules over all the world, give to you wisdom, intelligence, understanding, knowledge of his judgements, with patience. Farewell, children of love and peace. The Lord of glory and of all grace be with your spirit. Amen.

The Letter of Barnabas 21

Polycarp of Smyrna (*c.* 69–*c.* 155)

Polycarp was the Bishop of Smyrna (now Izmir in Turkey) and a leading figure in the church in Asia Minor. He knew the apostle John, the martyr Ignatius of Antioch, and also mid-second-century teachers such as Irenaeus. He negotiated the independence of his own church from the Bishop of Rome during a visit there. Soon after his return home he was arrested. He asked permission to pray before he was led away, and spent two hours praying for every Christian he had ever met, the great and the humble. Those who had come for him were sorry that they had to arrest such a wonderful old man.

Now may the God and Father of our Lord Jesus Christ, and may Jesus Christ himself also, the eternal high-priest and Son of God, build you up in faith and truth, and in gentleness, avoidance of anger, forbearance, long-suffering, patient endurance and purity; and may he grant you to inherit a place among his saints; may he grant this to us also so that we can be with you, and to everyone under heaven who will believe in our Lord Jesus Christ and in his Father who raised him from the dead.

From The Letter to the Philippians 12

In the stadium the magistrate tried to persuade him: 'Swear by Caesar as a God and I will release you, curse this Christ.' Polycarp replied, 'I have been his servant for eighty-six years and he has never mistreated me. Then how can I blaspheme the King who saved me?' . . . When he was tied to the stake, before they lit the fire, Polycarp looked up to heaven and said, 'O Lord God almighty, the Father of your beloved and blessed Son Jesus Christ, through whom we have our knowledge of you, the God of the angels and all the heavenly powers and of all creation and of all those righteous people who live in your presence; I bless you for giving me this day and this hour, so that I might inherit a place among the martyrs who have shared Christ's cup of suffering to bring them resurrection to imperishable and eternal life of soul and body in the Holy Spirit. Receive me into your presence today, as a valuable and acceptable sacrifice, as you have already told me I would be, dependable and true God. For this and everything I praise you, I thank you, I glorify you, through the eternal heavenly high-priest Jesus Christ, your beloved Son. Through him and with him and the Holy Spirit be glory both now and ever and for the ages to come. Amen.'

From The Letter from the Church in Smyrna on the Martyrdom of Saint Polycarp 7–8, 14

Justin Martyr (c. 100–c. 165)

Justin Martyr was the first Christian we know of to write a systematic philosophical defence of his faith, in his First and Second Apologies *and his* Dialogue with Trypho. *He also includes a full account of the Lord's Supper, by then known as the 'Eucharist' (from the Greek word for 'thanksgiving'). St Paul asked for everything to be done decently and in order; by Justin's time the service had a regular shape. He and some of his pupils were beheaded when they were reported to the authorities and refused to sacrifice to the Emperor as a god.*

On Sundays there is an assembly of all who live in towns or in the country, and the memoirs of the apostles or the writings of the prophets are read for as long as time allows. Then the reading is brought to an end, and the president delivers an address in which he admonishes and encourages us to imitate in our own lives the beautiful lessons we have heard read. Then we all stand up together and pray; when we have finished the prayer, as I have said, bread and wine and water are brought up; the president offers prayers and thanksgiving as best he can, and the people say 'Amen' as an expression of their agreement. Then follows the distribution of the food over which the prayer of thanksgiving has been recited; all present receive some of it, and the deacons carry some to those who are absent.

From The First Apology of Justin Martyr in Defence of the Christians[2]

Irenaeus of Lyons (*c.* 130–200)

Irenaeus, who was a disciple of Polycarp and therefore two generations from the apostles, wrote a long and systematic refutation of the heresies (mostly Gnostic) which were current in the Church of his time and which denied that Jesus was truly human. He taught that through prayer, Christians might participate in the nature of God: 'The Word is made human so that human beings may become gods.'

I appeal to you, Lord, God of Abraham, God of Isaac, God of Jacob and Israel, you the Father of our Lord Jesus Christ. Infinitely merciful as you are, it is your will that we should learn to know you. You made heaven and earth, you rule supreme over all that is. You are the true, the only God; there is no other god above you. Through our Lord Jesus Christ and the gifts of the Holy Spirit, grant that all who read what I have written here may know you, because you alone are God; let them draw strength from you; keep them from all teaching that is heretical, irreligious or godless.

Against Heresies 3.6.4[3]

O Lamb of God, you take away the sin of the world, look upon us and have mercy on us; you who are yourself both victim and priest, yourself both reward and redeemer. Keep safe from all evils those whom you have redeemed, O Saviour of the world. Amen.

The Old Gallican Sacramentary may contain words of Irenaeus:

Give perfection to beginners, O Father; give intelligence to the little ones; give aid to those who are running their course. Give sorrow to the negligent; give fervour of spirit to the lukewarm. Give to the perfect a good consummation; for the sake of Christ Jesus our Lord. Amen.

Hippolytus (*c.* 170–236)

In the Apostolic Tradition of St Hippolytus we have a complete eucharistic prayer which would have been used with little variation each time the service was said. He also gives a detailed rule for life within the Church, which marks the beginning of the Christian custom of having prayer at regular hours throughout the day, and he teaches about making the sign of the cross. The first two extracts are taken from his eucharistic prayer and the third is an evening prayer.

W e give you thanks, O God, through your beloved Servant, Jesus
Christ. It is he whom you have sent in these last times to save us
and redeem us, and be the messenger of your will. He is your Word,
inseparable from you, through whom you made all things and in whom
you take delight. You sent him from heaven into the Virgin's womb, where
he was conceived, and took flesh. Born of the Holy Spirit and the Virgin,
he was revealed as your Son. In fulfilment of your will he stretched out
his hands in suffering, to release from suffering those who place their hope
in you, and so he won for you a holy people. Of his own free choice he
was handed over to his passion in order to make an end of death and to
shatter the chains of the evil one; to trample underfoot the powers of hell
and to lead the righteous into light; to establish the boundaries of death
and to manifest the resurrection.[4]

E ternal God, to whom the hidden is as clearly known as the visible:
before you your people bow their heads, to you they submit their hard
hearts and unruly bodies. Send down blessing from your glorious dwelling
on these men and women, lend them a ready ear and answer their prayers.
Set them up firmly with your strong hand and protect them against all
evil passions. Preserve their bodies and souls, increase their faith and fear
and increase ours, through your only Son. Through him and with him
and with the Spirit may glory and power be yours, now and always and
for ever. Amen.[5]

W e thank you, O God, through your Child, Jesus Christ our Lord,
because you have enlightened us and revealed to us the light that
is incorruptible. The day's allotted span is over; we have reached the
beginning of the night. We have had our fill of that daylight which you
created for our pleasure. And now that evening has come and again we
have no lack of light, we praise your holiness and glory, through your only
Son, our Lord Jesus Christ. Through him the glory and power that are his
and the honour that is the Holy Spirit's are also yours, as they will be
throughout the unending succession of ages. Amen.[6]

Phos Hilaron (possibly second century)

*St Basil the Great writes in the fourth century: 'Our ancestors did not
think it right to accept the blessing of the lamplight in the evening in
silence. The moment it appeared, they would thank God for it. Who the*

author of this hymn of thanksgiving was we cannot say, but it is very old and the people still sing it.'

N ow, as the sun sets in the west,
soft lamplight glows as evening starts;
thus, light from light, God's Son all blest
comes from the immortal Father's heart;

We therefore sing our joyful songs
to Father, Holy Spirit, Son,
to whom in every age belongs
by right all praise from every tongue.

Lord Jesus, Son of God, from you
all life, all joy come forth this night;
the world, and each soft glowing hue,
reflect the glory of your light.[7]

Acts of the martyrs

Many accounts survive of those who died bravely for their faith during the persecutions of the first few Christian centuries. Here are some examples of the prayers which were on their lips when they died:

Afra of Augsburg (martyred *c.* 302)

She died in the persecution during Diocletian's reign.

L ord God almighty, Jesus Christ, you did not come to call the just; you came to call sinners to repentance. Your promise is clear; it admits of no doubt. You were so good as to say that as soon as a sinner turned away from his evil deeds, you would say no more about his sins. Accept, then, as a sign of my repentance, the sufferings I am now undergoing, and by this fire that is waiting to burn my body for a time, deliver me from the eternal fire that burns body and soul alike ... Thanks be to you, Lord Jesus Christ: in your mercy you have chosen me to be a victim for the glory of your name – you who offered yourself on the cross as a victim for the salvation of the whole world, you the innocent for us the guilty, you the good for us the wicked, you the blessed for us the cursed, you the sinless for all us sinners. To you I offer my sacrifice, to you who are one God with the Father and the Holy Spirit, with whom you live and reign, as you always will, age after age. Amen.[8]

Simeon bar Sabba'e (martyred between 339 and 344)

Simeon was Bishop of Seleucia in Persia. He died with several others in the persecution by the Persian King Sapor.

Simeon began to pray. He said: 'Give me this crown, Lord; you know how I long for it, for I have loved you with all my heart and all my being. When I see you, I shall be filled with joy and you will give me rest. I shall no longer have to live in this world and see my people suffering, your churches destroyed, your altars overthrown, your devoted clergy everywhere persecuted, the weak defiled, the lukewarm turned from the truth, and my flock that was so large reduced at the time of testing to a handful. I shall not see the many that seemed to be my friends undergo an inward change, become hostile and seek my death; or find those that were my friends for a while taken from me by persecution, at the very time when the killers are snapping their fingers at our people and lording it over them. Yet I mean to persevere in my vocation like a hero and to walk bravely along the path marked out for me, so that I shall still be an example to all your people in the east. I have had the first place at table, I will have the first place too when it comes to dying; I will be the first to give my blood. Then with my brethren I shall enter on that life in which there are no cares, no anxiety, no solicitude, a life where there is neither persecutor nor persecuted, neither oppressor nor oppressed, neither tyrant nor victim of tyranny. No threatening kings, no blustering prefects shall I see there. No one there will cite me before his tribunal or upset me with repeated menaces; there will be no one to do me violence or bully me. I shall stumble no more, when once I have gained a firm footing in you, the Way we all must walk in. My weary limbs will find their rest in you, for you, Anointed, are the Oil that is to anoint us. The grief in my heart will be forgotten when I drink of you, the Chalice of our salvation. The tears in my eyes you will wipe away, O Joy, O Consolation.'

Before his martyrdom, after celebrating the Eucharist with his friends, Simeon prayed:

Lord Jesus, you prayed for those who had crucified you and you taught us too to pray for our enemies. Stephen, your deacon, prayed for the people who had stoned him, and you received his spirit. Receive as well the souls of our brethren, receive my spirit with them. Set us among the martyrs who have received the garland in the west, among the holy apostles and the blessed prophets. Do not count it as a sin that these men persecute your people and kill our bodies, but grant them, Lord, the grace of conversion. May they come to know that you are God and realize that you are the Lord. Bless, Lord, the towns and cities in the east which you entrusted to my care. Protect all the faithful of these lands as you would the apple of your own eye. May they find shelter under the shadow of your wings until these troubles are over. Stay with them until the consummation of the world, as you promised that you would. Bless, Lord, this city, the city of our capture and our crowning. May your cross keep it true to the faith, now and for ever, age after age. Amen.[9]

Tertullian of Carthage (c. 160–c. 220)

Tertullian was a lawyer in Carthage. Western theology has tended to be culturally based in Roman law, with salvation described as acquittal by a law-court. His theology was mostly orthodox; his emphasis on the Holy Spirit was considered by some to be heretical, though today it might be called charismatic. Unlike other early Christian writers, Tertullian had little use for philosophy: 'What has Athens to do with Jerusalem?' he asked. His were the first Christian writings in Latin, and he gives us an insight into the worship of the early Church. He wrote an Apology *(a defence of Christianity against its enemies) and a book,* On Prayer.

Prayer is the spiritual offering which has abolished the ancient sacrifices ... We learn from the gospel what God has asked for. 'The hour will come,' we are told, 'when true worshippers will worship the Father in spirit and truth. God is spirit, and so this is the kind of worshipper he wants.' We are the true worshippers and the true priests: praying in spirit, we make our sacrifice of prayer in spirit, an offering which is God's own and acceptable to him . . . What will God deny to a prayer which proceeds from spirit and truth, seeing it is he who demands it? How great are the proofs of its efficacy which we read and hear and believe . . . It has no special grace to avert the experience of suffering, but it arms with endurance those who do suffer, who grieve, who are pained. It makes grace multiply in power, so that faith may know what it obtains from the Lord, while it understands what for God's name's sake it is suffering . . . It was Christ's wish for it to work no evil: he has conferred upon it all power concerning good. And so its only knowledge is how to call back the souls of the deceased from the very highway of death, to straighten the feeble, to heal the sick, to cleanse the devil-possessed, to open the bars of the prison, to loose the bands of the innocent. It also absolves sins, drives back temptations, quenches persecutions, strengthens the weak-hearted, delights the high-minded, brings home wayfarers, stills the waves, confounds robbers, feeds the poor, rules the rich, lifts up the fallen, supports the unstable, upholds them that stand.[10]

From On Prayer

Cyprian of Carthage (d. 258)

Christian leaders were faced with difficult decisions in an age when martyrdom was common. They taught that it was wrong to seek death unnecessarily, but the Christian must be prepared to accept it rather than deny their faith. Cyprian, Bishop of Carthage in North Africa, wrote a series of letters dealing with the question of whether those who had avoided being martyred could ever be welcomed back into the Church. He himself, when in disguise and about to be overtaken by a boat-load of Roman soldiers, turned his own boat around and told them, quite truthfully, 'A minute ago Cyprian was going that way!' His fellow bishops disagreed over whether this was a betrayal or not.

Prayer for All Needs

Let us pray to the Lord without duplicity, in tune with one another, entreating him with sighs and tears, as befits people in our position – placed as we are between the many, lamenting that they have fallen away, and the faithful remnant that fears it may do the same itself; between the weak, laid low in large numbers, and the few still standing firm. Let us pray that peace may very soon be restored to us, help reach us in our dangers, to draw us from our dark retreats, and God's gracious promises to his servants find fulfilment. May we see the Church restored and our salvation secured; after the rain, fair weather; after the darkness, light; after these storms and tempests, a gentle calm. Let us ask him to help us, because he loves us as a Father loves his children, and to give us the tokens of his divine power that are usual with him. So will our persecutors be stopped from blaspheming, those who have fallen away repent to some purpose, and the firm, unwavering faith of the steadfast be crowned with glory.

Letter 11.8[11]

Let us pray for those who have fallen away,
that they may recover their footing.
Let us pray for those standing firm,
that they may not be tempted to their downfall.
Let us pray for those of whose fall we have been told,
that they may admit the gravity of their sin
and realize that the remedy it calls for is anything but superficial.
Let us pray that when they have received full forgiveness, they may
   do penance,
and remembering their guilt, may decide to be patient for a time.

Letter 30.6 [12]

Prayer for Peace

We beg and beseech the God whom the enemies of the Church are forever provoking and irritating that he would tame their wild hearts. May their rage subside and calm return to their hearts; may their minds, clouded by the darkness their sins produce, repent and see the light; may they seek the bishop's prayers and not his blood.

Letter 59.18 [13]

Good God, may we confess your name to the end. May we emerge unsullied and glorious from the traps and dark powers of this world. As you have bound us together in love and peace, and as, together, we have persevered through times of hardship, may we also rejoice together in your heavenly kingdom.

From a letter written in the year of his martyrdom

Clement of Alexandria (c. 150–c. 215)

Alexandria in Egypt had the greatest university and the greatest library of the ancient world. It was important that Christians should send their best minds to the Catechetical School there, to prove that Christians could out-think the pagan philosophers. Clement went there from Athens as a pupil and eventually become the principal, and was recognized as one of the greatest philosophers in the tradition of Plato. Plato had taught that the things we see around us are all copies of invisible heavenly prototypes or ideas. Clement developed the concept that by prayer we can gain access to this ideal heavenly world.

B e kind, dear Teacher, to us your children. You are our Father, Defender of Israel; God the Son and God the Father, united as one Lord. Grant to us who obey your commands that we may become more perfectly like you, and know you to the utmost of our ability as a good God and a tolerant judge. Keep us all in your peace, citizens of heaven, having sailed calmly over the stormy waters of sin, wafted smoothly along by the wind of your Holy Spirit, your Wisdom beyond words. Night and day, until the last day; may we praise you with thanksgiving to the only Father and Son, Son and Father; the Son, our Teacher, together with the Holy Spirit. You are the one, in whom and for whom all things exist in unity, who has given us a share in eternal glory. All things exist for the one God, who is all goodness, all loveliness, all wise and all just. To God be glory, now and for ever and ever. Amen.

From The Tutor

A hymn to Christ the Saviour

B ridle of colts untamed, over our wills presiding;
Wing of unwandering birds, our flight securely guiding,
Rudder of youth unbending,
Firm against adverse shock;
Shepherd, with wisdom tending
Lambs of the royal flock:
Thy simple children bring
In one, that they may sing
In solemn lays
Their hymns of praise
With guileless lips to Christ their King.

From The Tutor, *translator unknown*

Origen of Alexandria (*c.* 185–254)

Origen was Clement's pupil and successor and, like his master, he used Greek philosophy to speculate on the Christian faith. He taught that the human spirit is deified by what it contemplates. Thus by the practice of contemplative prayer he held out the hope that we might become like God.

J esus, my feet are dirty. Come and slave for me; pour your water into your basin and come and wash my feet. I am overbold, I know, in asking this, but I dread what you threatened when you said: 'If I do not wash your feet, it means you have no companionship with me.' Wash my feet, then, because I do want to have companionship with you. And yet, why am I saying: 'Wash my feet'? It was all very well for Peter to say that, for in his case all that needed washing was his feet: he was clean through and through. My position is quite different: you may wash me now, but I shall still need that other washing you were thinking of, Lord, when you said: 'There is a baptism I must needs be baptized with.'

Sermon 5.2 on Isaiah[14]

Cyril of Jerusalem (*c.* 315–86)

Cyril, Bishop of Jerusalem, gives us an outline of how the church worshipped there in his day. His Catechisms are addressed to candidates who would be baptized on Holy Saturday, and he stresses the presence of Christ in the Eucharist.

God grant that all of you when you have finished the course of the fast, may remember what I say, and bringing forth fruit in good works, may stand blameless beside the Spiritual Bridegroom, and obtain the remission of your sins from God; to whom with the Son and Holy Spirit be the glory for ever. Amen.

Catechetical Lectures 3.16

The Desert Fathers

The third Christian century was a time of such great corruption and materialism in the Roman Empire that some Christians travelled into the Egyptian desert to meditate alone in silence. The greatest of these Desert Fathers was St Antony. His disciple Ammonas said that 'It was by silence that the saints grew.' But so many followers flocked out to learn from them that it was said that 'the desert was made a city'.

Antony of Egypt (251?–356)

God spoke to him through the Gospel read in Church: 'If you want to be perfect, go and sell all you have and give the proceeds to the poor. Take up your cross and follow me.' So Antony gave away all his possessions and went to live alone in the desert. But the discipline of his life of self-denial was in contrast to the luxury of the world around, and also to the wilder excesses of

self-punishment practised by other hermits, so more and more people made
their cells nearby to learn from him. He came out of his self-imposed isolation
for a while to form them into a loose-knit community with a common rule
of life, something which had never been seen before.

W hen the holy Abba Antony lived in the desert he was beset by
despair, and attacked by many sinful thoughts. He said to God,
'Lord, I want to be saved but these thoughts do not leave me alone; what
shall I do in my affliction? How can I be saved?' A short while afterwards,
when he got up to go out, Antony saw a man like himself sitting at his
work, getting up from his work to pray, then sitting down and plaiting a
rope, then getting up again to pray. It was an angel of the Lord sent to
correct and reassure him. He heard the angel saying to him, 'Do this and
you will be saved.' At these words, Antony was filled with joy and courage.
He did this, and he was saved.[15]

W hen the same Abba Antony thought about the depth of the judgements of God, he asked, 'Lord, how is it that some die when they
are young, while others drag on to extreme old age? Why are there those
who are poor and those who are rich? Why do wicked men prosper and
why are the just in need?' He heard a voice answering him, 'Antony, keep
your attention on yourself; these things are according to the judgement of
God, and it is not to your advantage to know anything about them.'[16]

The Sayings of the Desert Fathers

It was not to escape from the evil world that the first Christian hermits
went into the desert, but to confront evil head on. After prolonged fasting
they describe temptation by devils in various forms, but they were also
learning to deal with evil within themselves. For this reason many disciples
*approached the caves of the hermits to ask for teaching (*diakrisis*) in the*
spiritual life. Thus not only spiritual direction began in the desert, but so
did Christian monasticism, for communities of hermits began living near
to one another, learning from each other and at times praying together.
The monks were addressed as abba *which means 'father'. There were*
female hermits too, who were addressed as amma. *Even though some*
of them were quite young, they were called 'the elders'. The sayings or
apophthegms of the elders are collected together in the fifth-century
Apophthegmata, *and in Latin by John Cassian in his* Conferences *and*
Institutes.

Lord Jesus Christ, whose will all things obey: pardon what I have done and grant that I, a sinner, may sin no more. Lord, I believe that though I do not deserve it, you can cleanse me from all my sins. Lord, I know that man looks upon the face, but you see the heart. Send your Spirit into my inmost being, to take possession of my soul and body. Without you I cannot be saved; with you to protect me, I long for your salvation. And now I ask you for wisdom, deign of your great goodness to help and defend me. Guide my heart, almighty God, that I may remember your presence day and night.[17]

They asked abba Macarius, 'How should we pray?' And the old man replied, 'There is no need to speak much in prayer; often stretch out your hands and say, "Lord, as you will and as you know, have mercy on me." But if there is war in your soul, add, "Help me!" and because he knows what we need, he shows mercy on us.'[18]

Abba Lot went to see abba Joseph and he said to him, 'Abba, as far as I can, I say my little office, I fast a little, I pray and meditate, I live in peace and as far as I can I purify my thoughts. What else can I do?' Then the old man stood up and stretched his hands towards heaven; his fingers became like ten lamps of fire and he said to him, 'If you will, you can become all flame.'[19]

Some monks came to see abba Lucius and they said to him, 'We do not work with our hands; we obey Paul's command and pray without ceasing.' The old man said, 'Do you not eat or sleep?' They said, 'Yes, we do.' He said, 'Who prays for you while you are asleep? ... Excuse me, brothers, but you do not practise what you claim. I will show you how I pray without ceasing, though I work with my hands. With God's help, I collect a few palm-leaves and sit down and weave them, saying, "Have mercy upon me, O God, after thy great goodness; according to the multitude of thy mercies do away with mine offences."' He said to them, 'Is this prayer or not?' They said, 'Yes, it is.' And he continued, 'When I have worked and prayed in my heart all day, I make about sixteen pence. Two of these I put outside my door and with the rest I buy food. And he who finds the two coins outside the door prays for me while I eat and sleep. And so by the help of God I pray without ceasing.'[20]

An abba used to say, 'Do not pose as learned people in the wording of your prayer for often only childlike stammerings, simple and unadorned, are what have honoured our Father in heaven. Do not undertake to say heaps of words for fear that your mind may wander in its search for words.'[21]

An abba came to visit another abba. The latter cooked lentils for him and said, 'Let us make a short prayer first.' This 'short' prayer, in fact, lasted all night and, come morning, the visitor left and both forgot all about eating the dish of lentils.

A prayer of Abbot Isaiah: 'You possess strength, mercy, help, protection, forgiveness and patience; for who am I in the hands of ten evil ones from whom you have saved me? I have nothing to offer you for I am a sinner and unworthy of your gifts, and you have kept me from the hands of my enemies. But you are my Lord and my God, and yours is the glory, protection, mercy, help and power.'[22]

Pachomius (c. 290–346)

As opposed to hermits, who live on their own, some of the Christians of the Egyptian Desert lived in communities. Pachomius led a community who had separate cells and observed a rule of silence, but the cells were within a single enclosure and the members were organized as a monastic community. This type of monasticism is called cenobitic or coenobitic (from the Greek words koinos, *'common', and* bios, *'life') and is an attempt to combine the two monastic patterns of the solitary and the community.*

Pachomius used to say, 'One of the things we are commanded to do is to pray incessantly.'

Athanasius (c. 296–373)

Athanasius was born in Alexandria in Egypt and became its bishop. He believed that the teaching of Arius, that Jesus was only of a similar substance to the Father, destroyed the possibility of our redemption, for Christ cannot reconcile humans with God unless he is truly God and truly human. He defended the decision of the Council of Nicea in 325 that Jesus is of the same substance as the Father, and for this he was driven from his diocese into exile: at one time it seemed as if the whole world was against him – 'Athanasius contra mundum'. Eventually he was vindicated, and although the so-called 'Athanasian Creed' is not by him, its teaching is the same as his.

Anyone who wishes to understand the mind of the sacred writers must first cleanse his own life, and approach the saints by copying their deeds. Thus united to them in the fellowship of life, he will both understand the things revealed to them by God and, thenceforth escaping the peril that threatens sinners in the judgement, will receive that which is laid up for the saints in the kingdom of heaven. Of that reward it is written: 'Eye hath not seen nor ear heard, neither hath entered into the heart of man the things that God hath prepared' for them that live a godly life and love the God and Father in Christ Jesus our Lord, through whom and with whom be to the Father himself, with the Son himself, in the Holy Spirit, honour and might and glory to ages of ages of ages. Amen.[23]

Serapion (d. after 360)

Serapion, Bishop of Thmuis, was another disciple of St Antony.

We praise you, Father, invisible, giver of immortality. You are the source of life and light, the source of all grace and truth; you love us all and you love the poor, you seek reconciliation with all and draw them all to you by sending your dear Son to visit them, who now lives and reigns, with you, Father, and the Holy Spirit, one God for ever and ever. Amen.[24]

The First Prayer of Sundays

We ask for your help, Father of Christ, Lord of all that is, Creator of all the created, Maker of all that is made; we stretch out clean hands to you and lay bare our minds, Lord, before you. Have mercy, we pray you; spare us, be kind to us, improve us; fill us with virtue, faith and knowledge. Look at us, Lord; we bring our weaknesses for you to see. Be kind and merciful to all of us here gathered together; have pity on this people of yours and show them your favour, make them equitable, temperate and pure; send out angelic powers to make this your people – all that compose it – holy and noble. Send the Holy Spirit into our minds, I beg you, and grant that we may learn to understand the holy scriptures he inspired. May we interpret them correctly and fittingly, for the benefit of all the faithful here present. Through your only Son, Jesus Christ, in the Holy Spirit. Through him may glory and power be yours, now and age after age. Amen.[25]

Prayer for the Sick

W e pray for the sick; grant them health, and raise them up from their sickness and make them to have perfect health of body and soul, for you are the Saviour and Benefactor, you are Lord and King of all. Amen.

Eusebius of Caesarea (*c.* 260–*c.* 340)

Eusebius was educated at Caesarea Maritima on the coast of Palestine by Pamphilus, a disciple of Origen. When his tutor, whom he venerated, was martyred in one of the periodic persecutions, Eusebius fled to Tyre, then to Egypt where he spent some time in prison. Then the Emperor Constantine ordered tolerance of the Christians, and Eusebius became Bishop of Caesarea and one of Constantine's advisers. He wrote the history of the Church up until his own day, which he assembled from other writings, many of which are now lost.

T hanks be to God, the almighty, the king of the universe, for all his mercies; and heartfelt thanks to the Saviour and Redeemer of our souls, Jesus Christ, through whom we pray that peace from troubles outside and troubles in the heart may be kept for us stable and unshaken for ever. Let me now obediently sing aloud the new song, because after those terrifying darksome sights and stories I was now privileged to see and celebrate such things as in truth many righteous men and martyrs of God before us desired to see on earth and did not see, and to hear and did not hear. But they attained far better things in the heavens; whereas I, acknowledging that even my present lot is better than I deserve, have been more than amazed at the bountiful grace of its author, and am duly filled with wonder, worshipping him with my whole soul's strength.[26]

The Emperor Constantine the Great (274 or 288–337)

Proclaimed Emperor in York, Constantine defeated his enemies at the Battle of the Milvian Bridge. Eusebius reports that he saw the sign of the cross in the sky and heard the words, 'In this sign conquer'. From then on he was tolerant of Christianity, though he was not baptized until on his death-bed, which was not unusual at the time. Hoping that the Christian religion would unify the Roman Empire with the worship of one God, he was horrified to discover that Christians do not always agree between

themselves on what they believe, so he called the bishops together at Nicea
to produce a statement of what is essential to calling oneself a Christian.
This was one in a series of councils and controversies which split the early
Church over the relationship between Jesus and God, and between the
human and divine natures in Jesus. Yet in spite of their acrimony,
the disputants were all people of faith and prayer. It has been said that
the proof of the existence of the Holy Spirit is that the Church has arrived
at the truth in spite of its councils. Below is Constantine's letter summoning
the bishops to the Council of Nicea.

I continue to receive numerous letters from Christian leaders in every region. It is clear to me that many of you have become so inflamed with the spirit of enmity and hatred that you have forgotten your own salvation. Local synods are convened to resolve disagreements and disputes. But in some cases these synods fail to reach any conclusion; in other cases the agreements are ignored and flouted as soon as the synod is over. Your Saviour teaches you to practise unity and concord; but you have become masters of disunity and discord. In this way you bring disgrace on yourselves, and on your most holy religion. I therefore believe that under God I have a duty to impose unity on the church, using the imperial power which God has vested in me to put an end to all disputes. For this purpose I am convening a synod to which all Christian leaders will come. I will preside at this synod, listening to the beliefs and opinions of anyone who wishes to speak. I will then weigh up what I have heard, and issue my judgement. I accept this task with reluctance; I have not sought it, but your misbehaviour has forced it upon me. May the divine power of the great God keep you all in good health, both in spirit and in body, for many years.

From Eusebius' History of the Church[27]

The Early Western Church

One of the reasons why Constantine moved his capital to Byzantium, renaming it Constantinople, may have been to promote unity between the Eastern, Greek-speaking half of his empire and the Latin speakers of the West. But the Church was beginning to separate on the basis of language also.

Hilary of Poitiers (310/320–67)

Hilary came from a pagan background, but was dissatisfied with the teaching of the philosophers and longed to know God. He was converted by reading the Bible, and when he became a bishop, taught that there is a deeper spiritual meaning below the surface of the Scriptures, which is accessible to anyone reading with the same Spirit which inspired the original writers. He defended the doctrine of the Trinity, and became the leading Latin-speaking theologian of his day. He encouraged St Martin, an ex-soldier who had been converted when he divided his cloak with a beggar and was then told in a dream that the beggar had been Christ himself. Together they set up a monastery at Ligugé, before Martin moved on to Tours and established the beginnings of the parochial system. Martin wrote nothing, but Hilary was the first to write hymns in Latin, intended for congregational singing.

Keep, I pray, my faith unsullied, and till my spirit departs, grant that I may speak what I believe: so that I may always hold fast to what I professed in the creed, when I was baptized in the Father, and the Son, and the Holy Spirit. Let me adore you our Father, and your Son together with you; let me win the favour of your Holy Spirit, who is from you, through your only-begotten Son. For I have Jesus, a convincing witness to my faith, who says, 'Father, all mine are yours, and yours are mine.' My Lord Jesus Christ is my witness, abiding in you, and from you, and with you, for ever God: who is blessed for ever and ever. Amen.

On the Trinity XII.57

The chief service I owe you in my life, as I well know, O God, all-powerful Father, is that every word and thought of mine should speak of you. The power of speech that you have bestowed on me can give me no greater pleasure than to serve you by preaching and to show an ignorant world or a protesting heretic what you are: the Father, the Father whose only Son is God. But in saying this, I am merely saying what I want to do. If I am actually to do it, I must ask you for your help and mercy, ask you to fill with wind the sails I have hoisted for you and to carry me forward on my course – to breathe, that is, your Spirit into my faith and my confession of it, and to enable me to continue the preaching I have begun.

On the Trinity I.37[1]

Keep us, O Lord, from the vain strife of words, and grant to us a constant profession of the truth. Preserve us in the faith, true and undefiled; so that we may ever hold fast that which we professed when we were baptized into the name of the Father, and of the Son, and of the Holy Spirit; that we may have you for our Father, that we may abide in your Son, and in the fellowship of the Holy Spirit; through the same Jesus Christ our Lord. Amen.

Almighty God, bestow on us the meaning of words, the light of understanding, nobility of diction and faith in the truth. And grant that what we believe we may also speak. Amen.

Ambrose of Milan (c. 339–97)

Ambrose was the Roman prefect in charge of Milan. He led his troops into the cathedral there to quell a riot between opposing factions who could not agree on whom to elect as the next bishop. The story goes that in the horrified silence which greeted him, a child cried out, 'Ambrose for bishop!', and he was baptized, ordained and consecrated within a few days. Ambrose therefore brought great skill in Roman administration into the leadership of the Church.

Lord, teach us to seek you, and reveal yourself to us when we seek you. For we cannot seek you unless you first teach us, nor find you except you reveal yourself to us. Let us seek you in longing, and long for you in seeking; let us find you in love, and love you in finding, O Jesus Christ our Lord. Amen.

O splendour of God's glory bright,
  Who bringest forth the light from Light;
O Light, of light the fountain-spring;
O Day, our days illumining;

Come, very Sun of truth and love,
Come in thy radiance from above,
And shed the Holy Spirit's ray
On all we think or do to-day.

Teach us to work with all our might;
Put Satan's fierce assaults to flight;
Turn all to good that seems most ill;
Help us our calling to fulfil.[2]

O strength and stay upholding all creation,
  Who ever dost thyself unmoved abide,
Yet day by day the light in due gradation
From hour to hour through all its changes guide;

Grant to life's day a calm unclouded ending,
An eve untouched by shadows of decay,
The brightness of a holy death-bed blending
With dawning glories of the eternal day.

Hear us, O Father, gracious and forgiving,
Through Jesus Christ thy co-eternal Word,
Who with the Holy Ghost by all things living
Now and to endless ages art adored.[3]

O Lord, you have mercy on all, take away from me my sins, and
  mercifully set me ablaze with the fire of your Holy Spirit. Take away
from me the heart of stone, and give me a human heart, a heart to love
and adore you, a heart to delight in you, to follow and enjoy you, for
Christ's sake. Amen.

Jerome (c. 342–420)

*Saint Jerome moved to a cave next to that in which Jesus was born in
Bethlehem, so that he might immerse himself in the background that Jesus
knew, while he translated the Scriptures into Latin, creating what is known*

as the Vulgate version. He also wrote many letters to those who sought his advice, instructing those who could not join communities on how to live a life of prayer in their own homes, based on regular reading of the Bible and other devotional works.

O good Shepherd, seek me out, and bring me home to your fold again. Deal favourably with me according to your grace, till I may dwell in your house all the days of my life, and praise you for ever and ever with those who are there. Amen.

L ord, you have given us your word for a light to shine on our path. Inspire us to meditate on that word, and follow its teaching, that we may find in it the light which shines more and more until it is perfect day; through Jesus Christ our Lord. Amen.

Augustine of Hippo (354–430)

It was the teaching of Ambrose which brought Augustine of Hippo to the Christian faith. He saw the world as very evil and human nature as corrupt. His Confessions *tell his life's story in the form of a long prayer to God. He famously asserted that there must be 'in inessentials liberty, in essentials unity, and in all things love.' Below are some extracts from the* Confessions.

A lmighty God, in whom we live and move and have our being, you have made us for yourself, so that our hearts are restless till they rest in you; grant us purity of heart and strength of purpose, that no passion may hinder us from knowing your will, no weakness from doing it; but in your light may we see light clearly, and in your service find perfect freedom; through Jesus Christ our Lord. Amen.

B lessed are those who love you, O God; for they alone lose no one who is dear to them, if all are dear in you, who never can be lost; through Jesus Christ our Lord. Amen.

E ternal God, the light of the minds that know you, the joy of the hearts that love you, the strength of the wills that serve you; grant us so to know you that we may truly love you, so to love you that we may fully serve you, whom to serve is perfect freedom; through Jesus Christ our Lord. Amen.

Grant to us your servants that we may have, to our God, a heart of flame; to our neighbours, a heart of love; and to ourselves, a heart of steel.

Keep watch, dear Lord, with those who wake or watch or weep tonight, and give your angels charge over those who sleep. Tend those who are sick, Lord Christ; give rest to those who are weary; bless those who are dying; soothe those who are suffering; pity those who are afflicted; shield those who are joyous; and all, for your love's sake. Amen.

Late have I loved you, O Beauty so ancient and so new; late have I loved you; for you were within me, and I was outside; I sought you outside and my ugliness fell on those lovely things that you had made. You were with me, and I was not with you. I was kept from you by those things, yet had they not been in you, they would not have been at all. You called and cried to me to unstop my deaf ears: you sent forth the beams of your love to shine on me and heal my blindness: you wafted perfumes on me; I breathed them in and now I long for you: I tasted you, and now I hunger and thirst for you: you touched me, and now I burn for your peace.

O God, from whom to be turned is to fall, to whom to be turned is to rise, and in whom to stand is to abide for ever: grant us in all our duties your help, in all our perplexities your guidance, in all our dangers your protection, and in all our sorrows your peace, through Jesus Christ our Lord. Amen.

Monica (c. 331–87)

Monica was the mother of St Augustine. During his wild youth, when Augustine was praying, 'Lord make me chaste, but not yet,' his mother was praying that he might become a Christian. Her prayers were answered and her son became a great Christian teacher. It is significant that she was made a saint for no other distinction than that she prayed faithfully and patiently, when there seemed little likelihood of her request being granted. After Augustine was converted she prayed for her husband, who used to beat her, and he too was converted. In his Confessions, *Augustine describes a moving conversation about heaven with his mother by a window in Ostia, the port near Rome. A few days later she died there.*

May she therefore rest in peace with her husband, before or after whom she married none; whom she obeyed, bringing forth the fruit of patience, that she might gain him also for you. And inspire, my Lord God, inspire your servants my brother and sister Christians, and your children my superiors who with voice and heart and writings I serve, that as many of them as read these confessions may remember at your altar Monica, your handmaid, together with Patricius, her husband, through whom I was physically born into this world . . . In this way my mother's last request to me may, through my confessions more than through my prayers, be abundantly carried out for her through the prayers of many.

Augustine, Confessions 23.37

Niceta of Remesiana (d. *c.* 414)

There is a nice tradition, almost certainly untrue, that the Te Deum *was composed extempore in alternate verses by St Ambrose and St Augustine at the latter's baptism. It is now thought to be by Niceta of Remesiana.*

We praise thee, O God: we acknowledge thee to be the Lord.
    All the earth doth worship thee; the Father everlasting.
To thee all Angels cry aloud: the Heavens, and all the Powers
        therein.
To thee Cherubin: and Seraphin continually do cry
Holy, Holy, Holy; Lord God of Sabaoth;
heaven and earth are full of the Majesty of thy glory.
The glorious company of the Apostles praise thee.
The goodly fellowship of the Prophets praise thee.
The noble army of Martyrs praise thee.
The holy Church throughout all the world doth acknowledge thee;
the Father of an infinite Majesty;
thine honourable, true and only Son;
also the Holy Ghost, the Comforter.
Thou art the King of Glory, O Christ.
Thou art the everlasting Son of the Father.
When thou tookest upon thee to deliver man,
thou didst not abhor the Virgin's womb.
When thou hadst overcome the sharpness of death,
thou didst open the kingdom of heaven to all believers.
Thou sittest at the right hand of God in the Glory of the Father.

We believe that thou shalt come to be our Judge.
We therefore pray thee, help thy servants,
whom thou hast redeemed with thy precious blood.
Make them to be numbered with thy Saints in glory everlasting.
O Lord, save thy people; and bless thine heritage;
govern them and lift them up for ever.
Day by day we magnify thee;
and we worship thy name ever world without end.
Vouchsafe, O Lord to keep us this day without sin.
O Lord, have mercy upon us; have mercy upon us.
O Lord, let thy mercy lighten upon us; as our trust is in thee.
O Lord, in thee have I trusted; let me never be confounded.[4]

Fulgentius of Ruspe (468–533)

He was a member of the Roman civil service, but he gave this up to become a monk, and was then made bishop of a North African diocese. The local king and many of the clergy took the view of Arius against the Nicene Creed, and Fulgentius, who was a follower of Augustine, was twice banished to Sardinia.

We beseech thee, O God, the God of truth, that what we know not of things we ought to know thou wilt teach us; that what we know of truth, though wilt keep us therein; that what we are mistaken in, as men must be, thou wilt correct; that at whatsoever things we stumble, thou wilt yet establish us; and from all things that are false, and from all knowledge that would be hurtful, thou wilt evermore defend us, through Jesus Christ our Lord. Amen.

Adapted

Leo the Great (d. 461)

Leo was pope at a time of great disorder. He persuaded the Huns to withdraw beyond the Danube, and wrung concessions from the Vandals when they captured Rome. He saw this as a time when the Church needed strong central control, and he extended the power of the papacy over the whole of the Western Roman Empire, including North Africa.

Let us give thanks to God the Father, through his Son, in the Holy Spirit, who for his great mercy and his love for us has had pity on us, and when we were dead in sin, gave us new life in Christ, that together we might be a new Creation. Acknowledging our divinity, because we have become sharers in the divine nature through the birth of the Messiah, we submit ourselves to Christ, who will judge us in truth because he ransomed us in mercy, who with the Father and the Holy Spirit reigns for ever and ever. Amen.

On the Incarnation

M ay God grant us his grace through our prayers to carry out our promises; through Jesus Christ our Lord. Amen.

On the Passion

M ake us peacemakers, O Lord, that we may be called children of God and joint-heirs with Christ. May we never suffer calamities, never fear temptation. When the struggle is over, may we rest in the peace of God, the peace of utter tranquillity, through our Lord, who with the Father and the Holy Spirit lives and reigns for ever and ever. Amen.

Adapted from the Sermon on the Beatitudes

John Cassian (*c.* 360–435)

Cassian, having learnt about solitude from Evagrius and others in the Egyptian desert, brought monasticism into the West when he settled in Marseilles. He taught in his Institutes *and* Conferences *that meditation should consist in the repetition of a verse from Scripture, 'folding the recollection of God into the little space of meditation on one verse.'*

O God, be all my love, all my hope, all my striving; let my thoughts and words flow from you, my daily life be in you, and every breath I take be for you. Amen.

Adapted from Conferences 10

Benedict of Nursia (*c.* 480–*c.* 540)

Benedict sought to become a hermit in a cave at Subiaco, but found himself surrounded by other Christians wanting to learn from him. So he organized them into a community, bound together by the threefold vows of poverty, chastity and obedience, and organizing their daily life by the Rule of St Benedict, *which he based on an earlier anonymous* Rule of the Master.

This balanced physical labour and intellectual study, with corporate prayer at regular hours of the day, which he called the Opus Dei *('the work of God'), focusing on the reading of Scripture and the recitation of the Psalms, followed by meditation on what had been read. In his* Rule *he taught that the purpose of this 'Daily Office' is the praise of the Creator. This became the pattern for Western monasticism, and also for the daily prayer of many Christians who are not members of religious communities.*

G racious and holy Father, give us wisdom to perceive you, intelligence to understand you, diligence to seek you, patience to wait for you, eyes to behold you, a heart to meditate on you, and a life to proclaim you; through the power of the Spirit of Jesus Christ our Lord. Amen.

Boethius (*c.* 480–*c.* 524)

Anicius Manlius Torquatus Severinus Boethius was the son of a Roman consul, and studied Greek at Athens. There he gained the knowledge of the Greek philosophers which enabled him later to produce the translations and commentaries on the writings of Aristotle and Porphyry which became the standard textbooks on logic throughout the Middle Ages. He became consul while the Goths were occupying Rome, and later was chief minister to the Emperor Theodoric. But he was accused of treason and sent to prison, where he wrote his greatest work, The Consolations of Philosophy, *in which Philosophy personified comforts the author in his affliction by reminding him that the only thing that endures in life is virtue. After a year in prison he was executed, but his book became one of the most widely read for the next thousand years. He also wrote a number of short theological works defending the orthodox doctrine of the Trinity and the definition of the Council of Chalcedon that Jesus had two natures, human and divine, in one person.*

O God, whose reason rules the world,
who formed the starry heights above,
timeless, time's chain far forth you hurled,
unmoved, gave all things power to move.
Prevailed on by no outside cause
to fashion all reality;
ideas of love and mental laws
moulded the noble world we see.
Your nature perfect beauty, thus
you made the world in tenderness

with sights and sounds to conjure us
to love the source of loveliness.
You named the primal elements
of earth and water, air and fire,
and balanced out their influence
that none might lower be or higher.
O Father, give me power to climb
and wash in fountains filled with light,
weighed down no more by things of time,
lit by your shining in the night.
The sight of you begins our day,
with you its evening we shall spend;
you carry us, and lead the way,
the journey, and the journey's end.[5]

The Eastern Church

The Greek Church

The Eastern Emperors in Constantinople modelled their church on the pattern of the life of their court. Further councils of the Church were called, some recognized by the West and others not, which produced canons and creeds to govern the life and the faith of Christians.

John Chrysostom (*c.* 347–407)

Saint John Chrysostom, whose nickname means 'the golden tongued', preached in Constantinople sermons which by their eloquence made even Emperors tremble. He condemned the wealth which Christians were accumulating now that theirs was the official religion of the Empire. He was appointed Patriarch of Constantinople because the people demanded it, but the implacable hatred of the Empress Eudoxia led to his abduction while he was celebrating an Easter service, and his exile to Armenia. The poor people of Constantinople were becoming restless in their demands for his return, so the Emperor ordered that he travel on foot through the autumn rains to a distant fortress; as expected, he died on the journey.

God grant that we may live our lives here without trouble, and in security, and attain the joys of eternal life; by the grace of our Lord Jesus Christ and his love for us, to whom be glory and might, together with the Father and the Holy Spirit, now and always, and to the ages of ages. Amen.

Sermons on Matthew 90.4

O n this day of Christmas, the Word of God, being truly God, appeared in the form of a man, and turned all adoration to himself and away from competing claims for our attention. To him, then, who through the forest of lies has beaten a clear path for us, to Christ, to the Father, and to the Holy Spirit, we offer all praise, now and for ever. Amen.

Sermon on the Nativity

The Cappadocians

Basil the Great (Bishop of Caesarea), Gregory of Nyssa and Gregory of Nazianzus are known as the Cappadocian Fathers. The ikons show them wearing a distinctive white shawl covered in black crosses. In the region of Cappadocia, in the north of what we now call Turkey, there was a great flowering of Christianity, some of the worshippers meeting in the curious cave churches which can still be visited there. Their bishops became involved in the controversies over the Trinity and the person of Christ. The definitions they arrived at, enshrined in the Nicea-Constantinople creeds, were the only way to resolve the controversies of the time, and anyone choosing to disagree with them risked undermining the salvation which Jesus brought. For, even if the philosophical terms in which they are expressed seem outdated, the Cappadocian Fathers who argued for them knew that their experience of praying to God through Jesus depended on Christ being in some way at the same time both totally human and wholly God.

The teaching of all three is basically the same: 1. Everyone naturally desires God. 2. Divinization is a process of growth towards moral perfection, and knowledge of the transcendent God by action and contemplation. 3. Faith and conversion, as a result of our freewill, are essential for our growth towards God.

Macrina the Younger (c. 327–79)

Gregory Thaumaturgos (c. 213–270) was a disciple of Origen who was a zealous missionary in the region of Cappadocia. His nickname means 'the Wonder-worker'. He taught Macrina the Elder, who was the grandmother of Basil and Gregory of Nyssa and of Macrina the Younger, their sister. Gregory of Nyssa praised the amount of time his sister spent in prayer, saying that in consequence she had knees like a camel's. Below is Macrina's deathbed prayer.

O Lord, you have freed us from the fear of death. You have made the end of our life here into the beginning of true life for us. You give rest to our bodies for a time in sleep, and then you awaken them again with the sound of the last trumpet. Our earthly body, formed by your hands, you consign in trust to the earth, and then once more you reclaim it, transfiguring with immortality and grace whatever in us is mortal or deformed. You have opened for us the way to resurrection, and given to those that fear you the sign of the holy cross as their emblem, to destroy the enemy and to save our life. Eternal God, on you have I depended from my mother's womb, you have I loved with all the strength of my soul, to you have I dedicated my flesh and my soul from my youth until now. Set by my side an angel of light, to guide me to the place of repose, where are the waters of rest, among the holy Fathers. You have broken the fiery sword and restored to Paradise the thief who was crucified with you and implored your mercy: remember me also in your kingdom, for I too have been crucified with you ... Forgive me and accept my soul into your hands, spotless and undefiled, as incense in your sight.[1]

Basil the Great (330–79)

Basil was educated at Athens in the best of Greek and Christian learning, but went to settle as a hermit on the banks of the river Iris. He met his university friend Gregory of Nazianzus and they went on preaching tours together. Rejecting appeals from the Emperor Julian, who had also been at the university with them, to enter the life of the court, he only came out of seclusion to defend orthodoxy against the Arians in Cappadocian Caesarea (present-day Kayseri in Turkey, not to be confused with the two Caesareas in the Holy Land). He spent the last nine years of his life as Bishop of that city. In spite of his involvement in the bitter theological controversies of the age, he was revered for his holiness. Basil created a form of monasticism in which a group of brothers live around a local church and are engaged in care for their neighbours as well as the life of prayer. He taught that it is dangerous to seek perfection on one's own; yet the monastic life was much less rigorous than that taught in Egypt. This is the form that monasticism has followed ever since in the Eastern Church. The extensive monastic buildings at Caesarea included hospitals for the sick and hostels for the poor.

May the lawless person be confounded, the faithful exultant in the dogmas of truth, and the Lord glorified, the Lord to whom be glory and power, world without end. Amen.

Hexaemeron 9.6

O Lord our God, teach us, we pray, to ask you in the right way for the right blessings. Steer the vessel of our life towards yourself, the tranquil haven of all storm-tossed souls. Show us the course in which we should go. Renew a willing spirit within us. Let your Spirit curb our wayward senses, and guide and enable us towards that which is our true good, to keep your laws, and in all we do to rejoice always in your glorious and gladdening presence. For yours is the glory and praise from all your saints, for ever and ever. Amen.

O God, enlarge within us the sense of fellowship with all living things, and especially with our brothers and sisters the animals to whom you gave the earth as their home together with us. We remember with shame that we have dominated over them in the past with ruthless cruelty, so that the voice of the earth, which should have risen to you in song, has been instead a groan of pain. Teach us that they do not live only for our benefit, but for themselves and for you, and that they love the sweetness of life as much as we do. Amen.

Steer the ship of my life, good Lord, to your quiet harbour, where I can be safe from the storms of sin and conflict. Show me the course I should take. Renew in me the gift of discernment, so that I can always see the right direction in which I should go. And give me the strength and the courage to choose the right course, even when the sea is rough and the waves are high, knowing that through enduring hardship and danger in your name we shall find comfort and peace.[2]

Gregory of Nyssa (c. 330–95)

Gregory was Basil's younger brother and trained in rhetoric. Gregory of Nazianzus, his friend, persuaded him to be ordained, and Basil made him Bishop of Nyssa (present-day Nevsehir) in Cappadocia. He therefore brought skills of philosophy to the exposition of the faith. He had a holistic view of the human race, and believed there would be no true salvation until the whole of humanity is saved. Gregory emphasized the gulf between

Creator and creation but, unusually for a Greek, taught the importance
of using our feelings in approaching God.

Kindness flows from you, Lord, pure and continual.
   You had cast us off, as was only just, but mercifully you
      forgave us;
you hated us and you were reconciled to us, you cursed us and you
   blessed us;
you banished us from paradise, and you called us back again;
you took from us the fig-leaves that had made us so unseemly a
   garment,
and you put on us a cloak of great value;
you opened the prison-gates and gave the condemned a pardon;
you sprinkled us with clean water and washed away the dirt.[3]

Let us ... sing that joyful hymn
   which a voice inspired by the Spirit once sang in prophecy.
      My soul will rejoice in the Lord,
for he has given me salvation for my garment
and joy to wrap me round like a cloak;
he has set on my head a garland like a bridegroom's
and has dressed me like a bride in her finery.
There is no doubt who it is that dresses the bride in her finery:
it is, of course, Christ – he that is and was and will be.
Blessed is he, now and throughout the ages. Amen.[4]

Gregory of Nazianzus (329–89)

Gregory, who was born in the Cappadocian town of Nazianzus, became
a friend of Basil when they studied Greek literature together in Alexandria
and Athens. Basil made him Bishop of Sasima. Together with Gregory of
Nyssa they successfully opposed Arianism at the Councils of Constantinople
in 379 and 381. Gregory of Nazianzus was a deep and sensitive thinker,
and his prayers and poems are more personal than the writings of most
of the Fathers of the third century.

Christ, give me strength; your servant is not well.
   The tongue that praised you is made silent,
Struck dumb by the pain of sickness.
I cannot bear not to sing your praises.
O, make me well again, make me whole,

That I may again proclaim your greatness.
Do not forsake me, I beseech you.
Let me return now to your service.[5]

L ord, as I read the psalms let me hear you singing.
As I read your words, let me hear you speaking.
As I reflect on each page, let me see your image.
And as I seek to put your precepts into practice,
let my heart be filled with joy.[6]

W hile I sleep, O Lord,
let my heart not cease to worship you;
let my sleep be permeated by your presence,
while creation keeps watch,
singing psalms with the angels,
and taking up my soul into its paean of praise.[7]

Denys (Dionysius) the pseudo-Areopagite (c. 500)

An anonymous Christian whose writings purported to be by the Dionysius whom St Paul converted in Athens (Acts 17:34), and who is therefore known as Pseudo-Dionysius, or Denys, taught about Christian mysticism and has been widely influential. He probably lived at the end of the fifth century. He taught that the purpose of our existence is that the whole of creation should be united with God who created it. By this means the whole of creation will be perfected or divinized. There are three ways in which God can be known: 1. Cataphatic theology, which is by affirmations made about God based on his revelation in creation and Scripture. Through this we know that God is Trinity, and that there are nine orders of angels: seraphim, cherubim and thrones; dominations, powers and authorities; principalities, archangels and angels. 2. Symbolic theology, where through the sacraments we make statements about God by means of metaphor. 3. Apophatic theology, in which the only statements we can make about God are negative ones, describing God by what God is not. Apophatic mysticism has been a strong influence in Eastern spirituality, and most subsequent teachers have agreed with Denys that the three stages of purification, illumination and union describe the process we must all go through to approach God in prayer.

M ost exalted Trinity, divinity above all knowledge, whose goodness passes understanding, who guides Christians to divine wisdom; direct our way to the summit of your mystical oracles, most incomprehensible, most lucid and most exalted, where the simple and pure and unchangeable mysteries of theology are revealed in the darkness, clearer than light; a darkness that shines brighter than light, that invisibly and intangibly illuminates with splendours of inconceivable beauty the soul that sees not. Let this be my prayer.[8]

Maximus the Confessor (*c.* 580–662)

Maximus was an aristocrat who rose to become Imperial Secretary to the Emperor Heraclius; but he then joined a monastery at Chrysopolis and became in due time its abbot. He taught that Jesus became human so that we, through prayer, might become like God, and consequently Maximus became involved in the disputes about the nature of Christ. Because of his refusal to sign heretical statements he was exiled and eventually punished by having his tongue and right hand cut off. He died soon afterwards.

M ay all of us who call upon the name of our Lord Jesus Christ be delivered from the present delights and the future afflictions of the evil one by participating in the reality of the blessings held in store and already revealed to us in Christ our Lord himself, who alone with the Father and the Holy Spirit is praised by all creation. Amen.

From On the Lord's Prayer[9]

Symeon the New Theologian (949–1022)

He was groomed to become a civil servant of the Byzantine Emperors, but instead became a monk, and eventually abbot of the monastery of St Mamas at Constantinople. He taught that through meditation we can be 'deified', or share in the Divine Essence through grace. He was given his title because he was thought of as second only to Gregory Nazianzus among Byzantine teachers on prayer.

S it down alone and in silence. Lower your head, shut your eyes, breathe out gently and imagine yourself looking into your own heart. Carry your mind, i.e. your thoughts, from your head to your heart. As you breathe out, say, 'Lord Jesus Christ, have mercy on me.' Say it moving your lips gently, or simply say it in your mind. Try to put all other thoughts aside. Be calm, be patient, and repeat the process very frequently.[10]

From The Philokalia

Come, true light.
Come, life eternal.
Come, hidden mystery.
Come, treasure without name.
Come, reality beyond all words.
Come, person beyond all understanding.
Come, rejoicing without end.
Come, light that knows no evening.
Come, unfailing expectation of the saved.
Come, raising of the fallen.
Come, resurrection of the dead.
Come, all-powerful, for unceasingly you create,
refashion and change all things by your will alone.
Come, invisible whom none may touch and handle.
Come, for you continue always unmoved,
yet at every instant you are wholly in movement;
you draw near to us who lie in hell,
yet you remain higher than the heavens.
Come, for your name fills our hearts with longing and is ever on
    our lips;
yet who you are and what your nature is, we cannot say or know.
Come, Alone to the alone.
Come, for you are yourself the desire that is within me.
Come, the consolation of my humble soul.
Come, my joy, my endless delight.[11]

From Hymns of Divine Love

Hesychasts, the Jesus Prayer and *The Philokalia*

Hesuchia means 'quiet' in Greek. The world 'Hesychast' is normally used for those who seek inner quiet in prayer, traditionally in the Eastern Church by a method of meditation and the repetition of some version of the Jesus Prayer, which has been compared to the repetition of a mantra by the yoga teachers of Asia. But unlike yoga, the aim of Hesychasm is to come into closer personal contact with Jesus by shutting out distractions and obeying St Paul's instruction to 'Pray without ceasing.' Repetition of the phrase, 'Jesus Christ, Son of God, have mercy on me, a sinner, now and in the hour of my death', in time with slow breathing, while directing the eyes and the thoughts towards the centre of the body, has become the great contribution of the Eastern Orthodox Church to Christian prayer. It is also referred to as the 'Prayer of the Heart'. In time, the prayer may be simplified down to the words 'Jesus' as we breathe the life of Christ into ourselves, and 'mercy' as we breathe out his love to the world. The movement flowered in the fourteenth century with Nicephorus, Gregory of Sinai and Gregory Palamas, but it had developed earlier in writers such as Maximus the Confessor and Symeon the New Theologian. The Philokalia, one of the most famous collections of teaching on prayer in the Eastern Church, was compiled by Macarius of Corinth (1731–1805) and Nicodemus of the Holy Mountain (1749–1809). It contains complete works by more than thirty writers from the fourth to the fifteenth centuries, and is the source of much of the teaching on Hesychasm and the Prayer of the Heart.

Nicephoros of Mount Athos (late thirteenth century)

Called Nicephorus the Solitary, he lived on Mount Athos in Greece, a whole mountain peninsula covered in ancient monasteries, where even today women are not admitted and men can only visit under strict conditions. He teaches clearly how to use the Jesus Prayer.

If then from the first you enter through the mind into the place of the heart, as I have shown you, give thanks to God and praise him with transports of joy for all this work in you, which will teach you what you could not otherwise know. It is needful to learn this while your mind is in this condition, and not to keep silent, and so be fruitless. For your unceasing occupation ought to be to keep on saying: 'Lord Jesus, Son of God, have mercy on me.' This practice of continual recollection gives no handle or opportunity to the suggestions of the enemy, but leads us on day by day to more love and longing for God.[12]

Icons

The first thing which strikes a Western visitor to an Orthodox church is that the walls are covered with paintings of the saints and scenes from the Bible. The altar is divided from the rest of the church by a screen called an iconostasis. These are regarded as not just visual aids but sacraments of the presence of the communion of saints at every service. Yet from about 725 to 842 the Emperors ordered the destruction of all icons. This was partly because only the human nature of Christ could be represented, so there was a danger of separating it from his divinity; partly because they were thought to be a barrier to the conversion of the Muslims. John of Damascus wrote against the iconoclasts or icon-breakers. When they were restored on the first Sunday in Lent in 843 by the Patriarch Methodius, that day became thereafter the Feast of Orthodoxy. The painting of icons became a tradition that required careful study, following strict rules and accompanied by discipline and prayer. The composer John Tavener, a convert to Orthodoxy, describes his music as resembling an icon, which, following a long tradition, he describes as a window into eternity.

Eastern Liturgies

Eastern monasticism developed with a much less hierarchical organization than in the West. At the same time the corporate prayer of Christians in the Eastern half of the Roman Empire developed a richness of mystical symbolism in the worship of the Liturgy, especially the great Liturgies of St James, St Basil and St John Chrysostom. 'Orthodoxy' means 'right worship', and to Orthodox Christians, Christianity focuses on participation in the Liturgy, unchanged for centuries, in an atmosphere of mystery. It does not even matter if the words are in a strange language; the worshippers feel they have been in the presence of God and surrounded by the saints and angels.

The Liturgy of St James

Apart from the eucharistic services found in the Apostolic Constitutions *and in Serapion, the oldest of the Eastern liturgies is probably that attributed (nominally) to St James. Once widely used in the Eastern Church, it is now only found in the Syrian Church.*

Almighty God, whose glory the heavens are telling, the earth his power, and the sea his might, and whose greatness all feeling and thinking creatures everywhere herald; to you belongs glory, honour, might, greatness and magnificence now and for ever, to the ages of ages, through Jesus Christ our Lord. Amen.

O Lord our God, the bread from heaven, the food of the whole universe, I have sinned against heaven and before you, and I am not worthy to receive your most holy mysteries. But, in your compassion, grant me by your grace uncondemned to partake of your holy body and your precious blood, to remission of sins and life eternal. Amen.

Let all mortal flesh keep silence
And with fear and trembling stand;
Ponder nothing earthly-minded,
For with blessing in his hand
Christ our God to earth descendeth,
Our full homage to demand . . .[13]

From glory to glory advancing, we praise thee, O Lord;
Thy name with the Father and Spirit be ever adored.
From strength unto strength we go forward on Zion's highway,
To appear before God in the city of infinite day.
Thanksgiving, and glory and worship, and blessing and love,
One heart and one song have the saints upon earth and above.
Ever more, O Lord, to thy servants thy presence be nigh;
Ever fit us by service on earth for thy service on high.[14]

Remember O Lord the souls of those who have kept the faith, both those whom we remember and those whom we remember not, and grant them rest in the land of the living, in the joy of paradise, whence all pain and grief have fled away, where the light of your countenance shines for ever; and guide in peace, O Lord, the end of our lives so as to be Christian and well-pleasing to you; gathering us around your throne, when you will and as you will, only without shame and sin; through your only-begotten Son our Lord and Saviour Jesus Christ. Amen.

Grant, almighty God, that the words, which we have heard this day with our outward ears, may through thy grace be so grafted inwardly in our hearts, that they may bring forth in us the fruit of good living, to the honour and praise of thy name; through Jesus Christ our Lord. Amen.[15]

The Liturgy of St Basil the Great

Saint Basil borrowed The Liturgy of St James *from the church in Antioch to use in Cappadocia, and revised and shortened it. The Liturgy of St Basil is used in Orthodox churches now only in Lent and on the eves of Christmas, Epiphany and 1 January.*

O Lord, the helper of the helpless, the hope of those who are past hope, the saviour of the tempest-tossed, the harbour of the voyagers, the physician of the sick; you know each soul and our prayer, each home and its need; become to each one of us what we most dearly require, receiving us all into your kingdom, making us children of light; and pour on us your peace and love, O Lord our God. Amen.

Complete and perfected, so far as in us lies, is the mystery of your redeeming work, Christ our God. We have made the memorial of your death, we have seen the symbol of your resurrection, we have been filled with your unending life, we have tasted your inexhaustible joy, of which, we pray, you will count us worthy in the age to come, through the grace of God the Father who has no beginning, and of your holy, good and life-giving Spirit, now and always and for ever and ever. Amen.

The Liturgy of St John Chrysostom

Saint Basil's Liturgy *spread to Constantinople and throughout the Eastern Church, until it was replaced for most purposes by the shorter* Liturgy *which bears the name of Chrysostom, though it was compiled by various hands at the end of the fourth century.*

The Trisagion:

Holy God,
holy and strong,
holy and immortal,
have mercy on us.

The Cherubic Hymn:

We who in a mystery represent the cherubim and sing the thrice-holy hymn to the life-giving Trinity, let us now lay aside all earthly cares, that we may receive the king of all, invisibly escorted by the hosts of angels. Alleluia, alleluia, alleluia.

Before Communion:

Let us pay attention: holy things for those who are holy.
Only one is holy, only one is Lord,
Jesus Christ, in the glory of God the Father. Amen.

Before receiving Communion:

A t your mystical supper, Son of God, today receive me as a partaker; I will not speak of the mystery to your enemies; I will not let my lips touch your body with a Judas-kiss; but like the thief I will acknowledge you: Remember me when you come in your kingdom.

After Communion:

W e have seen the true light, we have received the heavenly Spirit, we have found the true faith, we worship the undivided Trinity: for the Trinity has saved us.

Intercession at Great Complines:

B e mindful, O Lord, of your people here before you, and of those who are absent through age, sickness or infirmity. Care for the infants, guide the young, support the aged, encourage the faint-hearted, collect the scattered, and bring back the wandering to your fold. Travel with the voyagers, defend the widows, shield the orphans, deliver the captives, heal the sick. Succour all who are in tribulation, necessity or distress. Remember for good all those who love us, and those who hate us, and those who have desired us, unworthy as we are, to pray for them. And those whom we have forgotten, Lord, remember. Grant unto each according to your merciful loving-kindness, and your eternal love; through Jesus Christ our Lord. Amen.

> *A Troparion is a short hymn celebrating the saint or event commemorated on that day in the Liturgy or the Daily Office. Below is the Troparion for Pentecost Sunday:*

B lessed are you, O Christ our God; you revealed your wisdom to simple fisherfolk, sending down upon them your Holy Spirit, and through them you caught the whole world in your net. Glory to you, Lover of humankind. Amen.

A lmighty God, who hast given us grace at this time with one accord to make our common supplication unto thee; and hast promised that when two or three are gathered together in thy name thou will grant their requests: Fulfil now, O Lord, the desires and petitions of thy humble servants, as may be most expedient for them, granting us in this world knowledge of thy truth, and in the world to come, life everlasting. Amen.

Prayer of the Third Antiphon[16]

Armenia

Gregory the Illuminator (c. 240–332) became a Christian in Cappadocia and went to spread the faith in Armenia. St Nerses and Isaac the Great were among his successors. The Armenian Orthodox Church, spread across the USSR and Turkey, suffered persecution well into the twentieth century, and their numbers were decimated. Nevertheless Armenian Christians have made a leading contribution to the arts and sciences around the world. Most people whose surnames end with '-an' are of Armenian origin.

Keep us in peace O Christ our God, under the protection of your holy and venerable Cross; save us from enemies visible and invisible and count us worthy to glorify you with thanksgiving, with the Father and the Holy Spirit now and ever and world without end. Amen.

The Dismissal from the Armenian Liturgy

Nerses (d. *c.* 373)

Nerses, a direct descendent of Gregory the Illuminator, was educated in Cappadocia and became an official in the royal court. When his wife died, however, he became a priest and was elected Catholicos (the head of the Armenian Church). He undertook reforms and founded many orphanages and hospitals. He criticized the dissolute life of the king and was deposed and exiled. The next king restored him to his position but later poisoned him during a meal.

Lord Jesus Christ, keeper and preserver of all things, may your right hand guard us by day and by night, when we sit at home, and when we walk abroad, when we lie down and when we rise up, that we may be kept from all evil; and have mercy upon us sinners. Amen.

Our God, you open your hand, and fill all things living with plenteousness; to you we commit all those who are dear to us; watch over them, we pray, and provide all things needful for their souls and bodies, now and for evermore; through Jesus Christ our Lord. Amen.

Russia

Vladimir's ambassadors to Byzantium (c. 988)

When Prince Vladimir (956–1015) conquered Kiev in 988 he looked for a new religion to unify his new empire, as the Emperor Constantine had done. He sent his ambassadors to the centre of each of the religions they could find, to report back which was the most suitable. It is said that the Russian Ambassadors attended worship in the great Basilica of Holy Wisdom in Constantinople, and reported that it was so like being in heaven that without a doubt this must become the religion of Russia. Although the Russian and Greek Orthodox are one church, the Slavonic language and the vastness and beauty of Russia give to prayer among this naturally religious people a distinct flavour.

The Icon of the Holy Trinity by St Andrei Rublev (?1370–?1430)

This famous image represents the three visitors to the home of Abraham in Genesis 18. Sometimes they are referred to as three and sometimes as one, 'the Lord', so Christians saw the story as a parable of the three persons in one God. The house behind one represents the Father, with his home in heaven, and the tree behind another reminds us of Jesus who died on the tree of the cross. The meal which Abraham spread before them has become a Eucharist, and there is an empty space at the table. Many Christians have meditated on this and have been able to visualize the Trinity inviting the worshipper to join the circle of their eternal love.

The Russian Contakion of the Departed

The Christian combination of grief and hope in the face of bereavement is summed up in The Troparion and Hymn at Funerals, *sometimes known as* The Russian Contakion of the Departed:

Give rest, O Saviour Christ, to the souls of your servants with the saints; where sorrow and pain are no more, neither sighing, but life eternal. You only are immortal, our creator. We are all mortal, formed from the earth, and to the earth we shall return; for when you made us you so declared: 'Dust you are, and to dust you shall return.' All of us go down to the dust, and weeping over the grave we sing, alleluia, alleluia, alleluia! Amen.

Tychon of Zadonsk (1724–83)

A much-admired and popular monk of the eighteenth century, Tychon moved among the peasants with whom he identified and rejected the fashionable aping of European culture by the upper classes. He was convinced that if they would keep to the Russian tradition of wrestling with God in prayer, their nation would prosper under God.

Since you came into the world for all people, O Saviour, therefore you came for me, for I am one of the people. Since you came into the world to save sinners, therefore you came to save me, for I am one of the sinners. Since you came to find those who are lost, therefore you came to find me, for I am one of the lost. O Lord, O my God and Creator! I should have come to you as a transgressor of your law ... But I was so proud and so stubborn that you had to come to me. You had to come down to earth as a tiny baby, enduring poverty, discomfort and danger, in order to reach me. You had to walk dusty lanes, enduring insults and persecution, in order to reach me. You had to suffer and die on a cross, in order to reach me. Forgive me my stubborn pride that I have put you to such trouble and such pain on my behalf ...

'And thy mercy will follow me all the days of my life': so that, being preserved by your grace, I shall offer you thanksgiving, face to face, with your chosen ones, and shall sing, and praise, and glorify you, with the Eternal Father and the Holy Ghost, for ever and ever. Amen.[17]

How shall I repay your generosity, O my Lover? How shall I repay you for all you have given me? If I had died a thousand times for your sake, it would be as nothing. You are my Lord, and I am just clay and ashes, a worthless sinner, who deserves to die thousands upon thousands of deaths. How shall I thank you, who suffered dishonour, insult, mockery, scourging, and death for my sake? How shall I, who has nothing, reward you who gave everything? I have ruined my own soul, which was given by you. And now the only merit my soul possesses is that which you have bestowed, in your forgiving love. The only thing I can return to you is my prayer, that time I devote each day speaking and listening to you. Receive my prayer, as a tiny token of my enormous gratitude.[18]

Theophan the Recluse (nineteenth century)

In the nineteenth century Theophan taught in Russia about the Prayer of the Heart and the Jesus Prayer, as they had been understood in fourteenth-century Greece.

The practice of the Jesus Prayer is simple. Stand before the Lord with the attention in the heart, and call to him: 'Lord Jesus Christ, Son of God, have mercy on me!' The essential part of this is not in the words but in faith, contrition, and self-surrender to the Lord. With these feelings one can stand before the Lord even without any words, and it will still be prayer.[19]

The Way of a Pilgrim

A great impression on the spiritual life in Russia, and other countries since they were translated, has been made by The Way of a Pilgrim *and* The Pilgrim Pursues his Way, *anonymous works which were much influenced by the* Philokalia *of the Greek Church.* The Way of a Pilgrim *was written sometime between 1853 and 1861 and describes a journey though Russia, but at the same time a spiritual pilgrimage in the hesychast tradition. The writer seeks guidance from a* starets, *a Russian holy man, spiritual director and guide.*

He turned to the teaching of Nicephorus and read, 'If after a few attempts you do not succeed in reaching the realm of your heart in the way you have been taught, do what I am about to say, and by God's help you will find what you seek. The faculty of pronouncing words lies in the throat. Reject all other thoughts (you can do this if you will) and allow that faculty to repeat only the following words constantly, "Lord Jesus Christ, have mercy on me." Compel yourself to do it always. If you succeed for a time, then without a doubt your heart also will open to prayer. We know it from experience. There you have the teaching of the holy Fathers on such cases,' said my *starets*, 'and therefore you ought from today onwards to carry out my directions with confidence, and repeat the Prayer of Jesus as often as possible. Here is a rosary. Take it, and to start with say the Prayer three thousand times a day. Whether you are standing or sitting, walking or lying down, continually repeat "Lord Jesus Christ, have mercy on me." Say it quietly and without hurry, but without fail exactly three thousand times a day without deliberately increasing or diminishing the number. God will help you and by this means you will reach also the unceasing activity of the heart . . .

'Now I give you my permission to say your Prayer as often as you wish and as often as you can. Try to devote every moment you are awake to the Prayer, call on the Name of Jesus Christ without counting the number of times, and submit yourself humbly to the will of God, looking to him for help. I am sure he will not forsake you, and that he will lead you into the right path.'

Under this guidance I spent the whole summer in ceaseless oral prayer to Jesus Christ, and I felt absolute peace in my soul. During sleep I often dreamed that I was saying the Prayer. And during the day if I happened to meet anyone, all men without exception were as dear to me as if they had been my nearest relations. But I did not concern myself with them much. All my ideas were quite calmed of their own accord. I thought of nothing whatever but my Prayer, my mind tended to listen to it, and my heart began of itself to feel at times a certain warmth and pleasure. If I happened to go to church the lengthy service of the monastery seemed short to me, and no longer wearied me as it had in time past. My lonely hut seemed like a splendid palace, and I knew not how to thank God for having sent to me, a lost sinner, so wholesome a guide and master.[20]

Fyodr Dostoevsky (1820–81)

In The Brothers Karamazov *the novelist Dostoevsky creates a fictional character called Father Zosima, who nonetheless is a perfect picture of the typical Russian* starets *or holy man.*

Young man, do not forget to say your prayers. If your prayer is sincere, there will be every time you pray a new feeling containing an idea in it, an idea you did not know before, which will give you fresh courage; you will then understand that prayer is education. Remember also: every day and whenever you can repeat to yourself, O Lord, have mercy upon all who appear before thee today. For thousands of people leave life on this earth every hour and every moment and their souls stand before God – and how many of them depart this life in solitude, unknown to anyone, in anguish and sorrow that no one feels sorry for them and does not even care whether they live or die. And so from the other end of the earth your prayer, too, will perhaps rise up to God that his soul may rest in peace though you knew him not nor he you. How deeply touching it will be to his soul, standing in fear before God, to feel at that moment that he has someone to utter a prayer for him, that there is one human being on earth left who loves him. And God also will look upon you both more benignly, for if you have had so much pity on him, how much greater will God's pity be on you, for God is infinitely more merciful and more loving than you. And he will forgive him for your sake . . .

At some ideas you stand perplexed, especially at the sight of men's sins, asking yourself whether to combat it by force or by humble love. Always decide: 'I will combat it by humble love.' If you make up your mind about that once and for all, you may be able to conquer the whole world.[21]

John of Kronstadt (1829–1908)

John Ilyitch Sergieff was born to a poor peasant family amid the majestic beauty of the extreme northern province of Arkhangelsk. He went to a seminary in Siberia and, rejecting the idea of becoming a monk and missionary in Siberia, he married and was appointed to the church in Kronstadt, a naval base near St Petersburg, where he served for the remainder of his life. He became famous for his passionate preaching and his holy celebration of the liturgy, for his practical activity in finding work for the poor, and for his ministry of healing. So many people wanted him to hear their confessions that eventually he told them all to shout them out at the same time, in the belief that in that way nobody could hear anybody else's sins, but God would hear them all!

O Lord, our most gracious Redeemer and King, dwell and reign within us, take possession of us by your Spirit, and reign where you have the right to reign, and spread your kingdom throughout the world; through Jesus Christ our Lord. Amen.

W e thank you, Lord and Master, for teaching us how to pray simply and sincerely to you and for hearing us when we so call upon you. We thank you for saving us from our sins and sorrows, and for directing all our ways this day. Lead us ever onwards to yourself; for the sake of Jesus Christ our Lord and Saviour. Amen.

L ord! grant me a simple, kind, open, believing, loving and generous heart, worthy of being your dwelling place, O most gracious one.[22]

From My Life in Christ

Lord! Teach me to bestow charity willingly, kindly, joyfully, and to believe that by bestowing it I do not lose, but gain, infinitely more than that which I give. Turn my eyes away from hard-hearted people who do not sympathize with the poor, who meet poverty with indifference, who judge, reproach, brand it with shameful names, and weaken my heart, so that I may not do good, so that I, too, may harden my heart against poverty. O my Lord, how many such people we meet with! . . . Lord, grant that every charity I bestow may be profitable, and may not do harm! Lord, accept yourself charity in the person of your poor people. Lord, deign to help me to build a house for the poor in this town, concerning which I have already many times prayed to you, the all-merciful, almighty, most wise, wonderful![23]

From My Life in Christ

The Syrian Orthodox Churches

Christians in Syria, many of them speaking the same Aramaic language as Jesus spoke, laid much greater emphasis on the humanity of Jesus than the more philosophical Greeks. They produced fine spiritual writers like Ephraim the Syrian, but they were often excommunicated by the rest of the Church during controversies over ineffable questions of the personality of Jesus.

May God by whose will the world and all creation have their being, and who wills the life of us all – may Christ, the true bridegroom, seal your marriage in the truth of his love. As he finds joy in his Church, so may you find your happiness in one another; that your union may abound in love and your coming together in purity. May his angel guide you, may his peace reign between you, that in all things you may be guarded and guided, so that you may give thanks to the Father who will bless you, the Son who will rejoice in you, and the Spirit who will protect you, now and for ever and world without end. Amen.

Marriage blessing

Glory to the Father, who has woven garments of glory for the resurrection; worship to the Son, who was clothed in them at his rising; thanksgiving to the Spirit, who keeps them for all the Saints; one nature in three, to God be praise.

To God be glory; to the angels honour; to Satan confusion; to the cross reverence; to the Church exaltation; to the departed quickening; to the penitent acceptance; to the sick and infirm recovery and healing; and to the four quarters of the world great peace and tranquillity; and on us who are weak and sinful may the compassion and mercies of our God come and overshadow us.

Monday Vespers

'Gloria in excelsis' (before the fifth century)

This extremely ancient hymn is based on the song of the angels in Luke 2:14. A text of it is found in The Apostolic Constitutions, *a version of the Syrian Orthodox liturgy dating from about 380. The traditional translation begins, 'Glory be to God on high'. Here is a modern translation:*

Glory in the highest heaven,
peace to people on the earth,
praise and worship now be given
for this baby's wondrous birth.
Gloria in excelsis deo, gloria in excelsis deo.

Author of this wondrous story,
Lord our God, and heaven's King,
you are due our praise and glory,
you it is to whom we sing:
Gloria in excelsis deo, gloria in excelsis deo.

Jesus Christ, forever living,
Son of God and God's true Lamb,
hear our prayer, our sins forgiving,
seated by the great I AM:
Gloria in excelsis deo, gloria in excelsis deo.

Father, Son and Holy Spirit,
you are holy one in three,
earth's creator dwelling in it,
now and through eternity.
Gloria in excelsis deo, gloria in excelsis deo.[24]

Ephrem the Syrian (c. 306–73)

Ephraim, Ephraem or Ephrem are variant spellings of this author's name.
He was born at Nisibis in Mesopotamia, which he left on its capture by
the Persians. Then he moved to Edessa, an important Christian centre
then in the north of Syria, now called Sanliurfa and in Turkey. His output
of poems and prose won him the name 'lyre of the Holy Spirit', and was
influential not only on the Syrian Church but also in translation on the
Greek Church.

Receive, O Lord, in heaven above
Our prayers and supplications pure;
Give us a heart all full of love
And steady courage to endure.

Thy holy name our mouths confess,
Our tongues are harps to praise thy grace;
Forgive our sins and wickedness,
Who in this vigil seek thy face.

Let not our song become a sigh,
A wail of anguish and despair;
In loving-kindness, Lord most high,
Receive to-night our evening prayer.

O raise us in that day, that we
May sing, where all thy Saints adore,
Praise to thy Father, and to thee,
And to thy Spirit, evermore. Amen.[25]

I have gathered pearls together to make a crown for the Son
in place of my sinful body.
Receive my offering, although you lack nothing;
I offer it because of my own lack. Whiten my stains!
This crown is made of spiritual pearls,
which are set in love, not in gold,
clasped in a mounting of faith;
let our praise be the hands that offer it to God!

From Seven Hymns on the Faith

G lory to you, Lord Jesus Christ! You built your cross as a bridge over
death, so that departed souls might pass from the realm of death to
the realm of life. Glory to you! You put on the body of a mortal man and
made it the source of life for all mortal human beings. You are alive! Your
murderers handled your life like farmers: they sowed it like grain deep in
the earth, for it to spring up and raise with itself a multitude of men. We
offer you the great, universal sacrifice of our love, and pour out before
you our richest hymns and prayers. For you offered your cross to God as
a sacrifice in order to make us all rich.

Adapted from The Sermon on our Lord 3–4.9

Rabbula of Edessa (d. 435)

*Rabbula was the bishop of the important Syrian town of Edessa, and
translated the New Testament into Syriac (the Peshitta version). This
prayer was for penitents to use before confession.*

M y thoughts confuse and cloud my mind. I am in despair because
my guilt is vaster than the ocean and my sins more numerous than
the waves of the sea. When I remember how I have fallen, I tremble at
the thought of your justice. I dare not look upwards, because my sins
reach as high as the heavens. The mere sight of the earth is an accusation
to me, because my offences exceed the number of its inhabitants. Have
pity on me, Lord.

What will become of me, Lord? How will I explain myself when I must
confess that there is nothing to show for the talents you bestowed on me?
Have pity.

I am determined that the fire of hell will not consume me, since you
have given your body and blood to feed me.

I refuse to be carried off to eternal damnation, for you have clothed me
with the garment of baptism.

Grant me the dew of your grace, Lord. Forgive my sins. But above all,
may the glory belong to you.[26]

Joseph Hazzayah (eighth century)

*Joseph the Visionary lived in what is now Iraq. He was a convert from
Zoroastrianism, and wrote a systematic exposition of the stages of the
spiritual life.*

F ashion in me, Lord, eyes within my eyes, so that with new eyes, I may contemplate your divine sacrifice. Create in me a pure heart, so that, through the power of your Spirit, I may inhale your salvation.

The Nestorians

Nestorius was born near the River Euphrates and became Bishop of Constantinople. He declared that it was heretical to call the Virgin Mary Theotokos, the 'Bearer-of-God', and although it is uncertain what he actually believed, he was condemned himself as a heretic. It was alleged that he asserted that there were two distinct persons, human and divine, in the one Jesus Christ. At the Council of Ephesus in 431 an Egyptian monk called Shenoudi hurled a silver-bound copy of the Gospels and hit Nestorius in the chest, exclaiming, 'Thus I confute the heretic with the Scriptures.' Some Christians today use methods of biblical argument which are scarcely more subtle. Nestorius was deposed, but the bishops who supported him formed an East Syrian Nestorian Church, based principally in what is now Iran and Iraq, though for a while they had an important school of theology at Edessa. They survive as a small group of so-called 'Assyrian Christians' in Kurdistan, though their beliefs today are not noticeably heretical. Their liturgy contains some useful prayers.

L ord, we acknowledge your grace which created us; we praise your love which cares for us; and we worship your greatness which makes us glad, Lord of our death and of our life. Amen.

O Lord, make your tranquillity to dwell amongst us, and your peace to abide in our hearts. May our voices proclaim your truth, and may your cross be the guardian of our souls. Account us worthy, O Lord, with the boldness which comes from you, to offer to you by your grace a pure and holy prayer through Jesus Christ our Lord. Amen.

W orthy of praise from every mouth,
        of confession from every tongue,
of worship from every creature,
is your glorious name, Father, Son, and Holy Spirit:
you created the world in your grace
and by your compassion you saved the world.
Ten thousand times ten thousand bow down and adore your
        majesty, O God,

singing and praising without ceasing and saying,
Holy, holy, holy, Lord God of hosts;
heaven and earth are full of your praises;
hosanna in the highest.

W ith earnest prayer we ask for the angel of peace and mercy,
from you, O Lord.
Night and day throughout our life,
we ask for continued peace for your Church,
from you, O Lord.
We ask for continual love, which is the perfect bond of unity,
confirmed by the Holy Spirit,
from you, O Lord.
We ask for forgiveness of sins
and those things which help our lives and bring pleasure to you,
from you, O Lord.
We ask the mercy and compassion of the Lord
continually and at all times,
from you, O Lord.

Nestorian Evening Office

China

*The Nestorian Christians spread their mission as far as China, where
they remained until Marco Polo met them. They translated the 'Gloria
in Excelsis' into Chinese a thousand years before it was translated into
English. They appointed no indigenous Chinese bishops, and a totally
expatriate leadership seems to have led to their decline.*

The Xi'an tablet (781)

*Xi'an is the city at the Chinese end of the Great Silk Road, so it was the
place where Mediterranean traders and travellers entered China. Today
many Western visitors go there to see the terracotta warriors, but very few
turn aside to visit the old Shaanxi Provincial Museum and search out the
Nestorian tablet. This seven-foot-high stone is carved mostly in Chinese
characters but also at one side in Syriac lettering. It contains a brief*

summary of Christian teaching; a description of the arrival of the first Nestorian missionaries in Xi'an in 635 and their welcome by the Tang emperor; and a history of the church there until 780.

In the beginning, the whole universe was in an absolute silence: the earth was formless and empty; while the Spirit of God was hovering over and it began uttering words. By the magic power in these words, everything in the world was created . . .

At this moment, our merciful Trinity God gave up his power over the world and became flesh. He came to earth to lead people to find their way back to God . . . By trusting God and being obedient, they could come to perfection. If they would ask earnestly and praise him loudly, people could hear his voice speaking to them, then do as they were told. The way to glory would be stored up for them . . .

Dai Zong, Su Zong's successor [as Tang emperor], believed God more and kept his words in his mind. Every Christmas, he prayed to heaven and praised God for victory and the success of God's will. He shared his food with the people in the Church. Thank God for sacrificing the beauty of Jesus Christ for salvation of many more people, and thank Jesus for giving up his body to take away our sins . . .

The Indian Syrian Churches

The Syrian Christians of India, known as the Malabar Church, claim to have been founded by St Thomas the Apostle. Because of divisions in Syria at the time of Nestorius, some of them are called Nestorians and others Jacobites, though there is nothing unorthodox in their theology today. Some have been received into the Roman Catholic Communion, while keeping their own liturgy and customs, and are called Malankarese; others, called Mar Thoma Christians, have formed closer links with the Anglican Church. They use various versions of the Syrian liturgies, in Syriac mixed with the local languages.

Strengthen for your service, Lord, the hands which have been stretched out to receive your holy things, that they may daily bring forth a harvest of good works to your glory. Grant that the ears which have heard the sound of your songs may be closed to the voice of clamour and dispute; that the eyes which have seen your great love may behold the fulfilment they hope for; that the tongues which have sung your praises may ever speak the truth; that the feet which have trodden your courts may walk in the light; and the bodies which have tasted your risen body may be restored to newness of life. And may your great love remain with us for ever, so that we may return abundant praise to your Majesty. Amen and Amen.

The Malabar Liturgy[27]

The Coptic Orthodox Church

The Coptic Church claims direct descent from Simon of Cyrene, who carried the cross for Jesus, and St Mark, who brought the gospel to Alexandria. Origen, Clement of Alexandria and Athanasius were all members of the Egyptian or Coptic Church. The Abyssinian Church in Ethiopia is closely related to the Copts.

God of love, through your only-begotten Son you have given us a new commandment, that we should love one another in the same way as you loved us, the unworthy and wandering: give to us your servants, in all the time of our life on the earth, a mind forgetful of past ill will, a pure conscience, and a heart to love our neighbours; through the same your Son our Saviour Jesus Christ.

Coptic Liturgy of St Cyril (fifth century)

O sovereign and almighty Lord, bless all your people and all your flock. Give peace, your help, your love to us, your servants the sheep of your fold, that we may be united in the bond of peace and love, one body and one spirit, in one hope of our calling, in your divine and boundless love; for the sake of Jesus Christ, the great Shepherd of the sheep. Amen.

Remember again, Lord, those who have asked us to remember them in the time of our prayer and our supplication when we make our requests to you, O Lord our God. Give rest to those who have fallen asleep before us, heal speedily those who are sick, for you are the life of us all, and the hope of us all, and the deliverer of us all, and the raiser-up of us all, and to you we send thanksgiving up to the highest heaven, for ever and ever. Amen.

Cyril of Alexandria (d. 444)

Cyril became Patriarch of Alexandria and added to its fame as a centre of learning. He became involved in the controversies over the nature of Christ, and insisted that Christ was God from the beginning. He therefore defended the use of the term Theotokos, *'the God-bearer', to describe the Virgin Mary. In the light of the Gospel account of her flight into Egypt, the Coptic Church has always shown a strong Marian devotion.*

Hail, O Trinity, holy and mystical,
in answer to whose call we have all assembled
    in this church of Mary,
the mother of God.
Hail Mary, mother of God,
the whole world's treasure, commanding its reverence,
lamp that will never cease to burn,
crowning glory of the virgin state,
mainstay of orthodox faith,
temple that none can demolish,
place that encompasses him whom no place encompasses,
both mother and virgin.
Thanks to you, he who comes in the name of the Lord
is called blessed in the holy Gospels.
Hail to you: to him that is not bounded by any place
you have given a place in your holy, virginal womb.
Thanks to you, the Trinity is glorified and the cross called precious
and given honour throughout the world.
Thanks to you the heavens rejoice,
    the angels and archangels keep festival,
the evil spirits are put to flight.
Thanks to you the Devil, who had tempted us, fell from heaven
and we who had fallen were taken back again.
Thanks to you the whole creation, ensnared by idolatry,
came to the knowledge of the truth.
Thanks to you, baptism was given to believers,
and oil to make them glad.
Thanks to you, churches have been built throughout the world
and the pagan peoples are on their way to conversion.
And again, thanks to you, God's only Son shed his light
on those who were living in darkness,

in the shadow of death.
Thanks to you, the prophets prophesied
and the apostles preached salvation to the Gentiles.
Thanks to you, the dead return to life
    and kings govern their people,
for the sake of the Holy Trinity.
Much praised is Mary, but what human tongue
can adequately declare her worth?
She is a mother and she is still a virgin.
The wonder of it dazes me.
And yet, who ever heard of an architect that built a temple
and was forbidden to enter it?
Who can claim to be slighted
if God calls his servant to be his mother?
The whole world therefore rejoices.

Papyri

Documents on papyrus (papyri) are well preserved in the dry Egyptian desert, so among them we have a number of prayers dating from the third and fourth centuries.[28]

Morning Prayer

Helper of men who turn to you,
Light of men in the dark,
Creator of all that grows from seed,
Promoter of all spiritual growth,
have mercy, Lord, on me
and make me a temple fit for yourself.
Do not scan my transgressions too closely,
for if you are quick to notice my offences,
I shall not dare to appear before you.
In your great mercy,
in your boundless compassion,
wash away my sins, through Jesus Christ,
your only Child, the truly holy,
the chief of our souls' healers.

Through him may all glory be given you,
all power and honour and praise,
throughout the unending succession of ages. Amen.

God eternal, all that is hidden is known to you,
all that will come to pass you see before it happens;
it is not your will that sinners should die:
you want them to repent and be saved.
Look, then, on this poor thing,
pitiful, sinful, your servant.

May none of God's wonderful works
keep silence, night or morning.
Bright stars, high mountains, the depths of the seas,
sources of rushing rivers:
may all these break into song as we sing
to Father, Son and Holy Spirit.
May all the angels in the heavens reply:
Amen! Amen! Amen!
Power, praise, honour, eternal glory
to God, the only Giver of grace.
Amen! Amen! Amen!

Inscriptions

Below is a selection of epitaphs carved on gravestones and inscriptions from buildings, from all over the early Christian world. They tell us a great deal about the faith of the ordinary Christians of the time.[29]

Christ bid you welcome.
May your spirit be at peace in Christ.
In the name of Christ Jesus.

Remember your servant Chrysis
and give her a place where there is light,
a place where she may find refreshment,
in Abraham's bosom, Isaac's, Jacob's.

O God the all-powerful, existing always,
    now and in the past and in the future,
Jesus Christ, Son of the living God:
remember that your servant Zoneïne
has ceased her labours and is at rest.
She was devout and loved your commandments.
Make her, then, fit to follow the lead
of Michael, your holy archangel, into the light,
into the bosom of Abraham, Isaac and Jacob,
the holy patriarchs.
Yours are glory and power
throughout the ages. Amen.

L et me come in,' she said, 'Lord, into your house, Anointed.'
    Quickly she had what she asked:
        God's light is now her possession.
Zosime, my holy sister, fallen in time of great danger,
sees them that died with her, died in that same holy combat,
        and seeing,
wonders to find them about her, rejoices to have them beside her.
Spirit so bold in only a girl amazes the fathers.
Vying with one another to welcome her to their numbers,
each would be foremost, clasping, embracing, giving ovation.
Great is the kingdom she sees
        and splendid the sights that she savours,
great her rejoicing because her merits have had their reward.
Death she despised, like you, Paul; like you she holds the garland;
she kept her faith, as you did, and ran the race to the end.

N o justice so great as that of the God who is merciful!
    She was born of the Holy Spirit, born for Christ's glory.
That she may be able to join the blessed and enter his service,
I pray you, God, to whom all is possible,
let her enter the paradise where all is light.
He that set up this inscription, in fulfilment of a vow, honours
the Father and the Son.

To Lucifera, gentlest of wives, a gentle reception.
Her departure was a great grief to her husband.
This inscription was put up to remind the brethren, as they read it,
to pray to God for her soul.
May she attain purity and holiness and find a welcome with him.

Hail to you who still have the consolation
of seeing the light of our Father
who is in heaven.
Pray that we may have rest
in Christ Jesus, our Lord,
and in his life-giving Spirit.
May you receive the grace
to spend your lives well before you leave this world;
for even I, poor thing that I am,
having lived the short space of life allotted to me,
possess my share of what God has promised us.

A dead man's prayer to the living

Magus, you were only a child, and blameless:
now you are with the innocents.
It is a life you can never lose.
How pleased you were when the Church's mother welcomed you
as you left this world.
Not a sigh, then, not a tear:
breast and eye be still.

Our Lord Jesus Christ, God's Son and Word, lives here.
Nothing evil may come inside.

Holy the God of the angels: the resurrection is his doing.
Holy the God of the prophets: the redemption is his doing.
Holy the God of the apostles: forgiveness is his doing.

God is eternal light.
May I die at peace with my God.
Lord, stay by our door.

The temple Solomon built, you say, was fairer.
    – In art as fair, but faith makes this one rarer,
for there the Law's thick veil was wrapped about
what's here, being open, stands more plainly out.
His temple shone with veined metallic light:
this, dyed with Christ's own blood, must shine more bright.
Gems, gold and cedar-wood? In vain they muster:
the cross sheds here a far more holy lustre.
Better a single day in your courts than a thousand anywhere else.
I would rather prostrate myself on the threshold of my God's house
than live with sinners in their tents,
for the Lord loves mercy and truth.

The Uniat Churches

Uniat churches are those which are in communion with the Roman Catholic Church but keep an Eastern Orthodox style of worship in their own languages. Their clergy are often married, baptism of children is by immersion, and both bread and wine are given in Communion. There are more than a dozen Uniat churches, which have united with Rome at different periods; the largest group is in the Ukraine.

The Maronite Uniat Church

A group of Syrian Orthodox Christians who at the time of the Crusades united with the Roman Catholics, the Maronites claim to take their name from St Maro in the fourth or fifth century. They mostly live in Lebanon, though Maronite communities are also found in Israel, Syria, Cyprus, Alexandria and the USA. Their liturgy derives from that of Antioch.

Holy Father, keep us in your truth; holy Son, protect us under the wings of your cross; Holy Spirit, make us temples and dwelling places for your glory; grant us your peace all the days of our lives, O Lord.[30]

O most glorious and exalted Lord, you are glorified in the heights above by ministers of fire and spirit in most holy fashion, yet in your love you wished to be glorified by us on earth as well, so that you might exalt our mortal race and make us like supernal beings and share your authority over creation. Free us, Lord, in your compassion from whatever cares may hinder us from worshipping you, and teach us to seek the kingdom and its righteousness, in accordance with your holy life-giving commandments; and may we become worthy of that kingdom along with the saints who have done your will, and may we sing your praises.[31]

Celtic Christianity

For many centuries the Celtic race occupied and ruled most of Western Europe. Their religion seems to have included a recognition of sacredness in many places, in the events of nature and of daily life, and this continued when they were converted to Christianity. Many of their prayers and songs have been passed on by word of mouth and only written down in the past century. Anglo-Saxon invaders drove them into the Celtic fringe of Brittany, Cornwall, Wales, Ireland and Scotland, but heroic Celtic missionaries spread the Christian faith, among them St David in Wales, St Patrick in Ireland, St Ninian among the Picts and St Columba from Ireland to the Scots in Scotland, whence it was taken into northern England. The monasteries became great centres of learning, and distinctive artistic styles emerged in carved crosses and illuminated manuscripts. The practical nature of Celtic Christianity led to Pelagius, a British or Irish Celt of the fourth or fifth century (whose Gaelic name was probably Morgan), being branded a heretic by St Augustine. Yet Celtic Christianity has enjoyed a revival in the twentieth century (see the section later in this book).

> *The following poem, about an Irish monk and his white cat, is an illustration of the saying* Laborare est orare *('To work is to pray').*

I and Pangur Bán, my cat,
'Tis a like task we are at;
Hunting mice is his delight,
Hunting words I sit all night.

Better far than praise of men
'Tis to sit with book and pen;
Pangur bears me no ill will,
He too plies his simple skill.

'Tis a merry thing to see
At our tasks how glad are we,
When at home we sit and find
Entertainment to our mind.

Oftentimes a mouse will stray
In the hero Pangur's way;
Oftentimes my keen thought set
Takes a meaning in its net.

'Gainst the wall he sets his eye
Full and fierce and sharp and sly;
'Gainst the wall of knowledge I
All my little wisdom try.

When a mouse darts from its den,
O how glad is Pangur then!
O what gladness do I prove
When I solve the doubts I love.

So in peace our tasks we ply,
Pangur Bán, my cat, and I;
In our arts we find our bliss,
I have mine and he has his.

Practice every day has made
Pangur perfect in his trade;
I get wisdom day and night,
Turning darkness into light.

Ninth-century manuscript of Reichenau[1]

Hail to you, glorious Lord!
May chancel and church praise you,
May plain and hillside praise you,
May the three springs praise you,
Two higher than the wind and one above the earth,
May darkness and light praise you,
May the cedar and sweet fruit-tree praise you.
Abraham praised you, the founder of faith,
May life everlasting praise you,
May the birds and the bees praise you,

May the stubble and the grass praise you.
Aaron and Moses praised you,
May male and female praise you,
May the seven days and the stars praise you,
May the lower and upper air praise you,
May books and letters praise you,
May the fish in the river praise you,
May thought and action praise you,
May the sand and the earth praise you,
May all the good things created praise you,
And I too shall praise you, Lord of glory,
Hail to you, glorious Lord!

Anonymous, tenth or eleventh century[2]

T he Lord Jesus Christ be near you to defend you,
 within you to refresh you,
around you to protect you,
before you to guide you,
behind you to justify you,
above you to bless you.

Tenth century

S hall I abandon, O King of mysteries, the soft comforts of home?
 Shall I turn my back on my native land,
    and my face towards the sea?
Shall I put myself wholly at your mercy, without silver,
    without a horse,
without fame and honour?
Shall I throw myself wholly on you, without sword and shield,
without food and drink, without a bed to lie on?
Shall I say farewell to my beautiful land,
placing myself under your yoke?
Shall I pour out my heart to you,
    confessing my manifold sins and begging forgiveness,
tears streaming down my cheeks?
Shall I leave the prints of my knees on the sandy beach,
a record of my final prayer in my native land?
Shall I then suffer every kind of wound that the sea can inflict?
Shall I take my tiny coracle across the wide sparkling ocean?

O King of the glorious heaven,
    shall I go of my own choice upon the sea?
O Christ, will you help me on the wild waves?

'A Pilgrim's Plea', attributed to St Brendan[3]

I wish, ancient and eternal King, to live in a hidden hut
in the wilderness.
A narrow blue stream beside it, and a clear pool
for washing away my sins by the grace of the Holy Spirit.
A beautiful wood all around,
where birds of every kind of voice can grow up and find shelter.
Facing southwards to catch the sun,
with fertile soil around it suitable for every kind of plant.
And virtuous young men to join me,
    humble and eager to serve you.
Twelve young men – three fours, four threes, two sixes, six pairs –
willing to do every kind of work.
A lovely church, with a white linen cloth over the altar,
a home for you from heaven.
A Bible surrounded by four candles, one for each of the gospels.
A special hut in which to gather for meals,
    talking cheerfully as we eat,
without sarcasm, without boasting, without any evil words.
Hens laying eggs for us to eat, leeks growing near the stream,
salmon and trout to catch, and bees providing honey.
Enough food and clothing given by you,
and enough time to sit and pray to you.

'A Hermit's Desire', attributed to St Kevin[4]

Lord of my heart, give me vision to inspire me,
that, working or resting, I may always think of you.
    Lord of my heart, give me light to guide me,
that, at home or abroad, I may always walk in your way.
Lord of my heart, give me wisdom to direct me,
that, thinking or acting, I may always discern right from wrong.
Lord of my heart, give me courage to strengthen me,
that, amongst friends or enemies,
    I may always proclaim your justice.
Lord of my heart, give me trust to console me,

that, hungry or well-fed, I may always rely on your mercy.
Lord of my heart, save me from empty praise,
that I may always boast of you.
Lord of my heart, save me from worldly wealth,
that I may always look to the riches of heaven.
Lord of my heart, save me from military prowess,
that I may always seek your protection.
Lord of my heart, save me from vain knowledge,
that I may always study your word.
Lord of my heart, save me from unnatural pleasures,
that I may always find joy in your wonderful creation.
Heart of my own heart, whatever may befall me,
rule over my thoughts and feelings, my words and action.[5]

D eep peace of the running water to you,
Deep peace of the flowing air to you,
Deep peace of the quiet earth to you,
Deep peace of the shining stars to you,
Deep peace of the Son of Peace to you.

Celtic Blessing, source unknown

Patrick (*c.* 389–*c.* 461)

Born somewhere in western Britain and taken to Ireland as a slave, Patrick escaped to Gaul and returned as a missionary. His Confessions *and his* Letter to Coroticus *are the chief sources for his life. See also under 'Breastplates' below.*

M ay the strength of God pilot us,
May the power of God preserve us,
May the wisdom of God instruct us,
May the hand of God protect us,
May the way of God direct us,
May the shield of God defend us,
May the host of God guard us against the snares of evil
and the temptations of the world.

May your angels, holy Son,
Guard our homes when day is done,
When at peace, our sleep is best:
Bid them watch us while we rest.

Prince of everything that is,
High Priest of the mysteries,
Let your angels, God supreme,
Tell us truth dressed as a dream.

May no terror and no fright
Spoil our slumber in the night;
Free from care our eyelids close;
Spirit, give us prompt repose.

We have laboured through the day:
Lift our burdens when we pray,
Then our souls in safety keep,
That our sleep be soft and deep.

'Evening Prayer', attributed to St Patrick[6]

Columbanus (*c.* 550–615)

Saint Columbanus was an Irish missionary to Gaul. He established monasteries in Burgundy, and the strict Monastic Rule *he wrote for them shows what the Celtic customs were, the continued use of which he defended at Rome and at a Gallican synod. His monks were expelled from Burgundy for criticising the royal court. They moved to Bregenz and then to Bobbio in north Italy. This became a great centre of Irish learning, and preserved many ancient documents, including the* Bobbio Missal *which shows the Irish way of worshipping in and around the eighth century.*

Grant me, O Lord, the lamp of love which never grows dim, that it may shine in me and warm my heart, and give light to others through my love for them, and by its brightness we may have a vision of the Holy City where the true and inextinguishable light shines, Jesus Christ our Lord. Amen.

I beg you, most loving Saviour, to reveal yourself to us, that knowing you we may desire you, that desiring you we may love you, that loving you we may ever hold you in our thoughts.[7]

O Lord God, destroy and root out whatever the Adversary plants in me, that with my sins destroyed you may sow understanding and good work in my mouth and heart; so that in act and in truth I may serve only you and know how to fulfil the commandments of Christ and to seek yourself. Give me memory, give me love, give me chastity, give me faith, give me all things which you know belong to the profit of my soul. O Lord, work good in me, and provide me with what you know that I need. Amen.[8]

Columba (*c.* 521–97)

Columcille (to give the Gaelic form of his name) was a member of the Irish nobility who was ordained a priest. He established several churches and monasteries in his native land. He went to Scotland (some say in penance because he had killed a man in some inter-tribal strife) and settled on Iona, the first island he came to where he could no longer look back and see Ireland. Here he established a community living a simple life. Missionaries were trained there who carried the gospel to the Scots and later into Northumbria. A visit to Iona today is not complete without walking to the isolated cell which Columba built himself, where he could meditate with only the sound of the sea and the wind and the cry of the sea-birds for company.

Almighty Father, Son and Holy Spirit, eternal ever-blessed gracious God; to me the least of saints, to me allow that I may keep a door in paradise. That I may keep even the smallest, the furthest, the darkest, coldest door, the door that is least used, the stiffest door. If so it but be in your house, O God, if so be that I can see your glory even from afar, and hear your voice O God, and know that I am with you, you O God, through Jesus Christ our Lord. Amen.

Lord, be a bright flame before me,
be a guiding star above me,
be a smooth path below me,
be a kindly shepherd behind me,
today and for evermore. Amen.

Alone with none but thee, my God,
I journey on my way.
What need I fear, when thou art near

O king of night and day?
More safe am I within thy hand
Than if a host did round me stand.

Translator unknown

Breastplates

There are several Celtic Lorica *or 'breastplate' prayers, taking the image of the armour of God from Ephesians 6:11–18. This, which is called 'St Patrick's Breastplate' or 'The Deer's Cry', is actually from the eighth century, several hundred years after St Patrick. This translation by Mrs C. F. Alexander is to be found in many hymnals.*

I bind this day to me for ever,
by power of faith, Christ's incarnation,
his baptism in the Jordan river,
his death on cross for my salvation:
his bursting from the spicèd tomb,
his riding up the heavenly way,
his coming at the day of doom,
I bind unto myself today . . .

I bind unto myself today
the power of God to hold and lead,
his eye to watch, his might to stay,
his ear to hearken to my need.
The wisdom of my God to teach,
his hand to guide, his shield to ward,
the word of God to give me speech,
his heavenly host to be my guard . . .

Christ be with me, Christ within me,
Christ behind me, Christ before me,
Christ beside me, Christ to win me,
Christ to comfort and restore me,
Christ beneath me, Christ above me,
Christ in quiet, Christ in danger,
Christ in hearts of all that love me,
Christ in mouth of friend and stranger.

I bind unto myself the name,
the strong name of the Trinity,
by invocation of the same,
the three in one, and one in three,
of whom all nature hath creation,
eternal Father, Spirit, Word.
Praise to the Lord of my salvation:
salvation is of Christ the Lord.

The Religious Songs of Connacht

*This collection was first published in 1906 by Douglas Hyde (1860–1949),
an Anglican who was the founder and president of the Gaelic League, and
the first President of independent Ireland (1938–45). The extracts below
are taken from the 1972 Irish University Press edition.*

O Patrick in the paradise
    Of God on high,
Who lookest on the poor man
        With a gracious eye,
See me come before thee
        Who am weak and bare,
O help me into Paradise
        To find thee there.[9]

May we lie down with God, and may God lie with us.
    A Person from God with us. The two hands of God with us.
The Three Marys with us.
God and Columcille with us.
Is it not strong the fortress in which we are!
Between Mary and her Son,
Brigit and her mantle,
Michael and his shield,
God and His right hand,
Going between us and every evil.
May we not lie down with evil,
May evil not lie down with us.
The protection of the Three Trees,
The tree of the Cross,

The tree of the blood,
The tree on which Christ was hanged
And from which He rose again alive.
O King of the *cathair* in heaven,
Keep the spirit of my soul
From the real-temptations of the adversary.

The 'Bed Confession'[10]

Breton

The Celtic people in the British Isles were known as Britons; in Gaul they were the Bretons who were pushed west into the Brittany peninsula.

Dear God, be good to me;
the sea is so large,
and my boat is so small.

Prayer of a Breton fisherman

Bridget (d. *c.* 523)

Little is known with certainty about the life of St Bridget, Bride or Brigid, as her name is variously spelt. The commonest tradition is that she was born near Dundalk to parents who had been baptized by St Patrick and founded Ireland's first nunnery at Cill-Dara, 'the Church of the Oak', now known as Kildare. One version even suggests that she was consecrated as a bishop. She is greatly venerated as 'the Mary of the Gael', though some of the devotion given to a pagan goddess with a similar name may have been transferred to the Christian saint.

We implore you, by the memory of your Cross's hallowed and most bitter anguish, make us fear you, make us love you, O Christ. Amen.

Carmina Gadelica

Alexander Carmichael was a Gaelic speaker who travelled extensively in the Western Highlands and the islands of the Inner and Outer Hebrides for the Customs and Excise Department. Between 1855 and 1899 he collected songs and prayers which were recited to him, and he published them with fascinating notes on the background as Ortha na Gaidheal/Carmina Gadelica.[11]

G od with me lying down,
   God with me rising up,
God with me in each ray of light,
Nor I a ray of joy without Him,
     Nor one ray without Him.
Christ with me sleeping,
Christ with me waking,
Christ with me watching,
Every day and night,
     Each day and night
God with me protecting,
The Lord with me directing,
The Spirit with me strengthening,
For ever and for evermore,
     Ever and evermore, Amen.
       Chief of chiefs, Amen.

       Vol. I, No. 2, taken down in 1866 from Mary Macrae on the Isle of Harris.

The Death Blessing

G od, omit not this woman from Thy covenant,
   And the many evils which she in the body committed,
That she cannot this night enumerate.
     The many evils that she in the body committed,
     that she cannot this night enumerate.
Be this soul on Thine own arm, O Christ,
Thou King of the City of Heaven,
And since Thine it was, O Christ, to buy the soul,
At the time of the balancing of the beam,
At the time of the bringing of judgment,
Be it now on Thine own right hand,
     oh! On Thine own right hand.
And be the holy Michael, king of angels,
Coming to meet the soul,
And leading it home
To the heaven of the Son of God.
     The Holy Michael, high king of angels,

Coming to meet the soul,
And leading it home
To the heaven of the Son of God.

Vol. I, No. 52

A prayer before travelling

L ife be in my speech,
Sense in what I say,
The bloom of cherries on my lips,
Till I come back again.

The love Christ Jesus gave
Be filling every heart for me,
The love Christ Jesus gave
Filling me for every one.

Traversing corries, traversing forests,
Traversing valleys long and wild.
The fair white Mary still uphold me,
The Shepherd Jesu be my shield,
The fair white Mary still uphold me,
The Shepherd Jesu be my shield.

Vol. I, No. 116

B e the peace of the Spirit mine this night,
Be the peace of the Son mine this night,
Be the peace of the Father mine this night,
The peace of all peace be mine this night,
Each morning and evening of my life. Amen.

Vol. III, No. 330

Dimma (seventh century)

The prayers of this obscure Irish monk were included in many early prayer collections.

For a sick brother

O Lord, holy Father, creator of the universe, author of its laws, you can bring the dead back to life, and heal those who are sick. We pray for our sick brother that he may feel your hand upon him, renewing his body and refreshing his soul. Show to him the affection in which you hold all your creatures.[12]

For a sinful brother

O God, you do not wish any sinner to die, but want all people to turn from their sins and live. We pray for our sinful brother, forgiving all his wrong-doing and turning his heart towards you. By his own merit he deserves only punishment, but in your mercy we pray that you will bestow upon him eternal life.[13]

For a brother in despair

O God, you rule over your creation with tenderness, offering fresh hope in the midst of the most terrible misery. We pray for our brother whose soul is blackened by despair, infusing him with the pure light of your love. As he curses the day he was born and yearns for oblivion, reveal to him the miracle of new birth which shall prepare him for the joys of heaven.[14]

Welsh Prayers (source unknown)

Grant us, O God, your protection; and in your protection, strength; and in strength, understanding; and in understanding, knowledge; and in knowledge, the knowledge of justice; and in the knowledge of justice, the love of justice; and in that love, the love of existence; and in the love of existence, the love of God, God and all goodness. Amen.

God the Sender, send us. God the Sent, come with us. God the Strengthener of those who go, empower us, that we may go with you and find those who will call you Father, Son and Holy Spirit. Amen.

The Mozarabic Sacramentary

This ancient Spanish liturgy is believed to retain traces of early Celtic worship – the Mozarabs were Christian subjects of a Moorish king.

As watchmen wait for the morning, so do our souls long for you, O Christ. Come with the dawning of the day, and make yourself known to us in the breaking of bread; for you are our God for ever and ever. Amen.

Grant us, O Lord, to pass this day in gladness and peace, without stumbling and without stain; that reaching the eventide victorious over all temptation, we may praise you, the eternal God, blessed, and governing all things, for ever and ever. Amen.

Jesus, our Master, meet us while we walk in the way, and long to reach the heavenly country; so that, following your light we may keep the way of righteousness, and never wander away into the darkness of this world's night, while you, who are the Way, the Truth, and the Life, are shining within us; for your own name's sake. Amen.

Look upon us and hear us, O Lord our God; and assist those endeavours to please you which you yourself have granted to us; as you have given the first act of will, so give the completion of the work; grant that we may be able to finish what you have granted us to wish to begin; through Jesus Christ our Lord. Amen.

O God, by making the evening to succeed the day, you have bestowed the gift of repose on human weakness. Grant, we pray, that while we enjoy those timely blessings we may acknowledge him from whom they come, Jesus Christ our Lord. Amen.

O God, by your great love for us you have reconciled earth to heaven through your only-begotten Son: grant that we, who by the darkness of our sins are turned aside from love for each other, may be filled with your Spirit shed abroad in us, and embrace our friends in you and our enemies for your sake; through Jesus Christ our Lord. Amen.

O God, you are peace everlasting, whose chosen reward is the gift of peace, and you have taught us that the peace-makers are your children. Pour your peace into our souls, that everything discordant may utterly vanish, and all that makes for peace be sweet to us for ever; through Jesus Christ our Lord. Amen.

John Scotus Eriugena (c. 810–c. 877)

John, an Irishman, travelled to Paris, where he was made head of the palace school. He translated the writings of Dionysius, Maximus the Confessor and Gregory of Nyssa into Latin, drawing the attention of the Western Church to the Eastern tradition of prayer, which had always been familiar to the Celts. He was an original thinker, and taught that God created the world through 'Platonic ideas' and that the whole world will in the end return to God. He also argued that for God, evil is non-existent, so that if sin is created by human beings, it carries its own punishment in itself. There is a tradition that he was later invited by King Alfred to become Abbot of Malmesbury.

O everlasting essence of things beyond space and time, and yet within them; you transcend yet pervade all things: manifest yourself to us, who feel after you, seeking you in the shadows of our ignorance. Stretch forth your hand to help us, for we cannot come to you without your aid. Reveal yourself to us, for we seek nothing but you; through Jesus Christ our Lord. Amen.

Anglo-Saxon Christianity

The Romano-British inhabitants of what would later be called England included a number of Christians, traces of whom are to be found in the mosaic face of Christ found at Hinton St Mary in Dorset; the legends of King Arthur; and at Lullingstone in Kent, which has the remains of the second oldest building in the world to be constructed specifically for Christian worship (after Dura-Europos in Mesopotamia). But Christian prayer was driven into the Celtic West by the invasion of the Anglo-Saxons.

Augustine of Canterbury (d. 604 or 605)

The young priest, Gregory, decided to become a missionary to the heathen English when he saw some fair-haired boys for sale in the slave market in Rome and made the famous pun, 'Not Angles but Angels'. Being made Pope prevented him from going in person, so he sent his friend Augustine to Canterbury in his place to convert the English, writing with very practical advice about how the worship in the new Ecclesia Anglicana was to be organized. The missionaries wanted to turn back when they heard what fierce savages the English were, but the Pope encouraged them. Augustine went first to the heathen king of Kent in his capital city of Canterbury, but lived outside the walls until the king was converted. Queen Bertha was a French Christian and had a bishop as her chaplain, but they had made no headway in converting the Anglo-Saxons until Augustine arrived. Soon King Ethelbert was baptized in St Martin's Church, and Augustine built the first cathedral inside the city. Christianity then quickly spread across south-east England, but Augustine failed to come to an agreement with the Celtic Christians beyond the borders of the Saxon lands. The following extract is a letter from Gregory to Augustine.

Augustine, my brother, you know the way we conduct services here in Rome; you were brought up with it. But if you find anything in the customs of the church in Gaul, or any other church, that would be more acceptable to God, make a careful selection from them, and teach what you can learn from other churches to the English, who are still young in the faith. We are not to love customs because they are associated with particular places, rather, we should love places because they have good customs there. So choose from every church those things which are devout, religious and good, and when you have combined them into a single service book, let the minds of the English people get used to it gradually.

From Bede's History of the English Church and People I.27

The Venerable Bede (672/3–735)

A monk of Wearmouth, he transferred to Jarrow, where he wrote the history of his abbey and expositions of the Bible which gave him a great reputation among his contemporaries. He also wrote The History of the English Church and People, *the major source for the events and personalities of the period when the Anglo-Saxon invaders were being converted.*

Good Jesus, as you have graciously allowed me here to drink in the sweetness of your word, so at the last, I pray, you will bring me into your presence, that I may listen to your voice which is the source of all wisdom, and watch your face for ever.[1]

Lord God, open my heart and illuminate it with the grace of your Holy Spirit. By this grace may I always seek to do what is pleasing to you; direct my thoughts and feelings so that I may at last come to the unending joys of heaven. Thus on earth may I keep your commandments, and so be worthy of your everlasting reward.

May your Spirit, O Christ, lead me in the right way, keeping me safe from all forces of evil and destruction. And, free from all malice, may I search diligently in your Holy Word to discover with the eyes of my mind your commandments. Finally, give me the strength of will to put those commandments into practice through all the days of my life.

O Christ, our Morning Star, Splendour of Light Eternal, shining with the glory of the rainbow, come and waken us from the greyness of our apathy and renew in us your gift of hope.

Caedmon (d. *c.* 680)

Bede reports that an attempt to reconcile the divergent traditions of Celtic and Roman Christianity was made at the Synod of Whitby in 664. Abbess Hilda seems to have been a powerful woman well able to issue orders to bishops, but she used her influence to persuade her fellow Celts to adopt the Roman customs. She also recognized the talent of Caedmon, a labourer in her Abbey, who received in a vision the gift of composing verses in praise of God. He thus became the first English Christian poet.

Endless praise now be given
    to God, King of heaven;
in his wisdom and might,
        and his works, we delight.
The great Father of glory
        began his strange story
in wonderful ways
        on the first of all days,
            and of all that came later
            he is the Creator!

First a roof he erected
    which safely protected
the children of earth –
    thus the heavens had their birth.
By the might of his hand
        he spread out the dry land –
a firm place fashioned well
        for the living to dwell.
            Endless praise now be given
            to God, King of heaven!²

Egbert of York (d. 766)

Egbert, a member of the Northumbrian royal family, was advised by Bede to apply to the Pope to be made Archbishop of York. When his own brother became King he was able to carry out many reforms, and founded a cathedral school where he himself taught theology, and Alcuin was one of his pupils. Egbert's Pontifical is a service book revealing details of how the Anglo-Saxon Church worshipped, and is a source for the English coronation service.

Lord Jesus Christ, you chose your apostles that they might preside over us as teachers; so also may you teach doctrine to our bishops, who occupy the place of your apostles, and bless and instruct them, that they may preserve their lives unharmed and pure into eternity. Amen.

Look down from heaven, O Lord, upon your flock and your lambs; bless their bodies and their souls; and grant that those who have received the sign of the cross on their foreheads at baptism, may be shown to belong to you on the day of judgement; through Jesus Christ our Lord. Amen.

'The Dream of the Rood' (c. 780)

'Rood' is the old English word for the cross. This poem is believed to be by Cynewulf, a poet in Northumbria.

Hear me! I tell of a marvellous dream
At midnight when men were all sleeping.
I dreamed I saw a tree most strange,
Lifted aloft and girded with light;
For bathed in gold was all that beacon.
At the foot of the cross gems flamed in beauty:
Five shone on the shoulder-beam.
Angels of the Lord, eternally lovely,
Watched over it; that was no wicked tree . . .
A long time I lay there and I looked
At the cross of our Saviour in sadness,
Till that wood of wonder spoke these words: –
'In the years of yore, that I yet remember,
On the forest's fringe they felled me.

Struck from my stem, the stern foes took me
And shaped me for a shameful show.
Bad men then bade me bear their felons.
So on their shoulders they shifted me,
Hoisted me on a hill and held me fast.
Then I beheld the Master of mankind
Coming with courage as if to climb me.
Since God forbad, I could not bend or break.
Earth trembled. Might was mine
To fell all his foes, but I stood fast.
The almighty God laid his garments by
And climbed the cross, constant in courage,
Fearless before folk, all souls to free . . .
I, the rood upreared, raised the royal One,
Lifted the Lord of heaven and dared not bow' . . .

May the Lord be my friend,
Who once on earth endured on the gallows-tree
Suffered here for the sins of men.
He has redeemed us, he has given us life
And a home in Heaven. Hope was renewed
With bliss and blessing for those who had been through burning.
The Son was successful in that expedition,
Mighty in victory, when with a mass,
A great crowd of souls came to God's kingdom.
The Almighty Ruler, to joy among the angels
And all the saints, who in heaven already
Lived in glory. Then the Lord,
Almighty God, came home to his own land.

The Book of Cerne (eighth century)

The Book of Cerne *is a collection of private prayers from the eighth century,
belonging to the Abbey of Cerne in Dorset. Many of the prayers are Celtic in
origin, although the book belonged to the Anglo-Saxon Bishop Aedelwald.*

May the right hand of the Lord keep us ever until our old age, the
grace of Christ continually defend us from the enemy. O Lord,
direct our hearts in the way of peace; through Jesus Christ our Lord. Amen.

May God the Father bless us; may Christ take care of us; the Holy Spirit enlighten us all the days of our life. The Lord be our defender and keeper of body and soul, both now and for ever, to the ages of ages. Amen.[3]

King Alfred the Great of Wessex (849–99)

By his defeat of the Danes, King Alfred the Great enabled the Christian kingdom in England to survive. A considerable scholar himself, he wrote poetry and, with the help of his advisers, translated works by Gregory the Great, Boethius and St Augustine from Latin into English. He had some success in founding and reforming monasteries and laid the foundations for the later establishment of new dioceses.

We pray to you, O Lord, who are the supreme Truth, and all truth is from you. We beseech you, O Lord, who are the highest Wisdom, and all the wise depend on you for their wisdom. You are the supreme Joy, and all who are happy owe it to you. You are the highest Good, and all goodness comes from you. You are the Light of minds, and all receive their understanding from you. We love you – indeed we love you above all things. We seek you, follow you, and are prepared to serve you. We desire to dwell under your power, for you are the King of all. Amen.

Lord God almighty, I pray you for your great mercy, and by the token of the holy rood, guide me to your will, to my soul's need, better than I can myself; and shield me against my foes, seen and unseen; and teach me to do your will, that I may love you inwardly before all things with a clean mind and a clean body. For you are my maker and redeemer, my help, my comfort, my trust and my hope. Praise and glory be to you now, ever and ever, world without end. Amen.

Dunstan (c. 908–88)

A reforming Abbot of Glastonbury in a time when monastic life had almost died out in England, he made it a centre of learning. He himself was a famous musician, metal-worker and illuminator of manuscripts. (In the margin of one of them he drew a tiny portrait of himself at prayer.) He became a minister to one king, was banished by the next, and under King Edgar was made Bishop of Worcester, then Bishop of London, and subsequently Archbishop of Canterbury. Together with King Edgar, Ethelwold, Bishop of Winchester, and Oswald, Archbishop of York, Dunstan reformed both church and state. Dunstan and Oswald ensured that Edgar was succeeded by King Edward the Martyr, who continued his predecessor's policies.

O Lord; O King, resplendent on the citadel of heaven,
   all hail continually;
and of your clemency upon your people still have mercy.
Lord, whom the hosts of cherubim in songs and hymns
with praise continually proclaim, upon us eternally have mercy.
The armies aloft, O Lord, sing high praise to you;
those to whom the seraphim reply, 'have mercy.'
O Christ, enthroned as king above,
whom the nine orders of angels in their beauty
        praise without ceasing,
upon us, your servants, ever have mercy.
O Christ, hymned by your one and only church
        throughout the world,
to whom the sun, and moon, and stars, the land and sea,
ever do service, have mercy.
O Christ, those holy ones, the heirs of the eternal country,
one and all with utter joy proclaim you in a most worthy strain:
have mercy upon us.
O Lord, O gentle son of Mary free;
O King of kings, blessed redeemer;
upon those who have been ransomed from the power of death,
by your own blood, ever have mercy.
O noblest unbegotten, yet begotten Son, having no beginning,
yet without effort (in the weakness of God) excelling all things,
upon this your people in your pity, Lord have mercy.
O sun of righteousness, in all unclouded glory,
        supreme dispenser of justice,
in that great day when you strictly judge all nations,
we earnestly beseech you, upon this your people,
who here stand before your presence,
in your pity, Lord, then have mercy on us.

Ethelwold (*c.* 908–84)

Ethelwold or Aethelwold was a monk at Glastonbury who became Abbot of Abingdon and finally Bishop of Winchester. He worked with Dunstan and Oswald to reform English Christianity after the depredations of the Danish invasions, and compiled the rule for monks known as the Regularis Concordia.

A prayer for an individual, for instance on a birthday:

O pen your heavens, O Lord, that thence your gifts may descend to him. Put forth your hand and touch his head. May he feel the touch of your hand, and receive the joy of the Holy Spirit, that he may remain blessed for evermore. Amen.

T he right hand of the Lord preserve me always to old age! The grace of Christ perpetually defend me from the enemy! Direct, Lord, my heart into the way of peace. Lord God, haste to deliver me, make haste to help me, O Lord. Amen.

Wulfstan (*c.* 1009–95)

Wulfstan or Wulstan was for twenty-five years a member of a monastery at Worcester, where he was so admired for his humility that he was elected Bishop by popular acclaim. He was so humble, however, that it was hard to persuade him to accept the post. Once enthroned he administered the diocese with great efficiency, and helped Archbishop Lanfranc to suppress the slave trade between England and Ireland. He was the only Saxon bishop whom William the Conqueror allowed to remain in place when he appointed Norman bishops to the other sees. Confusingly, an earlier Bishop of Worcester was also called Wulfstan; he combined the post with that of Archbishop of York, was a brilliant writer, and died in 1023. The following prayer was in an Anglo-Saxon prayer book carried around by the later Wulfstan.

O Lord, have mercy on me a sinner. Stablish my heart in your will. Grant me true repentance for my sins: right faith and true charity, patience in adversity and moderation in prosperity. Help me and all my friends and kinsmen, all who desire and trust in my prayers. Show mercy to all who have done me good and shown me the knowledge of good, and grant everlasting forgiveness to all who have spoken or thought evil against me. To you, my God, and to all your holy ones, be praise and glory for ever for all the benefits you have given me, and for all your mercies to me a sinner: for your name's sake. Amen.

The Medieval West

From the sixth to the twelfth centuries, following the collapse of the Roman Empire, it was the Christian Church which kept civilization and learning alive in Europe through what are sometimes called the Dark Ages.

Venantius Fortunatus (*c.* 525–*c.* 600)

A worldly man in his early years and a competent versifier in Latin, Fortunatus was brought up in Ravenna, where he would have been familiar with triumphal processions, each body of soldiers led by a banner or vexillum. At Ravenna Fortunatus was healed of an eye disease by some oil from a shrine to St Martin, so he showed his gratitude by a pilgrimage to the saint's tomb at Tours. He settled nearby at Poitiers, and when the Emperor gave the church there some fragments from the true cross he was stirred to write two hymns which take their place at the zenith of medieval Latin poetry. Fortunatus was then ordained priest and spent the last ten years of his life as Bishop of Poitiers.

Vexilla Regis Prodeunt

Abroad the regal banners fly,
Now shines the Cross's mystery;
Upon it life did death endure,
And yet by death did life procure.

That which the prophet-king of old
Hath in mysterious verse foretold,
Is now accomplished, whilst we see
God ruling nations from a tree.

Blest Tree, whose happy branches bore
The wealth that did the world restore;
The beam that did that body weigh
Which raised up hell's expected prey.

Hail Cross, our hope; on thee we call,
Who keep this mournful festival;
Grant to the just increase of grace,
And every sinner's crimes efface.

Blest Trinity, we praises sing
To thee, from whom all graces spring;
Celestial crowns on those bestow
Who conquer by the Cross below.[1]

Pange Lingua

S ing, my tongue, the glorious battle,
    Sing the ending of the fray;
Now above the Cross, the trophy,
Sound the loud triumphant lay:
Tell how Christ, the world's redeemer,
As a victim won the day.

God in pity saw man fallen,
Shamed and sunk in misery,
When he fell on death by tasting
Fruit of the forbidden tree;
Then another tree was chosen
Which the world from death should free . . .

Faithful Cross! above all other,
One and only noble tree!
None in foliage, none in blossom,
None in fruit thy peer may be;
Sweetest wood and sweetest iron!
Sweetest weight is hung on thee.

Bend thy boughs, O tree of glory!
Thy relaxing sinews bend;
For awhile the ancient rigour
That thy birth bestowed, suspend;

And the king of heavenly beauty
On thy bosom gently tend . . .[2]

Gregory the Great (540–604)

*Gregory was the son of a senator and became Prefect of the City of Rome,
before giving away his inherited wealth to charitable projects, including
the founding of the monastery of St Andrew in Rome, in which he himself
became a monk. He it was who sent Augustine to Canterbury to convert
the Angles of south-east England, after he had been elected Pope. He was
an able administrator, and made peace with the invading Lombards. His
instructions on the pastoral work of a bishop were highly regarded throughout the Middle Ages and were translated into English by King Alfred. He
was involved in drawing up the* Gregorian Sacramentary *(see below) and
in compiling the plainsong of the church services, which became known
as Gregorian Chant. Gregory asserted the authority of the Pope over the
other patriarchs; but he was a humble man and chose the title of 'servant
of the servants of God'.*

Lo, fainter now lie spread the shades of night,
and upward spread the trembling gleams of morn;
suppliant we bend before the Lord of light,
and pray at early dawn,
that this sweet charity may all our sin
forgive, and make our miseries to cease;
may grant us health, grant us the gift divine
of everlasting peace.
Father supreme, this grace on us confer;
and thou, O Son by an eternal birth!
With thee, coequal Spirit, comforter!
whose glory fills the earth.

Translator unknown

The Gelasian Sacramentary (fifth century)

*A sacramentary is a collection of prayers for use by priests when celebrating
the sacrament of the Mass.* The Gelasian Sacramentary, *although its
earliest manuscript dates from the eighth century, is probably the oldest,
being ascribed to the reign of Pope Gelasius I (492–6). This was the period
when the Collect came into full flower. It is a literary genre or poetic form*

with four parts: who we pray to, why we trust, what we pray for, and through whom. In many churches a special Collect is appointed to collect the thoughts of the worshippers together on the theme of the lections or readings. In the past children were set the task of learning the Collect of the day. Even today, many people find that even without any conscious effort, they know many of the most beautiful Collects by heart and can use them in their daily prayers.

Almighty and everlasting God, who art always more ready to hear, than we to pray, and art wont to give more than either we desire, or deserve; pour down upon us the abundance of thy mercy, forgiving us those things whereof our conscience is afraid, and giving us those good things which we are not worthy to ask, save through the merits and mediation of Jesus Christ thy Son our Lord. Amen.[3]

Almighty and everlasting God, who alone workest great marvels, send down upon our Bishops and Curates, and all congregations committed to their charge, the healthful Spirit of thy grace; and that they may truly please thee, pour upon them the continual dew of thy blessing. Grant this, O Lord, for the honour of our Advocate and Mediator Jesus Christ. Amen.[4]

Almighty God, who showest to them that be in error the light of thy truth, to the intent that they may return into the way of righteousness; Grant unto all them that are admitted into the fellowship of Christ's religion, that they may eschew those things that are contrary to their profession, and follow all such things as are agreeable to the same; through our Lord Jesus Christ Amen.[5]

Almighty and everlasting God, by whose Spirit the whole body of the Church is governed and sanctified: Receive our supplications and prayers which we offer before thee for all estates of men in thy holy Church, that every member of the same in his vocation and ministry, may truly and godly serve thee, through our Lord and Saviour Jesus Christ. Amen.[6]

Assist us mercifully, O Lord, in these our supplications and prayers, and dispose the way of thy servants, towards the attainment of everlasting salvation; that among all the changes and chances of this mortal life, they may ever be defended by thy most gracious and ready help; through Jesus Christ our Lord. Amen.[7]

Assist us mercifully with your help, O Lord God of our salvation, that we may enter with joy upon the contemplation of those mighty acts, whereby you have given us life and immortality; through Jesus Christ our Lord. Amen.[8]

Grant, we beseech thee, merciful Lord, to thy faithful people pardon and peace, that they may be cleansed from all their sins, and serve thee with a quiet mind; through Jesus Christ our Lord. Amen.[9]

Keep, we beseech thee, O Lord, thy Church with thy perpetual mercy. And because the frailty of man without thee cannot but fall, keep us ever by thy help from all things hurtful, and lead us to all things profitable to our salvation, through Jesus Christ our Lord Amen.[10]

Let thy merciful ears, O Lord, be open to the prayers of thy humble servants; and that they may obtain their petitions, make them to ask such things as shall please thee, through Jesus Christ our Lord. Amen.[11]

Lighten our darkness, we beseech thee, O Lord; and by your great mercy defend us from all perils and dangers of this night; for the love of thy only Son, our Saviour, Jesus Christ. Amen.[12]

Lord of all power and might, who art the author and giver of all good things; graft in our hearts the love of thy name, increase in us true religion, nourish us with all goodness, and of thy great mercy keep us in the same; through Jesus Christ our Lord. Amen.[13]

Lord, we beseech thee, grant thy people grace to withstand the temptations of the world, the flesh and the devil, and with pure hearts and minds to follow thee, the only God; through Jesus Christ our Lord. Amen.[14]

O almighty and most merciful God, of thy bountiful goodness keep us, we beseech thee, from all things that may hurt us; that we being ready both in body and soul, may cheerfully accomplish those things that thou wouldest have done, through Jesus Christ our Lord. Amen.[15]

O almighty God, who alone canst order the unruly wills and affections of sinful men; grant unto thy people, that they may love the thing which thou commandest, and desire that which thou dost promise, that so among the sundry and manifold changes of the world, our hearts may surely there be fixed, where true joys are to be found, through Jesus Christ our Lord. Amen.[16]

O God, forasmuch as without thee we are not able to please thee; mercifully grant that thy Holy Spirit may in all things direct, and rule our hearts; through Jesus Christ our Lord. Amen.[17]

O God, from whom all holy desires, all good counsels, and all just works do proceed; give unto thy servants that peace which the world cannot give, that both, our hearts may be set to obey thy commandments, and also that, by thee, we being defended from the fear of our enemies, may pass our time in rest and quietness, through the merits of Jesus Christ our Saviour. Amen.[18]

O God of unchangeable power and eternal light, look favourably on your whole church, that wonderful and sacred mystery; and by the tranquil operation of your perpetual providence, carry out the work of man's salvation; let the whole world feel and see that things which were cast down are being raised up, that those which had grown old are being made new, and that all things are returning to perfection; through him from whom they took their origin, even Jesus Christ our Lord. Amen.[19]

O King of glory, righteous Lord, who as on this day ascended in triumph above all the heavens, leave us not like orphans, but send us the Spirit of truth promised by the Father. Alleluia.[20]

O God, the strength of all them that put their trust in thee, mercifully accept our prayers, and because through the weakness of our mortal nature we can do no good thing without thee, grant us the help of thy grace, that in keeping of thy commandments we may please thee, both in will and deed, through Jesus Christ our Lord. Amen.[21]

O God, whose never-failing providence ordereth all things in heaven and earth; we humbly beseech thee to put away from us all hurtful things, and to give us those things which are profitable for us; through Jesus Christ our Lord. Amen.[22]

O God, who declarest thy almighty power most chiefly in showing mercy and pity, mercifully grant unto us such a measure of thy grace, that we, running the way of thy commandments, may obtain thy gracious promises, and be made partakers of thy heavenly treasure; through Jesus Christ our Lord. Amen.[23]

O God, who hast made this most sacred night to shine with illumination of the true light, grant, we beseech thee, that, as we have known the mystery of that light upon earth, we may also perfectly enjoy it in heaven; through the same Jesus Christ our Lord. Amen.[24]

O God, who hast prepared for them that love thee, such good things as pass man's understanding; Pour into our hearts such love towards thee, that we loving thee above all things, may obtain thy promises, which exceed all that we can desire; through Jesus Christ our Lord. Amen.[25]

O God, who makest us glad with the yearly remembrance of our redemption, grant that, as we joyfully receive thine only-begotten Son as our redeemer, we may also see him without fear when he cometh as our judge: even our Lord, who with thee and the Holy Spirit ever liveth, one God, world without end. Amen.[26]

O Lord, from whom all good things do come, grant to us thy humble servants, that by thy holy inspiration we may think those things that be good, and by thy merciful guiding may perform the same, through our Lord Jesus Christ our Lord. Amen.[27]

O Lord, raise up (we pray thee) thy power, and come among us, and with great might succour us; that whereas through our sins and wickedness, we are sore let and hindered in running the race that is set before us, thy bountiful grace and mercy may speedily help and deliver us, through the satisfaction of thy Son our Lord; to whom with thee and the Holy Ghost be honour and glory, world without end. Amen.[28]

O Lord, we beseech thee, let thy continual pity cleanse and defend thy Church; and because it cannot continue in safety without thy succour, preserve it evermore by thy help and goodness, through Jesus Christ our Lord. Amen.[29]

The Ambrosian Sacramentary (fifth century)

It is possible that these prayers come from Milan, but otherwise they are probably not connected with St Ambrose.

Almighty God, we give you thanks for surrounding us, as daylight fades, with the brightness of the vesper light, and we implore you of your great mercy that, as you enfold us with the radiance of this light, so you would shine into our hearts the brightness of your Holy Spirit; through Jesus Christ our Lord. Amen.[30]

Look down, O Lord, from your heavenly throne, illumine the darkness of this night with your celestial brightness, and from the children of light, banish the deeds of darkness; through Jesus Christ our Lord. Amen.

Compline

The Gregorian Sacramentary (c. 790)

In the eighth century, anxious that the Mass should be said in the same way throughout his kingdom, the Emperor Charlemagne asked Pope Hadrian I to send him a copy of the service books which his predecessor Gregory the Great had compiled. What arrived was incomplete, but by putting it together with a manuscript found at Padua and a supplement compiled probably by Alcuin, it is possible to gain an approximation to what was requested. If these prayers were composed at the time when the Vandals were attacking Rome, it explains the frequent return to the themes of suffering and peace.

Almighty and everlasting God, mercifully look upon our infirmities, and in all our dangers and necessities stretch forth thy right hand to help and defend us, through Jesus Christ our Lord. Amen.[31]

Almighty and everlasting God, who dost govern all things in heaven and earth; mercifully hear the supplications of thy people, and grant us thy peace all the days of our life, through Jesus Christ our Lord. Amen.[32]

Almighty God, who seest that we have no power of ourselves to help ourselves; keep us both outwardly in our bodies and inwardly in our souls, that we may be defended from all adversities which may happen to the body, and from all evil thoughts which may assault and hurt the soul; through Jesus Christ our Lord. Amen.[33]

Almighty and everliving God, in your tender love for the human race you sent your Son our Saviour Jesus Christ to take upon him our nature, and to suffer death upon the cross, giving us the example of his great humility: Mercifully grant that we may walk in the way of his suffering, and also share in his resurrection; through Jesus Christ our Lord, who lives and reigns with you and the Holy Spirit, one God, for ever and ever. Amen.[34]

Almighty God, we beseech thee graciously to behold this thy family, for which our Lord Jesus Christ was contented to be betrayed and given up into the hands of wicked men, and to suffer death upon the cross, who now liveth and reigneth with thee and the Holy Ghost, ever one God, world without end. Amen.[35]

Almighty God, who through thine only-begotten Son Jesus Christ, hast overcome death, and opened unto us the gate of everlasting life; we humbly beseech thee, that as by thy special grace preventing us, thou dost put into our minds good desires, so by thy continual help we may bring the same to good effect; through Jesus Christ our Lord, who liveth and reigneth with thee and the Holy Ghost, ever one God, world without end. Amen.[36]

Almighty and everlasting God, who hast given unto us thy servants grace, by the confession of a true faith, to acknowledge the glory of the eternal Trinity, and in the power of the divine majesty to worship the unity; we beseech thee, that thou wouldst keep us steadfast in this faith, and evermore defend us from all adversities, who livest and reignest one God word without end. Amen.[37]

God, who as at this time didst teach the hearts of thy faithful people by the sending to them the light of thy Holy Spirit, grant us by the same Spirit to have a right judgment in all things, and evermore to rejoice in his holy comfort; through the merits of Christ Jesus our Saviour, who liveth and reigneth with thee in the unity of the same Spirit, one God, world without end. Amen.[38]

Grant, we beseech thee, almighty God, that like as we do believe thy only begotten Son our Lord Jesus Christ to have ascended into the heavens; so we may also in heart and mind thither ascend, and with him continually dwell, who liveth and reigneth with thee and the Holy Ghost, one God, world without end. Amen.[39]

Grant, we beseech thee, almighty God, that we, who for our evil deeds do worthily deserve to be punished, by the comfort of thy grace may mercifully be relieved, through our Lord and Saviour Jesus Christ. Amen.[40]

Lord, we pray thee, that thy grace may always prevent and follow us; and make us continually to be given to all good works, through Jesus Christ our Lord. Amen.[41]

Lord, we beseech thee to keep thy household the Church in continual godliness, that through thy protection, it may be free from all adversities, and devoutly given to serve thee in all good works to the glory of thy name, through Jesus Christ our Lord. Amen.[42]

O God, our refuge and strength, who art the author of all godliness, be ready we beseech thee, to hear the devout prayers of thy Church; and grant that those things which we ask faithfully, we may obtain effectually, through Jesus Christ our Lord. Amen.[43]

O God, the protector of all that trust in thee, without whom nothing is strong, nothing is holy, increase and multiply upon us thy mercy, that thou being our ruler and guide, we may so pass through things temporal, that we finally lose not the things eternal: grant this, O heavenly Father, for Jesus Christ's sake, our Lord. Amen.[44]

O God, who knowest us to be set in the midst of so many and great dangers, that by reason of the frailty of our nature we cannot always stand upright; grant to us such strength and protection, as may support us in all dangers, and carry us through all temptations, through Jesus Christ our Lord. Amen.[45]

O God, whose nature and property is ever to have mercy and to forgive, receive our humble petitions, and though we be tied and bound with the chain of our sins, yet let the pitifulness of thy great mercy loose us; for the honour of Jesus Christ, our Mediator and Advocate. Amen.[46]

O Lord God, who seest that we put not our trust in any thing that we do; mercifully grant that by thy power we may be defended against all adversity, through Jesus Christ our Lord. Amen.[47]

O Lord, we beseech thee to keep thy Church and household continually in thy true religion, that they who do lean only upon the hope of thy heavenly grace, may evermore be defended by thy mighty power, through Jesus Christ our Lord. Amen.[48]

O Lord, we beseech thee mercifully to hear us, and grant that we, to whom thou hast given an hearty desire to pray, may by thy mighty aid be defended and comforted in all dangers and adversities, through Jesus Christ our Lord. Amen.[49]

O Lord, we beseech thee mercifully to receive the prayers of thy people which call upon thee, and grant that they may both perceive and know what things they ought to do, and also may have grace and power faithfully to fulfil the same, through Jesus Christ our Lord. Amen.[50]

O Lord, we beseech thee favourably to hear the prayers of thy people, that we who are justly punished for our offences, may be mercifully delivered by thy goodness, for the glory of thy name, through Jesus Christ our Saviour, who liveth and reigneth with thee and the Holy Ghost ever one God, world without end. Amen.[51]

O Lord, who never failest to help and govern them whom thou dost bring up in thy fear and love; keep us, we beseech thee, under the protection of thy good providence, and make us to have a perpetual fear and love of thy holy name, through Jesus Christ our Lord. Amen.[52]

P revent us, O Lord, in all our doings with thy most gracious favour, and further us with thy continual help; that in all our works begun, continued and ended in thee, we may glorify thy holy name, and finally by thy mercy obtain everlasting life; through Jesus Christ our Lord. Amen.[53]

S tir up, we beseech thee O Lord, the wills of thy faithful people, that they plenteously bringing forth the fruit of good works, may of thee be plenteously rewarded, through Jesus Christ our Lord. Amen.[54]

W e beseech thee, almighty God, look upon the hearty desires of thy humble servants, and stretch forth the right hand of thy majesty to be our defence against all our enemies, through Jesus Christ our Lord. Amen.[55]

W e beseech thee, almighty God, mercifully to look upon thy people; that by thy great goodness they may be governed and preserved evermore, both in body and soul, through Jesus Christ our Lord. Amen.[56]

The Leonine Sacramentary (before the seventh century)

An incomplete seventh-century collection of prayers in a library at Verona was attributed by its first editor to Pope Leo the Great (440–61).

A lmighty and merciful God, of whose only gift it cometh, that thy faithful people do unto thee true and laudable service; grant, we beseech thee, that we may so faithfully serve thee in this life, that we fail not finally to attain thy heavenly promises, through the merits of Jesus Christ our Lord. Amen.[57]

A lmighty God, giver of all good things, who by thy Holy Spirit hast appointed divers orders of ministers in thy Church, mercifully behold these thy servants now called to the office of priesthood, and replenish them so with the truth of thy doctrine, and adorn them with innocency of life, that both by word and good example they may faithfully serve thee in this office, to the glory of thy name, and the edification of thy Church, through the merits of our Saviour Jesus Christ, who liveth and reigneth with thee and the Holy Ghost, world without end. Amen.[58]

Almighty God, who didst wonderfully create man in thine own image, and didst yet more wonderfully restore him: grant, we beseech thee, that as thy Son our Lord Jesus Christ was made in the likeness of men, so we may be made partakers of the divine nature; through the same thy Son, who with thee and the Holy Ghost liveth and reigneth, one God, world without end. Amen.[59]

Almighty and everlasting God, give unto us the increase of faith, hope and charity; and that we may obtain that which thou dost promise, make us to love that which thou dost command, through Jesus Christ our Lord. Amen.[60]

Almighty God, who showest to them that be in error the light of thy truth, to the intent that they may return into the way of righteousness; grant unto all them that are admitted into the fellowship of Christ's religion, that they may eschew those things that are contrary to their profession, and follow all such things as are agreeable to the same; through our Lord Jesus Christ. Amen.[61]

Almighty God, you have taught us through your Son that love is the fulfilling of the law. Grant that we may love you with our whole heart and our neighbours as ourselves; through Jesus Christ our Lord. Amen.[62]

Be present, O merciful God, and protect us through the silent hours of this night, so that we who are wearied by the changes and chances of this fleeting world may repose upon your eternal changelessness; through Jesus Christ our Lord. Amen.

Compline[63]

Grant us, O Lord, not to mind earthly things, but to love things heavenly; and even now, while we are placed among things that are passing away, to cleave to those that shall abide; through Jesus Christ our Lord. Amen.

Grant, O Lord, we beseech thee, that the course of this world may be so peaceably ordered by thy governance, that thy Church may joyfully serve thee in all godly quietness, through Jesus Christ our Lord. Amen.[64]

Grant to us, Lord, we beseech thee, the spirit to think and do always such things as be rightful, that we, who cannot do anything that is good without thee, may by thee be enabled to live according to thy will; through Jesus Christ our Lord. Amen.[65]

O God, you divide the day from the night; separate our deeds from the darkness of sin, that we may continually live in your light, and reflect in all our deeds your eternal beauty. Amen.

O God, you give the day for work and the night for sleep; refresh our bodies and our minds through the quiet hours of the night, so that we may turn the eyes of our souls towards you, and dream of your eternal glory. Amen.

O Lord, we beseech thee, absolve thy people from their offences; that through thy bountiful goodness we may all be delivered from the bands of those sins, which by our frailty we have committed: grant this, O heavenly Father, for Jesus Christ's sake, our blessed Lord and Saviour. Amen.[66]

Remember, O Lord, what thou hast wrought in us, and not what we deserve; and as thou hast called us to thy service, make us worthy of our calling; through Jesus Christ our Lord. Amen.[67]

St Gregory (d. c. 638)

This Gregory was a bishop in Sicily, but very little is known about him.

O good Jesu, word of the Father, the brightness of the Father's glory, whom angels desire to behold; teach us to do your will; that guided by your good Spirit, we may come to that blessed city where there is everlasting day and all are of one spirit; where there is certain security and secure eternity and eternal tranquillity and quiet felicity and happy sweetness and sweet pleasantness; where you, with the Father and the Holy Spirit, are alive and reign, one God for ever and ever. Amen.

The Emperor Charlemagne (*c.* 742–814)

Charlemagne attempted to re-found a Holy Roman Empire in Europe, though Voltaire said it was 'neither holy, nor Roman, nor an empire'. Inheriting the Frankish kingdom of Pepin his father, he extended it by a series of military campaigns. In his first unsuccessful attempt to conquer Spain, Roland, one of his knights, was killed, and the story became a medieval romantic epic, The Song of Roland. Once he had built up the empire, Charlemagne proceeded to unite it by reforming the legal system and the church. His sponsorship of scholarship has been called the Carolingian Renaissance.

Most merciful God, incline your loving ears to our prayers, and illuminate the hearts of those you call, with the grace of the Holy Spirit, enabling them worthily to minister to your mysteries; to love you with an everlasting love, and to attain everlasting joys; through Jesus Christ our Lord. Amen.

Alcuin of York (*c.* 735–804)

Among the scholars whom Charlemagne recruited to help him was a monk from York called Alcuin. He became tutor to the royal family at the Emperor's palace, where he set up a library. Then he became Abbot of Tours, where he established a school. He wrote important theological works, educational textbooks, poetry, a history of York, and letters giving a picture of Carolingian society. He also revised the worship of the Church throughout the Empire, adding an appendix to The Gregorian Sacramentary. So he is the patron saint of liturgists, those who seek to develop the services of the Church to enable worshippers to pray better.

Christ, why do you allow wars and massacres on earth? By what mysterious judgement do you allow innocent people to be cruelly slaughtered? I cannot know. I can only find assurance in the promise that your people will find peace in heaven, where no one makes war. As gold is purified by fire, so you purify souls by these bodily tribulations, making them ready to be received above the stars in your heavenly home.[68]

Dear God, here on earth you are constantly seeking to change us. At times we wish to flee into the wilderness to avoid you. But let us learn to love the lasting things of heaven, rather than the dying things of earth. We must accept that time always brings change; and we pray that by your grace the change within our souls will make us worthy of your heavenly kingdom, where all time will cease.[69]

G ood Jesus, you have deigned to refresh our souls with the sweet stream of knowledge; grant that one day we may come to you, its source and spring.

H e lay with quiet heart in the stern asleep:
Waking, commanded both the winds and sea.
Christ, though this weary body slumber deep,
Grant that my heart may keep its watch with thee.
O Lamb of God that carried all our sin,
Guard thou my sleep against the enemy.[70]

Fulbert of Chartres (c. 960–1028)

Fulbert was appointed Chancellor of the cathedral school at Chartres, and his brilliance in every form of knowledge studied at the time brought crowds applying to be his pupils. When he was made Bishop of Chartres he advised kings and dukes and initiated an ambitious building pro-gramme, though only the crypt remains of Fulbert's cathedral. He also wrote the hymn 'Ye choirs of new Jerusalem'.

I come to you, dear Jesus, in my confusion, for I do not know what I should do, nor do I know how to be at peace. It was rash of me to have accepted a bishopric, for I fear I do my flock more harm than good. So I feel I should give up my position in favour of someone superior to me. And yet I remember that it was without the advantage of high birth or wealth that I rose to this great office. Thus I wonder if, in choosing someone of such humble origins and dire poverty, the Church was making your choice. Dear Lord, I will not resign my office as bishop without some sign from you, despite my many sins. Give me a sign.[71]

Anselm (c. 1033–1109)

A monk from the Abbey of Bec in Normandy, Anselm became Archbishop of Canterbury, and was in frequent conflict with successive kings. He reasoned carefully on what Jesus did on the cross – the doctrine of the atonement – and on the ontological argument for the existence of God. He wrote, 'Credo ut intelligam' ('I believe in order to understand').

Almighty and tender Lord Jesus Christ, just as I have asked you to love my friends so I ask the same for my enemies. You alone, Lord, are mighty. You alone are merciful. Whatever you make me desire for my enemies, give it to them. And give the same back to me. If I ever ask for them anything which is outside your perfect rule of love, whether through weakness, ignorance or malice, good Lord, do not give it to them and do not give it back to me. You who are the true light, lighten their darkness. You who are the whole truth, correct their errors. You who are the incarnate word, give life to their souls. Tender Lord Jesus, let me not be a stumbling block to them nor a rock of offence. My sin is sufficient to me, without harming others. I, a slave to sin, beg your mercy on my fellow slaves. Let them be reconciled with you, and through you reconciled to me.[72]

And you, Jesus, are you not also a mother? Are you not the mother who, like a hen, gathers her chickens under her wings? Truly, Lord, you are a mother; for both they who are in labour and they who are brought forth are accepted by you. You have died more than they, that they may labour to bear. It is by your death that they have been born, for if you had not been in labour, you could not have borne death; and if you had not died, you would not have brought forth. For longing to bear sons into life, you tasted of death, and by dying you begot them. You did this in your own self, your servants by your commands and help. You as the author, they as the ministers. So you, Lord God, are the great mother. Then both of you are mothers. Even if you are fathers, you are also mothers. For you have brought it about that those born to death should be reborn to life – you by your own act, you by his power. Therefore you are fathers by your effect and mothers by your affection. Fathers by your authority, mothers by your kindness. Fathers by your teaching, mothers by your mercy. Then you, Lord, are a mother, and you, Paul, are a mother too. If in quantity of affection you are unequal, yet in quality you are not unalike. Though in the greatness of your kindness you are not co-equal, yet in will you are of one heart. Although you have not equal fullness of mercy, yet in intention you are not unequal ... And you, my soul, dead in yourself, run under the wings of Jesus your mother and lament your griefs under his feathers. Ask that your wounds may be healed and that, comforted, you may live again.

Jesus, as a mother you gather your people to you: you are gentle with us like a mother with her children. In your love and tenderness, remake us. Often you weep over our sins and our pride: tenderly you draw us from hatred and judgment. In your love and tenderness, remake us. You comfort us in sorrow and bind up our wounds: in sickness you nurse us and with pure milk you feed us. In your love and tenderness, remake us. Jesus by your dying we are born to new life: by your anguish and labour we come forth in joy. In your love and tenderness, remake us. Despair turns to hope through your sweet goodness: through your gentleness we find comfort in fear. In your love and tenderness, remake us. Your warmth gives life to the dead; your touch makes sinners righteous. In your love and tenderness, remake us. In your compassion bring grace and forgiveness: for the beauty of heaven may your love prepare us. In your love and tenderness, remake us.

God of love, whose compassion never fails; we bring before you the griefs and perils of people and nations, the pains of the sick and injured, the sighing of prisoners and captives, the sorrows of the bereaved, the necessities of the homeless, the helplessness of the weak, the despair of the weary, the failing powers of the aged. Comfort and relieve them, O merciful Father, according to their several needs and your great mercy; for the sake of your Son our Saviour Jesus Christ. Amen.

Grant, O Lord God, that we may cleave to you without parting, worship you without wearying, serve you without failing, faithfully seek you, happily find you, for ever possess you, the one only God, blessed world without end. Amen.

Lord Jesus Christ, let me seek you by desiring you, and let me desire you by seeking you; let me find you by loving you, and love you in finding you. I confess, Lord, with thanksgiving, that you have made me in your image, so that I can remember you, think of you, and love you. But that image is so worn and blotted out by faults, and darkened by the smoke of sin, that it cannot do that for which it was made, unless you renew and refashion it. Lord, I am not trying to make my way to your height, for my understanding is in no way equal to that, but I do desire to understand a little of your truth which my heart already believes and loves. I do not seek to understand so that I can believe, but I believe so

that I may understand; and what is more, I believe that unless I do believe,
I shall not understand.[73]

O supreme and unapproachable light! O whole and blessed truth!
How far you are from me, who am so near to you! Everywhere you
are wholly present, yet I do not see you. In you I move, and in you I have
my being, and cannot come to you; you are within me, and around me,
and I do not feel you.

O Lord our God, grant us grace to desire you with our whole heart,
so that desiring you, we may seek you and find you; and so finding
you, may love you; and so loving you, may hate those sins which separate
us from you, for the sake of Jesus Christ our Lord. Amen.

Peter Abela·d (1079–1141)

Castrated on the orders of the guardian of his beloved Heloïse and con-
demned by St Bernard as a heretic, Peter Abelard learnt from his own
suffering that the cross reveals the love of God for us, and arouses in us
love for God. His lectures to the students at Paris drew large crowds. He
taught that it is the intention or purpose of an action which makes it right
or wrong, rather than the act itself.

Alone to sacrifice thou goest, Lord,
Giving thyself to death whom thou wilt slay.
For us thy wretched folk is any word,
Whose sins have brought thee to this agony?

For they are ours, O Lord, our deeds, our deeds.
Why must thou suffer torture for our sin?
Let our hearts suffer for thy passion, Lord,
That very suffering may thy mercy win.

This is that night of tears, the three days space,
Sorrow abiding of the eventide,
Until the day break with the risen Christ,
And hearts that sorrowed shall be satisfied.

So may our hearts share in thine anguish, Lord,
That they may sharers of thy glory be.
Heavy with weeping may the three days pass,
To win the laughter of thine Easter Day.[74]

O quanta qualia sunt illa sabbata

O what their joy and their glory must be,
Those endless Sabbaths the blessed ones see!
Crown for the valiant; to weary ones rest;
God shall be all, and in all ever blest . . .

We, where no trouble distraction can bring,
Safely the anthems of Sion shall sing;
While for thy grace, Lord, their voices of praise
Thy blessed people shall evermore raise . . .

Low before him with our praises we fall,
Of whom, and in whom, and through whom are all;
Of whom, the Father; and through whom, the Son;
In whom, the Spirit, with them ever one. Amen.[75]

Monastic Spirituality

The great monasteries grew up in this period as beacons of Christian culture in the darkness of paganism; they provided the only hospitality for travellers, the only medical treatment and rest for the sick, a centre for trade and an example of good agricultural practice. And because they followed the Benedictine spirituality, all this was done in the context of a routine of daily prayer. Everybody prayed, but it was the monks and nuns who taught them how to do it.

Often, however, the monks became lax, and there were frequent reformers who broke away from the Benedictine monasteries to pursue a purer life of prayer. One of the first and most influential of these centres of reformed Benedictine monasticism was at Cluny in central France. Berno, the abbot of Baume, was the first abbot of the new foundation.

Abbot Robert took several companions from the monastery he had founded at Molesme and founded a new monastery at Citeaux in 1098, which became the origin of the Cistercian order.

Leaving behind what he regarded as the slackness and worldliness of the religious orders of his time, Bruno (c. 1032–1101) led a few brothers into the mountainous district near Grenoble and built a collection of hermit huts at the Grand Chartreuse. Monasteries of the Carthusian order were called Charterhouses in England, and Hugh of Lincoln was an example of the great Christians they produced.

The Cistercian abbey of La Trappe was reformed by Abbot Armand-Joseph de Rancé (1626–1700) with a strict rule. The very strictness of the Trappists enabled them to survive the French Revolution in exile, when other Cistercian communities were almost obliterated.

William of Saint-Thierry (c. 1085–c. 1148)

William was a Cistercian who wrote The Golden Letter *for a group of Carthusians. He explains how we must move through the stages of faith, reason and love to approach God. Rational explanations of supernatural things are tools to be used and then left behind, not idolized as unchanging truths. Meditation on Scripture, through which we learn of God's existence, and meditation on the Word of God incarnate, through which we learn of God's love, must be left behind as we come ever closer to God. Human love reaches out and meets God who is love, and love transforms the human soul into the pattern of God. Within the love of the Trinity, human beings can become by grace what God is by nature.*

Loving you, O God, brings its own reward here on earth, as well as the eternal reward of heaven. And failure to love you, even when we can offer a thousand excuses, brings its own punishment. By becoming mirrors of your love, by wearing the mask of your likeness, and by allowing you to make us perfect, we can know the joy of heaven, even while we abide here on earth. Our consciences are sullied by our many sins; cleanse them, that we may reflect your infinite brightness.[1]

You alone are the Lord. To be ruled by you is for us salvation. For us to serve you is nothing else but to be saved by you! Now how is it we are saved by you, O Lord, from whom salvation comes and whose blessing is upon your people, if it is not in receiving from you the gift of loving you and being loved by you? That, Lord, is why you willed that the Son of your right hand, the Man whom you made strong for your own self, should be called Jesus, that is to say, Saviour, for he will save his people from their sins.[2]

Bernard of Clairvaux (1090–1153)

Bernard was born near Dijon and, despite his family's opposition, become a monk. He brought with him about thirty of his friends and relations, including five of his six brothers, to Citeaux, where the recently founded Cistercian order was nearing the point of closure. The sixth brother joined them later. A couple of years later the abbot, Stephen Harding, sent Bernard out to found a new house at Clairvaux, which soon became one of the chief centres of the order. The austerity of his life coupled with his charm of personality won him many supporters, and his writings On the Love of God *show him to be a deeply loving man of prayer.*

I will love you, O Lord my strength, my stony rock and my defence, my saviour, my one desire and love. My God, my helper, I will love you with all the power you have given me; not as much as you deserve to be loved, for that can never be, but as much as I am able to. Whatever I do, I never can discharge my debt to you, and I can love you only according to the power that you have given me. The more power to love you give me, the more I will love you; yet never, never, can I love you as much as you should be loved.

From On the Love of God

The Sweetness of Divine Love

Jesus, how sweet is the very thought of you! You fill my heart with joy. The sweetness of your love surpasses the sweetness of honey. Nothing sweeter than you can be described; no words can express the joy of your love. Only those who have tasted your love for themselves can comprehend it. In your love you listen to all my prayers, even when my wishes are childish, my words confused, and my thoughts foolish. And you answer my prayers, not according to my own misdirected desires, which would bring only bitter misery; but according to my real needs, which brings me sweet joy. Thank you, Jesus, for giving yourself to me.[3]

Christmas

Let your goodness, Lord, appear to us, that we, made in your image, conform ourselves to it. In our own strength we cannot imitate your majesty, power and wonder; nor is it fitting for us to try. But your mercy reaches from the heavens, through the clouds, to the earth below. You have come to us as a small child, but you have brought us the greatest of all gifts, the gift of eternal love. Caress us with your tiny hands, embrace us with your tiny arms, and pierce our hearts with your soft, sweet cries.[4]

Holy Week

You taught us, Lord, that the greatest love a man can show is to lay down his life for his friends. But your love was greater still, because you laid down your life for your enemies. It was while we were still enemies that you reconciled us to yourself by your death. What other love has ever been, or could ever be, like yours? You suffered unjustly for the sake of the unjust. You died at the hands of sinners for the sake of the sinful. You became a slave to tyrants, to set the oppressed free.[5]

Aelred of Rievaulx (*c.* 1109–67)

Abbot of the Yorkshire Cistercian monastery, he handled sensitively the issue of deep friendship between people of the same sex within a celibate community, and encouraged an intimate friendship with Jesus in prayer.

Lord, I sometimes wander away from you. But this is not because I am deliberately turning my back on you. It is because of the inconstancy of my mind. I weaken in my intention to give my whole soul to you. I fall back into thinking of myself as my own master. But when I wander from you, my life becomes a burden, and within me I find nothing but darkness and wretchedness, fear and anxiety. So I come back to you, and confess that I have sinned against you. And I know you will forgive me.[6]

O Lord Jesus, I will embrace you who became a little child for me. In my weakness I clasp you who became weak for me. A mere man, I embrace the God made man, the God who became a man as poor as I am, and came into Jerusalem seated on a humble donkey. I embrace you, O Lord, because your lowly state is my greatness, and your weakness is my strength. The foolishness of God is my wisdom.[7]

O Good Shepherd Jesus, good, gentle, tender Shepherd, behold a shepherd, poor and pitiful, a shepherd of your sheep indeed, but weak and clumsy and of little use, cries out to you. To you, I say, Good Shepherd, this shepherd, who is not good, makes his prayer. He cries to you, troubled on his own account, and troubled for your sheep.[8]

I ask you, by the power of your most sweet name, and by your holy manhood's mystery, to put away my sins and heal the languors of my soul, mindful only of your goodness, not of my ingratitude. Lord, may your good, sweet Spirit descend into my heart, and fashion there a dwelling for himself.[9]

My God, you know what a fool I am, my weakness is not hidden from your sight. Therefore, sweet Lord, I ask you not for gold, I ask you not for silver, nor for jewels, but only that you would give me wisdom, that I may know to rule your people well.[10]

O font of wisdom, send her from your throne of might, to be with me, to work with me, to act in me, to speak in me, to order all my thoughts and words and deeds and plans according to your will and to the glory of your name.[11]

Gilbert of Hoyland (d. *c.* 1170)

There were several well-known Gilberts in the Middle Ages. This one was the Abbot of the Cistercian monastery at Swineshead in Lincolnshire.

When, good Lord, will you manifest yourself to us in bright sunshine? Yes, we are slow to understand and slow to see. But we are quick to believe; and we believe that if you chose to reveal yourself to us, you could do so this very day. Dear Lord, please appear to us, at dawn or at dusk or at the height of day. Come to our table at mealtimes, that we may share our meals with you. Come to our bed, that we may share our rest with you. Come to us at our prayers, that we may rejoice and be glad.[12]

When we see dark grey clouds forming in the sky, we fear a mighty storm. In the same way when we see the darkness of our sin, we fear the storm of your wrath. But just as in truth rain brings new life to the earth, so you rain down mercy on our sinful souls, bringing forgiveness and peace. Be to us always like a mighty storm, raining down upon us the abundant waters of your mercy.[13]

The Victorines

The Abbey of St Victor in Paris produced among its canons in the twelfth century writers who gave systematic teaching on meditation. They showed how it was possible to remain natural and sincere in prayer, but at the same time to structure meditation in an orderly manner. The Victorines removed any false distinction between prayer and the intellectual search for understanding. Hugh of St Victor (d. 1142) came from Saxony; he clarified the distinction between reflection, meditation and contemplation. Reflection is idly thinking about God; meditation is a more structured thinking about God; and contemplation is not thinking about God at all, but enjoying wordless communion with God. Richard (d. 1173) came from Ireland or Scotland; he outlined six degrees of contemplation. These have been defined as simple awareness of things, which may lead to worship; the aesthetic stage, a deeper awareness of beauty and design in creation; the sacramental stage, when the inner reality of creatures is sought and perceived; purification; illumination; and ecstatic union with God. Adam of St Victor (d. between 1177 and 1192) composed many Latin sequences to be sung during the Mass.

Christmas

What is this jewel that is so precious?
I can see it has been quarried not by men, but by God.
It is you, dear Jesus.
You have been dug from the rocks of heaven itself
to be offered to me as a gift beyond price.

You shine in the darkness.
Every colour of the rainbow can be seen within you.
The whole earth is bathed in your light.

Infant Jesus, by being born as man
you have taken upon yourself the pain of death.
But such a jewel can never be destroyed.

You are immortal.
And by defying your own death, you shall deliver me from death.[14]

Easter

I see flames of orange, yellow and red
shooting upwards to the sky, piercing the whole clouds.
I see the clouds themselves chasing the flames upwards,
and I feel the air itself reaching for the heavens.

Down below I see great, grey rocks beating against the earth,
as if they were pushing their way down to hell.

At your resurrection that which is light and good rises up with you,
and that which is heavy and evil is pushed downwards.

At your resurrection goodness breaks from evil,
life breaks free from death.[15]

Whitsun

Who is this who smothers me with the most fragrant
    perfume?
Who is this who transforms my ugliness into perfect beauty?
Who is this who gives me the sweetest wine to drink, and the finest
    food to eat?
It is you, Holy Spirit. You turn me into a bride fit for Jesus Christ.
You give me wine and food fit for a wedding in heaven.
My heart was weary, but now it is eager for love.
My soul was sad, but now it is full of joy.
Jesus gave his life for me. Now you, Holy Spirit, give me to him.[16]

Hildegard of Bingen (1098–1179)

Hildegard was born to a noble family. Experiencing visions in her child-hood, she was brought up by Jutta, a recluse who lived on the Diessenberg. A community gathered round Jutta, organized on Benedictine lines. Having been admitted to the community at the age of eighteen, Hildegard succeeded Jutta as the Abbess. Some dozen years later she moved the community to Rupertsburg near Bingen on the River Rhine. There she carried on an influential correspondence, advising the Emperor Barbarossa, popes, kings, bishops and saints on a variety of matters; she also travelled widely in the Rhineland. She showed powers of scientific observation which were unusual for the time, and wrote many books, most of which were severely critical of the society of the time. Her most famous book was called Scivias, *probably an abbreviation for 'the science of life'. It is an account of her visions, and contains enigmatic prophesies of disaster. The revival of interest in recent years has focused on the books of songs which she wrote, together with the music to which they are to be sung.*

Jesus Christ, the love that gives love,
You are higher than the highest star;
You are deeper than the deepest sea;
You cherish us as your own family;
You embrace us as your own spouse;
You rule over us as your own subjects;
You welcome us as your dearest friend.
Let all the world worship you.[17]

Holy Spirit, the life that gives life.
You are the cause of all movement;
You are the breath of all creatures;
You are the salve that purifies our souls;
You are the ointment that heals our wounds;
You are the fire that warms our hearts;
You are the light that guides our feet.
Let all the world praise you.[18]

O eternal God,
Turn us into the arms and hands,
The legs and feet
Of your beloved Son, Jesus.
You gave birth to him in heaven
Before the creation of the earth.
You gave birth to us on earth,
To become his living body.
Make us worthy to be his limbs,
And so worthy to share
In his eternal bliss.[19]

Elizabeth of Schonau (d. 1184)

Also known as Elizabeth of the Trinity, she was a friend of Hildegard and, like her, she was a visionary.

O consuming fire, Spirit of love, descend within me and reproduce in me, as it were, an incarnation of the Word, that I may be to him another humanity wherein he renews his mystery.

Mechtild of Magdeburg (1210–80)

The Béguines were a lay women's community in Holland and North Germany who developed a life of corporate prayer while still very involved in serving the people round them. Their life together was somewhat austere, but they took no vows and were free to own property and to leave to get married. Mechtild received her first vision, of herself as the bride of Christ, at the age of twelve. In a search for an extreme austerity of life, she entered a Béguinage at Magdeburg, and on the advice of her confessor, she wrote an account of her visions, calling it The Flowing Light of the Godhead. *It consists mostly of poetic prayers, using erotic imagery for the unity between Christ and the believer. Later she joined a Cistercian convent and added a further volume.*

Lord, you are my lover, the object of my desire, you are like a stream flowing through my body, a sun shining on my face. Let me be your reflection.[20]

I cannot dance, O Lord, unless you lead me. If it is your will, I can leap with joy. But you must show me how to dance and sing by dancing and singing yourself! With you I will leap towards love, and from love I will leap to truth, and from truth I will leap to joy, and then I shall leap beyond all human senses. There I will remain and dance for evermore.[21]

Lord, I thank you that you have taken from me the sight of my eyes, and that now you serve me with the eyes of others. Lord, I thank you that you have taken from me the power of my hands, and that now you care for me by the hands of others. Lord, I pray for them. Reward them in your heavenly love, that they may faithfully serve and please you until death.[22]

O Lord, love me intensely, love me often and long!
For the more often you love me, the purer I become.
The more intensely you love me, the more beautiful I become.
The longer you love me, the holier I become.[23]

A h, dear love of God, always embrace this soul of mine,
For it pains me above all things when
    I am separated from you.
Ah love, do not allow me to grow cool,
For all my works are dead,
When I can feel you no longer.
Oh love, you sweeten both suffering and need;
You teach and console the true children of God.[24]

O burning mountain, O chosen sun,
O perfect moon, O fathomless well,
O unattainable height, O clearness beyond measure,
O wisdom without end, O mercy without limit,
O strength beyond resistance, O crown of all majesty,
The humblest being you created sings your praise.

Guigo the Carthusian (d. 1188)

*A superior of the Carthusians, Guigo was a teacher of prayer who saw
the material world as full of metaphors for our relationship with God.*

L ord, how much juice you can squeeze from a single grape.
How much water you can draw from a single well.
How great a fire you can kindle from a tiny spark.
How great a tree you can grow from a tiny seed.
My soul is so dry that by itself it cannot pray,
Yet you can squeeze from it the juice of a thousand prayers.
My soul is so parched that by itself it cannot love;
Yet you can draw from it boundless love for you and for my
    neighbour.
My soul is so cold that by itself it has no joy,
Yet you can light the fire of heavenly joy within me.
My soul is so feeble that by itself it has no faith;
Yet by your power my faith grows to a great height.

Thank you for prayer, for love, for joy, for faith;
Let me always be prayerful, loving, joyful, faithful.[25]

L ord you are invisible, except to the pure of heart.
I seek to understand true purity of heart
By reading the Scriptures and by meditating.
Lord, I have read your words and meditated on your person
For more years that I can remember.
I long to see you face to face.
It is the sight of you, Lord, that I have sought.
Over the years the fire of desire to see you
Has grown hotter and hotter.
As I have meditated, my soul has received greater light.
And the Scriptures excite my soul more than ever.
Lord, I do not dare to call you
To reveal yourself now or soon.
But give me a sign, a pledge
To ensure me that one day I will be rewarded.
Give me a single drop of heavenly rain
To assuage my spiritual thirst.[26]

Ludolf of Saxony (d. *c*. 1378)

Ludolf, after thirty years as a Dominican, joined the Carthusians in 1340 and was Prior of the Charterhouse at Koblenz for five years. After that he became an ordinary monk again and spent the rest of his life in prayer at Mainz and Strasburg. His Life of Christ, which contains meditations and prayers as well as biography, may have influenced Thomas à Kempis.

J esus, you let your side be opened by the spear so that there came forth blood and water; wound my heart with the spear of charity so that I may be made worthy of your sacraments which flow from your most holy side. In opening your side, Lord, you have opened the gate of life to your chosen ones.[27]

L ord Jesus Christ, by your glorious resurrection, in which you appeared alive and immortal to your disciples and faithful followers, by your forty days abiding and sweet converse, in which by many infallible proofs, speaking of things pertaining to the Kingdom of God, you comforted them and assured them of your actual resurrection, removing all doubt from their hearts; grant that we may be numbered among those appointed to be witnesses to your resurrection, not only by the words of our mouths, but by the evidence of our good works; to your honour and glory, for you are alive and reign, with the Father and the Holy Spirit, one God for ever and ever. Amen.

Anonymous medieval prayers

Many beautiful additions to the Latin liturgy were composed anonymously in the Middle Ages, including 'The Salve Regina', 'The Good Friday Reproaches', 'The Easter Exultet', 'The Anima Christi' and 'The Veni Creator Spiritus' (best known in the translation by Bishop Cosin, 'Come Holy Ghost, our souls inspire'). Their continuing popularity does not depend on their attachment to well-known names: rather, it shows how well they reflect the religious feelings of people at the time they were written, and of our own day also.

The Salve Regina

Hail, Queen, merciful mother; our life, our sweetness and our hope! We, the exiled children of Eve, call and sigh to you, lamenting and weeping in this vale of tears; therefore be our advocate, turn your merciful eyes towards us, and reveal to us, after our exile, Jesus, the blessèd fruit of your womb. O merciful, faithful, sweet Virgin Mary! Amen.

Eleventh century

The Good Friday Reproaches

Christ on the cross cries:
My people, what wrong have I done to you?
What good have I not done for you?
Listen to me. Is it nothing to you, all you who pass by?
Look and see if there is any sorrow like to my sorrow.

We adore you, O Christ, and we bless you,
because by your holy cross you have redeemed the world.

Probably tenth-century French

Requiem Mass, Introit

Rest eternal grant to them, O Lord, and may light perpetual shine upon them. You, O God, are praised in Zion, and to you the vow will be performed in Jerusalem. You hear our prayer, everyone shall come to you. Rest eternal grant to them, O Lord, and may light perpetual shine upon them.

The Easter Exultet

On this night we sing to Jesus, the true Lamb of God,
   who makes death to pass over all
   who are marked with his blood.
Alleluia, Christ is risen, let the heavens make it known!
Alleluia, all creation rejoice round God's throne,
    God's throne, God's throne,
alleluia, let the trumpet of peace now be blown!

On this night God leads us over by the power of his hand
out of slavery into freedom in his long-promised land.
Alleluia, Christ is risen, let the earth now be bright!
Alleluia, sin is powerless, and God brings us his light,
    his light, his light,
alleluia, sing to Jesus, who conquers death's night!

On this night the earth and heaven are wedded again –
may our candle shine for Jesus till he comes here to reign.
Alleluia, Christ is risen, Mother Church, sing his praise!
Alleluia, may he shine on our lives with his rays, his rays, his rays,
alleluia, serving Christ for the rest of our days.

Seventh century[28]

The Anima Christi

Soul of Christ, be my sanctification;
  body of Christ be my salvation;
blood of Christ fill all my veins;
water from Christ's side, wash out my stains;
passion of Christ, my comfort be;
O good Jesus, listen to me;
in your wounds I fain would hide,

ne'er to be parted from your side;
guard me should the foe assail me;
call me when my life shall fail me;
bid me come to you above,
with your saints to sing my love.

Fourteenth century[29]

The Veni Creator Spiritus

Come, O Creator Spirit, come,
And make within our hearts thy home;
To us thy grace celestial give,
Who of thy breathing move and live.

O Comforter, that name is thine,
Of God most high the gift divine.
The well of life, the fire of love,
Our souls' anointing from above.

Thou dost appear in sevenfold dower
The sign of God's almighty power.
The Father's promise, making rich
With saving truth our earthly speech.

Our senses with thy light inflame,
Our hearts to heavenly love reclaim;
Our bodies' poor infirmity
With strength perpetual fortify.

Our mortal foe afar repel,
Grant us henceforth in peace to dwell;
And so to us, with thee for guide,
No ill shall come, no harm betide.

May we by thee the Father learn,
And know the Son, and thee discern,
Who art of both; and thus adore
In perfect faith for evermore. Amen.[30]

The Breviary

Monks and nuns pray at fixed times of the day and night, known as the Canonical Hours. The services they use are called the Divine Office. The Night Office is called Matins, and the seven Day Hours are Lauds, Prime, Terce, Sext, None, Vespers and Compline. The prayers used at these services are collected in The Breviary, *which evolved over many centuries.*

Almighty and merciful God, you grant to your faithful people the grace by which we can make every path in this world into the strait and narrow way which leads to life eternal. Grant that we, who know that we have no strength of ourselves to help ourselves, and therefore put all our trust in your almighty power, may always conquer, by your grace, whatever may arise to fight against us; through Jesus Christ our Lord. Amen.

Almighty and everlasting God, grant that our wills may always be obedient to your will, and our hearts be honestly ready to serve you; for the sake of Jesus Christ our Lord. Amen.

Guide us, O Lord, waking, and guard us sleeping, that awake we may watch with Christ, and asleep we may rest in peace.

Compline

O God, mercifully grant that the fire of your love may burn up in us all the things which displease you, and make us fit to live in your heavenly Kingdom; for the sake of Jesus Christ our Saviour. Amen.

O God, the consolation of all those who are sorrowful, and the salvation of those who put their trust in you, grant us, in this mortal life, that peace for which we pray, and hereafter to enjoy your presence eternally; through our Lord Jesus Christ. Amen.

O Lord God, King of heaven and earth; arrange and sanctify, rule and govern, our hearts and our bodies, our thoughts, our works, and our words this day, according to your commandments, so that with your help, we may here and for ever be set free and saved; through Jesus Christ our Lord. Amen.

Visit our homes, O Lord, we pray, and drive far from them all the snares of the enemy; let your holy angels dwell therein to preserve us in peace; and may your blessing be upon us evermore; through Jesus Christ our Lord. Amen.

Compline

O Lord, guide and govern your Church, so that it may walk warily in peaceful times and boldly in times of trouble; through our Lord Jesus Christ. Amen.

The Franciscan Breviary

Books of Hours

Lay devotion flourished, and books of prayers ('Books of Hours') were produced and illuminated for rich people who wanted to pursue a regular pattern of prayer.

O Lord Jesu Christ, Son of the living God, we pray thee to set thy passion, cross and death between thy judgement and our souls, now and in the hour of our death. Vouchsafe to grant mercy and grace to the living, rest to the dead, to thy holy Church peace and concord, and to us sinners everlasting life and glory; for thou art alive and reignest, with the Father and the Holy Spirit, one God for ever and ever. Amen.[31]

God be in my head, and in my understanding;
God be in my eyes, and in my looking;
God be in my mouth, and in my speaking;
God be in my heart, and in my thinking;
God be at my end, and at my departing.[32]

Pilgrims and crusaders

In the fourth century a Spanish nun named Egeria gave an account of her enthusiastic pilgrimage to the Holy Land. In the second millennium the pilgrims were joined by others travelling as a penance for sins they had committed. If they went to the Shrine of St James at Compostella in Spain they wore the sign of a scallop shell; those returning with palm branches from Jerusalem were called 'palmers'.

The abbots of Cluny had established what was called 'The Truce of

God', consisting of days on which nobody was to fight. If anyone killed a man on one of these days, they had to atone by going on pilgrimage, and the Cluniacs provided refuges for them to shelter in on the way. But in the late eleventh century the Seljuk Turks drove out the tolerant Egyptian Muslim rulers of Palestine and attacked pilgrims on their way to the Holy Places. Pope Urban II, a Cluniac monk, preached a stirring appeal for Christians to defend the right of pilgrims to travel, and thus began the First Crusade. Terrible atrocities were committed in the name of Christianity during the Crusades, and irreparable damage was done to Christian relations with Muslims. At the same time, there was great bravery, and some whose prayer had been a formality learnt to be serious when they or their relations were away at the Crusades.

The Sultan sent his men to stay
   And guard the road in loyalty
The while the pilgrim folk marched by,
So that we passed secure from ills.
And then we climbed into the hills
And soon we reached the Montjoie's height.
Then in our hearts was great delight
To see Jerusalem. We felt
Such joy that on the ground we knelt,
As all who come there ought to do.
We saw the Mount of Olives, too,
The place whence started the procession
When the Lord God went to his passion.
We went next on our pilgrimage
To where God won his heritage,
The city. Those who rode first were
Allowed to kiss the Sepulchre;
The knights and those men who were mounted,
When they were with our troop, recounted
How Saladin showed and disclosed
That holy cross, the which was lost
During the battle, and saw fit
To have them kiss and worship it.
We others were on foot, and we
Saw all the things that we could see.
We saw in truth the monument
Wherein God's body evident

Was laid away when death he suffered.
There a few offerings were offered.
But since the Saracens would take
What offerings we chose to make
We offered little. But large share
We gave to the poor captives there,
The Franks and Syrians detained
In wretched bondage and enchained.[33]

Knights and chivalry

The Order of Knights Templar was founded to protect the site of the Temple in Jerusalem; the Hospitallers of St John were to provide hospitality and medical attention for the pilgrims. In spite of the terrible subsequent history of these orders, they were the inspiration for the movement of chivalry in the Middle Ages, for the ballads of the troubadours and jongleurs, and ultimately for the Romantic Movement of the nineteenth century.

In What Manner a Squire ought to be Received into the Order of Chivalry

At the beginning before a squire enters the order of chivalry he ought to confess him of his faults that he has done against God, and ought to receive chivalry with the intention that in it he will serve our Lord God which is glorious. And if he be clean from sin he ought to receive his Saviour [i.e. in Communion]. The day of some great feast such as Christmas, Easter, Whitsuntide or some other solemn day is proper for to make and dub a knight because, by reason of the honour of the feast, many people assemble in that place where the squire ought to be dubbed knight. And God ought to be adored and prayed that he give to him grace for to live well after the order of chivalry. The squire ought to keep the vigil of that feast in honour of the saint whose feast it is; and he ought to go to the church for to pray God, and ought to wake the night and be in his prayers. And he ought to hear the word of God and of the deeds of chivalry. For if he should otherwise hear jongleurs and ribalds that speak of corruption and of sin he should begin then to dishonour chivalry. On the morning after the feast at which he is to be dubbed he should cause a solemn mass to be sung. And the squire ought to come to the altar and offer to the priest, who holds the place of our Lord to whom he must undertake to submit himself to keep the honour of chivalry with all his power, saying 'In thy name, and with the intention to serve thee, and honour thee, my sovereign Lord God, and thy dear mother Mary, and all thy holy saints of paradise, I take this day this worthy order.' Then the prince or baron that will make the squire and dub him knight must have in himself the virtue and order of chivalry. For if the knight that maketh knights is not virtuous, how may he give that which he hath not? . . . The squire ought to kneel before the altar and lift up to God his eyes, corporal and spiritual, and his hands to heaven. And the knight ought to gird the squire with his sword in sign of chastity, justice and charity. The knight ought to kiss the squire and to give him a palm to remind him of that which he receives and promises . . . And after, when the knight spiritual, that is the priest, and the earthly knight have done what belongs to their office as touching the making of a new knight, the new knight ought to ride through the town and to show himself to the people to the end that all men know and see that he is newly made knight.

From The Book of the Order of Chivalry *by Ramón Lull*[34]

The Mystery Plays

The re-enactment of the Last Supper in the Eucharist or Mass is a form of drama. In the Middle Ages the Church supported re-enactments of the Bible stories, either in church or on carts around the streets of the town. These evolved into the Passion Plays of Oberammergau and many other places, processions such as that at Bruges, and the Mystery Plays in England. Parts of the Cycles from York, Chester, Wakefield and Coventry have survived. In this way, and through the stained-glass windows, the ordinary illiterate people of the Middle Ages probably knew more of the Bible than many educated people today.

This moral men may have in mind.
Ye hearers, take it of worth, old and young,
And forsake Pride, for he deceiveth you in the end;
And remember Beauty, Five Wits, Strength, and Discretion,
They all at the last do every man forsake,
Save his Good Deeds there doth he take.
But beware, for and they be small
Before God, he hath no help at all;
None excuse may be there for every man.
Alas, how shall he do then?

For after death amends may no man make,
For then mercy and pity doth him forsake.
If his reckoning be not clear when he doth come,
God will say: 'Ite, maledicti, in ignem eternum.'
And he that hath his account whole and sound,
High in heaven he shall be crowned;
Unto which place God bring us all thither,
That we may live body and soul together.
Thereto help the Trinity!
Amen, say ye, for saint charity.

From The Moral Play of Everyman[35]

The Albigensians

It has always been an attractive solution to the problem of evil to suppose that the Devil is as strong, or nearly as strong, as the Creator God. This dualism has emerged in Manichaeism and certain forms of Gnosticism, in the teachings of the tenth-century priest Bogomil in Bulgaria, and in the twelfth century in the town of Albi in Languedoc in southern France. Because of their emphasis on detachment from the evil world, the Albigensians were also known as 'Cathars', which roughly translates as 'Puritans'. The interrogation of the people of the Languedoc village of Montaillou by the court of their bishop, who knew they were influenced by the Cathar heresy, nonetheless gives a unique snapshot of everyday medieval life, showing how strong the life of prayer was among ordinary people in the Middle Ages.

Aude Fauré, when she realized she no longer believed in the real presence of the Body of Christ, turned to her nurse and said: 'Pray God to put in my heart to become a believer again.' And while the nurse prayed to God as best she could, Guillemette, servant in Aude Fauré's ostal, came in. 'Guillemette,' said Aude, 'pray to the Blessed Virgin Mary of Montgauzy and ask her to enlighten me that I may believe in God.' Guillemette, after having knelt, carried out her mistress's order. And when she had prayed, Aude was immediately enlightened, and believed firmly in God, and she still believes in him today, according to what she says.[36]

The Giving of the Lord's Prayer

The Elder: We pray the good Lord, who gave the disciples of Jesus Christ virtue and power to receive that holy prayer, to give you also grace to receive it for your salvation with power and with reverence for him.

The Elder shall then repeat the Lord's Prayer and the Believer shall repeat it after him. Then the Elder shall say:

This holy prayer we give to you, so that you may receive it from God and from the Church and from us; and that you may have power to say it at all times throughout your life, by day and by night, alone and with others; and that you may never eat or drink without first saying this prayer. If you fail to do so, then you must do a penance.

The Believer shall say: I receive this prayer from God and from you and from the Church.[37]

The Mendicant Orders or Friars

Dominic (1170–1221)

Saint Dominic was assistant to the Bishop of Osma in northern Spain when the Bishop was sent by the Pope on a mission to Languedoc to resist the Albigensians. Dominic stayed on and made it his life's work to convert the heretics. He formed his followers, the Dominicans, into a community of Little Brothers or Friars, the Order of Preachers, calling for an emphasis on study and learning to argue against the Cathars.

Thomas Aquinas (*c.* 1225–74)

The most distinguished theologian among the Dominicans was St Thomas Aquinas. His Summa Theologia *was the most complete work of systematic theology the Church had ever known. It teaches the importance of petition, (asking God for gifts and virtues), which, Aquinas taught, should be short and frequent. Aquinas was also devoted to the sacrament of the Eucharist, and compiled a complete liturgy for the new festival of Corpus Christi in honour of the sacramental Body of Christ.*

Lord, in a wonderful sacrament you have left us a memorial of your death and resurrection. Teach us so to reverence these sacred mysteries of your Body and Blood, that we may perceive within ourselves and show forth in our lives the fruits of our redemption, for you are alive and reign, Father, Son and Holy Spirit, for ever and ever. Amen.

Before Holy Communion

God, in this sacrament we come to your only Son, Jesus Christ.
Sick, we approach the physician;
unclean, we approach the fountain;

blind, we approach the light;
poor, we approach the monarch of all.
In your mercy, heal us,
cleanse us, enlighten us and clothe us,
so that we may receive the bread of angels
with reverence and humility,
repentance and love,
purity and faith,
for the good of our souls.
Make us members of Christ's body,
that one day we may see face to face
him whose presence here is veiled,
and who lives and reigns with you and the Holy Spirit,
one God for ever and ever. Amen.

Give us, O Lord, a steadfast heart, which no selfish desires may drag downwards; give us an unconquered heart, which no troubles can wear out; give us an upright heart, which no unworthy ambitions may tempt aside. Give us also, O Lord our God, understanding to know you, perseverance to seek you, wisdom to find you, and a faithfulness that may finally embrace you; through Jesus Christ our Lord. Amen.

Adoro te Devote

Godhead here in hiding, whom I do adore
Masked by these bare shadows, shape and nothing more,
See, Lord, at thy service low lies here a heart
Lost, all lost in wonder at the God thou art.

Seeing, touching, tasting are in thee deceived;
How says trusty hearing? That shall be believed;
What God's Son has told me, take for truth I do;
Truth himself speaks truly or there's nothing true.

On the cross thy godhead made no sign to men;
Here thy very manhood steals from human ken:
Both are my confession, both are my belief,
And I pray the prayer of the dying thief.

O thou our reminder of Christ crucified,
Living Bread, the life of us for whom he died,

Lend this life to me then: feed and feast my mind,
There be thou the sweetness man was meant to find.

Jesus whom I look at shrouded here below,
I beseech thee send me what I thirst for so,
Some day to gaze on thee face to face in light
And be blest for ever with thy glory's sight.[1]

The Stations of the Cross

Pilgrims to the Holy Land from the earliest times visited the sites where, as far as they could discover, the events of the Gospels had occurred, and there were devotional processions from one to another. So a route was worked out from the supposed site of Pilate's house to Calvary, and pilgrims would make stations or stopping-points to pray at intervals on the way. The present route and the fourteen stations developed slowly, but returning pilgrims, encouraged by the early friars, placed on the walls of their churches pictures of the various incidents which happened to Jesus as he made his way towards his crucifixion.

1. Jesus is condemned to death
2. Jesus receives the cross
3. Jesus falls for the first time
4. Jesus meets his Mother
5. Simon of Cyrene is made to carry the cross
6. Veronica wipes Jesus' face
7. Jesus falls for the second time
8. Jesus meets the women of Jerusalem
9. Jesus falls for the third time.
10. Jesus is stripped
11. Jesus is nailed to the cross
12. Jesus dies on the cross
13. His body is taken down from the cross
14. Jesus' body is laid in the tomb

Jesus, the Saviour of mankind, you were fastened to the cross with three nails, fasten our hearts to the same cross with the three nails of faith, hope and love.

Fr Adrian Parviliers sj (1619–78)

The Rosary

Traditionally it is said that the Rosary was first used by St Dominic in his preaching to counter the Albigensian heretics. It is more likely that the use of a string of beads to assist prayer was borrowed from the followers of Eastern religions and was promoted by the Cistercians and the Dominicans. In its traditional form every group of ten beads is counted off while reciting ten 'Hail Marys', preceded by the 'Our Father' and followed by 'Glory be to the Father'. Each of these fifteen 'decades' is recited whilst meditating on one of fifteen 'Mysteries'. The Mysteries are arranged in three 'chaplets', and normally only one chaplet is used at a time.

Hail Mary, full of grace, the Lord is with thee. Blessèd art thou among women, and blessèd is the fruit of thy womb, Jesus. Holy Mary, Mother of God, pray for us sinners, now and in the hour of our death.

The Joyful Mysteries
1. The Annunciation by Gabriel to Mary
2. The Visit of Mary to Elizabeth
3. The Birth of Christ
4. The Presentation in the Temple
5. Finding Jesus in the Temple at the age of twelve

The Sorrowful Mysteries
1. The Agony in Gethsemane
2. Jesus is Whipped by the Soldiers
3. The Crown of Thorns
4. Carrying the Cross
5. The Crucifixion

The Glorious Mysteries
1. The Resurrection
2. The Ascension
3. The Coming of the Holy Spirit at Pentecost
4. The Assumption of the Virgin Mary into Heaven
5. The Coronation of the Virgin Mary

Glory be to the Father, and to the Son, and to the Holy Ghost, as it was in the beginning, is now, and ever shall be. Amen.

The crucifix, beads and medal at the bottom of the Rosary are often used beforehand to say the Creed, the Lord's Prayer, three Hail Marys and the Gloria. Carlo Carretto argues strongly that the Rosary is not a form of

*prayer for beginners, but is the last stage before entering silent contem-
plation. The beads and the repetition may, however, be a great help to
those who want to pray when their mind is in turmoil, as a means of
achieving calm. For those who find the emphasis on the Virgin Mary
excessive, the Jesus Prayer may be used instead of the Hail Mary. In* Lord,
I Believe, *Austin Farrer develops an adaptation of the Rosary using the
Jesus Prayer to imagine that one is participating in the events of
the Gospels.*

Francis of Assisi (1181/2–1226)

*The new merchant classes were growing rich and powerful. Francis of
Assisi belonged to a rich family, but rejected his father's cloth business to
embrace Lady Poverty. So many sought to follow his example that he
formed them into a community of Little Brothers or Friars Minor. He told
them to 'Preach the gospel at all times; and if you must, use words.' His
introduction of live animals into the Christmas crib was an attempt to
show that Christ was born among the poor. His preaching to the birds
was a protest at the unwillingness of the rich to listen to him. He retreated
to Mount Alvernia to meditate, and so intense was his identification with
the crucified Jesus that wounds or 'stigmata' appeared on his hands, feet
and side.*

O most high, almighty, good Lord God: to you belong praise, glory,
honour and all blessing. Praise to my Lord God, with all his creatures:
and specially our brother the sun, who brings us the day and who brings
us the light. Fair is he, and shining with a very great splendour: O Lord,
it is you that he signifies to us. Praise to my Lord for our sister the moon:
and for the stars, which he has set clear and lovely in heaven. Praise to
my Lord for our brother the wind: and for air and cloud, calms, and all
weather, by which you uphold in life all creatures. Praise to my Lord for
our sister water: who is very serviceable to us, and humble, and precious,
and clean. Praise to my Lord for our brother fire, through whom you give
us light in the darkness: he is bright and pleasant and very mighty and
strong. Praise to my Lord for our mother the earth, which sustains
and keeps us; and brings forth divers fruits, and flowers of many colours,
and grass. Praise to my Lord for all those who pardon one another for his
love's sake: and who endure weakness and tribulation. Blessed are those
who peaceably shall endure; for you, O most highest, shall give them a
crown. Praise to my Lord for our sister the death of the body: blessed are

those who are found walking by your most holy will. Praise and bless the
Lord and give thanks to him and serve him with great humility. Alleluia,
alleluia![2]

M ay the power of your love, Lord Christ, fiery and sweet, so absorb
our hearts as to withdraw them from all that is under heaven;
grant that we may be ready to die for love of your love, as you died for
love of our love. Amen.

W e adore you, most holy Lord Jesus Christ, here, and in all your
churches throughout all the world; and we bless you, because, by
your holy cross, you have redeemed the world. Amen.

From St Francis' letter to the Chapter General and all the friars

G od almighty, eternal, righteous, and merciful, give to us poor sinners
to do for your sake all that we know of your will, and to will always
what pleases you, so that inwardly purified, enlightened, and kindled by
the fire of the Holy Spirit, we may follow in the footprints of your well-
beloved Son, our Lord Jesus Christ. Amen.

The Praises of the Trinity

H oly, holy, holy, Lord God almighty,
Who is and who was and who is to come.
Let us praise and exalt him above all for ever.
Worthy are you, O Lord our God, to receive praise, glory, honour
and blessing.
Let us praise and exalt him above all for ever.
Worthy is the lamb that was slain to receive power and divinity,
wisdom and strength, honour, glory, and blessing.
Let us praise and exalt him above all for ever.
Let us bless the Father, the Son, and the Holy Spirit.
Let us praise and exalt him above all for ever.
All the works of the Lord, now bless the Lord.
Let us praise and exalt him above all for ever.
Praise God, all of you his servants, and you that fear him, both
small and great.
Let us praise and exalt him above all for ever.
Let heaven and earth praise his glory,

and every creature that is in heaven, and on earth, and under the
   earth.
Let us praise and exalt him above all for ever.
Glory to the Father, and to the Son, and to the Holy Spirit,
as it was in the beginning, is now, and shall be for ever. Amen.

St Francis' Blessing of Brother Leo

*A parchment is reverently preserved at Assisi in St Francis' own hand-
writing, but it is worn and creased because it was kept in the breast of
Brother Leo's habit. In the margin Leo has written, 'Two years before his
death St Francis fasted on Mount La Verna in honour of the Blessed
Virgin Mary, Mother of the Lord, and of St Michael the Archangel. This
fast lasted from the Feast of the Assumption until the Feast of St Michael
in September. And the hand of the Lord rested upon him. And after the
vision and the words of the seraph, and the imprinting of the wounds of
Christ on his body, he wrote these praises on the other side of the parchment, and with his own hand gave thanks to God for the favour conferred
on him.' A little way below is added, 'Blessed Francis wrote this blessing
with his own hand for me, Brother Leo.'*

The lord bless you and keep you.
   May he show you his face and be merciful to you.
May he turn his countenance to you, and give you peace.
The Lord bless you, + Brother Leo.

On the other side of the parchment:

You alone are holy, Lord God, you do wonderful things.
   You are strong. You are great. You are the Most High.
You are the almighty King, the holy Father,
   King of heaven and earth.
You are Trinity and Unity, O Lord God, all goodness.
You are good, all good, the supreme good,
Lord God, living and true.
You are charity and love. You are wisdom.
You are humility. You are patience.
You are serenity. You are peace.
You are joy and gladness. You are justice and self-restraint.
You are our wealth, our treasure, and our satisfaction.
You are beauty. You are mercy.

You are our protector. You are our guardian and defender.
You are strength. You are refreshment.
You are our hope. You are our trust.
You are our delight. You are eternal life,
Great and wondrous Lord,
Almighty God,
Merciful Saviour.

'The Prayer of St Francis'

In spite of disagreements and periods of worldliness, the Franciscan Friars continued to bear witness to their founder's spirit of simplicity. It is in that spirit and to honour the saint (although it is not by him) that this much-loved prayer, first printed in France in 1913, is called 'The Prayer of St Francis'.

Lord, make me an instrument of thy peace. Where there is hatred let me sow love; where there is injury, pardon; where there is discord, union; where there is doubt, faith; where there is despair, hope; where there is darkness, light; where there is sadness, joy. Grant that I may seek not so much to be consoled, as to console; to be understood, as to understand; to be loved, as to love. For it is by giving that we receive; it is by losing that we find; it is by forgiving that we are forgiven; and it is by dying that we rise again to eternal life, in Jesus Christ our Lord. Amen.

Clare (1194–1253)

Inspired by the teaching of St Francis, St Clare came to join him, wishing to live a life like that of the brothers. At first Francis put her in a Benedictine convent, but when other women too wanted to lead a Franciscan life he asked Clare to be the first abbess of a new community for women. Not only did they have no private property, but some of the communities would not even own property in common, and they were rightly called the 'Poor Clares'.

I pray you, O most gentle Jesus, having redeemed me by baptism from original sin, so now by your precious blood, which is offered and received throughout the world, deliver me from all evils, past, present and to come. By your most cruel death give me a lively faith, a firm hope and perfect charity, so that I may love you with all my heart and all my soul and all my strength. Make me firm and steadfast in good works and grant me perseverance in your service so that I may be able to please you always.

Devotion to the Holy Name

It was the Franciscans who developed the cult of the Name of Jesus. The Gospels tell us that his name means 'God saves' and that the apostles worked miracles in his name. Also Jesus told us to pray in his name. The fifteenth-century Litany of the Holy Name was approved in the nineteenth century for use throughout the Roman Catholic Church. The Feast of the Holy Name has been celebrated on 14 January, the Second Sunday after Epiphany, the Sunday between 1 and 6 January and 7 August.

Jesu, dulcis memoria

Jesu, the very thought of thee
     With sweetness fills my breast;
But sweeter far thy face to see,
     And in thy presence rest.

Nor voice can sing, nor heart can frame,
     Nor can the memory find,
A sweeter sound than thy blest name,
     O Saviour of mankind!

O hope of every contrite heart,
     O joy of all the meek,
To those who fall, how kind thou art!
     How good to those who seek!

But what to those who find? Ah! this
     Nor tongue nor pen can show.
The love of Jesus! what it is,
     None but his loved ones know.

Jesu, our only joy be thou,
     As thou our prize wilt be;
Jesu, be thou our glory now,
     And through eternity.

Eleventh century[3]

Bonaventura (1217–74)

Saint Bonaventura became General of the Franciscans and, like St Denis, taught that there are three parts to the spiritual development of every Christian: The Way of Purgation, ridding oneself of sinful desires, which leads to peace; the Way of Illumination, which leads to truth; and the Way of Union, leading to love.

Crucifixion

O Lord, holy Father, show us what kind of man it is who is hanging for our sakes on the cross, whose suffering causes the rocks themselves to crack and crumble with compassion, whose death brings the dead back to life. Let my heart crack and crumble at the sight of him. Let my soul break apart with compassion for his suffering. Let it be shattered with grief at my sins for which he dies. And finally let it be softened with devoted love for him.[4]

Resurrection

Rise, beloved Christ, like a dove rising high in the sky,
its white feathers glistening in the sun.
Let us see your purity of soul.
Like a sparrow keeping constant watch over its nest of little ones,
watch over us day and night,
guarding us against all physical and spiritual danger.
Like a turtledove hiding its offspring from all attackers,
hide us from the attacks of the Devil.
Like a swallow, swooping down towards the earth,
swoop down upon us and touch us with your life-giving Spirit.[5]

For the Seven Gifts of the Spirit

Lord Jesus, as God's Spirit came down and rested upon you,
may the same Spirit rest upon us,
bestowing his sevenfold gifts.
First, grant us the gift of understanding,
by which your precepts may enlighten our minds.
Second, grant us counsel, by which we may follow
in your footsteps on the path of righteousness.

Third, grant us courage, by which we may ward
    off the Enemy's attacks.
Fourth, grant us knowledge, by which we can distinguish
    good from evil.
Fifth, grant us piety, by which we may acquire
    compassionate hearts.
Sixth, grant us fear, by which we may draw back from evil
and submit to what is good.
Seventh, grant us wisdom, that we may taste fully
the life-giving sweetness of your love.[6]

Jacapone da Todi (c. 1230–1306)

A young lawyer, addicted to luxury and with little interest in religion, da Todi married a deeply religious girl, who died soon afterwards as a result of an accident. Converted by the shock of his bereavement, he travelled around as an evangelist, writing poetry and eventually joining the Franciscan order. The 'Stabat Mater', about Mary watching Jesus on the cross, is attributed to him.

How the soul asks pardon for the offending and trying of love

Jesus, Lover dear and fair,
  Sweet thou art beyond compare . . .

Thou, O Love, wilt never leave us:
Though we sin, wilt never leave us,
Crowned with glory wilt receive us,
If our lot we humbly bear . . .

Sweet, O Love, so sweet thou art!
Towards thy realm aspires my heart;
Thirst and hunger straight depart,
Love, when once I taste thy fare . . .

On the Cross thou once didst show,
Love, that thou couldst love us so
That for us thou wast brought low,
Crucified in anguish there . . .

Thou art Love and Courtesy,
Nought ungracious dwells in thee;
Give, O Love, thyself to me,
Lest I perish in despair![7]

L ove, Love, O Love, thy touch so quickens me,
 Love, Love, O Love, I am no longer I:
Love, Love, O Love; thyself so utterly
   Thou giv'st me, Jesu, that I can but die.
Love, O Love, I am possessed of thee,
   Love, Love, my Love, O take me in a sigh!
   Love, glad and spent I lie.
      O Love, my Bliss,
      O Lover's Kiss!
   O quench my soul in Love![8]

Ramón Lull (*c.* 1235–*c.* 1315)

Ramón Lull was born in Palma on Majorca, and led a worldly life until he was converted at the age of thirty, when he became a Franciscan Tertiary. His mystical teaching aims at contemplation of God's perfection by purifying the memory, understanding and will; this results in action for the greater glory of God. He wrote hymns in his native Catalan as well as The Art of Contemplation *and* The Book of the Lover and the Beloved, *which is a dialogue between the soul (the Lover, or the Fool of Love) and Christ (the Beloved). Contrary to the crusading spirit of the age, he tried, as St Francis had done, to convert Muslims by loving service and preaching, but he was stoned to death by a crowd in North Africa. The extracts below are from* The Book of the Lover and the Beloved.

2. Long and perilous are the paths by which the Lover seeks his Beloved. They are peopled by cares, sighs and tears. They are lit up by love.

3. Many Lovers came together to love One only, their Beloved, who made them all to abound in love. And each declared his Beloved perfection, and his thoughts of Him were very pleasant, making him to suffer pain which brought delight.

4. The Lover wept and said, 'How long shall it be till the darkness of the world is past, that the mad rush of men towards hell may cease? When

comes the hour in which water, that flows downwards, shall change its nature and mount upwards? When shall the innocent be more in number than the guilty? Ah! When shall the Lover with joy lay down his life for the Beloved? And when shall the Beloved see the Lover grow faint for love of Him?'

72. The Lover entered a delightful meadow, and saw in the meadow many children who were pursuing butterflies, and trampling down the flowers; and, the more the children laboured to catch the butterflies, the higher did these fly. And the Lover, as he watched them, said: 'Such are they who with subtle reasoning attempt to comprehend the Beloved, who opens the doors to the simple and closes them to the subtle. And Faith reveals the secrets of the Beloved through the casement of love.'

73. 'Say, Fool of Love, why dost thou not speak, and what is this for which thou art thoughtful and perplexed?' The Lover answered: 'I am thinking of the beauties of my Beloved, and the likeness between the bliss and the sorrow which are brought me by the gifts of Love.'

74. 'Say, Fool, which was in being first, thy heart or thy love?' He answered and said: 'Both came into being together; for were it not so, the heart had not been made for love, nor love for reflection.'

77. Love called his lovers, and bade them ask of him the most desirable and pleasing gifts. And they asked of Love that he would clothe and adorn them after his own manner, that they might be more acceptable to the Beloved.

78. The Lover cried aloud to all men, and said: 'Love bids you ever love: in walking and sitting, in sleeping and waking, in buying and selling, in weeping and laughing, in speech and in silence, in gain and in loss – in short, in whatsoever you do, for this is Love's commandment.'[9]

Angela of Foligno (c. 1248–1309)

Angela lived almost her whole life in the Umbrian town of Foligno, and after the death of her husband she gave herself to a life of prayer. She never became a nun, but joined the Third Order of St Francis. Several of the religious orders, as well as communities of men and women, have a group of Tertiaries, who live in the world outside the convent but have a rule of life and meet to pray together when they can. Angela received frequent visions of the crucifixion of Jesus. Her confessor took down her accounts of them at her dictation, and the book is a supreme example of early Franciscan piety.

O Lord Jesus Christ, make me worthy to understand the profound mystery of your holy incarnation, which you have worked for our sake and for our salvation. Truly there is nothing so great and wonderful as this, that you, my God, who are the creator of all things, should become a creature, so that we should become like God. You have humbled yourself and made yourself small that we might be made mighty. You have taken the form of a servant, so that you might confer upon us a royal and divine beauty. You, who are beyond our understanding, have made yourself understandable to us in Jesus Christ. You, who are the uncreated God, have made yourself a creature for us. You, who are the untouchable One, have made yourself touchable to us. You, who are most high, make us capable of understanding your amazing love and the wonderful things you have done for us. Make us able to understand the mystery of your incarnation, the mystery of your life, example and doctrine, the mystery of your cross and Passion, the mystery of your resurrection and ascension. Blessed are you, O Lord, for coming to earth as a man. You were born that you might die, and in dying that you might procure our salvation. O marvellous and indescribable love! In you is all sweetness and joy! To contemplate your love is to exalt the soul above the world and to enable it to abide alone in joy and rest and tranquillity.

Catherine of Siena (1347 or 1333?–1380)

Saint Catherine of Siena joined a Dominican lay sisterhood when she was only sixteen, and gave herself to contemplation, serving the sick and poor, and converting sinners. Her letters and Dialogue *emphasize the unity of the Church as the means by which the blessings of Christ's death can reach the individual. God wishes to recreate the human race through his love. We become aware of God's love for us when we see it revealed in the cross. But first, we must know ourselves, said Catherine, so that we realize that we need to be recreated.*

Catherine: I know, Lord, that your will and my perfecting are to be sought in the sovereign love of yourself, so I want to fulfil this righteousness and to love you with this sovereign love as ardently as I may. But how must I set about it? I do not understand that sufficiently and I beseech you to enlighten me more.

Our Lord: Listen attentively with your whole mind. To love me perfectly three things are necessary. In the first place: To purify and direct the will in its temporal loves and bodily attachments so that nothing passing and perishable is loved except because of me . . .

In the second place: . . . Take my honour and my glory as the sole end of your thoughts, your actions, and all that you do; try always to worship me, whether it be by prayer, by words, or by deeds; do all you can to help your neighbour to have the same state of mind, so that everyone you meet may know, love, and worship me like you and with you . . .

In the third place: If you do that which I am going to tell you now, you will have reached a consummate perfection and nothing will be wanting in you. It is the attainment of an ardently desired and perseveringly sought disposition of the soul in which you are so closely united with me and your will so conformed to my perfect will that you never wish not only evil, but even the good that I do not wish; in every circumstance of this wretched life, whether spiritual or temporal interests are involved, whatever the difficulties, you possess your soul in peace and quietness, having always an unshakeable faith in me, your almighty God, knowing that I can love you more than you can love yourself and that I watch over you a thousand times more carefully than you can watch over yourself . . . I must not infringe the rights of your freedom; but I will transform you in myself, since you wish it, and make you one with me by making you share in my perfection, particularly in my tranquillity and my peace.

The Dialogue on Perfection[10]

Bernardino of Siena (1380–1444)

Bernardino was a Franciscan friar who preached eloquently in the cause of moral reform. He also attempted to negotiate reunion with the Greek Orthodox Church and promoted devotion to the Holy Name of Jesus.

O Lord Jesus, acknowledge what belongs to you in us, and take away from us all that is not of yours; for the sake of your honour and glory. Amen.

Italian Spiritual Writers

Dante Alighieri (1265–1321)

Dante, in his three great poems, combined the medieval understanding of Hell, Purgatory and Paradise with the newly rediscovered classical learning, and put it in the language of the ordinary people of his day.

O Light supreme, uplifted high above
Our power of grasping, grant, I pray, my mind
May yet be rendered able, through your love

To glimpse a little of your glory, and to find
The words with which those fragments may be told
Within these verses which I leave behind

That if my memory may yet be bold,
By future generations shall be known
Your splendour then as once it was of old . . .

Eternal light, eternally alone,
You smile to know yourself, and only might
You by yourself be ever fully known.

I see you as a ring of coloured light
Which, when my dazzled glance at last I raise,
And, as my eye accustoms to the sight,

Seems to contain a human form, ablaze
With the same colour as the light divine –
So strange I cannot tear away my gaze.

Geometry as yet cannot define
A circle's area as a square, we know
These are two systems which will not combine.

Nor does our language words enough bestow
With which the truths of heaven can be shown
In human terms created here below.

I could not fly so high, till from your throne
A flash of light showed what no words can prove:
What cannot be described may yet be known.

My fancy fails – you, God, are far above
My mind, which human weakness mars
Yet heart and will may still be turned by love –
The love that moves the sun and all the stars.

From Paradiso, Canto xxxiii[1]

Catherine of Genoa (1447–1510)

After ten years of unhappy marriage, Catherine, who came from a noble family of Genoa, had a religious conversion and began two practices which she continued for the rest of her life: daily Communion, and nursing the sick in the city's hospital. Her husband was then converted and worked with her until he died. Her Life and Teaching *was published after her death. It contains a 'Treatise on Purgatory' which, instead of the medieval idea of punishment, represents purgatory as a continuation of the suffering we begin in this life as the result of the tension between our love for God and love for self. This suffering is necessary until the love for self is completely eliminated, when it must end in perfect joy.*

Lord, I make you a present of myself. I do not know what to do with myself. So let me make this exchange: I will place myself entirely in your hands, if you will cover my ugliness with your beauty, and tame my unruliness with your love. Put out the flames of false passion in my heart, since these flames destroy all that is true within me. Make me always busy in your service. Lord, I want no special signs from you, nor am I looking for intense emotions in response to your love. I would rather be free of all emotion, than to run the danger of falling victim once again to false passion. Let my love for you be naked, without any emotional clothing.[2]

Vittoria Colonna (1490–1547)

She came from a famous Roman family and was distinguished not only for her writings but also for her friendship with the sculptor Michelangelo, who dedicated many of his religious sonnets to her.

Most tender Father, may your living fire purify us and your most clear light illuminate us, and by means of your love, without let or hindrance of mortal things, may we return to you in happiness and safety; through Jesus Christ, your Son, our Lord. Amen.

Teutonic Mysticism

Meister Eckhart (1260–1329)

Eckhart was a Dominican, born near Erfurt in Germany, who became a professor at Paris and then Cologne. He was a supporter of the Béguines, the new women's movement. He told the peasants that they were all aristocrats because God had made them so beautiful, and he criticised the merchant mentality of Cologne. His was a creation-centred theology; he combined cosmic mysticism with a prophetic concern for social justice. He taught a fourfold path on the approach to God: 1. The Via Positiva: *for Eckhart, prayer begins with our joy in the creation around us. 2. The* Via Negativa: *this is a question of Letting Go and Letting Be; Eckhart is not much interested in self-discipline and self-denial. 3. The* Via Creativa: *'What does God do all day long?' asked Eckhart, and replied, 'God gives birth.' So we must be creative in our prayer, and share the results of our meditation with others. 4. The* Via Transformativa: *building the new creation by way of compassion and social justice.*

O wonder of wonders! when I think of the union of my soul with you, O God! You make my soul flow out of herself in joyful ecstasy, for nothing but you can content her. A spring of divine love surges over my soul, sweeping her out of herself into you, O God, her original source.

Adapted from Tractate 2

Johann Tauler (c. 1300–1361)

Tauler was born in Strasbourg and entered the Dominican order at the age of fifteen. His sermons, printed a century and a half after his death, emphasize the equilibrium needed between the meditative journey inwards and the active duties of everyday life.

M ay Jesus Christ, the King of glory, help us to make the right use of all the myrrh (i.e. suffering) that God sends, and to offer to Him the true incense of our hearts; for his name's sake. Amen.

From A Sermon for the Epiphany

Heinrich Suso (*c.* 1295–1366)

Seuse (to give his German name) was born near Lake Constance and became a Dominican monk. He began to punish his body harshly, but soon realized that this was bringing him no nearer to God. He became the spiritual director to numerous Dominican nuns, one of whom wrote his life. Mysticism for Suso consisted in visions without images, which he described as immersion in the nothingness of God. All this is expressed in poetic language, so that Suso has been called the troubadour of German mysticism.

N ow indeed is my talk addressed to you, O love of my heart of hearts, to whom alone I have given the whole of myself, longing for this to be perpetuated for all ages. I give you thanks, my beloved, for these and the other innumerable benefits presented to me from your grace alone. May praise and glory be yours forever.

I entreat you with all my heart's burning desire 'by the bowels of your mercies' and by the power of your scarlet blood, which you poured out abundantly in your Passion for the redemption of the human race, that all those who may have determined to wed you, Eternal Wisdom, in the way that has been told, and who may have wished to worship you through the devout recitation of these prayers, or who may have laboured to make them known to the faithful, that you may bless all of them, I say, with your saving blessing, 'my King and my God.' For you are also that 'blessed fruit' long ago promised to the world, and in this you are singularly privileged, that 'whoever you will bless may himself be blessed'.

Therefore, my Father, bless these children, who are your lovers and your disciples, with the blessing of all the patriarchs and of every one of your elect who have been pleasing to you from the beginning, that in the end they may be gathered with joy to their happy number. May your lovable and glorious name, I pray, be invoked upon them, that it may be for them saving protection in all the different dangers of the life of this world. May your Eternal Wisdom direct them in what they must do, may the angel of peace keep them, and may health and prosperity of soul and body, smile upon them.

Give them, Lord, 'a place of penitence,' that through true contrition and pure confession and perfect satisfaction they may be turned before their death to you, their Creator, and may be fully reconciled to you, and, too, that by receiving your most sacred body as food for the journey they may be defended as they labour in their last agony, so that they may in no way be seized by 'sudden and unforeseen and unprepared death'.

Grant them, Lord, this grace 'because of your name,' so that as they now serve you through these devout offices, so in the last hour as they breathe out their life, they may be blessed by you, and by your sweetest mother, whom I call 'mother of mercy,' they may be led to the glorious kingdoms where in their celestial fatherland that holy 'troop of blessed spirits' may be made joyful with 'the plenteous wine of God's house' after their exile in this present wretchedness, looking upon you, 'the King of glory and the Lord of power in his beauty,' Jesus Christ, our Lord, who with the Father and the Holy Spirit lives and reigns, world without end.

Amen.[1]

I*n dulci jubilo*
Let us our homage show;
Our heart's joy reclineth
In praesipio,
And like a bright star shineth
Matris in gremio;
Alpha es et O.

O Jesu parvule,
My heart is sore for thee!
Hear me, I beseech thee,
O Puer optime!
My prayer let it reach thee,
O Princeps gloriae!
Trahe me post te!

O Patris caritas!
O nati lenitas!
Deep were we stained
Per nostra crimina;
But thou hast for us gained
Coelorum gaudia:
O that we were there!

Ubi sunt gaudia, where,
If that they be not there?
There are angels singing
Nova cantica;
There the bells are ringing
In Regis curiâ:
O, that we were there!²

'Devotio Moderna'

A movement of mystical piety which began in the Netherlands in the fourteenth century and spread across Europe, 'Devotio Moderna' arose in reaction against the mysticism of the monks and friars, and Eckhart and Tauler. Geert Groote (1340–84), the founder, was a lawyer and retired to a monastery near Arnhem, refusing the priesthood out of humility. He gathered the Brethren and the Sisters of the Common Life, united in voluntary obedience but without vows. Instead of long times spent in contemplation, he taught that we should spend a moment in meditation before we begin each new occupation during the working day and during the liturgy, but without allowing it to become a formal routine. He recommended loving devotion and contemplation of the person of Jesus. The movement grew in the fourteenth and fifteenth centuries, and continued into the nineteenth century, but its main importance was its influence, especially on Thomas à Kempis.

Thomas à Kempis (1380–1471)

Thomas was born near Cologne and spent his life in the Netherlands. His classic book The Imitation of Christ *comes from a monastic background, yet has been popular with all sorts of Christians because it teaches that it is possible for anyone to model their life on that of Jesus. 'The whole life of Christ was a cross and a martyrdom,' says Thomas, so that to follow in his steps means renouncing the world. Book 1 concerns growth in self-knowledge and detachment from the world and its priorities. Book 2 teaches that in our interior life we should follow the suffering of Jesus. Book 3 is a series of dialogues between the disciple and the living Christ, and Book 4 consists of further dialogues on the importance of careful preparation for receiving Holy Communion.*

With greatest devotion and ardent love, with all affection and fervour of heart I wish to receive you, O Lord, as many saints and devout persons, most pleasing to you in their holiness of life and most fervent in devotion, desired you in holy communion. O my God, everlasting love, my final good, my happiness unending, I long to receive you with as strong a desire and as worthy a reverence as any of the saints ever had or could have felt, and though I am not worthy to have all these sentiments of devotion, still I offer you the full affection of my heart as if I alone had all those most pleasing and ardent desires.

The Imitation of Christ 4.17

O most gracious God, from whom comes every good and perfect gift, work in us both to will and to do according to your good pleasure. Enlighten our minds that we may know you, and let us not be unfruitful in that knowledge. Lord, work in our hearts a true faith, a purifying hope, and an unfeigned love for you. Give us a full trust in you, zeal for you, reverence of all things that relate to you. Make us fearful to offend you, thankful for your mercies, humble under your corrections, devout in your service, and sorrowful for our sins. Grant that in all things we may behave ourselves so as befits a creature to his creator, a servant to his lord. Make us diligent in all our duties, watchful against all temptations, pure and temperate and moderate in your most lawful enjoyments, that they may never become a snare to us. Help us, O Lord, to act towards our neighbour that we may never transgress your royal law, of loving him as ourselves. Finally, O Lord, sanctify us throughout, that our whole spirit, soul, and body, may be preserved blameless unto the coming of our Lord Jesus Christ; to whom with you and the Holy Spirit be all honour and glory for ever. Amen.

Most gracious God, preserve us from the cares of this life, lest we should be too much entangled therein; also from the many necessities of the body, lest we should be ensnared by pleasure; and from whatever is an obstacle to the soul, lest, being broken with troubles, we should be overthrown. Give us strength to resist, patience to endure, and constancy to persevere; for the sake of Jesus Christ our Lord and Saviour. Amen.

Brother Lawrence (Nicolas Herman) (*c.* 1605–91)

Nicolas Herman was a soldier who became a hermit. On entering the Carmelite order as a lay brother he took the name Brother Lawrence, and was put in charge of the kitchen of their monastery in Paris. He wrote no book, but his papers and reports of conversations with him were collected after his death by the Abbé de Beaufort, the English translations having the title The Practice of the Presence of God. *This book has been of immense help and comfort to those who cannot go apart to pray by themselves as often as they would like, but find it possible to live a life of constant recollection in the midst of the noise and bustle of everyday business.*

'The time of business,' said he, 'does not with me differ from the time of prayer; and in the noise and clutter of my kitchen, while several persons are at the same time calling for different things, I possess God in as great tranquillity as if I were upon my knees at the Blessed Sacrament.'

From the Fourth Conversation

But when we are faithful to keep ourselves in his holy presence, and set him always before us, this not only hinders our offending him, and doing anything that may displease him, at least willfully, but it also begets in us a holy freedom, and if I may so speak, a familiarity with God, wherewith we ask, and that successfully, the graces we stand in need of. In fine, by often repeating these acts, they become habitual, and the presence of God is rendered as it were natural to us. Give him thanks, if you please, with me, for his great goodness towards me, which I can never sufficiently admire, for the many favours he has done to so miserable a sinner as I am. May all things praise him. Amen.

From the First Letter

Nicholas of Cusa (*c.* 1400–1464)

Nicholas was born at Cues on the River Moselle and became a Papal Legate, Bishop and Cardinal. He played an important part in the church politics of the time in the attempt to end the Great Schism which had led to two rival lines of Popes. He was also a philosopher, mathematician and mystic.

O Lord my God, I see you at the gate of paradise, and I do not know what I see, for I see nothing visible. The only thing I know is that I do not know what I see and can never know. You are infinity, and can only be approached by those who understand that they do not know you at all.

The Theologica Germanica (before 1516)

In 1516 Martin Luther discovered and published an anonymous manuscript, which he called Theologica Germanica *('The German Theology'). No details are known about the author, who taught that 'nothing burns in hell except self-will.'*

That we may deny ourselves, and forsake and renounce all things for God's sake, and give up our own wills, and die unto ourselves, and live unto God alone and to his will, may he help us, who gave up his will to his heavenly Father – Jesus Christ our Lord, to whom be blessing for ever and ever. Amen.

English Christianity Before the Reformation

The Sarum Rite

Many different forms of the Latin liturgy were found in different places, but the most influential in England was The Sarum Rite, *as used at Salisbury.*

Almighty God, unto whom all hearts be open, all desires known, and from whom no secrets are hid, cleanse the thoughts of our hearts by the inspiration of thy Holy Spirit, that we may perfectly love thee, and worthily magnify thy holy name; through Christ our Lord. Amen.[1]

Proficiscere, anima Christiana de hoc mundo!

Go forth upon thy journey, Christian soul!
Go from this world! Go, in the name of God,
the omnipotent Father, who created thee!
Go, in the name of Jesus Christ, our Lord,
Son of the living God, who bled for thee!
Go, in the name of the Holy Spirit, who
hath poured upon thee! Go, in the name
Of Angels and Archangels; in the name
Of Thrones and Dominations; in the name
Of Princedoms and of Powers; and in the name
Of Cherubim and Seraphim, go forth!
Go, in the name of Patriarchs and Prophets;
And of Apostles and Evangelists,
Of Martyrs and Confessors; in the name
Of holy Monks and Hermits; in the name

of holy Virgins; and all the Saints of God,
Both men and women, go! Go on thy course,
And may thy place today be found in peace,
And thy dwelling be the Holy Mount
Of Sion: – through the same, through Christ, our Lord.[2]

Incline your ear, O Lord, when we ask your mercy for the souls of your servants whom you have bidden to leave this world, that you would command them place in the kingdom of peace and light, and grant them the company of your saints; through Christ our Lord. Amen.[3]

O Lord Jesus Christ, son of the living God, who at this evening hour didst rest in the sepulchre, and didst thereby sanctify the grave to be a bed of hope to thy people: make us so to abound in sorrow for our sins, which were the cause of thy passion, that when our bodies lie in the dust, our souls may live with thee; who livest and reignest with the Father and the Holy Ghost, one God, world without end. Amen.[4]

O God, through the grace of your Holy Spirit, you pour your best gift of love into the hearts of your faithful people, grant unto us health, both of mind and body, that we may love you with our whole strength, and that today we may do those things which please you to your entire satisfaction, through Christ our Lord. Amen.[5]

We adore thee, O Christ, and we bless thee, because by thy holy Cross thou hast redeemed the world. O Saviour of the world: who by thy Cross and precious Blood hast redeemed us, save us and help us, we humbly beseech thee, O Lord.[6]

Thomas Bradwardine (c. 1290–1349)

Born in Chichester, he became confessor to King Edward III, and was one of the commissioners who sought to bring about peace between England, France and Scotland. He was made Archbishop of Canterbury and in the same year he died of the Black Death. He wrote books on mathematics and theological works about our need for God's grace.

M y God, I love you above all else, and I desire to end my life with you. Always and in all things with my whole heart and strength I seek you. If you do not give yourself to me, you give me nothing; if I do not find you, I find nothing. Grant, therefore, most gracious God, that I may always love you for your own sake more than anything else, and seek you always and everywhere in this present life, so that at the last I may find you and for ever hold fast to you in the life to come. Grant this for the sake of Jesus Christ our Lord. Amen.

The Prayer of the Most Noble Order of the Garter (1348)

The Order of the Garter is the senior British order of knighthood, founded by Edward III in about 1347, allegedly when he found a woman's garter on the floor at court. Its badge is a garter of dark blue velvet, with the motto of the order, Honi soit qui mal y pense *('Shame be to him who thinks evil of it') in gold letters. Membership is limited to 25 knights and to members of the royal family and foreign royalties. Appointments are made by the sovereign alone. St George's Chapel, Windsor, is the chapel of the order, and this is their prayer:*

O God, almighty Father, King of kings and Lord of all our rulers, grant that the hearts and minds of all who go out as leaders before us, the statesmen, the judges, the men of learning, and the men of wealth, may be so filled with the love of thy laws, and of that which is righteous and life-giving, that they may serve as a wholesome salt unto the earth, and be worthy stewards of thy good and perfect gifts; through Jesus Christ our Lord. Amen.

Richard Rolle (*c.* 1300–1349)

Richard Rolle was born in Yorkshire and studied at Oxford, but before completing his studies he left to become a hermit at various places, mostly in the north of England. His last few years were spent at Hampole near Doncaster. He wrote in Latin and English, in verse and prose, and in The Fire of Love *and* The Amendment of Life *he stands before us as an example of an ardently praying person. He described his own experience of prayer in terms of* calor, dulcor et canor, *'heat, sweetness and song'.*

My trewest tresowre sa trayturly was taken

My Truth and my Treasure so treacherously taken,
How bitter your bonds and how biting your bands,
How soon by your so-called servants forsaken,
When horrid men hurt your poor head with their hands.

The source of salvation was seized on so sore,
Then pulled out of prison to Pilate at prime.
Their battering blows then so bravely you bore;
The sinners just spat in your face with their slime.

My dear, my desire, you were dragged through the dirt,
Forced to carry your cross and wear cruel crown of thorn,
They harried your heels to your harm and your hurt,
To your hanging the back-breaking burden was born.

So sadly my Saviour in sorrow must die,
Stripped naked, then nailed to the cross all alone;
They horribly heaved up the gallows on high,
Then sank it in socket that stood in the stone.

My dearest, my darling, your death is displayed,
By ruffians roughly up-reared on the rood,
Your marvellous meekness, your mercy, have paid
For healing my hurt at the price of your blood.

You fought with our foe; when the warfare was won
Friends lovingly lowered you down to the ground,
So Mary your mother must succour her son;
All wept who were there, that so wide was your wound.

My peerless young prince, hear my cry when I call:
The meaning of this day may I never miss;
My deepest desire is to dwell in your hall –
In my breast you'll be buried, then bring me to bliss. Amen.[7]

The Cloud of Unknowing (fourteenth century)

*In England an important group of contemplatives emerged around the
fourteenth century. An anonymous writer in the East Midlands wrote that
between us and God there is a* Cloud of Unknowing. *It cannot be pierced*

by human knowledge, for God is unknowable. Only if we trample down
our desires and sin beneath a cloud of forgetting can the arrow of love
penetrate the cloud and bring us to God.

Y ou will ask me, perhaps, how you are to control yourself with due
care in the matter of food and drink and sleep and so on. My answer
is brief: 'Take what comes!' Do this thing without ceasing and without
care day by day, and you will know well enough, with a real discretion,
when to begin and when to stop in everything else. I cannot believe that
a soul who goes on in this work with complete abandon, day and night,
will make mistakes in mundane matters. If he does, he is, I think, the type
who always will get things wrong. Therefore, if I am able to give a vital
and wholehearted attention to this spiritual activity within my soul, I can
then view my eating and drinking, my sleep and conversation and so on
with comparative indifference. I would rather acquire a right discretion in
these matters by such indifference, than by giving them my close attention,
and weighing carefully all their pros and cons. Indeed, I could never bring
it about in such a way, for all I might do or say. Let men say what they
will: experience teaches. Therefore lift your heart up with this blind upsurge
of love, and consider now 'sin', and now 'God'. God you want to have;
sin you want to lose. You lack God: you know all about sin. Good God
help you now, for it is now that you have need of him.[8]

Julian of Norwich (*c.* 1342–1420)

Mother Julian lived as a recluse at Norwich, yet many people came to
learn about prayer from her. In a series of visions or 'Showings', Julian
sees that the whole universe is no greater, compared to the greatness of
God, than a hazelnut, yet God loves the creation with a mother's care.
We should pray even when we do not feel like it, because it is God who
is praying in us.

A lso in this he shewed me a little thing, the quantity of an hazel-nut,
in the palm of my hand; and it was as round as a ball. I looked
thereupon with eye of my understanding, and thought: *What may this be?*
And it was answered generally thus: *It is all that is made.* I marvelled how
it might last, for methought it might suddenly have fallen to naught for
littleness. And I was answered in my understanding: *It lasteth, and ever*
shall last for that God loveth it. And so all-thing hath the being by the love
of God.

In this little thing I saw three properties. The first is that God made it, the second is that God loveth it, the third, that God keepeth it. But what is to me verily the Maker, the Keeper, and the Lover, – I cannot tell; for till I am substantially oned to him, I may never have full rest nor very bliss: that is to say, till I be so fastened to him, that there is right nought that is made betwixt my God and me.[9]

After this our Lord shewed concerning prayer. In which shewing I see two conditions in our Lord's signifying: one is rightfulness, another is sure trust.

But yet oftentimes our trust is not full: for we are not sure that God heareth us, as we think because of our unworthiness, and because we feel right nought, (for we are as barren and dry oftentimes after our prayers as we were afore); and this, in our feeling our folly, is cause of our weakness. For thus have I felt in myself.

And all this brought our Lord suddenly to my mind, and shewed these words, and said: *I am ground of thy beseeching: first it is my will that thou have it; and after, I make thee to will it; and after, I make thee to beseech it and thou beseechest it. How should it then be that thou shouldst not have thy beseeching? . . .*

Full glad and merry is our Lord of our prayer; and he looketh thereafter and he willeth to have it because with his grace he maketh us like to himself, in condition as we are in kind: and so is his blissful will. Therefore he saith thus: *Pray inwardly, though thee thinketh it savour thee not: for it is profitable, though thou feel not, though thou see nought; yea, though thou think thou canst not. For in dryness and in barrenness, in sickness and in feebleness, then is thy prayer well-pleasant to me, though thou thinketh it savour thee nought but little. And so is all thy believing prayer in my sight.* For the meed and the endless thanks that he will give us, therefore he is covetous to have us pray continually in his sight. God accepteth the good-will and the travail of his servant, howsoever we feel: wherefore it pleaseth him that we work both in our prayers and in good living, by his help and his grace, reasonably with discretion keeping our powers turned to him, till when that we have him that we seek, in fulness of joy: that is, Jesus . . .

And also to prayer belongeth thanking. Thanking is a true inward knowing, with great reverence and lovely dread turning ourselves with all our mights unto the working that our good Lord stirreth us to, enjoying and thanking inwardly. And sometimes, for plenteousness it breaketh out with voice, and saith: *Good Lord, I thank thee! Blessed mayst thou be!* And sometime when the heart is dry and feeleth not, or else by temptation of our enemy, – then it is driven by reason and by grace to cry upon our Lord with voice, rehearing his blessed passion and his great goodness; and the virtue of our Lord's word turneth into the soul and quickeneth the heart and entereth it by his grace into true working, and maketh it pray right blissfully. And truly to enjoy our Lord, it is a full blissful thanking in his sight.[10]

And this word: *Thou shalt not be overcome*, was said full clearly and full mightily, for assuredness and comfort against all tribulations that may come. He said not: *Thou shalt not be tempested, thou shalt not be travailed, thou shalt not be afflicted*; but he said: *Thou shalt not be overcome*. God willeth that we take heed to these words, and that we be ever strong in sure trust, in weal and woe. For he loveth and enjoyeth us, and so willeth he that we love and enjoy him and mightily trust in him; and *all shall be well*.[11]

And from that time that it was shewed I desired oftentimes to learn what was our Lord's meaning. And fifteen years after, and more, I was answered in ghostly understanding, saying thus: *Wouldst thou learn thy Lord's meaning in this thing? Learn it well. Love was his meaning. Who shewed it thee? Love. What shewed he thee? Love. Wherefore shewed he it? For Love. Hold thee therein and thou shalt learn and know more in the same. But thou shalt never know nor learn therein other thing without end.* Thus was I learned that Love was our Lord's meaning.

And I saw full surely that ere God made us he loved us; which love was never slacked, nor ever shall be. And in this love he hath done all his works; and in this love he hath made all things profitable to us; and in this love our life is everlasting. In our making we had beginning; but the love wherein he made us was in him from without beginning: in which love we have our beginning. And all this shall we see in God, without end.[12]

Margery Kempe (*c.* 1373–after 1433)

Margery Kempe was a contemporary of Julian, and visited her in her cell. She was born at King's Lynn in Norfolk, married John Kempe and bore him fourteen children. After a period of madness she received a number of visions, and with her husband made a pilgrimage to Canterbury. Later, leaving her husband behind, she went on pilgrimage to the Holy Land and Compostella. Without fearing anyone, she condemned sin wherever she saw it. Her enemies then ensured that she was herself formally condemned. Undoubtedly she was psychologically disturbed, but she laid all her troubles before God in prayer, and wrote the prayers in her book. The Book of Margery Kempe was the first autobiography in English. In it she writes about the gift of tears: she regarded the ability to cry frequently as a blessing which God had given her, for her own benefit and for the benefit of those for whom she wept. She was also given a strong awareness of the presence of Jesus, and his love for herself and for the world. At the end of her life she devoted her time to nursing her invalid husband.

Lord I ask for your mercy. Chastise me for my sins and purge me of all evil, that I may be saved from everlasting damnation. I am willing, even happy, to endure any suffering here on earth, that I may be spared the torments of hell.[13]

Ah, dear God, I have not loved you for all my life, and now I bitterly regret the time when I ignored you. I ran away from you. Yet you ran after me, so now, for all my impurity, you have given me hope.[14]

Lord, make my eyes walls of tears, that when I receive your body tears of devotion may pour down my cheeks. You are my joy, Lord, my bliss and my comfort. You are all the treasure I have in this world. I want no earthly pleasures, I want only you. And so, dearest Lord, let your body which I now receive be your pledge that you will never forsake me, for all eternity.[15]

Ah, blessed Lord, I wish I knew how I might best love you and please you, and that my love were as sweet to you as your love is to me.[16]

Lord, why do you make me cry out loud, when I am in a public place? It causes them to condemn me as mad or stupid, and so they cannot see that I am really your most faithful servant. In particular, I beg you to prevent me from crying during sermons. When I cry listening to holy preaching, I have no choice but to run away, so my cries bar me from hearing your doctrines. And I fear that one day I will be arrested and put in prison, so I will hear no more sermons. If I must cry, please ensure that I only cry in the privacy of my bed-chamber.[17]

I thank you, Lord, for all the sins which I have not done, because you restrained me. I thank you for the sorrow I have felt for all the sins I have done. I thank you for all the people I have met, both friends and enemies. And I pray for them all, that they may all be your friends.[18]

Edmund Rich (*c.* 1180–1240)

Saint Edmund was born at Abingdon in Berkshire. He taught logic at Oxford, and St Edmund Hall in that University is believed to have been built on the site of his Oxford home. As Archbishop of Canterbury he attempted, without success, to resist royal mismanagement of the Church's property and the taxes imposed by the Pope, so he retired to Pontigny in self-imposed exile.

I nto thy hands, O Father and Lord, we commend this night our souls and our bodies, our parents and homes, friends and colleagues, neighbours and kindred, our benefactors and the faithful departed, all folk rightly believing, and all who need thy pity and protection: light us with thy holy grace, and suffer us never to be separated from thee, O Lord in Trinity, God everlasting; Amen.

L ord, since you exist, we exist. Since you are beautiful, we are beautiful. Since you are good, we are good. By our existence we honour you. By our beauty we glorify you. By our goodness we love you. Lord, through your power all things were made. Through your wisdom all things are governed. Through your grace all things are sustained. Give us power to serve you, wisdom to discern your laws, and grace to obey those at all times.

From The Mirror of Saint Edmund[19]

Richard of Wyche (1197–1253)

Born at Droitwich, he became chancellor of Canterbury under Archbishop Edmund Rich. King Henry III refused permission for Richard to be consecrated Bishop of Chichester, until the Pope threatened to excommunicate the King. Richard was a deeply spiritual man and an excellent administrator. The Prayer of St Richard of Chichester, which has recently been set to music by several composers, is now one of the most popular in the English language.

Praise to thee, Lord Jesus Christ, for all the benefits thou hast won for me, for all the pains and insults thou hast born for me. Most merciful redeemer, friend and brother, may I know thee more clearly, love thee more dearly, and follow thee more nearly, day by day. Amen.

King Henry VI (1421–71)

Henry became king when he was only one year old, and his tragic life included difficulties in France, civil war in England, mental breakdown, exile and imprisonment for three separate periods of time. Eventually he was murdered in the Tower of London. He was a deeply religious man, but too generous and trusting to be a good king. He spent many hours in prayer, and visited religious houses whenever he could. He was the founder of Eton College and of King's College, Cambridge. Of him Wordsworth wrote, 'Tax not the royal Saint with vain expense.' The architecture of great ecclesiastical buildings is a form of prayer in stone which has otherwise to remain unmentioned in this book.

Lord Jesu Christ, that madest me,
That boughtest me on rode-tree
And fore-ordainedst that I be,
Thou knowst what thou wouldst do with me;
Do with me now as pleaseth thee.
Amen, Jesu, for thy pity.

An anonymous verse in the Fairfax Manuscript

There appears in the fifteenth-century Fairfax Manuscript a song set to music by Sheryngham, with verses by Lydgate and an anonymous refrain. This is an example of the type of devotion which would have been popular at the time.

Ah gentle Jesu!'
'Who is that, that doth me call?'
'I, a sinner, that oft doth fall.'
'What wouldst thou have?'
'Mercy, Lord, of thee I crave.'
'Why, lov'st thou me?'
'Yea, my Maker I call thee.'
'Then leave thy sin, or I nil thee,

And think on this lesson that now I teach thee.'
'Ah, I will, I will, gentle Jesu.'

'Upon the cross nailed I was for thee,
Suffered death to pay thy ransom;
Forsake thy sin, man, for the love of me,
Be repentant, make plain confession;
To contrite hearts I do remission;
Be not despaired, for I am not vengeable;
Gain' ghostly en'mies think on my passion;
Why art thou froward, sith I am merciable?'
'Ah, gentle Jesu' . . .

'Lord, on all sinful, here kneeling on knee,
Thy death remembring of humble affection,
O Jesu, grant of thy benignity
That thy five wells plenteous of fusion,
Called thy five wounds by computation,
May wash us all, from surfeits reprovable.
Now for thy Mother's meek mediation,
At her request be to us merciable,
Ah, gentle Jesu.'

The Humanists

Alongside the development of mystical prayer in the Middle Ages went a growth in the power of the popes. This was challenged by a radical change in medieval thinking due to the rediscovery of Greek and Roman classical civilization, generally called the Renaissance. Together with this went a new study of the Bible in the original Greek and Hebrew languages, and of the writings of the early Christian Fathers. This led to a renewed emphasis on human experience, which naturally challenged the imposed doctrines of the medieval Church. The leading figure in this movement of Christian Humanism was Erasmus.

Desiderius Erasmus (c. 1466–1536)

Erasmus became an Augustinian canon near Gouda, and although he was given liberty to leave his monastery and was deeply satirical about monasticism, he never left the Roman Catholic Church or joined the Protestants. His depth of learning in the classics, as well as enabling him to publish sound Greek and Latin versions of the early Fathers and the New Testament, made him very critical of medieval scholasticism, and his humanism prepared the way for the Reformation. He several times visited England, where he was welcomed by Colet and stayed with Sir Thomas More. He emphasized free-will in opposition to Luther, and was at times rejected by both sides in the Reformation controversy, whereas his deepest wish was for peace.

O Lord Jesus Christ, the Way, the Truth and the Life, grant that we may never stray from you who are the Way, nor distrust you who are the Truth, nor rest in any thing other than you, who are the Life. Teach us by your Holy Spirit what to believe, what to do, and wherein to take our rest. For your own name's sake we ask it, O Jesus Christ our Lord. Amen.[1]

Hear our prayers, O Lord Jesu, the everlasting Wisdom of the Father; who givest unto us, in the days of our youth, aptness to learn: add, we pray thee, the furtherance of thy grace, so to learn knowledge and the liberal sciences that, by their help, we may attain to the fuller knowing of thee, whom to know is the height of blessedness; and by the example of thy boyhood, may duly increase in age, wisdom, and favour with God and man. Who livest and reignest with the Father and the Holy Ghost, world without end. Amen.[2]

Lord Jesus Christ,
you are the sun that always rises, but never sets.
You are the source of all life,
creating and sustaining every living thing.
You are the source of all food, material and spiritual,
nourishing us in both body and soul.
You are the light that dispels the clouds of error and doubt,
and goes before me every hour of the day,
guiding my thoughts and my actions.
May I walk in your light,
be nourished by your food,
be sustained by your mercy,
and be warmed by your love.[3]

Most merciful Saviour, whom to know, with the Father and the Holy Ghost, is life everlasting: increase the faith of thy servants, that we may never stray from thy truth; our obedience, that we may never swerve from thy commandments. Increase thy grace in us, that, alive in thee, we may fear nothing but thee, than whom nothing is more mighty; love nothing but thee, than whom nothing is more lovable; glory in nothing but thee, who art the glory of all the saints; and finally desire nothing but thee, who, with the Father and the Holy Ghost, art the full and perfect felicity for ever.[4]

John Colet (1466?–1519)

John was the son of the Lord Mayor of London, and studied Greek in France and Italy. He remained Dean of St Paul's in London from 1505 until he died, and spent his personal fortune on founding St Paul's School.

O merciful Father, who dost put away the sin of those who truly repent, we come before thy throne in the name of Jesus Christ, that for his sake alone, thou wilt have compassion upon us, and let not our sins be a cloud between thee and us. Amen.

Sir Thomas More (1478–1535)

A thorough education in the classics and in law led Thomas More to become a barrister and then a Member of Parliament. He thought of becoming a monk, but decided he was not called to celibacy. Yet his family life and his house at Chelsea, which was visited by all the great minds of Europe, were filled with regular and disciplined prayer. While he was acting as an envoy for Henry VIII in Flanders he wrote Utopia, *describing an ideal society living in natural obedience to God's laws. He wrote against Martin Luther and in favour of the veneration of saints and images and the punishment of heretics. In 1529 he was made Lord Chancellor, but he opposed the King's divorce, and he was imprisoned in the Tower for fifteen months, using it as an opportunity for prayer and penance and to write devotional books. He was beheaded on Tower Hill on 6 July 1535.*

Almighty God, have mercy on N. and N., and on all that bear me evil will, and would me harm, and their faults and mine together, by such easy, tender, merciful means, as thine infinite wisdom best can devise, vouchsafe to amend and redress, and make us saved souls in heaven together where we may ever live and love together with thee and thy blessed saints, O glorious Trinity, for the bitter passion of our sweet Saviour Christ.

O my sweet Saviour Christ, which in thine undeserved love towards mankind so kindly wouldst suffer the painful death of the cross, suffer me not to be cold nor lukewarm in love again towards thee.

Glorious God, give me grace to amend my life, and to have an eye to mine end without grudge of death, which to them that die in thee, good Lord, is the gate of a wealthy life. And give me, good Lord, an humble, lowly, quiet, peaceable, patient, charitable, kind, tender, and pitiful mind, with all my works and all my words and all my thoughts, to have a taste of thy holy, blessed Spirit. Give me, good Lord, a full faith, a firm hope, and a fervent charity, a love to thee incomparable above the love to myself. Give me, good Lord, a longing to be with thee, not for the avoiding of the calamities of this world, nor so much for the attaining of the joys of heaven, as for a very love of thee. And bear me, good Lord, thy love and favour, which thing my love to theeward, were it never so great, could not but thy great goodness deserve. These things, good Lord, that I pray for, give me thy grace to labour for. Amen.[5]

G ood and gracious Lord, as thou givest me grace to acknowledge my sins, so give me grace in both word and heart to repent them and utterly forsake them. And forgive me those sins which my pride blinds me from discerning. Glorious God, give me thy grace to turn my back on the things of this world, and to fix my heart solely on thee. Give me thy grace to amend my life, so that I can approach death without resentment, knowing that in thee it is the gateway to eternal riches. Glorious God, take from me all sinful fear, all sinful sorrow and self-pity, all sinful hope and all sinful desire. Instead give me such fear, such sorrow, such pity, such hope and such desire as may be profitable for my soul. Good Lord, give me this grace, in all my fear and agony, to find strength in that great fear and agony which thou, sweet Saviour, had on the Mount of Olives before thy bitter passion. Almighty God, take from me all desire for worldly praise, and all emotions of anger and revenge. Give me a humble, lowly, quiet, peaceable, patient, generous, kind, tender and compassionate mind. Grant me, good Lord, a full faith, a firm hope and a fervent love, that I may desire only that which gives thee pleasure and conforms to thy will. And, above all, look upon me with thy love and thy favour.[6]

Ludovicus Vives (Juan Luis Vives) (1492–1540)

Vives was born in Valencia, but King Henry VIII brought him over from Bruges to be tutor to Princess Mary. After opposing the King's divorce he was imprisoned, and on his release he lived mostly in Bruges. His prayers were quoted in many primers of devotion, both Catholic and Protestant, until well into the next century. He teaches that the events of daily life should be treated as parables to remind us of events in Scripture and of our own mortality.

G ive us grace, O our God, to listen to thy call, to obey thy voice, and to follow thy guiding. Thou leadest us to pleasures that never fade, to riches which no moth nor rust can corrupt or destroy. Unsearchable riches are in thy hand; O give us grace to know thy value of them and to covet them. Thou leadest us to fountains of living water. Suffer us not to wander or turn aside till we attain unto the pleasures which are at thy right hand for evermore. Establish, settle, strengthen us, that our goodness may not be like the early dew, which passeth away. But make us steadfast, immovable, always abounding in the work of the Lord, forasmuch as we know that our labour is not in vain in the Lord. Grant this, we beseech thee, for thy dear Son, Jesus Christ's sake. Amen.

O Lord, the author and persuader of peace, love and goodwill, soften our hard and steely hearts, warm our frozen and icy hearts, that we may wish well to one another, and may be the true disciples of Jesus Christ. And give us grace even now to begin to show forth that heavenly life wherein there is no hatred, but peace and love on all hands, one toward another; through Jesus Christ our Lord. Amen.[7]

The Protestant Reformation

The movement of protest which the humanists had begun remained for a while an attempt to reform the Roman Catholic Church from within. Some of the changes which were called for were achieved in the twentieth century at the Second Vatican Council. But when those calling for reform were expelled from the Church, they had little option other than to gather their followers into new, 'Protestant' churches. This led to a renewal in the life of prayer, as Protestants rediscovered the direct approach of the soul to God without needing any mediating priesthood.

William Tyndale (1494?–1536)

Whereas Wyclif's Bible was translated from the Latin Vulgate, the first to be translated into English directly from the Hebrew and Greek originals was that of William Tyndale or Tindale. He studied at Oxford and Cambridge, and told an opponent, 'If God spare my life, ere many years I will cause a boy that driveth the plough shall know more of the Scripture than thou dost.' But, receiving no support from the English church authorities for his translation project, he settled in Germany never to return, and it was there that his Bible was published. Many of the strong English phrases of Tyndale's version were retained unchanged in the King James Authorised Version. Tyndale was burnt at the stake near Brussels.

Almighty God, whose is the eternal only power, and other men's power but borrowed of thee: we beseech thee for those who hold office in this (*city, borough etc.*) that, holding it first from thee, they may use it for the general good and to thine honour; through Jesus Christ our Lord. Amen.[1]

Miles Coverdale (1488–1568)

Miles Coverdale was a priest in the house of Augustinian friars in Cambridge when he began his Bible translation. He preached sermons attacking confession and images, and was compelled to live abroad. His translation of the Bible was printed in Zurich. Many of his phrases have entered into common speech, and his version of the Psalms is included in The Book of Common Prayer *(1662).*

O give us patience and steadfastness in adversity, strengthen our weakness, comfort us in trouble and distress, help us to fight; grant unto us that in true obedience and contentation of mind we may give over our own wills unto thee our Father in all things, according to the example of thy beloved Son; that in adversity we grudge not, but offer up ourselves unto thee without contradiction . . . O give us a willing and cheerful mind, that we may gladly suffer and bear all things for thy sake.

O Lord Jesus Christ, draw thou our hearts unto thee; join them together in inseparable love, that we may abide in thee and thou in us, and that the everlasting covenant between us may stand sure for ever. Let the fiery darts of thy love pierce through all our slothful members and inward powers, that we, being happily wounded, may so become whole and sound. Let us have no lover but thyself alone; let us seek no joy nor comfort except in thee.

O God, give us patience when those who are wicked hurt us. O how impatient and angry we are when we think ourselves unjustly slandered, reviled and hurt! Christ suffers blows upon his cheek, the innocent for the guilty; yet we may not abide one rough word for his sake. O Lord, grant us virtue and patience, power and strength, that we may take all adversity with goodwill, and with a gentle mind overcome it. And if necessity and thy honour require us to speak, grant that we may do so with meekness and patience, that the truth and thy glory may be defended, and our patience and steadfast continuance perceived.

Christ is now risen again
From his death and all his pain:
Therefore will we merry be,
And rejoice with him gladly.
Kyrieleison.

Had he not risen again,
We had been lost, this is plain:
But since he is risen in deed,
Let us love him all with speed.
Kyrieleison.
Now is a time of gladness,
To sing of the Lord's goodness:
Therefore glad now will we be,
And rejoice in him only.
Kyrieleison.

Martin Luther (1483–1546)

Martin Luther was an Augustinian Canon, and so was obliged to recite the Daily Office. He fell ill and was unable to continue with this form of prayer, so when he recovered he thought he needed to complete all the hours of prayer he had missed while he was sick, and in the process he made himself ill again. So he realized that he could not earn his way into heaven by good works, and was justified by the grace of God, through faith alone. But he clung to a modified version of the medieval emphasis on the sacraments. When, in depression, he doubted his own salvation, he would strike the table and cry, 'But I have been baptized!' In 1517 he nailed his Ninety-Five Theses to the door of the Church in Wittenberg, calling for a debate on the practice of selling Indulgences, entitling the purchaser to a shorter time in Purgatory in return for a donation. He went on to attack the primacy of the Pope, the doctrine of transubstantiation, clerical celibacy, masses for the dead, religious orders, and the refusal of the wine of Communion to the lay people. Yet he saw himself as reforming the Roman Catholic Church, and not until he was excommunicated by the Pope in 1521 was he forced to start a new movement.

Behold, Lord, an empty vessel that needs to be filled. My Lord, fill it. I am weak in the faith; strengthen me. I am cold in love; warm me and make me fervent that my love may go out to my neighbour. I do not have a strong and firm faith; at times I doubt and am unable to trust you altogether. O Lord, help me. Strengthen my faith and trust in you. In you I have sealed the treasures of all I have. I am poor; you are rich and came to be merciful to the poor. I am a sinner; you are upright. With me there is an abundance of sin; in you is the fulness of righteousness. Therefore, I will remain with you, of whom I can receive, but to whom I may not give. Amen.

Come Lord Jesus be our guest,
And may our meal by thee be blest.

Attributed

O God, graciously comfort and tend all who are imprisoned, hungry, thirsty, naked, and miserable; also all widows, orphans, sick, and sorrowing. In brief, give us our daily bread, so that Christ may abide in us and we in him for ever, and that with him we may worthily bear the name of 'Christian.'

O my God, stand by me against all the world's wisdom and reason. Oh, do it! You must do it! You alone must do it! Not mine, but yours, is the cause. For myself, I have nothing to do with these great and earthly lords. I would prefer to have peaceful days, and to be out of this turmoil. But this cause is yours, O Lord; it is righteous and eternal. Stand by me, true and eternal God! I trust in no mortal being. God, O God! do you not hear me, O my God? Are you dead? No. You cannot die; you are only hiding yourself. Have you chosen me for this work? I ask you how I may be sure whether it is your will; for I would never have thought, in all my life, of undertaking anything against such great lords. Stand by me, O God, in the name of your dear Son, Jesus Christ. Christ shall be my Defence and Shelter, my Mighty Fortress, through the might and strength of your Holy Spirit. God help me. Amen.

Ah, dearest Jesus, holy Child,
Make thee a bed, soft, undefiled,
Within my heart, that it may be
A quiet chamber kept for thee.

Welcome to earth, thou noble guest,
Through whom e'en wicked men are blest!
Thou com'st to share our misery,
What can we render, Lord, to Thee!

Ah, Lord, who hast created all,
How hast thou made thee weak and small,
That thou must choose thy infant bed
Where ass and ox but lately fed!

Were earth a thousand times as fair
Beset with gold and jewels rare,
She yet were far too poor to be,
A narrow cradle, Lord, for thee.

For velvets soft and silken stuff
Thou hast but hay and straw so rough.
Whereon thou king, so rich and great.
As 'twere thy heaven, art throned in state.

Thus hath it pleased thee to make plain
The truth to us poor fools and vain.
That this world's honour, wealth and might
Are nought and worthless in thy sight . . .[2]

Ulrich Zwingli (1484–1531)

A Roman Catholic priest in Zurich, Zwingli had studied Greek, Hebrew and the writings of the early Church, and was an admirer of Erasmus. In 1519 he gave a series of lectures on the New Testament which caused controversy, and subsequently he condemned the doctrine of Purgatory, monasticism and the invocation of saints. But his desire for reform within the Roman Catholic Church seems to have been that shared by many loyal Catholics and was quite independent of Luther. However, when he questioned the control of believers by the Pope and the bishops, a public debate was called for, in which the city council gave Zwingli their support when he upheld sixty-seven theses. Clerical celibacy was abolished and Zwingli married. He now developed a purely symbolic view of the Eucharist, in which Christ is in no way present in the bread and wine, and was disappointed when Luther did not agree with him, so that any chance of a united Protestantism was lost. Much of Switzerland followed Zwingli, but the five Forest Cantons declared war on the Protestants, and Zwingli, carrying the banner as the chaplain, was killed.

When near to death from the plague in Zurich:

Help, Lord, help
In this need.
So let it be: Do what thou wilt.
I nothing lack.
Thy vessel I am: to make or break altogether.[3]

Philip Melancthon (1497–1560)

Philip Melancthon (his original surname was Schwarzerd) studied at Heidelberg and Tübingen and became professor of Greek at Wittenberg. More conciliatory than most other Protestant leaders, he found himself leader of the Reformation movement when Luther was imprisoned in the Wartburg. The principal author of the Augsburg Confession, the defining document of Lutheran doctrine, Melanchthon also wrote commentaries on Scripture which moved away from the medieval allegorical approach to a more classical and historical method.

Holy Spirit, almighty God, proceeding from the Father and the Son; Jesus the eternal Son, our Redeemer, has promised that you will kindle in us the true knowledge and love of God. Stir up in our hearts, we pray, true fear, true faith, that we may acknowledge the mercy which the Father of our Lord Jesus Christ hast promised unto us for his sake. Be our Comforter in all difficulties and dangers, and kindle divine love in our hearts, so that by true obedience, we may offer perpetual praise to you and to the Father of our Lord Jesus Christ, and to his blessed Son, our Saviour and Redeemer. Amen.

O God, the author of all good things in your holy Church, work mightily in all your servants, that we may be profitable to all, and bringers of your mercy and grace. Control us all, and so govern our thoughts and deeds, that we may serve you in righteousness and true holiness. Make us holy for that eternal life, which we, with all your creation, groaning together as if in childbirth, wait for and expect; through Jesus Christ our Lord.

To you, O Son of God, Lord Jesus Christ, we pray, as you pray to the eternal Father: make us one in him. Lighten our personal distress and that of our society. Receive us into the fellowship of those who believe. Turn our hearts, O Christ, to everlasting truth and healing harmony. Amen.

The Anabaptists

Arising from medieval prophetic mysticism and Zwinglian reform, the Anabaptists were a movement of independent congregations, which they called brotherhoods. They were determined to obey God only, rejecting the authority of the state or tradition. They refused to take oaths, or do military

service, or accept infant baptism, so they took their name from their
practice of re-baptizing those who joined them as adults. Their refusal to
compromise led to persecution and martyrdom, and in prison they
composed hymns which became the backbone of the movement.

F oremost, apply love
   Through which we overcome, while on this life's course;
It is the bond of perfection. Love is God himself,
It remains in eternity.[4]

Menno Simons (*c.* 496–1561)

Simons was a parish priest in Dutch Friesland, when in 1536 he left the
Roman Catholic Church to join the Anabaptists, who were suffering severe
persecution. He taught that only adult believers should be baptized, that
each church should be governed by its own congregation, and non-
resistance. His followers, known as the Mennonites, today number over
half a million, half of them in the United States of America, where their
pacifist witness has been impressive. Instead of military service they serve
the poor and needy around the world.

W e thank thee, Lord God and Father, Creator of heaven and earth,
   for all thy good gifts which we, O Father of lights, have received
of thee, and receive daily of thy liberal hand through Jesus Christ, the
dearly beloved Son, our Lord, thou who hast clothed our bodies with the
needed covering and hast satisfied them with the natural bread. We pray
thee humbly, as our dearly beloved Father, to look upon us, thy children,
persecuted for the sake of thy holy Gospel, and earnestly desirous, in our
weakness, to live devoutly in this world. Be pleased to keep us in thy Word
in fatherly fashion, in order that to the end of our days we may remain
constant in thy Word and Gospel, revealed by thee to the plain and simple,
and hidden to the wise ones of this world.[5]

M y God, where shall I wend my flight?
   Ah, help me on upon the way;
The foe surrounds both day and night
And fain my soul would rend and slay.
Lord God, thy Spirit give to me,
Then on thy ways I'll constant be,
And in Life's Book, eternally![6]

Thomas Münzer (*c.* 1490–1525)

Münzer was a priest who, under the influence of Luther, Huss and others, became a Protestant preacher. But his opposition to infant baptism won him the disapproval of Luther. He claimed the direct inspiration of the Holy Spirit, but he also preached revolt against the secular authorities. After being expelled from one town after another, he attempted to lead the Peasants' Revolt, but after it was defeated he was captured and executed. The serenity of his prayers is in marked contrast to his troubled life.

F aithful God, now that we have made a covenant with you, stay close beside us and guide us away from any sin or corruption. May the gentle flesh and the costly blood of your son Jesus Christ, symbolized in the bread and wine of Communion, be the seals of that covenant which can never be broken.[7]

J ust as a grain of wheat must die in the earth in order to bring forth a rich harvest, so your Son died on the cross to bring a rich harvest of love. Just as the harvest of wheat must be ground into flour to make bread, so the suffering of your Son brings us the bread of life. Just as bread gives our bodies strength for our daily work, so the risen body of your Son gives us strength to obey your laws.[8]

L oving God, we give thanks for the birth of your Son Jesus Christ, both in human form in Bethlehem and in spiritual form in our hearts. May he reign as king within every human heart, so that every town and village can live according to his joyful law of love.[9]

M erciful God, we know that we deserve to have your anger poured out upon us; yet in your infinite love you have chosen instead to pour out the grace of your Holy Spirit. May your Spirit so enlighten our hearts, that we may show the same merciful love to others that you have shown to us.[10]

Jean Calvin (1509–64)

Calvin was born in Picardy and trained for the priesthood, but while he was studying in Paris he had doubts about his vocation. In 1533 he had a religious experience, and felt that God was calling him to restore the

Church to its original purity. He went to Basle and published the first edition of his Institutes. *Guillaume Farel (1489–1565) pleaded with him to help organize the Reformation at Geneva. This he did by setting up a theocracy: every citizen without exception had to sign a personal profession of faith, and to receive Communion weekly; failure to do so was punished by exile. All pleasure was forbidden, including especially dancing and games. He taught that God has already predestined some to heaven and others to destruction. Although he had his opponents tortured and killed, he expounded the Bible with brilliance, and his influence spread through Presbyterian churches in many nations.*

M y God, Father and Saviour, since you have commanded us to work in order to meet our needs, sanctify our labour that it may bring nourishment to our souls as well as to our bodies. Make us constantly aware that our efforts are worthless unless guided by your light and strengthened by your hand. Make us faithful to the particular tasks for which you have bestowed upon us the necessary gifts, taking from us any envy or jealousy at the vocations of others. Give us a good heart to supply the needs of the poor, saving from any desire to exalt ourselves over those who receive our bounty. And if you should call us into greater poverty than we humanly desire, save us from any spirit of defiance or resentment but rather let us graciously and humbly receive the bounty of others. Above all may every temporal grace be matched by spiritual grace that in both body and soul we may live to your glory.

From The Christian Life[11]

O Lord God, who has given us the night for rest, I pray that in my sleep my soul may remain awake to you, steadfastly adhering to your love. As I lay aside my cares to relax and relieve my mind, may I not forget your infinite and unresting care for me. And in this way, let my conscience be at peace, so that when I rise tomorrow, I am refreshed in body, mind and soul.[12]

John Knox (c. 1513–72)

John Knox took minor orders in the Roman Catholic Church, maybe even the priesthood, but started a career as a notary. Influenced by George Wishart, he began to preach in favour of the Reformation at St Andrew's. He was captured by the French, and when released in France he went to England, became a chaplain to King Edward VI, and assisted in drawing up the 1552 Book of Common Prayer. *Fleeing from Queen Mary to*

Geneva, he met Jean Calvin, and, after a short return visit to Scotland, wrote The First Blast of the Trumpet against the Monstrous Regiment of Women. *This was aimed at Mary of Guise, the widow of James V of Scotland, who acted as regent while her daughter, Mary Queen of Scots, was not of age. The book argued that it was unscriptural for a woman to hold authority over men, a view not unknown among some Evangelicals today. This earned him the hostility of Queen Elizabeth I of England, but he became in effect the leader of the Reformed Church in Scotland, through times marked by executions and murders. His passionate, single-minded preaching stamped his personality on the events that he recorded in his* History of the Reformation in Scotland. *He compiled the first worship book for the Church of Scotland, called* The Book of Common Order.

Let thy mighty hand, O Lord God, and outstretched arm be our defence; thy mercy and loving-kindness in Jesus Christ, thy dear Son, our salvation; thy all-true word, our instruction; the grace of the life-giving Spirit, our comfort and consolation, unto the end and in the end.[13]

O heavenly Father, which art the fountain and full treasure of all goodness, we beseech thee to show thy mercies upon us thy children, and sanctify these gifts which we receive of thy merciful liberality, granting us grace to use them soberly and purely, according to thy blessed will; so that hereby we may acknowledge thee to be the author and giver of all good things; and, above all, that we may remember continually to seek the spiritual food of thy word, wherewith our souls may be nourished.

O God of all power, who hast called from death the great Shepherd of the sheep, our Lord Jesus, comfort and defend the flock which he hath redeemed by the blood of the eternal testament; increase the number of true preachers; mitigate and lighten the hearts of the ignorant; relieve the pains of such as be afflicted, but especially of those that suffer for the testimony of the truth, by the power of our Lord Jesus Christ. Amen.

The Lord sanctify and bless you; the Lord pour the riches of his grace upon you, that you may please him and live in holy love to your life's end. Amen.

Jacobus Arminius (Jacob Hermandzoon) (1560–1609)

Calling himself Arminius when writing in Latin, Hermandzoon studied in many of the great Reformed universities of Europe, but returned to Holland when he heard that most of his relatives had been massacred by the Spanish in their struggle against the Princes of Orange for control of Holland. Paradoxically, he was often accused afterwards of supporting the Spanish. He was appointed professor at Leyden, and was at once attacked because he could not agree with the doctrine of predestination taught by hard-line Calvinism. He believed that Christ died for all, not just for those who had been chosen by God in advance to be saved, and that human beings exercise freewill in choosing whether or not to accept salvation. His followers, after his death, summarized Arminianism in The Remonstrance, *which was condemned at the Synod of Dort. Calvinists have ever since condemned their opponents as Arminians, suspecting them of believing that we can pull ourselves up to heaven by our own bootstraps.*

O omnipotent and merciful God, the Father of our Lord Jesus Christ, we give you thanks for the infinite benefits you have conferred on us pitiable sinners. But first; we praise you that your Son Jesus Christ by your will should be the sacrificial victim and the price of redemption for our sins. Out of the whole human race you have collected for yourself a Church, by your word and Holy Spirit; you have taken us into the kingdom of light and of your Son. We thank you for calling our pleasant and delightful nation of Holland to know and confess your Son and to enjoy communion with him; and for preserving our native land in safety against the assaults of our adversaries. We thank you for establishing in our city this university as a seminary of true wisdom, piety and righteousness. Holy and indulgent God, continue these blessings on us for ever, and do not allow us, by our ingratitude, to be deprived of them. Rather increase them, and make firm the work which you have begun. May we always remember these things, and give eternal praise to your holy name for them, through our Lord Jesus Christ. Amen.

From A Homily on the Priesthood of Christ

Johann Kepler (1571–1630)

Educated at Tübingen and professor of mathematics at Graz, he was led to the discovery of his three laws of planetary motion by a mystical Protestant belief that the orderliness of creation expressed the nature of God.

O God, through the light of nature you have aroused in us a longing for the light of grace, so that we may be raised in the light of your majesty. To you I give thanks, Creator and Lord, that you allow me to rejoice in your works. Praise the Lord, you heavenly harmonies, and you who know the harmony that has been revealed. For everything exists from you, through you and in you, the perceptible world as well as the spiritual; that which we know and that which we do not know, for there is still much to learn.

Hermann of Wied (1477–1552)

As the Archbishop-Elector of Cologne, Hermann of Wied was the secular as well as the religious ruler of his principality. Initially opposed to Protestantism, he began to create a parallel movement in the Roman Catholic Church. Hermann's Consultations, *in which he outlined his policies and proposed a liturgy in the vernacular language, influenced Cranmer in compiling* The Book of Common Prayer. *He was excommunicated and deposed by the Pope and died a Lutheran.*

Let thy fatherly hand, we beseech thee, ever be over us; let thy Holy Spirit ever be with us and so lead us in the knowledge and obedience of thy word, that in the end we may obtain everlasting life; through Jesus Christ our Lord. Amen.

Have mercy upon us, most gentle Father, through thy Son our Lord Jesus Christ. Give, and increase thy Holy Spirit in us, who may teach us to acknowledge our sins truly and thoroughly, and to be pricked with a lively repentance of the same, and with true faith to apprehend and retain remission of them in Christ our Lord, that dying to sin daily more and more, we may serve and please thee in a new life, to the glory of thy name, and edifying of thy congregation. For we acknowledge that thou justly requirest these things of us, wherefore we desire to perform the same. Vouchsafe thou, O Father of heaven, which hast given us a will, to grant us also that we may study to do those things with all our hearts which pertain to our health, through our Lord Jesus Christ.[14]

Jacob Boehme (1575–1624)

Jacob Boehme was a German Lutheran shoemaker. In his writings he gives a religious significance to material things and has a deep sense of the tragedy of everything, but holds that the Creator can participate in the life of believers. Though unorthodox in his dualism and astrology, he was a great influence on many subsequent writers, although John Wesley complained that Boehme's prose was too obscure.

On Waking

Living Lord, you have watched over me, and put your hand on my head, during the long, dark hours of night. Your holy angels have protected me from all harm and pain. To you, Lord, I owe life itself. Continue to watch over me and bless me during the hours of day.[15]

On Rising

Rule over me this day, O God, leading me on the path of righteousness. Put your word in my mind and your truth in my heart, that this day I neither think nor feel anything except what is good and honest. Protect me from all lies and falsehood, helping me to discern deception wherever I meet it. Let my eyes always look straight ahead on the road you wish me to tread, that I might not be tempted by any distraction. And make my eyes pure, that no false desires may be awakened within me.[16]

At Bed-time

As I take off my dusty, dirty clothes, let me also be stripped of the sins I have committed this day. I confess, dear Lord, that in so many ways my thoughts and actions have been impure. Now I come before you, naked in body and bare in soul, to be washed clean. Let me rest tonight in your arms, and so may the dreams that pass through my mind be holy. And let me awake tomorrow, strong and eager to serve you.[17]

The English Reformation

It has been said that the Reformation on the Continent was a religious movement with political consequences and that in England it was a political movement with religious consequences.

King Henry VIII (1491–1547)

It is hard to discover what personal faith lies behind the public pronouncements of historical figures, which may have been written for them by others. King Henry was granted the title of 'Defender of the Faith' (which still appears on some British coins) by Pope Leo X for writing an Assertion of the Seven Sacraments, *and appears to have himself written the preface to* The King's Book, *a summary of medieval Roman Catholic doctrine arguing against the Reformers. Although he instituted political reforms, removing the control of church law and church revenues from the hands of a foreign Pope, which made the English Reformation possible in the next reign, he seems to have remained doctrinally a Roman Catholic until his death. It could be argued that, although Henry was undoubtedly a womanizer, his divorces were essentially a political matter in the attempt to ensure a legitimate male heir. These prayers are from* Henry VIII's Primer, *written for his personal devotional use.*

O merciful Lord God, heavenly Father, we render praise and thanks unto thee; that thou hast preserved us both this night, and all the times and days of our lives hitherto, under thy protection, and hast suffered us to live until this present hour. And we beseech thee heartily that thou wilt vouchsafe to receive us this day, and the residue of our whole lives, from henceforth into thy good keeping; ruling and governing us with thy Holy Spirit; that all manner of darkness and evil may be utterly chased and driven out of our hearts; and that we may walk in the light of thy truth; to thy glory and praise; and to the help and furtherance of our neighbours; through Jesus Christ our Lord and Saviour. Amen.

O most merciful Father, who by the mouth of our Saviour Jesus Christ hast said, 'Ask, and it shall be given you,' receive, we beseech thee, our supplication, and for thy Truth's sake hear us in thy righteousness. We make our prayers unto thee, most blessed Father, not trusting in our own righteousness, but in thy manifold mercies. Have mercy upon us, thy sinful children. Soften our hard hearts with the dew of thy grace. Fulfil thy promise made unto us by thy prophet. Take away from us our stony heart, and put a new spirit within us, and make us to walk after thy commandments. Lighten, O Father of lights, our blind hearts, blinded with error and ignorance. Lighten them with the true light of thy holy Word, that we may know thy will, love it, and live thereafter. Give us grace, O heavenly Father, to feel in our hearts thine infinite goodness and mercy and thine exceeding kindness set forth unto us in and by our Saviour Jesus Christ, whom thou hast given up to death to redeem us from everlasting death, and to make us thy children and heirs, brethren and inheritors together with thine only Son, our Lord Jesus Christ. Amen.

King Henry is traditionally supposed to have written the words and music of this anthem:

O Lord, the maker of all things, we pray thee now in this evening hour, to defend us through thy mercy from all deceit of our enemy. Let us not be deluded with dreams, but if we lie awake keep thou our hearts. Grant this petition, O Father, to whom with the Holy Ghost, always in heaven and earth, be all laud, praise and honour. Amen.

Thomas Cromwell (1485–1540)

Thomas Cromwell made himself useful to Cardinal Wolsey, taking the income of some small monasteries to found for him what later became Christ Church College, Oxford. But when Wolsey was disgraced – he died saying, 'Had I but served God as diligently as I have served the King, he would not have given me over in my grey hairs' – Cromwell transferred to King Henry VIII's service. He was responsible for the dissolution of the monasteries, which had grown very wealthy, the beginning of parish registers, and the requirement that there should be a Bible in every church. He arranged the marriage of the King with Ann of Cleves, with the aim of creating an alliance with the Protestant powers of Germany, but such was the King's disgust with the 'Flanders mare' that Cromwell was sentenced and beheaded, saying this prayer on the scaffold at Tower Hill:

O Lord Jesu, who art the only health of all men living, and the everlasting life of them which die in thy faith; I give myself wholly into thy will; being sure the thing cannot perish, which is committed unto thy mercy ... O Lord, into thy hands I commit my soul.

Thomas Cranmer (1489–1556)

Thomas Cranmer was a fellow of Jesus College, Cambridge when King Henry VIII was seeking a way to have his desired divorce accepted by the Church, and he suggested that as the Pope, who had waived the Church law to allow the marriage in the first place, was a virtual prisoner of the Queen's family, a debate in the universities of Europe might decide the matter. When the universities decided in Henry's favour, he appointed Cranmer Archbishop of Canterbury in gratitude. Cranmer accepted the office with great reluctance, but once appointed, he used it to further his own plans for a theological reformation in the Church. He had already secretly married. He compiled The Litany, *the first service in the vernacular, in 1544, when Henry was at war with the Scots and the French. It was not, however, until the boy King Edward VI was on the throne that he could pursue his aim of introducing Protestant theology to the Church of England.* The Book of Common Prayer *of 1549 and its more Protestant revision of 1552 were largely his own compositions. Cranmer influenced and was influenced by the changes in the English language at this time to produce some of the finest expressions of Christian prayer in the history of the nation. When Mary became Queen he was accused of high treason, sentenced and pardoned, but then tried for heresy. He signed a recantation, accepting transubstantiation and papal supremacy, but then withdrew it. He was burnt at the stake in Oxford, thrusting first into the flames the hand which had signed the recantation.*

O thou who in almighty power wast meek, and in perfect excellency wast lowly, grant unto us the same mind, that we may mourn over our evil will. Our bodies are frail and fading; our minds are blind and froward; all that we have which is our own is naught; if we have any good in us it is wholly thy gift. O Saviour, since thou, the Lord of heaven and earth, didst humble thyself, grant unto us true humility, and make us like thyself; and then, of thine infinite goodness, raise us to thine everlasting glory; who livest and reignest with the Father and the Holy Ghost for ever and for ever. Amen.

Before his death at the stake

O Father of heaven; O Son of God, Redeemer of the world; O Holy Ghost, proceeding from them both; three Persons, and one God; have mercy upon me, most wretched caitiff and miserable sinner. I have offended both heaven and earth, more grievously than any tongue can express. Whither then may I go, or whither should I flee for succour? To heaven I may be ashamed to lift up mine eyes, and in earth I find no refuge or succour. What shall I then do? Shall I despair? God forbid. O good God, thou art merciful, and refusest none that cometh unto thee for succour. To thee, therefore, do I run; to thee do I humble myself; saying, O Lord God, my sins be great, but yet have mercy upon me for thy great mercy. O God the Son, this great mystery was not wrought (that God became man) for few or small offences; nor thou didst not give thy Son unto death, O God the Father, for our little and small sins only, but for all the greatest sins of the world, so that the sinner return unto thee with a penitent heart, as I do here at this present. Wherefore have mercy upon me, O Lord, whose property is always to have mercy; for although my sins be great, yet thy mercy is greater. And I crave nothing, O Lord, for mine own merits, but for thy name's sake, that it may be glorified thereby.

The Litany (1544)

This responsive form of prayer, based on the Latin litanies then in use in England, was issued by Cranmer in 1544 to be used in the penitential processions ordered by Henry VIII when England was at war with Scotland and France.

O God, merciful Father, that despisest not the sighing of a contrite heart, nor the desire of such as be sorrowful; mercifully assist our prayers that we make before thee in all our troubles and adversities, whensoever they oppress us; and graciously hear us, that those evils, which the craft and subtlety of the devil or man worketh against us, be brought to nought, and by the providence of thy goodness they may be dispersed; that we thy servants, being hurt by no persecutions, may evermore give thanks unto thee in thy holy Church, through Jesus Christ our Lord.[1]

That it may please thee to give us true repentance, to forgive us all our sins, negligences and ignorances, and to endue us with the grace of thy Holy Spirit, to amend our lives according to thy holy word; we beseech thee to hear us, good Lord.[2]

The Order of Communion (1548)

As a first move towards the introduction of English in the Latin Mass, Cranmer published prayers to be used at the time when the congregation were receiving the bread and wine. So popular was the beautiful 'Prayer of Humble Access' that it has been included in almost every Anglican liturgy ever since, though nobody has been quite sure where to place it. In 1552 it was inserted in the middle of the Eucharistic Prayer, where it continued in 1662, with the result that the invitation to lift up one's heart and give thanks is followed by this prayer of great humility.

We do not presume to come to this thy table, O merciful Lord, trusting in our own righteousness, but in thy manifold and great mercies. We are not worthy so much as to gather up the crumbs under thy table. But thou art the same Lord, whose property is always to have mercy; grant us therefore, gracious Lord, so to eat the flesh of thy dear Son Jesus Christ, and to drink his blood in these holy mysteries, that we may evermore dwell in him, and he in us, and that our sinful bodies may be made clean by his body, and our souls washed through his most precious blood. Amen.

The Book of Common Prayer (1549)

Cranmer's reasons for compiling this can be found beautifully expressed in the Preface (renamed in 1662, 'Concerning the Service of the Church').

Almighty God, give us grace that we may cast away the works of darkness, and put upon us the armour of light, now in the time of this mortal life, in which thy Son Jesus Christ came to visit us in great humility, that in the last day, when he shall come again in his glorious Majesty to judge both the quick and the dead, we may rise to the life immortal, through him who liveth and reigneth with thee and the Holy Ghost, now and ever. Amen.

The First Sunday in Advent

Blessed Lord, who hast caused all Holy Scriptures to be written for our learning: grant that we may in such wise hear them, read, mark, learn, and inwardly digest them, that by patience, and comfort of thy holy Word, we may embrace, and ever hold fast the blessed hope of everlasting life, which thou hast given us in our Saviour Jesus Christ. Amen.

The Second Sunday in Advent

Almighty God, who hast given us thy only-begotten Son to take our nature upon him, and as at this time to be born of a pure Virgin: grant that we being regenerate, and made thy children by adoption and grace, may daily be renewed by thy Holy Spirit, through the same our Lord Jesus Christ, who liveth and reigneth with thee and the same Spirit, ever one God, world without end. Amen.

Christmas Day

Lord, who hast taught us that all our doings without charity are nothing worth: send thy Holy Ghost, and pour into our hearts that most excellent gift of charity, the very bond of peace and of all virtues, without which whosoever liveth is counted dead before thee: grant this for thine only Son Jesus Christ's sake. Amen.

Quinquagesima

Almighty and everlasting God, who hatest nothing that thou hast made, and dost forgive the sins of all them that are penitent: create and make in us new and contrite hearts, that we worthily lamenting our sins, and acknowledging our wretchedness, may obtain of thee, the God of all mercy, perfect remission and forgiveness; through Jesus Christ our Lord. Amen.

Ash Wednesday

O Lord, who for our sake didst fast forty days and forty nights: give us grace to use such abstinence, that, our flesh being subdued to the Spirit, we may ever obey thy godly motions in righteousness, and true holiness, to thy honour and glory, who livest and reignest with the Father and the Holy Ghost, one God, world without end. Amen.

The First Sunday in Lent

Almighty Father, who hast given thine only Son to die for our sins, and to rise again for our justification: grant us so to put away the leaven of malice and wickedness, that we may alway serve thee in pureness of living and truth; through the merits of the same thy Son Jesus Christ our Lord. Amen.

The First Sunday after Easter

Almighty God, who hast given thine only Son to be unto us both a sacrifice for sin, and also an ensample of godly life: give us grace that we may always most thankfully receive that his inestimable benefit, and also daily endeavour ourselves to follow the blessed steps of his most holy life; through the same Jesus Christ our Lord. Amen.

The Second Sunday after Easter

O God the King of glory, who hast exalted thine only Son Jesus Christ with great triumph unto thy kingdom in heaven: we beseech thee, leave us not comfortless; but send to us thine Holy Ghost to comfort us, and exalt us unto the same place whither our Saviour Christ is gone before, who liveth and reigneth with thee and the Holy Ghost, one God, world without end. Amen.

Sunday after Ascension Day

Almighty and everliving God, we most heartily thank thee, for that thou dost vouchsafe to feed us, who have duly received these holy mysteries, with the spiritual food of the most precious Body and Blood of thy Son our Saviour Jesus Christ; and dost assure us thereby of thy favour and goodness towards us; and that we are very members incorporate in the mystical body of thy Son, which is the blessed company of all faithful people; and are also heirs through hope of thy everlasting kingdom, by the merits of the most precious death and passion of thy dear Son. And we most humbly beseech thee, O heavenly Father, so to assist us with thy grace, that we may continue in that holy fellowship, and do all such good works as thou hast prepared for us to walk in; through Jesus Christ our Lord, to whom, with thee and the Holy Ghost, be all honour and glory, world without end. Amen.

Holy Communion

Almighty God, the fountain of all wisdom, who knowest our necessities before we ask, and our ignorance in asking: we beseech thee to have compassion upon our infirmities; and those things, which for our unworthiness we dare not, and for our blindness we cannot ask, vouchsafe to give us, for the worthiness of thy Son Jesus Christ our Lord Amen.

Holy Communion

Almighty God, who hast promised to hear the petitions of them that ask in thy Son's name: We beseech thee mercifully to incline thine ears to us that have made now our prayers and supplications unto thee; and grant, that those things, which we have faithfully asked according to thy will, may effectually be obtained, to the relief of our necessity, and to the setting forth of thy glory; through Jesus Christ our Lord. Amen.

Holy Communion

The Book of Common Prayer (1552)

Cranmer apparently regarded the 1549 book as a step on the way to the more Protestant revision of 1552. In that year an introduction was added to Morning and Evening Prayer, and alterations were made to most of the other services.

Almighty and most merciful Father; We have erred, and strayed from thy ways like lost sheep. We have followed too much the devices and desires of our own hearts. We have offended against thy holy laws. We have left undone those things which we ought to have done; And we have done those things which we ought not to have done; And there is no health in us. But thou, O Lord, have mercy upon us, miserable offenders. Spare thou them, O God, which confess their faults. Restore thou them that are penitent; According to thy promises declared unto mankind in Christ Jesu our Lord. And grant, O most merciful Father, for his sake; That we may hereafter live a godly, righteous, and sober life, To the glory of thy holy name. Amen.

The Absolution, or Remission of sins, to be pronounced by the Priest alone, standing; the people still kneeling.

Almighty God, the Father of our Lord Jesus Christ, who desireth not the death of a sinner, but rather that he may turn from his wickedness, and live; and hath given power, and commandment, to his Ministers, to declare and pronounce to his people, being penitent, the absolution and remission of their sins: He pardoneth and absolveth all them that truly repent, and unfeignedly believe his holy Gospel. Wherefore let us beseech him to grant us true repentance, and his Holy Spirit, that those things may please him, which we do at this present; and that the rest of our life hereafter may be pure and holy, so that at the last we may come to his eternal joy, through Jesus Christ our Lord.

The people shall answer here, and at the end of all other Prayers, 'Amen.'

Morning Prayer and Evening Prayer

Defend, O Lord, this thy child [or *this thy servant*] with thy heavenly grace, that he may continue thine for ever, and daily increase in thy Holy Spirit more and more, until he come unto thine everlasting kingdom; through Jesus Christ our Lord. Amen.

Confirmation

Nicholas Ridley (*c.* 1500–1555)

Ridley studied at the Sorbonne and in Louvain, as well as at Cambridge, where, after a short time as chaplain to Thomas Cranmer, he became Master of Pembroke Hall. He then became Bishop of Rochester and finally Bishop of London. He was sympathetic to the Reformation, and under Edward VI he openly promoted Protestantism at Cambridge and helped to compile the first Book of Common Prayer *in 1549. He preached on social injustice, and a sermon he preached to the King was partly instrumental in the foundation of Christ's Hospital (the Bluecoat School for orphans), St Thomas's Hospital, and the Bridewell as a home for vagrants, homeless children and petty criminals. He supported Lady Jane Grey's claim to the crown, and when Mary came to the throne he was removed from his bishopric. He was then excommunicated and burned at the stake with Hugh Latimer in Oxford, where the Martyrs' Memorial now stands.*

O heavenly Father, the author and fountain of all truth, the bottomless sea of all understanding, send, we beseech thee, thy Holy Spirit into our hearts, and lighten our understandings with the beams of thy heavenly grace. We ask this, O merciful Father, for thy dear Son our Saviour Jesus Christ's sake. Amen.

O heavenly Father, the Father of all wisdom, understanding, and true strength, I beseech thee, for thy only Son our Saviour Jesus Christ's sake, look mercifully upon me, wretched creature, and send thine Holy Spirit into my breast; that not only I may understand according to thy wisdom, how this temptation is to be borne off, and with what answer it is to be beaten back; but also, when I must join to fight in the field for the glory of thy holy name, that then I being strengthened with the defence of thy right hand, may manfully stand in the confession of thy faith, and of thy truth, and may continue in the same unto the end of my life; through the same our Lord Jesus Christ. Amen.

Written during his final imprisonment

Hugh Latimer (*c.* 1485–1555)

Hugh, the son of a yeoman farmer in Leicestershire, became a famous preacher with a down-to-earth style and a ready wit. Although he preached against social abuses and corruption in the Church, he was licensed to preach anywhere in England. He was rebuked for spreading Protestantism, but after the rift between Henry VIII and the Pope he became one of the King's advisors, and then Bishop of Worcester. He resigned rather than sign the Six Articles which condemned Reformation doctrine. For a while he was kept a prisoner in the Tower of London, but was released when Edward VI came to the throne, and soon became a popular court preacher. Under Queen Mary's reign, however, he was again arrested and sent to the Tower. In 1554, together with Cranmer and Ridley, he was taken to Oxford to debate transubstantiation and the Sacrifice of the Mass. Refusing to accept the medieval doctrine, he was excommunicated and burnt with Latimer. It shows remarkable faith and courage to be able to joke when one is being burnt at the stake. His last words were, 'Be of good comfort, Master Ridley, and play the man. We shall this day light such a candle by God's grace in England, as (I trust) shall never be put out.'

I f you will build a glorious church unto God, see first yourselves to be in charity with your neighbours, and suffer not them to be offended by your works. Then, when ye come into your parish-church, you bring with you the holy temple of God; as Saint Paul saith, 'You yourselves be the very holy temples of God:' and Christ saith by his prophet, 'In you will I rest, and intend to make my mansion and abiding place.'

From The Second Sermon on the Card

John Bradford (*c.* 1510–55)

Bradford was a native of Manchester and a Fellow of Pembroke Hall in Cambridge. Seeing some criminals being taken to execution, he exclaimed, 'But for the grace of God, there goes John Bradford.' In 1555 he was himself burnt at the stake in Smithfield.

O Lord, thou greatest and most true light, whence this light of the day and of the sun doth spring! O Light, which dost lighten every man that cometh into the world! O Light, which knowest no night nor evening, but art always a mid-day most clear and fair, without whom all is most dark darkness, by whom all be most resplendent! O thou wisdom of the eternal 'Father of mercies', lighten my mind, that I may only see those things that please thee, and may be blinded to all other things. Grant that I may walk in thy ways, and that nothing else may be light and pleasant unto me. Lighten my eyes, O Lord, that I sleep not in death.

Thomas Becon (*c.* 1513–67)

Becon was a priest in Norwich when he was arrested in about 1540 for preaching Protestant doctrines. When Edward VI became King, however, he was appointed Chaplain to the household of Archbishop Cranmer. He was exiled to Europe during the reign of Queen Mary, but under Elizabeth I returned to be a Canon of Canterbury. His earlier writings in particular are devotional in tone, moderate and basically Lutheran.

O Lord, give us grace not only to be hearers of the word, but also doers of the same; not only to love, but to live thy gospel; not only to profess, but also to practise thy blessed commandments, to the honour of thy holy name. Amen.

Heavenly Father, who watchest over thy faithful people and mightily defendest them, we thank thee that it has pleased thee to take care of us thy servants during the night past, and to give us needful sleep to refresh our bodies. We beseech thee to show the same goodness to us this day, so preserving and ruling over us that we may neither think, nor speak, nor do anything displeasing to thee, or hurtful to our neighbour, but that all our doings may be agreeable to thy most holy will, and may advance thy glory, so that, when thou shalt call us hence, we may be found the children, not of darkness, but of light; for the sake of Jesus Christ our Lord. Amen.

O Lord, heavenly Father, by whose divine ordinance the darkness covers the earth and brings unto us bodily rest and quietness, we render thee our hearty thanks for the loving-kindness which thou hast shown, in preserving us during the past day, and in giving us all things necessary for our health and comfort. And we beseech thee, for Jesus Christ's sake, to forgive us all the sins we have committed in thought, word, or deed, and that thou wilt shadow us this night under the wings of thy almighty power, and defend us from all power of the evil one. May our souls, whether sleeping or waking, wait upon thee, delight in thee, and evermore praise thee, so that when the light of day returns, we may rise with pure and thankful hearts, casting away the works of darkness and putting on the armour of light; through Jesus Christ. Amen.

King Edward VI (1537–53)

Here are two prayers from a 'Primer' published during the boy-king's reign. They were probably written for his personal use as he took his first steps in the life of prayer.

O merciful Lord God, heavenly Father, whether we sleep or wake, live or die, we are always thine, wherefore we beseech thee heartily that thou wilt vouchsafe to take care and charge of us, and not to suffer us to perish in the works of darkness, but to kindle the light of thy countenance in our hearts, that thy godly knowledge may daily increase in us through a right and pure faith, and that we may always be found to walk and live after thy will and pleasure; through Jesus Christ our Lord. Amen.

O Lord Jesus Christ, most true pastor and shepherd of our souls, we most humbly beseech thee mercifully to behold thy poor and scattered flock, whom thou hast purchased with thy most precious blood, and to send them such shepherds as may diligently seek the lost sheep, lovingly lay them on their shoulders and faithfully bring them home again to the fold. Vouchsafe ever to continue in thy Church good Bishops, learned preachers, faithful teachers, godly ministers, and diligent shepherds; even such as have a powerful and unfeigned zeal towards the setting forth of thy glory and the health of thy people. Endue them with thy holy Spirit, that they may be faithful, wise, and discreet servants, giving thy household meat in due season. Give them that wisdom which no man is able to resist, wherewith also they may be able to exhort with wholesome doctrine, and

The Counter-Reformation

The Roman Catholic Church, realizing that the Protestants were not just another minor schism within the Church, set about reforming abuses and discovered new ways to make a positive and successful presentation of the virtues of the Catholic faith. In the process many profound mystics arose, and much practical teaching on the life of prayer was published.

Ignatius Loyola (1491 or 1495–1556)

Ignatius Loyola formed the Jesuits as the mobile 'shock-troops' of the Counter-Reformation, to be deployed anywhere the Pope directed. His Spiritual Exercises *are intended as notes to guide a spiritual director who is leading someone else through an experience of meditation. To experience the whole process takes thirty days, and although flexibility is recommended, the strictest form would be a retreat in complete silence with a daily interview with the director, and four or five hours daily in prayer in addition to attending the daily services. The process begins with a consideration of the purpose of our life and our relationship with the rest of creation. This is followed by a week of meditation about sin and its consequences. Next comes a period for meditating on the events of Jesus' life, and another for thinking about his suffering and death. The final week is to experience the joy of the resurrection, and in conclusion to reflect on God's love for us and our response of love for God. Throughout, the person making the retreat is encouraged to think about the direction of their life and to make choices, and is helped to carry out the choices that have been made. Ignatius' motto was that everything should be done 'To the greater glory of God'.*

Dearest Lord, teach me to be generous;
teach me to serve you as you deserve;
to give and not to count the cost,
to fight and not to heed the wounds,

to toil and not to seek for rest,
to labour and not to ask for any reward,
save that of knowing that I do your will.

Lord Jesus Christ, fill us, we pray, with your light and life, that we may reveal your wondrous glory. Grant that your love may so fill our lives that we may count nothing too small to do for you, nothing too much to give and nothing too hard to bear.

Take, Lord, as your right, and receive as my gift, all my freedom, my memory, my mind and my will. Whatever I am and whatever I possess, you have given to me; I give it all back to you. Dispose of me, and the powers you gave me, according to your will. Give me only a love for you, and the gift of your grace; then I am rich enough, and ask for nothing more.

Lord, welcome into your calm and peaceful kingdom those who have departed out of this present life to be with you; grant them rest and a place with the spirits of the just; and give them the life that knows not age, the reward that passes not away; through Jesus Christ our Lord.

Francis Xavier (1506–52)

Born at Navarre, he met Ignatius Loyola while at Paris University, and was one of the original members of the Society of Jesus. He was invariably seasick, yet his missionary travels took him to Goa, Ceylon, Malacca and Japan, and he died on his way to China. He is credited with making 700,000 converts.

O God of all the nations of the earth, remember the multitudes who, though created in your image, have not known you, nor the dying of your Son their Saviour Jesus Christ; and grant that by the prayers and labours of your holy Church they may be delivered from all ignorance and unbelief, and brought to worship you; through him whom you have sent to be the Resurrection and the Life of all people, your Son Jesus Christ our Lord.

Teresa of Avila (1515–82)

Saint Teresa of Avila joined the Carmelite order when she was about twenty. Following her 'second conversion' in about 1555, she had frequent visions and raptures. Once she was sure these were not from the devil, she became convinced of God's leading, and in 1559 had a series of intense visions culminating in the impression that God was piercing her heart with a spear. She began to write her Life, *in which she compares the decreasing effort which has to be put into the life of prayer to watering a field from a well, a water-wheel, a stream and by the rain. The Way of Perfection contains a contemplation based on the Lord's Prayer. The Interior Castle pictures the soul progressing from the outer courtyard to the inmost rooms of its seven mansions. The first three concern the way of purification in prayer, when we eliminate selfishness, distraction and sin. The fourth is the prayer of recollection followed by the prayer of quiet. The fifth leads to the prayer of union and the spiritual betrothal. The soul is pictured as a silkworm emerging from its cocoon as a white butterfly. In the sixth mansion are afflictions resembling the dark nights of which her friend St John of the Cross speaks, but in the seventh comes the spiritual marriage and permanent union with God. Meanwhile she lived an active life, reforming the Carmelite order to which she belonged. Because her followers went barefoot, they were called the Discalced Carmelites. She persuaded St John of the Cross to begin a similar reform among the Carmelite friars. Together they taught about contemplative prayer, which goes beyond words in the silent contemplation of God's love.*

'Nada te turbe'

Let nothing disturb you;
nothing dismay you;
all things pass,
but God never changes.
Whoever has God lacks nothing:
if you have only God, you have more than enough.[1]

Christ has no other hands but your hands to do his work today;
no other feet but your feet to guide folk on his way;
no other lips but your lips to tell them why he died;
no other love but your love to win them to his side.[2]

Majestic King, for ever wise,
You melt my heart, which once was cold,
And when your beauty fills my eyes
It makes them young, which once were old.

Christ, my creator, hear my cry,
I am all yours, your call I hear,
My Saviour, Lover, yours am I,
My heart to yours be ever near.

Whether in life or death's last hour,
If sickness, pain or health you give,
Or shame, or honour, weakness, power,
Thankful is the life I live.[3]

My God, my life is sad:
Your face I cannot see.
With you it would be glad,
But if that cannot be –
I want to die.

In vain I cry, 'Be near!
Your voice I yearn to hear,
I wish to feel you here,
And that you would appear
Before my eye.'

When on my life's last day
You come into my heart,
That you may ever stay,
That we may never part –
I want to die.[4]

How is it, my God, that you have given me this hectic busy life when
I have so little time to enjoy your presence. Throughout the day
people are waiting to speak with me, and even at meals I have to continue
talking to people about their needs and problems. During sleep itself I am
still thinking and dreaming about the multitude of concerns that surround
me. I do all this not for my own sake, but for yours. To me my present
pattern of life is a torment; I only hope that for you it is truly a sacrifice
of love. I know that you are constantly beside me, yet I am usually so busy

that I ignore you. If you want me to remain so busy, please force me to think about and love you even in the midst of such hectic activity. If you do not want me so busy, please release me from it, showing how others can take over my responsibilities.[5]

O my Lord, since it seems you are determined to save me, I ask that you may do so quickly. And since you have decided to dwell within me, I ask that you clean your house, wiping away all the grime of sin.[6]

When I approached the altar to receive you in the blessed sacrament, my hair stood on end. Then my legs went weak, and I felt as if I were about to collapse under the weight of your majesty. In the tiny piece of bread you revealed to me your grandeur and your purity. Since I am so wretched and so filthy, I should have felt terrified of your presence. But instead I felt comforted and reassured by the knowledge that you, the King of kings, were about to give yourself in love to me.[7]

Saint Teresa's Last Words

My Lord, it is time to move on.
Well then, may your will be done.
O my Lord and my Spouse,
the hour that I have longed for has come.
It is time for us to meet one another.[8]

Queen Mary I of England (1516–58)

Mary Tudor was the daughter of King Henry VIII and his first wife, Catherine of Aragon. Her mother's disgrace and divorce embittered her childhood, as did her betrothal to the Dauphin of France and then to the Emperor Charles V, neither of which led to marriage. Her relations with Henry's subsequent wives were varied, but she was affectionate with Catherine Parr, and was given the next place in the succession to the throne after Edward VI, whom she succeeded in 1553. Unhappily married to Philip II of Spain, she was unable to have children. She refused to renounce her Roman Catholic faith in Edward's reign, and made it obligatory for everyone when she came to the throne, but at first she was lenient towards Protestants. After defeating Thomas Wyatt's plot against her, however, she signed the Heresy Bill and re-established the Bishops' courts which sent Cranmer, Latimer, Ridley, Hooper and others to the stake. To support her husband she declared war on France, and they were defeated at Saint-Quentin. But when Calais fell to the French again in 1558 she is reported to have said that when she died the word 'Calais' would be found written on her heart.

O merciful God, grant me to covet with a fervent mind those things which truly please thee, to search them wisely, to know them truly, and to fulfil them perfectly, to the laud and glory of thy name. Let that labour delight me, which is for thee, and let all the rest weary me, which is not in thee. My most loving Lord and God, give me a waking heart, that no curious thought withdraw me from thee; let it be so strong, that no unworthy affliction draw me backward; so stable, that no tribulation break it. Grant me wit to know thee, diligence to seek thee, a conversation to please thee, and finally, hope to embrace thee: for the sake of our only Saviour, Jesu Christ.[9]

John of the Cross (1542–91)

John came from a poor background, and worked in the hospital at Medina in Spain. In his spare time he studied at the Jesuit College, and when he was twenty-one he joined the Carmelite order. He studied the Bible and the German and Flemish mystics at the University of Salamanca, and then he met St Teresa. Under her influence John reformed the male side of the Carmelite order, but he was imprisoned and ill-treated. His union with God in prayer was complete and constant, and is described in his books, The Ascent of Mount Carmel, The Spiritual Canticle, The Living Flame of Love *and* The Dark Night of the Soul. *St John taught that every Christian who wants to know God must pass through the dark night of the senses, when we abandon all sensual satisfaction, and the dark night of the soul, when we learn to dispense with even the sense of the presence of God. His demand for self-abnegation in prayer is the most severe of any teacher, yet his sense of the love of God in the poems is overwhelming.*

D ear Lord, give me the truths which are veiled by the doctrines and articles of faith, which are masked by the pious words of sermons and books. Let my eyes penetrate the veil, and tear off the mask, that I can see your truth face to face.[10]

O flame of the Holy Spirit, you pierce the very substance of my soul and cauterize it with your heat. You love me so much, that you have put into my heart the hope and the knowledge of eternal life. Earlier my prayers never reached your ears, because my love was so weak and impure;

so, although I yearned for you, and begged you to warm my cold heart, you could not hear me. But now you have chosen to come to me, and my love burns with such passion that I know you hear my every prayer. I pray what you want me to pray; I desire what you want me to desire; I do what you want me to do. You have freed me to be your slave.[11]

Song of the Soul that is glad to know God by faith

How well I know that fountain's rushing flow
Although by night

Its deathless spring is hidden. Even so
Full well I guess from whence its sources flow
Though it be night.

Its origin (since it has none) none knows:
But that all origin from it arose
Although by night.

I know there is no other thing so fair
And earth and heaven drink refreshment there
Although by night.

Full well I know its depth no man can sound
And that no ford to cross it can be found
Though it be night.

Its clarity unclouded still shall be:
Out of it comes the light by which we see
Though it be night.

Flush with its banks the stream so proudly swells;
I know it waters nations, heavens, and hells
Though it be night.

The current that is nourished by this source
I know to be omnipotent in force
Although by night.

From source and current a new current swells;
Which neither of the other twain excels
Though it be night.

The external source hides in the Living Bread
That we with life eternal may be fed
Though it be night.

Here to all creatures it is crying, hark!
That they should drink their fill though in the dark,
For it is night.

This living fount which is to me so dear
Within the bread of life I see it clear
Though it be night.[12]

*Songs of the soul in rapture at having arrived at the height of perfection,
which is union with God by the road of spiritual negation*

Upon a gloomy night,
   With all my cares to loving ardours flushed,
(O venture of delight!)
With nobody in sight
I went abroad when all my house was hushed.

In safety, in disguise,
In darkness up the secret stair I crept,
(O happy enterprise)
Concealed from other eyes
When all my house at length in silence slept.

Upon that lucky night
In secrecy, inscrutable to sight,
I went without discerning
And with no other light
Except for that which in my heart was burning,

It lit and led me through
More certain than the light of noonday clear
To where One waited near
Whose presence well I knew,
There where no other presence might appear.

Oh night that was my guide!
Oh darkness dearer than the morning's pride,
Oh night that joined the lover

To the beloved bride
Transfiguring them each into the other.

Within my flowering breast
Which only for himself entire I save
He sank into his rest
And all my gifts I gave
Lulled by airs with which the cedars wave.

Over the ramparts fanned
While the fresh wind was fluttering his tresses,
With his serenest hand
My neck he wounded, and
Suspended every sense with its caresses.

Lost to myself I stayed
My face upon my lover having laid
From all endeavour ceasing:
And all my cares releasing
Threw them amongst the lilies there to fade.[13]

Mary Queen of Scots (1542–87)

The daughter of James V of Scotland, Mary became Queen when she was just a week old. Her life is too full of incident to give more than a summary. Betrothed to the Dauphin at the age of six, she was brought up in France until she married him when she was sixteen. A year later he came to the throne, and a year after that he died, leaving Mary dowager Queen of France. She returned to a Scotland torn between Catholics and Protestants. After protracted negotiations with Elizabeth of England, who wanted her to marry the Earl of Leicester, she married her cousin Lord Darnley. She bore him a son, the future James VI of Scotland and James I of England, but considered divorcing him after Darnley was involved in a conspiracy which murdered the Queen's secretary. Darnley was blown up, and three months later Mary married the Earl of Bothwell, who was suspected of being behind Darnley's murder. So unpopular was this that she was forced to abdicate. Escaping from prison, her army defeated, she threw herself on the mercy of Elizabeth of England. Fearing that she would lead a Catholic rebellion, Elizabeth imprisoned Mary again. Almost twenty years later Mary was executed in dubious circumstances. She was probably neither a papist plotter nor a Catholic martyr, but an extremely intelligent and cultured woman with a real spirituality, who had the misfortune to be a queen in troubled times.

O Lord my God, I hope in thee;
My dear Lord Jesus, set me free;
In chains, in pains,
I long for thee.
On bended knee
I adore thee, implore thee
To set me free.

Written in Latin just before her execution (translator unknown)

The Council of Trent (1545–63)

The need to counter the effects of the Reformation and the need for moral and administrative reform in the Roman Catholic Church led to a widespread demand from Catholics for a Universal Council. The Emperor Charles V was in favour of this move, but the Popes were mostly opposed. After many delays the Council of Trent was at last convened in 1545; its meetings continued until 1563. At first there were Protestant representatives present and an attempt at reconciliation was made, but the Council condemned Protestant ideas of justification and of the Eucharist, and upheld the doctrines of merit, the sacrifice of the Mass and transubstantiation, the denial of the wine chalice to lay-people, and the Index of forbidden books. The reforms within the Catholic Church proposed by Cardinal Guise were ruled out, and the Council refused to condemn the traditional practices of invocation of the saints, veneration of relics and images, and indulgences based on the doctrine of purgatory. Although opportunities of reform and reconciliation were missed, the Roman Catholic Church emerged with a stronger sense of discipline, a universal Latin liturgy in the 'Tridentine Mass', and a clearly defined system of doctrine, which gave an impulse to a growth of prayer all over the Catholic world.

Francis de Sales (1567–1622)

Francis de Sales was converted as a young man when he became convinced by Augustine's teaching on predestination, supported by Aquinas and emphasized by the Calvinists whom he met, and felt that he was certain to be damned. However, kneeling in a church in Paris, he heard Christ say, 'I do not call myself the one who condemns, my name is Jesus.' Francis became a priest and worked on the shores of Lake Geneva; eventually he was made Catholic Bishop of Calvinist Geneva. Some teachers on prayer say that everyone who is learning to pray should have a spiritual director to discuss their progress with. Francis spent the last twenty years of his life as a spiritual director, and writing two spiritual classics, The Introduction to the Devout Life *and* The Treatise on the Love of God. *The importance of these is that they teach that holiness is possible for people living ordinary lives in the world. He taught a form of meditation which makes use of the imagination. Salesian spirituality recommends the selection of a passage from the Bible, and after careful preparation, use of all the senses to imagine that you are physically present at the scene. The intellect is used to work out the application of the passage to the present day, and the will serves to make resolutions of practical response. The meditation is followed by a time of quiet to allow it to sink in.*

Our Creation

Preparation
Place yourself in the presence of God and ask him to inspire you.

Considerations
1. Consider that a few years ago you were not in the world at all, that you were nothing. O my soul, where was I then? The world had already lasted so long and I was not known.
2. God has raised you from this nothingness and made you what you are purely out of his goodness, for he had no need of you.
3. Consider what nature God has given you; the highest in the visible world, capable of eternal life and perfect union with himself.

Spiritual Acts and Resolutions
1. Humble yourself profoundly before God, saying from your heart with the Psalmist: *O Lord, I am as nothing before thee. Why hast thou been mindful of me to create me?* (Psalm 38:7; 8:5). Oh my soul, I was in an abyss of nothingness and would still be there had not God drawn me thence; and still there what could I have done?
2. Give thanks to God. O my great and good Creator, how much I owe to thee who in thy mercy hast willed to raise me from my nothingness to make me what I am. What can I possibly do to bless thy name worthily or thank thee enough for thy inestimable goodness?
3. Abase yourself. Alas, my Creator, instead of uniting myself to thee by loving service, my inordinate desires have made me a rebel and I have

cut myself off from thee by preferring sin, dishonouring thee as though thou wert not my Creator.

4. Cast yourself down before God. *Know, my soul, that the Lord is thy God:* he made thee; thou didst not make thyself. O God, *I am the work of thy hands* (Psalm 99:1).

5. From now on I will no longer exalt myself, for by myself I am nothing. What have I to glory in who am but dust and ashes, and even less than that! What have I to be proud of? In order to humble myself I will take the means necessary, bear with humiliations, and change my life. I will follow my Saviour, honouring the nature he has granted me, according to his will, in obedience, under the guidance of my spiritual director.

Conclusion
1. *Thanksgiving. Bless thy God, O my soul, and let all that is within me bless his holy name* (Psalm 102:1), for in his goodness he has lifted me from nothingness and in his mercy created me.

2. *Offering.* O my God, with all my heart I offer thee the being thou hast given me; I dedicate and consecrate it to thee.

3. *Petition.* Strengthen me, O God, in these desires and resolutions. O Blessed Virgin, recommend them to the mercy of thy Son.

Our Father. Hail Mary.
Your prayer completed, wander back in spirit among your considerations and gather a bouquet of spiritual thoughts to perfume your whole day.

From Introduction to the Devout Life[14]

Why we were created

You made me for yourself, O Lord, so that I might rejoice forever in the immensity of your glory. When shall I be worthy of that glory? When shall I praise you as I ought? I offer you, my Creator, all my desires and hopes; give me your blessing so that I may put them into practice, through Jesus Christ your Son who shed his blood for me on the cross.

The blessings of God

I have trampled on your blessings, Lord, misused your grace and ungratefully rejected your gifts. I will be faithful in prayer, receive the sacraments often, listen to your word, and do what you tell me to.

Heaven

Creator and Saviour, I thank you for your generosity in granting me the riches of your glory in eternity. Since you have guided me back into your ways, O Lord, I will never go astray again, but go straight ahead until I reach my eternal rest in that promised land of blessedness.

Robert Southwell (1561?–95)

During the Reformation controversies in England and Scotland both sides considered it a Christian action to put their opponents to death for their beliefs. Roman Catholics suffered as much as Protestants, and can boast of many glorious martyrs. Their suffering was increased by a suspicion, which lasted for many centuries, that they must be secret agents of a foreign power, usually Spain. There is great heroism to be found in the stories of those who remained loyal to their faith, met for secret masses, and hid in the priest-holes of country houses. Southwell was born near Norwich and was educated at Douai and Rome. He became a Jesuit priest, and was prefect of the English College in Rome. In spite of the dangers, he returned to England in 1584, and was hidden by Lord Vaux and then the Countess of Arundel. He spent most of his time in disguise or in hiding, but made many converts. In 1592 he was betrayed, tortured and thrown into the Tower of London. Three years later he was condemned for high treason, hanged and quartered at Tyburn.

The Nativity of Christ

Behold the father is his daughter's son,
The bird that built the nest is hatch'd therein,
The old of years an hour hath not outrun,
Eternal life to live doth now begin,
The word is dumb, the mirth of heaven doth weep,
Might feeble is, and force doth faintly creep.

O dying souls! behold your living spring!
O dazzled eyes! behold your son of grace!
Dull ears attend what word this word doth bring!
Up, heavy hearts, with joy your joy embrace!
From death, from dark, from deafness, from despairs,
This life, this light, this word, this joy repairs.

Gift better than himself God doth not know,
Gift better that his God no man can see;
This gift doth here the giver given bestow,
Gift to this gift let each receiver be:
God is my gift, himself he freely gave me.
God's gift am I, and none but God shall have me.

Man alter'd was by sin from man to beast;
Beast's food is hay, hay is all mortal flesh;
Now God is flesh, and lives in manger press'd,
As hay the brutest sinner to refresh:
Oh happy field wherein this fodder grew,
Whose taste doth us from beasts to men renew!

Jane Frances de Chantal (1572–1641)

Saint Jane took Francis de Sales as her spiritual director, and after her husband died she founded a convent for young women and widows who wanted to develop the life of prayer without enduring the rigorous asceticism of most other religious communities. By the time of her death there were eighty-six houses in her order.

O my Lord, I am in a dry land, all dried up and cracked by the violence of the north wind and the cold; but as you see, I ask for nothing more; you will send me both dew and warmth when it pleases you.

Augustine Baker (1575–1641)

Born in Abergavenny, he read law at Oxford and practised law in London. On his conversion to Roman Catholicism he became a member of Benedictine communities in Padua, Cambrai and Douai. He served as a missionary priest in Devonshire, and died in London of the plague. An abstract of his writings on prayer was published after his death as Sancta Sophia, *which became a classic.*

Exercises of Love

O my God, I love and desire to love thee, with a love pure and free from all respect of proper commodity and self-interest.

I love thee, my Lord, with a perseverant love, purposing by the help of thy holy grace and assistance never to be separated from thee by sin.

And if I were to live for millions of years, yet would I ever remain thy faithful servant and lover. I wish all creatures would adore and serve thee, and that infidels may be converted to thy faith, and all sinners to a good life; and all this only for thy supreme honour and glory.

I congratulate with thee, O my God, for the blessedness and all the perfections that are in thee, and which for all eternity thou hast ever had; as thy omnipotence and wisdom.

I congratulate with thee also, and am glad that thou hast need of no extrinsical thing, but art in thyself most rich and fully sufficient both for thyself and all creatures.

I likewise with thee, O my Lord, rejoice in the sweet ordinance and disposition of heaven and earth, and for all the things which are in the marvellous creation of this world, and for all the works which thou hast made, or shalt yet make unto the end of the world.

Exercises of Will

From this hour my purpose, through thy grace, is to accept and welcome all occurrences, whether pleasing or distasteful to sense, as coming from thy heavenly providence: this shall be my comfort and stay in all my afflictions; in dangers, security; and perfect rest of mind in expectation of future events. Thou alone, O my God, provide, determine, will and choose for me.

Hast not thou, O my God, provided for me thine own kingdom?

What, then, can make me dejected?

I offer unto thee my understanding, firmly to adhere to all divine verities revealed by thee to thy Church, renouncing all doubt or questioning of any of them; and herein my purpose irrevocable is, through thy grace, to live and die.

O that it would please thee that all mankind might know thee, and with a firm faith confess thee! My God, I do willingly offer unto thee my blood to seal this my faith, whensoever by thy providence an occasion shall be presented, hoping that then thou wilt be my strength and my salvation; and being assured that, whilst I hope in thee, I shall not be weakened.

Vincent de Paul (*c.* 1580–*c.* 1660)

A priest in south-western France, Vincent was captured by pirates and was kept for two years as a slave in Tunisia, so he knew about the plight of the needy at first hand. After he escaped, he decided to spend the rest of his life in caring for the needy. First he found a post as chaplain to the general in command of the galleys where prisoners were kept, and he set about improving their conditions. Then he founded Confraternities of men and women to perform acts of charity, and the Congregation of the Mission, commonly called the Lazarists or Vincentians, whose task was to carry out missions in country districts and train the clergy. Later he founded the Sisters of Charity, the first unenclosed women's order devoted entirely to the care of the poor and the sick.

Jesus said: 'He has sent me to preach good news to the poor.' Therefore we should be of the same mind and should imitate what Christ did, caring for the poor, consoling them, helping them and guiding them. Christ chose to be born in poverty and took poor men as his disciples; he himself became the servant of the poor and so shared their condition that whatever good or harm was done to the poor, he said he would consider done to himself. Since God loves the poor, he also loves the lovers of the poor: when someone loves another, he loves too those who love or serve that other. So we too hope that God will love us on account of the poor. We visit them then, we strive to concern ourselves with the weak and the needy, we so share their sufferings that with the apostle we feel we have become all things to all men. Therefore we must strive to be deeply involved in the cares and sorrows of our neighbour and pray to God to inspire us with compassion and pity, filling our hearts and keeping them full. The service of the poor is to be preferred to all else, and to be performed without delay. If at a time set aside for prayer, medicine or help has to be brought to some poor man, go and do what has to be done with an easy mind, offering it up to God as a prayer. Do not be put out by uneasiness or a sense of sin because of prayers interrupted by the service of the poor: for God is not neglected if prayers are put aside, if God's work is interrupted, in order that another such work may be completed. Therefore, when you leave prayer to help some poor man, remember this – that the work has been done for God. Charity takes precedence over any rules.[15]

Mary Ward (1585–1645)

A Yorkshire lass, brought up a Catholic in a Protestant country, Mary Ward entered the convent of the Poor Clares at Saint-Omer when she was twenty-one. Wanting to be more involved in service to others, she founded her own order modelled on the Jesuits, who became known as the Institute of the English Ladies. Their task was the education of women, an idea which some found shocking. She opened houses in many cities, including Liége, Cologne and Vienna, and then went to Rome to seek papal approval. But her project ran contrary to the instructions of Pius V that convents for women must be strictly enclosed; her community was suppressed and she was imprisoned in the Poor Clares convent at Munich. When released she returned to Rome, and a new pope gave approval to reopen her convents. She returned to England and opened convents in York and elsewhere, before she died.

O Parent of parents, and Friend of all friends, thou tookest me into thy care, and by degrees led me from all else that at length I might see and settle my love in thee. What had I ever done to please thee? Or what was there in me wherewith to serve thee? Much less could I ever deserve to be chosen by thee. O happy begun freedom, the beginning of all my good, and more worth to me at that time than the whole world besides. Had I never since hindered thy will and working in me, what degrees of grace should I now have had. It is more than nineteen years since, and where as yet am I? My Jesus, forgive me, remember what thou hast done for me, and whither thou hast brought me, and for this excess of goodness and love let me no more hinder thy will in me.[16]

O my God, how liberal you are and how rich are they to whom you will vouchsafe to be a friend. In your will I only found quiet rest. The most forcible motive of all to me to leave sin is that you forbid it, whom I love. If I ever see myself favoured by you, I cry out continually: 'You alone are important, I am nothing.' I will not take credit from you, to build myself up. Take me, all that I am, and do what you want with me. Without you I am nothing.[17]

N either life nor death, my God, but thy holy will be ever done in me. What pleaseth thee best, that do. Only this, let me no more offend thee, nor leave to do what thou wouldst have me.[18]

English Christianity after the Reformation

Matthew Parker (1504–75)

When Matthew Parker was at Cambridge, he became known as a moderate reformer in the Reformation controversies. During the reign of Edward VI he took advantage of the permission for clergy to marry. He lived in obscurity under Queen Mary, but was persuaded, somewhat reluctantly, by Queen Elizabeth I to become Archbishop of Canterbury. He was wise and tolerant, but tried to show that the Church of England was continuous with the Church of the past, by taking part in the drafting of The Bishops' Bible *and* The Thirty-nine Articles, *and insisting on clergy wearing a surplice, which was strongly opposed by the Puritans.*

What shall befall us hereafter we know not; but to God, who cares for all men, who will one day reveal the secrets of all hearts, we commit ourselves wholly, with all who are near and dear to us. And we beseech the same most merciful and Almighty God, that for the time to come we may so bear the reproach of Christ with unbroken courage, as ever to remember that here we have no continuing city, but may seek one to come, by the grace and mercy of our Lord Jesus Christ; to whom with the Father, and the Holy Ghost, be all honour and dominion, world without end. Amen.

Edmund Grindal (1519?–83)

The son of a Cumberland farmer, he was educated at Cambridge and became a Fellow of Pembroke Hall. Later he was chaplain to King Edward VI. Under Queen Mary he was exiled to Frankfurt. On his return he was made Bishop of London, then Archbishop of York and finally Archbishop of

Canterbury. He tried to reconcile the followers of John Knox and the Puritans with the Church of England.

G rant us, O Lord, such true repentance as may, through the blood of Jesus Christ our Saviour, blot out the stains of our sins and iniquities. Forgive us our sins, O Lord; forgive us our sins for thine infinite mercies' sake, and for the sake of Jesus Christ our Saviour. Amen.

W e know, O Lord, the weakness of ourselves, and how ready we are to fall from thee; suffer not therefore Satan to show his power and malice upon us; for we are not able to withstand his assaults. Arm us, O Lord, always with thy grace, and assist us with the Holy Spirit in all kinds of temptations; through Jesus Christ our Lord. Amen.

T ake from us, O God, the care of worldly vanities; make us content with necessaries. Keep our hearts from delighting in honours, treasures, and pleasures of this life, and engender in us a desire to be with thee in thy eternal kingdom. Give us, O Lord, such taste and feeling for thy unspeakable joys in heaven, that we may always long therefor, and saying, with all thy people, 'Hasten thy kingdom, O Lord take us to thee'; for the sake of Jesus Christ, who liveth and reigneth, ever one God, world without end. Amen.

James Pilkington (*c.* 1520–76)

Pilkington preached in favour of the Reformation at Cambridge, so he had to go into exile during Queen Mary's reign. Soon after her death he was made the first Protestant Bishop of Durham. He had to flee with his family when, during the Northern Rebellion of 1569, the rioters broke into Durham Cathedral.

G ive us new hearts, and renew thy Holy Spirit within, O Lord, that both the rulers of our land may faithfully minister justice, punish sin, defend and maintain the preaching of thy word, and that all ministers may diligently teach thy dearly beloved flock, purchased by the blood and of thine own, and only dear Son our Lord, and that all people may obediently learn and follow thy law, to the glory of thy holy Name; for Christ's sake, our only Lord and Saviour. Amen.

Hold us fast, O Lord of Hosts, that we fall not from thee; grant us thankful and obedient hearts; that we may increase daily in the love, knowledge, and fear of thee; increase our faith, and help our unbelief, that we, being provided for and relieved in all our needs by thy fatherly care and providence, as thou shalt think good, may live a godly life; to the praise and good example of thy people, and after this life may reign with thee for ever; through Christ our Saviour. Amen.

John Jewel (1522–71)

Jewel, a Fellow of Corpus Christi College in Oxford, became one of the intellectual leaders among those who wanted reform. Forced into exile during Queen Mary's reign, he was made Bishop of Salisbury when he returned. He wrote and preached strongly in favour of what came to be known as the Anglican Settlement – that position established during Elizabeth's reign in between Roman Catholicism and Calvinism, which has distinguished the Church of England ever since. In the process he argued ably with opponents on both sides, basing his arguments on the writers of the first six Christian centuries. In his Apologia Ecclesia Anglicana *Bishop Jewel wrote that the Church needed reforming, but worldwide assemblies like the Council of Trent were incapable of doing it, so that national churches had the right and the duty to reform themselves. Jewel's* Apologia *laid down the lines of Anglican controversy with Catholics and Puritans in the next century.*

O most merciful Father, we beseech thee, for thy mercy's sake, continue thy grace and favour towards us. Let not the sun of thy gospel ever go down out of our hearts; let thy truth abide and be established among us for ever. Help our unbelief, increase our faith, and give us hearts to consider the time of our visitation. Through faith clothe us with Christ, that he may live in us, and thy name may be glorified through us in all the world.

The God and Father of our Lord Jesus Christ open all our eyes, that we may see that blessed hope to which we are called; that we may altogether glorify the only true God and Jesus Christ, whom he hath sent down to us from heaven; to whom with the Father and the Holy Spirit be rendered all honour and glory to all eternity.

Queen Elizabeth I (1533–1603)

Prayer obviously played an important part in the lives of those at the court of the first Queen Elizabeth of England, and frequently they wrote their prayers down in dignified English for others to use also. The Virgin Queen cared strongly about the unity of her nation. She disliked Catholicism because the Catholics had declared her illegitimate, and she feared that the Calvinists, with their desire to abolish bishops, would before long threaten the monarchy. So she tried to steer a middle course, and at the beginning of her reign the Catholic Mass and the 1552 Book of Common Prayer were used side by side. But when Pope Pius V excommunicated Elizabeth and told her subjects they need no longer obey her, Elizabeth was afraid that a Catholic revolt would join the Spanish Armada which threatened to invade, and so she ordered the execution of Mary Queen of Scots. She compiled her Book of Devotions, however, for her own use, and it reveals a more vulnerable side to her character. Tired of fruitless theological disputes about what Jesus meant when he said of the Communion bread, 'This is my body', she wrote a verse which, though appalling poetry, is sound religious sense:

The Word it was that spake it;
He took the bread and brake it;
And what his word does make it,
That I believe and take it.

Give me, O eternal Father, a docile heart that I may know what is acceptable with thee. Send from heaven the spirit of thy wisdom and rule my heart by thine own command. Blessed is he whom thou dost instruct, O Lord, and make learned in thy will. Without this I lack the strength either to purpose well for myself or to be of service to others.

Most omnipotent, maker and guider of all, who alone searchest and fathomest our hearts, and dost truly discern that no malice of revenge, nor desire of bloodshed, nor greed of gain, hath bred our resolution: Prosper the work we humbly beseech thee, guide the journey, speed the victory, and make the return the advancement of thy glory, and safety of this realm. To these devout petitions, Lord, give thou thy blessed grant.

From a prayer composed by Queen Elizabeth at the departure of the fleet (1596)

From the time of Queen Elizabeth I

God grant to the living, grace; to the departed, rest; to the Church, the Queen, the Commonwealth, and all mankind, peace and concord; and to us and all his servants, life everlasting. Amen.[1]

Lady Jane Grey (1537–54)

During the final illness of King Edward VI, Lady Jane Grey was married against her will to Lord Guildford Dudley as part of a plan to ensure a Protestant succession. When the King died she reigned as Queen of England for ten days, but was rapidly succeeded by the Roman Catholic Queen Mary and made a prisoner in the Tower of London. After a rebellion failed to restore her to the throne, she was beheaded on Tower Hill. Amidst such a tragic life the serene faith of her prayer shines like a beacon.

O merciful God, consider my misery, best known unto thee; and be thou now unto me a strong tower of defence, I humbly require thee. Suffer me not to be tempted above my power, but either be thou a deliverer unto me out of this great misery, or else give me grace patiently to bear thy heavy hand and sharp correction. It was thy right hand that delivered the people of Israel out of the hands of Pharaoh, which for the space of four hundred years did oppress them, and keep them in bondage; let it therefore likewise seem good to thy fatherly goodness, to deliver me, sorrowful wretch, for whom thy Son Christ shed his precious blood on the cross, out of this miserable captivity and bondage, wherein I am now. How long wilt thou be absent? For ever? O Lord, hast thou forgotten to be gracious, and hast thou shut up thy loving kindness in displeasure? Wilt thou be no more entreated? Is thy mercy clear gone for ever, and thy promise come utterly to an end for evermore? Why dost thou make so long tarrying? Shall I despair of thy mercy? O God, far be that from me; I am thy workmanship, created in Christ Jesus. Give me grace therefore to tarry thy leisure, and patiently to bear thy works, assuredly knowing, that as thou canst, so thou wilt deliver me, when it shall please thee, nothing doubting or mistrusting thy goodness towards me; for thou knowest better what is good for me than I do. Therefore do with me in all things what thou wilt, and plague me what way thou wilt. Only, in the meantime, arm me, I beseech thee, with thy armour, that I may stand fast, my loins being girded about with verity, having on the breast-plate of righteousness, and shod with the shoes prepared by the gospel of peace; above all things, taking to me the shield of faith, wherewith I may be able to quench all the fiery darts of the wicked; and taking the helmet of salvation, and the sword of thy spirit, which is thy most holy word; praying always, with all manner of prayer and supplication, that I may refer myself wholly to thy will, abiding thy pleasure, and comforting myself in those troubles that it shall please thee to send me; seeing such troubles be profitable for me, and seeing I am assuredly persuaded that it cannot but be well all thou doest.[2]

Sir Francis Drake (1540–96)

Drake, a Devonshire sailor, was the first Englishman to see the Pacific Ocean and to circumnavigate the globe, in his ship The Golden Hind. *He was knighted by Queen Elizabeth I. Implacable foe of the Spanish Armada, he is said to have used this prayer on the day he sailed into Cadiz in 1537:*

O Lord God, when thou givest to thy servants to endeavour any great matter, grant us also to know that it is not the beginning, but the continuing of the same, until it be thoroughly finished, which yieldeth the true glory; through him that for the finishing of thy work laid down his life, our Redeemer, Jesus Christ. Amen.

Sir Walter Raleigh (1552–1618)

A Devonshire man who interrupted his university education to fight for the Huguenots in France, Raleigh later fought against the Spanish and the Irish. In the course of expeditions seeking unsuccessfully to found colonies in America he introduced tobacco and potatoes to Britain. His place in the Queen's favours was taken by the Earl of Essex and he was imprisoned in the Tower of London for his affair with Bessy Throckmorton, one of her maids of honour, whom he subsequently married. For three years he was a successful governor of the island of Jersey. He was falsely condemned following the intrigues at the end of Elizabeth's reign, and only when he reached the scaffold was his sentence suspended to perpetual imprisonment. He was released to lead an expedition up the Orinoco River, but because he burnt down a Spanish town, on his return the Spanish Ambassador demanded that the suspended sentence be carried out, and he was beheaded at Whitehall. His poetry, some of it written when he was a prisoner in the Tower, compares our life to the pilgrims who set off for the shrine of St James at Compostella, with a shell as their badge.

The Passionate Man's Pilgrimage

G ive me my scallop-shell of quiet;
My staff of faith to walk upon;
My scrip of joy, immortal diet;
My bottle of salvation;
My gown of glory (hope's true gage);
And thus I'll take my pilgrimage . . .

And this is my eternal plea,
To him that made heaven, earth and sea,
Seeing my flesh must die so soon,
And want a head to dine next noon,
Just at the stroke when my veins start and spread
Set on my soul an everlasting head.
Then am I ready like a palmer fit,
To tread those blest paths which before I writ.[3]

Edmund Spenser (*c.* 1552–99)

The son of a London tradesman and a distant relative of the Spencers of Althorpe, Edmund Spenser was educated at Merchant Taylors' School and Pembroke Hall, Cambridge. In spite of his friendship with many of the most eminent Elizabethans, he failed to win favour at court, though for his part in crushing rebellion in Ireland he was rewarded with a castle in County Cork, where he wrote his greatest work, The Faerie Queene, *which was also an attempt to win Elizabeth's favour. It was his wooing of his second wife, however, which raised his poetry to inspired heights in* The Epithalamion *and the sonnet sequence* Amoretti, *from which his Easter hymn is taken. In the Irish rebellion of 1598 his castle was burnt down, and although he escaped to London he died in the following year.*

M ost glorious Lord of Life! that, on this day,
Didst make thy triumph over death and sin;
And, having harrowed hell, didst bring away
Captivity thence captive, us to win:
This joyous day, dear Lord, with joy begin;
And grant that we, for whom thou diddest die,
Being with thy dear blood clean washed from sin,
May live for ever in felicity!
And that thy love we weighing worthily,

May likewise love thee for the same again;
And for thy sake, that all like dear didst buy,
With love may one another entertain!
So let us love, dear Love, like as we ought,
– Love is the lesson which the Lord us taught.

Sir Philip Sidney (1554–86)

He was born at Penshurst Place in Kent and travelled abroad after leaving university. He never rose to high office, leaving him time to write poetry, including Arcadia *and* Astrophel and Stella. *He was also a patron and encourager for other poets, including Spenser. At the end of his life he fought in Holland, was shot in the thigh and died from the infection.*

O all-seeing Light and eternal Life of all things, to whom nothing is either so great that it may resist, or so small that it is contemned; look upon my misery with thine eye of mercy, and let thine infinite power vouchsafe to limit out some proportion of deliverance unto me, as to thee shall seem most convenient. Let not injury, O Lord, triumph over me, and let my faults by thy hand be corrected, and make not mine enemy the minister of thy justice. But yet, O Lord, if, in thy wisdom, this be the aptest chastisement for my inexcusable folly; if this low bondage be fittest for my over-high desires; and the pride of my not enough humble heart be thus to be broken, O Lord, I yield unto thy will, and joyfully embrace what sorrow thou wilt have me suffer. Only this let me crave of thee . . . that thou wilt suffer some beams of thy majesty to shine into my mind, that it may still depend confidently on thee. Let calamity be the exercise, but not the overthrow of my virtue: let their power prevail, but prevail not to destruction . . . But, O Lord, let never their wickedness have such a hand, but that I may carry a pure mind in a pure body.[4]

Richard Hooker (c. 1554–1600)

Richard Hooker was born near Exeter. His most important posts were as a Fellow of Corpus Christi in Oxford and deputy professor of Hebrew there, and subsequently Master of the Temple in London, but he was also at different times rector of several country parishes. His Laws of Ecclesiastical Polity *defended the Elizabethan settlement of the Church of England against Puritans on the one hand and Roman Catholics on the other.*

The Puritans argued that nothing should be done, particularly in the organization of the Church, unless it was explicitly commanded by the Bible, which they regarded as a code of rules for all circumstances. Hooker replied that there is a natural law based upon divine reasonableness which even people without the Scriptures can observe in the universe. Based upon this, the Church as a growing organism will find new ways of organizing its life which are not mentioned in the Bible.

N ow the God of peace give you peaceable minds, and turn it to your everlasting comfort.

From A Learned Discourse of Justification

T o him which considereth the grievous and scandalous inconveniences whereunto they make themselves daily subject, with whom any blind and secret corner is judged a fit house of common prayer, the manifold confusions which they fall into where every man's private spirit and gift (as they term it) is the only Bishop that ordaineth him to this ministry; the irksome deformities whereby through endless and senseless effusions of indigested prayers they oftentimes disgrace in most unsufferable manner the worthiest part of Christian duty towards God, who herein are subject to no certain order, but pray both what and how they list: to him I say which weigheth duly all these things the reasons cannot be obscure, why God doth in public prayer so much respect the solemnity of places where, the authority and calling of persons by whom, and the precise appointment even with what words or sentences his name should be called on amongst his people. No man hath hitherto been so impious as plainly and directly to condemn prayer. The best stratagem that Satan hath, who knoweth his kingdom to be no one way more shaken than by the public devout prayers of God's Church, is by traducing the form and manner of them to bring them into contempt, and so to shake the force of all men's devotion towards them. From this and from no other forge hath proceeded a strange conceit, that to serve God with any set form of common prayer is superstitious.

From Laws of Ecclesiastical Polity, Book 5.25–26

Lancelot Andrewes (1555–1626)

A Fellow of Pembroke Hall, Cambridge, Lancelot Andrewes served as vicar of St Giles, Cripplegate in the City of London, and Prebendary of St Paul's Cathedral. Here his preaching attracted attention, and Queen Elizabeth I

offered him two bishoprics, which he declined, and he was made Dean of
Westminster. Under James I he became successively Bishop of Chichester,
Ely and Winchester. He was responsible for translating the Pentateuch
and the historical books of the Old Testament in the Authorised or King
James Version of the Bible. His was a classic Anglicanism which, reacting
against the Puritanism of his youth, he decided should be reasonable,
learned and Catholic. Andrewes' Preces Privatae was compiled for his
own use, and contains lists of people to pray for, with Greek and Latin
quotations from the Bible. The original manuscript is 'slubbered all over
with his pious hands and watered with his penitential tears'.

Almighty God, we will come into thy house, even upon the multitude
of thy mercies, and in thy fear will we worship toward thy holy
Temple. Hear the voice of our humble petitions, when we cry unto thee,
when we hold up our hands towards thy mercy-seat. Let thine eyes be
open, and let thine ears be attentive to hearken unto the prayer which thy
servants pray toward the place, whereof thou hast said, that thou wouldest
put thy name there; for the sake of Jesus Christ. Amen.

Be, Lord, within me to strengthen me, without me to preserve me, over
me to shelter me, beneath me to support me, before me to divert me,
behind me to bring me back, round about me to fortify me.

Blessed are you, O Lord, the God of our fathers, creator of the changes
of day and night, giving rest to the weary, renewing the strength of
those who are spent, bestowing upon us occasions of song in the evening.
As you have protected us in the day that is past, so be with us in the
coming night; keep us from every sin, every evil and every fear; for thou
are our light and salvation, and the strength of our life. To you be glory
for endless ages. Amen.[5]

Give unto us, O God, the girdle, the helmet, the breastplate, the shield,
the sandals, the sword – above all things, prayer. Grant unto us the
power and opportunity of well-doing, that before the day of our departure
may come, we may have wrought at least somewhat, whose good fruit may
remain; that we may behold thy presence in righteousness, and be satisfied
with thy glory; for Christ's sake. Amen.

Grant, O Lord, that Christ himself may be formed in us, that we may be made conformable to his image; that when we are lukewarm in prayer and stand in need of any grace or of heavenly consolation, we may remember his appearance in the presence of God; and his intercession for us; for his name's sake. Amen.

Lord lift thou up the light of thy countenance upon us, that in thy light we may see light, the light of thy grace today, the light of glory hereafter; through Jesus Christ our Lord. Amen.

O Lord God, perfect in us that which is lacking of thy gifts: of faith to increase it; of hope to stablish it; of love, to kindle it; and make us to fear but one thing only, the fearing aught more than thee, our Father, our Saviour, our Lord, for ever and ever. Amen.

O Lord, we pray for the universal Church, for all sections of thy Church throughout the world, for their truth, unity, and stability, that love may abound, and truth flourish in them all; we pray for all thy ministering servants that they may rightly divide the word of truth, that they may walk circumspectly; that teaching others they may themselves learn both the way and the truth. We pray for the people, that they make not themselves over-wise, but be persuaded by reason, and yield to the authority of their superiors. We pray for the kingdoms of the world, their stability and peace; for our own nation, kingdom, and empire, that they may abide in prosperity and happiness, and be delivered from all peril and disaster. For the King, O Lord, save him; O Lord, give him prosperity, compass him with the shield of truth and glory, speak good things unto him, in behalf of thy church and people. Unto all men everywhere give thy grace and thy blessing; through Jesus Christ. Amen.

O Lord God, mighty and merciful, hear our prayers touching every ill wherewith this world is beset, that thou remove it according to thy grace; for the afflicted, the sick, the destitute, the imprisoned and them that have no helper, that thou succour each according to his need; and for all in the captivity of sin, that thou deliver them at the supplications which we most humbly offer, in the name of Jesus Christ thy Son our Lord. Amen.[6]

O God, most glorious, most bountiful, accept, we humbly beseech thee, our praises and thanksgivings for thy holy Catholic Church, the mother of us all who bear the name of Christ; for the faith which it hath conveyed in safety to our time, and the mercies by which it hath enlarged and comforted the souls of men; for the virtues which it hath established upon earth, and the holy lives by which it glorifieth both the world and thee; to whom, O blessed Trinity, be ascribed all honour, might, majesty and dominion, now and for ever. Amen.[7]

To thee, O Christ, O Word of the Father, we offer up our lowly praises and unfeigned hearty thanks: who for love of our fallen race didst most wonderfully and humbly chose to be made man, and to take our nature as never more to lay it by; so that we might be born again by thy Spirit and restored in the image of God; to whom, one blessed Trinity, be ascribed all honour, might, majesty, and dominion, now and for ever. Amen.[8]

To thee, O Christ, O King exalted, we offer up our due praise and unfeigned hearty thanks for that thou hast sent down and dispersed abroad thine own Holy Spirit to restore and renew the spirit of men, to be the first dedication of thy Catholic Church on earth and the first publishing of the Gospel to all lands, the bond of unity, and giver of light and life; to whom with the Father and thee, one blessed Trinity, be ascribed all might, majesty, dominion and praise, now and for ever. Amen.[9]

Francis Bacon (1561–1626)

Bacon was a lawyer and Member of Parliament during the reign of Queen Elizabeth I, for whom he did useful work, but he did not rise to high office until James I made him Lord Chancellor. However, his rivals accused him of bribery and corruption, and he retired in disgrace. In his philosophical writings he argued that truth could only be discovered by experiment, and by turning from Aristotle's deductive method of reasoning to an inductive method he set the course for future science. He argued for the comprehensiveness of the Church of England, and published prayers and translations of the Psalms.

To God the Father, God the Son, God the Spirit, we pour forth most humble and hearty supplications, that he, remembering the calamities of mankind, and the pilgrimage of this our life in which we spend our days, would please to open to us new consolations out of the fountain of his goodness for the alleviating of our miseries. We humbly and earnestly ask that human things may not prejudice such as are divine, so that from the opening of the gates of sense, and the kindling of a greater natural light, nothing of incredulity or intellectual might may arise in our minds towards divine mysteries; but rather, O Lord, that our minds being thoroughly cleansed, and purged from fancy, and yet subject to the divine will, there may be given unto faith the things that are faith's, that so we may continually attain to a deeper knowledge and love of thee, who art the Fountain of Light, and dwellest in the light which no man can approach unto; through Jesus Christ our Lord. Amen.

O eternal God, and most merciful Father in Jesus Christ, whom thou hast made a covenant of grace and mercy within all those that come to thee in him: O stay not the course of thy mercies and loving-kindness towards us, but continually guide our feet in the paths of thy righteousness, and in the ways of thy commandments, that through thy grace we may be enabled to lead a godly, holy, sober, and Christian life in true sincerity and uprightness of heart before thee; and that, O Lord, not for any merits of ours, but only for the merits of thy Son our Saviour Jesus Christ.

William Shakespeare (1564–1616)

Passages of Shakespeare which seem puzzling on the page, in a good stage production can leap to life as brilliant dramatic effects. In particular, the reconstructed Globe Theatre in Southwark has revealed the interplay between actors and audience. As a good playwright Shakespeare never reveals his own beliefs, only those of his characters, but he probably shared the faith of his time, and in particular that 'there's a divinity that shapes our ends, rough-hew them how we will' (Hamlet), and it is the outworking of this Providence that is portrayed in the dramas.

O God, thy arm was here;
And not to us, but to thy arm alone,
Ascribe we all.

Henry V[10]

O Lord, that lends me life,
Lend me a heart replete with thankfulness!

Henry VI, Part 2

O thou, whose captain I account myself,
To thee I do commend my watchful soul,
Ere I let fall the windows of mine eyes;
Sleeping or waking, O defend me still.

Richard III[11]

O God! if my deep prayers cannot appease thee
But thou wilt be avenged on my misdeeds,
Yet execute thy wrath on me alone!

Richard III

Christopher Sutton (*c.* 1565–1629)

Christopher Sutton was a Canon of Westminster, then of Lincoln. His devotional books were very popular, and in Godly Meditations upon the Most Holy Sacrament of the Lord's Supper *he defended a doctrine of Christ's presence in the bread and wine mid-way between transubstantiation and the teachings of Zwingli.*

O Lord, cure our infirmities, pardon our offences, lighten our burdens, enrich our poverty; through Christ our Lord. Amen.

Lidley's Prayers (1566)

This prayer, taken from a sixteenth-century prayer collection, is sung to a beautiful anthem which was long thought to be by Richard Farrant, but is now believed to be by either John Hilton or Christopher Tye, or even an unfortunate composer whose name was Mudd.

L ord, for thy tender mercies' sake, lay not our sins to our charge, but forgive that which is past and give us grace to amend our sinful lives; to decline from sin and incline to virtue, that we may walk with a perfect heart before thee, now and evermore. Amen.

Thomas Campion (1567–1620)

Campion was born at Witham in Essex and became a successful physician. With Elizabethan versatility, he not only wrote masques and lyrics but himself set them to music. He saw nothing incongruous in publishing Divine and Moral Songs, *from which these are taken, in the same volume with* Light Conceits of Lovers.

View me, Lord, a Work of Thine

View me, Lord, a work of thine:
  Shall I then lie drown'd in night?
Might thy grace in me but shine,
I should seem made all of light.

But my soul still surfeits so
On the poisoned baits of sin,
That I strange and ugly grow,
All is dark and foul within.

Cleanse me, Lord, that I may kneel
At thine altar, pure and white:
They that once thy mercies feel,
Gaze no more on earth's delight.

Worldly joys like shadows fade,
When the heav'nly light appears;
But the cov'nants thou hast made,
Endless, know nor days, nor years.

In thy word, Lord, is my trust,
To thy mercies fast I fly.
Though I am but clay and dust,
Yet thy grace can lift me high.

Never Weather-beaten Sail

Never weather-beaten sail more willing bent to shore,
  Never tired pilgrim's limbs affected slumber more,
Than my wearied sprite now longs to fly out of my troubled breast.

O come quickly, sweetest Lord, and take my soul to rest.
Ever-blooming are the joys of heav'n's high paradise,
Cold age deafs not there our ears, nor vapour dims our eyes:
Glory there the sun outshines, whose beams the blessed only see;
O come quickly, glorious Lord, and raise my sprite to thee.

John Donne (1571–1631)

By the seventeenth century Anglicanism was gaining in self-confidence and was thinking out its own distinctive theology. In the reigns of Charles I and Charles II eloquent preachers and writers arose who, because they emphasized the Church as the creation of God, were called High Church-men. These 'Caroline Divines' happened to be all Cambridge scholars, but they were not an organized movement. They were a sudden flowering of the life of prayer in troubled times, all of them showing holiness of life, simplicity and discipline in prayer, and a devotion to scholarship and poetry.

John Donne's life falls into three sections. He was born the son of a Roman Catholic ironmonger in London, studied at Oxford and Cambridge, and took up law. He served as secretary to Sir Thomas Egerton, but was dismissed in disgrace and thrown into prison after secretly marrying his patron's niece, Ann More. During the second part of his life he had left the Roman Catholic Church but was not yet convinced of the truth of Anglicanism. He wrote passionate and erotic verse, and some flattering odes for members of the court who offered him hospitality and an income. But he was beginning to write religious poetry also, and after a long struggle with his conscience he was persuaded by King James I of England to seek ordination in the Church of England, and in 1621 he was made Dean of St Paul's Cathedral. The passion which he had previously expended on the flesh he now converted into love for God. This is shown in some of his greatest poems, his brilliant sermons, and his Devotions upon an Emergent Occasion, *when he was lying sick in bed and expected to die, from which comes the famous quotation, 'Ask not for whom the bell tolls . . .'*

Wilt thou forgive that sin where I begun,
      Which is my sin, though it were done before?
Wilt thou forgive that sin, through which I run,
And do run still: though still I do deplore?
When thou hast done, thou hast not done,
      For I have more.

Wilt thou forgive that sin by which I have won
Others to sin? and, made my sin their door?
Wilt thou forgive that sin which I did shun
A year, or two: but wallowed in, a score?
When thou hast done, thou hast not done,
For I have more.

I have a sin of fear, that when I have spun
My last thread, I shall perish on the shore;
Swear by thyself, that at my death thy Son
Shall shine as he shines now, and heretofore;
And, having done that, thou hast done,
I fear no more.

'A Hymn to God the Father'[12]

Batter my heart, three-person'd God; for you
As yet but knock, breathe, shine, and seek to mend;
That I may rise, and stand, o'erthrow me, and bend
Your force, to break, blow, burn and make me new.
I, like an usurp'd town, to another due,
Labour to admit you, but Oh, to no end.
Reason your viceroy in me, me should defend,
But is captiv'd, and proves weak or untrue.
Yet dearly I love you, and would be loved fain,
But am betroth'd unto your enemy.
Divorce me, untie, or break that knot again,
Take me to you, imprison me, for I
Except you enthral me, never shall be free,
Or ever chaste, except you ravish me.

From 'Holy Sonnets'

From needing danger, to be good,
From owing thee yesterday's tears today,
From trusting so much to thy blood,
That in that hope, we wound our soul away,
From bribing thee with alms, to excuse
Some sin more burdenous,
From light affecting, in religion, news,
From thinking us all soul, neglecting thus
Our mutual duties, Lord deliver us.

From 'A Litany'

S o, in his purple wrapped receive me Lord,
By these his thorns give me his other crown;
And as to others' souls I preached thy word,
Be this my text, my sermon to mine own,
Therefore that he may raise the Lord throws down.

From 'A Hymn to God my God, in my Sickness'

A ccept, O Lord God our Father, the spiritual sacrifices which we offer thee; this, of praise and thanksgiving, for thy great mercies already afforded to us; and this, of prayer, for the continuance and enlargement of them; and this, of the love of our hearts, as the only gift thou dost ask or desire; and all these, through the all-holy and atoning sacrifice of Jesus Christ thy Son our Saviour. Amen.

Adapted

A lmighty God, in this wondrous world thou dost manifest thy power and thy beauty: open the eyes of all to see that whatsoever has any being is a mirror wherein we may behold thee, the root and fountain of all being; through Jesus Christ our Lord. Amen.

B ring us, O Lord God, at our last awakening into the house and gate of heaven, to enter into that gate and dwell in that house where there shall be no darkness nor dazzling but one equal light; no noise nor silence but one equal music; no fears nor hopes but one equal possession; no ends nor beginnings but one equal eternity, in the habitations of thy majesty and thy glory, for ever and ever. Amen.

Adapted from Sermon 146

D ispel, O Lord, O Father of lights, all clouds of doubt, and the darkness about our earthly course, that in thy light we may see light, and come both to know thee as we are known, and to love as we are loved; through Jesus Christ our Lord. Amen.

Adapted from Sermon 21

L ord, teach thy people to love thy house best of all dwellings, thy scriptures best of all books, thy sacraments best of all gifts, the communion of saints best of all company: and that we may as one family and in one place give thanks and adore thy glory, help us to keep always thy day, the first of days, holy for thee, our Maker, our Resurrection, and our Life, God blessed for ever. Amen.

Adapted from Sermon 30

Ben Jonson (1572–1637)

Ben Jonson was born in Westminster and educated at Westminster School. After a time as a bricklayer and then a soldier, he joined a company of players. He killed a fellow-actor in a duel and was sent to prison, where he briefly converted to Roman Catholicism, but later returned to the Church of England. He wrote a number of plays, and Shakespeare was one of the cast in the first production of Every Man in his Humour. *He was most successful in writing the lyrics for songs, such as 'Drink to me only with thine eyes' in* Volpone.

To Heaven

Good and great God, can I not think of thee
But it must, straight, my melancholy be?
Is it interpreted in my disease
That, laden with my sins, I seek for ease?
O be thou witness, that the reins dost know
And hearts of all, if I be sad for show,
And judge me after, if I dare pretend
To aught but grace, or aim at other end.

As thou art all, so be thou all to me,
First, midst, and last, converted, one and three;
My faith, my hope, my love; and in this state
My judge, my witness, and my advocate.
Where have I been this while exil'd from thee,
And whither rap'd, now thou but stoop'st to me?
Dwell, dwell here still, O being everywhere,
How can I doubt to find thee ever, here?
I know my state, both full of shame and scorn
Conceiv'd in sin, and unto labour born,
Standing with fear, and must with horror fall,
And destin'd unto judgement, after all.
I feel my griefs too, and there scarce is ground

Upon my flesh t'inflict another wound.
Yet dare I not complain, or wish for death
With holy Paul, lest it be thought the breath
Of discontent; or that these prayers be
For weariness of life, not love of thee.

To God the Father

Hear me, O God!
A broken heart
Is my best part;
Use still thy rod,
That I may prove
Therein, thy Love.

If thou hadst not
Been stern to me,
But left me free,
I had forgot
My self and thee.

For sin's so sweet
As minds ill bent
Rarely repent,
Until they meet
Their punishment.

Who more can crave
Than thou hast done,
That gav'st a Son
To free a slave?
First made of nought,
With all since bought.

Sin, Death, and Hell
His glorious Name
Quite overcame,
Yet I rebel
And slight the same.

But I'll come in
Before my loss,
Me farther toss,
As sure to win
Under his Cross.

William Laud (1573–1645)

Laud, the son of a Reading tailor, became a Fellow and then President of St John's College, Oxford, then Dean of Gloucester. He was appointed Bishop of Bath and Wells, then Bishop of London, then Archbishop of Canterbury. He argued that the Roman Catholic Church and the Church of England are both parts of the same Catholic Church. He was, however, implacably opposed to the Puritans, and underestimated their popular support. He made the communion table rather than the pulpit the focus of the church, and wished to impose a general oath upholding the divine right of kings and swearing never to 'consent to alter the government of this Church by archbishops, deans and archdeacons, &c.' This 'etcetera oath' exposed him to ridicule, and he was impeached by the Long Parliament in a travesty of a trial, imprisoned in the Tower of London and executed on Tower Hill.

Give unto us, O Lord, we humbly beseech thee, a wise, a sober, a patient, an understanding, a devout, a religious, a courageous heart; a soul full of devotion to do thee service, strength against all temptations; through Jesus Christ our Lord. Amen.

Gracious Father, I humbly beseech thee for thy holy catholic church. Fill it with all truth, in all truth, with all peace. Where it is corrupt, purge it. Where it is in error, direct it. Where it is superstitious, rectify it. Where anything is amiss, reform it. Where it is right, strengthen and confirm it. Where it is in want, furnish it. Where it is divided and rent asunder, make up the breaches of it, O thou holy one of Israel.

From Works, *Vol. III*

Grant, Lord, that we may live in thy fear, die in thy favour, rest in thy peace, rise in thy power, and reign in thy glory; for thy own beloved Son's sake, Jesus Christ our Lord. Amen.

Lord, bless this Kingdom, we beseech thee, that religion may increase amongst us, that there may be peace within the gates, and plenty within the palaces of it. In peace, we beseech thee, so preserve it, that it corrupt not; in war, so defend it, that it suffer not; in plenty, so order it, that it riot not; in want, so pacify and moderate it, that it may patiently and peaceably seek thee, the only full supply both of men and states; that so it may continue a place and a people to do thee service to the end of time, through Jesus Christ our only Saviour and Redeemer. Amen.

M ost gracious God, we humbly beseech thee, as for this kingdom in general, so especially for the High Court of Parliament, under our most religious and gracious King at this time assembled: that thou wouldest be pleased to direct and prosper all their consultations to the advancement of thy glory, the good of thy Church, the safety, honour, and welfare of our Sovereign and his Dominions; that all things may be so ordered and settled by their endeavours, upon the best and surest foundations, that peace and happiness, truth and justice, religion and piety, may be established among us for all generations. These and all other necessaries, for them, for us, and thy whole Church, we humbly beg in the name and mediation of Jesus Christ, our most blessed Lord and Saviour. Amen.

In The Book of Common Prayer *(1662)*

T each me, O my Lord Jesus, instruct me, that I may learn from thee what I ought to teach concerning thee.

Joseph Hall (1574–1656)

Joseph Hall was a bishop with strong Puritan tendencies, who advocated a non-prelatical episcopacy. In The Art of Divine Meditation *he showed that Puritans could learn from the mystical and monastic teachers of prayer of earlier centuries. In spite of his sympathy for the Puritans, he was nonetheless imprisoned in the Tower and ejected from his post by the Puritan Parliament. He ended his days in poverty.*

I see man walketh in a vain shadow and disquieteth himself in vain; they are pitiful pleasures he enjoyeth while he forgetteth thee. I am as vain, make me more wise. O, let me see heaven and I know I shall never envy nor follow them. My times are in thine hands; I am no better than my fathers, a stranger on earth. As I speak of them, so the next, yea, this generation shall speak of me as one that was. My life is a bubble, a smoke, a shadow, a thought; I know it hath no abiding in this thoroughfare. O, suffer me not so mad as while I pass on the way I should forget the end. It is that other life that I must trust to. With thee it is that I shall continue.

From The Art of Divine Meditation

N ow howsoever in this or any other practice which may seem to carry with it a smack of superstition, our devotion may be groundless and unseasonable, yet nothing hinders but that we may take just and holy hints of raising up our hearts to our God; as when we do first look forth, and see the heavens over our heads, to think, *The heavens declare thy glory, O God.* When we see the day breaking, or the sun rising, *The day is thine, and the night is thine, thou hast prepared the light and the sun.* When the light shines in our faces, *Thou deckest thyself with light as with a garment;* or, *Light is sprung up for the righteous.* When we see our garden embellished with flowers, *The earth is full of the goodness of the Lord.* When we see a rough sea, *The waves of the sea rage horribly, and are mighty; but the Lord that dwelleth on high is mightier than they.* When we see the darkness of the night, *The darkness is no darkness unto thee.* When we rise up from our bed, or our seat, *Lord, thou knowest my down-sitting and my uprising; thou understandest my thoughts afar off.* When we wash our hands, *Wash thou me, O Lord, and I shall be whiter than snow.* When we are walking forth, *O hold thou up my goings in thy paths, that my footsteps slip not.* When we hear a passing bell, *O teach me to number my days, that I may apply my heart to wisdom;* or, *Lord, let me know my end, and the number of my days.*

From The Devout Soul; or Rules of Heavenly Devotion

Sir Jacob Astley (1579–1652)

Sir Jacob Astley used this prayer before the battle of Edgehill (1642). The last two lines are worth memorizing as a perfect example of an 'arrow prayer' to be used when there is no time for more. The whole prayer is not so well known.

L ord, help me today to realize that thou wilt be speaking to me through the events of the day,
through people, through things, and through all creation.
Give me ears, eyes and heart to perceive thee,
however veiled thy presence may be.
Give me insight to see through the exterior of things

to the interior truth.
Give me thy Spirit of discernment.
O Lord, thou knowest how busy I must be this day.
If I forget thee, do not thou forget me. Amen.

The Puritan *Prayers* of 1585

There has always been a strong Puritan streak in the British character. At its best, this results in a hunger after righteousness and purity of life; the downside is a tendency to condemn others and deny them any opportunity of taking pleasure in God's creation. But the term first began to be applied to those who struggled against the Elizabethan settlement and wanted a purified Church of England in which no ceremonies would be allowed which are not expressly commanded in the Bible. It is often loosely used to include the Independents, who wanted nothing to do with the established Church, and after they were expelled by the Act of Uniformity of 1662 it is more accurate to call them Nonconformists. In 1585 the Puritans proposed to Parliament a set of prayers which they found more acceptable than The Book of Common Prayer.

O merciful God, forasmuch as no council can stand, nor any can prosper, but only such as are gathered in thy name; we pray that thou wilt so incline the hearts of those who are elected to govern this nation, that their counsels may be subject in true obedience to thy holy word and will. Graft in them, we pray, good minds to conceive, free liberty to speak; and grant to all of us a ready and quiet consent to such wholesome laws and statutes, as may declare us to be thy people, and this nation to be prosperously ruled by thy good guiding and defence; through Jesus Christ our Lord. Amen.

Robert Sanderson (1587–1663)

Sanderson was made Professor of Divinity at Oxford, but was imprisoned for a while during the Civil War. In 1660 he became Bishop of Lincoln, and took an active part in the Savoy Conference which revised The Book of Common Prayer. *He was the author of the opening prayer in the new 'Forms of Prayer to be used at Sea', and of the Preface beginning: 'It hath been the wisdom of the Church of England, ever since the first compiling of her public liturgy, to keep the mean between the two extremes, of too much stiffness in refusing, and of too much easiness in admitting any variation from it . . .'*

O eternal Lord God, who alone spreadest out the heavens and rulest the raging of the sea; who hast compassed the waters with bounds until day and night come to an end; be pleased to receive into thy almighty and most gracious protection the persons of thy servants and the fleet in which they serve. Preserve us from the dangers of the sea, and from the violence of the enemy, that we may be a safeguard unto our most gracious Sovereign Lord, King Charles and his kingdoms, and a security for such as pass on the seas upon their lawful occasions; that the inhabitants of our island may in peace and quiet serve thee our God; and that we may return in safety to enjoy the blessings of the land, with the fruits of our labours; and with a thankful remembrance of thy mercies to praise and glorify thy holy name, through Jesus Christ our Lord. Amen.

From Forms of Prayer to be used at Sea

Robert Herrick (1591–1674)

Robert's father was a London goldsmith, and the boy was apprenticed to his uncle in the same trade. But he had the opportunity to go to Cambridge and was ordained. He was deprived of his Devon parish during the Commonwealth, but returned to it in 1662. His verse has a lightness of touch which has no rivals; but he seems to have seen nothing inconsistent in publishing at the same time as his religious verse poems about imaginary mistresses, 'Cherry ripe' and 'Gather ye rosebuds'.

No Coming to God Without Christ

Good and great God, how should I fear
To come to thee, if Christ not there;
Could I but think he would not be
Present to plead my cause for me;
To hell I'd rather run, than I
Would see thy face, and he not by.

Litany to The Holy Spirit

In the hour of my distress,
When temptations me oppress,
And when I my sins confess,
    Sweet Spirit comfort me.

When I lie within my bed,
Sick in heart and sick in head,
And with doubts discomforted,
   Sweet Spirit comfort me.
When the house doth sigh and weep,
And the world is drowned in sleep,
Yet mine eyes the watch do keep;
   Sweet Spirit comfort me . . .
When the priest his last hath prayed,
And I nod to what is said,
'Cause my speech is now decayed;
   Sweet Spirit comfort me.
When, God knows, I'm tossed about,
Either with despair, or doubt;
Yet before the glass be out,
   Sweet Spirit comfort me . . .
When the Judgement is revealed,
And that opened which was sealed,
When to thee I have appealed;
   Sweet Spirit comfort me.

His Prayer for Absolution

For those my unbaptized rhymes,
Writ in my wild unhallowed times;
For every sentence, clause and word,
That's not inlaid with thee (my Lord),
Forgive me, God, and blot each line
Out of my book, that is not thine.
But if, 'mongst all, thou find'st here one
Worthy thy benediction;
That one of all the rest, shall be
The glory of my work, and me.

His Wish to God

I would to God, that mine old age might have
Before my last, but here a living grave,
Some one poor alms-house; there to lie, or stir,
Ghost-like, as in my meaner sepulchre;

A little piggin, and a pipkin by,
To hold things fitting my necessity;
Which, rightly used, both in their time and place,
Might me excite to fore, and after-grace.
Thy cross, my Christ, fixed 'fore mine eyes should be,
Not to adore that, but to worship thee.
So, here the remnant of my days I'd spend,
Reading thy bible, and my book; so end.

Nicholas Ferrar (1592–1637)

Leaving his Fellowship at Cambridge on account of his health, Nicholas Ferrar travelled abroad for some years. On returning to his native London, he worked for six years as Deputy Treasurer of the Virginia Company before being elected to Parliament. The possibility of a brilliant career was given up, however, when he decided to settle at Little Gidding in Huntingdonshire and form a new type of religious community. He was ordained deacon but never priest. He invited his brother and brother-in-law with their families to live with him a life of prayer. Some thirty people took it in turns to recite the Psalms and read the Gospels every hour in the Chapel, and Nicholas himself frequently sat up all night continuing the vigil. King Charles I visited Little Gidding and was impressed by the life of the community; but the Puritans attacked it, and after Ferrar's death destroyed most of his papers and ended the community. A form of community has been re-established at Little Gidding in recent years, and it is still deeply moving, as T. S. Eliot puts it in his poem with that name, 'to kneel where prayer has been valid.'

A hymn for St John the Baptist's Day[13]

The holy faith we do profess;
Us to thy holy fellowship receive.
Our sins we heartily confess:
Thy pardon therefore let us have.
And as to us thy servant gives
Occasion thus to honour thee:
So also let our words and lives
As lights and guides to others be.

Thanksgiving for Community Life

Wonderful hath been thy goodness towards us: while the wise have been disappointed in their counsels, while those full of friends have been left desolate, while the men whose hands were mighty have found nothing, while the strong on every side have fallen, we, O Lord, have been by thy power raised up, by thine arm have we been strengthened, guided by thy counsels, and relieved by the favour of thy mercies. And that we might know that it was thy doing, by those ways and means which we thought not of, thou hast brought us into a wealthy place, and to these many comforts which we now enjoy.[14]

For George Herbert, during his Final Illness

O most mighty God, and merciful Father, we most humbly beseech thee, if it be thy good pleasure, to continue to us that singular benefit which thou hast given us in the friendship of thy servant, our dear brother, who now lieth on the bed of sickness. Let him abide with us yet awhile, for the furtherance of our faith. We have indeed deserved by our ingratitude, not only the loss of him, but whatever other opportunities thou hast given us for the attainment of our salvation. We do not deserve to be heard in our supplications; but thy mercies are above all thy works. In consideration whereof we prostrate ourselves in all humble earnestness, beseeching thee, if so it may seem good to thy Divine Majesty, that thou wilt hear us in this, who hast heard us in all the rest, and that thou wilt bring him back again from the gates of death; that thou wilt yet a while spare him, that he may live to thy honour and our comfort. Lord, thou hast willed that our delights should be in the saints on earth, and in such as excel in virtue: how then should we not be afflicted, and mourn when thou takest them away from us! Thou hast made him a great help, and furtherance of the best things amongst us; how then can we but esteem the loss of him, a chastisement from thy displeasure! O Lord, we beseech thee that it may not be so: we beseech thee, if it be thy good pleasure, restore unto us our dear brother, by restoring to him his health.[15]

After a Major Decision

I thank thee, O blessed Lord God, for of thee cometh this mind; it is not of myself, but from the inspiration of thy blessed Spirit.[16]

George Herbert (1593–1633)

George was a younger brother of Edward, Lord Herbert of Cherbury, and was made a Fellow of Trinity College, Cambridge, on account of his classical learning and his musical ability (he played the lute and viol and sang). He was appointed Public Orator of the University, and seemed destined to shine as a courtier. The influence of his friend Nicholas Ferrar, however, turned his interest to Divinity, and in 1630 he was ordained a priest in the Church of England. William Laud persuaded him to become rector of the country parish of Fugglestone with Bemerton, near Salisbury, where he stayed for the rest of his life. In The Country Parson *he gives simple and sage advice for the pastoral ministry which many ordinary parish priests have attempted to follow. In it he discovers a sense of vocation far higher than that of his worldly contemporaries. His poetry was written to be read at small gatherings of friends. On his death-bed he sent the collection known as* The Temple *to Nicholas Ferrar, leaving him to decide whether to burn or publish it. Yet many regard it as the greatest religious poetry in English, the metaphors or 'conceits' which were distinctive of the poetry of his time being much less convoluted than those of other 'metaphysical poets', and his deep faith was expressed in simple language. 'The God of love my shepherd is', 'Teach me my God and king' and 'Let all the world in every corner sing' are hymns which speak directly to the heart of the worshipper.*

Prayer

Prayer, the Church's banquet, Angels' age,
  God's breath in man returning to his birth,
The soul in paraphrase, heart in pilgrimage,
The Christian plummet sounding heaven and earth;
Engine against the Almighty, sinner's tower,
Reversèd thunder, Christ-side-piercing spear,
The six days' world transposing in an hour,
A kind of tune, which all things hear and fear.
Softness, and peace, and joy, and love, and bliss,
Exalted manna, gladness of the best,
Heaven in ordinary, man well drest,
The milky way, the bird of Paradise,
Church-bells beyond the stars heard, the soul's blood,
The land of spices, something understood.

Prayer

O f what an easy quick access,
   My blessed Lord, art thou! how suddenly
May our requests thine ear invade!
To show that state dislikes not easiness.
If I but lift mine eyes, my suit is made:
Thou canst no more not hear, than thou canst die.

Of what supreme almighty power
Is thy great arm which spans the east and west,
And tacks the centre to the sphere!
By it do all things live their measured hour:
We cannot ask the thing, which is not there,
Blaming the shallowness of our request.

Of what unmeasurable love
Art thou possessed, who, when thou couldst not die,
Wert fain to take our flesh and curse,
And for our sakes in person sin reprove;
That by destroying that which tied thy purse,
Thou mightst make way for liberality!

Since then these three wait on thy throne,
Ease, power, and love; I value prayer so,
That were I to leave all but one,
Wealth, fame, endowments, virtues, all should go.
I and dear prayer would together dwell,
And quickly gain, for each inch lost, an ell.

Easter

I got me flowers to straw thy way,
   I got me boughs off many a tree;
But thou wast up by break of day,
And brought'st thy sweets along with thee.

The Sun arising in the East,
Though he give light, & th'East perfume;
If they should offer to contest
With thy arising, they presume.

Can there be any day but this,
Though many suns to shine endeavour?
We count three hundred, but we miss:
There is but one, and that one ever.

Sin

Lord, with what care hast thou begirt us round!
  Parents first season us: then schoolmasters
Deliver us to laws; they send us bound
To rules of reason, holy messengers,
Pulpits and Sundays, sorrow dogging sin,
Afflictions sorted, anguish of all sizes,
Fine nets and stratagems to catch us in,
Bibles laid open, millions of surprises,
Blessings beforehand, ties of gratefulness,
The sound of glory ringing in our ears:
Without, our shame; within, our consciences;
Angels and grace, eternal hopes and fears.
Yet all these fences and their whole array
One cunning bosom-sin blows quite away.

Praise

King of glory, King of peace,
  I will love thee:
And that love may never cease,
  I will move thee.

Thou hast granted my request,
  Thou hast heard me:
Thou didst note my working breast,
  Thou hast spared me.

Wherefore with my utmost art
  I will sing thee,
And the cream of all my heart
  I will bring thee.

Though my sins against me cried,
  Thou didst clear me;

And alone, when they replied,
Thou didst hear me.

Sev'n whole days, not one in seven,
I will praise thee.
In my heart, though not in heaven,
I can raise thee.

Thou grew'st soft and moist with tears,
Thou relentedst:
And when Justice call'd for fears,
Thou dissentedst.

Small it is, in this poor sort
To enroll thee:
E'en eternity is too short
To extol thee.

Discipline

Throw away thy rod,
      Throw away thy wrath:
O my God,
Take the gentle path.

For my heart's desire
Unto thine is bent:
I aspire
To a full consent.

Not a word or look
I affect to own,
But by book,
And thy book alone.

Though I fail, I weep:
Though I halt in pace,
Yet I creep
To the throne of grace.

Then let wrath remove;
Love will do the deed;
For with love
Stony hearts will bleed.

Love is swift of foot;
Love's a man of war,
And can shoot,
And can hit from far.

Who can 'scape his bow?
That which wrought on thee,
Brought thee low,
Needs must work on me.

Throw away thy rod:
Though man frailties hath,
Thou art God:
Throw away thy wrath.

The Elixir

Teach me, my God and King,
In all things thee to see,
And what I do in any thing,
To do it as for thee:

Not rudely, as a beast,
To run into an action;
But still to make thee prepossessed
And give it his perfection.

A man that looks on glass,
On it may stay his eye;
Of if he pleaseth, through it pass,
And then the heav'n espy.

All may of thee partake:
Nothing can be so mean,
Which with his tincture 'For thy sake'
Will not grow bright and clean.

A servant with this clause
Makes drudgery divine:
Who sweeps a room, as for thy laws,
Makes that and th'action fine.

This is the famous stone
That turneth all to gold:
For that which God doth touch and own
Cannot for less be told.

Gratefulness

Thou that hast giv'n so much to me,
  Give one thing more, a grateful heart.
See how thy beggar works on thee
By art.

He makes thy gifts occasion more,
And says, If he in this be cross'd,
All thou hast giv'n him heretofore
Is lost.

But thou didst reckon, when at first
Thy word our hearts and hands did crave,
What it would come to at the worst
To save.

Perpetual knockings at thy door,
Tears sullying thy transparent rooms,
Gift upon gift, much would have more,
And comes.

This not withstanding, thou wentst on,
And didst allow us all our noise:
Nay, thou hast made a sigh and groan
Thy joys.

Not that thou hast not still above
Much better tunes, than groans can make;
But that these country airs thy love
Did take.

Wherefore I cry, and cry again;
And in no quiet canst thou be,
Till I a thankful heart obtain
Of thee:

Not thankful, when it pleaseth me;
As if thy blessings had spare days:
But such a heart, whose pulse may be
Thy praise.

Love

L ove bade me welcome; yet my soul drew back
Guilty of dust and sin.
But quick-eyed Love, observing me grow slack
From my first entrance in,
Drew nearer to me, sweetly questioning,
If I lacked anything.

'A guest', I answered, 'worthy to be here.'
Love said, 'You shall be he.'
'I the unkind, ungrateful? Ah my dear,
I cannot look on thee.'
Love took my hand, and smiling did reply,
'Who made the eyes but I?'

'Truth, Lord, but I have marred them; let my shame
Go where it doth deserve.'
'And know you not', says Love, 'who bore the blame?'
'My dear, then I will serve.'
'You must sit down', says Love, 'and taste my meat.'
So I did sit and eat.

John Cosin (1594–1672)

*Cosin was a rector in County Durham, and was asked by King Charles I
to compile a book of prayers for Queen Henrietta Maria's maids of honour.
A Collection of Private Devotions (1627) was the result, but it did nothing
to ingratiate him with the Puritans, who already opposed him because he
was a personal friend of William Laud. He was elected Master of Peterhouse
in Cambridge, then Dean of Peterborough, but the Long Parliament
deprived him of these positions because of his 'popish innovations'. He
fled to Paris, where he ministered to members of the exiled Queen's household, and became a friend of the Huguenots. After the Restoration of the
monarchy he was made Bishop of Durham, and tried in vain to bring
about a reconciliation between the Church of England and the Puritans*

*at the Savoy Conference of 1661. He liked dignified ceremonial and contrib-
uted to* The Book of Common Prayer *of 1662.*

Almighty God, our heavenly Father, who hast purchased to thyself an universal Church by the precious blood of thy dear Son, mercifully look upon the same, and at this time so guide and govern the minds of thy servants, the bishops and pastors of thy flock, that they may lay hands suddenly on no man, but faithfully and wisely make choice of fit persons to serve in the sacred ministry of thy Church. And to those which shall be ordained to any holy function give thy grace and heavenly benediction; that both by their life and doctrine they may set forth thy glory and set forward the salvation of all men; through Jesus Christ our Lord. Amen.[17]

Be thou a light unto mine eyes, music to mine ears, sweetness to my taste, and a full contentment to my heart. Be thou my sunshine in the day, my food at the table, my repose in the night, my clothing in nakedness, and my succour in all necessities. Lord Jesu, I give thee my body, my soul, my substance, my fame, my friends, my liberty, and my life. Dispose of me and of all that is mine, as it seemeth best to thee and to the glory of thy blessed name.[18]

I am now not mine, but thine. Therefore claim me as thy right, keep me as thy charge, and love me as thy child. Fight for me when I am assaulted, heal me when I am wounded, and revive me when I am destroyed.[19]

Lord, let me be obedient without arguing, humble without feigning, patient without grudging, pure without corruption, merry without lightness, sad without mistrust, sober without dullness, true without doubleness, fearing thee without desperation, and trusting in thee without presumption.[20]

Merciful Lord, of thy abundant goodness towards us thou hast made the day wherein to work, and ordained the night wherein to take our rest; grant us such rest of body, that we may have a waking soul. Let no vain and wandering fancy trouble us; let our spiritual enemies have no power over us, but let our minds be set wholly upon thy presence, to love, and fear, and rest in thee alone, that being refreshed with moderate and sober sleep, we may rise up again, with cheerful strength and gladness, to serve thee in all good works; through Jesus Christ our Lord. Amen.

O most gracious Jesus, our Lord and our God, who bore our sins in thine own body on the tree, that we, being dead to sin, might live unto righteousness: have mercy upon us, we beseech thee, both now and at the hour of our death; and grant unto us thy humble servants, with all other Christian people that have this thy blessed passion in devout remembrance, a godly and peaceful life in this present world; and through thy grace, eternal glory in the world to come; where with the Father and the Holy Spirit, thou livest and reignest ever one God, world without end. Amen.

O God, whose blessed Son was manifested, that he might destroy the works of the devil, and make us the sons of God and heirs of eternal life: grant us, we beseech thee, that having this hope, we may purify ourselves, even as he is pure; that when he shall appear in power and great glory we may be made like unto him in his eternal and glorious kingdom; where with thee, O Father, and thee, O Holy Spirit, he liveth and reigneth ever one God, world without end. Amen.[21]

O Lord Jesu Christ, who at thy first coming didst send thy messenger to prepare thy way before thee; grant that the ministers and stewards of thy mysteries may likewise so make ready and prepare thy way, by turning the hearts of the disobedient to the wisdom of the just, that at thy second coming to judge the world, we may be found an acceptable people in thy sight, who livest and reignest with the Father and the Holy Spirit, ever one God, world without end. Amen.[22]

O God, the Father of lights, from whom cometh down every good and perfect gift; mercifully accept our thanksgivings, and look upon our frailty and infirmity, and grant us such health of body as thou knowest to be needful for us; that both in body and soul, we may evermore serve thee with all our strength and might; through Jesus Christ our Lord. Amen.

Oliver Cromwell (1599–1658)

The most vehement advocate of applying Puritan principles to national life was Oliver Cromwell, Member of Parliament for his birthplace of Huntingdon, then for Cambridge, where he had graduated, and cavalry commander at the Battle of Edgehill. As leader of the Independents, who would make no compromise with King Charles I, Cromwell led his New Model Army which defeated the King at Naseby. At first content merely to strip the King of some of his powers, royalist plots and rebellions persuaded Cromwell to press for the prosecution and eventual execution of the King. He was the chairman of the Council of State in the new Commonwealth. He defeated the Scots royalists at the Battle of Worcester, which effectively ended the Civil War. As Lord Protector he reorganized the Church of England on Calvinist lines, but with a limited degree of toleration.

Strengthen us, O God, to relieve the oppressed, to hear the groans of poor prisoners, to reform the abuses of all professions; that many be made not poor to make a few rich; for Jesus Christ's sake.[23]

Lord, though I am a miserable and wretched creature, I am in covenant with thee through grace. And I may, I will, come to thee for thy People. Thou hast made me, though very unworthy, a mean instrument to do them some good, and thee service; and many of them have set too high a value upon me, though others wish and would be glad of my death. Lord, however thou do dispose of me, continue and go on to do good for them. Give them consistency of judgement, one heart, and mutual love; and go on to deliver them, and with the work of reformation; and make the Name of Christ glorious in the world. Teach those who look too much on thy instruments, to depend more upon thyself. Pardon such as desire to trample upon the dust of a poor worm, for they are thy People too. And pardon the folly of this short prayer; even for Jesus Christ's sake. And give us a good night, if it be thy pleasure. Amen.

Oliver Cromwell's prayer on his death-bed[24]

Edward Reynolds (1599–1676)

Reynolds was a preacher who was sympathetic to the Puritans during the Commonwealth, but was ejected from his post as Dean of Christ Church in Oxford because he was not wholehearted enough in his support. At the restoration of the monarchy he was made Bishop of Norwich, and worked hard to reconcile the Presbyterians with the Episcopalians. His contribution to The Book of Common Prayer *was the popular and comprehensive 'General Thanksgiving', which many congregations used to be able to recite from memory.*

Almighty God, father of all mercies, we thine unworthy servants do give thee most humble and hearty thanks for all thy goodness and loving-kindness to us, and to all men; we bless thee for our creation, preservation, and all the blessings of this life: but above all, for thine inestimable love in the redemption of the world by our Lord Jesus Christ; for the means of grace, and for the hope of glory. And, we beseech thee, give us that due sense of all thy mercies, that our hearts may be unfeignedly thankful, and that we show forth thy praise, not only with our lips, but in our lives; by giving up ourselves to thy service, and by walking before thee in holiness and righteousness all our days; through Jesus Christ our Lord, to whom with thee and the Holy Ghost be all honour and glory, world without end. Amen.

Anonymous sixteenth-century prayers

Merciful and loving Father, we beseech thee with all our hearts to pour out upon our enemies whatsoever things thou knowest will do them good; and chiefly a sound and uncorrupt mind to know thee and love thee with their whole heart, and love us thy children for thy sake. Let not their first hating of us turn to their harm. Lord, we desire their amendment and our own. Separate them not from us by punishing them, but join and knit them to us by thy favourable dealing with them. And seeing that we are all ordained to be citizens of one Eternal City, let us prepare ourselves for it here already by mutual love through Jesus Christ our Lord. Amen.

Almighty God, maker of all things, thou hast placed thy creatures necessary for our use in diverse lands: grant that all peoples and nations, needing one another, may be knit together in one bond of mutual service, to share their diverse riches; through Jesus Christ our Lord. Amen.[25]

Pietism

Under the influence of Johann Arndt, whom he revered, Philipp Spener (1635–1705) sought to inject new life into what he regarded as the formal Lutheranism of his time, with its emphasis on correct doctrine. Beginning with meetings in his own home, and proclaiming the universal priesthood of all the faithful, he established a network of circles for prayer and Bible reading. Philip Gerhard's hymns expressed the depth of sentiment which characterized the movement, which attracted the name of Pietism. When A. H. Francke (1663–1727) attacked the Lutheran theologians in Leipzig, demanding that lectures be turned into devotional meetings, and rejecting all philosophy and doctrine, he was forced to leave, and a new university was founded at Halle, which became the centre of the movement. At Halle, however, Pietism developed into a rigid system of penance, grace and rebirth, whereas at Herrnhut, under Count von Zinzendorf, Spener's godson, it emphasized personal devotion to the Redeemer. The intense emotions in the words to much of the vocal music of J. S. Bach (1685–1750) show the power of Pietism, and in this form it influenced early Methodism and renewal movements in many countries.

Johann Arndt (1555–1621)

Arndt was a disciple of Melanchthon who became pastor at Badeborn. He was a Lutheran who was opposed by Calvinists, so he moved to Quedlinburg and then Brunswick. His Four Books of True Christianity *turned away from the prevalent image of the lawcourt in describing the forgiveness brought by the death of Jesus, preferring to stress its effects in the human heart.*

Ah, Lord, to whom all hearts are open, you can pilot the ship of our souls far better than we can. Stand up, Lord, and command the stormy wind and the troubled sea of our hearts to be still, and at peace in you, so that we may look up to you undisturbed, and rest in union with you, our Lord. Do not let us be carried hither and thither by wandering thoughts, but, forgetting all else, let us see and hear you alone. Renew our spirits; kindle in us your light, that it may shine within us, and our hearts may burn in love and adoration for you. Let your Holy Spirit dwell in us continually, and make us your temples and sanctuary. Fill us with divine love and light and life, with devout and heavenly thoughts, with comfort and strength, with joy and peace. Amen.

Bestow on me, O Lord, a genial spirit and unwearied forbearance; a mild, loving, patient heart; kindly looks, pleasant, cordial speech and manners in the exchanges of daily life; that I may give offence to none, but insofar as I can, may live in charity with everyone.

Gracious and gentle and condescending God, God of peace, Father of mercy, God of all comfort; see, I lament before you the evil of my heart; I acknowledge that I am too much disposed to anger, jealousy, and revenge, to ambition and pride, which often give rise to discord and bitter feelings between me and others. Too often in this way I have offended and grieved you, my long-suffering Father, as well as my neighbours. Oh! forgive me this sin, and allow me to share in the blessing which you have promised to the peacemakers, who shall be called the children of God.

Johann Freylinghausen (1670–1739)

Johann Freylinghausen's Spiritual Songbook *was the most popular hymn-book of the Pietists, sanctifying erotic language to describe the love of the Christian for the Saviour.*

Who is Like You?

Who is like you,
Jesus, sweet Jesus?

You are the light of those who are spiritually lost.
You are the life of those who are spiritually dead.
You are the liberation of those who are imprisoned by guilt.

You are the glory of those who hate themselves.
You are the guardian of those who are paralysed by fear.
You are the guide of those who are bewildered by falsehood.

You are the peace of those who are in turmoil.
You are the prince of those who yearn to be led.
You are the priest of those who seek the truth.[1]

May Your Spirit Guide My Mind

May your Spirit guide my mind,
May its lethargy be healed,
May my mind be set to find
Christ in everything revealed.

Spirit, stimulate my soul,
Lift its listless muscle-tone,
With my soul in your control,
Christ in everything is known.

May your Spirit melt my heart,
Cold as ice and hard as steel;
Warm my heart till by your art
Christ in everything I feel.[2]

Gerhard Tersteegen (1697–1769)

Tersteegen was born near Düsseldorf and converted at the age of twenty among some Pietists. He then lived in solitude and earned his living as a ribbon weaver, until he was able to establish a Pilgrim's Hut at Otterbeck, where he gathered a small community and devoted himself to spiritual direction and leading meetings. He published much and is chiefly remembered for his hymns.

Lo, God is here! let us adore,
And own how dreadful is this place!
Let all within us feel his power,
And silent bow before his face;
Who know his power, his grace who prove,
Serve him with awe, with reverence love.

Lo, God is here! him day and night
Rejoicing choirs of angels sing;
To him, enthroned above all height,
The hosts of heaven their praises bring:
Disdain not, Lord, our meaner song,
Who praise thee with a faltering tongue.

Being of beings! may our praise
Thy courts with grateful fragrance fill;
Still may we stand before thy face,
Still hear and do thy sovereign will;
To thee may all our thoughts arise
A true and ceaseless sacrifice.[3]

Let your love so warm our souls, O Lord, that we may gladly surrender ourselves with all we are and have unto you. Let your love fall as fire from heaven upon the altar of our hearts; teach us to guard it heedfully by continual devotion and quietness of mind, and to cherish with anxious care every spark of its holy flame, with which your good Spirit would quicken us, so that neither height, nor depth, things present, nor things to come, may ever separate us therefrom. Strengthen our souls, animate our cold hearts with your warmth and tenderness, that we may no more live as in a dream, but walk before you as pilgrims in earnest to reach their home. And grant us all at last to meet with your holy saints before your throne, and there rejoice in your love. Amen.

God, you are in your holy temple, let all that is in me be still in your presence: still in my tongue, in my will, in all my desires and thoughts; I will cease from any sort of activity: O how precious in the sight of God is a gentle and quiet spirit silent in his presence.

Scots Protestants

The Scottish Reformation had its own martyrs – Resby, Crawar, Patrick Hamilton and Wishart among them – and although it started on Lutheran lines, finally, under the influence of Knox and others, it took on a Calvinistic form, so that now the established Church north of the border is the Presbyterian Church of Scotland, and the Episcopalians are a minority.

The Scottish Metrical Psalter (1595)

The Church of Scotland continued to develop its worship according to its own genius, and produced several revisions of John Knox's Book of Common Prayer. The central feature of their services was the singing of the psalms, in a translation into metrical verse, to the wonderful Metrical Psalm tunes. The Scottish Metrical Psalter of 1595 contained a Collect based on each of the psalms.

Gracious Lord, who art not the God of confusion or discord, but the God of concord and of peace; join our hearts and affections in such sort together that we may walk as brethren in thy house, in brotherly charity and love, and as members of the body of Christ. Let the oil of sanctification, that is, thy Holy Spirit, inflame us, and the dew of thy blessing continually fall upon us, that we may obtain life eternal; through the same Jesus Christ.[1]

Merciful Lord, the comforter and deliverer of poor captives; thou seest the great extremities whereunto thy poor Church is brought, and how she is on all sides exposed to the slavery and mockery of thine enemies and ours, scoffing and taunting both us and thy praises. O God, turn back thy wrath upon them, and hear us who mourn and sigh for our deliverance; that, the tyrants our persecutors being overthrown, we may freely sing thy praises and lauds in thy house; in the name of Jesus Christ, our Lord.[2]

O good God, suffer never that in any wise we shall set thee aside, to put our trust or confidence in princes, or in the children of men; but let us continually have all our trust and confidence fixed upon thee, for unto such thou art a sure rock and refuge. Lead them, Lord, that walk in darkness; deliver the oppressed; enlarge thy kingdom, which all thy chosen children that are redeemed by the blood of thy Son, most earnestly thirst for; and that for the same Jesus Christ's sake.[3]

Samuel Rutherford (1600–1661)

A bad start, when he was dismissed from his professorship at Edinburgh for fornication, led Samuel Rutherford to a fervent religion. He was minister of Amwoth, then a professor of Divinity at St Andrews. He was one of the Scots representatives at the Westminster Assembly and argued strongly there for Presbyterianism. He favoured religious persecution of those with whom he disagreed and was against the divine right of kings, and was charged with high treason, but he received the citation on his death-bed. His letters contain lyrical passages which pass almost unnoticed into prayer.

A little of God would make my soul bank-full. Oh that I had but Christ's odd off-fallings; that he would let but the meanest of his love-rays and love-beams fall from him, so as I might gather and carry them with me! I would not be ill to please with Christ, and veiled visions of Christ; neither would I be dainty in seeing and enjoying of him: a kiss of Christ blown over his shoulder, the parings and crumbs of glory that fall under his table in heaven, a shower like a thin May-mist of his love, would make me green, and sappy, and joyful ... Oh that my Lord Jesus would rue upon me, and give me but the meanest alms of felt and believed salvation! ... Oh, what pain is it, that time and sin should be so many thousand miles betwixt a loved and longed-for Lord and a dwining and love-sick soul, who would rather than all the world have lodging with Christ! Oh, let this bit of love of ours, this inch and half-span length of heavenly longing, meet with thy infinite love![4]

Robert Leighton (1611–84)

When Robert Leighton was Bishop of Dunblane, he worked hard to bring about a reconciliation between the Presbyterians and the Episcopalians.

He threatened to resign in protest at the persecution of the Presbyterian
Covenanters, but King Charles II reassured him and appointed him Arch-
bishop of Glasgow in 1670. He finally resigned in 1674 when his strenuous
efforts to achieve an understanding only rendered him unacceptable to
either side.

G rant, O Lord, that I may be so ravished in the wonder of thy love
that I may forget myself and all things; may feel neither prosperity
nor adversity; may not fear to suffer all the pain in the world rather than
be parted from thee. O let me find thee more inwardly and verily present
with me than I am with myself; and make me most circumspect how I do
use myself in the presence of thee, my holy Lord.

D eliver, O most merciful God, those little ones of thy flock who have
fallen into sin. Remember not their offences, but set them free from
the snare of the enemy. Prosper with the help of thy Holy Spirit the
endeavours of all who are seeking to train them for good. Grant that
following after humility and being made partakers of thy heavenly wisdom,
they may be strengthened to the performance of thy will and may be
restored to the perfect fellowship of thy saints; through Jesus Christ our
Lord. Amen.

The Scottish *Book of Common Prayer* (1637)

King Charles I continued trying to impose The Book of Common Prayer
on an unwilling Scotland, and instructed a committee of Scottish bishops
to draw up a revision. Archbishop Laud made many alterations to their
draft, and it was never widely accepted, but it influenced revision in
England and the later Scottish Episcopalian prayer books.

G rant, O Lord, that as we are baptized into the death of thy blessed
Son our Saviour Jesus Christ; so by continual mortifying our corrupt
affections, we may be buried with him, and that through the grave and
gate of death we may pass to our joyful resurrection, for his merits, who
died and was buried, and rose again for us, thy Son Jesus Christ our Lord.
Amen.[5]

A lmighty God, the giver of all good gifts, who of thy divine providence
hast appointed divers orders in thy Church; give thy grace, we humbly
beseech thee, to all those, who are to be called to any office and adminis-

tration in the same; and so replenish them with the truth of thy doctrine, and endue them with innocency of life, that they may faithfully serve before thee, to the glory of thy great name, and the benefit of thy holy Church, through Jesus Christ our Lord. Amen.[6]

The Seventeenth Century

Listing authors chronologically by the century in which they were born is for convenience, even though many of them may have done their most important work in the following century.

King Charles I (1600–1649)

King Charles was a saintly man but not a wise king. His dignity at the time of his trial and execution entitle him, however, to be numbered among the noble army of martyrs. After spending two hours in prayer, he remarked to Sir Thomas Herbert, the night before he died, 'Herbert, this is my second marriage day; I would be as trim today as may be; for before night I hope to be spoused to my blessed Jesus ... I fear not death! Death is not terrible to me. I bless my God I am prepared.' In his speech from the scaffold he said, 'In troth, sirs, my conscience in religion I think is very well known to the world, and therefore I declare before you all, that I die a Christian according to the profession of the Church of England as I found it left me by my father ... I have a good cause, and I have a gracious God. I will say no more ... I shall say but very short prayers, and then thrust out my hands.'

Almighty and most merciful Father, look down upon us, thy unworthy servants, who here prostrate ourselves before the footstool of thy throne of grace. Look upon us, O Father, through the mediation and in the merits of Jesus Christ, in whom only thou art well pleased, for of ourselves we are not worthy to stand before thee. As in sin we were born, so we have broken thy commandments, by thought, words, and works. We confess, O Lord, that it is thy mercy which endureth for ever, thy compassion which never fails, which is the cause that we have not been consumed. With thee there is mercy and plenteous redemption; in the multitude of thy mercies and by the merits of Jesus Christ, enter not into judgment with thy servants, but be thou merciful unto us, and wash away all our sins with that precious blood which our Saviour shed for us. Purify our hearts by thy Holy Spirit, and as thou dost add days to our lives, so good Lord, we beseech thee, to add repentance to our days, that when we have passed this mortal life we may be partakers of thine everlasting Kingdom; through the merits of Jesus Christ our Lord. Amen.

Devotion to the Sacred Heart

Saint Jean Eudes (1601–80) was born in Normandy and at first was a member of the Oratory, an order which St Philip Neri started in Italy, and which Cardinal Newman later established in England, though the French Oratory was begun by Pierre de Bérulle. Eudes cared for the victims of two outbreaks of plague, and then conducted missions for ten years. Eventually he left the Oratory to set up his own 'Congregation of Jesus and Mary', out of which grew several other orders involved in care for the needy. But his claim to fame is to have begun devotion to the Sacred Heart of Jesus, and later to the heart of Mary also. Saint Margaret Mary Alacoque (1647–90) promoted this cult as a corrective to the merciless picture of God which was prevalent at the time. The artistic representations of the Sacred Heart may not be to everyone's taste, but as a visual symbol for the Saviour's love it has inspired a history of devotion.

Act of Consecration to the Sacred Heart of Jesus

I, N. N., give myself and consecrate to the Sacred Heart of our Lord Jesus Christ, my person and my life, my actions, pains and sufferings, so that I may be unwilling to make use of any part of my being save to honour, love, and glorify the Sacred Heart. This is my unchanging purpose, namely, to be all his, and to do all things for the love of him at the same time renouncing with all my heart whatever is displeasing to him. I therefore take you, O Sacred Heart, to be the only object of my love, the guardian of my life, my assurance of salvation, the remedy of my weakness and inconstancy, the atonement for all the faults of my life, and my sure refuge at the hour of death. Be then, O Heart of goodness, my justification before God our Father, and turn away from me his justified anger. O Heart of love, I put all my confidence in you, for I fear everything from my own wickedness and frailty, but I hope for all things from your goodness and bounty. Consume in me all that displeases you or resists your holy will; let your pure love imprint itself so deeply on my heart, that I shall never be able to forget or to be separated from you. May I obtain from your loving kindness the grace of having my name written on your heart, for in you I desire to place all my happiness and all my glory, living and dying in your true service.

St Margaret Mary Alacoque

L ove of the heart of Jesus, inflame my heart.
Charity of the heart of Jesus, flow into my heart.
Strength of the heart of Jesus, support my heart.
Mercy of the heart of Jesus, pardon my heart.
Patience of the heart of Jesus, grow not weary of my heart.
Kingdom of the heart of Jesus, be in my heart.
Wisdom of the heart of Jesus, teach my heart.
Will of the heart of Jesus, guide my heart.
Zeal of the heart of Jesus, consume my heart.
Immaculate Virgin Mary, pray for me to the heart of Jesus.[1]

The Book of Common Prayer (1604)

During the reign of Elizabeth the 1552 Book of Common Prayer *remained compulsory, with a few small changes in the rubrics (the 'stage-directions' or instructions to the ministers, so called because they were printed in red). James I was greeted with a petition from a thousand Puritans asking for changes in the Prayer Book, and a conference to hear their complaints was held at Hampton Court in 1603–4. Few of their grievances were righted; the great achievement of the Hampton Court Conference was to order a new translation of the Bible. The result was the 'King James Version' of the Bible, often called the 'Authorized Version', from the title page inscription, 'Appointed to be read in Churches', though it never received any formal authorization. This translation, together with the works of Shakespeare, shaped the language of the English-speaking people for centuries, including, for better or worse, the language in which they thought it appropriate to pray. The only changes made to* The Book of Common Prayer *in 1604 were in the rubrics and the addition of six Thanksgivings and a final section for the catechism - a summary of Christian belief to be learnt by those being confirmed by 'echoing' questions with prepared answers.*

O God our heavenly Father, who by thy gracious providence dost cause the former and latter rain to descend upon the earth, that it may bring forth fruit for the use of man; we give thee humble thanks that it hath pleased thee in our great necessity to send us at the last a joyful rain upon thine inheritance, and to refresh it when it was dry, to the great comfort of us thy unworthy servants, and to the glory of thy holy name, through thy mercies in Jesus Christ our Lord. Amen.

O almighty God, who art a strong tower of defence unto thy servants against the face of their enemies; we yield thee praise and thanksgiving for our deliverance from those great and apparent dangers wherewith we were compassed. We acknowledge it thy goodness that we were not delivered over as a prey unto them; beseeching thee still to continue such thy mercies towards us, that all the world may know that thou art our saviour and mighty deliverer, through Jesus Christ our Lord. Amen.

Sir Thomas Browne (1605–82)

Sir Thomas Browne studied medicine at Oxford, Montpellier and Padua, and received a doctorate from Leyden. He settled in Norwich and practised as a physician there for the rest of his life. Because of his travels he was much more broad-minded than most Englishmen of his day. He wrote Hydriotaphia, or Urn-Burial, *an account of funeral practices in many countries, favouring cremation and opposing elaborate memorials. But his most famous work was his earliest,* Religio Medici, *a confession of the faith of a doctor. His was a tolerant faith, which he thought required that we should use our intellects, and he said he would make salvation no narrower than Christ did.*

The night is come, like to the day.
Depart not thou, great God, away.
Let not my sins, black as the night,
Eclipse the lustre of thy light.
Keep still in my horizon; for to me
The sun makes not the day, but thee.
Thou whose nature cannot sleep,
On my temples sentry keep.
Guard me 'gainst those watchful foes,
Whose eyes are open while mine close.
Let no dreams my head infest,
But such as Jacob's temples blest.

While I do rest, my soul advance:
Make my sleep a holy trance:
That I may, my rest being wrought,
Awake into some holy thought,
And with as active vigour run
My course, as doth the nimble sun.
Sleep is a death; O make me try,
By sleeping, what it is to die!
And as gently lay my head
On my grave, as now my bed.
Howe'er I rest, great God, let me
Awake again at last with thee.
And thus assured, behold I lie
Securely, or to wake or die.
These are my drowsy days; in vain
I do now wake to sleep again:
O come that hour, when I shall never
Sleep again, but wake for ever!

From Religio Medici

Henry Hammond (1605–60)

Hammond became the incumbent of Penshurst in Kent. During the Civil War he was deprived of his living, and spent his time relieving the poverty of other deprived clergy, and raising funds to pay for the training of the next generation of candidates for ordination. He was respected for his personal devotion and self-discipline, and for his writings.

O holy Jesus, who camest down from heaven and wast pleased to pay the ransom on the cross for us, on purpose that thou mightest redeem us from all iniquity, and purify unto thyself a peculiar people, zealous of good works, we beseech thee to write thy law in our hearts that we may see it, that we may know thee, and the power of thy resurrection, and express it in turning our foot from our iniquities, that thou mayest rule in our hearts by faith, and that we, being dead unto sin and living unto righteousness, may have our fruit unto holiness, may grow in grace, and in the practical knowledge of thee. Amen.

Jean-Jacques Olier (1608–57)

Olier went blind when studying in Rome, and was cured and converted on a pilgrimage to Loreto. He was ordained and conducted missions and founded seminaries in several places before he settled at Saint-Sulpice in Paris. Here he trained many priests, and formed them into a society of secular priests leading a common way of life. He also instigated social reforms in the depressed neighbourhood, relieving distress among the poor and opposing duelling among the rich. The method of prayer taught by the priests from Saint-Sulpice is a simple sequence of 1. Adoration (Jesus before my eyes); 2. Communion (Jesus drawn into my heart); and 3. Cooperation (Jesus in my hands).

O Jesus living in Mary,
Come and live in thy servants,
In the spirit of thy sanctity,
In the fulness of thy strength,
In the reality of thy virtues,
In the perfection of thy ways,
In the communion of thy mysteries,
Be Lord over every opposing power,
In thine own Spirit, to the glory of the Father. Amen.

Thomas Fuller (1608–61)

Successively curate of St Benet's, Cambridge, rector of Broadwindsor, Dorset, curate of Waltham Abbey and rector of Cranford, Fuller is chiefly remembered for his biographical writings. He compiled a Church History of Britain *and* Worthies of England, *published posthumously and generally known as 'Fuller's Worthies'.* The Poems and Translations of Thomas Fuller DD *is less well known, but it contains a number of personal prayers.*

Lord, what particulars we pray for, we know not, we dare not, we humbly tender a blank into the hands of almighty God; write therein, Lord, what thou wilt, where thou wilt, by whom thou wilt.

Hard is my heart, Lord, to my grief, I feel;
Be thou the loadstone, it shall be the steel.

Lord, teach me the art of patience whilst I am well, and give me the use of it when I am sick. In that day either lighten my burden or strengthen my back. Make me, who so often in my health have discovered my weakness presuming on my own strength, to be strong in my sickness when I solely rely on thy assistance.

B efore I commit a sin it seems to me so shallow, that I may wade through it dry-shod from any guiltiness. But when I have committed it, it often seems so deep that I cannot escape without drowning. Thus I am always in the extremities; either my sins are so small that they need not my repentance, or so great that they cannot obtain thy pardon. Lend me, O Lord, a reed out of thy sanctuary, truly to measure the dimension of my offences. But oh! as thou revealest to me more of my misery, reveal also more of thy mercy.

From Good Thoughts in Bad Times

John Milton (1608–74)

While still a student at Christ's College, Cambridge, Milton wrote his acclaimed Ode on the Morning of Christ's Nativity; *it was followed soon after by* L'Allegro *and* Il Penseroso, *and the masque of* Comus. Lycidas *is both a lament on the death of a friend and a bitter attack on corruption of the clergy, a constant theme in his writings. When his wife left him soon after their marriage he wrote a passionate pamphlet in favour of divorce, arguing that the sanctity of marriage was an invention of the clergy. When he was accused for publishing this without a licence he responded with* Areopagitica, *an argument against censorship. He rejected the established Church and joined the Presbyterians, but, falling out with them, he became an Independent. Having supported Oliver Cromwell, he disagreed with his plans for an established Presbyterian Church. By this time he was completely blind, but his greatest works were the three religious poems of these final years,* Paradise Lost, Paradise Regained *and* Samson Agonistes, *in which the blind hero defying the world has autobiographical implications.*

Adam and Eve's Prayer

T hou also madest the night,
    Maker Omnipotent, and thou the day,
Which we in our appointed work employed
Have finished, happy in our mutual help

And mutual love, the crown of all our bliss,
Ordained by thee, and this delicious place,
For us too large, where thy abundance wants
Partakers, and uncropt falls to the ground.
But thou hast promised from us two a race
To fill the earth, who shall with us extol
Thy goodness infinite, both when we wake,
And when we seek, as now, thy gift of sleep.

From Paradise Lost, *Book IV, lines 724–35.*

On his Blindness

When I consider how my light is spent
Ere half my days, in this dark world and wide;
And that one talent which is death to hide,
Lodged with me useless, though my soul more bent
To serve therewith my Maker, and present
My true account, less he returning chide;
Doth God exact day-labour, light denied,
I fondly ask? But Patience, to prevent
That murmur, soon replies, God doth not need
Either man's work or his own gifts; who best
Bear his mild yoke, they serve him best: his state
Is kingly; thousands at his bidding speed,
And post o'er land and ocean without rest;
They also serve who only stand and wait.

Vouchsafe to us, though unworthy, a plenteous out-pouring of thy
Spirit to refresh thy heritage; for thy kingdom is now at hand, and
thou art standing at the door. Hear us, we beseech thee, O Lord. Amen.

Richard Alleine (1611–81) and Joseph Alleine (1634–68)

*One of the most inspiring services to come out of Methodism is the annual
renewal of the Covenant. But John Wesley in 1747 wrote that it was the
work of Richard and Joseph Alleine, two apparently unrelated Puritan
preachers of a century earlier. Richard was rector of Batcombe in Somerset
for twenty years, and was dearly loved by his parishioners. Finding reluc-*

tantly that his Puritan principles would not allow him to follow the Act of Uniformity in 1662, he was ejected from his living and he became a nonconformist preacher at Frome, where he was so respected that the vicar of Frome preached at his funeral.

When Joseph was eleven his eldest brother, a clergyman, died. After this Joseph was, as he put it, 'born again', and he begged to be educated to continue his brother's ministry. This he did, turning down other offers, as assistant at the large parish church of Taunton. Ejected in 1662, he became an itinerant preacher, frequently imprisoned for breaching the Five-Mile Act. One of his fellow workers was the grandfather of Samuel Wesley. He is described as the best-loved Puritan other than Richard Baxter. Both the Alleines wrote books which sold in tens of thousands.

O most dreadful God, for the Passion of thy Son, I beseech thee accept of thy poor Prodigal no prostrating himself at thy door ... of thine infinite grace thou hast promised mercy to me in Christ, if I will but turn to thee with all my heart: therefore upon the call of thy Gospel, I am now come in, and throwing down my weapons, submit myself with thee, that I should put away mine idols, and be at defiance with all thine enemies which I acknowledge I have wickedly sided with against thee, I here from the bottom of my heart renounce them all, firmly covenanting with thee, not to allow myself in any known sin ...

And since thou hast appointed the Lord Jesus Christ, the only means of coming unto thee, I do here upon the bended knee of my soul accept of him as the only new and living way, by which sinners may have access to thee, and do here solemnly join myself in a Marriage Covenant to him ...

And since thou hast told me that I must suffer if I will reign, I do here covenant with thee to take my lot, as it falls, with thee ...

Only because through the frailty of my flesh, I am subject to many failings; I am bold humbly to protest, that unallowed miscarriages, contrary to the settled bent and resolution of my heart, shall not make void this Covenant, for so thou hast said.

Now almighty God, searcher of hearts, thou knowest that I make this Covenant with thee this day, without any known guile or reservation, beseeching thee, that if thou espiest any flaw or falsehood therein, thou wouldst discover it to me, and help me to do it aright ...

O dreadful Jehovah the Lord God, omnipotent, Father, Son and Holy Ghost, thou art now become my covenant friend, and I through thine infinite grace, am become thy covenant servant, Amen. So be it. And the covenant which I have made on earth, let it be ratified in heaven.[2]

Lord God, Holy Father, since you have called us through Christ
to share in this gracious Covenant
we take upon ourselves with joy the yoke of obedience,
and, for love of you, engage ourselves
to seek and do your perfect will.
We are no longer our own, but yours.

I am no longer my own, but yours.
Put me to what you will, rank me with whom you will;
put me to doing, put me to suffering;
let me be employed for you or laid aside for you,
exalted for you or brought low for you;
let me be full, let me be empty;
let me have all things, let me have nothing;
I freely and wholeheartedly yield all things
to your pleasure and disposal.
And now, glorious and blessed God,
Father, Son, and Holy Spirit,
you are mine and I am yours.
So be it.
And the Covenant now made on earth,
let it be ratified in heaven. Amen.

From John Wesley's version[3]

Jeremy Taylor (1613–67)

*A native of Cambridge and successively Fellow in that University and at
Oxford, Jeremy Taylor became chaplain to King Charles I and then a
chaplain in the Royalist army. After a short imprisonment, he went to
Wales as chaplain to Lord Carbery at Golden Grove, where he wrote
several profound books in beautiful prose, most famously* The Rule and
Exercise of Holy Living *and* The Rule and Exercise of Holy Dying. *He
then went to Ireland, where he was appointed Bishop of Down and Connor
and vice-chancellor of Dublin University.*

O Lord, I have sinn'd, and the black number swells
To such a dismal sum,
That should my stony heart and eyes,
And this whole sinful trunk a flood become,
And melt to tears, their drops could not suffice

To count my score,
Much less to pay.
But thou, my God, hast blood in store,
Yet, since the balsam of thy blood,
Although it can, will do no good,
Unless the wound be cleans'd in tears before;
Thou in whose sweet, but pensive face,
Laughter could never steal a place,
Teach but my heart and eyes
To melt away,
And then one drop of balsam will suffice.

Almighty God, Father of our Lord Jesus Christ, who hast sent thy Son to take upon him our nature, and hast made him to become the Son of man, that we might become the sons of God: grant that we, being conformed to his humility and sufferings, may be partakers of his resurrection; through the same Jesus Christ our Lord.

Be pleased, O Lord, to remember my friends, all that have prayed for me, and all that have done me good. Do thou good to them, and return all their kindness double into their own bosom, rewarding them with blessings, and sanctifying them with thy graces, and bringing them to glory.[4]

Bless thy servant (my wife or husband) with health of body and of spirit. Let the hand of thy blessing be upon his head, night and day, and support him in all necessities, strengthen him in all temptations, comfort him in all his sorrows, and let him be thy servant in all changes; and make us both to dwell with thee for ever in thy favour, in the light of thy countenance, and in thy glory.[5]

Blessed be thy name, O Jesu, Son of the most high God; blessed be the sorrow thou sufferedst when thy holy hands and feet were nailed to the tree; and blessed thy love when, the fullness of pain accomplished, thou didst give thy soul into the hands of the Father; so by thy cross and precious blood redeeming all the world, all longing souls departed and the numberless unborn; who now livest and reignest in the glory of the eternal Trinity for ever and ever.[6]

Grant, O Lord, that in thy wounds we may find our safety, in thy stripes our cure, in thy pain our peace, in thy cross our victory, in thy resurrection our triumph: and a crown of righteousness in the glories of thy eternal kingdom.

Guide us, O Lord, in all the changes and varieties of the world; that we may have evenness and tranquillity of spirit: that we may not murmur in adversity nor in prosperity wax proud, but in serene faith resign our souls to thy divinest will; through Jesus Christ our Lord.

Lord Jesus, come quickly; my heart is desirous of thy presence, and would entertain thee, not as a guest, but as an inhabitant, as the Lord of all my faculties. Enter in and take possession, and dwell with me for ever, that I also may dwell in the heart of my dearest Lord, which was opened for me with a spear and love.[7]

O almighty God who fillest all things with plenty, teach me to use thy creatures soberly and temperately, that I may not, with loads of meat or drinks, make my spirit unapt for the performance of my duty, or my body healthless, or my affections sensual and unholy. In the strength of thy provisions may I cheerfully and actively and diligently serve thee; that I may worthily feast at thy table here, and through thy grace, be admitted to thy table hereafter.[8]

Remember all them that do the Lord's work in the ministry and conduct of souls. Give them, we beseech thee, O Father, great gifts and great holiness; that wisely and charitably, diligently and zealously, prudently and acceptably, they may be guides to the blind, comforters to the sad and weary, that they may strengthen the weak and confirm the strong, separate the worthless from the precious, boldly rebuke sin, patiently suffer for the truth, and be exemplary in their lives; that in all their actions and sermons, in their discipline and ministrations, they may advance the good of souls, and the honour of our Lord Jesus Christ; grant this for the sake of thy Son our Lord. Amen.

Teach us to pray often, that we may pray oftener.

Richard Crashaw (c. 1613–49)

Richard was the son of William Crashaw, a Puritan poet and clergyman, but already at Cambridge his sympathy for the Roman Catholics prevented his ordination, and when he refused to sign the Covenant he lost his Fellowship. He went to Paris, where he became a Roman Catholic and lived in great poverty, until Queen Henrietta Maria recommended him for a small living at Loreto; but he died soon afterwards.

Lord, when the sense of thy sweet grace
Sends up my soul to seek thy face,
Thy blessed eyes breed such desire,
I die in love's delicious fire.
O love, I am thy sacrifice.
Be still triumphant, blessed eyes.
Still shine in me, fair suns! that I
Still may behold, though still I die.

Though still I die, I live again;
Still longing so to be still slain,
So gainful is such loss of breath,
I die even in desire of death.
Still live in me this loving strife
Of living death and dying strife,
For while thou sweetly slayest me
Dead to myself, I live in thee.

Welcome, all wonders in one sight!
Eternity shut in a span.
Summer in winter, day in night.
Heaven in earth, and God in Man;
Great little one! whose all-embracing birth
Lifts earth to heaven, stoops heav'n to earth.

Welcome, though not to gold nor silk,
To more then Caesar's birthright is;
Two sister-seas of Virgin-milk,
With many a rarely-temper'd kiss
That breathes at once both Maid and Mother,
Warms in the one, cools in the other.

She sings thy tears asleep, and dips
Her kisses in thy weeping eye,
She spreads the red leaves of thy lips,
That in their buds yet blushing lie,
She 'gainst those mother-diamonds tries
The points of her young eagle's eyes.

From 'The Nativity'

Peter Gunning (1614–84)

During Cromwell's Commonwealth, Gunning continued to hold Prayer Book services at Exeter House in the Strand in London. After the restoration of the monarchy he was made a professor in Cambridge, then Bishop of Chichester and finally Bishop of Ely. He took an active part in the Savoy Conference which revised The Book of Common Prayer, *and is considered to have drafted the 'Prayer for All Conditions of Men', which, from its regular use at Morning and Evening Prayer for many centuries, must have shaped the attitudes of thousands as to what should be included in our intercessions.*

O God, the creator and preserver of all mankind, we humbly beseech thee for all sorts and conditions of men; that thou wouldest be pleased to make thy ways known unto them, thy saving health unto all nations. More especially we pray for the good estate of the catholic Church; that it may be so guided and governed by thy good spirit, that all who profess and call themselves Christians may be led into the way of truth, and hold the faith in unity of spirit, in the bond of peace, and in righteousness of life. Finally, we commend to thy fatherly goodness all those who are any ways afflicted or distressed in mind, body or estate; [especially those for whom our prayers are desired], that it may please thee to comfort and relieve them, according to their several necessities, giving them patience under their sufferings, and a happy issue out of all their afflictions. And this we beg for Jesus Christ His sake. Amen.

Richard Baxter (1615–91)

Richard Baxter was pastor of a church in Kidderminster in Cromwell's time, but found the demands of the 1662 Act of Uniformity, that he should use nothing but The Book of Common Prayer, *too restrictive. Reluctantly he left the established Church and became the leader of the moderate or 'Presbyterian' nonconformists. He attempted to reconcile those who dis-*

agreed on religious matters in his day, and is one of the most attractive members of the Puritan faction, the very opposite of the usual picture of a narrow killjoy. In The Saints' Everlasting Rest *he wrote that Christians should enjoy the beauty of nature, music and poetry, to prepare them to long for the even greater delights of heavenly bliss.*

Lord, it belongs not to my care,
Whether I die or live;
To love and serve thee is my share,
And this thy grace must give.

If life be long I will be glad,
That I may long obey;
If short – yet why should I be sad
To soar to endless day?

Christ leads me through no darker rooms
Than he went through before;
He that unto God's kingdom comes,
Must enter by this door.

Come, Lord, when grace has made me meet
Thy blessed face to see;
For if thy work on earth be sweet,
What will thy glory be!

Then I shall end my sad complaints,
And weary, sinful days;
And join with the triumphant saints,
To sing Jehovah's praise.

My knowledge of that life is small,
The eye of faith is dim;
But 'tis enough that Christ knows all,
And I shall be with him.

Keep us, O Lord, while we tarry on this earth, in a serious seeking after thee, and in an affectionate walking with thee, every day of our lives; that when thou comest, we may be found not hiding our talent, nor serving the flesh, nor yet asleep with our lamp unfurnished, but waiting and longing for our Lord, our glorious King, for ever and ever.

Adapted from The Saints' Everlasting Rest

Most gracious God, who hast given us Christ and with him all that is necessary to life and godliness: we thankfully take this our food as the gift of thy bounty, procured by his merits. Bless it to the nourishment and strength of our frail bodies to fit us for thy cheerful service.

From Instructions for a Holy Life

John Evelyn (1620–1706)

Evelyn served, for three days only, in the King's army in 1642, but this was enough to make it wiser for him to travel on the Continent for a while. While in Paris he married the British Ambassador's daughter, who was only twelve. After the Restoration of the monarchy he spent much time at court, and recorded his impressions of the people and events in his famous Diary. *He played a part in the plans to rebuild St Paul's Cathedral. The* Diary *reveals the thoughts of an honest, God-fearing, down-to-earth Christian. This is a prayer on the death of a child.*

May we become as this little child who now follows the Child Jesus, that Lamb of God, in a white robe whithersoever he goes; even so, Lord Jesus, thou gavest him to us, thou hast taken him from us. Blessed be the name of the Lord. Blessed be our God for ever and ever. Amen.

Henry Vaughan (1621–95)

Henry Vaughan was a Welsh physician. He acknowledged his debt to the poems of George Herbert. His published collections include The Mount of Olives, *a collection of prayers, and* Silex Scintillans, *a collection of poems. The death of his twin brother gave a new intensity to Henry's verse.*

Abide with us, O most blessed and merciful Saviour, for it is toward evening and the day is far spent. As long as thou art present with us, we are in the light. When thou art present all is brightness, all is sweetness. We discourse with thee, watch with thee, live with thee and lie down with thee. Abide then with us, O thou whom our soul loveth, thou Sun of righteousness with healing under thy wings arise in our hearts; make thy light then to shine in darkness as a perfect day in the dead of night.

Peace

M y soul, there is a country
Far beyond the stars,
Where stands a wingèd Sentry
All skilful in the wars:
There above noise and danger
Sweet Peace sits crowned with smiles,
And One born in a manger
Commands the beauteous files.
He is thy gracious friend,
And (O my soul awake!)
Did in pure love descend
To die here for thy sake.
If thou canst get but thither,
There grows the flow'r of Peace,
The Rose that cannot wither,
Thy fortress, and thy ease;
Leave then thy foolish ranges;
For none can thee secure,
But one, who never changes,
Thy God, thy life, thy cure.

They are all gone into the world of light!

T hey are all gone into the world of light!
And I alone sit ling'ring here;
Their very memory is fair and bright,
And my sad thoughts doth clear . . .

O Father of eternal life, and all
Created glories under thee!
Resume thy spirit from this world of thrall
Into true liberty.

Either disperse these mists, which blot and fill
My perspective[9] (still) as they pass,
Or else remove me hence unto that hill,
where I shall need no glass.

The Pursuit

Lord! what a busy restless thing
Hast thou made man!
Each day and hour he is on wing,
Rests not a span;
Then having lost the sun and light
By clouds surprised
He keeps a commerce in the night
With air disguised;
Hadst thou given to this active dust
A state untired,
The lost son had not left the husk
Nor home desired;
That was thy secret, and it is
Thy mercy too,
For when all fails to bring to bliss,
Then, this must do.
Ah! Lord! and what a purchase will that be
To take us sick, that sound would not take thee!

Blaise Pascal (1623–62)

Pascal was born in Clermont-Ferrand, but when his mother died the family moved to Paris, where his father, no mean mathematician himself, personally undertook his children's education. Blaise shone at an early age in Euclidian geometry and conics, and with his father conducted experiments leading to the development of the barometer, the hydraulic press and the syringe. He patented a calculating machine and laid the foundations for probability theory and integral calculus. Then at the age of thirty-one he had two experiences which revealed to him that his life had been too intellectual. He gave up mathematics and social life, and joined his sister in the Jansenist retreat at Port-Royal. Jansenism was in a sense a Roman Catholic equivalent of Puritanism, so he argued against the Jesuits of the Sorbonne, who had condemned the Jansenists as heretics. His eighteen pamphlets in exemplary French prose, collected as Provincial Letters, *failed to save the Jansenists but undermined the Jesuit reliance on jargon and casuistry. After his death the notes were discovered which he had started for a book defending the Christian faith, and these were published as the* Pensées. *He described his feelings about the majesty of God revealed in the world of nature as 'vertigo'. But he was sceptical about the power of human reason: God reveals himself in 'the order of charity'. He correctly distinguished between the faith to which the Christian is called, and the certainty which is claimed by the scientist about measurable events, but which is never possible in more profound matters. He explained faith from his researches into probability in the passage which came to be known as 'Pascal's gamble'. Nobody can prove certainly that God either does or does not exist, so if we believe he does and are mistaken, we have nothing to lose. But if we decide he does not and meet him when we die, we might have an eternity of regret, so faith in God is the better bet.*

Pascal's conversion[10]

The year of grace 1654,
Monday, 23 November, Feast of Saint Clement,
Pope and Martyr . . .
From about half-past-ten in the evening until
half-past-midnight,
FIRE
'God of Abraham, God of Isaac, God of Jacob',
not of philosophers and scholars,
Certainty, certainty, heartfelt, joy, peace.
God of Jesus Christ.
God of Jesus Christ.
'My God and your God,'
'Thy God shall be my God.'
The world forgotten, and everything except God.
He can only be found by the ways taught in the Gospels.
Greatness of the human soul.
'O righteous Father, the world had not known thee,
but I have known thee.'
Joy, joy, joy, tears of joy.
I have cut myself off from him.
'They have forsaken me, the fountain of living waters.'
My God wilt thou forsake me?
Let me not be cut off from him for ever!
'And this is life eternal, that they might know thee, the only true
    God,
and Jesus Christ whom thou hast sent.'

Jesus Christ.

Jesus Christ.

I have cut myself off from him, shunned him, decried him, crucified
him.

Let me never be cut off from him!

We cling to him only by the ways taught in the Gospel.

Sweet and total renunciation.

Total submission to Jesus Christ and to my director,

Eternal joy in return for one day's trial on earth.

'I will not forget your word.'

Meditations on the Good Use of Sickness

Lord, you are good and gentle in all your ways; and your mercy is so
great that not only the blessings but also the misfortunes of your
people are channels of your compassion. Grant that I may turn to you as
a Father in my present condition since the change in my own state from
health to sickness brings no change to you. You are always the same, and
you are my loving Father in times of trouble and in times of joy alike.[11]

O my Saviour, since I share in some small way your sufferings, fill me
to the brim with the glory which your sufferings won for mankind.
Let me share in some small way the joy of your risen life.[12]

O Lord, let me not henceforth desire health or life except to spend
them for you, with you and in you. You alone know what is good
for me; do therefore what seems best to you. Give to me or take from me;
conform my will to yours; and grant that with humble and perfect submission and in holy confidence I may receive the orders of your eternal
providence, and may equally adore all that comes to me from you; through
Jesus Christ our Lord.

George Fox (1624–91)

*How the Society of Friends came to be known as Quakers is a matter of
dispute. Some say it was because ecstatic trembling broke out at the early
meetings; some say it was a name taken over from an earlier group; while
some say it was given to George Fox by Justice Bennett when Fox told him
to 'tremble at the word of the Lord.' To this day they bear witness to silence*

in worship, pacifism and simplicity of life. George Fox was born in Leicester-shire and was apprenticed to a Nottingham shoemaker. At the age of nineteen he rebelled against family and friends, social convention and the state-controlled church. He interrupted church services all over the country, acknowledging no authority except the Bible and the 'Inner Light' which he said was in everyone. Priests, lawyers and soldiers were all abhorrent to him. He called his followers the 'Friends of the Truth', and travelled around Britain, to the Caribbean, North America and Holland spreading his message, for which he and his numerous followers were often imprisoned.

The Lord preserve them all out of the world (in which there is trouble) in Christ Jesus, in whom there is peace, life, love, and unity. Amen.

From The Autobiography

O Lord, baptize our hearts into a sense of the conditions and needs of all men.

Samuel Crossman (1624–83)

A Suffolk man, Crossman graduated from Pembroke College, Cambridge, and was appointed to the living of Little Henny in Essex. But this was during the Commonwealth, and at the restoration of the monarchy he was ejected as a nonconformist. However, he made his peace with the established Church and went on to become Dean of Bristol. 'My Song is Love Unknown' is one of the most poignant Passiontide hymns ever written.

. . . Here might I stay and sing,
    No story so divine;
Never was love, dear King,
    Never was grief like thine!
    This is my Friend,
    In whose sweet praise
I all my days
    Could gladly spend.

John Bunyan (1628–88)

'The tinker of Bedford' (actually, he inherited his father's trade of working in brass) seems to have read no books other than the Bible, The Book of Common Prayer, *Foxe's* Book of Martyrs *and two or three more. He*

joined an Independent congregation and became a popular preacher. After the restoration of the monarchy he was imprisoned for refusing to conform to the established Church, and Grace Abounding to the Chief of Sinners *was written while he was in Bedford Jail between 1660 and 1672. He was imprisoned again in 1676 and, during those six months of confinement, he wrote the first version of* Pilgrim's Progress. *The book's simple parables and direct imagery have encouraged millions to see their progress in Christ as a pilgrimage, and many of the phrases have passed into the heart of the English language. Bunyan's hymns 'He who would valiant be' and 'He that is down need fear no fall' are in many hymn-books. After his release from prison he enlarged* Pilgrim's Progress, *wrote* The Holy War *and continued to preach.*

The Shepherd-boy's Song in the Valley of Humiliation

He that is down needs fear no fall,
  He that is low, no pride:
He that is humble ever shall
Have God to be his guide.
I am content with what I have,
Little be it or much:
And, Lord, contentment still I crave;
Because thou savest such.
Fulness to such a burden is
That go on pilgrimage:
Here little, and hereafter bliss
Is best from age to age.

From Pilgrim's Progress, Part II

Isaac Barrow (1630–77)

Isaac Barrow, although he was from a Royalist family, entered Trinity College, Cambridge, at the age of thirteen during the period when the Puritans ruled the country, and became a Fellow. He travelled abroad until the restoration of the monarchy, when he was ordained and appointed Professor of Greek at Cambridge. Soon afterwards he was also appointed Professor of Mathematics, but he resigned this chair six years later so that his brilliant pupil, Isaac Newton, could take his place, while Barrow concentrated on theology, to which he brought an incisive mathematician's mind. He was a popular preacher, and King Charles II appointed him as his chaplain and Master of Trinity.

O blessed Saviour, draw us; draw us by the cords of thy love; draw us by the sense of thy goodness; draw us by thyself; draw us by the unspotted purity and beauty of thy example; draw us by the merit of thy precious death and by the power of thy Holy Spirit; draw us, good Lord, and we shall run after thee. Amen.

John Dryden (1631–1700)

Dryden was Poet Laureate, and wrote successful verse plays, satires and translations. He led English poetry out of the conceits of the Metaphysical poets towards the more formal neoclassical style of the next century. His religious allegiance was, to say the least, flexible. Born in a vicarage, he wrote a poem to honour Oliver Cromwell, followed closely by one to welcome King Charles II. Religio Laici *celebrated Anglicanism, but under James II he wrote* The Hind *and the* Panther *in honour of Roman Catholicism, to which he had converted.*

A Paraphrase of 'Veni Creator Spiritus'

Creator Spirit, by whose aid
The world's foundations first were laid,
Come visit ev'ry pious mind;
Come pour thy joys on humankind:
From sin and sorrow set us free;
And make thy temples worthy thee.
O, source of uncreated light,
The Father's promised Paraclete!
Thrice holy fount, thrice holy fire,
Our hearts with heav'nly love inspire;
Come, and thy sacred unction bring
To sanctify us, while we sing!
Plenteous of grace, descend from high,
Rich in thy sev'n-fold energy!
Thou strength of his almighty hand,
Whose pow'r does heav'n and earth command:
Proceeding Spirit, our defence,
Who dost the gift of tongues dispense,
And crown'st thy gift, with eloquence!
Refine and purge our earthy parts;

But, oh, inflame and fire our hearts!
Our frailties help, our vice control;
Submit the senses to the soul;
And when rebellious they are grown,
Then, lay thy hand, and hold 'em down.
Chase from our minds th'infernal foe;
And peace, the fruit of love, bestow:
And, lest our feet should step astray,
Protect, and guide us in the way.
Make us eternal truths receive,
And practise, all that we believe:
Give us thy self, that we may see
The Father and the Son, by thee.
Immortal honour, endless fame
Attend th'almighty Father's name:
The saviour Son be glorified,
Who for lost man's redemption died:
And equal adoration be
Eternal Paraclete, to thee.

Thomas Traherne (c. 1636–74)

*The son of a Herefordshire shoemaker, Traherne became rector of Cred-
enhill, and then went to the court as chaplain to the Lord Keeper of the
Great Seal. Most of his poetry, and his great prose work* Centuries, *were
not published until the beginning of the twentieth century. Of all the
Christian mystics, he is the most affirming of the value to God of the
natural world, the human body, and us as God's children. He did not
ignore the fact of sin, and the necessity of the cross, but his emphasis was
far more on 'felicity'. In one series of meditations he wrote: 'Your enjoyment
of the world is never right, till every morning you awake in heaven; see
yourself in your Father's palace; and look upon the skies, the earth, and
the air as celestial joys: having such a reverent esteem of all, as if you were
among the angels.'*

O Lord, I wonder at thy love,
  Which did my infancy so early move:
But more at that which did forbear
And move so long, though slighted many a year.

But most of all, at last that thou
Thyself shouldst me convert, I scarce know how.[13]

O adorable Trinity! What hast thou done for me? Thou hast made me the end of all things, and all the end of me. I in all, and all in me. In every soul whom thou hast created, thou hast given me the similitude of thyself to enjoy! Could my desires have aspired unto such treasures? Could my wisdom have devised such sublime enjoyments? Oh! Thou hast done more for us than we could ask or think. I praise and admire, and rejoice in thee: who are infinitely infinite in all thy doings.[14]

O God, who in the church of thy dear Son hast advanced us to the fellowship of the crowned saints, to inward room and seat in their hearts even as in thine: set us so steadfastly to follow them in humble boldness of love, that we may be found worthy to share the glory which they have eternally from thee; through Jesus Christ our Lord. Amen.[15]

The Non-Jurors

King James II of England was received into the Roman Catholic Church in 1670, and in spite of some opposition, he ascended the throne in 1685. He proceeded to make it possible for Catholics to be appointed to offices from which they had been excluded. When he demanded that a Declaration of Liberty of Conscience be read in all churches, William Sancroft, the Archbishop of Canterbury, saw this as an attempt to destroy the Church of England. He and seven other bishops refused to carry out the order, and were imprisoned in the Tower of London. They were acquitted and released, but when Prince William of Orange invaded, King James fled to France, and the Prince was crowned as King William II.

Yet eight bishops, some 400 priests and a few lay people – the so-called Non-Jurors – refused to swear the oath of allegiance to William, arguing that they had already sworn an oath to James which they could not break, however much they disagreed with him. They were deprived of their positions and others were appointed to succeed them, by act of Parliament. They continued to worship with a dignified liturgy privately and illegally, and to proclaim the sanctity of oaths, the divine right of kings, and the Church as a spiritual society with its own laws. They produced some fine devotional writers, but by the end of the eighteenth century they had died out as a separate movement.

O thou who hast foretold that thou wilt return again, to judgment, in an hour that we are not aware of; grant us grace to watch and pray always; that whether thou shalt come at even, or at midnight, or at the cock-crowing, or in the morning, thou mayest find us in the number of those servants who shall be blessed for watching for their Lord; for thy Name's sake. Amen.

The Non-Jurors' Prayer Book (1734)

Thomas Ken (1637–1711)

Thomas Ken taught at Winchester College, where he wrote a manual of devotion to teach the boys how to pray, and the hymns 'Awake, my soul, and with the sun' and 'Glory to thee my God this night'. King Charles II made him Bishop of Bath and Wells, even though he refused to receive the royal mistress Nell Gwyn in his house. Although he was also critical of James II, he regarded him as the true king, and refused to take the oath of allegiance to William and Mary. He was deposed, and lived in retirement, mostly at Longleat House, refusing to return to his bishopric when it was offered back to him. In his will he wrote: 'I die in the Holy Catholic and Apostolic Faith, professed by the whole Church, before the disunion of East and West: more particularly I die in the communion of the Church of England, as it stands distinguished from all Papal and Puritan Innovations.'

Lord, sanctify us wholly, that our whole spirit, soul, and body may become thy temple. Oh, do thou dwell in us, and be thou our God, and we will be thy servants, through Jesus Christ. Amen.

O our God, amidst the deplorable division of thy Church O let us never widen its breaches, but give us universal charity to all who are called by thy name. O deliver us from the sins and errors, from the schisms and heresies of the age. O give us grace daily to pray for the peace of thy Church, and earnestly to seek it and to excite all we can to praise and to love thee; through Jesus Christ, our one Saviour and Redeemer. Amen.

From Directions for Prayers, *for the priests of his diocese to teach illiterate parishioners to learn by heart:*

Going to Bed

I will lay me down in peace, and take my rest;
for it is thou, Lord, only, that makest me dwell in safety.

Rising from Bed

I laid me down and slept, and rose up again,
for thou Lord, sustained me:
all love, all glory, be to thee.

Going or Coming

Lord, bless my going out and coming in,
from this time forth, for evermore.

Meals

Lord, grant that whether I eat or drink, or whatever I do,
I may do all to thy glory.

Work

Prosper thou the works of my hands, O Lord;
O, prosper thou my handiwork.

At the Market

Lord, give me grace to use this world so as not to abuse it.
Lord, grant that I may never go beyond or defraud my brother
in any matter; for thou art the avenger of all such.

At Any Time

Wherever I am, whatever I do, thou, Lord, seest me:
O, keep me in thy fear all day long.
Lord, give me grace to keep always a conscience
void of offence towards thee and towards men.
Lord, teach me so to number my days,

that I may apply my heart to wisdom.
O, let my mouth be filled with thy praise,
that I may sing of thy glory and honour all the day long.

Evening Hymn

Glory to thee, my God, this night
For all the blessings of the light;
Keep me, O keep me, King of Kings,
Beneath thy own almighty wings;

Forgive me, Lord, for thy dear Son,
The ill that I this day have done,
That with the world, myself, and thee,
I, ere I sleep, at peace may be.

Teach me to live, that I may dread
The grave as little as my bed;
Teach me to die, that so I may
Rise glorious at the awful day.

O may my soul on thee repose,
And may sweet sleep mine eyelids close,
Sleep that may me more vigorous make
To serve my God when I awake;

When in the night I sleepless lie,
My soul with heavenly thoughts supply;
Let no ill dreams disturb my rest,
No powers of darkness me molest.

Thou, my blest guardian, whilst I sleep
Close to my bed thy vigils keep;
Divine love into me instil,
Stop all the avenues of ill.

Praise God, from whom all blessings flow,
Praise him, all creatures here below,
Praise him above, ye heavenly host,
Praise Father, Son, and Holy Ghost.[16]

O God, make the door of this house wide enough to receive all who need human love and fellowship; narrow enough to shut out all envy, pride and strife. Make its threshold smooth enough to be no stumbling-block to children, nor to straying feet, but rugged and strong enough to turn back the tempter's power. God make the door of this house the gateway to thine eternal kingdom.

Inscription on St Stephen's Church, Walbrook, London

Blessing and honour, thanksgiving and praise
more than we can utter, more than we can conceive,
 be unto thee,
O most adorable Trinity, Father, Son, and Holy Ghost,
by all angels, all men, all creatures,
for ever and ever. Amen and Amen.
To God the Father, who first loved us,
and made us accepted in the Beloved:
To God the Son, who loved us,
and washed us from our sins in His own blood:
To God the Holy Ghost,
who sheds the love of God abroad in our hearts
be all love and all glory for time and eternity. Amen.

William Penn (1644–1718)

Penn was sent down from Christ Church College in Oxford in 1661 for refusal to conform with the newly re-established Anglicanism. After some years of travel he became a Quaker, and wrote pamphlets attacking the doctrines of the Trinity, the atonement and the Calvinistic understanding of justification. For this he was imprisoned in the Tower of London, where he wrote the spiritual classic No Cross, No Crown: 'No pain, no palm; no thorns, no throne; no gall, no glory; no cross, no crown.' After his release he sailed to America and set up the colony of Pennsylvania, with a constitution which allowed freedom of religion to all monotheists.

Lord, help me not to despise or oppose what I do not understand.

John Mason (1645–94)

John Mason was born in Northamptonshire and became rector of Water Stratford in Buckinghamshire. Below is one of a number of moving and deeply spiritual hymns that he wrote. Sadly, he became increasingly disturbed, and towards the end of his life preached on no subject other than that the reign of Christ had already begun. When he died the noisy crowd of his followers, who had camped on the 'Holy Ground' near the village, refused for many years to believe that he was dead, even though his successor had the body exhumed and exhibited to them.

How shall I sing that majesty
Which angels do admire?
Let dust in dust and silence lie;
Sing, sing, ye heavenly choir.
Thousands of thousands stand around
Thy throne, O God most high;
Ten thousand times ten thousand sound
Thy praise; but who am I?

Thy brightness unto them appears,
Whilst I thy footsteps trace;
A sound of God comes to my ears,
But they behold thy face.
They sing because thou art their sun;
Lord, send a beam on me;
For where heaven is but once begun
There alleluias be.

Enlighten with faith's light my heart,
Inflame it with love's fire;
Then shall I sing and bear a part
With that celestial choir.
I shall, I fear, be dark and cold,
With all my fire and light;
Yet when thou dost accept their gold,
Lord, treasure up my mite.

How great a being, Lord, is thine,
Which doth all beings keep!
Thy knowledge is the only line
To sound so vast a deep.

Thou art a sea without a shore,
A sun without a sphere;
Thy time is now and evermore,
Thy place is everywhere.

Jeanne-Marie Bouvier de la Motte Guyon (1648–1717)

A wealthy widow at the age of twenty-eight, Madame Guyon devoted her time to spreading her ideas on the spiritual life. In 1685 she published A Short and Very Simple Method of Prayer. *Her teaching about the wordless contemplation of God was based on the Spanish and German mystics. She was impulsive in her writings, which she never reread, and almost childish in her inability to realize how she might be misunderstood. She was conscious of the omnipresent God, and felt that the mystical union of the human and divine wills could be achieved simply by sinking into the divine, so that the individual had no longer any consciousness of itself as a separate entity. Pure love meant stripping away any independence which might cause a separation between the soul and God. By simplicity in prayer, consoled by the presence of God, she sought a state of 'holy indifference' where the soul wills nothing apart from the will of God. The Archbishop of Paris, frustrated in his attempt to marry his great-nephew to Madame Guyon's daughter, had her imprisoned in 1688 on suspicion that her teaching was a new heresy which he named Quietism. Following her release in the same year she met François Fénélon, who defended her teaching. But when Quietism was banned by Rome she was again imprisoned, this time in the Bastille from 1699 until 1703. After that she spent her retirement at Blois, where Catholics who continued to support her and also many Protestants came to visit her.*

Give no place to despondency. This is a dangerous temptation from our enemy the devil. Melancholy shrinks and withers the heart, and makes it unfit to receive the effects of God's grace. It magnifies material objects, and gives them a false colouring, so making your burdens too heavy to bear ... A sad outward appearance is more likely to put other people off than to attract them to piety. You should serve God with a certain joyousness of spirit, with freedom and openness, which makes it obvious that for you 'his yoke is easy,' it is neither a burden nor an inconvenience. If you want to please God, be useful to other people, and happy in yourself, you must give up this melancholy disposition. It is better to divert your mind with innocent recreation, than to leave room for melancholy . . . Let the desire to please and honour God arouse and inspire your spirit, by means of an outward appearance of sweetness, humility, cordiality and cheerfulness.

François Fénélon (1651–1715)

Fénélon was already a distinguished preacher and spiritual director when he met Madame Guyon. He changed his opinion of her teachings on the prayer of quiet and the union of love, which he now supported, regarding them as traditional. But when he was made Archbishop of Cambrai in 1695 they were condemned by Bossuet. He wrote an Explanation of the Maxims of the Saints on the Interior Life. *His teaching was that we can love God for himself alone, not seeking a reward. Then the desire to please God is so strong that we would even abandon hope of eternity if it were necessary in order to do so. In this state of disinterested love, the soul is quiet, unaware of itself and its actions because its attention is entirely turned to God. There is obviously a danger in this Quietism that it might be misunderstood to suggest that our actions, whether of charity or sin, are unimportant. So his book was condemned by Rome. Fénélon accepted this ruling, remained in his diocese, and diverted his writing to opposing free-thinkers and the Jansenists. Yet when his book was translated, he had more influence in England and other Protestant countries over the next couple of centuries than any other Catholic.*

Lord, I know not what I ought to ask of you; you only know what I need; you love me better than I know how to love myself. Father, give to me, your child, that which I myself know not how to ask. I dare not ask for crosses or consolations. I simply present myself before you, I open up my heart to you. Behold my needs which I know not myself, and see and do according to your tender mercy. Smite, or heal, depress me, or raise me up: I adore all your purposes without knowing them: I am silent: I offer in sacrifice: I yield myself to you. I would have no other desire than to accomplish your will. Teach me to pray: pray in me, yourself; for Christ's sake. Amen.

O Lord, you know the weakness and misery of your creatures. We have nothing, but what matter – so long as we have you, so long as we can see you with certainty of finding all that is not to be found in ourselves. So help us, Lord, to seek; through Jesus Christ. Amen.

Y ou know better than I how much I love you, Lord. You know it and I know it not, for nothing is more hidden from me than the depths of my own heart. I desire to love you; I fear that I do not love you enough. I beseech you to grant me the fullness of pure love. Behold my desire; you have given it to me. Behold in your creature what you have placed there. O God, you love me enough to inspire me to love you for ever; behold not my sins. Behold your mercy and my love.

The Westminster Confession (1647–8)

The Westminster Assembly was set up by the Long Parliament in 1643 to reform the English Church. It contained representatives of a wide spectrum of Christian opinion, although the bishops, from loyalty to the King, hardly ever attended. The Solemn League and Covenant, signed in 1643, aimed to unite the churches of the British Isles on a Presbyterian pattern and to defend democracy. Scottish Presbyterian representatives were then included in the Westminster Assembly. Together they drew up a statement of faith, The Westminster Confession, *which became a standard statement of Presbyterianism throughout the English-speaking world.*

Q What is the chief end of man?
A. Man's chief end is to glorify God, and to enjoy him for ever.

From 'The Shorter Catechism'

O God, who hast so greatly loved us, long sought us, and mercifully redeemed us; give us grace that in everything we may yield ourselves, our wills and our works, a continual thankoffering unto thee; through Jesus Christ our Lord. Amen.

The Whole Duty of Man (c. 1658)

This anonymous book of Christian devotional and ethical instruction was for a long time the most popular among Puritans and Royalists alike. Its moral standards are very high, but not unattainable.

O blessed Lord, whom without faith it is impossible to please; let thy Spirit, I beseech thee, work in me such a faith as may be acceptable in thy sight even such as worketh by love. O let me not rest in a dead, ineffectual faith, but grant that it may be such as may show itself by my works; that it may be that victorious faith, which may enable me to overcome the world, and conform me to the image of that Christ, on whom I believe.

O Lord, who art the hope of all the ends of the earth, let me never be destitute of a well-grounded hope, nor yet possessed with a vain presumption: suffer me not to think thou wilt either be reconciled to my sins, or reject my repentance; but give me, I beseech thee, such a hope as may be answerable to the only ground of hope, thy promises, and such as may both encourage and enable me to purify myself from all filthiness, both of flesh and spirit; that so, it may indeed become to me an anchor of the soul both sure and steadfast.

Lord, thou art pleased to require my heart, and thou only hast a right to it. O let me not be so sacrilegiously unjust, as to alienate any part of it, but enable me to render it up whole and entire to thee. But, O my God, if thou seest fit, be pleased to let me taste of the joys, those ravishments of thy love, wherewith thy saints have been so transported. But if in this I know not what I ask, if I may not choose my place in thy kingdom, yet, O Lord, deny me not to drink of thy cup; let me have such a sincerity and degree of love, as may make me endure anything for thy sake; such a perfect love as may cast out all fear and sloth, that nothing may seem to me too grievous to suffer, or too difficult to do, in obedience to thee.

O merciful God, thy wisdom is infinite to choose, and thy love forward to dispense good things to us: O let me always fully and entirely resign myself to thy disposal, have no desires of my own, but a perfect satisfaction in thy choice for me; that so, in whatsoever state I am, I may be therein content; Lord, grant I may never look murmuring on my own condition, nor with envy on other men's. And, to that end, I beseech thee purge my heart of all covetous affections.

Matthew Henry (1662–1714)

Matthew Henry began to study law but soon changed to theology. He became a Nonconformist minister in Chester, and wrote many devotional works and sermons. It is principally on his Exposition of the Old and New Testaments, *a commentary on the whole Bible, that his reputation rests, for its practical common sense, thoughtfulness and memorable turn of phrase.*

O Lord, lift up the light of thy countenance upon us; let peace rule in our hearts, and may it be our strength and our song, in the house of our pilgrimage. We commit ourselves to thy care and keeping this day. Let thy grace be mighty in us, and sufficient for us, and let it work in us both to will and to do of thine own good pleasure, and grant us strength for all the duties of the day. Keep us from sin. Give us the rule over our own spirits, and keep us from speaking unadvisedly with our lips. May we live together in peace and holy love, and do thou command thy blessing upon us, even life for evermore. Prepare us for all the events of the day, for we know not what a day may bring forth. Give us grace to deny ourselves; to take up our cross daily, and to follow in the steps of our Lord and Master, Jesus Christ our Lord. Amen.

The Book of Common Prayer (1662)

When Charles II returned to the throne, after the Commonwealth period in which The Book of Common Prayer *was not used, he received petitions from the Puritans asking that, if it were to be used again, many changes should be made in a Calvinistic direction. The bishops offered a list of changes which they would not object to. A conference was called at the Savoy, both Houses of Parliament discussed it, and with the approval of the convocations of the clergy, a revised book was issued in 1662, which has been the regular usage of the Church of England ever since. The changes were not, however, very great, and when its use was enforced by the Act of Uniformity on St Bartholomew's Day in that year, many Puritans felt unable to remain in the Church of England and set up their own Nonconformist congregations. There had been many divisions in the Christian Church before, but nearly always a whole geographical area broke away – 'to each region its own religion'. Now, for the first time, neighbours in the same street went to pray in different congregations.*

And we also bless thy holy name for all thy servants departed this life in thy faith and fear; beseeching thee to give us grace so to follow their good examples, that with them we may be partakers of thy heavenly kingdom. Grant this, O Father, for Jesus Christ's sake our only mediator and advocate. Amen.

Added to 'The Holy Communion'

See also Cosin (p. 254), Gunning (p. 280), Reynolds (p. 257), Sanderson (p. 243) and the Scottish Book of Common Prayer (1637) (p. 265).

Edmund Gibson (1669–1748)

An expert in ecclesiastical law, Edmund Gibson became Bishop of Lincoln and then Bishop of London. He laboured for reform in the Church and tolerance of the Methodists, Independents and Quakers.

Continue thy gracious protection to us, Lord, this night. Defend us from all dangers, and from the fear of them, that we may enjoy such refreshing sleep as may fit us for the duties of the coming day. And grant us grace always to live so close to thee that we may never be afraid to die, so that, living or dying, we may be completely thine, in Jesus Christ our Lord. Amen.

Adapted from Morning and Evening Prayer for a Family

Joseph Addison (1672–1719)

The son of the Dean of Lichfield, Addison became a Fellow at Oxford, and published translations of classical poetry and studies of English poets. He then began a diplomatic and political career. Richard Steele had been a schoolfriend of his at Charterhouse, and Addison contributed to Steele's magazine The Tatler, *before together they founded* The Spectator. *Addison edited 274 issues of the magazine.*

How are thy Servants blest

How are thy servants blest, O Lord!
How sure is their defence!
Eternal wisdom is their guide,
Their help omnipotence . . .

In midst of dangers, fears and death,
Thy goodness I'll adore;
And praise thee for thy mercies past,
And humbly hope for more.

My life, if thou preserv'st my life,
Thy sacrifice shall be;

And death, if death must be my doom,
Shall join my soul to thee.

When all thy Mercies

W hen all thy mercies, O my God,
   My rising soul surveys;
Transported with the view, I'm lost
In wonder, love, and praise:

O how shall words with equal warmth
The gratitude declare
That glows within my ravished heart!
But thou canst read it there . . .

Unnumbered comforts to my soul
Thy tender care bestowed,
Before my infant heart conceived
From whom those comforts flowed.

When in the slipp'ry paths of youth
With heedless steps I ran,
Thine arm unseen conveyed me safe
And led me up to man; . . .

Ten thousand thousand precious gifts
My daily thanks employ,
Nor is the least a cheerful heart,
That tastes those gifts with joy . . .

Through all eternity, to thee
A grateful song I'll raise;
But O eternity's too short
To utter all thy praise![17]

Isaac Watts (1674–1748)

The author of many of the best-loved hymns in the English language was born in Southampton. Although a benefactor offered him a chance to go to university, he preferred the Dissenting Academy at Stoke Newington. He became pastor of the Independent congregation at Mark Lane, London, but his health failed, and after ten years he retired to Stoke Newington.

At the time the only songs allowed in most Nonconformist churches were the metrical Psalms. The hymns of Isaac Watts transformed Christian worship throughout the world. They include 'Jesus shall reign where'er the sun', 'O God, our help in ages past' and 'When I survey the wondrous cross'. He also wrote a Guide to Prayer *which outlines eight parts to prayer: Invocation, Adoration, Confession, Petition, Pleading, Self-dedication, Thanksgiving and Blessing God. It also describes 'the Use and Abuse of Book Prayers'.*

God of the morning, at whose voice
The cheerful sun makes haste to rise,
And like a giant doth rejoice
To run his journey through the skies;

O, like the sun, may I fulfil
The appointed duties of the day,
With ready mind and active will
March on, and keep my heavenly way.

Give me thy counsel for my guide,
And then receive me to thy bliss:
All my desires and hopes beside
Are faint and cold, compared with this.

Lord of the worlds above,
How pleasant and how fair
The dwellings of thy love,
Thy earthly temples, are!
To thine abode
My heart aspires,
With warm desires
To see my God;

O happy souls that pray
Where God appoints to hear!
O happy men that pay
Their constant service there!
They praise thee still;
And happy they
That love the way
To Zion's hill.

They go from strength to strength
Through this dark vale of tears,
Till each arrives at length,
Till each in heaven appears:
O glorious seat!
When God our King
Shall thither bring
Our willing feet.

The heavens declare thy glory, Lord;
  In every star thy wisdom shines;
But when our eyes behold thy word,
We read thy name in fairer lines.

Sun, moon, and stars convey thy praise
Round the whole earth, and never stand;
So, when thy truth began its race,
It touched and glanced on every land.

Nor shall thy spreading Gospel rest
Till through the world thy truth has run;
Till Christ has all the nations blest
That see the light or feel the sun.

Great Sun of Righteousness, arise;
Bless the dark world with heavenly light;
Thy Gospel makes the simple wise,
Thy laws are pure, thy judgements right;

Thy noblest wonders here we view,
In souls renewed and sins forgiven;
Lord, cleanse my sins, my soul renew,
And make thy word my guide to heaven.

From all that dwell below the skies
  Let the Creator's praise arise:
Let the Redeemer's name be sung
Through every land by every tongue.

Eternal are thy mercies, Lord;
Eternal truth attends thy word;

Thy praise shall sound from shore to shore,
Till suns shall rise and set no more.

Jean Pierre de Caussade (1675–1751)

In 1693 de Caussade joined the Jesuit order in Toulouse; he travelled widely and was a popular preacher. He taught contemplation, recollection and attention to God, basing his ideas on Francis de Sales, and so rehabilitated mysticism at a time when many feared the exaggerations of the Quietists. His letters to a group of nuns at Nancy were collected under the title of Self-abandonment to the Divine Providence. *He reassured his readers that they did not have to struggle with pious practices to come close to Jesus; they would find him close to them in their daily lives: in a famous phrase, in 'the sacrament of the present moment'. All that is required is waiting on God, discerning his presence, and cooperation with his will.*

Forgive me, divine Love, for speaking only of my shortcomings and not having yet understood what it means to let your will be done, not having allowed myself to be poured into that mould. I have been through all your galleries and admired all your paintings, but I have not yet surrendered myself sufficiently to be worthy to receive the strokes of your brush. Now I have at last found you, beloved Master, my Healer, my Lord, blessed Love! I will be your disciple and learn only from you. I return like a prodigal son, starving for your bread. I will cease to traffic in ideas and works of piety, using them only in obedience to you in this as in all things, and not for my own satisfaction. I will devote myself exclusively to the duty of the present moment to love you, to fulfil my obligations and to let your will be done.[18]

O unknown Love! We are inclined to think that your marvels are over, and that all we can do is to copy the ancient Scriptures and quote your words from the past. We fail to see that your inexhaustible action is the source of new thoughts, new sufferings, new actions, new leaders, new prophets, new apostles, new saints, who have no need to copy each other's lives and writings, but live in perpetual self-abandonment to your operations. We hear perpetually of the 'early centuries' and the 'times of the saints'. What a way to talk! Are not all times and all events the successive results of your grace, pouring itself forth on all instants of time,

filling them and sanctifying them? Your divine action will continue until
the world ends to shed its glory on those souls who abandon themselves
to your providence without reserve.[19]

L ord, may your kingdom come into my heart to sanctify me, nourish
me and purify me. How insignificant is the passing moment to the eye
without faith! But how important each moment is to the eye enlightened by
faith! How can we deem insignificant anything which has been caused by
you? Every moment and every event is guided by you, and so contains your
infinite greatness. So, Lord, I glorify you in everything that happens to
me. In whatever manner you make me live and die, I am content. Events
please me for their own sake, regardless of their consequences, because
your action lies behind them. Everything is heaven to me, because all my
moments manifest your love.[20]

L ord, must it always be that so many people remain ignorant of your
providence? Must you, as it were, shower your favours on their heads,
while they refuse to accept your infinite generosity? We would think a
person absurdly foolish if he refused to breathe the open air, or to drink
the water which he needs. Yet why may that same person not find you in
the air, the water and everything else around him? Must I resign myself
to possessing so great a treasure from you, while I watch other souls die
of spiritual poverty? Must I see them dry up like desert plants, while your
living waters are all around them?[21]

William Law (1686–1761)

*William Law was a Fellow of Emmanuel College, Cambridge, but refused
to take the oath of allegiance to George I. He became tutor at Putney to
the father of Edward Gibbon (who wrote* The Decline and Fall of the
Roman Empire*), then retired to King's Cliffe where he organized schools
and almshouses and led a life of great simplicity and devotion. Law's A
Serious Call to a Devout and Holy Life earnestly recommends a life of
moral virtue and meditation; his later works have a more mystical tendency, emphasizing the love of God already within us.*

O God, in whom nothing can live but as it lives in love, grant us the
spirit of love which does not want to be rewarded, honoured or

esteemed, but only to become the blessing and happiness of everything that wants it; love which is the very joy of life, and thine own goodness and truth within the soul; who thyself art love, and by love our redeemer, from eternity to eternity.

Grant us, O Lord Christ, to desire to have thee as our saviour, not in the next world, but in this; that thou wilt change and alter all that is within us, as thou didst help the blind to see and the lame to walk; that thy tempers may be formed and begotten in our hearts, thy humility and self-denial, thy love of the Father, the desire of doing his will and seeking only his honour; that so the kingdom of God may be in us now, and our possession for ever, world without end. Amen.

Alexander Pope (1688–1744)

Crippled at the age of twelve by tuberculosis of the spine, and largely self-educated, Pope published An Essay on Criticism *and* The Rape of the Lock *while still in his twenties, then turned to translating Homer. His own variable health may have added to the sharpness of his satire, but also to the nobility of much of his verse, and his appreciation of the suffering of Christ.*

Thou art my God, sole object of my love;
Not for hope of endless joys above;
Not for the fear of endless pains below,
Which they who love thee must not undergo.
For me, and such as me, thou deignst to bear
An ignominious cross, the nails, the spear;
A thorny crown transpierced thy sacred brow,
While bloody sweats from every member flow.
For me in tortures thou resignst thy breath,
Embraced me on the cross, and saved me by death.
And can these sufferings fail my heart to move?
Such as then was, and is, thy love to me,
Such is, and shall be still, my love to thee –
To thee, Redeemer! mercy's sacred spring!
My God, my Father, Maker, and my King!

Richard Challoner (1691–1781)

Richard's father was a Protestant wine-cooper of Lewes in Sussex, but his mother was Roman Catholic, and he was sent to Douai to study for the priesthood. After twenty-eight years as a missioner and spiritual director in London, he was made a bishop with the title of Vicar Apostolic of London. He translated Francis de Sales's Introduction to the Devout Life *and wrote several books of meditations modelled on it. His most famous book was* The Garden of the Soul.

O my God, I believe in thee, do thou strengthen my faith. All my hopes are in thee, do thou secure them. I love thee with my whole heart, teach me to love thee daily more and more. I am sorry that I have offended thee, do thou increase my sorrow.

I adore thee as my first beginning. I aspire after thee as my last end. I give thee thanks as my constant benefactor. I call upon thee as my sovereign protector.

Vouchsafe, O my God, to conduct me by thy wisdom, to restrain me by thy justice, to comfort me by thy mercy, to defend me by thy power.

To thee I desire to consecrate all my thoughts, words, actions, and sufferings; that henceforward I may think of thee, speak of thee, and willingly refer all my actions to thy greater glory, and suffer willingly whatever thou shalt appoint.

Lord, I desire that in all things thy will may be done, because it is thy will, and in the manner that thou willest.

I beg of thee to enlighten my understanding, to enflame my will, to purify my body, and to sanctify my soul.

From The Garden of the Soul

O Jesus, our adorable Saviour, behold us prostrate at thy feet, imploring thy mercy for ourselves and for the souls of all the faithful departed. Vouchsafe to apply to us the infinite merits of thy Passion, on which we are about to meditate. Grant that while we trace this path of sighs and tears, our hearts may be so touched with contrition and repentance that we may be ready to embrace with joy all the crosses and sufferings and humiliations of this our life and pilgrimage.

From Stations of the Cross

O Jesus, we devoutly embrace that honoured cross where thou didst love us even unto death. In that death we place all our confidence. Henceforth let us live only for thee; and in dying for thee let us die loving thee, and in thy sacred arms.

From Stations of the Cross

John Byrom (1692–1763)

John Byrom, author of the carol 'Christians Awake', which he composed for his daughter Dolly, was born in Broughton near Manchester. He studied medicine at Montpellier but returned to England to teach a system of shorthand which he had invented, and which he taught to John Wesley.

The Desponding Soul's Wish: Desiderium

M y spirit longeth for thee,
Within my troubled breast,
Although I be unworthy
Of so divine a guest.

Of so divine a guest,
Unworthy though I be,
Yet has my heart no rest,
Unless it come from thee.

Unless it come from thee,
In vain I look around;
In all that I can see,
No rest is to be found.

No rest is to be found,
But in thy blessed love;
O let my wish be crowned,
And send it from above.

The Answer

C heer up, desponding soul,
Thy longing, pleased, I see;
'Tis part of that great whole
Wherewith I longed for thee.

Wherewith I longed for thee,
And left my Father's throne;
From death to set thee free,
To claim thee for my own.

To claim thee for my own
I suffered on the cross:
O were my love but known,
No soul could fear its loss.

No soul could fear its loss,
But, filled with love divine,
Would die on its own cross,
And rise for ever mine.

From Miscellaneous Poems *(1773)*

Joseph Butler (1692–1752)

Joseph Butler was brought up a Presbyterian, but after ordination in the Church of England was made preacher at the Rolls Chapel in London, where he delivered an influential series of sermons. His lasting legacy was a book prepared while he was rector of Stanhope in County Durham, The Analogy of Religion, Natural and Revealed, to the Constitution and Course of Nature. *Many Deists saw the regularity and order of nature as the work of a remote creator who had no interest in human affairs. Butler argued convincingly that the revealed Christian religion was analogous to the world of nature in its logical order and regularity, and that human nature had been created with the basic properties of self-love, benevolence and conscience; it is more natural, therefore, to follow these than the pursuit of pleasure. Butler's* Analogy *was for many years required reading for candidates for ordination.*

O almighty God, inspire us with this divine principle; kill in us all the seeds of envy and ill-will; and help us, by cultivating within ourselves the love of our neighbour, to improve in the love of thee. Thou hast placed us in various kindreds, friendships, and relations, as the school of discipleship for our affections: help us, by the due exercise of them, to improve to perfection; till all partial affection be lost in that entire universal one, and thou, O God, shalt be all in all. Amen.

Methodism

One reaction against the formality of the eighteenth century was the Methodist Movement.

Susanna Wesley (1669–1742)

Susanna was the wife of the Revd Samuel Wesley (1662–1735), the rector of Epworth in Lincolnshire, and mother of John and Charles.

Enable me, O God, to collect and compose my thoughts before an immediate approach to you in prayer. May I be careful to have my mind in order when I take upon myself the honour to speak to the Sovereign Lord of the universe, remembering that upon the temper of my soul depends, in very great measure, my success. You are infinitely too great to be trifled with, too wise to be imposed on by a mock devotion, and abhor a sacrifice without a heart. Help me to entertain an habitual sense of your perfections, as an admirable help against cold and formal performances. Save me from engaging in rash and precipitate prayers and from abrupt breaking away to follow business or pleasure as though I had never prayed.

God, I give you the praise for days well spent. But I am yet unsatisfied, because I do not enjoy enough of you. I apprehend myself at too great a distance from you. I would have my soul more closely united to you by faith and love. You know Lord that I would love you above all things. You made me, you know my desires, my expectations. My joys all centre in you and it is you that I desire. It is your favour, your acceptance, the communications of your grace that I earnestly wish for more than anything in the world. I rejoice in your essential glory and blessedness. I rejoice in my relation to you, that you are my Father, my Lord and my God. I thank you that you have brought me so far. I will beware of despairing of your mercy for the time which is yet to come, and will give you the glory of your free grace.

John Wesley (1703–91)

John was the fifteenth child of Samuel and Susanna Wesley. As a Fellow of Lincoln College, Oxford, he gathered round him a group of Christian friends who were so methodical in their practice of daily prayer and holiness of life that they were derisively called 'Methodists'. He went as a missionary with the SPG (the Society for the Propagation of the Gospel in Foreign Parts) to the American state of Georgia, preaching to the British people who had settled there but were without clergy. Preaching against slavery and gin did not make him popular, and two years later he returned. Some Moravians persuaded him that he still lacked the faith which is necessary for us to be saved. He was attending a meeting in Albemarle Street, London, and reading Luther's Preface to his Commentary on Romans *when he felt his heart 'strangely warmed'. Feeling called to evangelize, and finding the churches closed to him, he became an open-air preacher, travelling an average of 8,000 miles a year on horseback, and reaching large sections of the population with whom the Church had lost touch. He arranged annual conferences for lay preachers, and the congregations were organized into class-meetings, and continued to receive Communion in their parish churches. The British Government refused to appoint bishops for America, who might have claimed seats in the House of Lords, so Wesley took it upon himself to ordain ministers, although he was not a bishop. His contributions to Christian thought include his balance between the two great commandments of love for God and love for the neighbour, hence between mysticism and activism, and his emphases on preaching, frequent Holy Communion, extempore prayer, perfection and assurance.*

Deliver me, O God, from a slothful mind, from all lukewarmness, and all dejection of spirit. I know these cannot but deaden my love to thee; mercifully free my heart from them, and give me a lively, zealous, active, and cheerful spirit; that I may vigorously perform whatever thou commandest, thankfully suffer whatever thou choosest for me, and be ever ardent to obey in all things thy holy love.

Fix thou our steps, O Lord, that we stagger not at the uneven motions of the world, but steadily go on to our glorious home; neither censuring our journey by the weather we meet with, nor turning out of the way for anything that befalls us. The winds are often rough, and our own weight presses us downwards. Reach forth, O Lord, thy hand, thy saving hand, and speedily deliver us. Teach us, O Lord, to use this transitory life as pilgrims returning to their beloved home; that we may take what our journey requires, and not think of settling in a foreign country.

Forgive them all, O Lord: our sins of omission and our sins of commission; the sins of our youth and the sins of our riper years; the sins of our souls and the sins of our bodies; our secret and our more open sins; our sins of ignorance and surprise, and our more deliberate and presumptuous sins; the sins we have done to please others; the sins we know and remember, and the sins we have forgotten; the sins we have striven to hide from others and the sins by which we have made others offend; forgive them, O Lord, forgive them all for his sake, who died for our sins and rose for our justification, and now stands at thy right hand to make intercession for us, Jesus Christ our Lord.

Jesus, poor, unknown and despised, have mercy on us, and let us not be ashamed to follow you. Jesus, accused, and wrongfully condemned, teach us to bear insults patiently, and let us not seek our own glory. Jesus, crowned with thorns and hailed in derision; buffeted, overwhelmed with injuries, griefs and humiliations; Jesus, hanging on the accursed tree, bowing the head, giving up the ghost, have mercy on us, and conform our whole lives to your spirit. Amen.

Let us adore the Father, the God of love; who created us; who continually preserves and sustains us; who has loved us with an everlasting love and given us the light of the knowledge of the glory of God in the face of Jesus Christ. Let us glory in the grace of our Lord Jesus Christ. Though he was rich, yet for our sakes he became poor; he was tempted in all points as we are, yet without sin; he became obedient to death, death on a cross; he was dead and is alive for ever; he has opened the kingdom of heaven to all who trust in him. Let us rejoice in the fellowship of the Holy Spirit, the Lord, the giver of life; by whom we are born into the family of God; whose witness confirms us, whose wisdom teaches us; whose power enables us. All praise to you, Holy Trinity, for you live and reign, one God for ever and ever. Amen.

Wesley's Table Grace

B e present at our table, Lord;
Be here and everywhere adored.
Thy creatures bless, and grant that we
May feast in paradise with thee.

Communion Hymn

A uthor of life divine,
Who hast a table spread,
Furnished with mystic Wine
And everlasting Bread,
Preserve the life thyself hast given,
And feed and train us up for heaven.

Our needy souls sustain
With fresh supplies of love,
Till all thy life we gain,
And all thy fulness prove,
And, strengthened by thy perfect grace,
Behold without a veil thy face.

Charles Wesley (1707–88)

Charles was the eighteenth child of Samuel Wesley and the brother of John Wesley. He went with his brother to Georgia from 1735 to 1736, where he served as secretary to the Governor. Like John, he was influenced by the Moravians on his return to London, and was converted on Whitsunday 1738. Charles then spent seventeen years as a travelling preacher, before settling at the City Road Chapel in London. He wrote over 5,500 hymns and knew their importance in evangelism and in teaching Christians to pray. To mention 'Jesu, lover of my soul', 'Love divine, all loves excelling' and 'Lo! he comes with clouds descending', together with 'Hark how all the welkin rings' – later changed to 'Hark the herald angels sing' – gives some idea of his influence. He remained loyal to the Church of England and was irritated by John's ordinations.

S hepherd divine, our wants relieve
In this our evil day;
To all thy tempted followers give
The power to watch and pray.

Long as our fiery trials last,
Long as the cross we bear,
O let our souls on thee be cast
In never-ceasing prayer.

The Spirit's interceding grace
Give us in faith to claim;
To wrestle till we see thy face,
And know thy hidden name.

Till thou thy perfect love impart,
Till thou thyself bestow,
Be this the cry of every heart,
'I will not let thee go.'

I will not let thee go, unless
Thou tell thy name to me;
With all thy great salvation bless,
And make me all like thee.

Then let me on the mountain-top
Behold thy open face;
Where faith in sight is swallowed up,
And prayer in endless praise.[1]

Wrestling Jacob

Come, O thou traveller unknown,
Whom still I hold, but cannot see,
My company before is gone,
And I alone am left with thee;
With thee all night I mean to stay
And wrestle till the break of day . . .

Yield to me now, for I am weak,
But confident in self-despair;
Speak to my heart, in blessings speak,
Be conquered by my instant prayer!
Speak, or thou never hence shalt move, –
And tell me, if thy name is Love?

'Tis Love! 'tis Love! Thou diedst for me!
I hear thy whisper in my heart!
The morning breaks, the shadows flee;
Pure universal Love thou art!
To me, to all, thy bowels move;
Thy nature and thy name is Love!

My prayer hath power with God; the grace
Unspeakable I now receive;
Through faith I see thee face to face,
I see thee face to face, and live:
In vain I have not wept and strove;
Thy nature and thy name is Love . . .

And Can it Be?

And can it be that I should gain
An interest in the Saviour's blood?
Died he for me, who caused his pain?
For me, who him to death pursued?
Amazing love! how can it be
That thou, my God, shouldst die for me? . . .

Long my imprisoned spirit lay
Fast bound in sin and nature's night:
Thine eye diffused a quickening ray;
I woke; the dungeon flamed with light;
My chains fell off, my heart was free,
I rose, went forth, and followed Thee.

Jesu, Lover of my Soul

Jesu, Lover of my soul,
Let me to thy bosom fly,
While the nearer waters roll,
While the tempest still is high:
Hide me, O my Saviour, hide
Till the storm of life is past,
Safe into the haven guide,
O receive my soul at last! . . .

Wilt thou not regard my call?
Wilt thou not accept my prayer?
Lo! I sink, I faint, I fall –
Lo! on thee I cast my care!
Reach me out thy gracious hand:
While I of thy strength receive,
Hoping against hope I stand,
Dying, and behold I live! . . .

Love Divine

Love Divine, all loves excelling,
Joy of heav'n, to earth come down,
Fix in us thy humble dwelling,
All thy faithful mercies crown.

Jesu, thou art all compassion,
Pure unbounded love thou art;
Visit us with thy salvation,
Enter every trembling heart,

Come, almighty to deliver,
Let us all thy grace receive;
Suddenly return, and never,
Never more thy temples leave.

Thee we would be always blessing,
Serve thee as thy hosts above;
Pray, and praise thee, without ceasing,
Glory in thy perfect love.

Finish then thy new creation,
Pure and spotless let us be;
Let us see thy great salvation,
Perfectly restored in thee.

Changed from glory into glory,
Till in heav'n we take our place,
Till we cast our crowns before thee,
Lost in wonder, love, and praise.

George Whitefield (1717–40)

George Whitefield was a Gloucester man who was influenced by the Wesleys and followed them to Georgia, where he founded an orphanage. When he returned to England he began preaching in the open air and attracted large crowds; he also raised considerable sums for his orphanage. He was possibly a better preacher than the Wesleys, but his theology was narrow and Calvinist, and he disputed their offer of free salvation. The churches he founded through the patronage of Selina, Countess of Huntingdon – 'the Countess of Huntingdon's Connexion' – did not survive, although the Calvinistic Methodists of Wales trace their origins to Whitefield, and his influence in America was enormous.

I bless God his Spirit has convinced me of our eternal election by the Father through the Son, of our free justification through faith in his blood, of our sanctification as the consequence of that, and of our final perseverance and glorification as the result of all. These I am persuaded God has joined together; these, neither men nor devils shall ever be able to put asunder.

Early American Christianity

Edward Taylor (c. 1684)

The Pilgrim Fathers sailed to Massachusetts in 1620 in search of liberty to pray in their own way without interference from any state. The thirteen states of the eastern seaboard were settled by a variety of peoples, but the original Puritans were a strong influence.

Here is a feast that's a feast indeed. It excels the most sumptuous and magnificent feast of the most magnificent monarch that ever breathed on earth. The guests are saints sparklingly adorned in the vestments of glorifying grace. The waiters are the all gloriously holy angels of light. The authors, the everlasting King of Glory. The occasion, the wedding and marriage of his only Son, to his bride the souls of his elect, the church of the first born whose names are written in heaven. And the entertainment itself, and this is most rich and royal, the manna of heaven, angels' bread, the bread of life, the water of life, the fruits of 'the Tree of Life in the middest of the paradise of God' (Rev. 2:7). Spiritual dainties: Oh! the sweet heart-ravishing melodies, musics, and songs of a spiritual nature with which Christ entertains souls hereat, what tongue of man or angel is able to relate? It is as it were the very suburbs of glory.[1]

Jonathan Edwards (1703–58)

Edwards was a Congregationalist pastor in the Puritan Calvinist tradition. A revival spread across the United States, referred to as the Great Awakening, encouraged by the preaching of Jonathan Edwards and George Whitefield. Edwards argued with the opponents of revivalism that the 'affections' are the work of the Holy Spirit; yet at the same time he argued with the enthusiasts, declaring that the affections, including emotion, pas-

sion and will, moved a person to accept the divine majesty, and must be tested to see whether they are of God. Love, he said, is the chief affection.

T is to be feared that some have gone too far towards directing the Spirit of the Lord, and marking out his footsteps for him, and limiting him to certain steps and methods. Experience plainly shows, that God's Spirit is unsearchable and untraceable, in some of the best of Christians, in the method of his operations, in their conversion. Nor does the Spirit of God proceed discernibly in the steps of a particular established scheme, one half so often as is imagined.

From Religious Affections[2]

The Diary of David Brainerd (1743)

Jonathan Edwards edited and published the diary of his friend Brainerd, who had been a missionary to the Native Americans.

O ne morning, while I was walking in a solitary place, as usual, I at once saw that all my contrivances and projects to effect or procure deliverance and salvation for myself were utterly in vain; I was brought quite to a stand, as finding myself totally lost . . . While I remained in this state, my notions respecting my duties were quite different from what I had ever entertained in times past. Before this, the more I did in duty the more hard I thought it would be for God to cast me off . . . Now I saw that there was no necessary connection between my prayers and the bestowment of divine mercy . . . I saw that I had been heaping up my devotions before God, fasting, praying, etc., pretending, and indeed really thinking sometimes, that I was aiming at the glory of God; whereas I never once truly intended it, but only for my own happiness . . . the whole was nothing but self-worship, and an horrid abuse of God . . . I continued, as I remember, in this state of mind, from Friday morning till the Sabbath evening following (July 12, 1739), when I was walking again in the same solitary place . . . I thought that the spirit of God had quite left me; but still was not distressed; yet disconsolate, as if there was nothing on heaven and earth could make me happy. Having been thus endeavouring to pray – though, as I thought, very stupid and senseless – for nearly half an hour; then, as I was walking in a dark, thick grove, unspeakable glory seemed to open to the view and apprehension of my soul. I do not mean any external brightness, for I saw no such thing; nor do I intend any imagination of a body of light, somewhere in the third heavens, or any thing of that nature; but it was a new inward apprehension or view that I had of God, such as I never had before, nor any thing which had the least resemblance to it. I stood still; wondered; and admired! ... My soul rejoiced with joy unspeakable, to see such a God, such a glorious divine Being; and I was inwardly pleased and satisfied, that he should be God over all for ever and ever. My soul was so captivated and delighted with the excellency, loveliness, greatness. and other perfections of God, that I was even swallowed up in him; at least to that degree, that I had no thought (as I remember) at first, about my own salvation, and scarce reflected that there was such a creature as myself.[3]

William Ellery Channing (1780–1842)

Channing graduated from Harvard and became pastor of the Congregational Church in Federal Street, Boston. Some time later there was a division between conservative and liberal Congregationalists in America. The conservatives argued for a Calvinistic view of the total depravity of the human race. Channing took the liberal cause and preached against the doctrines of the Trinity, the atonement and total depravity as they were presented by his opponents. He was therefore called a Unitarian, but he regarded himself as belonging 'not to a sect, but to the community of free minds'. He 'desired to escape the narrow walls of a particular church'.

O God, animate us to cheerfulness. May we have a joyful sense of our blessings, learn to look on the bright circumstances of our lot, and maintain a perpetual contentedness under thy allotments. Fortify our minds against disappointment and calamity. Preserve us from despondency, from yielding to dejection. Teach us that no evil is intolerable but a guilty conscience, and that nothing can hurt us, if, with true loyalty of affection, we keep thy commandments and take refuge in thee; through Jesus Christ our Lord. Amen.

The Eighteenth Century

The eighteenth century was one of great formality in behaviour and rationalism in philosophy. Religion was marked by Deism, the belief in a remote creator uninterested in his creation, the watch-maker who has wound up the watch and then forgotten about it. But as will be seen here, beneath the formal exterior, heart-felt prayer was being offered.

Count Nicholas Ludwig von Zinzendorf (1700–1760)

Nikolaus Ludwig Graf von Zinzendorf was born in Dresden, and when some of the Bohemian Brethren settled on his lands at Herrnhut, he devoted himself to caring for them and the work of evangelism. He was appointed a bishop, and the group were called the 'Brüdergemeinde', or more commonly 'Moravians'. Theirs was a non-dogmatic but very emotional faith, under the influence of the Pietists. They opened a church in London where John Wesley was converted, and he translated several of Zinzendorf's hymns.

Lord, when my eye confronts my heart, and I realize that you have filled my heart with your love, I am breathless with amazement. Once my heart was so small in its vision, so narrow in its compassion, so weak in its zeal for truth. Then you chose to enter my heart, and now in my heart I can see you, I can love all your people, and I have courage to proclaim the truth of your gospel to anyone and everyone. Like wax before a fire, my heart has melted under the heat of your love.

O Thou to Whose All-Searching Sight

O thou to whose all-searching sight
The darkness shineth as the light,
Search, prove my heart; it pants for thee;
O, burst these bonds, and set it free!

Wash out its stains, refine its dross,
Nail my affections to the Cross;
Hallow each thought; let all within
Be clean, as thou, my Lord, art clean!

If in this darksome wild I stray,
Be thou my light, be thou my way;
No foes, no violence I fear,
No fraud, while thou, my God, art near.

When rising floods my soul o'erflow,
When sinks my heart in waves of woe,
Jesus, thy timely aid impart,
And raise my head, and cheer my heart.

Saviour, where'er thy steps I see,
Dauntless, untired, I follow thee!
Oh, let thy hand support me still,
And lead me to thy holy hill!

If rough and thorny be the way,
My strength proportion to my day.
Till toil, and grief, and pain shall cease,
Where all is calm, and joy, and peace.[1]

Jesu, geh' voran

Jesus, still lead on,
　　Till our rest be won,
And, although the way be cheerless
We will follow calm and fearless;
Guide us by thy hand
To our fatherland.

If the way be drear,
If the foe be near,
Let not faithless fears o'ertake us,
Let not faith and hope forsake us;
For, through many a foe,
To our home we go.

Jesus, still lead on,
Till our rest be won;
Heavenly leader, still direct us,
Still support, console, protect us,
Till we safely stand
In our fatherland.[2]

Philip Doddridge (1702–51)

Doddridge was a dissenting minister in Northampton. He had a wide friend-ship, and believed that love of Christ is a surer test of orthodoxy than any precise formulation of words. His hymns are all pervaded by joy: 'Hark the glad sound', 'O happy day' and 'My God, and is thy table spread'.

My God, and is thy table spread?
And doth thy cup with love o'erflow?
Thither be all thy children led,
And let them all its sweetness know.

Hail, sacred feast, which Jesus makes!
Rich banquet of his flesh and blood!
Thrice happy he, who here partakes
That sacred stream, that heavenly food!

Why are its dainties all in vain
Before unwilling hearts displayed?
Was not for you the victim slain?
Are you forbid the children's bread?

O let thy table honoured be,
And furnished well with joyful guests;
And may each soul salvation see,
That here its sacred pledges tastes.

Let crowds approach with hearts prepared;
With hearts inflamed let all attend;
Now, when we leave our Father's board,
The pleasure or the profit end.

Revive thy dying churches, Lord,
And bid our drooping graces live;
And more that energy afford,
A Saviour's blood alone can give.[3]

Dr Samuel Johnson (1709–84)

The famous dictionary writer and scholar of Lichfield, whose life is described by Boswell, showed in his personal religion a deep sense of unworthiness, a strong faith, and a fear of enthusiasm.

Compiling the Dictionary

O God, who hast hitherto supported me, enable me to proceed in this labour, and in the whole task of my present state; that when I shall render up, at the last day, an account of the talent committed to me, I may receive pardon.

On starting his magazine The Rambler

Almighty God, the giver of all good things, without whose help all labour is ineffectual, and without whose grace all wisdom is folly; grant, I beseech thee, that in this my undertaking, thy Holy Spirit may not be withheld from me, but that I may promote thy glory, and the salvation both of myself and others; grant this O Lord, for the sake of Jesus Christ. Lord bless me. So be it.

Prayed during a farewell visit to a friend

Almighty and most merciful Father, whose loving kindness is over all thy works; behold, visit and relieve this thy servant who is grieved with sickness. Grant that the sense of her weakness may add strength to her faith, and seriousness to her repentance. And grant that, by the help of thy Holy Spirit, after the pains and labours of this short life, we may all obtain everlasting happiness, through Jesus Christ our Lord: for whose sake hear our prayers.

A prayer for New Year's Day

Almighty God, by whose mercy my life has continued for another year, I pray that, as my years increase, my sins may not increase. As age advances, let me become more open, more faithful and more trusting in thee. Let me not be distracted by lesser things from what is truly important. And if I become infirm as I grow old, may I not be overwhelmed by self-pity or bitterness. Continue and increase thy loving kindness towards me, so that, when thou dost finally call me to thyself, I may enter into eternal happiness with thee, through Jesus Christ my Lord.[4]

O Lord, our heavenly Father, without whom all purposes frustrate, all efforts are vain, grant us the assistance of the Holy Spirit, that we may not sorrow as those without hope, but may now return to the duties of our present life with humble confidence in thy protection, and so govern our thoughts and actions that no business or work may ever withdraw our minds from thee, but that in the changes of this life we may fix our hearts upon the reward which thou hast promised to them that serve thee, and that whatsoever things are true, whatsoever things are honest, whatsoever things are just, whatsoever things are pure, whatsoever things are lovely, whatsoever things are of good report, wherein there is virtue, wherein there is praise, we may think upon and do, and obtain mercy, consolation, and everlasting happiness. Grant this, O Lord, for the sake of Jesus Christ. Amen.

On his wife's death, which plunged him into lasting depression

O Lord, governor of heaven and earth, in whose hands are embodied and departed spirits, if thou hast ordained the souls of the dead to minister to the living, and appointed my departed wife to have care of me, grant that I may enjoy the good effects of her attention and ministration, whether exercised by appearance, impulses, dreams, or in any other manner agreeable to thy government; forgive my presumption, enlighten my ignorance, and however meaner agents are employed, grant me the blessed influences of thy Holy Spirit, through Jesus Christ our Lord.

A month after his wife's death

O Lord, our heavenly Father, almighty and most merciful God, in whose hands are life and death, who givest and takest away, castest down and raisest up, look with mercy on the affliction of thy unworthy servant, turn away thine anger from me, and speak peace to my troubled soul. Grant me the assistance and comfort of thy Holy Spirit, that I may remember with thankfulness the blessings so long enjoyed by me in the society of my departed wife. Make me so to think on her precepts and example, that I may imitate whatever was in her life acceptable in thy sight, and avoid all by which she offended thee. Forgive me, O merciful Lord, all my sins, and enable me to begin and perfect that reformation which I promised her, and to persevere in that resolution, which she implored thee to continue, in the purposes which I recorded in thy sight, when she lay dead before me, in obedience to thy laws, and faith in thy word. And now, O Lord, release me from my sorrow, fill me with just hopes, true faith, and holy consolations, and enable me to do my duty in that state of life to which thou hast been pleased to call me, without disturbance from fruitless grief, or tumultuous imaginations; that in all my thoughts, words, and actions, I may glorify thy Holy Name, and finally obtain, what I hope thou hast granted to thy departed servant, everlasting joy and felicity, through our Lord Jesus Christ. Amen.[5]

Two years after his wife's death

Almighty God, vouchsafe to sanctify unto me the reflections and resolutions of this day, let not my sorrow be unprofitable; let not my resolutions be vain. Grant that my grief may produce true repentance, so that I may live to please thee, and when the time shall come that I must die like her whom thou hast taken from me, grant me eternal happiness in thy presence.

The Accession Service of King George I (1714)

Whenever a new monarch succeeds to the throne a service is added to The Book of Common Prayer *for use on the anniversary of their accession. In 1714 a prayer was included concerning political unity in a divided nation, but it has often been used to pray for unity in a divided Church.*

O God, the Father of our Lord Jesus Christ, our only Saviour, the Prince of Peace: give us grace seriously to lay to heart the great dangers we are in by our unhappy divisions. Take away all hatred and prejudice, and whatsoever else may hinder us from godly union and concord: that, as there is but one Body, and one Spirit, and one hope of our calling, one Lord, one faith, one baptism, one God and Father of us all, so we may henceforth be all of one heart, and of one soul, united in one holy bond of truth and peace, of faith and charity, and may with one mind and one mouth glorify thee; through Jesus Christ our Lord. Amen.

Christopher Smart (1722–71)

Smart suffered from insanity, but showed the type of internal logic and flashes of insight which make many people wonder whether it is in fact the person in the asylum who is sane, and all those outside it mad. As a student at Pembroke College, Cambridge, he drank too much, wrote a poem to the barmaid at the Mitre, put on a play, and got into debt. Soon after being elected a Fellow he secretly married and was arrested for debt. He went to London and attempted a literary career, but according to Dr Johnson, he had to be carried home from the tavern every night. In 1757 he was detained in St Luke's Hospital for the Insane.

Dr Johnson said: 'Madness frequently discovers itself merely by unnecessary deviation from the usual modes of the world. My poor friend Smart showed the disturbance of his mind by falling upon his knees and saying his prayers in the street, or in any other unusual place. Now although, rationally speaking, it is greater madness not to pray at all, than to pray as Smart did, I am afraid there are so many who do not pray, that their understanding is not called in question . . . I did not think he ought to be shut up. His infirmities were not noxious to society. He insisted on people praying with him; and I'd as lief pray with Kit Smart as any one else.'

Smart moved to Mr Potter's Madhouse at Bethnal Green, where he wrote his extraordinary poem 'Jubilate Agno', part of which was set to music by Benjamin Britten as 'Rejoice in the Lamb'. How many singers note the pun in 'H is aspirate/a spirit'? After his release he published the very long and beautiful 'Song to David'. He was arrested for debt again and died in prison.

Extracts from 'Jubilate Agno'

Rejoice in God, O ye Tongues;
give the glory to the Lord, and the Lamb.
Nations, and languages, and every Creature,
in which is the breath of Life.
Let man and beast appear before him,
and magnify his name together.

Let David bless with the Bear – The beginning of victory to the Lord
– to the Lord the perfection of excellence – Hallelujah from the heart
of God, and from the hand of the artist inimitable, and from the echo
of the heavenly harp in sweetness magnifical and mighty . . .

For I am under the same accusation with my Saviour –
For they said, he is besides himself.
For the officers of the peace are at variance with me,
and the watchman smites me with his staff.
For I am in twelve hardships,
but he that was born of a virgin shall deliver me out of all.

For H is a spirit and therefore he is God.
For K is king and therefore he is God.
For L is love and therefore he is God.
For M is music and therefore he is God.

For the trumpet of God is a blessed intelligence
and so are all the instruments in heaven.
For God the Father almighty plays upon the harp
of stupendous magnitude and melody.
For at that time malignity ceases
and the devils themselves are at peace.
For this time is perceptible to man
by a remarkable stillness and serenity of soul.

Extracts from 'A Song to David'

Strong is the lion – like a coal
His eye-ball – like a bastion's mole
His chest against the foes:
Strong, the gier-eagle on his sail,
Strong against tide, th'enormous whale
Emerges, as he goes.

But stronger still, in earth and air,
And in the sea, the man of pray'r;
And far beneath the tide;
And in the seat to faith assigned,
Where ask is have, where seek is find,
Where knock is open wide.

Beauteous the moon full on the lawn;
And beauteous, when the veil's withdrawn,
The virgin to her spouse:
Beauteous the temple decked and filled

When to the heav'n of heav'ns they build
Their heart-directed vows.

Glorious the sun in mid career;
Glorious th'assembled fires appear;
Glorious the comet's train:
Glorious the trumpet and alarm;
Glorious th'almighty stretched out arm;
Glorious th'enraptured main:

Glorious the northern lights astream;
Glorious the song, when God's the theme;
Glorious the thunder's roar:
Glorious hosanna from the den;
Glorious the catholic amen;
Glorious the martyr's gore:

Glorious – more glorious is the crown
Of him that brought salvation down
By meekness, called thy Son;
Thou at stupendous truth believed,
And now the matchless deed's achieved,
DETERMINED, DARED, and DONE.

The Nativity of Our Lord and Saviour

Where is this stupendous stranger?
Swains of Solyma advise,
Lead me to my Master's manger,
Shew me where my Saviour lies.

O most Mighty! O most Holy!
Far beyond the seraph's thought,
Art thou then so mean and lowly,
As unheeded prophets taught?

O the magnitude of meekness!
Worth from worth immortal sprung;
O the strength of infant weakness,
If eternal is so young!

If so young and thus eternal,
Michael tune the shepherd's reed,
Where the scenes are ever vernal.
And the loves be love indeed!

See the God blasphemed and doubted
In the schools of Greece and Rome,
See the powers of darkness routed,
Taken at their utmost gloom.

Nature's decorations glisten
Far above their usual trim;
Birds on box and laurels listen,
As so near the cherubs hymn.

Boreas now no longer winters
On the desolated coast;
Oaks no more are riven in splinters
By the whirlwind and his host.

Spinks and ouzels sing sublimely,
'We too have a Saviour born'.
Whiter blossoms burst untimely
On the blest Mosaic thorn.

God all-bounteous, all creative,
Whom no ills from good dissuade,
Is incarnate and a native
Of the very world he made.

Père Nicholas Grou (1731–1803)

This Jesuit priest began his ministry as a teacher at the Jesuit college at La Flèche, and ended it in England. His writings on prayer were at one time very popular in France and in Britain, but are possibly rather dry for modern tastes.

O my divine Master, teach me to hold myself in silence before you, to adore you in the depths of my being, to wait upon you always and never to ask anything of you but the fulfilment of your will. Teach me to let you act in my soul, and form in it the simple prayer that says little but includes everything. Grant me this favour for the glory of your name.

Augustus Toplady (1740–78)

Local tradition in the parish of Blagdon, Somerset, points out the cleft in a rock in Burrington Combe where Augustus Toplady, the curate at the parish church, sheltering from a storm, wrote 'Rock of Ages, Cleft for Me' on a scrap of paper he happened to be carrying. Although there is no other confirmation for this story, it may explain the appeal of the hymn to those who wish to pray for protection.

Rock of ages, cleft for me,
Let me hide myself in thee;
Let the water and the blood,
From thy riven side which flowed,
Be of sin the double cure:
Cleanse me from its guilt and power.

Not the labours of my hands
Can fulfil thy law's demands;
Could my zeal no respite know.
Could my tears for ever flow,
All for sin could not atone:
Thou must save, and thou alone

Nothing in my hand I bring,
Simply to thy cross I cling;
Naked, come to thee for dress;
Helpless, look to thee for grace;
Foul, I to the fountain fly;
Wash me, Saviour, or I die.

While I draw this fleeting breath,
When my eyelids close in death,
When I soar through tracts unknown,
See thee on thy judgement throne;
Rock of ages, cleft for me,
Let me hide myself in thee

Johann Wolfgang von Goethe (1749–1832)

Born in Frankfurt-am-Main, Goethe is regarded as the greatest German poet. His administrative duties at the court of Weimar helped to discipline his genius. It would be pantheism to suggest that God is no more than a force in nature; this poem, on the contrary, expresses the conviction of many Christians that God, who is greater than the universe he created, reveals himself in a multitude of ways.

In a Thousand Forms

Although a thousand forms may seek to hide you,
Yet, All-Beloved, yet, I know you well.
Though wrapped in magic veils your look belied you,
All-Present One, at once I know you well.

In the clear reach of the young cedar's branches,
All-Beautiful-Growing One, I know you well.
In the clear crystal flood beneath the arches,
All-Soothing One, truly I know you well.

Where fountains climb up high to their unfolding,
All-Playful, with what joy I know you well.
Where cloudshapes shift with no shape ever holding,
All-Multiple-Folded One, I know you well.

On fields spread out like flowery bales unbound,
All-Starred-With-Lovely-Hues, I know you well.
Where ivy's thousand arms clasp up and round,
O All-Embracing One, I know you well.

When on the mountain peaks dawn catches fire,
All-Joyful-Making One, I greet you well.
Then as pure heaven opens, rounder, higher,
Enlarger-Of-All-Hearts, I breathe you well.

What I may know, by thought or outward valour,
From you, All-Teacher, I have learned it well.
And as I name the Hundred Names of Allah,
In each an echo rings, and names you well.[6]

William Blake (1757–1827)

William Blake was born in London, the son of an Irish stocking-maker. He describes how, on his way back from a walk in the woods near Dulwich, he saw a vision of angels in an oak tree, and counted this as the beginning of his spiritual life. He was apprenticed to an engraver, and after studying at the Royal Academy School he began to produce watercolours, and then to engrave by a new process pictures which could be printed from copper plates. Among his earliest published poems were the two series, Songs of Innocence *and* Songs of Experience, *which need to be read in parallel: God resembles both the Lamb and the Tiger. He was a sworn opponent of rationalism and materialism: 'Mock on, mock on, Voltaire, Rousseau,/ Mock on, mock on; 'tis all in vain;/ You throw the dust against the wind,/ And the wind blows it back again.' His answer was to reassert the power of emotion and feeling, and this is shown in the strange symbolism of the poetic books. Intellectually he was far from orthodox, but many Christians believe that his passion was the work of God. Perhaps not many of those who enthusiastically sing 'And did those feet . . .' realize what is meant by the 'arrows of desire', and that the dark Satanic mills are probably not just the industrial revolution, which was only just beginning, but also the chop-logic intellectualism of the philosophers and the moralism of Christians. Arguably his greatest work of art is also his greatest contribution to our thinking about God: the wonderful series of illustrations to the Book of Job.*

The Divine Image

To Mercy Pity Peace and Love
All pray in their distress:
And to these virtues of delight
Return their thankfulness.

For Mercy Pity Peace and Love,
Is God our father dear:
And Mercy Pity Peace and Love,
Is Man his child and care.

For Mercy has a human heart
Pity, a human face:
And Love, the human form divine,
And Peace, the human dress.

Then every man of every clime,
That prays in his distress,
Prays to the human form divine
Love Mercy Pity Peace,

And all must love the human form.
In heathen, turk or jew,
Where Mercy, Love and Pity dwell,
There God is dwelling too.

Auguries of Innocence

To see the world in a grain of sand,
   And a heaven in a wild flower;
Hold infinity in the palm of your hand.
And eternity in an hour.

The Garden of Love

I went to the Garden of Love,
  And saw what I never had seen;
A Chapel was built in the midst,
Where I used to play on the green.

And the gates of this Chapel were shut,
And 'Thou shalt not' writ over the door;
So I turned to the Garden of Love
That so many sweet flowers bore.

And I saw it was filled with graves,
And tombstones where flowers should be;
And priests in black gowns were walking their rounds,
And binding with briars my joys and desires.

The Gates of Paradise (Introduction)

Mutual forgiveness of each vice,
   Such are the Gates of Paradise,
Against the Accuser's chief desire,
Who walked among the stones of fire.
Jehovah's fingers wrote the Law.
He wept; then rose in zeal and awe,
And, in the midst of Sinai's heat,
Hid it beneath his Mercy-seat.
O Christians! Christians! tell me why
You rear it on your altars high!

The Everlasting Gospel

T he Vision of Christ that thou dost see,
  Is my vision's greatest enemy.
Thine is the Friend of all Mankind,
Mine speaks in Parables to the blind.
Thine loves the same world that mine hates,
Thy heaven-doors are my hell-gates.
Socrates taught what Melitus
Loathed as a nation's bitterest curse.
And Caiaphas was, in his own mind,
A benefactor to mankind.
Doth read the Bible day and night,
But thou readest black where I read white.

The Death of Christ

J esus said, 'Would'st thou love one who had never died
  For thee, or ever die for one who had not died for thee?'
And if God dieth not for man, and giveth not Himself
Eternally for man, man could not exist, for man is love,
As God is love. Every kindness to another is a little Death
In the Divine Image, nor can man exist but by brotherhood.

To the Christian

I give you the end of a golden string:
  Only wind it into a ball, –
It will lead you in at Heaven's gate,
Built in Jerusalem's wall.

O Saviour, pour upon me thy spirit of meekness and love, annihilate
  the selfhood in me, be thou all my life. Guide thou my hand which
trembles exceedingly upon the rock of ages.

Lord Horatio Nelson (1758–1805)

*A lifelong sailor, Lord Nelson became a national hero by defeating the
French fleet during the French revolutionary wars, notably at the Battle
of the Nile, but lost his right arm and the sight of his right eye. His final*

victory was over the French off Cape Trafalgar, but he was killed by a sniper's bullet in the hour of victory. This is his prayer on the eve of the Battle of Trafalgar:

May the great God whom I worship grant to my country, and for the benefit of Europe in general, a great and glorious victory; and may no misconduct in anyone tarnish it; and may humanity after victory be the predominant feature in the British Fleet. For myself, individually, I commit my life to him that made me, and may his blessing alight on my endeavours for serving my country faithfully. To him I resign myself and the just cause which it is entrusted to me to defend. Amen. Amen. Amen.

Elizabeth of France (1764–94)

Madame Elizabeth was the sister of King Louis XVI, and, like him, she was guillotined.

I know not, O my God, what may befall me today, but I am well convinced that nothing will happen which thou hast not foreseen and ordained from eternity. I adore thy eternal and impenetrable designs, I submit to them for thy love, I sacrifice myself in union with the sacrifice of Jesus Christ my divine Saviour. I ask in his holy name for patience and resignation in my sufferings, and perfect conformity of my will to thine in all things, past, present and to come. My God, I have nothing worthy of thy acceptance to offer thee, I know nothing, I can do nothing. I have but my heart to give thee; I may be deprived of health, reputation and even life, but my heart is my own. I consecrate it to thee, hoping never to resume it and desiring not to live if not for thee. Amen.[7]

James Montgomery (1771–1854)

James Montgomery was the son of a Moravian pastor in Irvine. After trying various occupations he started the Sheffield Iris *newspaper, writing against injustice and slavery. He edited a hymn-book for the Church of England parish he had joined in Sheffield, and was taken to court under a law forbidding hymns 'of human composition'. The Archbishop of York had the law repealed in 1821 – thanks to Montgomery it is now legal to sing hymns in the Church of England! He was fined and spent three months in prison for printing a seditious ballad, and later served six months for describing a riot. Many of his deeply religious poems have passed into the hymn-books, including the carol 'Angels from the realms of glory'.*

Lord, teach us how to pray aright
With reverence and with fear;
Though dust and ashes in thy sight,
We may, we must, draw near.

We perish if we cease from prayer:
O grant us power to pray
And, when to meet thee we prepare,
Lord, meet us by the way.

God of all grace, we bring to thee
A broken, contrite heart;
Give what thine eye delights to see,
Truth in the inward part;

Faith in the only Sacrifice
That can for sin atone,
To cast our hopes, to fix our eyes,
On Christ, on Christ alone;

Patience to watch and wait and weep,
Though mercy long delay.
Courage our fainting souls to keep,
And trust thee though thou slay.

Give these, and then thy will be done;
Thus, strengthened with all might,
We, through thy Spirit and thy Son,
Shall pray, and pray aright.

Prayer is the Soul's Sincere Desire

Prayer is the soul's sincere desire,
Uttered or unexpressed;
The motion of a hidden fire
That trembles in the breast.

Prayer is the burden of a sigh,
The falling of a tear,

The upward glancing of an eye
When none but God is near.

Prayer is the simplest form of speech
That infant lips can try;
Prayer the sublimest strains that reach
The Majesty on high.

Prayer is the contrite sinner's voice,
Returning from his ways,
While angels in their songs rejoice,
And cry, 'Behold, he prays!'

Prayer is the Christian's vital breath,
The Christian's native air,
His watchword at the gates of death:
He enters heaven with prayer.

The saints in prayer appear as one
In word, in deed, and mind,
While with the Father and the Son
Sweet fellowship they find.

O thou by whom we come to God,
The Life, the Truth, the Way,
The path of prayer thyself hast trod:
Lord, teach us how to pray.

Samuel Taylor Coleridge (1772–1834)

Coleridge's importance as a poet is linked with his friendships with Southey and the Wordsworths. The Ancient Mariner and Kubla Khan are signs of what he was capable of, but his later years were ruined by opium, as indicated in his 'Ode to Dejection'. At one time he was an itinerant preacher for the Unitarians, and this fragment of religious verse is worth quoting if only for its closing lines.

My Baptismal Birth-day

God's child in Christ adopted, Christ my all,
What that earth boasts were not lost cheaply, rather

Than forfeit that blest name by which I call
The holy one, the almighty God, my Father?
Father! In Christ we live, and Christ in thee;
Eternal thou, and everlasting we.
The heir of heaven, henceforth I fear not death:
In Christ I live, in Christ I draw the breath
Of the true life. Let then earth, sea, and sky
Make war against me! On my front I show
Their mighty Master's seal. In vain they try
To end my life, that can but end its woe.
Is that a death-bed where the Christian lies?
Yes! But not his – 'tis Death itself there dies.

Hartley Coleridge (1796–1849)

The eldest son of Samuel Taylor Coleridge also wrote some touching poetry, and also failed to achieve his potential through intemperance.

Whate'er is good to wish, ask that of heaven,
　　Though it be what thou canst not hope to see;
Pray to be perfect though the material leaven
Forbid the spirit so on earth to be;
But if for any wish thou dar'st not pray,
Then pray to God to cast that wish away.

Jane Austen (1775–1817)

The fifth of a Hampshire clergyman's seven children, Jane Austen published four of her six great novels anonymously, and the other two were not published until after she had died. She wrote almost in secret, hiding the paper under a folder if she heard the door creak as somebody entered the room. Yet her wit and amused tolerance of human behaviour made her a unique observer of the society of her time, and one of the world's greatest novelists.

Incline us, O God, to think humbly of ourselves, to be saved only in the examination of our own conduct, to consider our fellow-creatures with kindness, and to judge of all they say and do with the charity which we would desire from them ourselves; through Jesus Christ our Lord. Amen.

Give us grace, almighty Father, to address thee with all our hearts as well as with our lips. Thou art everywhere present: from thee no secrets can be hidden. Teach us to fix our thoughts on thee, reverently and with love, so that our prayers are not in vain, but are acceptable to thee, now and always; through Jesus Christ our Lord.

Grant us grace, almighty Father, so to pray as to deserve to be heard.

Ebenezer Elliott (1781–1849)

Elliott was a Sheffield iron merchant, and was a passionate agitator for the repeal of the Corn Laws, which kept the price of wheat artificially high, to the benefit of the landowners and the starvation of the poor. He believed in the power of the press to bring about social reforms, and wrote his best-known hymn as a counterblast to 'God save the King'.

When wilt thou save the people?
O God of mercy, when?
The people, Lord, the people,
Not crowns and thrones, but men!
Flowers of thy heart, O God, are they;
Let them not pass like weeds away,
Their heritage a sunless day:
God save the people!

Shall crime bring crime for ever,
Strength aiding still the strong?
Is it thy will, O Father,
That man shall toil for wrong?
'No,' say thy mountains; 'No,' thy skies;
Man's clouded sun shall brightly rise,
And songs be heard instead of sighs:
God save the people!

When wilt thou save the people?
O God of mercy, when?
The people, Lord, the people,
Not crowns and thrones, but men!
God save the people; thine they are,

Thy children, as thy angels fair;
From vice, oppression and despair
God save the people!

Jean-Baptiste Marie Vianney (1786–1859)

Jean-Baptiste Marie Vianney served for forty years as the priest of the obscure country parish of Ars near Lyons. People came from all over France to make their confessions in his hearing and to receive his spiritual guidance, from peasants to ministers of the government. His own devotion was to the Mass and the presence of Christ in the consecrated wafer in the tabernacle. He had great compassion and insight, and skill in guiding penitents. Six thousand people attended his funeral, yet he wrote no book. All that survives is the recollections of his friends:

An old peasant used to sit for long periods of time silently in the church. The Curé asked him what he did and he replied: 'Well, I look at God, and God looks at me, and we're happy together.'

I love you, O my God, and my only desire is to love you until the last breath of my life. I love you, and I would rather die loving you, than live without loving you. I love you, Lord, and the only grace I ask is to love you eternally. My God, if my tongue cannot say in every moment that I love you, I want my heart to repeat it to you as often as I draw breath.

My Jesus, from all eternity you were pleased to give yourself to us in love. And you planted within us a deep spiritual desire that can only be satisfied by yourself.

My Jesus, how good it is to love you. Let me be like your disciples on Mount Tabor, seeing nothing else but you. Let us be like two bosom friends, neither of whom can ever bear to offend the other.

We can only be satisfied by setting our hearts, imperfect as they are, on you. We are made to love you; you created us as your lovers.

Charles Blomfield (1786–1857)

After fourteen years as a parish priest, Blomfield became Bishop of Chester and then Bishop of London. Following the Industrial Revolution, thousands of souls had flocked into the cities, and there were no churches for them to worship in or clergy to minister to them. While Blomfield was Bishop over 200 new churches were built in his diocese, mostly at his instigation. But it was too late; the English working classes had lost the habit of church-going.

O God, by whom the world is governed and preserved, we thine unworthy creatures, under a thankful sense of thy providential care, draw nigh unto thee to offer our morning sacrifice of prayer and praise. We thank thee that thou hast protected us from all the dangers of the night. Continue thy goodness to us through this day, and preserve us from all dangers both of body and soul. May we remember that every day is thy gift, and to be used both in thy service and in doing the work of our salvation. Enable us to resist all evil, and dispose us to follow the guidance of thy good Spirit, not trusting to our own strength or wisdom, but looking to thee for grace to establish us in every good work and word; through Jesus Christ thy Son our Lord. Amen.

Thomas Arnold (1795–1842)

Thomas Arnold was appointed headmaster of Rugby School in 1828, and aimed to make it an example to other public schools in providing a truly Christian education for the sons of the new middle classes. He saw no difference between the sacred and the secular, and published Principles of Church Reform *and several volumes of sermons.*

Let thy blessing, O Lord, rest upon all who work in education. Teach them to seek after truth, and enable them to attain it; but grant that as they increase in the knowledge of earthly things, they may grow in the knowledge of thee, whom to know is life eternal; through Jesus Christ our Lord. Amen.

O Lord, preserve us this day and strengthen us to bear whatever thou shalt see fit to lay on us, whether pain, sickness, danger or distress; through Jesus Christ our Lord. Amen.

O Lord, we have a busy world around us. Eye, ear, and thought will be needed for all our work to be done in the world. Now ere we again enter upon it on the morrow we would commit eye, ear and thought to thee. Do thou bless them and keep their work thine, that as through thy natural laws our hearts beat and our blood flows without any thought of ours for them, so our spiritual life may hold on its course at those times when our minds cannot consciously turn to thee to commit each particular thought to thy service; hear our prayer for our Redeemer's sake. Amen.

Used before he entered Rugby School every day

Louis Felici sj (*c.* 1797)

In reaction to Protestant attacks on the doctrine of transubstantiation, the Roman Catholic Church began to emphasize the adoration of the sacrament, not only in the Mass but in the Sunday evening service of Benediction. The consecrated wafer is exposed in a monstrance, and the Divine Praises – the text of which has been altered several times since it was first written by Louis Felici – are sung just before it is replaced in the tabernacle. Even those Protestants who believe that this is not what the eucharistic bread was intended for may agree that it is a beautiful service, and would have no problems with this version of the Divine Praises.

B lessèd be God. Blessèd be his holy name. Blessèd be the holy and undivided Trinity. Blessèd be God the Father, maker of heaven and earth. Blessèd be the holy name of Jesus. Blessèd be Jesus Christ in his death and resurrection; on his throne of glory; in the Sacrament of his body and blood. Blessèd be the Holy Spirit, the giver and sustainer of life. Blessèd be God in the Virgin Mary, Mother of our Lord and God. Blessèd be God in the angels and saints. Blessèd be God. Amen.

The Evangelical and Missionary Revival

The sense of revival and return to the teachings of the gospel was not limited to Methodism. It reinvigorated dormant congregations in many denominations and drove men and women, at the cost of their lives in many cases, to go forth to proclaim the gospel to the nations.

John Newton (1725–1807)

The young John Newton was captured by the press-gang and compelled to serve in the British Navy, where he had an adventurous career. In 1748 he was converted, and soon obtained the post of surveyor of tides at Liverpool. He was influenced at this time by George Whitefield, and studied Latin, Hebrew, Greek and Syriac. He was ordained in 1764 and made curate of Olney, where with William Cowper he wrote the Olney Hymns. *Among his most popular hymns are 'Glorious things of thee are spoken' and 'How sweet the name of Jesus sounds'. For the last twenty-seven years of his life he was rector of St Mary Wolnoth in London, and he supported William Wilberforce in his campaign against slavery.*

Come, My Soul, Thy Suit Prepare

Come, my soul, thy suit prepare:
Jesus loves to answer prayer;
He himself has bid thee pray,
Therefore will not say thee nay.

Thou art coming to a King:
Large petitions with thee bring;
For his grace and power are such
None can ever ask too much.

With my burden I begin:
Lord, remove this load of sin;

Let thy Blood, for sinners spilt,
Set my conscience free from guilt.

Lord, I come to thee for rest;
Take possession of my breast;
There thy blood-bought right maintain
And without a rival reign.

While I am a pilgrim here,
Let thy love my spirit cheer;
Be my guide, my guard, my friend,
Lead me to my journey's end.

J esus! my Shepherd, Husband, Friend,
My Prophet, Priest, and King,
My Lord, my Life, my Way, my End,
Accept the praise I bring.

Weak is the effort of my heart,
And cold my warmest thought;
But when I see thee as thou art,
I'll praise thee as I ought.

Till then I would thy love proclaim
With every fleeting breath;
And may the music of thy name
Refresh my soul in death.

From 'How sweet the name of Jesus sounds'

Great Shepherd of Thy People Hear

G reat Shepherd of thy people, hear,
Thy presence now display;
As thou hast given a place for prayer,
So give us hearts to pray.

Within these walls let holy peace
And love and concord dwell
Here give the troubled conscience ease,
The wounded spirit heal.

May we in faith receive thy word,
In faith present our prayers,
And in the presence of our Lord
Unbosom all our cares.

The hearing ear, the seeing eye,
The contrite heart, bestow;
And shine upon us from on high,
That we in grace may grow.

Henry Venn (1725–97)

*Henry Venn made a deep impression as vicar of Huddersfield in Yorkshire,
and by his book* The Complete Duty of Man *he influenced many to take
a more earnest approach to Christian life. This was the beginning of the
Evangelical Revival, and after he retired from Huddersfield due to bad
health, he took a living in Huntingdonshire, from where he was able to
influence many at Cambridge University. His son John Venn (1759–1813)
became the rector of Clapham, and the group of like-minded Evangelicals
who gathered round them, including William Wilberforce and Hannah
More, became known as the Clapham Sect. Henry Venn was one of the
founders of the Church Missionary Society. It seems strange to find a
prominent Evangelical lamenting his unemotional nature.*

Thy miracles of love, no joy to me impart;
In me no tender passions move, O my unfeeling heart!

When, Lord, to thee I turn, nailed to th'accursed tree,
With no transporting love I burn, although thou diedst for me!

When I my sins recall, to pass before my eye,
Scarce one bewailing tear will fall; I scarce can heave one sigh!

Thy promises I lay close to my pained breast;
Fain would I hope: – hope flees away; and still I find no rest!

Thus dark must I walk on, in fear and misery;
And never shall my bosom glow with fervent love to thee?

Unclose, unclose these eyes! pour in the longed-for day!
Before me bid thy glory rise! My darkness chase away![1]

William Cowper (1731–1800)

The son of a Hertfordshire rector, William Cowper became a barrister but began to suffer suicidal mental breakdowns. He was comforted in the home of a retired clergyman in Huntingdon. When the clergyman died, Cowper moved to Olney with the widow, Mary Unwin. John Newton persuaded hm to write hymns, and some of his best verse is among the sixty-seven he contributed to the Olney Hymns: *'God moves in a mysterious way', 'Hark my soul it is the Lord', 'O for a closer walk with God', and 'Jesus, where'er thy people meet'. His increasing insanity prevented him from marrying Mrs Unwin, but she cared for him and persuaded him to write secular poetry also, including* The Ballad of John Gilpin. *It has been said that Cowper's hymns are written with 'the pen of misery dipped in the ink of despair', yet his flashes of insight into the love of God make them an encouragement for all who seek to pray out of the pit of depression.*

Jesus, Where'er Thy People Meet

Jesus, where'er thy people meet,
There they behold thy mercy-seat;
Where'er they seek thee thou art found,
And every place is hallowed ground.

For thou, within no walls confined,
Inhabitest the humble mind;
Such ever bring thee when they come,
And, going, take thee to their home.

Dear Shepherd of thy chosen few,
Thy former mercies here renew;
Here to the waiting hearts proclaim
The sweetness of thy saving name.

Here may we prove the power of prayer
To strengthen faith and sweeten care,
To teach our faint desires to rise,
And bring all heaven before our eyes.

Lord, we are few, but thou art near;
Nor short thine arm, nor deaf thine ear:
O rend the heavens, come quickly down,
And make a thousand hearts thine own.

Far from the World, O Lord, I Flee

Far from the world, O Lord, I flee,
From strife and tumult far;
From scenes, where Satan wages still
His most successful war.

The calm retreat, the silent shade,
With pray'r and praise agree;
And seem by thy sweet bounty made,
For those who follow thee.

There if thy Spirit touch the soul,
And grace her mean abode;
Oh with what peace, and joy, and love
She communes with her God!

There like the nightingale she pours
Her solitary lays;
Nor asks a witness of her song,
Nor thirsts for human praise.

Author and Guardian of my life,
Sweet source of light divine;
And (all harmonious names in one)
My Saviour; thou art mine!

What thanks I owe thee, and what love
A boundless, endless store;
Shall echo thro' the realms above,
When times shall be no more.

Hark, My Soul! It is the Lord

Hark, my soul! it is the Lord;
'Tis thy Saviour, hear his word
Jesus speaks, and speaks to thee:
'Say, poor sinner, lov'st thou me?

'I delivered thee when bound,
And, when wounded, healed thy wound;
Sought thee wandering, set thee right
Turned thy darkness into light.

'Can a woman's tender care
Cease towards the child she bare?
Yes, she may forgetful be,
Yet will I remember thee.

'Mine is an unchanging love,
Higher than the heights above,
Deeper than the depths beneath,
Free and faithful, strong as death.

'Thou shalt see my glory soon,
When the work of grace is done;
Partner of my throne shalt be;
Say, poor sinner, lov'st thou me?'

Lord, it is my chief complaint
That my love is weak and faint;
Yet I love thee, and adore;
O for grace to love thee more!

Charles Simeon (1759–1836)

On ordination in 1783 Simeon moved from his position as a Fellow of King's College, Cambridge, to become vicar of Holy Trinity Church in the same town, where he remained until his death. He became a leading light in the Evangelical movement, and was a supporter of the British and Foreign Bible Society and one of the founders of the Church Missionary Society. A phrase in his writings serves as a motto for all those distressed by religious controversy: 'Truth does not lie in either extreme taken on its own, nor yet midway between them: truth lies in both extremes held together in tension.' A guest wrote that 'Mr Simeon invariably rose every morning, though it was the winter session, at four o'clock; and after lighting his fire, he devoted the first four hours of the day to private prayer, and the devotional study of Scripture.' He loved The Book of Common Prayer *and said of the blessing: 'In pronouncing it, I do not do it as a mere finale, but I feel that I am actually dispensing peace from God, and at God's command. I know not the individuals to whom my benediction is a blessing; but I know that I am the appointed instrument by whom God is conveying the blessing to those who are able to receive it.'*

What is before us, we know not, whether we shall live or die; but this we know, that all things are ordered and sure. Everything is ordered with unerring wisdom and unbounded love, by thee, our God, who art love. Grant us in all things to see thy hand; through Jesus Christ our Lord. Amen.

William Wilberforce (1759–1833)

The Member of Parliament for Hull in Yorkshire, where he was born, Wilberforce read the New Testament assiduously and was converted to Evangelicalism. John Newton persuaded him that it would be a waste of his talents to be ordained, and he promoted Christian causes in Parliament instead. He was appalled at the injustice of slavery, and after many setbacks he pushed through Parliament Bills to abolish the slave trade in 1807 and to emancipate all slaves in 1833. He settled in Clapham, where he became the acknowledged leader of 'the Clapham Sect'. Together they helped found the Church Missionary Society in 1798 and the British and Foreign Bible Society in 1803. Wilberforce's most influential book was A Practical View of the Prevailing Religious System of Professed Christians, *published in 1797, which was largely responsible for the earnest transformation of English society from the dissipations of the previous century to what we call Victorian morality.*

Sunday Morning

O Lord God, who, though unseen by our bodily eyes, art continually about out bed, and about our path, and seest all our ways, in whom we live and move and have our being, who art the Author of all the various comforts, which we here enjoy, and to whom we look for all future benefits, we desire now to bow down before thee. Let thy Holy Spirit, we beseech thee, help our infirmities, that we may worship thee in Spirit and in truth. We approach thee in the name of Jesus Christ, the great Mediator between God and man . . .[2]

Sunday Evening

. . . Bless those who labour in thy word and doctrine. May they be the honoured instruments of turning many from sin to righteousness, that so we may not in this highly-favoured land have a name to live while we are dead, and have the form of godliness without the power. We pray to thee for all the dark corners of the earth, for all who are suffering under the evils of slavery, or from injustice or cruelty of any kind ... Oh, do thou grant that the reign of the Prince of peace may be more established, that the knowledge of the Lord may cover the earth, as the waters cover the sea ...[3]

William Carey (1761–1834)

William Carey was apprenticed to a cobbler in Northamptonshire, and following his conversion he continued cobbling by night, ran a school by day and was pastor of a Baptist congregation, meanwhile teaching himself Latin, Greek, Hebrew, Dutch and French. At the ministers' meeting in Nottingham he called for people to share the good news about Jesus with the people of India who had not heard of him. 'Expect great things from God,' he said, 'and attempt great things for God.' This led to the formation of the Baptist Missionary Society, and he himself sailed for India, and while running an indigo factory at Malda he preached in two hundred villages and translated the New Testament into Bengali. Moving to Serampore, he had it printed there. He was then appointed professor of Sanskrit, Bengali and Marathi at a newly opened college in Calcutta. He translated the whole Bible into Bengali, and portions of it into twenty-four other languages. He also campaigned successfully for the abolition of suttee, the custom of burning widows on their husband's funeral pyre. This prayer based on Carey's words was written for the inauguration of the Church of South India.

O God, who to an expectant and united Church didst grant at Pentecost the gift of the Holy Spirit, and hast wonderfully brought into one fold those who now worship thee here: Grant, we beseech thee, the help of the same Spirit in all our life and worship, that we may expect great things from thee, and attempt great things for thee, and being one in thee may show to the world that thou didst send Jesus Christ our Lord, to whom, with thee and the Holy Spirit, be all honour and glory, world without end. Amen.[4]

Henry Martyn (1781–1812)

Henry Martyn met Charles Simeon at Cambridge, where he was a Fellow, and was inspired by him to seek ordination and go to Calcutta as a chaplain with the East India Company. Unlike some chaplains, he did not limit his ministry to Europeans, but learnt local languages and shared the gospel with the Indian people. He translated the New Testament into Hindustani, Persian and Arabic, the Psalms into Persian and The Book of Common Prayer *into Hindustani. He died at Tokat in Turkey on his way home and was buried by the Armenian clergy there.*

O send thy light and thy truth, that we may live alway near to thee, our God. Let us feel thy love, that we may be as it were already in heaven, that we may do all our work as the angels do theirs. Let us be ready for every work, be ready to go out or come in, to stay or to depart, just as thou shalt appoint. Lord, let us have no will of our own, or consider our true happiness as depending in the slightest degree on anything that can befall us outwardly, but as consisting altogether in conformity to thy will; through Jesus Christ our Lord. Amen.

Lord, I am blind and helpless, stupid and ignorant. Cause me to hear; cause me to know; teach me to do; lead me.

Reginald Heber (1783–1826)

A Shropshire vicar who in 1823 accepted the bishopric of Calcutta, which at that time covered most of Asia and Australasia, he worked tirelessly for the spread of the gospel, and was dead within three years of his arrival. He is best remembered for his hymns, 'Brightest and best of the sons of the morning', 'Holy, holy, holy, Lord God almighty', and 'From Greenland's icy mountains'.

O Lord Jesus Christ, who (as at this time) didst burst the prison-house of the grave, and open to all that believe in thy Name the gate of a glorious resurrection, let the light of thy truth, we beseech thee, shine on all that dwell in darkness. Have mercy on the great land of India. Bless all the rulers and peoples of that land. Bless, guide, and enlighten all who are inquiring after truth, and hasten the time, if it be thy gracious will, when the knowledge of thy Name shall cover the world as the waters cover the sea; for thine honour and glory. Amen.

God, that Madest Earth and Heaven

God, that madest earth and heaven,
Darkness and light,
Who the day for toil hast given,
For rest the night;
May thine angel-guards defend us,
Slumber sweet thy mercy send us,
Holy dreams and hopes attend us,
This livelong night.

I Praised the Earth

I praised the earth, in beauty seen
With garlands gay of various green;
I praised the sea, whose ample field
Shone glorious as a silver shield;
And earth and ocean seemed to say
'Our beauties are but for a day!'

I praised the sun, whose chariot rolled
On wheels of amber and of gold;
I praised the moon, whose softer eye
Gleamed sweetly through the summer sky –
And moon and sun in answer said,
'Our days of light are numberèd!'

O God! O good beyond compare!
If thus thy meaner works are fair;
If thus thy bounties gild the span
Of ruined earth and sinful man;
How glorious must the mansion be
Where thy redeemed shall dwell with thee!

Lord Shaftesbury (1801–85)

Anthony Ashley Cooper, seventh Earl of Shaftesbury, entered Parliament as a member of the Conservative Party and devoted himself to caring for the working classes. After visiting the London slums for himself, he had the Ten Hours' Bill and the Factory Act passed by Parliament. He fought for protection for women and children working in the coal mines, and for

the boy chimney-sweeps for whom he introduced the Climbing Boys Act.
Among the many Evangelical societies he supported was the British and
Foreign Bible Society, whose president he was for many years. He hated
ritualism and attacked rationalism.

O God, the Father of the forsaken, the help of the weak, supplier of the needy, who hast diffused and proportioned thy gifts to body and soul, in such sort that all may acknowledge and perform the joyous duty of mutual service; who teachest us that love towards the race of men is the bond of perfectness, and the imitation of thy blessed self; open our eyes and touch our hearts, that we may see and do, both for this world and for that which is to come, the things which belong to our peace. Strengthen us in the work we have undertaken; give us counsel and wisdom, perseverance, faith and zeal, and in thine own good time, and according to thy pleasure, prosper the issue. Pour into us a spirit of humility. Let nothing be done but in devout obedience to thy will, thankfulness for thine unspeakable mercies, and love to thine adorable Son Christ Jesus, who with thee, O Father, and the Holy Ghost, ever liveth one God, world without end. Amen.

George Edward Lynch Cotton (1813–66)

George Cotton was a schoolmaster at Rugby School under Thomas Arnold.
In Tom Brown's Schooldays *he is portrayed as 'the Young Master'. He*
became head of Marlborough College, which he raised to become one of
the best schools in the country. In 1858 he was appointed Bishop of Calcutta,
where he founded schools for the children of the poorer Anglo-Indians and
Eurasians. Eight years later he was drowned in the Ganges.

O God, who hast made of one blood all nations for to dwell on the face of the whole earth, and didst send thy blessed Son to preach peace to them that are far off, and to them that are nigh; grant that all the peoples of the world may feel after thee and find thee, and hasten, O Lord, the fulfilment of thy promise to pour out thy Spirit upon all flesh; through Jesus Christ our Lord. Amen.

David Livingstone (1813–73)

David Livingstone was born in Blantyre in Lanarkshire and worked in a
cotton factory, educating himself by reading every book he could lay hands
on. He felt called to become a missionary to China, and after studying

medicine in Edinburgh he joined the London Missionary Society, but was prevented by the political situation and went instead to what is now Botswana. He was popular among the Africans for his medical work and schools, but realized that the majority of Africans would only be able to hear the gospel if the continent was opened up for trade. He therefore embarked on a series of explorations, winning great fame in England, and appealing in the Senate House in Cambridge for missionary workers, which led to the formation of the Universities Mission to Central Africa. He was discovered exhausted by H. M. Stanley, the American journalist, and died in Africa two years later.

O Jesus, fill me with thy love now, and I beseech thee, accept me, and use me a little for thy glory. O do, do, I beseech thee, accept me and my service, and take thou all the glory.

Robert Milman (1816–76)

With a doctorate in Divinity from Oxford, Milman served humbly as a vicar in Chaddleworth, then Lambourn, then Great Marlow. While there he lectured in the Anglo-Catholic theological college at Cuddesdon. He was then appointed Bishop of Calcutta, where he was energetic and fluent in languages, and laboured for co-operation between the high-church and low-church missionaries, and between Europeans and Indians, inviting them together to his home.

O great Lord of the harvest, send forth, we beseech thee, labourers into the harvest of the world, that the grain which is even now ripe may not fall and perish through our neglect. Pour forth thy sanctifying Spirit on our fellow Christians abroad, and thy converting grace on those who are living in darkness. Raise up, we beseech thee, a devout ministry among the native believers, that, all thy people being knit together in one body, in love, thy church may grow up into the measure of the stature of the fulness of Christ; through him who died, and rose again for us all, the same Jesus Christ our Lord. Amen.

B lessed Jesus, Lord of the harvest, send forth, we beseech thee, labourers into thy harvest, and by thy Holy Spirit, stir the hearts of many, that they may be ready to spend and be spent in thy service, and if it please thee, so to lose their life in this world, that they may gather fruit unto life eternal; Lord Jesus, lover of souls. Amen.

The Nineteenth Century

Frederick Denison Maurice (1805–72)

F. D. Maurice completed a course at Cambridge University, but because he refused to subscribe to the Thirty-Nine Articles, in those days he was not allowed to graduate. As he wrestled with his faith, however, he gradually came to accept the Anglican position, and after graduating from Oxford he was ordained. From a curacy in Warwickshire he went to be chaplain at Guy's Hospital, then Professor of English Literature and History, and finally the first Professor of Theology at King's College, London. Seeking to apply Christian principles to social reform, he formed the Christian Socialist movement. His views, which were regarded as radical then, would now be seen as a rather old-fashioned concern for the poor. Similarly, in theology he was forced to resign from King's College for opposing the popular view of endless punishment after death. He pointed out that in the New Testament 'eternity' has nothing to do with time, a view which now would be widely accepted. His influence in the twentieth century has been greater than in his own time.

O eternal Father, we believe that in thy Son thou art satisfied with our race. We believe that thou hast created us in Him, and that thou lookest upon us as we really are, not as we are made by the unbelief which separates us from thee and from our brethren. Only thus, do we find that peace which thy Son left His disciples. We believe that in Christ thou wilt restore all things. Use us, each one of us, we humbly beseech thee, to work with thee in thy purpose of restoration, blotting out our sins, that we may serve thee day by day with free hearts, thy free Spirit dwelling and working within us to thy honour and glory.

Before we go to rest, we would commit ourselves to God's care through Christ, beseeching him to forgive us for all our sins of this day past, and to keep alive His grace in our hearts, and to cleanse us from all sin, pride, harshness and selfishness, and give us the spirit of meekness, humility, firmness, and love. O Lord, keep thyself present to us ever, and perfect thy strength in our weakness. Take us and ours under thy blessed care this night and evermore; through Jesus Christ our Lord. Amen.

Most blessed and glorious Trinity, three Persons in one God, teach us to worship and adore that absolute Trinity, that perfect Unity. And that we may adore thee, that our worship may not be a mockery, make us to know that we are one in Christ, as the Father is one with the Son, and the Son with the Father. Suffer us not to look upon our sectarianism as if it were a destiny. Help us to regard it as a rebellion against thee. Help us to see all distinctions more clearly in the light of thy everlasting love. Help us to recognize the truth of every effort to express something of that which passes knowledge. Help us to feel and confess the feebleness of our own efforts. So may thy holy name embrace us more and more. So may all creatures in heaven and earth and under the earth at last glorify thee throughout all ages. Amen.

James Martineau (1805–1900)

James Martineau was a Unitarian minister in Dublin and Liverpool, then professor and principal of Manchester New College. He was a brilliant philosopher, and argued strongly that it was still possible, in the light of Darwinism, to accept the Argument from Design for belief in God.

Almighty God, who hast created us in thine own image, grant us grace fearlessly to contend against evil and to make no peace with oppression; and, that we may reverently use our freedom, help us to employ it in the maintenance of justice in our communities and among the nations, to the glory of thy holy name; through Jesus Christ our Lord, who lives and reigns with thee and the Holy Spirit, one God, now and for ever. Amen.

O God, thine eye is over all thy children, and thou hast called them to a kingdom not of this world; send forth thy Holy Spirit into all the dark places of life, to still the noise of our strife and the tumult of the people; carry faith to the doubting, hope to the fearful, strength to the weak, light to the mourners, and more and more increase the pure in heart who see their God; through Jesus Christ our Lord. Amen.

O searcher of hearts, thou knowest us better than we know ourselves, and seest the sins which our sinfulness hides from us. Yet even our own conscience beareth witness against us, that we often slumber on our appointed watch; that we talk not always lovingly with each other, and humbly with thee; and we withhold that entire sacrifice of ourselves to thy perfect will; without which we are not crucified with Christ, or sharers in his redemption. Oh, look upon our contrition, and lift up our weakness, and let the dayspring yet arise within our hearts, and bring us healing, strength, and joy. Day by day may we grow in faith, in self-denial, in charity, in heavenly-mindedness. And then, mingle us at last with the mighty host of thy redeemed for evermore. Amen.

Alfred Lord Tennyson (1809–92)

Tennyson was the fourth son of a Lincolnshire rector; his first book of poetry was published when he was twenty-one. Three years later he published early versions of 'The Lotus Eaters' and 'The Lady of Shallott'; he improved and republished them nine years later. His college friend Arthur Hallam died young at this time, and Tennyson began writing the elegies which he would later collect as In Memoriam. *This explores optimistically the religious dilemma of the Victorians, confident in their civilization but uncertain because of the challenges which science was making to their faith. It was published in 1850, the year when he married, was made Poet Laureate and moved to the Isle of Wight. He later wrote verse novels and drama, but it was the Arthurian* Idylls of the King *which made him a hero to all, even Queen Victoria herself. His last poem, 'Crossing the Bar', was an expression of confidence in the face of death.*

Strong Son of God, immortal Love,
Whom we, that have not seen thy face,
By faith, and faith alone, embrace,
Believing where we cannot prove;

Thine are these orbs of light and shade;
Thou madest Life in man and brute;
Thou madest Death; and lo, thy foot
Is on the skull which thou hast made.

Thou wilt not leave us in the dust:
Thou madest man, he knows not why.
He thinks he was not made to die;
And thou hast made him: thou art just.

Thou seemest human and divine,
The highest, holiest manhood, thou:
Our wills are ours, we know not how;
Our wills are ours, to make them thine.

Our little systems have their day,
They have their day and cease to be:
They are but broken lights of thee,
And thou, O Lord, art more than they.

We have but faith: we cannot know;
For knowledge is of things we see;
And yet we trust it comes from thee,
A beam in darkness: let it grow ...

Forgive my grief for one removed,
Thy creature, whom I found so fair.
I trust he lives in thee, and there
I find him worthier to be loved.

Forgive these wild and wandering cries,
Confusions of a wasted youth;
Forgive them where they fail in truth,
And in thy wisdom make me wise.

From In Memoriam A. H. H.

Speak to him thou for he hears, and spirit with Spirit can meet –
Closer is he than breathing, and nearer than hands and feet.

From The Higher Pantheism

More things are wrought by prayer
Than this world dreams of. Wherefore, let thy voice
Rise like a fountain for me night and day.
For what are men better than sheep and goats
That nourish a blind life within the brain,
If, knowing God, they lift not hands of prayer

Both for themselves and those who call them friend?
For so the whole round earth is every way
Bound by gold chains about the feet of God.

From The Passing of Arthur

William Ewart Gladstone (1809–98)

Under the influence of a strongly Evangelical mother, Gladstone hoped to be ordained when he left Oxford, but his father persuaded him to pursue a political career instead. He had been influenced by the Oxford Movement and remained a High Church Anglican for the rest of his life. He became Chancellor of the Exchequer on several occasions, and then several times Prime Minister. Initially in favour of the establishment of the Church, he changed his mind and pushed through disestablishment in Ireland as a preliminary move towards Irish Home Rule, though he died having failed in this. His Christian beliefs influenced his politics and his personal life: he received Communion every week, ate little and slept less, and was generous to good causes.

Go forth with us, O Lord, from this thy holy house; cast about us the fence which the evil one cannot pass, and clothe us in the armour which his darts cannot pierce. Send down upon us thy love and light and calm, wherein, as in a cloud, we may continually dwell and worship thee for evermore, through Jesus Christ our Lord. Amen.

Henry Alford (1810–71)

A Fellow of Trinity College, Cambridge, Alford served as vicar of Wymeswold in Leicestershire, then as minister of Quebec Chapel, Marylebone, and from 1857 as Dean of Canterbury Cathedral. He edited the works of John Donne, published an edition of the Greek New Testament and wrote several hymns, including 'Come, ye thankful people, come' and 'Ten thousand times ten thousand'.

O God, thou hast commanded us to walk in the Spirit and not to fulfil the lusts of the flesh; make us perfect, we pray, in love, that we may conquer our natural selfishness and give ourselves to others. Fill our hearts with thy joy, and garrison them with thy peace; make us long-suffering and gentle, and thus subdue our hasty and angry tempers; give us faithfulness, meekness and self-control; that so crucifying the flesh with

its affections and lusts, we may bring forth the fruit of the Spirit to thy
praise and glory; through Jesus Christ our Lord. Amen.

O Lord, give us more charity, more self-denial, more likeness to thee.
Teach us to sacrifice our comforts to others, and our likings for the
sake of doing good. Make us kindly in thought, gentle in word, generous
in deed. Teach us that it is better to give than to receive, better to forget
ourselves than to put ourselves forward, better to minister than to be
ministered unto. And unto thee, the God of Love, be all glory and praise,
both now and for evermore. Amen.

O God, grant unto us that we be not unwise, but understanding thy
will; not slothful, but diligent in thy work; that we run not as uncer-
tainly, nor fight thy battles as those that beat the air. Whatsoever our hand
findeth to do, may we do it with our might; that when thou shalt call thy
labourers to give them their reward, we may so have run that we may
obtain; so have fought the good fight, as to receive the crown of eternal
life; through Jesus Christ our Lord. Amen.

Søren Aaby Kierkegaard (1813–55)

*Kierkegaard, the greatest Existentialist philosopher, spent most of his life
in Copenhagen, and because he wrote in Danish his works were unknown
outside Denmark in his lifetime, but subsequently they were widely
influential on European philosophers, even those who called themselves
Existentialists but moved in the direction of atheism. Kierkegaard studied
Lutheran theology and Hegel's dialectic, and reacted against them both.
Both scientific liberalism and church dogma only increased his natural
gloom. What was important for him was not objective history, but the
subjective existence of the individual standing before the Jesus of faith.*

From your hand, O Lord, we receive everything. You stretch your
powerful hand, and turn worldly wisdom into holy folly. You open
your gentle hand, and offer the gift of inward peace. If sometimes it seems
that your arm is shortened, then you increase our faith and trust, so that
we may reach out to you. And if sometimes it seems that you withdraw
your hand from us, then we know that it is only to conceal the eternal
blessing which you have promised – that we may yearn even more fervently
for that blessing.[1]

O Lord Jesus Christ, I long to live in your presence, to see your human form and to watch you walking on earth. I do not want to see you through the darkened glass of tradition, nor through the eyes of today's values and prejudices. I want to see you as you were, as you are, and as you always will be. I want to see you as an offence to human pride, as a man of humility, walking amongst the lowliest of men, and yet as the saviour and redeemer of the human race.[2]

Teach us, O God not to torture ourselves, not to make martyrs of ourselves through stifling reflection; but rather teach us to breathe deeply in faith, through Jesus, our Lord.

Lord, give us weak eyes for things which are of no account and clear eyes for all your truth.

God our heavenly Father, when the thought of you wakes in our hearts, let its awakening not be like a startled bird that flies about in fear; let it be like a child waking up from its sleep with a heavenly smile.

Charles John Vaughan (1816–97)

Charles Vaughan was educated at Rugby under Thomas Arnold, and became headmaster of Harrow School. While he was successively Vicar of Doncaster, Master of the Temple and Dean of Llandaff in Wales, he trained young men for ordination, so that over 450 of 'Vaughan's Doves' were grateful for the education he had given them.

Lord, that which we have prayed against this morning, suffer us not to have done before the evening.

O Lord God, give us grace to set a good example to all amongst whom we live, to be just and true in all our dealings, to be strict and conscientious in the discharge of every duty, pure and temperate in all enjoyment, kind and charitable and courteous toward all men; that so the mind of Jesus Christ may be formed in us, and all men take knowledge of us that we are his disciples; through the same Jesus Christ our Lord.

S et before our minds and hearts, O heavenly Father, the example of our Lord Jesus Christ, who, when he was upon earth, found his refreshment in doing the will of him that sent him, and in finishing his work. When many are coming and going, and there is little leisure, give us grace to remember him who knew neither impatience of spirit nor confusion of work, but in the midst of all his labours held communion with thee, and even upon earth was still in heaven; where now he reigneth with thee and the Holy Spirit world without end.

Mrs Cecil Frances Alexander (1818–95)

Fanny Humphreys was the daughter of a Marines captain in County Wicklow. It was customary in many families for children to learn by heart the collect of the day from The Book of Common Prayer *every Sunday. Her godchildren complained that this was a dreary duty, so she used to turn each prayer into verse. In 1848 she published these as* Hymns for Little Children. *In 1850 she married a poor clergyman, William Alexander, and it was not until 1867 that he was made a bishop. After she had died he became Archbishop of Armagh in 1896 – in other words, she knew less about the rich man in his castle than she did about the poor man at the gate. Among her well-known hymns are 'All things bright and beautiful', 'Once in Royal David's City', 'There is a green hill far away' and the translation of St Patrick's Breastplate, 'I bind unto myself this day'.*

O oft forsaken, oft denied,
Forgive our shame, wash out our sin;
Look on us from thy Father's side
And let that sweet look win.

Hear when we call thee from the deep,
Still walk beside us on the shore,
Give hands to work, and eyes to weep,
And hearts to love thee more.[3]

Henry Allon (1818–92)

Allon was the pastor of Union Congregational Chapel in Islington and secretary of Cheshunt College, where he had himself trained for the ministry. He edited several hymnals for the Congregational Church, and 'Saviour of the World' appears for the first time in one of them. It is presumed that he wrote it himself.

Saviour of the World

J esus, Saviour of the world, come to us in thy mercy:
we look to thee to save and help us.
By thy cross and thy life laid down thou didst set thy people free:
we look to thee to save and help us.
When they were ready to perish thou savedst thy disciples:
we look to thee to come to our help.
In the greatness of thy mercy loose us from our chains:
forgive the sins of all thy people.
Make thyself known as our Saviour and mighty deliverer:
save and help us that we may praise thee.
Come now and dwell with us Lord Christ Jesus:
hear our prayer and be with us always.
And when thou comest in thy glory,
make us to be one with thee,
and to share the life of thy kingdom. Amen.

Emily Brontë (1818–48)

*Those who enjoy the novels of the Brontë sisters may not realize that their
personal, questioning faith comes out most strongly in their poetry. These
were the last lines written by Emily Brontë before her death.*

N o coward soul is mine,
No trembler in the world's storm-troubled sphere:
I see Heaven's glories shine,
And faith shines equal, arming me from fear.

O God within my breast,
Almighty, ever-present Deity!
Life – that in me has rest,
As I – undying Life – have power in thee!

Vain are the thousand creeds
That move men's hearts: unutterably vain;
Worthless as withered weeds,
Or idlest froth amid the boundless main,

To waken doubt in one
Holding so fast by thine infinity;

So surely anchored on
The steadfast rock of immortality.

With wide-embracing love
Thy Spirit animates eternal years,
Pervades and broods above;
Changes, sustains, dissolves, creates and rears.

Though earth and man were gone,
And suns and universes cease to be,
And thou wert left alone,
Every existence would exist in thee.

There is not room for death,
Nor atom that his might could render void;
Thou – thou art Being and Breath,
And what thou art may never be destroyed.

Anne Brontë (1820–49)

While faith is with me, I am blest;
  It turns my darkest night to day.
But, while I clasp it to my breast,
I often feel it slide away.

What shall I do if all my love,
My hopes, my toil, are cast away?
And if there be no God above
To hear and bless me when I pray?

Oh, help me, God! For thou alone
Canst my distracted soul relieve.
Forsake it not: it is thine own,
Though weak, yet longing to believe.

Oppressed with Sin and Woe

Oppressed with sin and woe,
  A burdened heart I bear;
Opposed by many a mighty foe,
Yet I will not despair.

With this polluted heart,
I dare to come to thee –
Holy and mighty as thou art –
For thou wilt pardon me.

I feel that I am weak,
And prone to every sin;
But thou, who giv'st to those who seek,
Wilt give me strength within.

I need not fear my foes;
I need not yield to care;
I need not sink beneath my woes,
For thou wilt answer prayer.

In my Redeemer's name,
I give myself to thee;
And, all unworthy as I am,
My God will cherish me.

Charles Kingsley (1819–75)

Charles Kingsley was a social reformer, poet and novelist. For most of his life he was vicar of Eversley in Hampshire. Under the influence of F. D. Maurice and Thomas Carlyle, he became a leading member of the Christian Socialist movement, though through the cooperative movement, education and better housing rather than radical politics, he sought to improve the lot of the people. He was considered an exponent of what was called 'Muscular Christianity', and opposed all forms of asceticism. A thoughtless jibe from Kingsley led Cardinal Newman to defend himself by writing the Apologia pro Vita Sua. *Kingsley's popular novels included* Westward Ho! *and* The Water Babies.

Grant, O God, that we may wait patiently, as servants standing before their lord, to know thy will; that we may welcome all truth, under whatever outward forms it may be uttered; that we may bless every good deed, by whomsoever it may be done; that we may rise above all party strife to the contemplation of the eternal Truth and Goodness; through Jesus Christ our Saviour. Amen.

Lift up our hearts, O Christ, above the false shows of things, above laziness and fear, above custom and fashion, up to the everlasting

Truth which is thee thyself; so that we may live joyfully and freely, in the faith that thou art our king and our saviour, our example and our judge; and that, so long as we are loyal to thee, all will be well with us in this world and in all worlds to come, O Jesus Christ our Lord. Amen.

O Christ, give us patience, and faith, and hope as we kneel at the foot of thy cross, and hold fast to it. Teach us by thy cross, that however ill the world may go, the Father so loved us that he spared not thee. Amen.

O God, grant that looking upon the face of the Lord, as into a glass, we may be changed into his likeness, from glory to glory. Take out of us all pride and vanity, boasting and forwardness; and give us the true courage which shows itself by gentleness; the true wisdom which shows itself by simplicity; and the true power which shows itself by modesty.

William Bright (1824–1901)

William Bright was an Oxford professor of church history and a writer of hymns, including 'And now, O Father, mindful of the love that bought us once for all on Calvary's tree'. His volume of Ancient Collects *is the source of many of those felicitous phrases which remain in the memory long after the intercessions are completed.*

Grant us, we beseech thee, O Lord, the aid of thy Holy Spirit, that, whatever by his teaching we know to be our duty, we may by his grace be enabled to perform; through Jesus Christ our Lord.

O almighty God, from whom every good prayer cometh, and who pourest out on all who desire it the spirit of grace and supplication, deliver us, when we draw nigh to thee, from coldness of heart and wanderings of mind, that with steadfast thoughts and kindled affections we may worship thee in spirit and in truth; through Jesus Christ our Lord. Amen.

O God, who hast brought us near to an innumerable company of angels, and to the spirits of just men made perfect: grant us during our earthly pilgrimage to abide in their fellowship, and in our heavenly country to become partakers of their joy; through Jesus Christ our Lord. Amen.

O God, who makest us glad with the weekly remembrance of the glorious resurrection of thy Son our Lord: vouchsafe us this day such a blessing through thy worship, that the days which follow it may be spent in thy favour, through the same Jesus Christ our Lord. Amen.

O God, by whom the meek are guided in judgement, and light riseth up in the darkness for the godly; grant us, in all our doubts and uncertainties, the grace to ask what thou wouldst have us do; that the Spirit of Wisdom may save us from all false choices and that in thy light we may see light, and in thy straight path may not stumble; through Jesus Christ our Lord.

O Lord, without whom our labour is but lost, and with whom the weakest go forth as the mighty; be present to all works in thy Church which are undertaken according to thy will, (especially . . .), and grant to thy labourers a pure intention, patient faith, sufficient success upon earth, and the bliss of serving thee in heaven; through Jesus Christ our Lord. Amen.[4]

O Lord and Saviour Christ, who camest not to strive nor to cry, but to let thy words fall as the drops that water the earth; grant all who contend for the faith once delivered, never to injure it by clamour and impatience; but speaking thy precious truth in love, so to present it that it may be loved, and that thy goodness and thy beauty may be seen in it; who livest and reignest with the Father and the Holy Ghost, ever one God, world without end. Amen.

Brooke Foss Westcott (1825–1901)

Westcott was a pupil at King Edward's School, Birmingham, at the same time as J. B. Lightfoot and E. W. Benson. While he was Regius Professor of Divinity at Cambridge he prepared with F. J. A. Hort what was for a long time the definitive edition of the Greek New Testament. His lectures at Cambridge were turned into his three great commentaries on the Gospel of John, the Epistles of John and the Epistle to the Hebrews. He inspired the foundation of the Cambridge Clergy Training School, now 'Westcott House', and the Cambridge Mission to Delhi. When he was appointed Bishop of Durham he mediated in the coal strike of 1892.

Behold, O Lord God, our strivings after a truer and more abiding order. Give us visions that bring back a lost glory to the earth, and dreams that foreshadow the better order which you have prepared for us. Scatter every excuse of frailty and unworthiness: consecrate us all with a heavenly mission: open to us a clearer prospect of our work. Give us strength according to our day gladly to welcome and gratefully to fulfil it; through Jesus Christ our Lord. Amen.

Glory to thee, O God, the Father, the Maker of the world: Glory be to thee, O God, the Son, the Redeemer of mankind: Glory to thee, O God, the Holy Ghost, the sanctifier of thy people.

O Lord God, in whom we live and move and have our being, open our eyes that we may behold thy fatherly presence ever about us. Draw our hearts to thee with the power of love. Teach us in nothing to be anxious; and when we have done what thou hast given us to do, help us, O God our Saviour, to leave the issue to thy wisdom. Take from us all doubt and distrust. Lift our thoughts up to thee, and make us know that all things are possible to us, in and through thy Son our redeemer, Jesus Christ our Lord. Amen.

Almighty God, who hast sent the spirit of truth unto us to guide us into all truth, so rule our lives by thy power, that we may be truthful in word, deed, and thought. O keep us, most merciful Saviour, with thy gracious protection, that no fear or hope may ever make us false in act or speech. Cast out from us whatsoever loveth or maketh a lie, and bring us all to the perfect freedom of thy truth; through Jesus Christ our Lord. Amen.

John Ellerton (1826–93)

Although he never rose to any position higher than that of incumbent of a Church of England parish, John Ellerton will be remembered for the many hymns he wrote or translated, including 'Saviour, again to thy dear name we raise' and 'O Strength and Stay, upholding all creation'. 'The day thou gavest' sums up the amazing spread of Christian prayer as the Christian Church continues to grow at a fantastic rate worldwide.

The day thou gavest, Lord, is ended,
the darkness falls at thy behest;
to thee our morning hymns ascended,
thy praise shall sanctify our rest.

We thank thee that thy Church unsleeping,
while earth rolls onward into light,
through all the world her watch is keeping,
and rests not now by day or night.

As o'er each continent and island
the dawn leads on another day,
the voice of prayer is never silent,
nor dies the strain of praise away.

The sun that bids us rest is waking
our brethren 'neath the western sky,
and hour by hour fresh lips are making
thy wondrous doings heard on high.

So be it, Lord; thy throne shall never,
like earth's proud empires, pass away;
thy kingdom stands, and grows for ever,
till all thy creatures own thy sway.

George Ridding (1828–1904)

George Ridding was the first bishop of the new diocese of Southwell in Nottinghamshire. His Litany of Remembrance *was first published in 1905. Its challenging words are a fruitful source for self-examination.*

The Southwell Litany

Let us pray. O Lord, open our minds to see ourselves as thou seest us, or even as others see us and we see others, and from all unwillingness to know our infirmities,
save us and help us, **we humbly beseech thee, O Lord.**

From moral weakness of spirit; from timidity; from hesitation; from fear of others and dread of responsibility, strengthen us with the courage to speak the truth in love and self-control; and alike from the weakness of hasty violence and weakness of moral cowardice,
save us and help us, **we humbly beseech thee, O Lord.**

From weakness of judgement; from the indecision that can make no choice and the irresolution that carries no choice into act; and from losing opportunities to serve thee;
save us and help us, **we humbly beseech thee, O Lord.**

From infirmity of purpose; from want of earnest care and interest; from the sluggishness of indolence, and the slackness of indifference; and from all spiritual deadness of heart;
save us and help us, **we humbly beseech thee, O Lord.**

From dullness of conscience; from feeble sense of duty; from thoughtless disregard of consequences to others; from a low idea of the obligations of our Christian calling; and from all half-heartedness in our service for thee;
save us and help us, **we humbly beseech thee, O Lord.**

From weariness in continuing struggles; from despondency in failure and disappointment; from overburdened sense of unworthiness; from morbid fancies of imaginary back-slidings; raise us to a lively hope and trust in thy presence and mercy, in the power of faith and prayer; and from all exaggerated fears and vexations,
save us and help us, **we humbly beseech thee, O Lord.**

From self-conceit and vanity and boasting; from delight in supposed success and superiority, raise us to the modesty and humility of true sense and taste and reality; and from all the harms and hindrances of offensive manners and self-assertion,
save us and help us, **we humbly beseech thee, O Lord.**

From affectation and untruth, conscious or unconscious; from pretence and acting a part which is hypocrisy; from impulsive self-adaptation to the moment in unreality to please persons or make circumstances easy, strengthen us to simplicity; and from all false appearances,
save us and help us, **we humbly beseech thee, O Lord.**

From love of flattery; from over-ready belief in praise; from dislike of criticism; from the comfort of self-deception in persuading ourselves that others think better than the truth of us,
save us and help us, **we humbly beseech thee, O Lord.**

From all love of display and sacrifice to popularity; from thought of ourselves and forgetfulness of thee in our worship; hold our minds in

spiritual reverence; and in all our words and works from all self-glorification,
save us and help us, **we humbly beseech thee, O Lord.**

From pride and self-will; from desire to have our own way in all things; from overweening love of our own ideas and blindness to the value of others; from resentment against opposition and contempt for the claims of others; enlarge the generosity of our hearts and enlighten the fairness of our judgements; and from all selfish arbitrariness of temper,
save us and help us, **we humbly beseech thee, O Lord.**

From all jealousy, whether of equals or superiors; from grudging others success; from impatience of submission and eagerness for authority; give us the spirit of brotherhood to share loyally with fellow-workers in all true proportions; and from all insubordination to law, order and authority,
save us and help us, **we humbly beseech thee, O Lord.**

From all hasty utterances of impatience; from the retort of irritation and the taunt of sarcasm; from all infirmity of temper in provoking or being provoked; from love of unkind gossip, and from all idle words that may do hurt,
save us and help us, **we humbly beseech thee, O Lord.**

In all times of temptation to follow pleasure, to leave duty for amusement, to indulge in distraction and dissipation, in dishonesty and debt, to degrade our high calling and forget our Christian vows, and in all times of frailty in our flesh,
save us and help us, **we humbly beseech thee, O Lord.**

In all times of ignorance and perplexity as to what is right and best to do, direct us, O Lord, with wisdom to judge aright, order our ways and overrule our circumstances as thou canst in thy good Providence; and in our mistakes and misunderstandings,
save us and help us, **we humbly beseech thee, O Lord.**

In times of doubts and questionings, when our belief is perplexed by new learning, new thought, when our faith is strained by creeds, by doctrines, by mysteries beyond our understanding, give us the faithfulness of learners and the courage of believers in thee; alike from

stubborn rejection of new revelations, and from hasty assurance that we are wiser than our forefathers,
save us and help us, **we humbly beseech thee, O Lord.**

From strife and partisanship and division among thy people, from magnifying our certainties to condemn all differences, from all arrogance in our dealings with others,
save us and help us, **we humbly beseech thee, O Lord.**

Give us knowledge of ourselves, our powers and weaknesses, our spirit, our sympathy, our imagination, our knowledge, our truth; teach us by the standard of thy Word, by the judgements of others, by examinations of ourselves; give us earnest desire to strengthen ourselves continually by study, by diligence, by prayer and meditation; and from all fancies, delusions, and prejudices of habit, or temper, or society,
save us and help us, **we humbly beseech thee, O Lord.**

Give us true knowledge of other people in their differences from us and in their likenesses to us, that we may deal with their real selves, measuring their feelings by our own, but patiently considering their varied lives and thoughts and circumstances; and in all our relations to them, from false judgements of our own, from misplaced trust and distrust, from misplaced giving and refusing, from misplaced praise and rebuke,
save us and help us, **we humbly beseech thee, O Lord.**

Chiefly, O Lord, we beseech thee, give us knowledge of thee, to see thee in all thy works, always to feel thy presence near, to hear and know thy call. May thy Spirit be our spirit, our words thy words, and thy will our will, and in all shortcomings and infirmities may we have sure faith in thee,
save us and help us, **we humbly beseech thee, O Lord.**

Finally, O Lord, we humbly beseech thee, blot out our past transgressions, heal the evils of our past negligences and ignorances, make us amend our past mistakes and misunderstandings; uplift our hearts to new love, new energy and devotion, that we may be unburdened from the grief and shame of past faithlessness to go forth in thy strength to persevere through success and failure, through good report and evil report, even to the end; and in all time of our tribulation, in all time of our prosperity,
save us and help us, **we humbly beseech thee, O Lord.**[5]

Edward White Benson (1829–96)

Edward White Benson was born in Birmingham and educated at King Edward's School, where he became a lifelong friend of J. B. Lightfoot. He was an assistant master at Rugby School, then the first head of the new Wellington College. He was made Bishop of Truro, where he was the first to introduce the Service of Nine Lessons and Carols. Later he became Archbishop of Canterbury. His most inspired action was to revive the defunct Court of the Archbishop of Canterbury, so that the saintly Bishop King of Lincoln, who had been accused of illegal Anglo-Catholic ceremonial, could be declared not guilty without having to go before a secular court.

O God, who on the day of Pentecost didst send down tongues of fire on the heads of thy holy Apostles, to teach them and lead them unto all truth, giving them boldness with fervent zeal to preach the Gospel to all nations; raise up, we pray thee, thy power and come among thy people, and with great might succour us. Bless, O Lord, all thy servants everywhere; give the Holy Spirit to all who teach and all who learn; send forth men and women full of faith and of the Holy Ghost, mighty in the Scriptures, and able ministers of the New Testament. Let thy ministers be examples to their flock in word, in conversation, in charity, in spirit, in faith, in purity; workmen that need not be ashamed, rightly dividing the word of truth, prepared and willing to endure affliction, to do the work of evangelists, and to make full proof of their ministry; and upon the seed of thy Word sown by them pour down, O Lord, we beseech thee, the continual dew of thy heavenly blessing, that it may take root downwards, and bear fruit upwards, to thy honour and glory, and to a joyful ingathering of a spiritual harvest of souls at the great day of harvest, to glorify for ever thy holy Name; through Jesus Christ our Lord. Amen.

O Lord we beseech thee to raise up for the work of the ministry faithful and able men, counting it all joy to spend and be spent for the sake of thy dear Son, and for the souls for which he shed his most precious blood upon the cross, and we pray thee to fit them for their holy function by thy bountiful grace and heavenly benediction; through Jesus Christ our Lord, who liveth and reigneth with thee and the Holy Ghost, one God, world without end. Amen.

Written on the death of his young son Martin in 1877

O God, to me who am left to mourn his departure, grant that I may not sorrow as one without hope for my beloved who sleeps in you; but, as always remembering his courage, and the love that united us on earth, I may begin again with new courage to serve you more fervently who are the only source of true love and true fortitude; that when I have passed a few more days in this valley of tears and this shadow of death, supported by your rod and staff, I may see him face to face, in those pastures and beside those waters of comfort where I believe he already walks with you. O Shepherd of the sheep, have pity on this darkened soul of mine.

Christina Rossetti (1830–94)

Christina Rossetti was the daughter of a poet, Gabriele Rossetti, and the sister of another, Dante Gabriel Rossetti. Although she was educated at home and was an invalid most of her life, her poetry is technically brilliant, with wide-ranging emotional and imaginative scope. She was a high Anglican, and broke off her engagement when her fiancé returned to the Roman Catholic faith. The Christmas carols 'In the bleak midwinter' and 'Love came down at Christmas' are the best-known items in her extensive output.

Lord Jesus, merciful and patient, grant us grace, I beseech thee, ever to teach in a teachable spirit; learning along with those we teach, and learning from them whenever thou so pleasest. Word of God, speak to us, what thou wilt. Wisdom of God, instruct us, instruct by us, if and whom thou wilt. Eternal truth, reveal thyself to us, reveal thyself by us, in whatsoever measure thou wilt; that we and they may all be taught by God.

O God the Holy Ghost who art light unto thine elect, evermore enlighten us. Thou who art fire of love, evermore enkindle us. Thou who art lord and giver of life, evermore live in us. Thou who bestowest sevenfold grace, evermore replenish us. As the wind is thy symbol, so forward our goings. As the dove, so launch us heavenwards. As water, so purify our spirits. As a cloud, so abate our temptations. As dew, so revive our languor. As fire, so purge out our dross.

O Lord Jesus Christ, thou art as the shadow of a mighty rock in a weary land. Thou beholdest thy weak creatures weary of labour, weary of pleasure, weary of hope deferred, weary of self; in thy abundant compassion and fellow-feeling with us, and unutterable tenderness, bring us, we pray, to thy eternal rest for ever and ever. Amen.

O merciful Lord Jesus, forget not me, as I have forgotten thee.

I Have No Wit, No Words, No Tears

I have no wit, no words, no tears;
My heart within me like a stone
Is numbed too much for hopes or fears.
Look right, look left, I dwell alone;
I lift mine eyes, but dimmed with grief
No everlasting hills I see;
My life is in the falling leaf.
O Jesus, quicken me.
My life is like a faded leaf
My harvest dwindled to a husk:
Truly my life is void and brief
And tedious in the barren dusk:
My life is like a frozen thing,
No bud nor greenness can I see,
Yet rise it shall – the sap of Spring,
O Jesus, rise in me.

Good Friday

Am I a stone and not a sheep
That I can stand, O Christ, beneath thy cross,
To number drop by drop thy blood's slow loss,
And yet not weep?
Not so those women loved
Who with exceeding grief lamented thee;
Not so fallen Peter weeping bitterly;
Not so the thief was moved;
Not so the sun and moon
Which hid their faces in a starless sky,

A horror of great darkness at broad noon
I, only I.
Yet give not o'er,
But seek thy sheep, true shepherd of the flock,
Greater than Moses, turn and look once more
And smite a rock.

Lord Salisbury (1830–1903)

Robert Cecil was three times Prime Minister in the nineteenth century and steered the British Government through some difficult times. He opposed the disestablishment of the Irish Church, and took a position on the Public Worship Regulation Act which brought him into conflict with members of his own party.

O God, the God of all righteousness mercy and love, give us all grace and strength to conceive and execute whatever may be for thine honour and the welfare of the nation, that we may become at last, through the merits and intercession of our common redeemer, a great and a happy, because a wise and understanding people; to thy honour and glory. Amen.

Eugène Bersier (1831–89)

Calvinists have for a long time been a significant minority in French Christianity. Wars between Catholics and Protestants, climaxing in the massacre of the latter on St Bartholomew's Day in 1572, were resolved by the tolerance shown in the Edict of Nantes of 1598. But in 1685 the edict was revoked, and many Huguenots (as they were nicknamed) fled the country. The Revd Eugène Bersier was a minister in the French Reformed Church who served at l'Eglise de l'Etoile in Paris.

Father, you are love, and you see all the suffering, injustice and misery, which reign in this world. Have pity, we implore you, on the work of your hands. Look mercifully on the poor, the oppressed, and all who are heavy laden with error, labour and sorrow. Fill our hearts with deep compassion for those who suffer, and hasten the coming of your kingdom of justice and truth, through Jesus Christ our Lord. Amen.

O God, from whom we have received life and all earthly blessings, vouchsafe to give unto us each day what we need. Give unto all of us strength to perform faithfully our appointed tasks; bless the work of our hands and of our minds. Grant that we may ever serve you, in sickness and in health, in necessity and in abundance; sanctify our joys and our trials, and give us grace to seek first your kingdom and its righteousness, in the sure and certain faith that all else shall be added unto us through Jesus Christ, your Son, our Lord and Saviour. Amen.

O God, you know our hearts, and you see our temptations and struggles. Have pity on us, deliver us from the sins which make war upon our souls. You are all-powerful, and we are weak and erring. Faithful God, our trust is in you. Deliver us from the bondage of evil, and grant that we may hereafter be your devoted servants, serving you in the freedom of holy love; for Jesus Christ's sake. Amen.

Charles George Gordon (1833–85)

Every age needs its heroes, but although General 'Chinese' Gordon was admired by the Victorians for his great courage, especially in his last campaign in the Sudan, he was what we today would call a 'religious nutter'. Having volunteered to take a colleague's place in an unpopular posting as military engineer on the remote Seychelles Islands, he became convinced that they were the site of the biblical Garden of Eden, and that the coco-de-mer was the forbidden fruit. He published these conclusions later in an article, during which he also argued that the site of Calvary was outside the present walls of Jerusalem. The Garden Tomb was later opened up near to 'Gordon's Calvary'.

O Lord God, grant us always, whatever the world may say, to content ourselves with what thou wilt say, and to care only for thine approval, which will outweigh all world's; for Jesus Christ's sake.

Charles Haddon Spurgeon (1834–92)

Spurgeon was descended from generations of Independent ministers, but experienced a personal conversion, became a Baptist, and was given the appointment of Baptist pastor at Waterbeach at the age of seventeen. When he was twenty he went to Southwark, where his sermons attracted so many people that a new Metropolitan Tabernacle had to be built for him at Newington Causeway. He also founded a college to train others in preaching. His life was not without controversy, but his sermons have been read by many for their shrewd common sense and humorous choice of illustrations.

New Year

O sweet Lord Jesus, thou art the present portion of thy people, favour us this year with such a sense of thy preciousness, that from its first to its last day we may be glad and rejoice in thee. Let January open with joy in the Lord, and December close with gladness in Jesus.[6]

L ord, accept me; I here present myself, praying to live only in thee and to thee. Let me be as the bullock which stands between the plough and the altar, to work or to be sacrificed; and let my motto be, 'Ready for either'.[7]

O my Saviour, let me not fall by little and little, or think myself able to bear the indulgence of any known sin because it seems so insignificant. Keep me from sinful beginnings, lest they lead me on to sorrowful endings.

T hou glorious Bridegroom of our hearts,
Thy present smile a heaven imparts:
Oh, lift the veil, if veil there be,
Let every saint thy beauties see![8]

On a paper found in his desk when he died

N o cross, no crown; no loss, no gain;
They, too, must suffer who would reign.
He best can part with life without a sigh,
Whose daily living is to daily die.
Youth pleads for age, age pleads for rest,
Who pleads for heaven will plead the best.

Frances Ridley Havergal (1836–79)

Frances was the daughter of an Anglican clergyman who was an eminent church musician and composer, as well as a powerful preacher. She herself was fluent in several languages, was an accomplished pianist and composer, and had a prodigious memory. But her intellect stood in the way of her conversion until at last she gave up her soul to the Saviour. She then became busy with evangelism, good works and singing. She also wrote poetry: 'Writing is praying with me,' she said. Still there was a further act of consecration which she needed to make, after which she felt the assurance that God had accepted her. Her best-known hymn and her commentary on it entitled Kept for the Master's Use, *reiterate this connection between offering and acceptance which she found in her own relationship with God, and which has influenced that of countless others who have sung it and come to deeper commitment by doing so.*

Take my life, and let it be
Consecrated, Lord, to thee;
Take my moments and my days,
Let them flow in ceaseless praise.
Take my hands, and let them move
At the impulse of thy love.
Take my feet, and let them be
Swift and beautiful for thee.
Take my voice, and let me sing
Always, only, for my King.
Take my lips, and let them be
Filled with messages from thee.
Take my silver and my gold,
Not a mite would I withhold.
Take my intellect, and use
Every power as thou shalt choose.
Take my will, and make it thine;
It shall be no longer mine.
Take my heart, it is thine own;
It shall be thy royal throne.
Take my love: my Lord, I pour
At thy feet its treasure store.
Take myself, and I will be,
Ever, only, all for thee.

Handley Carr Glyn Moule (1841–1920)

Handley Moule, the Dean of Trinity College, Cambridge, resigned that post to become the first Principal of Ridley Hall, the Evangelical theological college there, and then succeeded B. F. Westcott as Bishop of Durham. Evangelicals had emphasized that salvation is a free gift of God's grace, but then had been disheartened by their failure in the struggle to achieve sanctification of life. The annual Keswick Conventions were teaching that holiness, too, is a free gift which need only be accepted without any need for struggle. Moule, having at first opposed it, became the scholarly spokesman for this new Holiness Movement, and while there were obvious dangers in the teaching (which were attacked by another prominent Evangelical, Bishop Ryle of Liverpool), Moule was aware of these and carefully compared the words of Scripture with his own spiritual experience, especially in his Commentary on Romans.

Heavenly Father, receive our evening sacrifice of praise, and confession, and prayer, we beseech thee. We thank thee for all the known and unknown mercies of another day, for all the blessings of this life, for all the means of grace, for all the riches of thy salvation, and for the hope of glory, that blessed hope, the coming of our Lord Jesus Christ and our gathering together unto him. We are one day nearer to that day. Teach us to live every day as those whose citizenship is in heaven, and who are looking from thence for a Saviour, the Lord Jesus Christ. Amen.

Merciful Father, we commend to thee the worship and ordinances of this day. Bless all our souls, keep our hearts and thoughts in thy house of prayer. Speak to us through thy holy Word, which liveth and abideth for ever. Pour the continual dew of thy blessing on all thy ministers; for the sake of Jesus Christ our Lord. Amen.

Palm Sunday

As on this day we keep the special memory of our Redeemer's entry into the city, so grant, O Lord, that now and ever he may triumph in our hearts. Let the king of grace and glory enter in, and let us lay ourselves and all we are in full joyful homage before him; through the same Jesus Christ our Lord.

The blessing of the Lord rest and remain upon all his people, in every land and of every tongue;

The Lord meet in mercy all who seek him;
The Lord comfort all who suffer and mourn;
The Lord hasten his coming, and give us his people peace by all means.

William H. M. H. Aitken (1841–1927)

The Revd William Hay Macdowell Hunter Aitken was a successful evangel-
ist, and visited the United States and Canada to conduct missions. From
1900 he was a Canon Residentiary of Norwich Cathedral.

O Lord, take our minds and think through them; take our lips and
speak through them; take our lives and live out your life; take our
hearts and set them on fire with love for thee; and guide us ever by thy
Holy Spirit, through Jesus Christ our Lord. Amen.[9]

John Wordsworth (1843–1911)

John Wordsworth was the son of Christopher Wordsworth, the hymn-writer
and Bishop of Lincoln, and thus the great nephew of the poet William
Wordsworth. John was a brilliant Latin scholar and spent much of his life
producing an accurate edition of the Vulgate translation of the Bible. He
was a friend of Archbishop Benson, and when he was made Bishop of
Salisbury he laboured to bring about reunion between the Church
of England and the Swedish Lutheran Church, and also the Old Catholic
Church which had broken with Rome over the issue of Papal infallibility.

O eternal Lord God, who holdest all souls in life: we beseech thee to
shed forth upon thy whole church in paradise and on earth the bright
beams of thy light and heavenly comfort; and grant that we, following the
good example of those who have served thee here and are at rest, may at
the last enter with them into the fullness of thine unending joy; through
Jesus Christ our Lord. Amen.

Henry Scott Holland (1847–1918)

Henry Scott Holland was a canon of St Paul's Cathedral in London from
1884 until 1910, when he went to Oxford to become Regius Professor of
Divinity. He wrote the first article, on 'Faith', for the liberal Anglo-Catholic
collection Lux Mundi, *and was a leading advocate of the Christian Social*

Union. He was the author of the hymn 'Judge eternal, throned in splen-
dour', and of the famous meditation often quoted at funerals, 'Death is
nothing at all . . .' which is said to have been left as a letter for his wife
to read when he had died.

Our God, may we lay hold of thy cross, as of a staff that can stand
unshaken when the floods run high. It is this world and not another,
this world with all its miseries – its ruin and its sin – that thou hast entered
to redeem by thine agony and bloody sweat. Amen.

O Lord Jesus, thou, whom we, by our sins, have robbed of that good
gift of joy, which might have been thine! Thou, whom we have
forbidden to partake of flesh and blood, except at the bitter cost of that
agony and blood-sweat! O holy, merciful, all-forgiving redeemer, teach us
more worthily to repent of the terror and horror of our fall, by the memory
of that innocent gladness with which we should have gone with thee to
the altar of God, to offer there, no sorrow-stricken, death-stained, sin-worn
sacrifice, but the unshrinking homage of a spotless heart!

St Augustine's College, Canterbury, *Manual of Offices* (1848)

St Augustine's College was formed in 1848 to train missionaries. The
memorial boards in the chapel show how many of those who trained there
lost their lives in the first few years after going abroad, from sickness or
in local rebellions.

O Lord our Saviour, who hast warned us that thou wilt require much
from those to whom much is given; grant that we, whose lot is cast
in so goodly a heritage, may strive together the more abundantly, by prayer,
by giving, and by all other appointed means, to extend to others what we
so richly enjoy; and as we have entered into the labours of others, so to
labour that others may enter into ours, to the fulfilment of thy holy will,
and the salvation of the whole human race; through Jesus Christ our Lord.
Amen.

Oscar Wilde (1854–1900)

Oscar Wilde was born in Dublin and was a brilliant classical scholar at
Trinity College there and at Oxford. He was attracted by the romanticism
of the Pre-Raphaelite painters, and critical of hypocritical morality. The

Picture of Dorian Gray, *and a succession of brilliant plays culminating in* The Importance of Being Earnest *dissected the humbug in society with an affectionate and witty scalpel. He was happily married and loved his two sons, and yet he was convicted of homosexuality. To read 'The Ballad of Reading Gaol' is to doubt whether imprisonment, with its corrosive effect on the soul, is appropriate for more than a handful of criminals. The sincerity of the prayer in 'E Tenebris' may also make us ashamed of the pain we inflict on those who are different.*

E Tenebris

Come down O Christ, and help me! reach thy hand,
For I am drowning in a stormier sea
Than Simon on thy lake of Galilee:
The wine of life is spilt upon the sand,
My heart is as some famine murdered land
Whence all good things have perished utterly,
And well I know my soul in Hell must lie
If I this night before God's throne should stand.
'He sleeps perchance, or rideth to the chase,
Like Baal, when his prophets howled that name
From morn to night on Carmel's smitten height.'
Nay, peace, I shall behold, before the night,
The feet of brass, the robe more white than flame,
The wounded hands, the weary human face.

The Anglo-Catholic Revival

With slovenly standards in church life and the challenges to faith from scientific discoveries in the mid-nineteenth century, a need for church reform was felt. Historical studies and the romantic movement had made Christians aware of what they regarded as an ideal strength and purity of church life in the early centuries and the Middle Ages. There were too many Anglican bishops in Ireland, claiming an income and a seat in the House of Lords when there were few Anglicans living in their dioceses, so the Government planned to suppress ten Irish bishoprics. This was seen as unjustified interference from the State by those who gave high importance to the independence of the Church as a society created by God – the High Churchmen. Centred mostly in Oxford, they started what became known as the Oxford Movement.

Keble, Newman and Pusey were regarded as leaders, and they published the writings of the early Fathers and the Caroline divines. Although Henry Manning, John Henry Newman and Frederick Faber were received into the Roman Catholic Church, many Anglo-Catholics remained in the Church of England, and their emphasis on personal prayer and holiness influenced all wings of that church and many Nonconformists also. At the beginning of the movement, the dignity of their simple worship, with candles on the altar and robed choirs, shocked many, and they were attacked and persecuted. In the next generation, this turned into the ritualist movement, with attempts to reconstruct what they mistakenly regarded as medieval English traditions of worship. Nevertheless, the rediscovery by the Oxford Movement of dignified ceremonial, of earlier writings on prayer, and of the value of monks and nuns in the religious life even of Protestant churches, has left church life irreversibly changed throughout the world.

John Keble (1792–1866)

John Keble became a Fellow at Oxford when he was only nineteen, but resigned twelve years later to become his father's curate in a country parish among the Cotswold Hills. There he wrote the series of poems called The Christian Year, *which became immensely popular and influential during the Victorian period. In 1831 he was appointed Professor of Poetry at Oxford. Keble's University sermon in 1833 on 'National Apostasy' is regarded as the beginning of the Oxford Movement. He defended belief in the Real Presence of Jesus in the Holy Communion, and encouraged the clergy to take a high view of their duties, including praying for their parishioners by daily use of Morning and Evening Prayer. Keble's hymns still in regular use include 'New every morning is the love' and 'Blest are the pure in heart'.*

'In choirs and places where they sing, here followeth the anthem'

Lord, make my heart a place where angels sing!
For surely thoughts low-breathed by thee
Are angels gliding near on noiseless wing;
And where a home they see
Swept clean, and garnished with adoring joy,
They enter in and dwell,
And teach that heart to swell
With heavenly melody, their own untired employ.

From 'New Every Morning'

Only, O Lord, in thy dear love
Fit us for perfect rest above;
And help us, this and every day
To live more nearly as we pray.

Evening Hymn

Sun of my soul, thou Saviour dear,
It is not night if thou be near.
O may no earth-born cloud arise
To hide thee from thy servant's eyes.

When the soft dews of kindly sleep
My wearied eyelids gently steep,

Be my last thought, how sweet to rest
For ever on my Saviour's breast.

Abide with me from morn till eve,
For without thee I cannot live;
Abide with me when night is nigh,
For without thee I dare not die.

If some poor wand'ring child of thine
Have spurned to-day the voice divine,
Now, Lord, the gracious work begin;
Let him no more lie down in sin.

Watch by the sick; enrich the poor
With blessings from thy boundless store;
Be every mourner's sleep to-night
Like infant's slumbers, pure and light.

Come near and bless us when we wake,
Ere through the world our way we take;
Till in the ocean of thy love
We lose ourselves in heaven above.

Vouchsafe, we pray, almighty God, to grant to the whole Christian people unity, peace and true concord, both visible and invisible, when you will and as you will; through Jesus Christ our Lord. Amen.[1]

Edward Bouverie Pusey (1800–1882)

Pusey spent his entire life from the age of twenty-eight as Professor of Hebrew and Canon of Christ Church in Oxford. He contributed learned papers on the discipline of fasting, and on baptismal regeneration, to the series of 'Tracts for the Times' which gave rise to the Tractarian Movement. When Newman joined the Roman Catholic Church, Pusey became the leader of the Anglo-Catholics or Puseyites. He preached and wrote extensively on the Church of England as part of the worldwide catholic Church, and on the Real Presence of Christ in the Holy Communion. But his most profound contribution to the life of prayer in his time was probably his involvement in and encouragement of the translation of the Fathers of the early Church, and the revival of monasticism and sacramental confession.

Good Jesu, too late have I loved thee, nor ever yet have I wholly followed thee; make me now at last wholly to love thee, and out of the fullness of thine infinite love give me all the love I might have had, had I always loved thee. O dearest Lord, too late have I loved thee, too late have I loved thee, too late is it always, not always to have loved thee wholly. Now, too, I cannot love thee as I would. O dearest Lord, who art love, give me of thine own love, that therewith I may wholly love thee.

Christmas

Good Jesu, born as at this time, a little child for love of us; be thou born in me, that I may be a little child in love of thee; and hang on thy love as on my mother's bosom, trustfully, lovingly, peacefully; hushing all my cares in love of thee.

During Holy Week

Make me cheerful under every cross, for love of thy cross; take from me all which displeases thee, or hinders thy love in me, that I may deeply love thee. Melt me with thy love, that I may be all love, and with my whole being love thee.

Good Jesu, who gavest thyself for me, give me of the fullness of thy love, that for all thy love, with thy love, I may love thee.

At Pentecost

Good Jesu, fountain of love: fill me with thy love, absorb me into thy love, compass me with thy love, that I may see all things in the light of thy love, receive all things as tokens of thy love, speak of all things in words breathing of thy love, win through thy love others to thy love, be kindled, day by day, with a new glow of thy love, until I be fitted to enter into thine everlasting love, to adore thy love and love to adore thee, my God and my all. Even so, come, Lord Jesu!

Grant Lord, that I may not, for one moment, admit willingly into my soul any thought contrary to thy love.

Most loving Lord, give me a childlike love of thee, which may cast out all fear. Amen.

John Henry Newman (1801–90)

Newman was a Fellow of Oriel College in Oxford, and vicar of St Mary's Church there. He was preparing a study of the Church in the fourth century when he made a tour of southern Europe and met vigorous Roman Catholicism. On his return he became the leader of the Oxford Movement, seeking to restore to the Church of England an awareness that it is part of a worldwide Church which is continuous with that of the first few centuries. His Parochial and Plain Sermons *in St Mary's made a deep impression with their simple but profound spirituality. He wrote many of the 'Tracts for the Times', arguing for a middle way between 'Popery and Dissent'. They encountered so much opposition that he began to doubt his position in the Church of England and gradually withdrew to the village of Littlemore, where in 1845 he was received into the Roman Catholic Church.*

His Essay on the Development of Christian Doctrine, *published at this time, together with* The Grammar of Assent *in 1870, showed how theology can change while remaining true to its origins, and developed his psychology of faith. The* Apologia pro Vita Sua *was a frank autobiography written as a response to a controversy with Charles Kingsley. He established the Birmingham Oratory, and was for a while rector of Dublin University, writing the seminal* Idea of a University. *But although he was made a Cardinal, his relationship with Rome was almost as strained as had been his place in the Church of England, perhaps because he was at heart a romantic poet. His hymn 'Lead, kindly light' and the visionary poem 'The Dream of Gerontius' have moved generations of Christians of all denominations. 'The Dream of Gerontius' was written in 1865, when he thought he was dying.*

Lead, kindly light, amid the encircling gloom,
  Lead thou me on;
The night is dark, and I am far from home;
Lead thou me on.
Keep thou my feet; I do not ask to see
The distant scene: one step enough for me.

I was not ever thus, nor prayed that thou
Shouldst lead me on;
I loved to choose and see my path; but now
Lead thou me on.
I loved the garish day, and, spite of fears,
Pride ruled my will: remember not past years.

So long thy power hath blest me, sure it still
Will lead me on
O'er moor and fen, o'er crag and torrent, till
The night is gone,
And with the morn those angel faces smile
Which I have loved long since, and lost awhile.

D ear Jesus, help me to spread your fragrance everywhere I go. Flood
my soul with your spirit and life. Penetrate and possess my whole
being so utterly that my life may only be a radiance of yours.

Adapted

A prayer about old age

O Lord, support us all the day long of this troublous life, until the
shades lengthen, and the evening comes, the busy world is hushed,
the fever of life is over, and our work is done. Then Lord in thy mercy
grant us safe lodging, a holy rest, and peace at the last, through Jesus
Christ our Lord. Amen.[2]

O Lord, bright as is the sun, and the sky, and the clouds; green as are
the leaves and the fields; sweet as is the singing of the birds; we
know that they are not all, and we will not take up with a part for the
whole. They proceed from a centre of love and goodness, which is thee
thyself; but they are not thy fulness; they speak of heaven, but they are
not heaven; they are but as stray beams and dim reflections of thine image;
they are but the crumbs from the table. Shine forth, O Lord, as when on
thy Nativity thy angels visited the shepherds; let thy glory blossom forth
as bloom and foliage on the trees.[3]

S tay with me, and then I shall begin to shine as thou shinest: so to shine
as to be a light to others. The light, O Jesus, will be all from thee. None
of it will be mine. No merit to me. It will be thou who shinest through
me upon others. O let me thus praise thee, in the way which thou dost
love best, by shining on all those around me. Give light to them as well
as to me; light them with me, through me. Teach me to show forth thy
praise, thy truth, thy will. Make me preach thee without preaching – not
by words, but by my example and by the catching force, the sympathetic
influence, of what I do – by my visible resemblance to thy saints, and the
evident fulness of the love which my heart bears to thee.

Gerontius

J esu, Maria – I am near to death,
     And thou art calling me; I know it now.
Not by the token of this faltering breath,
This chill at heart, this dampness on my brow, –
(Jesu, have mercy! Mary, pray for me!)
'Tis this new feeling, never felt before,
(Be with me, Lord, in my extremity!)
That I am going, that I am no more.
'Tis this strange innermost abandonment,
(Lover of souls! great God! I look to thee,)
This emptying out of each constituent
And natural force, by which I come to be . . .

F irmly I believe and truly
     God is Three, and God is One;
And I next acknowledge duly
Manhood taken by the Son.

And I trust and hope most fully
In that manhood crucified;
And each thought and deed unruly
Do to death, as he has died.

Simply to his grace and wholly
Light and life and strength belong,
And I love, supremely, solely,
Him the holy, Him the strong . . .

First Choir of Angelicals

P raise to the Holiest in the height,
     And in the depth be praise:
In all His words most wonderful;
Most sure in all His ways! . . .

Richard Hurrell Froude (1803–36)

A close friend of Newman's, Froude too was a Fellow of Oriel College, Oxford. They travelled in Europe together, and Froude collaborated with Newman and Keble in the early stages of the Tractarian Movement. When he died tragically young of consumption, Newman contributed a preface to his posthumously published works. These contained extracts from his diary, revealing that he had been punishing his body severely as part of his prayer. This, and his devotion to the Virgin Mary, advocacy of clerical celibacy and other unguarded remarks led to the beginning of the storm of opposition to the Tractarians which broke Newman's heart.

Save us, O Lord, from the snares of a double mind. Deliver us from all cowardly neutralities. Make us to go in the paths of thy commandments, and to trust for our defence in thy mighty arm alone; through Jesus Christ our Lord.

Richard Chenevix Trench (1807–86)

R. C. Trench was Professor of Divinity at King's College, London, then Dean of Westminster before being appointed Archbishop of Dublin. He opposed Prime Minister Gladstone's proposals to disestablish the Irish Church. His Notes on the Parables *and* Notes on the Miracles *stimulated a renewed interest in the Gospels, and he wrote many volumes of sermons and poetry.*

If there had anywhere appeared in space
Another place of refuge, where to flee,
Our hearts had taken refuge in that place,
And not with thee.

For we against creation's bars had beat
Like prisoned eagles, through great worlds had sought
Though but a foot of ground to plant our feet,
Where thou wert not.

And only when we found in earth and air,
In heaven or hell, that such might nowhere be –
That we could not flee from thee anywhere,
We fled to thee.

Prayer

Lord, what a change within us one short hour
Spent in thy presence will prevail to make!
What heavy burdens from our bosoms take;
What parched grounds refresh as with a shower.
We kneel – and all around us seems to lower,
We rise – and all, the distant and the near,
Stands forth in sunny outline brave and clear;
We kneel: how weak! – we rise: how full of power!
Why, therefore, should we do ourselves this wrong,
Or others – that we are not always strong?
That we are ever overborne with care;
That we should ever weak or heartless be,
Anxious or troubled, while with us is prayer,
And joy, and strength, and courage, are with thee?

John Mason Neale (1818–66)

*While still an undergraduate, J. M. Neale founded the Cambridge Camden
Society for the study of church art and architecture. It later changed its
name to the Ecclesiological Society, and greatly influenced the revival of
the Gothic style as the norm in designing churches. He was four times
rioted against as an alleged ritualist, and his disputes with the church
authorities damaged his health. He gratefully accepted a post as warden
of an almshouse for thirty old people, Sackville College in East Grinstead.
Here he founded the Sisterhood of St Margaret, who would devote their
time to the education of girls and the care of the sick. Although they met
with violent opposition at first, they are now one of the most respected
religious orders in the Church of England. But it is as a hymn-writer that
J. M. Neale is famous. 'O happy band of pilgrims' is his best-known
original composition and 'Jerusalem the golden' is the most familiar of his
many translations – he was fluent in around twenty languages. Burnt out
by hard work, he died while still not fifty years old.*

Oh! give thy servants patience to be still and hear thy will, courage to
venture wholly on thine arm that will not harm, the wisdom that
will never let us stray out of our way, the love that now afflicting knoweth
best when we should rest.

N ot for our land alone we pray,
　　Though that above the rest;
The realms and islands far away,
O let them all be blest.[4]

William John Butler (1818–94)

William Butler's first incumbency was the parish of Wantage, where he remained for thirty-four years, an example of the High Church understanding of what a parish priest should be. He founded a convent there, and the Community of St Mary the Virgin, usually known as the Wantage sisters, grew into one of the largest of the Anglican religious orders. Butler went on to become Dean of Lincoln.

A lmighty and everlasting God, who dost govern all things in heaven and earth, mercifully hear the supplications of us thy servants; and grant to this parish/diocese (and place in which we live) all things needful for its spiritual welfare: schools wherein to bring up the young in thy faith and fear; ministers to labour in this portion of thy vineyard; churches complete in the beauty of holiness. Strengthen and confirm the faithful, protect and guide the children; visit and relieve the sick and afflicted; turn and soften the wicked; rouse the careless; recover the fallen; restore the penitent; remove all hindrances to the advancement of thy truth; and bring all to be of one heart and mind within the fold of thy holy Church; to the honour and glory of thy blessed name, through Jesus Christ our Lord. Amen.

Richard Meux Benson (1824–1915)

R. M. Benson was a disciple of Pusey, and the founder of the Society of St John the Evangelist at Cowley in Oxford (the 'Cowley Fathers'), which was the first men's religious community in the Church of England since the Reformation. He taught the importance of daily meditation on Scripture in the context of the liturgy, and that all prayer is the work of the Holy Spirit, enabling us to share in the prayer of Jesus Christ.

This prayer, for those going on retreat, reminds us of the influence which the growth of the retreat movement has had on the life of prayer in the nineteenth and twentieth centuries, with Christians and those seeking a faith staying for anything from a day to several weeks in a monastery, convent or retreat house to be quiet with the Lord.

O Lord Jesus Christ, who saidst to thy apostles, 'Come ye apart into a desert place and rest awhile,' for there were many coming and going: grant, we pray, to thy servants when they gather together in retreat, that they may rest awhile with thee. May they so seek thee, whom their souls desire to love, that they may both find thee and be found by thee. And grant such love and such wisdom to accompany the words which shall be spoken in thy name, that they may not fall to the ground, but may be helpful in leading us onward through the toils of our pilgrimage to that rest, which remaineth to the people of God; where, nevertheless, they rest not day and night from thy perfect service; who with the Father and the Holy Spirit art alive and reignest, one God, for ever and ever. Amen.

From The Intercessory Manual

Almighty God, look mercifully upon the world, which thou hast re-deemed by the blood of thy dear Son, and incline the hearts of many to offer themselves for the sacred ministry of thy Church; so that by their labours thy light may shine in the darkness, and the coming of thy kingdom may be hastened by the perfecting of thine elect, through the same Jesus Christ our Lord. Amen.

O blessed Saviour, who wast pleased thyself to be reckoned among the craftsmen, bless all those who labour with their hands, that their work may be done for thy honour and rewarded with thy approval; for thine own Name's sake. Amen.

O God, who art everywhere present, look down with thy mercy upon those who are absent from among us. Give thy holy angels charge over them, and grant that they may be kept safe in body, soul and spirit, and presented faultless before the presence of thy glory with exceeding joy, through Jesus Christ our Lord. Amen.

O God of all the nations of the earth, remember the multitudes of the heathen, who, though created in thine image, are perishing in their ignorance; and grant that, by the prayers and labours of thy holy church, they may be delivered from all superstition and unbelief, and brought to worship thee; through him whom thou hast sent to be our salvation, the resurrection and the life of all the faithful, thy Son Jesus Christ our Lord. Amen.

Edward King (1829–1910)

Edward King was Principal of Cuddesdon Theological College, then Bishop of Lincoln, and was recognized as a saint in his own lifetime. His Spiritual Letters convey a sense of holiness without narrowness. An attempt was made to prosecute him for high church practices, but when Archbishop Benson decided in his favour, it put an end to the practice of taking matters of church ritual before the civil courts.

O blessed Jesus, our Lord and our Master, who wast pleased to thirst for our souls, grant that we may not be satisfied with the pleasures of this lower life, but even thirst for the salvation of the souls thou didst die to save, and, above all, to thirst for thee; grant this for thine own Name's sake. Amen.

I thank thee, O God; for the pleasures thou hast given me through my senses: for the glory of the thunder, for the mystery of music, the singing of birds and the laughter of children. I thank thee for the delights of colour, the awe of the sunset, the wild roses in the hedgerows, the smile of friendship. I thank thee for the sweetness of flowers and the scent of hay. Truly, O Lord, the earth is full of thy riches.

Adapted

Henry Parry Liddon (1829–90)

Henry Parry Liddon was a Canon of St Paul's Cathedral, London, and compiled a book entitled Hours of Prayer for Daily Use throughout the Year in 1856, encouraging the clergy to model their private prayer on the seven services of the ancient Breviaries.

O thou true Light, that lightest every man that cometh into the world, do thou in thy mercy touch the hearts and lighten the understanding of all who are preparing for thy service, that they may readily acknowledge and cheerfully obey all that thou wouldst have them believe and practise, to the benefit of thy people and their own salvation; who livest and reignest God for ever and ever. Amen.

O God, who makest thine angels spirits and thy ministers a flame of fire, vouchsafe, we beseech thee, to stir up and confirm the sacred grace in all stewards of thy mysteries, that as ministering spirits they may gather out of thy kingdom all things that offend, and may kindle in the hearts of all, that fire which thou camest to send upon the earth; who with the Father and the Holy Ghost, livest and reignest, ever world without end. Amen.

Francis Paget (1851–1911)

Francis Paget was Bishop of Oxford, and wrote an article on Sacraments in Lux Mundi, *a collection of essays which reinterpreted Tractarian principles in the light of new knowledge.*

Almighty God, from whom all thoughts of truth and peace proceed: kindle, we pray thee, in every heart the true love of peace, and guide with thy pure and peaceable wisdom those who take counsel for the nations of the earth; that in tranquillity thy kingdom may go forward, till the earth is filled with the knowledge of thy love; through Jesus Christ our Lord. Amen.

William Holden Hutton (1860–1930)

Hutton's entire career was divided between a Fellowship at Oxford, where he was a history tutor for twenty-five years; a canonry at Peterborough; and the deanery of Winchester. Dean Hutton wrote this prayer for Winchester Cathedral.

God of our fathers, who of old moved thy servants the founders of this church to build a house of prayer for the offering of eternal praises to thine honour; grant to us, and to all who herein call upon thy holy name from age to age, that by the offering of our lives, and the praises of our lips, we may ever seek the advancement of thy glory and the increase of thy kingdom; through Jesus Christ our Lord. Amen.

Farnham Hostel (1860)

At the time of the Oxford Movement, to be ordained in the Church of England, men had to have a degree from Oxford or Cambridge, though it could be in any subject and no special Christian training was given. The Bishop of London set up, in his residence in Farnham Castle, an early training scheme.

O God, the God of all goodness and grace, who art worthy of a greater love than we can either give or understand, fill our hearts, we beseech thee, with such love towards thee, that nothing may seem too hard for us to do or to suffer in obedience to thy will; and grant that thus loving thee, we may become daily more like unto thee, and finally obtain the crown of life which thou hast promised to those that love thee; through Jesus Christ our Lord. Amen.[5]

Walter Howard Frere (1863–1938)

Dr Frere was the Superior of the Church of England monastic Community of the Resurrection at Mirfield, and then Bishop of Truro. He revised F. Procter's History of the Book of Common Prayer, *thenceforth known as 'Procter and Frere', and he advocated the traditional English, or Sarum, ceremonial rather than the contemporary Roman version. He worked for the reunion of the Church, especially with the Eastern Orthodox, and took part in the Malines Conversations with the Roman Catholic Church.*

M y God, I desire to love thee perfectly, with all my heart which thou madest for thyself, with all my mind which only thou canst satisfy, with all my soul which fain would soar to thee, with all my strength, my feeble strength, which shrinks before so great a task, and yet can choose naught else but spend itself in loving thee. Claim thou my heart, fill thou my mind, uplift my soul, and reinforce my strength, that where I fail thou mayest succeed in me, and make me love thee perfectly.

O God, the Father of all, inspire us, we pray, with such love, truth and equity, that in all our dealings one with another we may remember that we are one family in thee, for the sake of Jesus Christ our Lord. Amen.[6]

Nineteenth-Century Roman Catholicism

Frederick William Faber (1814–63)

Faber was an Evangelical who was influenced by Pusey, Keble, Newman and the other Tractarians while an undergraduate at Oxford. He was ordained in the Church of England, but followed Newman into the Roman Catholic Church, and joined Newman's Oratory in Birmingham. He was sent to London to start a branch house, and the Brompton Oratory became extremely popular, mainly as a result of Father Faber's preaching and his devotional books. His hymns, such as 'Hark! hark, my soul! Angelic songs are swelling', are redolent with the emotionalism of Victorian times, and he had a deep love for God and for people, especially the poor: 'There's a wideness in God's mercy,' he wrote, 'like the wideness of the sea.' Immersed in the spirituality of the French Counter-Reformation, he preached a form of devotion for lay people based on self-denial, the sacraments and the love of God.

My God! my God! and can it be?

My God! my God! and can it be
    That I should sin so lightly now,
And think no more of evil thoughts
    Than of the wind that waves the bough?

I walk the earth with lightsome step,
    Smile at the sunshine, breathe the air,
Do my own will, nor ever heed
    Gethsemane and thy long prayer.

Shall it be always thus, O Lord?
    Wilt thou not work this hour in me

The grace thy Passion merited,
   Hatred of self, and love of thee!

Ever when tempted, make me see,
   Beneath the olives' moon-pierced shade,
My God, alone, outstretched, and bruised,
   And bleeding, on the earth he made;

And make me feel it was my sin,
   As though no other sins there were,
That was to him who bears the world
   A load that he could scarcely bear.

Sweet Saviour, bless us ere we go

S weet Saviour, bless us ere we go;
   Thy word into our minds instil
And make our lukewarm hearts to glow
   With lowly love and fervent will.
Through life's long day and death's dark night;
O gentle Jesus, be our Light.

The day is done, its hours have run,
   And thou hast taken count of all;
The scanty triumphs grace hath won,
   The broken vow, the frequent fall.

Grant us, dear Lord, from evil ways
   True absolution and release;
And bless us, more than in past days,
   With purity and inward peace.

Do more than pardon; give us joy,
   Sweet fear and sober liberty,
And loving hearts without alloy,
   That only long to be like thee.

Labour is sweet, for thou hast toiled,
   And care is light, for thou hast cared;
Let not our works with self be soiled,
   Nor in unsimple ways ensnared.

For all we love, the poor, the sad,
    The sinful, – unto thee we call;
Oh let thy mercy make us glad;
    Thou art our Jesus and our All.

My God, how wonderful thou art

My God, how wonderful thou art,
    Thy majesty how bright,
How beautiful thy mercy-seat,
    In depths of burning light!

How dread are thine eternal years,
    O everlasting Lord,
By prostrate spirits day and night
    Incessantly adored!

How wonderful, how beautiful,
    The sight of thee must be,
Thine endless wisdom, boundless power,
    And aweful purity!

O, how I fear thee, living God,
    With deepest, tenderest fears,
And worship thee with trembling hope,
    And penitential tears!

Yet I may love thee too, O Lord,
    Almighty as thou art,
For thou hast stooped to ask of me
    The love of my poor heart.

No earthly father loves like thee,
    No mother, e'er so mild,
Bears and forbears as thou hast done
    With me thy sinful child.

Father of Jesus, love's reward,
    What rapture will it be
Prostrate before thy throne to lie,
    And gaze and gaze on thee!

Gerard Manley Hopkins (1844–89)

Hopkins was born at Stratford in London, and studied at Balliol College in Oxford, where he was influenced by the Tractarians. He followed New-man into the Roman Catholic Church in 1866, and became a Jesuit. He taught at Stoneyhurst School, then became the professor of Greek at University College, Dublin. An exceptionally sensitive and compassionate poet, he invented what he called 'sprung rhythm', in which the pattern of stresses is more important than the number of syllables. None of his verse was published in his lifetime, but his friend Robert Bridges, whom he had met in Oxford, brought out a full edition in 1918.

Pied Beauty

Glory be to God for dappled things –
For skies of couple-colour as a brinded cow;
For rose-moles all in stipple upon trout that swim;
Fresh-firecoal chestnut-falls; finches' wings;
Landscape plotted and pieced – fold, fallow, and plough;
And all trades; their gear and tackle and trim.

All things counter, original, spare, strange;
Whatever is fickle; freckled (who knows how?)
With swift, slow; sweet, sour; adazzle, dim;
He fathers-forth whose beauty is past change:
Praise him.

Thee, God, I come from

Thee, God, I come from, to thee go,
All day long I like fountain flow
From thy hand out, swayed about
Mote-like in thy mighty glow.

What I know of thee I bless,
As acknowledging thy stress
On my being and as seeing
Something of thy holiness.

Once I turned from thee and hid,
Bound on what thou hadst forbid;
Sow the wind I would; I sinned:
I repent of what I did.

Bad I am, but yet thy child.
Father, be thou reconciled.
Spare thou me, since I see
With thy might that thou art mild.

I have life left with me still
And thy purpose to fulfil;
Yea a debt to pay thee yet:
Help me, sir, and so I will.

But thou bidst, and just thou art,
Me shew mercy from my heart
Towards my brother, every other
Man my mate and counterpart . . .

Christmas

Moonless darkness stands between.
Past, O Past, no more be seen!
But the Bethlehem star may lead me
To the sight of him who freed me
From the self that I have been.
Make me pure, Lord: thou art holy;
Make me meek, Lord: thou wert lowly;
Now beginning, and alway:
Now begin, on Christmas Day.[1]

Bernadette of Lourdes (1844–79)

Marie Bernarde Soubirous was the oldest of six children of a poor miller. When she was fourteen the Virgin Mary appeared to her eighteen times near her home in Lourdes, saying to her, 'I am the Immaculate Conception.' A miraculous spring of water was revealed to her. This met a need among Christians at the time for a place of pilgrimage associated with miracles and visions, but Bernadette, as she was affectionately called, escaped from the publicity by joining a convent at Nevers. The Roman Catholic Church has set stringent standards for the examination of alleged healings at Lourdes, but even those who feel culturally estranged from the Marian devotion there cannot deny the effect that a pilgrimage to Lourdes has on the faithful, or the sincerity of the devout girl who began it all.

Christ Jesus, we beg you by your loneliness, not that you may spare us affliction, but that you may not abandon us in it. When we encounter affliction, teach us to see you in it as our sole comforter. Let affliction strengthen our faith, fortify our hope, and purify our love. Grant us the grace to see how we can use our affliction to your glory, and to desire no other comforter but you, our Saviour, Strengthener and Friend. Amen.

Adapted

Alice Meynell (1847–1922)

Alice Meynell was born in Barnes, south London, and was a convert to the Roman Catholic faith. She married Wilfred Meynell, who, like her, was an author with a growing reputation, and together they edited several literary magazines. She contributed essays and studies of contemporary authors to other magazines also. Her poetry was admired by many who did not share her faith.

Thou art the Way

Thou art the Way
   Hadst thou been nothing but the goal
  I cannot say
If thou hadst ever met my soul.

I cannot see –
I, child of process – if there lies
  An end for me
Full of repose, full of replies.

I'll not reproach
The road that winds, my feet that err.
  Access, Approach
Art thou, Time, Way, and Wayfarer.

The Unknown God

One of the crowd went up,
  And knelt before the Paten and the Cup,
Received the Lord, returned in peace, and prayed
Close to my side. Then in my heart I said:

O Christ, in this man's life –
This stranger who is thine – in all his strife,
All his felicity, his good and ill,
In the assaulted stronghold of his will,

I do confess thee here
Alive within this life; I know thee near
Within this lonely conscience, closed away,
Within this brother's solitary day,

Christ in his unknown heart,
His intellect unknown – this love, this art,
This battle and this peace, this destiny,
That I shall never know, look upon me!

Christ in his numbered breath,
Christ in his beating heart and in his death,
Christ in his mystery! From that secret place
And from that separate dwelling, give me grace.

Francis Thompson (1859–1907)

Francis Thompson was born in Preston and began to train for the Roman Catholic priesthood at Ushaw. He neither completed this nor a time of studying medicine at Manchester. He lived in poverty in London selling matches or newspapers, and addicted to opium, before he was discovered by Wilfrid and Alice Meynell, to whom he had submitted some poems. They arranged for him to be looked after at Storrington Priory in Sussex, and cared for him until his death from tuberculosis. His most popular poem, 'The Hound of Heaven', written at Storrington, may be semi-autobiographical, but it resonates for many Christians with our own experience of fleeing from the love of God. The phrase in another poem of his about 'the many-splendoured thing' deserves to be remembered in its original context, rather than as the title of a movie, for it makes of every town we live in a sacred place.

The Kingdom of God

O world invisible, we view thee,
    O world intangible, we touch thee,
O world unknowable, we know thee,
Inapprehensible, we clutch thee!

Does the fish soar to find the ocean,
The eagle plunge to find the air –
That we ask of the stars in motion
If they have rumour of thee there?

Not where the wheeling systems darken,
And our benumbed conceiving soars! –
The drift of pinions, would we hearken,
Beats at our own clay-shuttered doors.

The angels keep their ancient places; –
Turn but a stone, and start a wing!
'Tis ye, 'tis your estranged faces,
That miss the many-splendoured thing.

But (when so sad thou canst not sadder)
Cry; – and upon thy so sore loss
Shall shine the traffic of Jacob's ladder
Pitched betwixt Heaven and Charing Cross.

Yea, in the night, my soul, my daughter,
Cry, – clinging heaven by the hems;
And lo, Christ walking on the water,
Not of Genesareth, but Thames!

Charles de Foucauld (1858–1916)

*Charles de Foucauld was a cavalry officer who became a Trappist monk,
then a servant of the Poor Clares in Nazareth and Jerusalem, a priest and
finally a hermit who lived among and served the Tuareg people in the
Algerian mountains on the fringes of the Sahara desert. He was trusted
by them, but was ultimately assassinated. He drew up a rule for two
religious orders which were actually begun after his death: the Little Sisters
and the Little Brothers, who have adapted to the local way of life wherever
they have been established, in humble service to the poor.*

My Father, I abandon myself to you. Do with me as you will. Whatever you may do with me I thank you. I am prepared for anything.
I accept everything, provided your will is fulfilled in me and in all creatures.
I ask for nothing more, my God. I place my soul in your hands. I give it
to you, my God, with all the love of my heart, because I love you. And

for me it is a necessity of love, this gift of myself, this placing of myself in your hands without reserve in boundless confidence, because you are my Father.

O Lord, grant us faith, the faith that removes the mask from the world and manifests God in all things; the faith that shows us Christ where our eyes see only a poor person; that shows us the Saviour where we feel only pain. O Lord, grant us the faith that inspires us to undertake everything that God wants without hesitation, without shame, without fear, and without ever retreating; the faith that knows how to go through life with calm, peace and profound joy, and that makes the soul completely indifferent to everything that is not you, O Jesus Christ our Lord. Amen.

O Lord, guide my thoughts and my words. It is not that I lack subjects for meditation. On the contrary, I am crushed with the weight of them. How many are your mercies God – mercies yesterday and today, and at every moment of my life, from before my birth, from before time itself began! I am plunged deep in mercies; I drown in them; they cover me, wrapping me round on every side. Lord Jesus, we should all sing of your mercies – we, who were all created for everlasting glory and redeemed by your blood. But if we all have cause to sing your praises, how much more cause have I? From childhood I have been surrounded by so many graces. My saintly mother taught me to know you, to love you, and, as soon as I could speak, to pray to you. Despite so many blessings I drifted away from you for many years. I withdrew further and further from you, and my life became a death in your eyes. I enjoyed numerous worldly pleasures, and thought I was alive. But beneath the surface there was deep sadness, disgust, boredom, restlessness. Whenever I was alone a great melancholy came over me. Yet, how good you are to me. You slowly and patiently destroyed my worldly attachments. You broke down everything that prevented me from living for you. You showed me the futility and falsehood of my life in the world. Then you planted in my heart a tender seedling of love, so gradually my heart turned back to you. You gave me a taste for prayer, a trust in your word, a desire to imitate you. Now I am overwhelmed by your blessings. O beloved Bridegroom there is nothing that you have not done for me. Now tell me what you want of me, how you expect me to serve you. Create in my thoughts, words and actions that which will give true glory to you.[2]

P overty, humility, penitence – you, dear Jesus, know that I long to practise these virtues to the degree and in the way which you want. But what are that way and degree? Until now I have always thought that I should practise them by imitating you as closely as possible, by making myself follow, as far as I could, the way in which you yourself practised them. Now I fear I might be mistaken. While yours is the best and most perfect way, perhaps you are not calling me to a perfect life, and so will not let me follow you so closely. Indeed, if I look at myself, there is such a gap between my wretchedness and true perfection, that I am certainly unworthy to be counted amongst those close disciples who tread in your footsteps. And yet you have heaped so many blessings on me that it would seem ungrateful not to strive for perfection. To be content with imperfection would seem like a rejection of your generosity. I find it hard to believe that, in giving yourself so freely to me, you do not want me to give myself wholly to you. My only desire is to be and to do what pleases you. Enlighten my mind that I may always conform to your will.[3]

Inspired by the Lord's Prayer

O ur Father. O God, how good you are to allow us to call you 'our Father'! Not only do you allow it, you command it. What gratitude, what joy, what love, and above all, what confidence it inspires in me. And since you are so good to me. I should be good to others. You are Father to all people, so I should feel like a loving brother towards everyone, however wicked he may be. Our Father, our Father, teach me to have your name continually on my lips.

Who art in heaven. Why did you choose this qualification rather than any other – such as 'righteous Father', or 'holy Father'? It was doubtless O God, that my soul might be uplifted from the very beginning of this prayer, high above this poor world, and placed at the outset where it ought to be, in heaven which is its native land. It was also to put me at the outset into a state of joy, remembering that you, O God, love me and care for me for all eternity.

Hallowed be thy name. What is it, O Lord, that I am expressing in these words? I am expressing the whole object of my desires, the whole aim and purpose of my life. I want to hallow your name in all my thoughts, words and actions. And this means that I want to imitate your Son, Jesus, since he hallowed your name in his every thought, word and action.

Thy kingdom come. In these simple words, I am asking that you reveal the fullness of your glory, and that you make all people holy. Your kingdom will come when all people acknowledge you as Master, seeking with all their minds to obey you, with all their hearts to love you, and with all their energies to serve you. So in saying those words, I am committing myself to spread the knowledge of your glory to all mankind.

Thy will be done, on earth as it is in heaven. These words show me to what extent every offence against you, and every sinful act of one person against another, cause you pain and grief. With feelings far deeper and far greater than we could ever understand, you desire all people to be reconciled with you and with one another. You desire earth to be a mirror of heaven. So when people strive to break that mirror through their sinfulness, your heart breaks. Yet equally, for the same reasons, you experience great joy at even the least act of goodness. And your heart is filled with fatherly pleasure whenever any person turns to you in prayer.

Give us this day our daily bread. You desire me, O Lord, to look to you for my every need. And in looking to you, I know that you will provide me with bread to eat, clothes to wear, and a warm place to rest. But it is not only material bread which you provide; you give also spiritual bread. Whenever I eat the bread of Holy Communion, I am reminded that your Son gave his body to die on the cross, to give me spiritual food for all eternity. And in this phrase, I note that it is not 'me' for whom I pray, but 'us'. You do not want me ever to pray selfishly, but always to pray for other's needs, because only through such mutual charity do I become fit to receive the true bread of eternal life.

Forgive us our trespasses as we forgive. Having spoken to you so intimately as 'our Father' – having climbed so high, I now realize how low I really am. I remember how I fail to obey your will or work for your kingdom. And so I say, 'Father, forgive me'. With my whole soul I see how horrible are my sins to you, how they disgust and insult you, and what a price your Son had to pay to redeem me from them. I realize how much pain I have caused you; and in that realization I feel pain myself, crying with remorse at what I have done. At the same time I recognize that I have no right to ask your forgiveness for my sins, unless I forgive others their sins. And, of course, the sins which others commit against me are as nothing compared with the sins I have committed against you. Thus in truth I am asking that all mankind might be forgiven.

Lead us not into temptation. This is a cry suitable for every hour and every minute of my life – a cry for help. I am so beset by temptation that it is impossible for me to accomplish the smallest good deed unless I call for help continually. Indeed my every prayer is in truth a call for help.

Deliver us from evil. If you were to deliver all people from evil then they would all be saints, glorifying you in their holiness. Thus your purpose and my desire would be wholly fulfilled, that you would reign as King over the whole world. But it is not fit for me to worry about the evil of others, unless I first turn inwards to my own soul. I ask only that your purpose be accomplished in me.

Thérèse of Lisieux (1873–97)

Although she was still too young, Thérèse begged to be admitted to the local Carmelite convent, where she was soon made mistress of the novices. She was a first-rate story-teller, and was persuaded to write her autobiography. When it was circulated to other convents after her early death, as was the custom, it quickly became a spiritual classic. She felt that her mission in life was to call others to her 'Little Way' of childlike loving simplicity and the almost playful trust in God which she shows in her own prayers. She encouraged others 'not to attribute to ourselves the virtues . . . not to be discouraged by our faults'.

Jesus, I don't know how to intensify this petition of mine; if I tried to, I might find myself sinking under the weight of my own presumption. My excuse is that I'm just a child, and children don't always weigh their words. But a parent who is enthroned and has great resources at his disposal is ready to humour the caprices of the child he loves, even to the point of fondness, even to the point of weakness. And here am I, a child, the child of Holy Church, that Mother who is also a Queen because she is a King's bride. Child-like, I'm not concerned with riches or honour, even with the glory of heaven; I quite realise that that belongs to my elder brothers, the Angels and the Saints. The reflection of the jewels in my Mother's crown will be glory enough for me; it's love I ask for, love is all the skill I have. Sensational acts of piety are not for me; not for me to preach the gospel, or to shed my blood as a martyr, but I see now that all that doesn't matter; my elder brothers will do the work for me, while I, as the baby of the family, stay close to the King's throne, the Queen's throne, and go on loving on behalf of my brothers, out on the battle-field.

But this love of mine, how to shew it? Love needs to be proved by action. Well, even a little child can scatter flowers, to scent the throne-room with their fragrance; even a little child can sing, in its shrill treble, the great canticle of Love. That shall be my life, to scatter flowers – to miss no single opportunity of making some small sacrifice, here by a smiling look, there by a kindly word, always doing the tiniest things right, and doing it for love. I shall suffer all that I have to suffer – yes, and enjoy all my enjoyments too – in the spirit of love, so that I shall always be scattering flowers before your throne; nothing that comes my way but shall yield up its petals in your honour. And, as I scatter my flowers, I shall be singing; how could one be sad when occupied so pleasantly? I shall be singing, even when I have to pluck my flowers from a thorn-bush; never in better voice than when the thorns are longest and sharpest. I don't ask what use they will be to you, Jesus, these flowers, this music of mine; I know that you will take pleasure in this fragrant shower of worthless petals, in these songs of love in which a worthless heart like mine sings itself out. And because they will give pleasure to you, the Church triumphant in heaven will smile upon them too; will take these flowers so bruised by love and pass them on into your divine hands. And so the Church in heaven, ready to take part in the childish game I am playing, will begin scattering these flowers, now hallowed by your touch beyond all recognition; will scatter them on the souls in Purgatory, to abate their sufferings, scatter them on the Church Militant, and give her the strength for fresh conquests.

Yes, Jesus, I do love you; I do love the Church, my Mother. And it sticks in my mind that 'the slightest movement of a disinterested love has more value than all the other acts of a human soul put together' (St John of the Cross, *Spiritual Canticle*, commentary on Stephen, xxix). But is mine a disinterested love? Or are these wide-ranging aspirations of mine no better than a dream, a fond illusion? If so, Jesus, make it known to me; I only want to be told the truth. If my longings are presumptuous, make them fade away; why should I suffer needless torment? And yet, I don't think I shall really regret having aspired to the highest levels of love, even if it doesn't mean attaining them hereafter; unless, after death, the memory of all my earthly hopes disappears by some miracle, that memory will always be my consolation; to have suffered like that, to have been a fool for your sake like that, will be something dearer to me than any reward I could have expected in heaven. Let me go on, during my exile,

Nineteenth-Century Scots Protestants

Horatius Bonar (1808–89)

Bonar was born in Edinburgh and was a Church of Scotland Minister at Kelso, but nearly a third of the ministers of that church had broken away in 1843 to form the Free Church of Scotland, and Bonar joined them in 1866 to become minister of the Chalmers Memorial Church in Edinburgh. His well-known hymns include 'I heard the voice of Jesus say'.

Thy way, not mine, O Lord,
However dark it be;
Lead me by thine own hand,
Choose out the path for me.
Smooth let it be or rough,
It will be still the best;
Winding or straight, it leads
Right onward to thy rest.
Choose thou for me my friends,
My sickness or my health;
Choose thou my cares for me,
My poverty or wealth.
Not mine, not mine the choice
In things or great or small;
Be thou my guide, my strength,
My wisdom, and my all.

The Lord's Supper

Here, O my Lord, I see thee face to face;
Here would I touch and handle things unseen;
Here grasp with firmer hand the eternal grace,
And all my weariness upon thee lean.

Here would I feed upon the bread of God;
Here drink with thee the royal wine of heaven;
Here would I lay aside each earthly load,
Here taste afresh the calm of sin forgiven.

Alexander Campbell Fraser (1819–1914)

A minister in the Free Church of Scotland, he was appointed professor of philosophy at Edinburgh University.

Write upon our hearts, O Lord God, the lessons of your holy word, and grant that we may all be doers of the same, and not forgetful hearers only; through Jesus Christ our Lord. Amen.[1]

May God grant that we who have worshipped him in his church may be witnesses to him in his world.[2]

George Macdonald (1824–1905)

George Macdonald was born and educated in Aberdeenshire, but became a Congregationalist minister in England. Bad health caused him to resign and concentrate on writing poetry and novels such as David Elginbrod *and* Lilith. *But he is chiefly remembered for* At the back of the North Wind *and other children's books.*

I would go near thee – but I cannot press
Into thy presence – it helps not to presume.
Thy doors are deeds.

Lord, teach us to understand that your Son died to save us, not from suffering, but from ourselves; not from injustice, far less from justice, but from being unjust. He died that we might live – but live as he lives, by dying as he died who died to himself.

O son of man, to right my lot
Nought but thy presence can avail;
Yet on the road thy wheels are not,
Nor on the sea thy sail.

My fancied ways why should'st thou heed?
Thou com'st down thine own secret stair
Com'st down to answer all my need,
Yea, every bygone prayer!

F ather, into thy hands I give the heart
Which left thee but to learn how good thou art.

W hen I look back upon my life nigh spent,
Nigh spent, although the stream as yet flows on,
I more of follies than of sins repent,
Less for offence than love's shortcomings moan.
With self, O Father, leave me not alone –
Leave not with the beguiler the beguiled;
Besmirched and ragged, Lord, take back thine own:
A fool I bring thee to be made a child.

Robert Louis Stevenson (1850–94)

*R. L. Stevenson was born in Edinburgh, the son and grandson of engineers
to the Board of Lighthouses. After one session in which he attempted to
study engineering, he turned to law and qualified as an advocate. But his
interest was in literature. He travelled, chiefly in France, and wrote* Travels
with a Donkey in the Cevennes. *It was in France that he met a divorcée,
Fanny Osbourne; he followed her to America and married her in 1880.
When they returned to Europe, with Fanny's son by her first marriage,
Robert began his struggle with tuberculosis and a wretched peripatetic
existence. It was only in the last five years, which the three of them spent
on Samoa, that he found peace, and it was during this time that most of
his prayers were written. Meanwhile he had soared to fame with* Treasure
Island, Kidnapped, Catriona, The Master of Ballantrae, Dr Jekyll and
Mr Hyde, Virginibus Puerisque *and* A Child's Garden of Verses.

G ive us grace and strength to forbear and to persevere. Offenders
ourselves, give us the grace to accept and to forgive offenders. Forgetful ourselves, help us to bear cheerfully the forgetfulness of others. Give
us courage and gaiety and a quiet mind. Spare to us our friends, soften
to us our enemies. Bless us, if it may be, in all our innocent endeavours.
If it may not, give us the strength to encounter that which is to come,
that we be brave in peril, constant in tribulation, temperate in wrath, and

in all changes of fortune, and, down to the gates of death, loyal and loving one to another. As the clay to the potter, as the windmill to the wind, as children of their sire, we beseech of thee this help and mercy.

Grant to us, O Lord, the royalty of inward happiness, and the serenity which comes from living close to thee. Daily renew in us the sense of joy, and let the eternal Spirit of the Father dwell in our souls and bodies, filling every corner of our hearts with light and grace; so that, bearing about with us the infection of good courage, we may be diffusers of life, and may meet all ills and cross accidents with gallant and high-hearted happiness, giving thee thanks always for all things.

Grant that we here before thee may be set free from the fear of vicissi-tude and the fear of death, may finish what remains before us of our course without dishonour to ourselves or hurt to others; and, when the day comes, may die in peace. Deliver us from fear and favour, from mean hopes and cheap pleasures. Have mercy on each in his deficiency; let him be not cast down. Support the stumbling on the way, and give at last rest to the weary.

Written and read to his family on the eve of his unanticipated death

Lord, go with each of us to rest; if any awake, temper to them the dark hours of watching; and when the day returns, return to us, our sun and comforter, and call us up with morning faces and with morning hearts, eager to labour, eager to be happy, if happiness should be our portion, and if the day be marked for sorrow, strong to endure it.

George Henry Somerset Walpole (1854–1929)

Walpole was the Episcopalian Bishop of Edinburgh. This prayer was adapted in the American Episcopal Book of Common Prayer *(1979).*

O God, you prepared your disciples for the coming of the Spirit through the teaching of your Son Jesus Christ: make the hearts and minds of your servants ready to receive the blessing of the Holy Spirit, that they may filled with the strength of his presence; through Jesus Christ our Lord. Amen.

American Christianity in the Nineteenth Century

The Shakers

During a Quaker revival in England in 1747, James and Jane Wardley formed a new community, nicknamed the Shakers from their habit of trembling when in ecstasy. They were succeeded by 'Mother Ann' who was regarded as the second coming of Christ in the sense that the male principle in Christ had been Jesus, and she was supposed to be the female principle in Christ. As a result of persecution she took eight followers to America and settled near Albany, New York. Their plain dress and community life soon attracted converts, and at one time there were 5,000 Shakers, but as they encouraged, though did not insist on, celibacy, they were fated to die out. In their worship they would hang the chairs on pegs on the wall to clear the floor for religious dance. The tune to their best-known song is sung in England to new words: 'The Lord of the Dance'.

'Tis a gift to be simple, 'tis a gift to be free,
'Tis a gift to come down where we ought to be,
And when we find ourselves in the place just right
'Twill be in the valley of love and delight.
When true simplicity is gained
To bow and to bend we shan't be ashamed,
To turn, turn, shall be our delight,
Till by turning, turning we come round right.

John Greenleaf Whittier (1807–92)

Whittier worked as a journalist until he was twenty-five, when he gave himself completely to the anti-slavery movement. He wrote many poems in the cause of freedom for slaves, and was a victim of mob-violence in consequence. He was a Quaker, and was appalled at the noisy 'camp-meetings', where, in a tent taken from town to town, the enthusiastic revivalism of the Great Awakening was preached. It is a sign of the unifying effects of Christian song that his best-known hymn, in which he called for the Quaker virtue of silence, has been taken up enthusiastically by the very denominations that he attacked.

Dear Lord and Father of mankind,
forgive our foolish ways;
re-clothe us in our rightful mind,
in purer lives thy service find,
in deeper reverence praise.

In simple trust like theirs who heard,
beside the Syrian sea,
the gracious calling of the Lord,
let us, like them, without a word
rise up and follow thee.

O Sabbath rest by Galilee!
O calm of hills above,
where Jesus knelt to share with thee
the silence of eternity,
interpreted by love!

With that deep hush subduing all
Our words and works that drown
The tender whisper of thy call,
As noiseless let thy blessing fall
As fell thy manna down.

Drop thy still dews of quietness,
till all our strivings cease;
take from our souls the strain and stress,
and let our ordered lives confess
the beauty of thy peace;

Breathe through the heats of our desire
thy coolness and thy balm;
let sense be dumb, let flesh retire;
speak through the earthquake, wind, and fire,
O still small voice of calm.

All that I feel of pity thou hast known
Before I was; my best is all thy own.
From thy great heart of goodness mine but draws
Wishes and prayers; but thou, O Lord, wilt do,
In thine own time, by ways I cannot see,
All that I feel when I am nearest thee!

Immortal Love for ever full,
for ever flowing free,
for ever shared, for ever whole,
a never-ebbing sea! . . .

Through him the first fond prayers are said
our lips of childhood frame.
the last low whispers of our dead
are burdened with his name.

Alone, O Love ineffable,
thy saving name is given;
to turn aside from thee is hell,
to walk with thee is heaven.

Henry Ward Beecher (1813–27)

Henry Ward Beecher was a Congregationalist minister in Brooklyn, New York, where he preached to huge congregations, proclaiming the gospel, promoting temperance, and opposing slavery. His church raised a volunteer regiment during the Civil War, but afterwards he worked hard for reconciliation. His sister, Harriet Beecher Stowe, wrote Uncle Tom's Cabin.

We rejoice that in all time men have found a refuge in thee, and that prayer is the voice of love, the voice of pleading, and the voice of thanksgiving. Our souls overflow toward thee like a cup when full; nor can we forbear; nor shall we search to see if our prayers have been registered, or whether of the things asked we have received much, or more, or anything. That we have had permission to feel ourselves in thy presence, to take upon ourselves something of the light of thy countenance, to have a consciousness that thy thoughts are upon us, to experience the inspiration of the Holy Spirit in any measure – this is an answer to prayer transcending all things that we can think of. We are glad that we can glorify thee, that we can rejoice in thee, that it does make a difference to thee what we do, and that thou dost enfold us in a consciousness of thy sympathy with us, of how much thou art to us, and of what we are to thee.

Walt Whitman (1819–91)

Whitman's early career consisted of short spells as a clerk, a printer, a teacher and a journalist. In order to look after his brother, who had been wounded in the Civil War, he became a volunteer nurse, but the experience left him a shattered man. He was given a government clerkship but was dismissed from it for publishing 'an indecent book', Leaves of Grass. What shocked his readers was that he sought to find a transcendent meaning in the events of contemporary life.

O thou transcendent,
Nameless, the fibre and the breath,
Light of the light, shedding forth universes, thou centre of them,
Thou mightier centre of the true, the good, the loving,
Thou moral, spiritual fountain – affection's source – thou reservoir,
(O pensive soul of me – O thirst unsatisfied – waitest not there?
Waitest not haply for us somewhere there the Comrade perfect?)
Thou pulse – thou motive of the stars, suns, systems,
That, circling, move in order, safe, harmonious,
Athwart the shapeless vastnesses of space,
How should I think, how breathe a single breath, how speak, if, out
    of myself,
I could not launch, to those, superior universes?

From Passage to India, *Book XXVII*

Away O Soul, hoist instantly the anchor!
Cut the hawsers – haul out – shake out every sail!
Sail forth – steer for the deep waters only;
Reckless O Soul, exploring, I with thee, and thou with me,
For we are bound where mariner has not yet dared to go,
And we will risk the ship, ourselves and all.
O my brave Soul.
O farther, farther sail!
O daring joy, but safe! are they not all the seas of God?
O farther, farther, farther sail!

From 'The Explorers'

Philips Brooks (1835–93)

Born in Boston, Massachusetts, Philips Brooks became rector of the Prot-
estant Episcopal Church of Holy Trinity, Boston, and in 1891 Bishop of
Massachusetts, having in the meanwhile studied at Harvard and held a
rectorship in Philadelphia. He was influenced by the liberal Christianity
of writers such as F. D. Maurice, and became one of the leading preachers
of his generation. After the Civil War he visited the Holy Land in search
of peace, and when he rode out from Jerusalem to Bethlehem at night, he
wrote the carol 'O little town of Bethlehem' for his Sunday school class.

O holy child of Bethlehem,
　Descend to us, we pray;
Cast out our sin, and enter in:
Be born in us today.
We hear the Christmas angels
The great glad tidings tell:
O come to us, abide with us,
Our Lord Emmanuel.

O Lord, I do not pray for tasks equal to my strength: I ask for
　strength equal to my tasks.

Dwight Lyman Moody (1837–99)

Dwight Moody was the son of a bricklayer in Massachusetts. Dwight moved
to Chicago where he prospered in business. He began evangelism through
his local Sunday school, and during the Civil War worked under the
YMCA evangelizing the wounded. When he was organizing Sunday school
teachers' conventions in Chicago he met a young musician called Ira David
Sankey (1840–1908). Like William Booth, the founder of the Salvation
Army, they did not see why the devil should have all the best tunes, and
compiled a book of popular songs which made a direct emotional appeal
to the singers. It was so successful during the many missions they conducted
in the United States and in Great Britain that 'Sankey and Moody' came
to describe a style of music, and a style of evangelism with large meetings,
direct appeals for conversion through powerful preaching, and enquirers'
rooms where those who had responded could be followed up.

U se me, then, my Saviour, for whatever purpose, and in whatever way,
　thou mayest require. Here is my poor heart, an empty vessel; fill it
with thy grace. Here is my sinful and troubled soul; quicken it and refresh
it with thy love. Take my heart for thine abode; my mouth to spread abroad

the glory of thy name; my love and all my powers, for the advancement of thy believing people; and never suffer the steadfastness and confidence of my faith to abate; so that at all times I may be enabled from the heart to say, 'Jesus needs me, and I am his.'

William Reed Huntingdon (1838–1909)

William Reed Huntingdon was an Episcopal rector in New York. Prayers from his Materia Ritualis *have been adapted in the Episcopal* Book of Common Prayer *(1979).*

Almighty God, whose most dear Son went not up to joy but first he suffered pain, and entered not into glory before he was crucified: mercifully grant that we, walking in the way of the cross, may find it none other than the way of life and peace; through Jesus Christ our Lord. Amen.

O God, the King eternal, whose light divides the day from the night and turns the shadow of death into the morning: drive far from us all wrong desires, incline our hearts to keep your law, and guide our feet into the way of peace; that having done your will with cheerfulness during the day, we may, when night comes, rejoice to give you thanks; through Jesus Christ our Lord. Amen.[1]

Rossiter Worthington Raymond (1840–1918)

It has proved difficult to discover who is the author of this prayer, but in Alice Robson's Undying Life *it is attributed to Rossiter Raymond, who was a mining engineer and writer.*

We seem to give back the dead to you, Lord, who gave them to us. But as you did not lose them in giving, so do we not lose them by their return. Not as the world gives do you give, O Lover of souls. What you give you do not take away, for what is yours is ours also if we are yours. And life is eternal and love is immortal, and death is only a horizon, and a horizon is nothing, save the limit of our sight. Lift us up, strong Son of God, that we may see further; cleanse our eyes that we may see more clearly; draw us closer to yourself that we may know ourselves to be nearer to our loved ones who are with you. And while you prepare a place for us, prepare us also for that happy place, that where you are we may be also, for ever and ever. Amen.

William James (1842–1910)

William James was born in New York, the brother of the novelist Henry James. He graduated in medicine from Harvard, where he became professor of philosophy and then psychology. He described himself as a radical empiricist: beliefs are true if and because they work. The Varieties of Religious Experience comprises his Gifford Lectures in Edinburgh. In it he argues that some Christians are once-born and grow gradually into faith, whereas others are twice-born and come to faith through a sudden conversion experience. Aware that many evangelicals were claiming that only they met the requirement of Christ that we must be born again, he argued that both types of religious experience are equally valid, so long as we start afresh on the basis of God's grace and not our own achievements.

M any reasons have been given why we should not pray, whilst others are given why we should. But in all this very little is said of the reason why we do pray. The reason why we pray is simply that we cannot help praying.

Frank Mason North (1850–1935)

North was a Methodist Episcopal Church leader in New York, and was influential in turning the focus of his denomination away from individualism to united social action.

W here cross the crowded ways of life,
  Where sound the cries of race and clan,
Above the noise of selfish strife
We hear thy voice, O Son of man.

In haunts of wretchedness and need,
On shadowed thresholds dark with fears,
From paths where hide the lure of greed,
We catch the vision of thy tears,

O Master, from the mountain side,
Make haste to heal these hearts of pain;
Among these restless throngs abide,
O tread the city's streets again;

Till sons of men shall learn thy love,
And follow where thy feet have trod;
Till glorious from thy heav'n above,
Shall come the city of our God.

George Zabriskie Sr (1852–1931)

George Zabriskie was a New York lawyer; his grandson is a retired priest of the Episcopal Church. He wrote this prayer for lawyers, which was adapted in the American Episcopal Book of Common Prayer *(1979).*

Almighty God, you sit in the throne judging right: we humbly beseech you to bless the courts of justice and the magistrates in all this land; and give to them the spirit of wisdom and understanding, that they may discern the truth, and impartially administer the law in the fear of you alone; through him who shall come to be our Judge, your Son our Saviour Jesus Christ. Amen.

Joseph Scriven (c. 1855)

Joseph Scriven was born in Co. Down, Ireland, and graduated from Trinity College, Dublin. He became estranged from his Congregationalist parents when he was influenced by the Plymouth Brethren. When his fiancée was drowned on the eve of their wedding, he emigrated to Canada. He was twenty-five and was to battle with depression for the rest of his life. He worked as a schoolmaster and helped the poor. His well-known hymn was wrought in the furnace of his own suffering.

What a friend we have in Jesus, all our sins and griefs to bear!
What a privilege to carry ev'rything to God in prayer!
Oh, what peace we often forfeit, O what needless pain we bear,
All because we do not carry ev'rything to God in prayer!

Have we trials and temptations? Is there trouble anywhere?
We should never be discouraged: take it to the Lord in prayer!
Can we find a friend so faithful, who will all our sorrows share?
Jesus knows our ev'ry weakness – take it to the Lord in prayer!

Are we weak and heavy laden, cumbered with a load of care?
Precious Saviour, still our refuge – take it to the Lord in prayer!
Do thy friends despise, forsake thee? Take it to the Lord in prayer!
In his arms he'll take and shield thee, thou wilt find a solace there.

John Wallace Suter (1859–1942)

John Wallace Suter was a liturgist and a rector in Massachusetts. This prayer was adapted in the American Episcopal Book of Common Prayer *(1979).*

O God, whose blessed Son made himself known to his disciples in the breaking of bread: open the eyes of our faith, that we may behold him in all his redeeming works, who lives and reigns with you, in the unity of the Holy Spirit, one God, now and for ever. Amen.[2]

Walter Rauschenbusch (1861–1918)

A Baptist minister and professor of theology, Professor Rauschenbush emphasized that Christians should be involved in the struggle for economic and social justice in contrast to the narrow emphasis on personal salvation which was prevalent. He published For God and People: Prayers for Social Awakening.

O God, we thank thee for this universe, our great home; for its vastness and its riches, and for the manifoldness of the life which teems upon it and of which we are part. We praise thee for the arching sky and the blessed winds, for the driving clouds, and the constellations on high. We praise thee for the salt sea and the running water, for the everlasting hills, for the trees, and for the grass under our feet. We thank thee for our senses by which we can see the splendour of the morning, and hear the jubilant songs of love, and smell the breath of the springtime. Grant us, we pray thee, a heart wide open to all this joy and beauty, and save our souls from being so steeped in care or so darkened by passion that we pass heedless and unseeing when even the thornbush by the wayside is aflame with the glory of God. Enlarge within us the sense of fellowship with all the living things, our little brothers, to whom thou hast given this earth as their home in common with us. We remember with shame that in the past we have exercised the high dominion of man with ruthless cruelty, so that the voice of the Earth, which should have gone up to thee in song, has been a groan of travail. May we realize that they live, not for us alone, but for themselves and for thee, and that they love the sweetness of life, even as we, and serve thee in their place better than we in ours. When our use of this world is over and we make room for others, may we not leave anything ravished by our greed or spoiled by our ignorance, but may we hand on our common heritage fairer and sweeter through our use of it, undiminished in fertility and joy, that so our bodies may return in peace to the great mother who nourished them and our spirits may round the circle of a perfect life in thee.

O Christ, thou hast bidden us pray for the coming of thy Father's kingdom, in which his righteous will shall be done on earth. We have treasured thy words, but we have forgotten their meaning, and thy great hope has grown dim in thy Church. We bless thee for the inspired souls of all ages who saw afar the shining city of God, and by faith left the profit of the present to follow their vision. We rejoice that to-day the hope of these lonely hearts is becoming the clear faith of millions. Help us, O Lord, in the courage of faith to seize what has now come so near, that the glad day of God may dawn at last. As we have mastered nature that we might gain wealth, help us now to master the social relations of mankind that we may gain justice and a world of brothers. For what shall it profit our nation if it gain numbers and riches, and lose the sense of the living God and the joy of human brotherhood? Make us determined to live by truth and not by lies, to found our common life on the eternal foundations of righteousness and love, and no longer to prop the tottering house of wrong by legalised cruelty and force. Help us to make the welfare of all the supreme law of our land, that so our commonwealth may be built strong and secure on the love of all its citizens. Cast down the throne of Mammon who ever grinds the life of men, and set up thy throne, O Christ, for thou didst die that men might live. Show thy erring children at last the way to the City of Love, and fulfil the longings of the prophets of humanity. Our Master, once more we make thy faith our prayer: 'Thy Kingdom come!'

Charles Henry Brent (1862–1929)

Bishop Brent was born in Canada; he went as a missionary bishop of the Philippines and then became Episcopal bishop of Western New York. He was chief chaplain to the US Expeditionary Forces in Europe from 1917 to 1919, and was concerned to promote Christian unity.

L ord Jesus Christ, you stretched out your arms of love on the hard wood of the cross that everyone might come within the reach of your saving embrace: so clothe us in your Spirit that we, reaching forth our hands in love, may bring those who do not know you to the knowledge and love of you; for the honour of your name. Amen.[3]

O God, who hast folded back the mantle of the night to clothe us in the golden glory of the day, chase from our hearts all gloomy thoughts, and make us glad with the brightness of hope, that we may effectively aspire to unwon virtues, through Jesus Christ our Lord. Amen.

P rosper the labours of all Churches bearing the name of Christ and striving to further righteousness and faith in Him. Help us to place thy truth above our conception of it and joyfully to recognize the presence of thy Holy Spirit wherever he may choose to dwell among men. Teach us wherein we are sectarian in our intentions, and give us grace humbly to confess our fault to those whom in past days our Communion has driven from its fellowship by ecclesiastical tyranny, spiritual barrenness or moral inefficiency, that we may become worthy and competent to bind up in the Church the wounds of which we are guilty, and hasten the day when there shall be one fold under one Shepherd, Jesus Christ our Lord.

The prayer of an unknown Confederate soldier (1865)

I asked for strength that I might achieve;
I was made weak that I might learn humbly to obey.
I asked for health that I might do greater things;
I was given infirmity that I might do better things.
I asked for riches that I might be happy;
I was given poverty that I might be wise.
I asked for power that I might have the praise of men;
I was given weakness that I might feel the need of God.

I asked for all things that I might enjoy life;
I was given life that I might enjoy all things.
I got nothing that I had asked for,
but everything that I had hoped for.
Almost despite myself my unspoken prayers were answered;
I am, among all men, most richly blessed.

William Thomas Manning (1866–1949)

*This prayer conveys the distinctive American emphasis on loving our neigh-
bours, and contains phrases which are associated with Bishop Manning
of New York, though whether he wrote the whole prayer is uncertain.*

Blessed Lord, by word and example you have shown us the meaning
of neighbourliness and the way of love: grant that we may learn to
recognise as our neighbour every fellow human being who needs our help,
and to serve them with a love that is costly and unselfish, like your own
love for us. We ask this for your name's sake, O Jesus Christ our Lord.
Amen.

Charles Lewis Slattery (1867–1930)

Slattery was Bishop of Massachusetts.

Almighty God, we remember before you today your faithful servant *N.*;
and we pray that, having opened to *him* the gates of larger life, you
will receive *him* more and more into your joyful service, that, with all who
have faithfully served you in the past, *he* may share in the eternal victory
of Jesus Christ our Lord; who lives and reigns with you, in the unity of
the Holy Spirit, one God for ever and ever. Amen.[4]

The Early Twentieth Century

Percy Dearmer (1867–1936)

Dearmer's Parson's Handbook *set out to adapt medieval ceremonial to the services of* The Book of Common Prayer, *and the decoration of many parish churches is derived from his recommendations. He was also one of the editors of* The English Hymnal, Songs of Praise *and* The Oxford Book of Carols, *and wrote or translated many well-known hymns and carols.*

God, our Shepherd, give to the Church a new vision and a new charity, new wisdom and fresh understanding, the revival of her brightness and the renewal of her unity; that the eternal message of thy Son, undefiled by the traditions of men, may be hailed as the good news of the new age; through him who maketh all things new, Jesus Christ our Lord.

Jesus, good above all other,
Gentle Child of gentle Mother,
In a stable born our Brother,
Give us grace to persevere.

Amy Carmichael (1867–1951)

A missionary in India, where she spent the last fifty years of her life, Amy Carmichael founded the inter-denominational Dohnavur Fellowship in Tamil Nadu, to save children from moral danger and abuse. Initially, most who came had been destined for a life of prostitution in the local temples. A hospital was also built to serve the surrounding community, and the work of both home and hospital continues today.

Before the winds that blow do cease,
Teach me to dwell within thy calm;
Before the pain has passed in peace,
Give me, my God, to sing a psalm.
Let me not lose the chance to prove
The fullness of enabling love.
O love of God, do this for me:
Maintain a constant victory.
Before I leave the desert land
For meadows of immortal flowers,
Lead me where streams at thy command
Flow by the borders of the hours,
That when the thirsty come, I may
show them the fountains in the way.
O love of God do this for me:
Maintain a constant victory.[1]

He said, 'I will forget the dying faces
The empty places –
They shall be filled again;
O voices mourning deep within me cease.'
Vain, vain the word: vain, vain;
Not in forgetting lieth peace.

He said, 'I will crowd action upon action,
The strife of faction
Shall stir my spirit to flame;
O tears that drown the fire of manhood, cease.'
Vain, vain the word: vain, vain;
Not in endeavour lieth peace.

He said, 'I will withdraw me and be quiet,
Why meddle in earth's riot?
Shut be my door to pain.
Desire thou dost befool me; thou shalt cease.'
Vain, vain the word: vain, vain;
Not in aloofness lieth peace.

He said, 'I will submit; I am defeated;
God hath depleted

My rich life of its gain.
O futile murmurings; why will ye not cease?'
Vain, vain the word: vain, vain;
Not in submission lieth peace.

He said, 'I will accept the breaking sorrow
Which God tomorrow
Will to his son explain.'
Then did the turmoil deep within him cease.
Not vain the word, not vain:
For in acceptance lieth peace.[2]

Edward Lambe Parsons (1868–1960)

Parsons was Bishop of California.

Almighty God our heavenly Father, guide the nations of the world into the way of justice and truth, and establish among them that peace which is the fruit of righteousness, that they may become the kingdom of our Lord and Saviour Jesus Christ. Amen.[3]

Heavenly Father, whose blessed Son came not to be served but to serve: bless all who, following in his steps, give themselves to the service of others; that with wisdom, patience and courage, they may minister in his name to the suffering, the friendless and the needy; for the love of him who laid down his life for us, your Son our Saviour Jesus Christ, who lives and reigns with you and the Holy Spirit, one God for ever and ever. Amen.[4]

G. K. Chesterton (1874–1963)

Converted to the Roman Catholic Church in 1922, Gilbert Keith Chesterton was the most successful apologist for his faith in his generation. One has only to mention Orthodoxy, *the 'Father Brown' stories and his life of Saint Francis of Assisi to remember his sharp insights and robust humour. He was also critical of the imperialistic nationalism of his contemporaries.*

O God of earth and altar,
Bow down and hear our cry,
Our earthly rulers falter,
Our people drift and die;

The walls of gold entomb us,
The swords of scorn divide,
Take not thy thunder from us,
But take away our pride.

From all that terror teaches,
From lies of tongue and pen,
From all the easy speeches
That comfort cruel men,
From sale and profanation
Of honour and the sword,
From sleep and from damnation,
Deliver us, good Lord!

Tie in a living tether
The prince and priest and thrall,
Bind all our lives together,
Smite us and save us all;
In ire and exultation
Aflame with faith, and free,
Lift up a living nation,
A single sword to thee.[5]

George Wallace Briggs (1875–1959)

G. W. Briggs was a Canon of Worcester Cathedral. He compiled a book called The Daily Service *which was published by Oxford University Press in 1936, and collaborated with Milner-White in* Daily Prayer, *which, when published by Penguin Books as a paperback, made a collection of beautiful ancient prayers available to a wide readership. In the Preface they wrote that 'It has become evident that our national history might almost be written in terms of prayer.'*

Go thou with us, O Lord, as we enter into thy holy house; and go thou with us, as we return to take up the common duties of life. In worship and in work alike let us know thy presence near us; till work itself be worship, and our every thought be to thy praise; through Jesus Christ our Saviour. Amen.[6]

H oly Father, who hast shown us that the brave bearing of the cross is the beginning of wearing thy crown: help us by thy grace to bear patiently our pains and disappointments, as thy beloved Son bore his; and to present them to thee as the pure gift of our faithfulness to our crucified Lord; who now reigneth with thee and the Holy Ghost, God, for ever and ever. Amen.[7]

L ord, make us apt to teach, but more apt to learn; that we may not only desire to reveal to others what thou hast revealed to us, but with humble and thankful heart to learn of them what they have learned of thee; for Jesus Christ's sake. Amen.[8]

O God, who by thy Son Jesus Christ hast set up an earth a kingdom of holiness, to measure its strength against all others: make faith to prevail over fear, and righteousness over force, and truth over the lie, and love and concord over all things; through the same Jesus Christ our Lord. Amen.[9]

O God, give thy people grace to use aright thy holy day; that it may be a day of mercy to the heavy-laden, a day of resurrection to newness and fulness of life; a day to worship thee in the fellowship of the faithful; through Jesus Christ our Lord. Amen.[10]

O Holy Spirit, giver of light and life, impart to us thoughts higher than our own thoughts, and prayers better than our own prayers, and powers beyond our own powers, that we may spend and be spent in the ways of love and goodness, after the perfect image of our Lord Jesus Christ. Amen.[11]

S et a watch, O Lord, upon our tongue: that we never speak the cruel word which is untrue; or, being true, is not the whole truth; or being wholly true, is merciless; for the love of Jesus Christ our Lord. Amen.[12]

Albert Schweitzer (1875–1965)

Winner of the Nobel Peace Prize, Schweitzer broke fresh ground in so many fields of human thought that, even if you disagree with him, it is impossible to ignore him. In the organ music of Bach he attempted to

*show a symbolic method by which themes were composed. In the study
of the Gospels he pointed out the importance to Jesus of apocalyptic
– proclaiming the end of the age. In mission he trained in medicine
and worked in an isolated situation at Lambaréné, recording his experiences in his book,* On the Edge of the Primeval Forest. *His ethical teaching
centred on 'reverence for life'.*

O heavenly Father,
protect and bless all things that have breath;
guard them from all evil
and let them sleep in peace.[13]

William Edwin Orchard (1877–1955)

*William Orchard was a Presbyterian minister at the Kingsweigh House
Church in London. Subsequently he became a Roman Catholic priest.*

O God, we ask you not to lift us out of life, but to prove your power
within it; not for tasks more suited to our strength, but for strength
more suited to our tasks. Give us the vision that moves, the strength that
endures, the grace of Jesus Christ, who wore our flesh like a monarch's
robe, and walked our earthly life like a conqueror in triumph; we ask it
for his sake. Amen.[14]

E ternal God, thou makest all things new, and abidest for ever the same:
grant us to begin this year in thy faith, and to continue it in thy favour;
that, being guided in all our doings, and guarded all our days, we may
spend our lives in thy service, and finally, by thy grace, attain the glory of
everlasting life; through Jesus Christ our Lord. Amen.

O God, forgive the poverty, the pettiness, Lord, the childish folly of
our prayers. Listen, not to our words, but to the groanings that
cannot be uttered; hearken, not to our petitions, but to the crying of our
need. So often we pray for that which is already ours, neglected and
unappropriated; so often for that which never can be ours; so often for
that which we must win ourselves; and then labour endlessly for that which
can only come to us in prayer . . . O give us to love thy will, and seek thy
kingdom first of all. Sweep away our fears, our compromise, our weakness,
lest at last we be found fighting against thee. Amen.

Harry Emerson Fosdick (1878–1969)

Fosdick was born in Buffalo, New York, and was ordained to the Baptist ministry. He was appointed a professor at the Union Theological Seminary in New York. He became known as an outstanding preacher during his ministry from 1926 to 1946 at the interdenominational Riverside Church in New York. He was regarded as a modernist, and opposed fundamentalism. Among his many popular books, The Meaning of Prayer *was frequently reprinted, and helped many by its daily readings on 'The Naturalness of Prayer', 'Hindrances and Difficulties' and 'Unanswered Prayer'.*

God of grace and God of glory,
come among us in your power:
crown your ancient church's story,
bring her bud to glorious flower.
Grant us wisdom,
grant us courage
for the facing of this hour.

See the hosts of evil round us
scorn your Christ, attack his ways!
Fears and doubts too long have bound us –
free our hearts to work and praise.
Grant us wisdom,
grant us courage
for the living of these days.

Save us from weak resignation
to the evils we deplore:
let the search for your salvation
be our glory evermore.
Grant us wisdom,
grant us courage
serving you whom we adore;

Heal your children's warring madness,
bend our pride to your control:
shame our wanton, selfish gladness,
rich in things and poor in soul.
Grant us wisdom,
grant us courage
lest we miss our kingdom's goal.[15]

Pierre Teilhard de Chardin (1881–1955)

A Jesuit priest from the Auvergne and a professor of geology at the Catholic Institute in Paris, Teilhard de Chardin was one of the scientists involved in the discovery of the skull of an early hominid in China, which was called Peking Man. He was given high academic honours for his scientific work, but his religious writings were disapproved of by his superiors, and they forbade him to publish them during his lifetime. The Phenomenon of Man *argues that* Homo sapiens *is the climax of biological evolution, which is now replaced by the evolution of human society. In* Le Milieu Divin *he suggests that God acts within and through the processes of evolution towards an Omega Point, when all things are summed up in Christ. His other writings show a deeply spiritual man who finds God at work, during his travels, in the beauty and complexity of the world around him.*

Te igitur . . .

Since today, Lord, I your Priest have neither bread nor wine nor altar, I shall spread my hands over the whole universe and take its immensity as the matter of my sacrifice.

Is not the infinite circle of things the one final Host that it is your will to transmute?

The seething cauldron in which the activities of all living and cosmic substance are brewed together – is not that the bitter cup that you seek to sanctify? . . .

The whole world is concentrated, is exalted, in expectation of union with God . . . and yet it is pulled up short by an impassable barrier. Nothing can attain Christ except he take it up and enfold it.

Thus the universe groans, caught between its passionate desire and its impotence.

Today, Lord, I can feel so strongly within me the cry of the weary multitude, seeking to win, in the divine, its right order and its repose.

I seem to hear, rising up from all creatures – both those that are imprisoned in inert matter, and those who are opening their eyes to the light of life, from those, too, who move and act in freedom – the universal lament: 'Show your pity for us, O you our priest, and, if it be in your power, give us our fulfilment by giving us our God!'

Who, then, will utter, over the formless mass of the world, the words that will give it *one* soul? What voice will overthrow the obstacle between God and creation which prevents *this* One from meeting with that other? . . .

Take up in your hands, Lord, and bless this universe that is destined to sustain and fulfil the plenitude of your being among us.

Make this universe ready to be united with you: and that this may be so, intensify the magnetism that comes down from your heart to draw to it the dust of which we are made.

When that moment comes, Almighty Father, I shall concentrate in myself all the aspiration that rises up towards you from these lower spheres – I shall feel the full force of the yearning that seeks expression in my words – I shall look beyond the white host, accepting its domination, and with all the strength of my desire and my prayer, with all my power, over every substance and every development, I shall pronounce the words: *Hoc est corpus meum.*

The divine work is accomplished . . .

The universe assumes the form of Christ – but, O mystery! the man we see is Christ crucified. The sacramental bread is made out of grains of wheat which have been pressed out and ground in the mill: and the dough has been slowly kneaded. Your hands, Jesus, have broken the bread before they hallow it.

Who shall describe, Lord, the violence suffered by the universe from the moment it falls under your sovereign power? . . .

May the blood of the Lord Jesus – the blood which is infused into creatures and the blood which is shed and spread out over all, the blood of endeavour and the blood of renouncement – mingle with the pain of the world.

Hic est calix sanguinis mei.

From The Mass on the World *or* The Priest[16]

Pope John XXIII (1881–1963)

Angelo Giuseppi Roncale, born to a peasant family in north Italy, served as a sergeant in the medical corps and then as a chaplain during the First World War. In 1944 he was Papal Nuncio to newly liberated France, and spoke in favour of the controversial worker-priests. He then became Patriarch of Venice, and was elected Pope in 1958 on the twelfth ballot. It is said that it was regarded as a safe appointment of an old man who would make no changes before he died, but he called the Second Vatican Council, with an aim of promoting Christian unity, and thereby brought about a massive updating of Roman Catholic attitudes and procedures.

O sweet Child of Bethlehem, grant that we may share with all our hearts in this profound mystery of Christmas. Put into our hearts this peace for which we sometimes seek so desperately and which you alone can give us. Help us to know one another better, and to live as children of the same Father. Reveal to us also your beauty, holiness and purity. Awaken in our hearts love and gratitude for your infinite goodness. Join us all together in your love. And give us your heavenly peace. Amen.[17]

O God, we are conscious that many centuries of blindness have blinded our eyes so that we no longer see the beauty of thy chosen people, nor recognize in their faces the features of our privileged brethren. We realize that the mark of Cain stands upon our foreheads. Across the centuries our brother Abel has lain in the blood which we drew or which we caused to be shed by forgetting thy love. Forgive us for the curse we falsely attached to their name as Jews. Forgive us for crucifying thee a second time in their flesh. For we knew not what we did.[18]

William Temple (1881–1944)

William Temple was headmaster of Repton School, Bishop of Manchester and Archbishop successively of York and Canterbury. His Readings in Saint John's Gospel *reveal his deep learning and his devotional approach to Scripture. He was an advocate of social reform and of Christian unity. His prayers arose out of his pastoral concerns.*

M ay the love of the Lord Jesus draw us to himself, may the power of the Lord Jesus strengthen us in his service; may the joy of the Lord Jesus fill our souls. May the blessing of God almighty, the Father, the Son, and the Holy Spirit, be amongst you and remain with you always. Amen.[19]

L ord Jesus Christ, who prayed for your disciples that they might be one, even as you are one with the Father; draw us to yourself, that in common love and obedience to you we may be united to one another, in the fellowship of the one Spirit, that the world may believe that you are Lord, to the glory of God the Father. Amen.[20]

O God, the King of righteousness, lead us, we pray, in the ways of justice and of peace. Inspire us to break down all oppression and wrong, to gain for every one their due reward, and from every one their due service; that each may live for all, and all may care for each, in the name of Jesus Christ our Lord. Amen.[21]

O God of love, we pray thee to give us love: love in our thinking, love in our speaking, love in our doing, and love in the hidden places of our souls; love of our neighbours, near and far; love of our friends, old and new; love of those whom we find it hard to bear, and love of those who find it hard to bear with us; love of those with whom we work, and love of those with whom we take our ease; love in joy, love in sorrow; love in life and love in death; that so at length we may be worthy to dwell with thee, who art eternal Love, Father, Son and Holy Spirit, for ever and ever. Amen.[22]

Kahlil Gibran (1883–1931)

The author of The Prophet *was born in the Maronite Christian hamlet of Bsharri on the slopes of Mount Lebanon. His family emigrated to the United States when he was twelve, and settled in Boston. In 1912 he moved to New York City, where he lived for the rest of his life. The popularity of his writings probably derives from his gift of making a Middle Eastern mystical understanding of life accessible to ordinary people of the Western world. His images, language and insights are very beautiful, and his* Jesus: The Son of Man *shows the influence on him of the person of Christ and his Christian background, though the development of his thought, like that of William Blake who influenced him, may not have been entirely in line with Christian orthodoxy.*

A Priestess said, Speak to us of Prayer.
And he answered, saying:
You pray in your distress and in your need;
would that you might pray also in the fullness of your joy
and in your days of abundance.
For what is prayer but the expansion of yourself into the living
ether?
And if it is for your comfort to pour your darkness into space,
it is also for your delight to pour forth the dawning of your heart.

And if you cannot but weep when your soul summons you to
    prayer,
she should spur you again and yet again, though weeping,
until you shall come laughing.
When you pray you rise to meet in the air
those who are praying at that very hour,
and whom save in prayer you may not meet.
Therefore let your visit to that temple invisible
be for naught but ecstasy and sweet communion.
For if you should enter the temple
for no other purpose than asking you shall not receive:
And if you should enter into it to humble yourself
you shall not be lifted:
Or even if you should enter into it to beg for the good of
    others
you shall not be heard.
It is enough that you enter the temple invisible.
I cannot teach you how to pray in words.
God listens not to your words
save when he himself utters them through your lips.
And I cannot teach you
the prayer of the seas and the forests and the mountains.
But you who are born of the mountains and the forests
and the seas can find their prayer in your heart,
And if you but listen in the stillness of the night
you shall hear them saying in silence:
'Our God, who art our winged self,
it is thy will in us that willeth.
It is thy desire in us that desireth.
It is thy urge in us that would turn our nights,
which are thine, into days, which are thine also.'

And look into space; you shall see Him walking in the cloud,
outstretching his arms in the lightning and descending in rain.
You shall see him smiling in flowers,
then rising and waving his hands in trees.[23]

Master, Master of Light,
Whose eye dwells in the seeking fingers of the blind,
You are still despised and mocked,
A man too weak and infirm to be God,
A God too much man to call forth adoration.
Their mass and their hymn,
Their sacrament and their rosary, are for their imprisoned self.
You are their yet distant self, their far-off cry, and their passion.
But Master, Sky-heart, Knight of our fairer dream,
You do still tread this day,
Nor bows nor spears shall stay your steps;
You walk through all our arrows.
You smile down upon us,
And though you are the youngest of us all
You father us all.[24]

Geoffrey Anketell Studdert-Kennedy (1883–1929)

'Woodbine Willie', as he was known to all the troops to whom he was a chaplain in the hell which was the trenches of the First World War, from the brand of cigarettes he gave them, said the name was 'the symbol/ Of unpaid – unpayable debt,/ For the men to whom I owed God's Peace,/ I put off with a cigarette.' He was a vicar in Worcester before and after the war, and then moved to London, but travelled around speaking to large gatherings and supporting the Industrial Christian Fellowship. Some of his poems are in dialect, and some are too long to quote here, but almost all are heart-rending in their compassion.

The Comrade God

Thou who dost dwell in depths of timeless being,
Watching the years as moments passing by,
Seeing the things that lie beyond our seeing,
Constant, unchanged, as æons dawn and die.

Thou who canst count the stars upon their courses,
Holding them all in the hollow of thy hand,
Lord of the world with its myriad of forces
Seeing the hills as single grains of sand;

Art thou so great that this our bitter crying
Sounds in thine ears like sorrow of a child?
Hast thou looked down on centuries of sighing,
And, like a heartless mother, only smiled?

Since in thy sight to-day is as to-morrow,
And while we strive thy victory is won,
Hast thou no tears to shed upon our sorrow?
Art thou a staring splendour like the sun?

Dost thou not heed the helpless sparrow's falling?
Canst thou not see the tears that women weep?
Canst thou not hear thy little children calling?
Dost thou not watch above them as they sleep?

Then, O my God, thou art too great to love me,
Since thou dost reign beyond the reach of tears,
Calm and serene as the cruel stars above me,
High and remote from human hopes and fears.

Only in Him can I find home to hide me,
who on the Cross was slain to rise again;
Only with Him, my Comrade God, beside me,
Can I go forth to war with sin and pain.[25]

Prayer before an Attack

It ain't as I 'opes 'E'll keep me safe
While the other blokes goes down,
It ain't as I wants to leave this world
And wear an 'ero's crown.
It ain't for that as I says my prayers
When I goes to the attack,
But I pray that whatever comes my way
I may never turn me back.
I leaves the matter o' life and death
To the Father who knows what's best,
And I prays that I still may play the man
Whether I turns east or west.
I'd sooner that it were east, ye know,
To Blighty and my gal Sue;

I'd sooner be there, wi' the gold in 'er 'air,
And the skies be'ind all blue.
But still I pray I may do my bit,
And then, if I must turn west,
I'll be unashamed when my name is named.
And I'll find a soldier's rest.[26]

Eric Milner-White (1884–1964)

The service of Nine Lessons with Carols was first drawn up by Archbishop Benson when he was Bishop of Truro, based on the three readings at each of the morning offices on the triple feast of Christmas in the medieval church. In 1918 Eric Milner-White, the Dean of King's College, Cambridge, adapted it and wrote the Bidding Prayer. When it began to be broadcast regularly by the BBC it became an essential part of Christmas for many listeners. Milner-White went on to become Dean of York, and his books of prayers contain many of the most beautiful and memorable writings in the genre.

Almighty Father, who by thy Son Jesus Christ hast poured upon us thy best gift of love, to be the bond of perfectness in the families of men, and the means to bring man and wife and child to thine everlasting mansions; bless, we beseech thee, the homes of our land, that in them love may abound and happiness abide, by faith in thee; through the same Jesus Christ our Lord. Amen.[27]

Blessed Lord, lifting up holy hands perpetually for all mankind; breathe by thy Spirit such love into the prayers we offer, that they may be taken into thine, and prevail with thine; to the glory of thy holy name. Amen.[28]

Direct, O God, with thine own loving wisdom our schools of thought and science; that they may more and more unveil the wondrous things of thy law, and draw all to adore thee with mind and heart and soul; through Jesus Christ our Lord. Amen.[29]

God, who hast made every calling acceptable to thyself, if only thy glory be intended in it: give us day by day the desire to do our work, of what sort soever it be, for thine honour; and the joy of rendering it to thee well done; through Jesus Christ our Lord. Amen.[30]

Grant us, O Lord, the peace of claiming thee in death as our Father, because we have served thee in life as our God; for Jesus Christ's sake. Amen.[31]

Lord, this is thy feast, prepared by thy longing, spread at thy command, attended at thine invitation, blessed by thine own Word, distributed by thine own hand, the undying memorial of thy sacrifice upon the cross, the full gift of thine everlasting love, and its perpetuation till time shall end. Lord, this is Bread of heaven, Bread of life, that, those who eat it never shall hunger more. And this the cup of pardon, healing, gladness, strength, that those who drink it, never thirst again. Amen.[32]

Grant, O Lord God, that what we have heard with our ears and sung with our lips, we may believe in our hearts and practise in our lives; for Jesus Christ's sake. Amen.[33]

O Lord Jesus Christ, who didst take into thine arms the children brought to thee for blessing: bless always and in all places the children of thy Church, and thy Church in telling them of thee, that they may grow into thy likeness, keeping innocency, obedient to thy will and happy in thy house; for thy tender mercy's sake. Amen.[34]

O God, who dost begin and sustain all progress up to thee in thy kingdom: bless our Universities and Schools, that they may convey to thy children thy best gifts of truth and godliness, and prepare them for the perfect citizenship alike of earth and heaven; through Jesus Christ our Lord. Amen.[35]

O God, mighty to save, infinite in compassion towards the nations that know thee not, and the tongues which cannot speak thy name: we humbly thank thee that thou hast made the Church of thy dear Son the chariot of the gospel, to tell it out among the nations that thou art King, and to bear thy love to the world's end: and for all who counted not their lives dear to them on this employment, and for all peoples newly praising thee, we praise and bless thee, Father, Son and Holy Spirit, one God for ever and ever. Amen.[36]

O God, who wouldest fold both heaven and earth in a single peace: let the design of thy great love lighten upon the waste of our wraths and sorrows; and give peace to thy Church, peace among nations, peace in our dwellings, and peace in our hearts; through thy Son our Saviour, Jesus Christ our Lord. Amen.[37]

O Lord Christ, Lamb of God, Lord of Lords, call us, who are called to be saints, along the way of thy Cross; draw us, who would draw nearer our King, to the foot of thy Cross; cleanse us, who are not worthy to approach, with the pardon of thy Cross; instruct us, the ignorant and blind, in the school of thy Cross; arm us, for the battles of holiness, by the might of thy Cross; bring us, in the fellowship of thy sufferings, to the victory of thy Cross; and seal us in the kingdom of thy glory among the servants of thy Cross, O crucified Lord, who with the Father and the Holy Spirit livest and reignest, one God, almighty, eternal, world without end. Amen.[38]

O God, thou Lord of the vineyard, who wouldest not that any should stand idle in the market place: hear our prayer for those who are without employment or assurance of livelihood; and in thy loving wisdom, declare to us the counsels to help and heal all our distresses; through Jesus Christ our Lord. Amen.[39]

O Lord, our shepherd and guide, grant us to walk through the valley of the shadow of death fearing no evil, lacking nothing, accompanied by thee, who thyself hast passed that way and made it light, and now livest and reignest in the glory of the eternal Trinity, world without end. Amen.[40]

P rosper our industries, we pray thee, God most high, that our land may be full with all manner of store, and that there be no complaining in our streets: and as thy glorious Son our Lord plied tool and trade on earth, so give to all that labour pride in their work, a just reward, and joy both in supplying need and serving thee; through the same Jesus Christ our Lord. Amen.[41]

W e beseech thee, O Lord our God, to set the peace of heaven within the hearts of men, that it may bind the nations also in a covenant which cannot be broken; through Jesus Christ our Lord. Amen.[42]

Beloved in Christ, at this Christmas-tide let it be our care and delight to hear again the message of the angels, and in heart and mind to go even unto Bethlehem and see this thing which is come to pass, and the Babe lying in a manger. Therefore let us read and mark in Holy Scripture the tale of the loving purposes of God from the first days of our disobedience unto the glorious Redemption brought us by this Holy Child. But first, let us pray for the needs of the whole world; for peace on earth and goodwill among all his people; for unity and brotherhood within the Church he came to build, and especially in this our diocese. And because this would rejoice his heart, let us remember, in his name, the poor and helpless, the cold, the hungry, and the oppressed; the sick and them that mourn, the lonely and the unloved, the aged and the little children; all those who know not the Lord Jesus, or who love him not, or who by sin have grieved his heart of love. Lastly, let us remember before God all those who rejoice with us, but upon another shore, and in a greater light, that multitude which no man can number, whose hope was in the Word made flesh, and with whom in the Lord Jesus we are one for evermore. These prayers and praises let us humbly offer up to the Throne of Heaven, in the words which Christ himself hath taught us. Our Father . . .[43]

Karl Barth (1886–1968)

The distinguished Swiss theologian proclaimed in his monumental Church Dogmatics *that God cannot be known by human reason, unless we accept the revelation of himself which he gives through grace. He supported the 'Confessing Church' in Germany by speaking out strongly against Nazism, and was forced to resign his professorship at Bonn and return to Switzerland. Later he preached to the men detained in Basle prison, and each sermon concluded with a prayer.*

O Lord our God, you know who we are; men with good consciences and with bad, persons who are content and those who are discontented, the certain and the uncertain, Christians by conviction and Christians by convention, those who believe and those who half-believe, those who disbelieve. And you know where we have come from: from the circle of relatives, acquaintances and friends, or from the greatest loneliness; from a life of quiet prosperity, or from manifold confusion and distress; from family relationships that are well ordered or from those disordered, or under stress; from the inner circle of the Christian community or from its outer edge. But now we all stand before you, in all our differences, yet alike in that we are all in the wrong with you and with one another, that we must all one day die, that we would be lost without your grace, but also in that your grace is promised and made available to us all in your dear Son, Jesus Christ.[44]

O Lord, our Father! We have gathered here at the turn of the year because we do not want to be alone but want to be with each other, and together be united with you. Our hearts are filled with sombre thoughts as we reflect on our misdeeds of the past year. And our ears are deafened by the voices of the radio and in the newspapers, with their numerous predictions for the coming year. Instead we want to hear your word, your voice, your assurance, your guidance. We know that you are in our midst, and are eager to give us all that we need, whether we ask or not. On this night we ask for one thing only: that you collect our scattered thoughts, getting rid of the confused and defiant thoughts that may distract us, and thus enable us to concentrate on your limitless generosity to us. You were abundantly generous to us last year, and will be no less generous to us next year, and in every year to come. Fill us with gratitude to you.[45]

John Baillie (1886–1960)

Baillie was a Scot who taught in North America, working tirelessly to establish better relations between the Christian denominations. He was elected as president of the World Council of Churches, and published several books of prayers.

I praise thee for the life that stirs within me:
I praise thee for the bright and beautiful world into which I go:
I praise thee for earth and sea and sky, for scudding cloud and
    singing bird:
I praise thee for the work thou hast given me to do:
I praise thee for all that thou hast given me to fill my leisure hours:
I praise thee for my friends:
I praise thee for music and books and good company and all pure
    pleasures.[46]

Teach me, O God, so to use all the circumstances of my life today that they may bring forth in me the fruits of holiness rather than the fruits of sin.

Let me use disappointments as material for patience:

Let me use success as material for thankfulness:

Let me use suspense as material for perseverance:

Let me use danger as material for courage:

Let me use reproach as material for longsuffering:

Let me use praise as material for humility.

Let me use pleasure as material for temperance:

Let me use pains as material for endurance.[47]

Toyohiko Kagawa (1888–1960)

Kagawa was a Japanese convert to Christianity, educated at Princeton, who devoted his life thereafter to working in the slums of Kobe, supporting the labour movement, agricultural collectives, the anti-war movement, women's suffrage, and the movement towards democracy. Prayer can be quite subversive in any culture.

Great God, our Father: as we call to mind the scene of Christ's suffering in Gethsemane, our hearts are filled with penitence and shame that we foolishly waste our time in idleness and that we make no progress in the Christian life from day to day ... We are ashamed that war and lust flourish and grow more rampant every day. Forgive us for our cruel indifference to the cross, and pardon us that, like the bystanders of old, we merely stand and gaze in idle curiosity upon the piteous scene. O teach us, we beseech thee, the good news of thy forgiveness. Cause humanity, degenerate as it is, to live anew, and hasten the day when the whole world shall be born again.[48]

T. S. Eliot (1888–1965)

Born into a Unitarian family at St Louis, Missouri, and educated at Harvard, Thomas Stearns Eliot came to Oxford on a travelling scholarship for a year and stayed in England for the rest of his life. He was baptized and confirmed, and became a British citizen in 1927, and his poetry from then on is infused with the faith of an Anglo-Catholic. His poetry seemed difficult at first, partly because it is full of allusions to writers such as

Lancelot Andrewes and Julian of Norwich, who were not well known at the time. The plays for performance in church, The Rock *and* Murder in the Cathedral, *are the clearest statement of his Christian beliefs: 'The last temptation is the greatest treason:/ to do the right deed for the wrong reason.' He believed that verse should be written in modern idiom without romantic rhetoric, and his greatest work is probably* The Four Quartets. *Try reading 'Little Gidding' in the chapel at Little Gidding in Hunting-donshire.*

LORD, shall we not bring these gifts to Your Service?
Shall we not bring to Your service all our powers
For life, for dignity, grace and order,
And intellectual pleasures of the senses?
The LORD who created must wish us to create
And employ our creation again in His service
Which is already His service in creating.[49]

Martin P. G. Leonard (1889–1963)

The Provost of Glasgow wrote a book of prayers and services for use by the Boy Scout movement, in which this popular prayer appears, though its authorship has sometimes been attributed to others.

O Jesu, Master Carpenter, who at the last through wood and nails purchased our whole redemption; wield well thy tools in this thy workshop, that we who come to thee rough-hewn may be fashioned to a nobler beauty by thy hand; for thy name's sake, O Jesus Christ our Lord. Amen.[50]

Reinhold Niebuhr (1892–1971)

Professor of Applied Christianity at the Union Theological Seminary in New York, he sought to make Christianity a prophetic religion, speaking out about the culture of the times. He was enormously influential, and his most famous prayer has been used by Alcoholics Anonymous.

God, give us grace to accept with serenity the things that cannot be changed, the courage to change the things that should be changed, and the wisdom to distinguish the one from the other.[51]

O God, who hast bound us together in this bundle of life, give us grace to understand how our lives depend upon the courage, the industry, the honesty and the integrity of our fellow-men; that we may be mindful of their needs, grateful for their faithfulness, and faithful in our responsibilities to them; through Jesus Christ our Lord.[52]

Sadhu Sundar Singh (1889–c. 1929)

Sundar Singh was a Sikh who converted to Christianity following a vision. He wore the robes of a Sadhu, or Hindu holy man, and attempted to present Christianity in terms of Indian cultural traditions. B. H. Streeter wrote that trying to gather an account of the Sadhu's preaching on his visits to England, out of several people's recollections, gave him an insight into the process of writing down the sayings of Jesus in the Gospels. His biography was written by C. F. Andrews, famous as a friend of Mahatma Ghandi.

D ear Master, your varied blessings and gifts have filled my heart to overflowing with gratitude and praise. But the praise of heart and tongue are not enough for me until I prove by my deeds that my life is devoted to your service. I thank and praise you because you have brought me, unworthy though I am, out of death into life and made me rejoice in your fellowship and love. I do not know myself as I ought to, nor my need of you, but Father, you know well those whom you have created and what we need. Nor can I love myself in the way that you love me. To love myself truly is to love with heart and soul that boundless love which gave me being; and you are that love. You have therefore given me only one heart, that it might be fixed on only one beloved, on you, who created it. Master, to be seated at your feet is better far than to sit upon the highest throne of earth, for it means to be enthroned for ever in the eternal kingdom. And now, on the altar of these holy feet I offer myself as a sacrifice. Graciously accept me, and wherever and however you choose, use me in your service. For you are mine, and I belong to you, who took this handful of dust and made me in your own image and gave me the right to become your son. All honour and glory and praise and thanksgiving be to you for ever and ever. Amen.

M y Lord God, my all in all, Life of my life, and Spirit of my spirit, look in mercy on me and so fill me with your Holy Spirit that my heart has no room for love of anything but you. I ask from you no other gift but yourself, for you are the giver of life and all its blessings. From you I ask not for the world or its treasures, neither do I beg for heaven. I desire and long for you alone, and where you are, there is heaven. The hunger and the thirst of this heart of mine can be satisfied only with you who gave me birth. O my Creator! You have created my heart for yourself alone, and not for another, therefore this my heart can find no rest or ease except in you; in you who both created it and set in it this very longing for rest. Take away then from my heart everything that is opposed to you, and enter and abide and rule there for ever. Amen.

Leslie Weatherhead (1893–1975)

Leslie Weatherhead was the minister at the Congregationalist City Temple in London for almost thirty years. He was one of the first to show that the insights of psychology could be helpful in the Christian ministry of healing. Books such as A Plain Man looks at the Cross *enabled some to feel what Jesus has done for us. In* A Private House of Prayer *he responded to requests for guidance in prayer by imagining our daily prayer as a house with seven rooms, with sample prayers to be said in each room.*

F rom the cowardice that shrinks from new truth,
from the laziness that is content with half-truths,
from the arrogance which thinks it knows all truth,
O God of Truth, deliver us. Amen.[53]

Room 1: Affirmation of God's Presence. As I bow in the quiet room I have made in my heart, O Lord, let the hush of thy presence fall upon me.

Room 2: Adoration and Praise. I turn my thoughts quietly, O God, away from self to thee. I adore thee. I praise thee. I thank thee. I here turn from this feverish life to think of thy holiness – thy love – thy serenity – thy joy – thy mighty purposefulness – thy wisdom – thy beauty – thy truth – thy final omnipotence. Slowly I murmur these great words about thee and let their feeling and significance sink into the deep places of my mind.

Room 3: Confession and Forgiveness. Dear Lord, forgive me in that so much of my religion is concerned with myself. I want harmony with thee. I want peace of mind. I want health of body – and so I pray. Forgive me, for I have made thee the means and myself the end. I know it will take long to wean me from this terrible self-concern, but O God, help me, for hell can be nothing else but a life on which self is the centre. Can I ever abandon self as men a sinking ship, only to find that the waves will bear them up and a divine hand will rescue them? My salvation can come only from thee, O Lord. Leave me not. Forgive and uphold me and make me truly thine in utter committal to thee.

Room 4: Relaxation. Help me now to be quiet, relaxed and receptive, accepting the thought of thy healing grace at work, deep within my nature.

Room 5: Petition. I pray, O Lord, that today I may know with keener awareness that I am in thy hands; well or ill, happy or sad, at work or at play, with others or alone, may I become increasingly conscious that I dwell within thy purposeful providence.

Illness does not mean punishment or thy disfavour. Fun is not 'secular'. The trifles of my life do not forfeit thine interest in me.

Grant me the sense of thy presence, born of thine indwelling and of thine enfolding love, and let me increasingly pause to recollect that, in every circumstance, I live within thy life and am always the object of thy care.

Room 6: Intercession. I lift up my heart, O God, for all who are the prey of anxious fears, who cannot get their minds off themselves and for whom every demand made on them fills them with foreboding, and with the feeling that they cannot cope with all that is required of them.

Give them the comfort of knowing that this feeling is illness, not coward-ice; that millions have felt as they feel, that there is a way through this dark valley, and light at the end of it.

Lead them to those who can help them and understand them and show them the pathway to health and happiness. Comfort and sustain them by the loving presence of the Saviour who knows and understands all our woe and fear, and give them enough courage to face each day, and rest their minds in the thought that thou wilt see them through.

Room 7: Meditation. Come, in this quiet moment of meditation; call me again, lead me in thy way for me, let the assurance of thy friendship take away my fears. Let every shadow make me look up into thy blessed face. Let me rise up now and follow thee.

From A Private House of Prayer [54]

C. S. Lewis (1898–1963)

Clive Staples Lewis, lecturer at Oxford and professor of English at Cambridge, wrote the story of his own life in Surprised by Joy. *He became widely known through his radio talks and popular books as one who could explain traditional Christian beliefs in a simple, rational way; they helped many to come to faith and strengthened the faith of new Christians. His 'Narnia' books for children use the extended metaphor of Aslan the lion to represent Christ, and the space-travel trilogy also uses fiction to convey Christian truth.* Letters to Malcolm, Chiefly on Prayer *explores the purpose and difficulties of prayer in the form of one half of a witty dialogue.* Shadowlands *has made his thinking and the story of his marriage to Joy Davidson known to an even wider public.*

The Apologist's Evening Prayer

From all my lame defeats and oh! much more
From all the victories that I seemed to score;
From cleverness shot forth on thy behalf
At which, while angels weep, the audience laugh;
From all my proofs of thy divinity,
Thou, who wouldst give no sign, deliver me.

Thoughts are but coins. Let me not trust, instead
Of thee, their thin-worn image of thy head.
From all my thoughts, even from my thoughts of thee,
O thou fair Silence, fall, and set me free.
Lord of the narrow gate and the needle's eye,
Take from me all my trumpery lest I die.[55]

Footnote to All Prayers

He whom I bow to only knows to whom I bow
When I attempt the ineffable name, murmuring thou,
And dream of Pheidian fancies and embrace in heart
Symbols (I know) which cannot be the thing thou art.
Thus always, taken at their word, all prayers blaspheme
Worshipping with frail images a folk-lore dream,
And all men in their praying, self-deceived, address
The coinage of their own unquiet thoughts, unless
Thou in magnetic mercy to thyself divert

Our arrows, aimed unskilfully, beyond desert;
And all men are idolators, crying unheard
To a deaf idol, if thou take them at their word.
Take not, oh Lord, our literal sense. Lord, in thy great,
Unbroken speech our limping metaphor translate.[56]

e e cummings (1894–1962)

Immediately recognizable by their idiosyncratic use of small and capital letters (which in this case contrast the small 'i' with the big 'You'), the poems of Edward Estlyn Cummings are perfectly crafted, as in this sonnet:

i thank You God for most this amazing
day: for the leaping greenly spirits of trees
and a blue true dream of sky; and for everything
which is natural which is infinite which is yes

(i who have died am alive again today,
and this is the sun's birthday; this is the birth
day of life and of love and wings: and of the gay
great happening illimitably earth)

how should tasting touching hearing seeing
breathing any – lifted from the no
of all nothing – human merely being
doubt unimaginable You?
(now the ears of my ears awake and
now the eyes of my eyes are opened)[57]

Queen Salote of Tonga (1900–1965)

She was educated in New Zealand, and Queen from 1918. She is remembered in Britain for her colourful presence at the 1953 coronation, but in her own islands for the reunion between the Tongan Free Church and the Methodist Church in 1924, for which she was largely responsible.

God, our Heavenly Father, we draw near to thee with thankful hearts because of all thy great love for us. We thank thee most of all for the gift of thy dear Son, in whom alone we may be one. We are different one from another in race and language, in material things, in gifts, in opportunities, but each of us has a human heart, knowing joy and sorrow, pleasure and pain. We are one in our need of thy forgiveness, thy strength, thy love; make us one in our common response to thee, that bound by a common love and freed from selfish aims we may work for the good of all and the advancement of thy kingdom. Through Jesus Christ, our Lord.

Dom Gregory Dix (1901–52)

A monk of the Anglican Benedictine Abbey of Nashdom in Buckingham-shire, Dom Gregory Dix influenced the revision of all subsequent versions of the Holy Communion, which followed the fourfold pattern of the Last Supper, where Jesus took bread and wine, gave thanks, broke and gave. He gives a lyrical description of the centrality of Holy Communion in the history of Christian prayer.

'Do this in remembrance of me'

Was ever another command so obeyed? For century after century, spreading slowly to every continent and country and among every race on earth, this action has been done, in every conceivable human circumstance, for every conceivable human need from infancy and before it to extreme old age and after it, from the pinnacles of earthly greatness to the refuge of fugitives in the caves and dens of the earth. Men have found no better thing than this to do for kings at their crowning and for criminals going to the scaffold; for armies in triumph or for a bride and bridegroom in a little country church; for the proclamation of a dogma or for a good crop of wheat; for the wisdom of the Parliament of a mighty nation or for a sick old woman afraid to die; for a schoolboy sitting an examination or for Columbus setting out to discover America; for the famine of whole provinces or for the soul of a dead lover; in thankfulness because my father did not die of pneumonia; for a village headman much tempted to return to fetish because the yams had failed; because the Turk was at the gates of Vienna; for the repentance of Margaret; for the settle-ment of a strike; for a son for a barren woman; for Captain so-and-so, wounded and prisoner of war; while the lions roared in the nearby amphi-theatre; on the beach at Dunkirk; while the hiss of scythes in the thick June grass came faintly through the windows of the church; tremulously, by an old monk on the fiftieth anniversary of his vows; furtively, by an exiled bishop who had hewn timber all day in a prison camp near

Murmansk; gorgeously, for the canonisation of Saint Joan of Arc – one could fill many pages with the reasons why men have done this, and not tell a hundredth part of them. And best of all, week by week and month by month, on a hundred thousand successive Sundays, faithfully, unfailingly, across all the parishes of Christendom, the pastors have done this just to *make* the *plebs sancta Dei* – the holy common people of God.[58]

Peter Marshall (1902–49)

Peter Marshall was a Scot who emigrated to the USA and was ordained as a Presbyterian minister. He was made a chaplain to the Senate and said prayers every day before their sessions. The simplicity and sincerity of these prayers won him many admirers before his early death, since when his widow Catherine has published them, and many other devotional books in her own right.

Our Father, sometimes thou dost seem so far away, as if thou art a God in hiding, as if thou art determined to elude all who seek thee. Yet we know that thou art far more willing to be found than we are to seek. Thou hast promised 'If with all thy heart ye truly seek me, ye shall ever surely find me'. And hast thou not assured us that thou art with us always?[59]

Help us now to be as aware of thy nearness as we are of the material things of every day. Help us to recognize thy voice with as much assurance as we recognize the sounds of the world around us. We would find thee now in the privacy of our hearts, in the quiet of this moment. We would know, our Father, that thou art near us and beside us; that thou dost love us and art interested in all that we do, art concerned about all our affairs. May we become aware of thy companionship, of him who walks beside us. At times when we feel forsaken, may we know the presence of the Holy Spirit who brings comfort to all human hearts, when we are willing to surrender ourselves. May we be convinced that even before we reach up to thee, thou art reaching down to us.[60]

In the name of Jesus Christ, who was never in a hurry, we pray, O God, that thou wilt slow us down, for we know that we live too fast. With all of eternity before us, make us take time to live – time to get acquainted with thee, time to enjoy thy blessings, and time to know each other.[61]

Alan Paton (1903–88)

It was because of his experience as principal of the Diepkloof Reformatory for young offenders that Alan Paton developed a deep concern for the racial situation in South Africa, which he expressed in the novel Cry, the Beloved Country. *He collected his prayers in* Instrument of thy Peace.

O Lord, open my eyes
    that I may see the need of others,
open my ears that I may hear their cries,
open my heart so that they need not be without succour.
Let me not be afraid to defend the weak
because of the anger of the strong,
nor afraid to defend the poor
because of the anger of the rich.
Show me where love and hope and faith are needed,
and use me to bring them to these places.
Open my eyes and ears that I may, this coming day,
be able to do some work of peace for thee.[62]

Give us courage, O Lord, to stand up and be counted, to stand up for others who cannot stand up for themselves. To stand up for ourselves when it is needful to do so. Let us fear nothing more than we fear thee. Let us love nothing more than we love thee, for then we shall fear nothing also. Let us have no other God before thee, whether nation or party or state or church. Let us seek no other peace but the peace which is thine, and make us its instruments, opening our eyes and our ears and our hearts, so that we should know always what work of peace we should do for thee.[63]

Help me, O Lord, to be more loving. Help me, O Lord, not to be afraid to love the outcast, the leper, the unmarried pregnant woman, the traitor to the State, the man out of prison. Help me by my love to restore the faith of the disillusioned, the disappointed, the early bereaved. Help me by my love to be the witness of your love. And may I this coming day be able to do some work of peace for you.[64]

Oliver Warner (1903–76)

Oliver Warner was a naval historian, a publisher's reader and a prolific author.

A prayer for racial harmony

Father, you have made us all in your likeness and you love all whom you have made; suffer not our family to separate itself from you by building barriers of race or colour. As your Son our Saviour was born of a Hebrew mother, but rejoiced in the faith of a Syrian woman and of a Roman soldier, welcomed the Greeks who sought him, and suffered a man from Africa to carry his cross; so teach us to regard the members of all races as fellow heirs of the kingdom of Jesus Christ our Lord. Amen.[65]

Dag Hammarskjøld (1905–61)

The Secretary-General of the United Nations died in an aeroplane crash, and in his apartment was found a manuscript which he described as 'negotiations with myself – and with God'. It was published under the title Markings.

Night is drawing nigh –
For all that has been – Thanks!
For all that shall be – Yes![66]

Thou takest the pen – and the lines dance. Thou takest the flute – and the notes shimmer. Thou takest the brush and the colours sing. So all things have meaning and beauty in that space beyond time where thou art. How then can I hold back anything from thee?[67]

Dietrich Bonhoeffer (1906–45)

Bonhoeffer was a pastor of the German Lutheran Church. He left Germany in 1933 in protest against Nazi anti-Jewish legislation, and ministered to the German congregation in Forest Hill, south London. In 1935 he returned to head the pastoral seminary of the German Confessing Church – the section which refused to compromise with Hitler. His involvement with the plot to assassinate Hitler led to his arrest in 1943. Hanged in 1945, he is widely revered as a martyr. In his Ethics *and* Letters and Papers from Prison *he coined the phrase 'religionless Christianity', and laid the foundations of the post-war reinterpretation of the gospel in a way that would be meaningful to contemporary people.*

Prayer in Time of Distress

O Lord God,
   great distress has come upon me;
my cares threaten to crush me,
and I do not know what to do.
Give me strength to bear what you send,
and do not let fear rule over me;
Take a father's care of my wife and children.

O merciful God,
forgive me all the sins that I have committed
against you and against my fellow men.
I trust in your grace
and commit my life wholly into your hands.
Do with me according to your will
and as is best for me.
Whether I live or die, I am with you,
and you, my God, are with me.
Lord, I wait for your salvation
and for your kingdom.
Amen.[68]

William Barclay (1907–78)

After thirteen years as a Church of Scotland Minister in the parish of Renfrew, William Barclay concentrated on his writing, speaking and broadcasting as a lecturer and then professor at Trinity College in Glasgow. His New Testament Wordbook *and his* Daily Study Bible *grew out of his articles in the* British Weekly, *and as well as helping many ordinary Christians to grow in understanding of the Scriptures and to read them regularly, they have provided illustrations for thousands of preachers. His books on prayer are equally down-to-earth and practical, concealing deep learning under an easy manner.*

Eternal and everblessed God, we remember this day
the unseen cloud of witnesses who compass us about.
We remember the blessed dead who do rest from their labours,
and whose works do follow them.
And we give thee thanks for all of them.
For parents who gave us life; who tended and cared for us
in years when we were helpless to help ourselves;
who toiled and sacrificed to give to us our chance in life;
at whose knees we learned to pray,
and from whose lips we first heard the name of Jesus:
We give thee thanks, O God.
For teachers who taught us;
For ministers of thy gospel who instructed us in thy truth
　　　and in thy faith;
For all those who have been an example to us
　　　of what life should be;
For those whose influence on us will never cease,
　　　and whose names will never depart from our memory:
We give thee thanks, O God.
For the saints, the prophets and the martyrs;
For those who lived and died for the faith;
And, above all else, for Jesus, the captain of our salvation
　　　and the author and finisher of our faith:
We give thee thanks, O God.
Grant unto us in our day and generation
　　　to walk worthily of the heritage into which we have entered:
　　　through Jesus Christ our Lord. Amen.[69]

O God, our Father, who ever makest the light to shine out of the darkness, we thank thee for waking us to see the light of this new day. Grant unto us to waste none of its hours; to soil none of its moments; to neglect none of its opportunities; to fail in none of its duties. And bring us to the evening time undefeated by any temptation, and at peace with ourselves, at peace with our fellow-men, and at peace with thee. This we ask for thy love's sake. Amen.[70]

O God, our Father, give us the humility which realizes its ignorance; admits its mistakes; recognizes its need; welcomes advice; accepts rebuke. Save us from pride in our knowledge, and make us to think of the great ocean of truth all undiscovered before us. Save us from pride in our achievement, and make us to remember all that we still have to do. Save us from pride in our performance, and make us to remember how far short of perfection our best must still fall. Help us in the days ahead, to study with diligence; to learn with eagerness. And give us a retentive memory to remember that which we have learned; and a resolute will to put it into action. Amen.[71]

O God, our Father, we thank thee for this sacrament. For all who down the centuries at this table have found the light that never fades, the joy that no one takes from them, the forgiveness of their sins, the love which is thy love, the presence of their Lord; we thank thee. Amen.[72]

Giovanni Guareschi (1908–68)

Born in Parma, he became the editor of a Milan magazine, Bertoldo, before becoming a prisoner of war. Guareschi returned to journalism after the war, but became internationally famous for a series of books chronicling the rivalry between a parish priest and the town's communist mayor. Like the parables of Jesus, these stories make a challenging point by means of humour; in this case, that anyone who comes to know Jesus well, and is totally honest in expressing their desires to him, will not need too much imagination to work out what his response to them would be. In this extract the priest, after preaching against communism, has just been attacked and beaten, but it was too dark to identify his attacker.

D on Camillo . . . had gone into the church to discuss the matter with the Lord, as was his habit in moments of perplexity.

'What should I do?' Don Camillo asked.

'Anoint your back with a little oil beaten up in water and hold your tongue,' the Lord had replied from above the altar. 'We must forgive those who offend us. That is the rule.'

'Very true, Lord,' agreed Don Camillo, 'but on this occasion we are discussing blows, not offences.'

'And what do you mean by that? Surely you are not trying to tell me that injuries done to the body are more painful than those aimed at the spirit?'

'I see your point, Lord. But you should also bear in mind that in the beating of me, who am your minister, an injury has been done to yourself also. I am really more concerned on your behalf than on my own.'

'And was not I a greater minister of God than you are? And did I not forgive those who nailed me to the Cross?'

'There is never any use in arguing with you!' Don Camillo had exclaimed. 'You are always in the right. Your will be done. We must forgive, all the same, don't forget that if those ruffians, encouraged by my silence, should crack my skull, the responsibility will lie with you. I could cite several passages from the Old Testament . . .'

'Don Camillo, are you proposing to instruct me in the Old Testament? As for this business, I assume full responsibility. Moreover, strictly between Ourselves, the beating has done you no harm. It may teach you to let politics alone in my house.'

. . . While he sat in the confessional, Don Camillo discerned through the grille the countenance of the local leader of the extreme leftists, Peppone . . .

. . . 'For example, two months ago I gave you a hiding.'

'That was serious indeed,' replied Don Camillo, 'since in assaulting a minister of God, you have attacked God himself.'

'But I have repented,' exclaimed Peppone. 'And moreover, it was not as God's minister that I beat you, but as my political adversary. In any case, I did it in a moment of weakness.'

. . . Don Camillo let him off with a score of Paters and Aves. Then, while Peppone was kneeling at the altar rails performing his penance, Don Camillo went and knelt before the crucifix.

'Lord,' he said. 'You must forgive me, but I am going to beat him up for you.'

'You are going to do nothing of the kind,' replied he Lord. 'I have forgiven him and you must forgive him also. All things considered, he is not a bad soul.'

. . . 'Let me at least break this candle on his shoulders. Dear Lord, what, after all, is a candle?'

'No,' replied the Lord. 'Your hands were made for blessing, not for striking.'

Don Camillo sighed heavily . . . he found himself exactly behind Peppone who, on his knees, was apparently absorbed in prayer.

'Lord,' groaned Don Camillo, clasping his hands and gazing at the crucifix. 'My hands were made for blessing, but not my feet.'

'There is something in that,' replied the Lord from above the altar, 'but all the same, Don Camillo, bear it in mind: only one!'[73]

Daniel Thambyrajah Niles (1908–70)

President of the World Council of Churches, Chairman of the East Asia Christian Conference, and President of the Methodist Church of Ceylon, D. T. Niles revealed to the West that winsome and statesmanlike leadership of the world Church could come from Christians deeply rooted in non-Western cultures. These words are set in the EACC Hymnal to one of the tuneful and rhythmical Tamil lyrics which are so distinctive of South Indian and Sri Lankan Christianity.

Praise God from whom all blessings flow:
 Praise him.
Alleluia in the highest, for ever praise him,
Praise God from whom all blessings flow.
Clap your hands, rejoicing;
Strike your harps, resounding;
Raise your voice, recalling
Every mercy falling.
Praise God from whom all blessings flow.[74]

Southwark Diocese (1910)

A special form of prayer was sanctioned in 1910 for use in the Church of England Diocese of Southwark, which had been formed in 1905 to cover South London, from which this blessing is taken.

May the Lord of his great mercy bless you, and give you understanding of his wisdom and grace; may he nourish you with the riches of the Catholic Faith, and make you to persevere in all good works; may he keep your steps from wandering, and direct you into the paths of love and peace; and may the blessing of God almighty, the Father, the Son, and the Holy Spirit, be upon you and remain with you always. Amen.

The Boy's Prayer Book (1913)

The author of this prayer cannot have envisaged that the coming century would see the growing importance of new forms of communication, and the importance of praying for those who work in the media.

Almighty God, who proclaimed the eternal truth by the voice of prophets and evangelists: direct and bless, we pray, those who in this our generation speak where many listen and write what many read; that they may do their part in making the heart of the people wise, its mind sound, and its will righteous; to the honour of Jesus Christ our Lord. Amen.[75]

Chao Tzu-chen (1931)

A children's hymn set to a Chinese tune.

Jesus loves both great and small.
children, though, especially;
Jesus called them one and all:
'Let the children come to me.'

Children in his circling arm
gather, happy at his knee,
and he holds them free from harm:
'Let the children come to me.'

Jesus' loving heart is kind,
blessing our humility;
grown-ups need a childlike mind;
'Let the children come to me.'

All of us need simple faith,
trusting with simplicity,
then he'll welcome us at death:
'Let my children come to me!'[76]

Ernest Yang Yin-liu (1934)

Set in the hymn-book of the Chinese Church to the ancient verse tune, 'All red the river'.

As the compass-needle's arms
point to North, South, East and West,

so the cross, through life's alarms,
helps us choose the way that's best.
Thank you, Lord, that you provide
this clear compass-cross to guide.

Where life's meaning is obscure,
through the valley of deep shade,
eyes are blind and hearts unsure;
Christ, our Sun, shine through to aid,
showing where before us lies
journey's end in paradise.

Transitory earthly things
break like bubbles in the breeze,
hopes dry up like desert springs,
plans may crash like rootless trees.
Drench dry land, O Lord, with rain,
till we bear the harvest grain.

Countless voices seek to guide,
many paths there are to choose,
if we turn to either side
firm ground soon our feet will lose.
Take us by the hand, we pray,
lead us on the narrow way.

Lord, through dusty ways ahead,
save the stumbling, here below,
be on every path we tread,
show lost sheep which way to go.
Guide us through the sheepfold's door,
till we come to joy once more.[77]

Prayers from Two World Wars

War Prayers (1914–18)

Special prayers were published to be used during the First World War.

O Lord God, our heavenly Father, regard, we pray, with thy divine pity the pains of all thy children; and grant that the Passion of our Lord and his infinite love may make fruitful for good the tribulations of the innocent, the sufferings of the sick, and the sorrows of the bereaved; through him who suffered in our flesh and died for our sake, the same thy Son Jesus Christ our Lord. Amen.

Toc H

Toc H, formed at Talbot House in Belgium by the Revd 'Tubby' Clayton during the 1914–18 war, is a fellowship and service organization which has published books of prayers. This one is adapted from a prayer used in Balliol Boys' Club, and is used by courtesy of Toc H.

O eternal God, who watchest over us all; grant that the friendships formed between us here may neither through sin be broken, nor hereafter through worldly cares be forgotten; but that bound together across the world by the unseen chain of thy love, we may be drawn nearer to thee and nearer to each other, through Jesus Christ our Lord. Amen.

Ravensbrück Concentration Camp (1945)

O Lord, remember not only the men and women of goodwill, but also those of ill will. But do not remember all the suffering they have inflicted; remember the fruits we have bought, thanks to this suffering – our comradeship, our loyalty, our humility, our courage, our generosity, the greatness of heart which has grown out of all this, and when they come to judgement, let all the fruits which we have born be their forgiveness. Amen.

Found beside a dead child

Peace Prayers (1946)

Almighty and eternal God, who hast entrusted the minds of men with the science and skill which can greatly bless or wholly destroy: Grant them also a new stature of spirit to match thy trust; that they may use their many inventions to thy glory and the benefit of mankind; through Jesus Christ our Lord. Amen.

Coventry Cathedral (1962)

The medieval cathedral at Coventry was destroyed by German bombs. When the new cathedral was built on an adjacent site, the ruins of the old were left, containing a simple altar with a cross made from charred timbers from the burnt-out roof, and the words, 'Father forgive.' The message of reconciliation, which comes when we realize that we all need forgiveness, was carried around the world, together with the cross of nails which was also made from the remains of the cathedral roof.

All have sinned and fallen short of the glory of God.
The hatred which divides nation from nation,
race from race, class from class,
Father forgive.
The covetous desires of people and nations
to possess what is not their own,
Father forgive.
The greed which exploits the work of human hands,
and lays waste the earth,

Father forgive.
Our envy of the welfare and happiness of others,
Father forgive.
Our indifference to the plight of the imprisoned,
the homeless, the refugee,
Father forgive.
The lust which dishonours the bodies of men, women and children,
Father forgive.
The pride which leads to trust in ourselves and not in God,
Father forgive.
Be kind to one another, tenderhearted, forgiving one another,
as God in Christ forgave you.[1]

May God in the plenitude of his love pour upon you the torrents of his grace, bless you and keep you in his holy fear, prepare you for a happy eternity, and receive you at last into immortal glory.[2]

Black Worship

African slaves taken to North America kept alive many of their cultural traditions, and when they heard the Christian gospel they interpreted it in their own cultural context, with an emphasis on the liberation of slaves after the example of the exodus from Egypt. They joined denominations which gave them freedom to develop this, but in their own manner, often in secrecy away from their masters' eyes. When slavery was abolished, the black Christians came into the open and many founded independent churches. During the 1914–18 war many African-Americans migrated to the cities, and created storefront churches in the ghettoes. Thomas Dorsey and Mahalia Jackson led the rise of black gospel music, and to be caught up in the singing was identified with being in the presence of the Holy Spirit. Later Black Power movements proclaimed that the God of the Bible was the power which was winning their freedom from discrimination.

The songs of Bob Marley expressed similar feelings for the Caribbean population in Britain.

Spirituals

The songs of the slaves on the plantations, longing to cross the water, ambiguously whether to heaven or back to an Africa many of them had never seen, have become so much a part of everybody's folk religion that Sir Michael Tippett used them in the place of Bach's chorales in his oratorio A Child of our Time.

And I Couldn't Hear Nobody Pray

And I couldn't hear nobody pray, and I couldn't hear nobody pray;

O way down yonder by myself, and I couldn't hear nobody pray.
In the valley on my knees,
With my burden and my Saviour, O Lord!
And I couldn't hear nobody pray, and I couldn't hear nobody pray;
O way down yonder by myself, and I couldn't hear nobody pray.

Ev'ry Time I Feel the Spirit

Ev'ry time I feel the Spirit movin' in my heart I will pray,
O, ev'ry time I feel the Spirit movin' in my heart I will pray,
Upon the mountains my Lord spoke,
Out of his mouth came fire and smoke,
An' all around me look so shine,
Asked my Lord if all was mine.
O ev'ry time I feel the Spirit movin' in my heart I will pray.

It's Me, It's Me, O Lord

It's me, it's me, O Lord, standin' in the need of prayer,
It's me, it's me, O Lord, standin' in the need of prayer.
Not my brother, nor my sister, but it's me, O Lord,
standin' in the need of prayer,
Not my brother, nor my sister, but it's me, O Lord,
standin' in the need of prayer.
It's me, it's me, O Lord, standin' in the need of prayer,
It's me, it's me, O Lord, standin' in the need of prayer.

My Lord, What a Morning

My Lord, what a morning, my Lord, what a morning,
My Lord, what a morning, when the stars begin to fall!
You'll hear the trumpet sound,
To wake the nations underground,
Lookin' to my God's right hand,
When the stars begin to fall.
My Lord, what a morning, my Lord, what a morning,
My Lord, what a morning, when the stars begin to fall!

Nobody Knows the Trouble I See

Nobody knows the trouble I see, nobody knows but Jesus;
Nobody knows the trouble I see, Glory, Hallelujah!
Sometimes I'm up, sometimes I'm down, O yes, Lord!
Sometimes I'm almost to the groun', O yes Lord.
Nobody knows the trouble I see, nobody knows but Jesus;
Nobody knows the trouble I see, Glory, Hallelujah!

Oh, Wasn't That a Wide River?

Oh, wasn't that a wide river, river of Jordan, Lord?
Wide river, there's one more river to cross.
Old River Jordan is so wide, (one more river to cross),
I don't know how to get on the other side,
    (one more river to cross).
Oh, wasn't that a wide river, river of Jordan, Lord?
Wide river, there's one more river to cross.

Trials dark on every hand

Trials dark on every hand, and we cannot understand
All the ways that God would lead us to that Blessed Promise
    Land.
But he guides us with his eye and we'll follow till we die.
For we'll understand it better by and by.
    By and by, when the morning comes,
    All the saints of God are gathered home.
    We'll tell the story how we overcome.
    For we'll understand it better by and by.[1]

James Weldon Johnson (1871–1938)

Born in Jacksonville, Florida, James Weldon Johnson was an attorney, then an American consul in Venezuela and Nicaragua, and finally professor of creative literature at Fisk University. He was secretary of the National Association for the Advancement of Colored People. In God's Trombones *he tried to capture what he regarded as a vanishing tradition of black preaching.*

Listen, Lord. A Prayer.

O Lord, we come this morning
Knee-bowed and body-bent
Before thy throne of grace.
O Lord – this morning –
Bow our hearts beneath our knees,
And our knees in some lonesome valley.
We come this morning –
Like empty pitchers to a full fountain,
With no merits of our own.
O Lord – open up a window of heaven,
And lean out far over the battlements of glory,
And listen this morning.

Lord, have mercy on proud and dying sinners –
Sinners hanging over the mouth of hell,
Who seem to love their distance well.
Lord – ride by this morning –
Mount your milk-white horse,
And ride-a this morning –
And in your ride, ride by old hell,
Ride by the dingy gates of hell,
And stop poor sinners in their headlong plunge.

And now, Lord, this man of God
Who breaks the bread of life this morning –
Shadow him in the hollow of thy hand
And keep him out of the gunshot of the devil.
Take him, Lord – this morning –
Wash him with hyssop inside and out,
Hang him up and drain him dry of sin.
Pin his ear to the wisdom post,
And make his words sledge-hammers of truth –
Beating on the iron heart of sin.
Lord God, this morning –
Put his eye to the telescope of eternity,
And let him look upon the paper walls of time.
Lord, turpentine his imagination,
Put perpetual motion in his arms,

Fill him full of the dynamite of thy power,
Anoint him all over with the oil of thy salvation,
And set his tongue on fire.

And now, O Lord –
When I've done drunk my last cup of sorrow –
When I've been called everything but a child of God –
When I've done travelling up the rough side of the mountain –
O – Mary's Baby –
When I start down the steep and slippery steps of death –
When this old world begin to rock beneath my feet –
Lower me to my dusty grave in peace
To wait for that great gittin' up morning – Amen.[2]

Martin Luther King (1929–68)

Both his father and his grandfather were Baptist pastors, so Martin Luther King, born in Atlanta, Georgia, felt called to follow in their footsteps. He gained a doctorate of philosophy from Boston University in the theology of Paul Tillich, then went to be a pastor in Montgomery, Alabama. When a black woman was arrested for refusing to surrender her seat on the bus to a white passenger, King led the successful boycott of the bus company, and from then on became the acknowledged leader of the civil rights movement. He based his method of non-violent direct action on Ghandi's example, and stressed the need for black voters to register. He was imprisoned twice, but was supported by the Kennedy and Johnson administrations, and was awarded the Nobel Peace Prize. In 1968 he was assassinated by a white gunman in Memphis, Tennessee. Does his dream of a just America help us to understand some of the 'visions' which are reported as part of the prayer experience?

And now to him who is able to keep us from falling, and lift us from the dark valley of despair to the bright mountain of hope, from the midnight of desperation to the day break of joy; to him be power and authority, for ever and ever.[3]

I have a dream that my four little children will one day live in a nation where they will not be judged by the colour of their skin but by the content of their character. I have a dream today. I have a dream that one day the state of Alabama, whose governor's lips are presently dripping with the words of interposition and nullification, will be transformed into a situation where little black boys and black girls will be able to join hands with little white boys and white girls and walk together as sisters and brothers. I have a dream today.[4]

Desmond Mpilo Tutu (1931–)

An outspoken opponent of apartheid, Desmond Tutu has also condemned violence as a means of seeking to overcome injustice. Bishop of Lesotho, Secretary-general of the South African Council of Churches, the first black Bishop of Johannesburg, and Archbishop of Capetown, he continued to preach a simple message of the love of God. He may be found to have changed the way the human race resolves conflicts by his development of the Truth and Reconciliation Commission, which he chaired after his retirement.

B less our beautiful land, O Lord,
with its wonderful variety of people,
of races, cultures and languages.
May we be a nation
of laughter and joy,
of justice and reconciliation,
of peace and unity,
of compassion, caring and sharing.
We pray this prayer for a true patriotism,
in the powerful name of Jesus our Lord.[5]

Gospel music

Forget the commercialized version of the record producers: go to a black church and experience the power of the gospel singing, where the whole congregation seems to have an inborn sense of rhythm and harmony, and ask yourself, Is not this the work of the Holy Spirit?

Can't Nobody Do Me Like Jesus

C an't nobody do me like Jesus,
Can't nobody do me like the Lord.
Can't nobody do me like Jesus,
He's my, he's my friend.

He picked me up, turned me around,
He picked me up, turned me around,
He picked me up, turned me around,
He's my, he's my friend.[6]

Soon and Very Soon

Soon and very soon, we are going to see the King;
Soon and very soon, we are going to see the King;
Soon and very soon, we are going to see the King;
Hallelujah, hallelujah! We're going to see the King.[7]

I Don't Know What the Future Holds

I don't know what the future holds, I don't know about today,
But I know who holds my hand, and I know who leads the way.
Come what may from day to day! I will never fret
For the Lord's been good to me, and he's never failed me yet.
Tomorrow might find me broke without a dime,
But I don't worry 'cause he's gonna step right in on time.
I might be friendless, left all by myself,
But as long as I got a friend in the Lord, I don't need nobody else.

When the Glory of the Lord Fills His Holy Temple

When the glory of the Lord fills his holy temple he will lift us
    high,
    And on angels' wings, we'll rise to the pure and holy,
When his glory fills this place.
When his glory, when his glory, when his glory fills this place.
When his glory, when his glory, when his glory fills this place.
Let the glory of the Lord fill this holy temple, let him lift us high,
And on angels' wings, we'll rise to the pure and holy,
Let thy Spirit fill this place.
Let thy glory, let thy glory, let thy glory fill this place.
Let thy glory, let thy glory, let thy glory fill this place.
Let thy glory fill this place.[8]

The Pentecostal and Charismatic Movements, and the Healing Ministry

Prayer would be impossible without the work of the Holy Spirit within us. Jesus promised a Comforter to lead us into all truth; St Paul welcomed the gifts of the Spirit, but warned that they must be used to create unity, not division, between Christians. But for too long the majority of Christians treated the Spirit merely as 'that gentle voice we hear, soft as the breath of even', and failed to claim the power that the Spirit gives to change lives and move mountains. There were always exceptions: Tertullian and the Montanists, the Wesleyan Revival, the Irvingites and the Holiness Movement with which Jonathan Edwards was connected.

But with Charles Parham and the Topeka Kansas Bible School in 1901, and the Hansa Street Mission in Los Angeles between 1906 and 1909, out of which grew the Assemblies of God and the Elim and Holiness Churches, together with Demos Shakarian and the Full Gospel Business Fellowship International in 1912, we begin to find a renewed emphasis on the power and the gifts of the Spirit, and the experience called Baptism in the Spirit, which led into the Pentecostal Movement of the twentieth century. David du Plessis, a South African Pentecostalist, was asked why, when he visited Europe and America, he preached in main-stream churches rather than his own denomination, and replied, 'Because more blessed than healing the sick is to raise the dead!'

Renewal in the Holy Spirit began to spread through all denominations, now usually called the charismatic movement, from St Paul's word for gifts. There are also Christians, some of them quoted here, who have been deeply influenced by renewal but would not accept the label 'charismatic'. As the emphasis now is on extempore prayer and tongues, it is not possible to include many written prayers, though the publication of worship songs has become a flood.

Praying in tongues

There is nothing particularly mysterious about tongues. They are not language, and they have no syntax: they cannot be translated (interpretation of tongues is not translation). There are many tape-recordings of tongue-speaking, and they all manifest the same pattern of strings of syllables, sounds taken from a variety of sources, put together haphazardly in units which have a sentence-like shape with rhythm and melody. There is nothing specifically Christian and probably nothing specifically religious about tongues. Indeed from a purely phenomeno-logical point of view, they represent a regression to a kind of 'baby talk'. What then is their religious significance, and have they a value in the life of prayer? The New Testament throws considerable light on the place of tongues in spirituality, and presents a very balanced and sane view of the issue. To pray in tongues, St Paul says, is to pray in a way which is not normally intelligible either to others or to oneself (1 Corinthians 14:2, 14). It is not ecstasy, and it is subject to control and to discipline, both external (of the local church) and internal (within the individual). Indeed at the time of the Montanist heresy, it was regarded as a mark of orthodox spirituality that the person possessed of spiritual gifts retained his own consciousness. Today the situation is the same: speaking in tongues is frequently a quiet, matter-of-fact unemotional activity, often pursued and practised in private.

Kenneth Leech[1]

Of course they experience a certain freeing of their prayer, and a certain uplift in their hearts; but essentially what they discover is a new depth of trust in God, a greater assurance that the peace of Christ is really there in their hearts. And this is a very important factor in spiritual as well as psychological growth. As a result of receiving and using this gift, the range of their response to God's grace in prayer and in their whole lives is, sometimes dramatically increased, allowing them a far greater involvement in all the 'moods' of God's Spirit, from the most intense joy and exuberant praise, to utter silence before God, and sometimes acute agony, in union with the suffering of Christ.

Simon Tugwell[2]

So tongues is a gift to use in the praise of God, not given to all but apparently very widespread. Its association with praise – 'speaking in tongues and magnifying God' (Acts 10:46) – involves moving beyond the restrictions of the mind. When one prays in tongues, the mind remains barren (1 Corinthians 14:14). It can therefore be a means of setting free the personality to glorify God, freed from the tyranny of mental concepts, set free in the power of the Spirit.

Kenneth Leech[3]

Merlin Robert Carothers (1924–)

Drafted into the US Army, Merlin Carothers was imprisoned for absence without leave and stealing a car. He eventually became Chaplain of the same unit, having on the way experienced the Baptism in the Spirit. His first book, Prison to Praise, *makes the apparently shocking claim that God works miracles when we praise him for everything that happens to us.*

One evening ... I began to laugh ... I felt God speaking: 'Are you glad that Jesus died for your sins?'

'Yes, Lord, I'm glad, I'm glad' ...

God said: 'It really makes you glad that they took my Son and drove nails into his hands. It really makes you glad, doesn't it? It makes you glad that they took my Son and drove nails through his feet. It really makes you glad that they drove a spear through his side and the blood flowed down his body and dripped on the ground. It makes you very happy and you laugh with great joy because they did this to my Son, doesn't it?'

Everything became very silent. I didn't know how to answer ... Finally I had to say: 'Yes, Lord, it does. I don't understand it, Father, but I am glad' ...

Then to my great relief I heard him say: 'Yes, my son, I want you to be glad! ... Now listen, my son. For the rest of your life when anything ever happens to you that is less difficult than what they did to my Son, I want you to be just as glad as you were when I first asked you if you were glad Christ died for you' ...

The next morning I was sitting on the edge of my bed when I heard a voice: 'What are you doing?'

'I'm sitting here wishing I didn't have to get up!'

'I thought we made an agreement last night.'

'But Lord, I didn't know you meant things like this!'

'Remember what I said, "in everything".'

I said: 'But Lord, I've got to be honest with you. I've been sitting on the edge of my bed every morning for twenty years wishing I didn't have to get up . . .'

But the Spirit said: 'You are supposed to be thankful that it is time to get up.'

'Lord, that's a little beyond my comprehension.'

The Lord is always very patient and kind: 'Are you willing to be made willing?'

'Yes, Lord, I am' . . .

For many years I had suffered with painful headaches. I seldom complained about it, I just thanked God that I wasn't as bad off as some people. One day he said: 'Why don't you try praising me *for* the headache?'

'*For* it?'

'Yes, *for* it.'

I began to lift up my thoughts in thanksgiving that God was giving me this headache as an opportunity to increase the power of Christ in my life. The headache got worse. I continued to thank God, but with every thought of praise came increased pain. I realised that Satan and the Spirit of Christ were at war. The pain reached an overwhelming state; I held on to thoughts of praise and thanks and suddenly I was being flooded with joy. Joy seemed to pour over every cell of my body. I had never experienced such power of joy! I was certain that if I took a step I would rise clear up into the air. And the headache was completely gone![4]

Graham Kendrick (1950–)

A member of the Ichthus Christian Fellowship, which originated as part of the house church movement in South-east London, Graham Kendrick inspired many when he led the worship at the annual Spring Harvest weeks at coastal holiday camps, and his hymns have become modern classics which are sung well beyond the charismatic churches. He is a co-founder of the 'March for Jesus' prayer walks which have spread worldwide.

From heaven you came, helpless babe,
entered our world, your glory veiled,
not to be served but to serve,
and give your life that we might live.

This is our God, the Servant King, he calls us now to follow him,
to bring our lives as a daily offering of worship to the Servant
    King.[5]

J esus, stand among us at the meeting of our lives,
  be our sweet agreement at the meeting of our eyes;
O Jesus, we love you, so we gather here,
join our hearts in unity and take away our fear.[6]

L ord, the light of your love is shining,
  in the midst of the darkness shining:
Jesus, Light of the world, shine upon us;
set us free by the truth you now bring us –
shine on me, shine on me.
Shine Jesus, shine, fill this land with the Father's glory;
blaze, Spirit, blaze, set our hearts on fire.
Flow, river, flow, flood the nations with grace and mercy;
send forth your word, Lord, and let there be light![7]

Anonymous worship songs

H oly, holy, holy is the Lord,
  Holy is the Lord God almighty!
Holy, holy, holy is the Lord,
Holy is the Lord God almighty!
Who was, and is, and is to come!
Holy, holy, holy is the Lord.

G ive me joy in my heart, keep me praising,
  give me joy in my heart, I pray,
Give me joy in my heart, keep me praising,
keep me praising till the break of day.
Sing hosanna, sing hosanna, sing hosanna to the King of kings!
Sing hosanna, sing hosanna, sing hosanna to the King!

David Watson (1933–84)

David Watson led a small congregation at St Michael le Belfry, in the shadow of York Minster, until it grew into a mecca for those who wanted to experience Spirit-filled worship. There and on his worldwide travels he took the blessings of the Charismatic Movement and shared them with many who hungered for a Christianity which would have its roots in the mainstream churches, but far from being a dead survival from the past, would give them a present experience of God at work in their lives. He welcomed the charismatic gifts, especially that of healing, but was fully aware of the danger that they could become divisive. His charm influenced many at the missions which he led; and then he was diagnosed with cancer. It was a personal struggle for him, but even more for his followers, to deepen their understanding of God's healing until it embraced death as the final healing of all ills.

If you lack the assurance of a personal relationship with God through Jesus Christ, pray this prayer quietly on your own. Don't be in a hurry, take time, and be still in God's presence before you pray.

Lord Jesus Christ,
I admit that I have sinned and gone my own way.
I need your forgiveness.
Thank you for your love, especially in dying on the cross to take away
     my sin.
I am willing for you to lead and direct my life.
And now I come to you, Lord Jesus.
I ask you to be my Saviour and Friend and Lord for ever.
Amen.[8]

There is, of course, a great variety in prayer and we must not always be asking God for things. Some people find the word ACTS a mnemonic for the most basic forms of prayer.

Adoration:. . . First, there is the 'sacrifice of praise to God, that is, the fruit of lips that acknowledge his name'. It is good therefore, to begin prayer by quietly reflecting on the presence of God, and then praising him for his nature and his goodness towards us. You may find that some of the psalms are particularly helpful, or else hymns or spiritual songs. Time spent worshipping God with a sacrifice of praise will be time when our relationship with him is considerably enriched. Secondly, there is the sacrifice of possessions . . . Thirdly, there is the sacrifice of our persons . . .

Confession: The commonest hindrance to prayer is unconfessed sin: 'If I had cherished iniquity in my heart, the Lord would not have listened.' Further, confession needs to be specific. It is one thing to acknowledge, in formal Prayer Book language, that we are 'miserable offenders', it is another thing to say, 'Lord, I confess that I was unkind to Jane this morning, selfish with Tom this afternoon, etc.' . . . God never wants us to stay guilty; as soon as we confess our guilt he releases us from our debt. This is how our love for him grows. It is when we are forgiven much that we can love much.

Thanksgiving:. . . If prayer becomes dull, or if you feel discouraged or depressed, consciously start thanking God for all the positive aspects of your life and situation, and even for his promised control in your trials and difficulties. Genuine gratitude is a marvellous way of healing and strengthening all relationships, not least our relationship with God.

Supplication: Be definite in your prayer requests. 'Nothing is too great for his power; nothing is too small for his love' . . . This form of prayer is like unpacking a suitcase. Many people are worn out by the heavy burdens they have to carry. Worry today is a killer. But in prayer we should unpack that suitcase, and bring each need before our heavenly Father: 'Lord, here is my work . . . and my family . . . and my need for guidance.' As one Dutch Christian, Corrie ten Boom, once put it, 'Travel with a round face and an empty suitcase!'[9]

Prayer for healing

There are many types of healing of body, mind and spirit, but from the first Christians have prayed for healing and, often to their surprise, have seen results.

Dorothy Kerin (1889–1963)

Before charismatic healing became common in Britain, she experienced more than one miraculous cure herself, and gave her home at Burrswood in Kent as a centre where medical treatment and prayer ministry could be practised side by side.

A Little Way of Prayer

Let us by an act of the will place ourselves in the presence of our Divine Lord, and with an act of faith ask that he will empty us of self and of all desire save that his most blessed will may be done, and that it may illumine our hearts and minds. We can then gather together ourselves and all those for whom our prayers have been asked, and hold all silently up to him, making no special request – neither asking nor beseeching – but just resting, with them, in him, desiring nothing but that our Lord may be glorified in all. In this most simple way of approach he does make known his most blessed will for us. 'For so he giveth himself to his beloved in quietness.'[10]

Prayer for use by those who will be laying hands on others

And now O God, I give myself to you.
Empty me of all that is not of you,
Cleanse me from all unrighteousness,
And, according to your will,
Take my hands and use them for your glory.

In the name of God Most High, and through his infinite love and power, may release from all sickness and infirmity to be given to you *[and those for whom you pray]*.
(The words in italics may be used if a person receives the laying on of hands on behalf of someone else.)

In the name of Jesus Christ, may the healing power of the Holy Spirit make you whole, and keep you entire, working in you according to his most loving will.

John Wimber (1934–97)

John Wimber, with his healing missions, taught Evangelicals how to make healing part of their power evangelism, while avoiding some of the dangers of those who made extravagant claims about miraculous healing.

Isn't he beautiful, isn't he?
Prince of Peace, Son of God,
Isn't he wonderful, isn't he?
Counsellor, almighty God, isn't he?
Yes you are![11]

Francis S. MacNutt (1925–)

A former Dominican priest, MacNutt is probably the best-known Roman Catholic in the healing ministry today.

The idea behind inner healing is simply that we can ask Jesus Christ to walk back to the time we were hurt and to free us from the effects of that wound in the present. This involves two things then:

(1) Bringing to light the things that have hurt us. Usually this is best done with another person; even the talking out of the problem is in itself a healing process.

(2) Praying the Lord to heal the binding effects of the hurtful incidents of the past ... Jesus, as Lord of time, is able to do what we cannot: he can heal those wounds of the past that still cause us suffering.

The most I was ever able to do as a counsellor was to help the person bring to the foreground of consciousness the things that were buried in the past, so that he could consciously cope with them in the present. Now I am discovering that the Lord can heal these wounds – sometimes immediately – and can bring the counselling process to its completion in a deep healing. At times, these hurts may seem slight to an adult mind, but we must be sensitive to see things as a child would. I remember once praying for a woman whose complaint was that her inner life was always bleak and boring, even though her professional life was in itself full and exciting. When we finally found what had caused her to shut off the flow of life it was an incident that happened when she was ten years old.[12]

Christian counselling

Dr Frank Lake in his Clinical Theology *showed how the insights of Freud and others could be used in the service of the gospel, and many others have written books on counselling from a Christian perspective. This prayer is by Dr Roger Hurding, a psychotherapist who is visiting lecturer in Pastoral Studies at Trinity College, Bristol, and the author of* Roots and Shoots.

Lord Christ, I thank you for your love so strong
May that love flow through me to others
May I be patient when change comes slowly
May I be kind when life seems harsh
May I be gentle when others feel bruised

May I be humble when things go well
May I be peaceful when anger rises within
May I forgive when wronged
May I rejoice when the truth is discovered
Love never fails, but I do
May I hope when things seem hopeless
May I persevere when the way is hard.[13]

Twentieth-Century Liturgies

The Scottish Episcopalian *Book of Common Prayer* (1912)

Unconstrained by the requirement of parliamentary approval for any changes in their prayer book, which made liturgical revision so difficult in the Church of England, the Scottish Episcopalians pioneered the adaptation of the old book to new circumstances.

Almighty God, we beseech thee with thy gracious favour to behold our universities, colleges and schools, that knowledge may be increased among us, and all good learning flourish and abound. Bless all who teach and all who learn; and grant that in humility of heart they may ever look to thee, the fountain of all wisdom; through Jesus Christ our Lord. Amen.

At times of Industrial Unrest and Strikes

O God, who hast ordained that we should live and work together as thy children: remove, we beseech thee, from those who are now at variance, all spirit of strife and all occasion of bitterness, that seeking only what is just and equal, they may grow together in love and harmony, to their own well-being, and the prosperity of all; through Jesus Christ our Lord. Amen.

O Lord God almighty, whose glory cherubim and seraphim and all the hosts of heaven with ceaseless voice do proclaim: hear and accept, we humbly beseech thee, the praises of thy Church below; and pour down upon thy ministers in choir and sanctuary such a spirit of faith, reverence, and joy as shall lift both their hymns and their lives to thee; through Jesus Christ our Lord. Amen.

O God our Saviour, who willest that all men should be saved and come to the knowledge of the truth, prosper, we beseech thee, our brethren who labour in distant lands. Protect them in all perils by land and sea, support them in loneliness and in the hour of trial; give them grace to bear faithful witness unto thee, and endue them with burning zeal and love, that they may turn many to righteousness and finally obtain a crown of glory; through Jesus Christ. Amen.

Almighty God, whose blessed Son Jesus Christ went about doing good and healing all manner of sickness and disease among the people; continue, we beseech thee, this his gracious work among us in the hospitals and infirmaries of our land; console and heal the sufferers, grant to the physicians and surgeons wisdom and skill, and to the nurses diligence and patience. Prosper their work, O Lord, and vouchsafe thy blessing to all who give of their substance for its maintenance; through Jesus Christ our Lord. Amen.

The Prayer Book as proposed in 1928

It had proved impossible to compel the Anglo-Catholics to use only those services contained in The Book of Common Prayer *unchanged since 1662, so the Church of England decided to revise it, in the hope of creating a type of worship which would be acceptable to all and could be enforced. The revisions passed the newly created Church Assembly, but were rejected by Parliament. After a second failed attempt, the bishops were reduced to turning a blind eye to services which they had proposed but were technically illegal. Yet several great new prayers were composed for the new book.*[1]

Almighty God, from whom all thoughts of truth and peace proceed: kindle, we pray thee, in the hearts of all men the true love of peace; and guide with thy pure and peaceable wisdom those who take counsel for the nations of the earth; that in tranquillity thy kingdom may go forward, till the earth is filled with the knowledge of thy love; through Jesus Christ our Lord. Amen.

Almighty God, Father of all mercies and giver of all comfort: deal graciously, we pray thee, with those who mourn, that casting every care on thee, they may know the consolation of thy love; through Jesus Christ our Lord. Amen.

H eavenly Father, who in thy Son Jesus Christ hast given us a true faith and a sure hope: help us, we pray thee, to live as those who believe and trust in the communion of saints, the forgiveness of sins, and the resurrection to life everlasting, and strengthen this faith and hope in us all the days of our life: through the love of thy Son, Jesus Christ our Saviour. Amen.

O God of our Fathers, bless these thy servants, and sow the seed of eternal life in our hearts; that whatsoever in thy holy word they shall profitably learn, they may in deed fulfil the same; that so, obeying thy will, and always being in safety under thy protection, they may abide in thy love unto their lives' end; through Jesus Christ our Lord. Amen.

O Father of all, we pray for those whom we love, but see no longer. Grant them thy peace; let light perpetual shine upon them; and in thy loving wisdom and almighty power work in them the good purpose of thy perfect will; through Jesus Christ our Lord. Amen.

O God, who by the passion of thy blessed Son hast made the instru- ment of shameful death to be unto us the means of life and peace: grant us so to glory in the Cross of Christ that we may gladly suffer shame and loss; for the sake of the same thy Son our Lord. Amen.

M ay the almighty and merciful Lord grant unto you pardon and remission of all your sins, time for amendment of life, and the grace and strength of the Holy Spirit. Amen.

G o forth into the world in peace; be of good courage; hold fast that which is good; render to no man evil for evil; strengthen the faint- hearted; support the weak; help the afflicted; honour all men; love and serve the Lord; rejoicing in the power of the Holy Spirit. And the blessing of God almighty, the Father, the Son, and the Holy Ghost, be upon you, and remain with you for ever. Amen.

The Scottish Episcopalian *Book of Common Prayer* (1929)[2]

Almighty God, whose will it is to restore all things in thy beloved Son, the king of all: govern the hearts and minds of those in authority, and bring the families of the nations, divided and torn apart by the ravages of sin, to be subject to his just and gentle rule; who is alive and reigns with thee and the Holy Spirit, one God, world without end. Amen.

Almighty God, who at the baptism of thy blessed Son Jesus Christ in the river Jordan didst reveal the glory of his divine nature: let the light of his presence shine in our hearts, and his glory be shown forth in our lives; through the same Jesus Christ our Lord. Amen.

O Lord God, our heavenly Father, regard, we pray, with thy divine pity the pains of all thy children; and grant that the passion of our Lord and his infinite love may make fruitful for good the tribulations of the innocent, the sufferings of the sick, and the sorrows of the bereaved; through him who suffered in our flesh and died for our sake, the same thy Son our Saviour Jesus Christ. Amen.

O almighty God, the God of the spirits of all flesh: multiply, we pray, to those who sleep in Jesus, the manifold blessings of thy love, that the good work which thou hast begun in them may be perfected unto the day of Jesus Christ. And of thy mercy, O heavenly Father, vouchsafe that we, who now serve thee here on earth, may together with them be partakers of the inheritance of the saints in light; for the sake of the same thy Son Jesus Christ our Lord and Saviour. Amen.

Almighty God, who sent thy Holy Spirit to be the life and light of thy Church: open our hearts to the riches of his grace, that we may bring forth the fruit of the Spirit in love and joy and peace; through Jesus Christ our Lord. Amen.

A Book of Common Prayer (South Africa, 1954)[3]

Heavenly Father, from whose care we learn our pattern of parenthood, give to those who have the care of children the spirit of wisdom, patience and love; so that the homes in which they grow up may be to them an image of your kingdom, and the care of their parents a likeness of your love; for Jesus Christ's sake. Amen.

Adapted

O God, the Father of all mankind, we beseech thee so to inspire the people of this land with the spirit of justice, truth, and love, that in all our dealings one with another we may show forth our brotherhood in thee, for the sake of Jesus Christ our Lord.

O God, the maker and redeemer of all believers: grant to the soul of thy servant – all the unsearchable benefits of thy Son's passion; that in the day of his appearing *he/she*, and all the faithful departed, may be manifested as thy children; through the same Jesus Christ our Lord, who liveth and reigneth with thee and the Holy Ghost, one God world without end.

O Almighty God, who by thy holy apostle hast taught us to set our affection on things above: grant us so to labour in this life as ever to be mindful of our citizenship in those heavenly places whither our Saviour Christ is gone before; to whom with thee, O Father, and thee, O Holy Ghost, be all honour and glory, world without end.

The Church of Ireland *Book of Common Prayer* (1960)[4]

Grant, O Lord, to all who are bereaved, the spirit of faith and courage, that they may have the strength to meet the days to come with steadfastness and patience; not sorrowing as those without hope, but in thankful remembrance of thy great goodness in past years, and in the sure expectation of a joyful reunion in the heavenly places; and this we ask in the name of Jesus Christ our Lord.

Almighty God, who alone art without variableness or shadow of turning, and hast safely brought us through the changes of time to the beginning of another year: we beseech thee to pardon the sins that we have committed in the year which is past; and give us grace that we may spend the remainder of our days to thy honour and glory, through Jesus Christ our Lord.

The Book of Common Worship
of the Church of South India (1963)

In 1947 the United Church of South India was formed by the reunion of the Anglican, Methodist and United Churches, the last being itself a union of Presbyterian, Congregational, Dutch Reformed, Lutheran and Calvinist Churches. As well as setting an example which older churches have yet to follow, they pioneered new, culturally appropriate, forms of worship in their Book of Common Worship *and its successors.*

Those who feed and clothe us

O thou to whom belong earth and sea, and all that lives and grows in them: we commend to thee those who till the land, or tend living creatures for the feeding or clothing of mankind, or fish in the seas or inland waters, and those who in laboratory or office study and direct their work; that the full harvest of land and water may be brought in, and all may rejoice and praise thy name; through Jesus Christ our Lord. Amen.[5]

O God, our Father, by whose mercy and might the world turns safely into darkness and returns again to light: we commend to thy care and keeping all the concerns of the day. We give into thy hands our unfinished tasks, our unsolved problems, and our unfulfilled hopes; knowing that only that which thou dost bless shall prosper. To thy great love and protection we commit each other and those we love, knowing that thou alone art our sure Defender.[6]

Modern Collects, Church of the Province of South Africa (1971)

Almighty God, in Christ you make all things new. Transform the poverty of our nature by the riches of your grace, and in the renewal of our lives make known your heavenly glory; through Jesus Christ our Lord. Amen.[7]

Book of Common Prayer of the Church of India, Pakistan, Burma and Ceylon (1978)

May the cross of the Son of God, who is mightier than all the powers of evil, abide with you in your going out and your coming in! From the wrath of evil people, from the temptations of the devil, from all low passions that beguile the soul and body, may it guard, protect and deliver you: and may the blessing of God almighty, the Father, the Son and the Holy Spirit, be among you and remain with you always. Amen.[8]

The American Episcopal *Book of Common Prayer* (1979)

Following the separation of the Episcopal Church in the United States from the Church of England, the same principle was invoked which led the English at the Reformation to assert the right and duty of the local church to revise its worship. These revisions, at first conservative, replacing the name of the King with that of the President, by 1979 became innovative and created many prayers of great beauty.

Most gracious God, by whose knowledge the depths are broken up and the clouds drop down the dew: we yield thee hearty thanks and praise for the return of seedtime and harvest, for the increase of the ground and the gathering in of its fruits, and for all the other blessings of thy merciful providence bestowed upon this nation and people. And we pray, give us a just sense of these great mercies, such as may appear in our lives by a humble, holy, and obedient walking before thee all our days; through Jesus Christ our Lord, to whom, with thee and the Holy Spirit, be all glory and honour, for ever and ever. Amen.[9]

Lord God, whose blessed Son our Saviour gave his back to the smiters and did not hide his face from shame: give us grace to endure the sufferings of this present time with sure confidence in the glory that shall be revealed; through Jesus Christ our Lord. Amen.[10]

For all who have died in the communion of your Church, and those whose faith is known to you alone, that, with all the saints, they may have rest in that place where there is no pain or grief, but life eternal, we pray to you, O Lord.

Lord, have mercy (*or* Kyrie eleison).

Rejoicing in the fellowship of [the ever-blessed Virgin Mary, *(blessed N.,)* and] all the saints, let us commend ourselves, and one another, and all our life to Christ our God.

I nto your hands, O Lord, we commend the soul of your servant *N.* Acknowledge, we humbly beseech you, a sheep of your own fold, a lamb of your own flock, a sinner of your own redeeming. Receive *him* into the arms of your mercy, into the blessed rest of everlasting peace, and into the glorious company of the saints in light. Amen.

O God, you made us in your image and redeemed us through Jesus your Son: look with compassion on the whole human family; take away the arrogance and hatred which infect our hearts; break down the walls that separate us; unite us in bonds of love; and work through our struggle and confusion to accomplish your purposes on earth; that, in your good time, all nations and races may serve you in harmony around your heavenly throne; through Jesus Christ our Lord. Amen.

O God our Father, whose Son forgave his enemies while he was suffer-ing shame and death: strengthen those who suffer for the sake of conscience; when they are accused, save them from speaking in hate; when they are rejected, save them from bitterness; when they are imprisoned, save them from despair; and to us your servants, give grace to respect their witness and to discern the truth, that our society may be cleansed and strengthened. This we ask for the sake of Jesus Christ, our merciful and righteous Judge. Amen.

H eavenly Father, in your word you have given us a vision of that holy City to which the nations of the world bring their glory: behold and visit, we pray, the cities of the earth. Renew the ties of mutual regard which form our civic life. Send us honest and able leaders. Enable us to eliminate poverty, prejudice, and oppression, that peace may prevail with righteousness, and justice with order, and that men and women from different cultures and with differing talents may find with one another the fulfilment of their humanity; through Jesus Christ our Lord. Amen.

Lord Jesus, for our sake you were condemned as a criminal: visit our jails and prisons with your pity and judgement. Remember all prisoners, and bring the guilty to repentance and amendment of life according to your will, and give them hope for their future. When any are held unjustly, bring them release; forgive us, and teach us to improve our justice. Remember those who work in these institutions; keep them humane and compassionate; and save them from becoming brutal or callous. And since what we do for those in prison, O Lord, we do for you, constrain us to improve their lot. All this we ask for your mercy's sake. Amen.

Almighty God, in giving us dominion over things on earth, you made us fellow workers in your creation: give us wisdom and reverence so to use the resources of nature, that no one may suffer from our abuse of them, and that generations yet to come may continue to praise you for your bounty; through Jesus Christ our Lord. Amen.

Almighty and everlasting God, you made the universe with all its marvellous order, its atoms, worlds and galaxies, and the infinite complexity of living creatures: grant that, as we probe the mysteries of your creation, we may come to know you more truly, and more surely fulfil our role in your eternal purpose; in the name of Jesus Christ our Lord. Amen.

O God, who created all peoples in your image, we thank you for the wonderful diversity of races and cultures in this world. Enrich our lives by ever-widening circles of fellowship, and show us your presence in those who differ most from us, until our knowledge of your love is made perfect in our love for all your children; through Jesus Christ our Lord. Amen.

The Taizé Community

Brother Roger arrived alone, aged twenty-five, in the village of Taizé in Burgundy in 1940. He wanted to create a community which would establish reconciliation between Christians and thereby throughout divided humanity. He started out by giving shelter to refugees, notably to Jews. Other brothers came to share his work, at first from different Protestant backgrounds, but Catholic brothers soon joined them. Now the community

*includes brothers from over twenty-five countries and from every continent.
In 1949 they made a lifelong commitment to living together in celibacy
and great simplicity. From 1957 onwards the Taizé community developed
a ministry to young people from all over Europe, and now many other
countries also. As the number of young visitors increased year by year,
living in tents or huts and sharing the life of the community in work and
in prayer, one extension after another was added to the chapel. Now the
atmosphere is electric, as thousands of young people squat in silence by
candlelight on the floor of what looks like a vast aircraft hangar. In this
factory the work of God is being done, as people from different nations in
East and West, who have previously been enemies, learn to meet at the
foot of the cross in love and shared forgiveness. Because so many languages
are represented, to avoid translation most of the music is repetitive chant-
ing, often in Latin, which comes back into its own as a shared language.
These chants have inspired congregations around the world in creating a
mood of devotion.*

B less the Lord, my soul, and bless God's holy name.
Bless the Lord, my soul, who leads me into life.

B *onum est confidere in Domino, bonum sperare in Domino.*

C *onfitemini Domino quoniam bonus,*
Confitemini Domino Alleluia.

I n the Lord I'll be ever thankful, in the Lord I will rejoice!
Look to God, do not be afraid, lift up your voices, the Lord is
near,
lift up your voices, the Lord is near.

L ord Jesus Christ, your light shines within us.
Let not my doubts nor my darkness speak to me.
Lord Jesus Christ, your light is shines within us.
Let my heart always welcome your love.

J *ubilate Deo, omnis terra. Servite Domino in laetitia.*
Alleluia, alleluia, in laetitia. Alleluia, alleluia, in laetitia.

J ubilate Deo, Jubilate Deo. Alleluia.

L audate Dominum, Laudate Dominum,
  omnes gentes, Alleluia!

O adoramus te O Christe.

O ur darkness is never darkness in your sight:
  the deepest night is clear as the daylight.

S tay with me, remain here with me,
  watch and pray, watch and pray.

U bi caritas et amor, ubi caritas Deus ibi est.

V eni Sancte Spiritus.

W ait for the Lord, whose day is near.
  Wait for the Lord: keep watch, take heart!

W ithin our darkest night, you kindle the fire
  that never dies away, that never dies away.

The Alternative Service Book (1980)

The ASB consolidated the progress made towards modern language worship in the Church of England, and although its style was criticized in places, masterpieces of devotional prose were produced.[12]

A lmighty God, we thank you for the gift of your holy word. May it be a lantern to our feet, a light to our paths, and a strength to our lives. Take us and use us to love and serve all men in the power of the Holy Spirit and in the name of your Son, Jesus Christ our Lord. Amen.

Father of all, we give you thanks and praise, that when we were still far off you met us in your Son and brought us home. Dying and living, he declared your love, gave us grace, and opened the gate of glory. May we who share Christ's body live his risen life; we who drink his cup bring life to others; we whom the Spirit lights give light to the world. Keep us firm in the hope you have set before us, so we and all your children shall be free, and the whole earth live to praise your name; through Jesus Christ our Lord. Amen.

Most merciful Lord, your love compels us to come in. Our hands were unclean, our hearts were unprepared; we were not fit even to eat the crumbs from under your table. But you, Lord, are the God of our salvation, and share your bread with sinners. So cleanse and feed us with the precious body and blood of your Son, that he may live in us and we in him; and that we, with the whole company of Christ, may sit and eat in your kingdom. Amen.

Lent, Holy Week and Easter: Services and Prayers (1984)

This book provides additional services for use in the forty days before Easter.[13]

Loving Father, we thank you for feeding us at the supper of your Son. Sustain us with your Spirit, that we may serve you here on earth, until our joy is complete in heaven and we share the eternal banquet with Jesus Christ our Lord. Amen.

The Book of Alternative Services of the Anglican Church of Canada (1985)[14]

Let us pray to God the Holy Spirit, saying:
Come, Holy Spirit, come.
Come Holy Spirit, creator, and renew the face of earth.
Come, Holy Spirit, come.
Come Holy Spirit, counsellor,
and touch our lips that we may proclaim your word.
Come Holy Spirit, come.

Come Holy Spirit, power from on high:
make us agents of peace and ministers of wholeness.
Come Holy Spirit, come.
Come Holy Spirit, breath of God,
give life to the dry bones of this evil age,
and make us a living people, holy and free.
Come Holy Spirit, come.
Come Holy Spirit, wisdom and truth:
strengthen us in the risk of faith.
Come Holy Spirit, come.

Creator of the fruitful earth, you have made us stewards of all things. Give us grateful hearts for all your goodness, and steadfast wills to use your bounty well, that the whole human family, today and in generations to come, may with us give thanks for the riches of your creation. We ask this in the name of Jesus Christ the Lord.

Eternal God, comfort of the afflicted and healer of the broken, you have fed us this day at the table of life and hope. Teach us the ways of gentleness and peace, that all the world may acknowledge the kingdom of your Son Jesus Christ our Lord.

Heavenly Father, renew the life of your Church by the power of this sacrament. May the breaking of bread and the teaching of the apostles keep us united in your love, in the name of Jesus Christ the Lord.

Merciful God, we have been gathered at the table of your Son. Hear our prayer for all our sisters and brothers in faith who suffer for truth, justice and freedom. Strengthen their witness and keep them, with us, under the protection of your wings. We ask this in the name of Jesus Christ the Lord.

A Kenyan Revised Liturgy for Holy Communion (1987)[15]

Almighty God, you bring to light things hidden in darkness, and know the shadows of our hearts; cleanse and renew us by your Spirit, that we may walk in the light and glorify your name, through Jesus Christ, the light of the world. Amen.

Almighty God, our great Elder,
we have sat at your feet,
learnt from your word,
and eaten from your table.
We give you thanks and praise
for accepting us into your family.
Send us out with your blessing,
to live and to witness for you
in the power of your Spirit,
through Jesus Christ, your First Born. Amen.

The people accompany their first three responses with a sweep of the arm towards the west end of the church, and their final response with a sweep towards the east end.

All our problems
We send to the setting sun.
All our difficulties
We send to the setting sun.
All the devil's works
We send to the setting sun.
All our hopes
We set on the Risen Son.
Christ the Sun of righteousness shine upon you
and scatter the darkness from before your path;
and the blessing of God almighty, Father, Son and Holy Spirit,
be among you and remain with you always. Amen.

Almighty God,
Creator of the living and the non-living,
you marvellously made us in your image;
but we have corrupted ourselves

and damaged your likeness,
by rejecting your love
and hurting our neighbour.
We are desperately sorry
and heartily repent of our sins.
Cleanse us and forgive us
by the sacrifice of your Son;
Remake us and lead us
by your Spirit, the Comforter.
We only dare to ask this
through Jesus Christ our Lord. Amen.

Almighty God, whose steadfast love is as great as the heavens are high above the earth, remove our sins from us, as far as the east is from the west, strengthen our life in his kingdom and keep us upright until the last day; through Jesus Christ our merciful high priest.

Amen. Thank you, Father, for forgiveness.
We come to your table as your children,
not presuming but assured,
not trusting ourselves but your Word:
we hunger and thirst for righteousness,
and ask for our hearts to be satisfied
with the body and blood of your Son,
Jesus Christ the Righteous. Amen.

A New Zealand Prayer Book/ He Karakia Mihinare o Aotearoa (1989)[16]

Draw your Church together, O God, into one great company of disciples, together following our Lord Jesus Christ into every walk of life, together serving him in his mission to the world, and together witnessing to his love on every continent and island. Amen.

Almighty God, you give seed for us to sow, and bread for us to eat; make us thankful for what we have received; make us able to do those generous things which supply your people's needs; so all the world may give you thanks and glory. Amen.

The peace of God be with you all.
In God's justice is our peace.
Brothers and sisters, Christ calls us to live in unity.
We seek to live in the Spirit of Christ.

Save us, Jesus, from hurrying away, because we do not wish to help, because we know not how to help, because we dare not. Inspire us to use our lives serving one another. Amen.

Jesus said, There is joy among the angels of God
over one sinner who repents.
Come to me all who labour and are heavy laden
and I will give you rest.
God has promised forgiveness to all who truly repent,
turn to Christ in faith, and are themselves forgiving.
In silence we call to mind our sins.

Silence.

Let us confess our sins.
Merciful God,
we have sinned
in what we have thought and said,
in the wrong we have done
and in the good we have not done.
We have sinned in ignorance:
we have sinned in weakness:
we have sinned through our own deliberate fault.
We are truly sorry.
We repent and turn to you.
Forgive us, for our Saviour Christ's sake,
and renew our lives to the glory of your name. Amen.

The Absolution is declared by the presiding priest.
Through the cross of Christ God have mercy on you,
pardon you and set you free.
Know that you are forgiven and be at peace.
God strengthen you in all goodness
and keep you in life eternal. Amen.

Ever-loving God, your care for us is greater even than a mother's love for her child; teach us to value a mother's love and see in it an expression of your grace, that we may ever feel more deeply your love for us in Christ Jesus our Saviour. Amen.

The Promise of his Glory: Services and Prayers for the Season from All Saints to Candlemas (1991)[17]

Gracious Father, our eyes have seen the King in his beauty; by this living bread and saving cup let his likeness be formed in us and grow until the end of time; through Christ our Lord. Amen.

May God keep you in all your days.
May Christ shield you in all your ways.
May the Spirit bring you healing and peace.
May the Holy Trinity drive all darkness from you
and pour upon you blessing and light. Amen.

May God give to you and to all those whom you love his comfort and his peace, his light and his joy, in this world and the next; and the blessing of God almighty, the Father, the Son, and the Holy Spirit, be upon you and remain with you always. Amen.[18]

We have not held out the word of life in a dark and twisted world.
Lord have mercy.
Lord, have mercy.
We have failed to share our bread with the hungry.
Christ, have mercy.
Christ, have mercy.
We have closed our hearts to the love of God.
Lord, have mercy.
Lord, have mercy.

God in the night
God at my right
God all the day
God with me stay
God in my heart
Never depart
God with thy might
Keep us in light
Through this dark night. Amen.

O Lord God, whose mercies are sure and full and ever new: grant us the greatest of them all, the Spirit of your dear Son; that in the day of judgement we may be presented to you if not blameless, yet forgiven, if not successful, yet faithful, if not holy, yet persevering, deserving nothing, but accepted in him who pleads our cause and redeemed our lives, even Jesus Christ our Lord. Amen.

Celebrating Common Prayer (1992)

'The fundamental purpose of Celebrating Common Prayer – The Daily Office SSF *is this: to help the Church as a whole to pray together daily in a reflective and structured way. This was always Cranner's intention in* The Book of Common Prayer. *Although his version of Morning and Evening Prayer has long provided a non-eucharistic form of public worship on Sundays and has done much to characterise Anglican public worship, it has only rather patchily achieved his other purpose of being the regular worship attended by the whole congregation and offered day by day in parish churches throughout the land. For many regular Sunday worshippers, personal prayer during the week is unstructured and haphazard. This places even more burdens on the Sunday act of worship, which has to do the task of nourishing and sustaining reflective prayer during the week as well as celebrating and proclaiming the risen life of Christ in word and sacrament. A pattern of daily prayer which complements eucharistic worship, such as this book, offers a major resource to the Church. I hope many Christians will use it to engage in a common pattern of daily prayer which will unite us all in prayer and praise and allow us to feed on a common diet of psalmody and canticle.' – From the Foreword by the Archbishop of Canterbury.*[19]

May the risen Lord Jesus watch over us and renew us as he renews the whole of creation. May our hearts and lives echo his love. Amen.

Restore us again, O God of hosts, show us the light of your countenance and we shall be saved. Bless us and keep us, this night and always. Amen.

May the love of the Word made flesh enfold us, his joy fill our lives, his peace be in our hearts; and the blessing of God be with us this night and always. Amen.

May God bless us, that in us may be found love and humility, obedience and thanksgiving, discipline, gentleness and peace. Amen.

Almighty God, as we stand at the foot of the cross of your Son, help us to see and know your love for us, so that in humility, love and joy we may place at his feet all that we have and all that we are, through Jesus Christ our Saviour. Amen.

As we sing your love, O Lord, establish your covenant with us and anoint us with the seal of your Spirit, that we may praise your faithfulness and proclaim your righteousness from age to age; through Jesus Christ our Lord. Amen.

A Prayer Book for Australia (1995)[20]

Living God, in this holy meal you fill us with new hope. May the power of your love, which we have known in word and sacrament, continue your saving work among us, give us courage for our pilgrimage, and bring us to the joys you promise. Amen.

Gracious God, we humbly thank you for all your gifts so freely bestowed on us, for life and health and safety, for freedom to work and leisure to rest, and for all that is beautiful in creation and in human life. But, above all, we thank you for our Saviour, Jesus Christ, for his death and resurrection, for the gift of your Spirit, and for the hope of glory. Fill our hearts with all joy and peace in believing; through Jesus Christ our Lord. Amen.

L et us pray that we will be joined together in working for reconciliation,
and the healing of our ancient land and its peoples.
Forgive us for remaining silent and bound by fear.
Give us the courage to speak and act with justice.
Forgive us for our arrogance in closing our eyes
to other peoples and cultures.
Enable us to know your redeeming love.
Forgive us for disfiguring the earth and despoiling its bounty.
Come, Holy Spirit, renew the whole creation.
Forgive us for despising the cultures of others,
and taking away their self-respect.
Give us grace to bind one another's wounds.
Forgive us for not listening to the griefs
of all who are oppressed in this land, especially . . .*
Draw us together as one people.
Forgive us for our prejudice and indifference
towards those whose ways differ from our ways.
Strengthen us to live with respect and compassion for one another.

Particular prayers for forgiveness will often be appropriate.[21]

G od our creator, you have made each one of us in every part. Bless *us* through and through, that we may delight to serve you to the full. Bless *our* eyes, that we may discern the beauty you give. Bless *our* ears, that we may hear you in the music of sounds. Bless *our* sense of smell, that your fragrance may fill *our* being. Bless *our* lips, that we may speak your truth, and sing your joy. Bless *our* hands, that they may play, write and touch as you guide them. Bless *our* feet, that they may be messengers of your peace. Bless *our* imaginations, that we may be fired with wonder in your truth. Bless *our* hearts, that they may be filled with your love. Bless *us* through and through, that we may delight to serve you to the full, through Jesus Christ, who took our nature to make us whole. Amen.

Heavenly Father, give us wisdom and understanding. As we listen to your Word, may we know you better, love you more, and learn to please you in all we do; through Jesus Christ our Lord. Amen.

Gracious God, in baptism you make us one family in Christ your Son, one in the sharing of his body and blood, one in the communion of his Spirit. Help us to grow in love for one another and come to the full maturity of the body of Christ. Most loving God, you send us into the world you love. Give us grace to go thankfully and with courage in the power of your Spirit.

All thanks and praise to you, loving Father, for sending your only Son to be our Saviour. He took upon himself our human nature, shared our joy and our tears, bore all our sickness, and carried all our sorrows. He brought us through death to the life of his glorious resurrection, giving for our frailty eternal strength, and restoring us in your perfect image.

Father of all mercies, for your gifts of healing and forgiveness, for grace to love and care for one another, for your hidden blessings, and for all you have in store for us, we give you thanks, through Jesus Christ our Lord. Amen.

Patterns for Worship (1995)

A source book of prayers and other material for use when compiling new liturgies for local use.[22]

Living God, Father of light, Hope of nations, Friend of sinners, Builder of the city that is to come; your love is made visible in Jesus Christ, you bring home the lost, restore the sinner and give dignity to the despised. In the face of Jesus Christ your light shines out, flooding lives with goodness and truth, gathering into one a divided and broken humanity. Amen.

Patterns for Worship 13P18

The Companion to the Lectionary (1996)

Whereas some Methodist churches in Britain will use nothing but extempore prayer, others choose from the Methodist Service Book *and a variety of other liturgical resources. For some years the Epworth Press has published an annual volume of such material called* Companion to the Lectionary.

Everlasting peace:
Soon, Lord, soon.
Nations walking in your way:
Soon, Lord, soon.
Disputes settled according to your will:
Soon, Lord, soon.
Swords becoming ploughs:
Soon, Lord, soon.
Neighbours caring for each other as for themselves:
Soon, Lord, soon.
your will being done on earth as it is in heaven:
Soon, Lord, soon. Amen

Loving God, you spoke to us and we did not listen.
'I am sending you', said God.
We looked around to see who would go,
then as realisation dawned,
we made off in the opposite direction. So we pray:
Forgive us, and send us.
'I need workers', said God.
We looked around to see who would respond,
then, making our excuses,
we tried to tiptoe gently away. So we pray:
Forgive us, and empower us.
'You must be wise as serpents', said Jesus.
We looked around, startled and amazed.
We did not expect to bring intelligence
into reading the gospel! So we pray:
Forgive us, and embolden us.
'Be innocent as doves', said Jesus.
We looked around at those we must face –
challenged to be accepting, gentle, peaceful. So we pray:
Forgive us, and inspire us.[23]

The Sacramentary

Following the decision of the Second Vatican Council to allow the Mass to be said in the vernacular, the whole of the Missal and all the associated services were revised by the Vatican, and committees were set up to supervise the translation into different language groups. The International Commission on English in the Liturgy coordinates the services in all the English-speaking nations. Faithful Catholics feel the loss of knowing that anywhere they went they would hear the familiar sound of the Latin, most of which they had learnt to understand. But the gain has been a great number of prayers of very great beauty which everybody can make their own, and the process of revision is on-going.[24]

Preface of Marriage

F ather, all-powerful and ever-living God,
we do well always and everywhere to give you thanks.
You created man in love to share your divine life.
We see his high destiny in the love of husband and wife,
which bears the imprint of your own divine love.
Love is man's origin,
love is his constant calling,
love is his fulfilment in heaven.
The love of man and woman
is made holy in the sacrament of marriage,
and becomes the mirror of your everlasting love.
Through Christ the choirs of angels
and all the saints
praise and worship your glory.
May our voices blend with theirs
as we join in their unending hymn:
Holy, holy, holy . . .

Prayer of Self-Dedication to Jesus Christ

L ord Jesus Christ,
take all my freedom,
my memory, my understanding, and my will.
All that I have and cherish
you have given me.

I surrender it all to be guided by your will.
Your grace and your love are wealth enough for me.
Give me these, Lord Jesus,
and I ask for nothing more.

Opening Prayer, First Sunday of Advent, Year B

Rend the heavens and come down,
O God of all the ages!
Rouse us from sleep,
deliver us from our heedless ways,
and form us into a watchful people,
that, at the advent of your Son,
he may find us doing what is right,
mindful of all you command;
Grant this through him whose coming is certain,
whose day draws near:
your Son, our Lord Jesus Christ,
who lives and reigns with you in the unity of the Holy Spirit,
God for ever and ever.

Opening Prayer, Christmas, Mass at midnight

Good and gracious God,
on this holy night you gave us your Son.
the Lord of the universe, wrapped in swaddling clothes,
the Saviour of all, lying in a manger.
On this holy night
draw us into the mystery of your love.
Join our voices with the heavenly host,
that we may sing your glory on high
Give us a place among the shepherds,
that we may find the one for whom we have waited,
Jesus Christ, your Word made flesh,
who lives and reigns with you in the unity of the Holy Spirit.
in the splendour of eternal light.
God for ever and ever.

Opening Prayer, Third Sunday of Lent, Year A

O God, living and true,
look upon your people,
whose dry and stony hearts are parched with thirst.
Unseal the living water of your Spirit;
let it become within us an ever-flowing spring,
leaping up to eternal life;
Thus may we worship you in spirit and in truth
through Christ, our deliverance and hope,
who lives and reigns with you in the unity of the Holy Spirit,
holy and mighty God for ever and ever.

Opening Prayer, Sixth Sunday in Ordinary Time, Year C

O God,
who alone can satisfy our deepest hungers,
protect us from the lure of wealth and power;
move our hearts to seek first your kingdom,
that ours may be the security and joy
of those who place their trust in you.
We make our prayer through our Lord Jesus Christ, your Son,
who lives and reigns with you in the unity of the Holy Spirit,
God for ever and ever.

Common Worship (1997)

The beginning of a new generation of revised liturgy to be used in the Church of England in the new millennium.[25]

God of truth, whose servant Janani Luwum walked in the light, and in his death defied the powers of darkness: free us from fear of those who kill the body, that we too may walk as children of light, through him who overcame darkness by the power of the cross, Jesus Christ your Son our Lord, who is alive and reigns with you, in the unity of the Holy Spirit, one God, now and for ever.

Collect for the commemoration of Janani Luwum, Archbishop of Uganda, Martyr, 1977.

17 February

Heavenly Father, whose Son grew in wisdom and stature in the home of Joseph the carpenter of Nazareth, and on the wood of the cross perfected the work of the world's salvation: help us, strengthened by this sacrament of his passion, to count the wisdom of the world as foolishness, and to walk with him in simplicity and trust; through Jesus Christ our Lord. Amen.

Collect for the feast of Joseph of Nazareth, 19 March.

Merciful God, who, when your Church on earth was torn apart by the ravages of sin, raised up men and women in this land who witnessed to their faith with courage and constancy: give to your Church that peace which is your will, and grant that those who have been divided on earth may be reconciled in heaven, and share together in the vision of your glory; through Jesus Christ your Son our Lord, who is alive and reigns with you, in the unity of the Holy Spirit, one God, now and for ever.

Collect for the commemoration of English Saints and Martyrs of the Reformation era, 4 May

Feminist Spirituality

Jesus was the first feminist, because, in contrast to the patriarchal society around him, he treated women as human beings of equal worth with men, and revealed his resurrection first to women. The twentieth century will be remembered as the period when the process was begun of attempting to recover that balance. As always in justice movements, prayer has been the essential foundation.

Janet Morley

Janet Morley has written many inspiring words for worship for the charity Christian Aid. She first compiled All Desires Known *to support those women who were seeking ordination to the priesthood in the Church of England, and were suffering insults and calumny in the process. She produced challenging turns of phrase which make many of these collects far superior to the traditional ones. They will probably be remembered and used long after the controversy is forgotten.*

God our deliverer, whose approaching birth still shakes the foundations of our world, may we so wait for your coming with eagerness and hope that we embrace without terror the labour pangs of the new age, through Jesus Christ. Amen.

Christ our victim, whose beauty was disfigured and whose body torn upon the cross; open wide your arms to embrace our tortured world, that we may not turn away our eyes, but abandon ourselves to your mercy. Amen.

God of terror and joy, you arise to shake the earth. Open our graves and give us back the past; so that all that has been buried may be freed and forgiven, and our lives may return to you through the risen Christ. Amen.

God our lover, in whose arms we are held, and by whose passion we are known; require of us also that love which is filled with longing, delights in the truth, and costs not less than everything, through Jesus Christ. Amen.

God whose Holy name defies our definition, but whose will is known in freeing the oppressed, make us to be one with all who cry for justice; that we who speak your praise may struggle for your truth, through Jesus Christ. Amen.

Hidden God, whose wisdom compels our love and unsettles all our values; fill us with desire to search for her truth, that we may transform the world becoming fools for her sake, through Jesus Christ. Amen.

May the God who dances in creation, who embraces us with human love, who shakes our lives like thunder, bless us and drive us out with power to fill the world with her justice.

O God, before whose face we are not made righteous even by being right; free us from the need to justify ourselves by our own anxious striving, that we may be abandoned to faith in you alone, through Jesus Christ. Amen.

O God our disturber, whose speech is pregnant with power and whose word will be fulfilled; may we know ourselves unsatisfied with all that distorts your truth, and make our hearts attentive to your liberating voice, in Jesus Christ. Amen.

O God our mystery, you bring us to life, call us to freedom, and move between us with love. May we so participate in the dance of your trinity, that our lives may resonate with you, now and for ever. Amen.

O God, the source of all insight, whose coming was revealed to the nations not among men of power but in a woman's lap; give us grace to seek you where you may be found, that the wisdom of this world may be humbled and discover your unexpected joy, through Jesus Christ. Amen.

O God who brought us to birth, and in whose arms we die, in our grief and shock contain and comfort us; embrace us with your love, give us hope in our confusion, and grace to let go into new life, through Jesus Christ. Amen.

O God whose word is life, and whose delight is to answer our cry, give us faith like the Syro-Phoenician woman who refused to remain an outsider; that we too may have the wit to argue and demand that our daughters be made whole, through Jesus Christ. Amen.

S pirit of integrity, you drive us into the desert to search out our truth. Give us clarity to know what is right, and courage to reject what is strategic; that we may abandon the false innocence of failing to choose at all, but may follow the purposes of Jesus Christ. Amen.

O God, you have searched us out and known us, and all that we are is open to you. We confess that we have sinned: we have used our power to dominate and our weakness to manipulate; we have evaded responsibility and failed to confront evil; we have denied dignity to ourselves and to our sisters (each other), and fallen into despair.

We turn to you, O God;
we renounce evil;
we claim your love;
we choose to be made whole.

In turn, around the circle, we say for each other: 'Woman/man, your sins are forgiven; be at peace.' This can be accompanied by a gesture such as taking hands, or making the sign of the cross on the forehead.[1]

Victoria Walton, for the Saskatchewan
Christian Feminist Network

O flaming Spirit of love,
we cry to you in the midst of the struggles of our lives!
O sacred fire, empower us!
Together we release our anger and our rage.
Transform them into the power of your compassion.
O sacred fire, empower us!

Together we release our fears.
Transform them into courage.
O sacred fire, empower us!
Together we release our despair.
Transform it into hope.
O sacred fire, empower us!
Together we release our doubts.
Transform them into wisdom.
O sacred fire, empower us!
We offer to you our broken sisterhood.
We offer to you our broken brotherhood.
Help us remember the wholeness that you intended.
O God of fire,
burn within us,
heal us, strengthen us,
remake us,
empower us with your passion for justice!
Amen.[2]

Christ Church Cathedral, Vancouver

Holy and compassionate God:
so direct our strength
and inspire our weakness
that we may enter with power
into the movement of your whole creation
towards wholeness, justice and peace. Amen.[3]

The Twentieth-Century Celtic Revival

The down-to-earth prayers of the ancient Celts resonate with a desire in our own days for a faith rooted in the natural world, and sanctifying ordinary life. Following the rediscovery of ancient texts, many contemporary Christians are writing prayers and songs in the Celtic style.

George Fielden Macleod (1895–1991)

George Macleod was a Church of Scotland minister in Edinburgh and then Glasgow, and in 1938 he founded the Iona Community on the island where St Columba had lived. The community steadily grew larger, meeting in the summer on the island and renovating the ruined abbey, and spearheading evangelism and social action in inner-city parishes when they dispersed. MacLeod became Moderator of the Church of Scotland, and favoured the controversial proposal, which failed, to introduce bishops to the government of the kirk in order to facilitate reunion with the Church of England. As a well-known speaker, broadcaster and writer, his political views were strongly Left wing. In 1967 he was made a life peer, as Baron MacLeod of Fuinary.

The Church at Home

Let us pray for our own church,
the place where we were brought up –
the place where we now worship;
Let us remember its achievements;
Children, in all the dross of false teaching.
still clutching the gold;
going about forgiving
because they know they are forgiven;
going about fearless

because they know evil is conquered;
And ourselves.
forgiving and fearless because of what we did learn there,
all the dross swept away;
And old folk not afraid of crossing the bourne,
and sorrowing folk bereaved of dear ones,
but not bitter,
because they know the empty chair
is not empty for always,
because there will be a meeting again.
And young folk,
tempted of passion or of acquisitiveness,
who have been stayed from lust or from dishonesty
because of what they did learn
in the all too faulty fellowship of the church at home;
We bless You, O God, for that church at home.
Let us remember its frailties.
It is often too frail for the modern storm,
is that church at home.
Too conformist to a world that's dying.
Too respectable for the drunkard
or the wretch to feel at home.
Too keen about its money to accuse an acquisitive society.
Too concerned about its own internal peace
to say the scarifying word about the Cross
as the way of peace for the world.
We ask You, Lord,
so to invade that church at home
that it becomes careless of dollars and pounds,
more careful of drunkards,
more courageous for peace,
more acquisitive of love.
And just because each one of us is that church at home,
help us to view again
our attitude to money in the light of Your poverty,
our attitude to drunkards and the lecherous
in the light of Your love for them,
our attitude to war
in the light of Your so strange way of dealing with it.

Lest, when we speak so critically
of the frailty of our church at home,
in our walks we should confront You, Lord Christ,
suddenly at the bend of the road
and not escape Your silent gaze at us,
Your silent gaze at each one of us
so clearly saying:
'You are the cause of the frailty of the church at home.'[1]

The Iona Community

In recent years the Iona Community has also become a centre for development of a distinctive style of worship based on its Celtic roots, which has inspired many.

eader: Let us pray.
You keep us waiting.
You, the God of all time,
Want us to wait
For the right time in which to discover
Who we are, where we must go,
Who will be with us, and what we must do.
All: So, thank you . . . for the waiting time.

Leader: You keep us looking.
You, the God of all space,
Want us to look in the right and wrong places
For signs of hope,
For people who are hopeless,
For visions of a better world which will appear
Among the disappointments of the world we know.
All: So, thank you . . . for the looking time.

Leader: You keep us loving.
You, the God whose name is love,
Want us to be like you –
To love the loveless and the unlovely and the unlovable;
To love without jealousy or design or threat;
And, most difficult of all,
To love ourselves.
All: So, thank you . . . for the loving time.

Leader: And in all this,
You keep us.
Through hard questions with no easy answers;
Through failing where we hoped to succeed
and making an impact when we felt we were useless;
Through the patience and the dreams and the love of others;
And through Jesus Christ and his Spirit,
you keep us.
All: So, thank you . . . for the keeping time,
and for now,
and for ever.
Amen.[2]

L *eader:* In the beginning, God made the world:
Women: Made it and mothered it,
Men: Shaped it and fathered it;
Women: Filled it with seeds and signs of fertility,
Men: Filled it with love and its folk with ability.
Leader: All that is green, blue, deep and growing,
All: God's is the hand that created you.
Leader: All that is tender, firm, fragrant and curious;
All: God's is the hand that created you.
Leader: All that crawls, flies, swims, walks or is motionless,
All: God's is the hand that created you.
Leader: All that speaks, sings, cries, laughs or keeps silence,
All: God's is the hand that created you.
Leader: All that suffers, lacks, limps or longs for an end,
All: God's is the hand that created you.
Leader: The world belongs to the Lord,
All: The earth and all its people are his.[3]

Margaret (1920–87) and Ian Fraser (1917–)

*Margaret and Ian Fraser helped into being Scottish Churches House, a
house of the Churches Together, in the 1960s.*

L ord God,
whose son was content to die
to bring new life,

have mercy on your church
which will do anything you ask,
anything at all:
except die
and be reborn.

Lord Christ,
forbid us unity
which leaves us where we are
and as we are:
welded into one company
but extracted from the battle;
engaged to be yours
but not found at your side.

Holy Spirit of God –
reach deeper than our inertia and fears:
release us into the freedom of the children of God.[4]

From Wind and Fire

David Adam (1936–)

David Adam is the vicar of Lindisfarne, where St Cuthbert lived in the
seventh century, and has composed many contemporary prayers in Celtic
idiom.

The Lord of the empty tomb, the conqueror of gloom,
come to you.
The Lord in the garden walking, the Lord to Mary talking,
come to you.
The Lord in the upper room, dispelling fear and doom,
come to you.
The Lord on the road to Emmaus, the Lord giving hope to Thomas,
come to you.
The Lord appearing on the shore, giving us life for evermore,
come to you.[5]

B lessed are you, Creator and giver of peace. Peace be upon us; peace be upon this place; peace be upon this day. The deep, deep peace of God, which the world cannot give, be upon us and remain with us always.[6]

Anjela Duval (1905–81)

Anjela Duval, as the only surviving child, inherited the family smallholding in the Leger River valley in France, and worked on the land until her old age. She had only four years of primary schooling, but in her forties she began writing poetry in the Breton language.

Prayer for a New Year

L ord! Father of the Universe
And Father of all Creatures
Spirit and Matter
Today hear if she asks
The least of your children
Who loves you from the depths of her heart
Her happiness to live forever . . .
Before you like a child before his father
With neither pain nor suspicion
I start a new Year
In the beginning of the springtime.
What will I be? I am in your hands.
Respectful? . . . Yes. Obedient? Hardly . . .
But may Your Will be done
And may a morsel of wisdom descend on my old age
So that my time will not be empty or vain
Give me Love and Enlightenment
Sufficient to share with others who
Stumble and grope on the Way
The Way so narrow that leads to Eternity . . .
Amen.[7]

Prayers by Indigenous Peoples

Prayers from Africa

All you big things, bless the Lord
Mount Kilimanjaro and Lake Victoria
The Rift Valley and the Serengeti Plain
Fat baobabs and shady mango trees
All eucalyptus and tamarind trees
Bless the Lord
Praise and extol him for ever and ever.
All you tiny things, bless the Lord
Busy black ants and hopping fleas
Wriggling tadpoles and mosquito larvae
Flying locusts and water drops
Pollen dust and tsetse flies
Millet seeds and dried dagaa
Bless the Lord
Praise and extol him for ever and ever.

An African canticle

Great is, O King, our happiness
in your kingdom, you, our King.
We dance before you, our King,
By the strength of your kingdom.
May our feet be made strong;
Let us dance before you, eternal.
Give praise, all angels,
To him above who is worthy of praise.

A prayer in a sacred dance of the Zulu Nazarite Church

O great Chief, light a candle in my heart, that I may see what is in it, and sweep the rubbish from your dwelling place.

An African schoolgirl's prayer

O Chief of chiefs, we kneel before you in humble adoration. Like the bird in the branches we praise your heavenly glory. Like the village sharpening stone, you are always available and never exhausted. Remove, we pray, our sins that hide your face. You know that we are poor and simple; that we are often hungry while we work. Send rain at the right time for our gardens so that our food may not fail. Protect us from the cold and danger by night. Help us to stay healthy so that we may rejoice in our strength. May our villages be filled with children. Set us free from the fear of the fetish and the witch doctor and from all sorts of superstitions. Save the people, especially the Christian boys and girls in the villages, from the evil that surrounds them. All this we ask in the name of Jesus Christ your Son.

A prayer from Zaire

The sun has disappeared.
I have switched off the light,
and my wife and children are asleep.
The animals in the forest are full of fear,
and so are the people on their mats.
They prefer the day with your sun to the night.
But I still know that your moon is there,
and your eyes and also your hands.
Thus I am not afraid.
This day again
you led us wonderfully.
Everybody went to his mat
satisfied and full.
Renew us during our sleep,
that in the morning
we may come afresh to our daily jobs.
Be with our brothers far away in Asia
who may be getting up now. Amen.

Prayer of a young Ghanaian Christian

G od in Heaven, you have helped my life to grow like a tree. Now, something has happened. Satan, like a bird, has carried in one twig of his own choosing after another. Before I knew it he had built a dwelling place and was living in it. Tonight, my Father, I am throwing out both the bird and the nest.

Prayer of a Nigerian Christian

S eed we bring
Lord, to you, please bless them, O Lord!
Gardens we bring
Lord, to you, please bless them, O Lord!
Hoes we bring
Lord, to you, please bless them, O Lord!
Knives we bring
Lord, to you, please bless them, O Lord!
Hands we bring
Lord, to you, please bless them, O Lord!
Ourselves we bring
Lord, to you, please bless us, O Lord!

East African hymn used at seed consecration services

A Native American Prayer

Black Elk (1863–1950)

Black Elk was a native American of the Lakota tribe; he was born near the Little Powder River in Dakota Territory, which is now southeast Wyoming. His family were medicine people, and he began to hear voices and see visions from the age of five; from the age of eighteen he was recognized as a holy man and a healer. When his people were restricted to the Reservations, he longed for wider horizons and joined Buffalo Bill's Wild West Show, travelling across the United States and to Europe; one of the conditions was that every Indian should be baptized a Christian. While not wishing to adopt the white man's culture, he was fascinated by the person of Jesus and his teachings. Nevertheless he returned to his reservation and was a leader in a revival of native religion, which was ended by the massacre of his people at Wounded Knee. He was given the name of Nicholas when he was baptized into the Roman Catholic Church in 1904; he identified the Christian God with Wakan-Tanka, the sacred mystery at the heart of the native religion, and was selected to become a catechist. He dictated accounts of his beliefs to researchers, and his prayers have become a model of how the Christian faith can without compromise be expressed through the terms of the ancient wisdom.

He he he hey *(four times)*. Grandfather, the Great Spirit, you have been always, and before you no one has been. There is no other one to pray to but you. You, yourself, everything that you see, everything has been made by you. The star nations all over the universe you have finished. The four quarters of the earth you have finished. The day, and in that day everything you have made on earth, everything you have done. Grandfather, Great Spirit, lean close to the earth so you may hear the voice I send . . .[1]

Prayers from Asia

God stir the soil,
Run the ploughshare deep,
Cut the furrows round and round,
Overturn the hard, dry ground,
Spare no strength nor toil,
Even though I weep.
In the loose, fresh mangled earth
Sow new seed.
Free of withered vine and weed
Bring fair flowers to birth.

Prayer from Singapore, Church Mission Society

Prayers by Chinese Christian Women

Prayer when opening a door
I pray thee, Lord, to open the door of my heart to receive thee within my heart.

When washing clothes
I pray thee, Lord, to wash my heart, making me white as snow.

When sweeping floors
I pray thee, Lord, to sweep away my heart's uncleanness, that my heart may always be pure.

When pouring oil
I pray thee, Lord, to give me wisdom like the wise virgins
who always had oil in their vessels.

When posting a letter
I pray thee, Lord, to add to me faith upon faith,
that I may always have communication with thee.

When lighting lamps
I pray thee, Lord, to make my deeds excellent like lamps before
    others,
and more, to place thy true light within my heart.

When watering flowers
I pray thee, Lord, to send down spiritual rain into my heart,
to germinate the good seed there.

When boiling water for tea
I pray thee, Lord, to send down spiritual fire
to burn away the coldness of my heart
and that I may always be hot-hearted in serving thee.

Prayers by Chinese Christian Men

Prayer on building a wall
I pray thee, Lord, to make my faith as firmly established
as a house built upon a rock,
so that neither rain, flood nor wind can ever destroy it.

On pruning a tree
I pray thee, Lord, to purge me and take away my selfishness
and sinful thoughts, that I may bring forth more fruits of the Spirit.

On tending sheep
I pray thee, Lord, to protect me from evil and keep me from want,
daily carrying me in thine arms like a lamb.

On winnowing grain
I pray thee, Lord, to winnow away the chaff from my heart
and make it like the true wheat,
fit to be garnered in thy barn.

On sowing seed
I pray thee, Lord, to sow the good seed of virtue in my heart,
letting it grow by day and night
and bring forth a hundredfold.

On writing a book
I pray thee, Lord, by the precious blood of Jesus,
to pay my debt of sin and write my name in heaven,
making me free in body and soul.

On planing wood
I pray thee, Lord, to make me smooth and straight,
fit to be a useful vessel, pleasing to the Lord.

On drawing water
I pray thee, Lord, to give living water to quench my thirst,
and wash away the stains from my heart.

Lord, let me rest the ladder of gratitude against your cross and,
mounting, kiss your feet.

Prayer of an Indian Christian

O heavenly Father, open wide the sluice gates into my heart
that I may receive your living water and be fruitful.

Prayer of a Punjabi Christian

A prayer from Australia

Bapa (Father), Ngandi (Mother),
You gave us the dreaming.
You have always spoken to us through our belief.
You then made your love clear to us
in the message of Jesus.
We thank you for your care.
You own us, you are our hope!
Make us strong as we face the problem of change.
Help the people of Australia to listen
to us and respect our belief.

We can only know ourselves in our culture.
Make the knowledge of you grow strong in all people,
so that you can find a home in us,
and we can make a home for everyone in our land.

Anne Pattel-Gray[2]

See also under Anonymous Prayers, p.581ff.

Twentieth-Century
Roman Catholic Spirituality

The changes in the 'unchanging' Roman Catholic Church in the twentieth century have been astonishing. Grass-roots movements like the Young Christian Workers, groups such as Focolare, and courses such as Cursillos, have all changed the spirituality of Catholics today. The effects of the Second Vatican Council, in vernacular liturgy and in many other spheres, are still being felt. Working among the poor in South America has led to the rise of Liberation Theology, and the 'base communities' have developed their own spirituality by reflecting on their personal experience and, in the light of that, interpreting the Scriptures.

Helder Pessoa Câmara (1909–)

Helder Câmara, the Archbishop of Olinda and Recife in north-east Brazil, has been an outspoken champion of the poor. He has argued for non-violent social change in his own country, and through his participation in the Second Vatican Council, in the Roman Catholic Church throughout the world. He received the Martin Luther King Jr Peace Prize in 1970 and the People's Prize in 1973.

Aren't you going too far, Lord . . .
with your respect for human freedom?
Your love extends to all creatures.
But you reserve your special love
for the small, the simple, the poor.
Then how can you bear to see
these millions
of your sons and daughters
living in subhuman conditions
owing to the selfishness

and ambition
of unjust and oppressive minorities?
By now you must have realized
that your cataclysms –
floods and droughts,
volcanic eruptions,
typhoons,
earthquakes –
affect the little ones most of all,
whose life is already
subhuman.
Isn't it bad enough
for them to be crushed
by diseases or human weakness?
How are we to explain
what comes from you?
Is it sufficient to say
that you have given us brains
and teach us how to overcome
natural disasters?[1]

Carlo Carretto (1910–88)

A leading priest in the Catholic Action movement in Italy, Carretto went to Algeria to the place where Charles de Foucauld had been murdered, and set up as a shoemaker serving the local Arabs and sharing their lifestyle and poverty. For long periods he would retreat to de Foucauld's cave in a mountainside two days' donkey-ride from his cobbler's shop.

Mary and Joseph, you it is who are masters of faith, perfect examples to inspire us, correct our course and support our weakness.

Just as you were beside Jesus, you are still beside us to accompany us to eternal life, to teach us to be small and poor in our work, humble and hidden in life, courageous in trial, faithful in prayer, ardent in love.

And when the hour of our death comes and dawn rises over our friendly night, our eyes, as they scan the sky, may pick out the same star that was in your sky when Jesus came upon earth.[2]

Frances Caryll Houselander (1901–54)

Caryll Houselander was born in England, and during her teens she abandoned the Catholic Faith into which she had been baptized. In her autobiography, A Rocking-Horse Catholic, *she describes how, after attending art school, working at various jobs and exploring different religions, she returned to Catholicism in the 1920s. She was a mystic, and the author of many books.*[3]

D escend,
Holy Spirit of Life!
Come down into our hearts,
that we may live.
Descend into emptiness,
that emptiness
may be filled.
Descend into the dust,
that the dust may flower.
Descend into the dark,
that the light
may shine in the darkness.
Amen.

B e born in us,
Incarnate Love.
Take our flesh and blood,
and give us Your humanity;
take our eyes, and give us your vision;
take our minds,
and give us Your pure thought;
take our feet and set them in your path;
take our hands,
and fold them in Your prayer;
take our hearts
and give them Your will to love.

B y your heaviness and fear
in Gethsemane,
comfort the oppressed
and those who are afraid.

By Your loneliness,
facing the Passion
while the Apostles slept,
comfort those who face evil alone
while the world sleeps.
By Your persistent prayer,
in anguish of anticipation,
strengthen those
who shrink from the unknown.
By your humility,
taking the comfort of angels,
give us grace to help
and to be helped by one another,
and in one another
to comfort You, Jesus Christ.
Amen.

Nail our hands
in Your hands
to the Cross.
Make us take and hold
the hard thing.
Nail our feet,
in Your feet
to the Cross,
that they may never
wander away from You.
Make our promises and our vows,
nails that hold us fast,
that even the dead weight of sin,
dragging on the nails
in our last weakness,
may not separate us from You,
but may make us one with You
in Your redeeming love.
Amen.

Gerard W. Hughes (1924–)

Trainer of the novices at the Jesuit House in Harborne, Birmingham, Fr Gerard Hughes sj wrote a best-seller in God of Surprises, *which inspired non-Catholic as well as Catholic readers. He followed this with* Walk to Jerusalem *and, more recently,* God of Compassion.[4]

O God, Father and Mother of all, from whom we come, to whom we go, enlighten our minds and hearts, so that recognizing your goodness in our own lives, we may become your goodness. We ask this through Jesus Christ our Lord. Amen.

God, lover of all that you have created, whose living Spirit is in all, batter down the defences of our minds and hearts with the waves of your compassion, so that surrendering to you, we may be delivered from our imprisoning self-interest into the expanse of your kingdom. We ask you this through Jesus Christ our Lord. Amen.

Deliver us, Lord, from triumphalism in all its forms. Whenever we encounter anyone of a different faith, or of no faith, help us to tread warily and reverently, for you have been there before us and your living Spirit is in every heart. We ask you this through Jesus Christ our Lord. Amen.

Lord, we thank you for the gift of hearing. Help us to use this gift so that as individuals, as groups, and as a nation, we may learn to listen without judging, without condemning, and to pardon and forgive as you pardon and forgive us. We ask you this through Jesus Christ our Lord. Amen.

Lord, you did not cling to your equality with God, but emptied yourself to assume the condition of a slave. Root out from our hearts all desire for power and influence over others, plant in its place love and delight in serving you by listening and responding to the needs of others. We ask you this through Jesus Christ our Lord. Amen.

Lord, deliver us from searching for our ultimate security in any created thing, in any theory, system or organisation, sacred or secular. Show yourself to us, our light, our refuge, our salvation, so that we may recognise you in all things and worship you always in spirit and in truth. We ask you this through Jesus Christ our Lord. Amen.

J esus, light of the world, be the light and joy of my life. Dispel the darkness of my fears and break down the barriers of my prejudice, so that I may recognise that which is of you in everyone I meet, and live grateful for your presence within us and amongst us. Amen.

Pope John Paul II (1920–)

Karol Jozef Wojtyla, born and educated in Poland, became professor of moral theology at the Universities of Lublin and Crakow. The author of plays, poems and several other books, he was made cardinal in 1967 and became the first non-Italian pope in 450 years when he was elected in 1978. His pontificate has been notable for his links with former communist countries, and his many journeys to almost every nation under heaven, kissing the tarmac and preaching to huge audiences.

T o you, creator of nature and humanity, of truth and beauty, I pray:
    Hear my voice, for it is the voice of the victims of all wars and
    violence among individuals and nations.
Hear my voice, for it is the voice of all children who suffer and who
    will suffer when people put their faith in weapons and war.
Hear my voice when I beg you to instil into the hearts of all human
    beings the vision of peace, the strength of justice and the joy of
    fellowship.
Hear my voice, for I speak for the multitudes in every country and in
    every period of history who do not want war and are ready to
    walk the road of peace.
Hear my voice and grant insight and strength so that we may always
    respond to hatred with love, to injustice with total dedication to
    justice, to need with the sharing of self, to war with peace.
O God, hear my voice, and grant to the world your everlasting peace.

Spoken during his visit to Hiroshima in 1981

Merciful Love, we pray to you, do not fail!
Merciful Love, we pray to you, be tireless!
Be constantly greater than every evil,
which is in man and in the world.
Be constantly greater than that evil
which has increased in our country and in our generation!
Be more powerful with the power of the crucified King!
'Blessed be his kingdom which is coming.'[6]

Let us ask the Lord to strengthen in all Christians faith in Christ,
the Saviour of the world. Listen to us, O Lord.
Let us ask the Lord to sustain and guide Christians with his gifts
along the way to full unity. Listen to us, O Lord.
Let us ask the Lord for the gift of unity and peace for the world.
Listen to us, O Lord.
Let us pray: We ask you, O Lord, for the gifts of your Spirit. Enable
us to penetrate the depths of the whole truth, and grant that
we may share with others the goods you put at our disposal.
Teach us to overcome divisions. Send your Spirit to lead to full
unity all your sons and daughters in full charity, in obedience
to your will, through Christ our Lord. Amen.[7]

Anthony de Mello (1931–87)

*Father de Mello was a Jesuit priest who applied the spiritual methods of
the East in retreats to train Christians in prayer. His profound teaching is
interspersed with memorable stories revealing a delicious sense of humour.*

Exercise 21: The Empty Chair

I developed this exercise as a result of hearing the story of a priest who
went to visit a patient in his home. He noticed an empty chair at the
patient's bedside and asked what it was doing there. The patient said, 'I
had placed Jesus on that chair and was talking to him before you arrived
. . . For years I found it extremely difficult to pray until a friend explained
to me that prayer was a matter of talking to Jesus. He told me to place
an empty chair nearby, to imagine Jesus sitting on that chair, and to speak
with him and listen to what he says to me in reply. I've had no difficulty
praying ever since.'

Some days later, so the story goes, the daughter of the patient came to the rectory to inform the priest that her father had died. She said, 'I left him alone for a couple of hours. He seemed so peaceful. When I got back to the room I found him dead. I noticed a strange thing, though: his head was resting not on the bed but on a chair that was beside his bed.'

Try this exercise yourself right now, even though at first it might seem childish to you:

Imagine you see Jesus sitting close to you. In doing this you are putting your imagination at the service of your faith. Jesus isn't here in the way you are imagining him, but he certainly is here and your imagination helps to make you aware of this. Now speak to Jesus . . . If no one is around, speak out in a soft voice . . .

Listen to what Jesus says to you in reply . . . or what you imagine him to say . . .[8]

Thomas Merton (1915–68)

Merton was born in France of New Zealand and American parents. After converting to Roman Catholicism he joined the Trappist order of Cistercian monks in Kentucky. His autobiography The Seven Storey Mountain *led many to vocations to become monks, but Merton himself found a tension between his desire for solitude and living in a community. He was set free to travel and write books. His interest in Eastern mysticism took him to a conference in Bangkok, where he was accidentally electrocuted by a faulty fan.*

On Becoming a Monk

How far have I to go to find you in whom I have already arrived? From now, O my God, it is to you alone that I can talk, because nobody else will understand. I cannot bring any other man on this earth into the cloud where I dwell in your light, that is, your darkness, where I am lost and abashed. I cannot explain to any other man the anguish which is your joy, nor the loss which is the possession of you, nor the distance from all things which is the arrival in you, nor the death which is the birth in you because I do not know anything about it myself and all I know is that I wish it were over – I wish it were begun.

You have contradicted everything. You have left me in no-man's land.

You have got me walking up and down all day under those trees, saying to me over and over again: 'Solitude, solitude'. And you have turned me around and thrown the whole world in my lap. You have told me, 'Leave all things and follow me', and then you have tied half of New York to my foot like a ball and chain. You have got me kneeling behind the pillar with my mind making a noise like a bank. Is that contemplation?

Before I went to make my solemn vows on the Feast of St Joseph, in the thirty-third year of my age, being a cleric in minor orders – before I went to make my solemn vows, this is what it looked like to me. It seemed to me that you were almost asking me to give up all aspirations for solitude and for a contemplative life. You were asking me for obedience to superiors who will, I am morally certain, either make me write or teach philosophy or take charge of a dozen material responsibilities around the monastery, and I may even end up as a retreat master preaching four sermons a day to the seculars who come to the house. And even if I have no special job at all, I will always be on the run from two in the morning to seven at night.[9]

For Unity of Faiths

O God, we are one with you. You have made us one with you. You have taught us that if we are open to one another, you dwell in us. Help us to preserve this openness and to fight for it with all our hearts. Help us to realize that there can be no understanding where there is mutual rejection. O God, in accepting one another wholeheartedly, fully, completely, we accept you, and we thank you, and we adore you, and we love you with our whole being, because our being is in your being, our spirit is rooted in your spirit. Fill us then with love, and let us be bound together with love as we go our diverse ways, united in this one spirit which makes you present in the world, and which makes you witness to the ultimate reality that is love. Love has overcome. Love is victorious.[10]

Henri Josef Machiel Nouwen (1932–96)

A Dutch priest, and trained in the United States in clinical psychology, Henri Nouwen's many books spoke in a simple, non-judgmental way to readers, especially those who had suffered psychologically, who were more attuned to the language of therapy than to that of religion. He was a brilliant teacher at Harvard University, using his whole body to convey his meaning, but when he went to one of Jean Vanier's 'L'Arche' communi-

ties of people with developmental disabilities in Toronto, he was forced to
confront his own homosexuality and suffered a mental breakdown. It was
while he was recovering from this that he penned some of his most profound
writings about the certainty of being loved and embraced by God.

O Lord, how hard it is to accept your way. You come to me as a small, powerless child born away from home. You live for me as a stranger in your own land. You die for me as a criminal outside the walls of the city, rejected by your own people, misunderstood by your friends, and feeling abandoned by your God. I am trying to overcome the feelings of alienation and separation which continue to assail me. But I wonder now if my deep sense of homelessness does not bring me closer to you than my occasional feelings of belonging. I do not have to run away from those experiences that are closest to yours. Every time I feel this way I have an occasion to be grateful and to embrace you better and taste more fully your joy and peace. Come, Lord Jesus, and be with me where I feel poorest. I trust that this is the place where you will find your manger and bring your light. Come, Lord Jesus, come.[11]

D ear Lord, awaken the people of the earth and their leaders to the realization of the madness of the nuclear arms race. Today we mourn the dead of past wars, but will there be anyone to mourn the dead of the next one? O Lord, turn us away from our foolish race to self-destruction; let us see that more and more weaponry indeed means more of a chance to use it. Please, Lord, let the great talents you have given to your creatures not fall into the hands of the powers and principalities for whom death is the means as well as the goal. Let us see that the resources hidden in your earth are for feeding each other, healing each other, offering shelter to each other, making this world a place where men, women, and children of all races and nations can live together in peace. Give us new prophets who can speak openly, directly, convincingly, and lovingly to kings, presidents, senators, church leaders, and all men and women of good will, prophets who can make us wage peace instead of war. Lord, make haste to help us. Do not come too late![12]

Hoob Oosterhuis (1933–)

Hoob Oosterhuis is a Jesuit priest who has been for most of his ministry a chaplain to students in Amsterdam. He was involved in the revision of the liturgy in Dutch, and several of his volumes of prayers and poems have been translated into English.

You wait for us
until we are open to you.
We wait for your word
To make us receptive.
Attune us to your voice,
to your silence,
speak and bring your Son to us –
Jesus, the word of your peace.
Your word is near,
O Lord our God,
your grace is near.
Come to us, then,
Do not let us be deaf to you,
but make us receptive and open
to Jesus Christ your Son,
who will come to look for us and save us
today and every day
for ever and ever.[19]

Michel Quoist (1921–)

Quoist's book, Prayers of Life, *opened many people's eyes to the possibility of praying in everyday words about the people and objects we see in front of us in the city: the telephone, the office block, the delinquent, the baldhead . . .*

And so all men run after time, Lord.
They pass through life running –
hurried, jostled, overburdened, frantic, and they never get there.
They haven't time.
In spite of all their efforts they're still short of time,
of a great deal of time.
Lord, you must have made a mistake in your calculations.

There is a big mistake somewhere.
The hours are too short,
The days are too short,
Our lives are too short.

You who are beyond time, Lord, you smile to see us fighting it.
And you know what you are doing.
You make no mistakes in your distribution of time to men.
You give each one time to do what you want him to do.

But we must not lose time
waste time,
kill time,
For time is a gift that you give us,
But a perishable gift,
A gift that does not keep.

Lord, I have time,
I have plenty of time,
All the time that you give me,
The years of my life,
The days of my years,
The hours of my days,
They are all mine.
Mine to fill, quietly, calmly,
But to fill completely, up to the brim,
To offer them to you, that of their insipid water
You may make a rich wine
such as you made once in Cana of Galilee.

I am not asking you tonight, Lord,
for time to do this and then that,
But your grace to do conscientiously,
in the time that you give me, what you want me to do.[14]

Brother Roger of Taizé (1915–)

*Roger Brother is a Swiss, born in Provence, the son of a Protestant pastor.
The founder of the Taizé Community, he is also the author of many books
and the annual Taizé newsletter.*

C hrist, Saviour of all life, you come to us always. Welcoming you in the peace of our nights, in the silence of our days, in the beauty of creation, in the hours of great combat within, welcoming you is knowing that you will be with us in every situation, always. Amen.[15]

R isen Christ, today, tomorrow and every day, your Spirit lives within us. Sometimes we feel we understand so little. But remaining in your presence, wherever we are, is prayer. And perhaps close to you, O Christ, silence is often all there is to prayer. And then we sense that, our whole life long, we move forward when trust in you guides every step, when a trusting heart is at the beginning of everything.[16]

Mother Teresa of Calcutta (1910–97)

Can there be anybody who does not know of the little Albanian nun who lived among the poorest of the poor in the slums of Calcutta, and found Christ in the poor old men and women she brought into her convent to give them 'a good death'? And yet it was largely because Malcolm Muggeridge, who was not at that time a believer, discovered her and told the world her story, that she became so famous. Is it possible that there are hundreds more twentieth-century missionaries who are just as saintly, but have received no publicity? Those who visited her reported that her charitable work was firmly grounded in a disciplined life of community prayer and a worldwide network of prayer supporters.

M y secret is quite simple. I pray and through my prayer I become one in love with Christ, and see that praying to him is to love him, and that means to fulfil his words. Remember the words of Saint Matthew's Gospel:

I was hungry and you gave me no food,
I was thirsty and you gave me no drink,
I was a stranger and you did not welcome me,
naked and you did not clothe me,
sick and in prison and you did not visit me.[17]

My poor ones in the world's slums are like the suffering Christ. In them God's Son lives and dies, and through them God shows me his true face. Prayer for me means becoming twenty-four hours a day at one with the will of Jesus to live for him, through him and with him.

If we pray
  we will believe
If we believe
  we will love
If we love
  we will serve.
Only then can we put
  our love for God
  into living action
Through service of Christ
  in the distressing
  disguise of the Poor.[18]

Lord, make me a saint according to your own heart, meek and humble.[19]

Make us worthy, Lord, to serve our fellow men throughout the world who live and die in poverty and hunger. Give them, through our hands, this day their daily bread, and by our understanding love, give peace and joy.

Ecumenical Spirituality Today

Jesus prayed for his disciples 'That they may all be one, in the same way as you, Father, and I are one.' The fulfilment of that prayer will require the resolving of many historical disagreements between different groups of Christians. The twentieth century has been marked by those who have laboured to bring this to pass. Not all are agreed that this will involve a structural unity of organization; some prefer to look for mutual understanding and agreement to work alongside. Between these two positions is the hope for an organic unity which does not require uniformity. The first step is to pray together; when this has happened, the inspiration to overcome our unhappy divisions has been renewed.

The World Council of Churches

Growing out of the Kikuyu Conference of Missionaries in 1913, the Faith and Order conferences and the Life and Work movement, the WCC was set up in 1948 as a 'fellowship of Churches which accept our Lord Jesus Christ as God and Saviour'. It contains representatives of most Protestant Churches, many Orthodox, and a few Pentecostals, but not Roman Catholics, Quakers, nor many of the more Evangelical denominations. From its headquarters in Geneva comes a regular supply of prayer material, and the worship material produced for their regular assemblies shows how Christians of different traditions can pray together in new ways.

O God, to those who have hunger give bread, and to us who have bread give the hunger for justice.[1]

Turn us, God,
when we are tempted to mock one another,
when we laugh at another's hopes and dreams,
when we break the bruised reed or quench the dimly burning wick.

Turn us, God,
> until we know the joy of the last becoming first, and the first last,
> until we live the truth

that those who lose their life for the sake of the gospel will find it.
> Amen.[2]

E verything is ready, Jesus Christ.
    We sit around your table in hope,
and wait for the moment
of eating and drinking with you.
> *Response:* **Lord have mercy.**

Your hands break the bread;
you hold it out for us to eat,
even those of us who betray you.
> *Response:* **Lord have mercy.**

You take the cup and give thanks,
the cup of our salvation,
the cup of the costly shedding of your blood.
> *Response:* **Lord have mercy.**

But we wait for the meal at our different tables.
We each claim you as our host, but not together.
We are not willing to share the one loaf.
We are not willing to drink from a common cup.
> even your loaf, even your cup.
> *Response:* **Lord have mercy.**

What will we do as we grieve?
Wehat will we do as we await the day
> of gathering as one around your table?

What will we do to prepare for your meal?
> *Response:* **Lord have mercy.**

We will share the loaf and the cup with those who have none.
We will gather together from the North, the South, the East and the
> West,
> poor and rich together in community,
> each one taking care of the other,
> giving and receiving as a sign of your grace.

Be present as we eat together, Jesus Christ. Amen.[3]

The Lima Liturgy

The Lima Liturgy was prepared for the Faith and Order Commission of the World Council of Churches following a series of reports on the agreement between the member churches of the WCC, from Orthodox to Protestant, on Baptism, Eucharist and Ministry. The final report was published at a conference in Lima, Peru, and the Liturgy is intended to be a Eucharist which any member church could use.[4]

I n faith let us pray to God our Father, his Son Jesus Christ, and the Holy Spirit.
Kyrie eleison.

For the Church of God throughout the world, let us invoke the Spirit.
Kyrie eleison.

For the leaders of the nations, that they may establish and defend justice and peace, let us pray for the wisdom of God.
Kyrie eleison.

For those who suffer oppression or violence, let us invoke the power of the Deliverer.
Kyrie eleison.

That the churches may discover again their visible unity in the one baptism which incorporates them in Christ, let us pray for the love of Christ.
Kyrie eleison.

That the churches may attain communion in the eucharist around one table, let us pray for the strength of Christ.
Kyrie eleison.

That the churches may recognize each other's ministries in the service of their one Lord, let us pray for the peace of Christ.
Kyrie eleison.

(*Free prayer of the congregation may follow.*)

Into your hands, O Lord, we commend all for whom we pray, trusting in your mercy; through your Son, Jesus Christ, our Lord. **Amen.**

T ruly it is right and good to glorify you, at all times and in all places, to offer you our thanksgiving O Lord, Holy Father, Almighty and Everlasting God. Through your living word you created all things, and pronounced them good; you made human beings in your own image, to share your life and reflect your glory. When the time had fully come, you gave Christ to us as the Way, the Truth and the Life. He accepted baptism and consecration as your Servant to announce the good news to the poor. At the last supper, Christ bequeathed to us the Eucharist, that we should celebrate the memorial of the cross and resurrection, and receive his presence as food. To all the redeemed, Christ gave the royal priesthood and, in loving his brothers and sisters, chooses those who share in the ministry, that they may feed the Church with your Word and enable it to live by your Sacraments.

The Council of Churches for Britain and Ireland

The British Council of Churches was created in 1942 with Archbishop William Temple as its first President. Its successor, the Council of Churches for Britain and Ireland, was inaugurated in 1990, as a result of the 'Not Strangers but Pilgrims' Inter-Church Process of 'prayer, reflection and debate together on the nature and purpose of the Church in the light of its mission'. The Council of Churches for Britain and Ireland, due shortly to be re-named Churches Together in Britain and Ireland, continues to publish material for prayer for unity. At the crucial Swanwick Conference of 1987 the 'Pilgrim Prayer' summed up this movement of the churches together:

L ord God, we thank you
For calling us into the company
Of those who trust in Christ
And seek to obey his will.
May your Spirit guide and strengthen us
In mission and service to your world
For we are strangers no longer
But pilgrims together on the way to your Kingdom
Amen.[5]

Christian Aid

Beginning in Britain after the Second World War as Inter-Church Aid to help churches in other countries to care for refugees, Christian Aid has become one of the world's largest aid agencies, and publishes much challenging and inspiring worship material for its supporters.

T ake our hatreds, make them into handshakes.
Take our prejudices, make them into peace-offerings.
Take our misunderstandings; make them into music.
Take our divisions; turn them into dances.
Take our helplessness; make us hope,
for you never withdraw the forces of your love.[6]

M ay the God who binds up the brokenhearted, who proclaims freedom to those held captive by poverty, and promises justice to all who mourn its loss, bless you with beauty instead of ashes, the oil of gladness in place of grief, and instead of your spirit of despair, a garment of unending praise; through Jesus Christ our Lord. Amen.[7]

The Women's World Day of Prayer (1993)

Material for the annual day of prayer is produced by the women of a different country each year, and used all over the world; much of it is excellent. But it was when the editor of this anthology attended a Women's World Day of Prayer service in the USA and found he was expected to thank God aloud for the privilege of bearing children, and ask to be made a good wife and mother, that he first realized the hurtfulness of using non-inclusive language, which implies that some of those present were forgotten about when the service was compiled!

L ord, we thank you for our world – for its infinite varieties of people, colours, races and cultures, for the endless opportunities of making new relationships, venturing across new frontiers, creating new things, discovering new truths, healing the hurt and the broken. Forgive us for our narrowness of vision which sees only the clouds and misses the rainbow. Amen.[8]

The Daily Office of the Joint Liturgical Group

The Joint Liturgical Group's Daily Office was offered as a supplement to private prayer and public worship, in all the member churches of the British Council of Churches.

I n darkness and in light,
in trouble and in joy,
help us to trust your love,
   to serve your purpose, and
   to praise your name,
through Jesus Christ our Lord. Amen.[9]

Pentecost 6

A lmighty God,
you have chosen us as your own
and you give us new life in Christ.
Fill us with his spirit of compassion and love,
and may his peace always reign in our hearts.
We ask this in his name and for his sake.[10]

Pentecost 14

A lmighty God,
you have taught us through your Son
that love is the fulfilling of the law.
Grant that we may love you with our whole heart
and our neighbours as ourselves;
through Jesus Christ our Lord.[11]

The Corrymeela Community

This is the members' prayer of a mixed community of Roman Catholics and Protestants, founded in 1965 and committed to bringing peace and reconciliation in Northern Ireland.

G od, we believe that you have called us together
to broaden our experience of you and of each other.
We believe that we have been called to help
in healing the many wounds of society

and in reconciling people to each other and to God.
Help us as individuals or together,
to work, in love, for peace, and never to lose heart.
We commit ourselves to each other – in joy and sorrow.
We commit ourselves to all who share our belief in reconciliation –
to support and stand by them.
We commit ourselves to the way of justice and peace –
in thought and deed.
We commit ourselves to you – as our guide and friend.[12]

The Churches' National Housing Commission

A combination of charities and pressure groups dealing with the problem of homelessness in Britain. Homelessness is now commonplace in First and Third World countries and in many societies, the churches are at the forefront in tackling this social evil, but the scale of the problem remains daunting.

Y ou asked for our hands that you might use them for your
     purpose,
**We gave them for a moment then withdrew them for the work
     was hard.**
You asked for our mouths to speak out against injustice,
We gave you a whisper that we might not be accused.
You asked for our eyes to see the pain of poverty,
We closed them for we did not want to see.
You asked for our ears, that we might hear the cries of the
     oppressed,
We did not listen for it was too hard.
You asked for our lives that you might work through us,
We gave a small part that we might not get too involved.
Forgive us for the times we have washed our hands of people,
walked away when they needed us, offered half measure,
O God, our Father and Mother, forgive us.
We believe in one God, author of life, Creator of the universe.
We believe in the Son, Jesus Christ our Lord,
who came into the world to seek the lost
and to redeem the whole of creation.
We believe in the Holy Spirit, the Giver of Life,

who renews us and helps us grow in the likeness of Christ.
We believe we are created to be faithful servants
who will not waver or be crushed,
who, by praying, working, and standing together
can bring justice and truth to the whole earth.[13]

More Contemporary Prayers

'Anna'

The unique and mould-breaking book by 'Fynn', Mister God, This is Anna, fits into no categories. All our thought about God is split apart and fitted together again in a totally new language through the mind of a small child. If you are willing to have your heart broken and your mental horizons exploded as Anna hurls herself into your arms, read the book. Meanwhile here are some samples of her style of prayer.

'A in't you gonna say your prayers?' she asked.
'Well, yes,' I replied, 'when I get to bed.'
'I want to say mine now with you,' she said. So we both got down on our knees and she talked while I listened.

I've been to church many times, and heard many prayers, but none like this. I can't remember much about her prayer except that it started off with 'Dear Mister God, this is Anna talking,' and she went on in such a familiar way of talking to Mister God that I had the creepy feeling that if I dared look behind me he would be standing there. I remember her saying, 'Thank you for letting Fynn love me,' and I remember being kissed goodnight, but how I got to bed I don't know . . .

She started to say, 'What is the question to the answer, "In the middle of sex"?'

I reached out my hand and silenced her question with a finger on her lips. 'The question is,' I said, '"Where is Mister God?"'

She bit my finger – hard – and looked at me. Her eyes said, 'That's for keeping me waiting.' Her lips said 'Yes'.

I lay back again on the deck of the barge and thought about what I had said. The more I thought about it the more did I come to the conclusion that it really wasn't bad at all, in fact it was pretty good.

I liked it. At least it prevented all the fuss and pother of pointing up there and saying that's where God is, or pointing out among the stars and saying that God is there! Yes, indeed, I liked it very much – only –.

The 'only' didn't get resolved for quite a few days. Even then 'teacher' had to lead me gently by the hand and explain in words that this idiot could understand. You see, I had got to the point where I could, without any undue hesitation, give the question to the answers, 'In the worm's middle', 'In my middle', 'In your middle.' I'd even stopped getting het up about the question to the answer, 'In the tramcar's middle.' The question was 'Where is Mister God?' So far so good. Everything in the garden was lovely, except perhaps for one tiny, irrelevant and unimportant fact. I was ringed about with an unclimbable, impenetrable, couldn't-see-the-top-of range of mountains. The names of these towering peaks were: The worm's in the GROUND, I'm HERE; you're THERE; the tramcar's moving DOWN the street. I had got stuck with all these multitudinous and varied things which had got 'middles' in which Mister God was! The whole universe it seemed was strewn and littered about with sundry THERES and various HERES. Instead of some whole and big Mister God sitting around in a heaven of umpteen dimensions, I was now faced with a vast assortment of little Mister Gods inhabiting the middles of everything! Perhaps all these middles contained bits of Mister God which had to be put together like some gigantic jigsaw puzzle . . .

As for my problem about the HERES and the THERES, the explanation went like this:

'Where are you?' she had said.

'Here, of course', I replied.

'Where's me then?'

'There!'

'Where do you know about me?'

'Inside myself someplace.'

'Then you know my middle in your middle.'

'Yes, I suppose so.'

'Then you know Mister God in my middle in your middle, and everything you know, every person you know, you know in your middle. Every person and everything that you know has got Mister God in their middle and so you have got their Mister God in your middle too – It's easy.'

When Mr William of Occam said, 'It is vain to do with more what can be done with less', he had invented his famous razor, but it was Anna who sharpened it! . . .

She smiled. 'Fynn, there ain't no different churches in heaven, cos everybody in heaven is inside themselves.'

Then she went on:

'It's the outside bits that make all the different churches and synagogues and temples and things like that. Fynn, Mister God said "I am", and that's what he wants us all to say – that's the hard bit.'

My head went up and down in bewildered agreement.

'"I am" . . . that's the hard bit. "I am." Really get around to saying that and you're home, really mean it and you're full up, you're all inside. You don't have to want things outside you to fill up the gaps inside you. You don't leave bits of you hanging around on objects in shop-windows, in catalogues or on advertising hoardings. Wherever you go you take your whole self with you, you don't leave bits lying around to get stamped on, you're all of a piece, you're what Mister God wants you to be. An "I am", like he is. Hell's bells!'[1]

Metropolitan Anthony of Sourozh (1914–)

Orthodox Christianity seems to enter the bloodstream of those who live in Greece, Russia and the other nations of Eastern Christendom. Travelling in exile, they and their descendants continue to worship with the Liturgy as their parents knew it in their home country. Many who are not of Orthodox stock are so deeply moved by the beauty of holiness that they either convert to Orthodoxy or visit their churches whenever they can. Yet under the unchanging exterior, there are many gentle movements of renewal. Born Anthony Bloom in Switzerland, where his father was a Russian diplomat, and brought up in Persia and Paris, where he became a medical doctor, Metropolitan Anthony has been resident in London for most of his life, and has been a popular television speaker. To meet him is to see how tenuous is the boundary between everyday life and the Liturgy for the Orthodox, so that all is caught up into worship.

O Lord, I know not what to ask of thee; thou alone knowest what are my true needs. Thou lovest me more than I know how to love myself. Help me to see my real needs which are concealed from me. I dare not ask either a cross or consolation. I can only wait on thee. My heart is open to thee. Visit and help me for thy great mercy's sake, strike me and heal me, cast me down and raise me up. I worship in silence thy holy will and thine inscrutable ways. I offer myself as a sacrifice to thee. I put all my trust in thee. I have no other desire than to fulfil thy will. Teach me how to pray, pray thou thyself in me. Amen.[2]

The old lady said 'These fourteen years I have been praying the Jesus Prayer almost continually, and never have I perceived God's presence at all.' So I blundered out what I thought. I said 'If you speak all the time, you don't give God a chance to place a word in.' She said 'What shall I do?' I said 'Go to your room after breakfast, put it right, place your armchair in a strategic position that will leave behind your back all the dark corners which are always in an old lady's room into which things are pushed so as not to be seen. Light your little lamp before the ikon that you have and first of all take stock of your room. Just sit, look round, and try to see where you live, because I am sure that if you have prayed all these fourteen years it is a long time since you have seen your room. And then take your knitting and for fifteen minutes knit before the face of God, but I forbid you to say one word of prayer. You just knit and try to enjoy the peace of your room.'

She didn't think it was very pious advice but she took it. After a while she came to see me and said 'You know, it works.' I said 'What works, what happens?' because I was very curious to know how my advice worked. And she said 'I did just what you advised me to do. I got up, washed, put my room right, had breakfast, came back, made sure that nothing was there that would worry me, and then I settled in my armchair and thought "Oh how nice, I have fifteen minutes during which I can do nothing without being guilty!" and I looked round and for the first time after years I thought "Goodness what a nice room I live in – a window opening onto the garden, a nice shaped room, enough space for me, the things I have collected for years".' Then she said 'I felt so quiet because the room was so peaceful. There was a clock ticking but it didn't disturb the silence, its ticking just underlined the fact that everything was so still and after a while I remembered that I must knit before the face of God, and so I began to knit. And I became more and more aware of the silence. The needles hit the armrest of my chair, the clock was ticking peacefully, there was nothing to bother about, I had no need of straining myself, and then I perceived that this silence was not simply an absence of noise, but that the silence had substance. It was not absence of something but presence of something. The silence had a density, a richness, and it began to pervade me. The silence around began to come and meet the silence in me.' And then in the end she said something very beautiful which I have found later in the French writer, Georges Bernanos. She said 'All of a sudden I perceived that the silence was a presence. At the heart of the silence there was Him who is all stillness, all peace, all poise.'

After that she lived for about ten more years and she said that she could always find the silence when she was quiet and silent herself. This does not mean that she stopped praying, it means that she could sustain this contemplative silence for a while, then her mind began to quiver and she turned to vocal prayer until the mind was still and settled again, then she dropped out of words into silence as before.

The workshops of the monastery were manned by young Russian peasants who used to come for one year, for two years, in order to make some money, really farthing added to farthing, in order to go back to their villages with a few pounds, perhaps, at the utmost to be able to start a family by marrying, by building a hut and by buying enough to start their crops. One day other monks, who were in charge of other workshops, said 'Father Silouan, how is it that the people who work in your workshops work so well while you never supervise them, while we spend our time looking after them and they try continuously to cheat us in their work?' Father Silouan said 'I don't know. I can only tell you what I do about it. When I come in the morning, I never come without having prayed for these people and I come with my heart filled with compassion and with love for them, and when I walk into the workshop I have tears in my soul for love of them. And then I give them the task they have to perform in the day and as long as they will work I will pray for them, so I go into my cell and I begin to pray about each of them individually. I take my stand before God and I say "O Lord, remember Nicholas. He is young, he is just twenty, he has left in his village his wife, who is even younger than he, and their first child. Can you imagine the misery there is there that he has had to leave them because they could not survive on his work at home. Protect them in his absence. Shield them against every evil. Give him the courage to struggle though this year and go back to the joy of a meeting, with enough money, but also enough courage, to face the difficulties".' And he said 'In the beginning I prayed with tears of compassion for Nicholas, for his young wife, for the little child, but as I was praying the sense of the divine presence began to grow on me and at a certain moment it grew so powerful that I lost sight of Nicholas, his wife, his child, his needs, their village, and I could be aware only of God, and I was drawn by the sense of the divine presence deeper and deeper, until of a sudden, at the heart of this presence, I met the divine love holding Nicholas, his wife, and his child, and now it was with the love of God that I began to pray for them again, but again I was drawn into the deep and in the depths of this I again found the divine love. And so', he said, 'I spend my days, praying for each of them in turn, one after the other and when the day is over I go, I say a few words to them, we pray together and they go to their rest. And I go back to fulfil my monastic office.'

Here you can see how contemplative prayer, compassion, active prayer was an effort and a struggle, because it was not just saying 'Remember O Lord, him, him and him.' It was hours and hours spent just praying with compassion, praying with love, both blending together.[3]

Angela Ashwin (1949–)

These prayers are all from Angela Ashwin's The Book of a Thousand Prayers.[4]

Abba, Father,
I am here,
for you,
for myself,
for the world,
for this moment,
I am here . . .

This day, Lord, may I dream your dreams,
this day, Lord, may I reflect your love,
this day, Lord, may I do your work,
this day, Lord, may I taste your peace.

May the song of your Spirit soothe us,
your gentle arms cradle us,
your tenderness ease our tiredness
and your welcome enfold our weariness,
this night
and all our nights.

Lord, cleanse and sweeten the springs of my being,
that your freedom and light
may flow into my conscious mind
and into my hidden, unconscious self.

S ave me, Lord, from the distraction
of trying to impress others,
and from the dangers of having done so.
Help me to enjoy praise for work well done,
and then to pass it on to you.
Teach me to learn from criticism,
and give me the wisdom
not to put myself at the centre of the universe.

L ove of Jesus, fill us,
Joy of Jesus, surprise us,
Peace of Jesus, flood us,
Light of Jesus, transform us,
Touch of Jesus, warm us,
Strength of Jesus, encourage us.
O Saviour, in your agony, forgive us,
in your wounds, hide us,
and in your risen life take us with you,
for your love's sake.

Eddie Askew (1927–)

In his series of books published by the Leprosy Mission (for whom he worked for fifteen years in India and then in London) and illustrated with his own drawings, Eddie Askew has provided a style of praying which many people have found that they could make their own. They originated in a series of monthly newsletters circulated to Leprosy Mission staff worldwide.

L ord, teach me to pray.
It sounds exciting, put like that.
It sounds real. An exploration.
A chance to do more than catalogue
and list the things I want,
to an eternal Father Christmas.
The chance of meeting you,
of drawing closer to the love that made me.
and keeps me, and knows me.
And, Lord, it's only just begun.

There is so much more of you,
of love, the limitless expanse of knowing you.
I could be frightened, Lord, in this wide country.
It could be lonely, but you are here, with me.

The chance of learning about myself,
of facing up to what I am.
Admitting my resentments,
bringing my anger to you, my disappointments, my frustration.
And finding that when I do,
when I stop struggling and shouting
and let go
you are still there.
Still loving.

Sometimes, Lord, often –
I don't know what to say to you.
But I still come, in quiet
for the comfort of two friends
sitting in silence.
And it's then, Lord, that I learn most from you.
When my mind slows down,
and my heart stops racing.
When I let go and wait in the quiet,
realizing that all the things I was going to ask for
you know already.
Then, Lord, without words,
in the stillness
you are there . . .
And I love you.
Lord, teach me to pray.[5]

The Church Mission Society

Founded in 1799 as the Society for Missions in Africa and the East, then until recently known as the Church Missionary Society, the CMS sees itself as a voluntary society, with members committed to the task of sending mission partners to pioneer evangelism and supporting the Church in other lands in service to the needy. The way this has been applied has been modified as circumstances changed, but the vision has remained the same.

CMS has its roll-call of heroes and martyrs too, and now shares a head-quarters with USPG. The Society has provided a variety of literature to help its members pray for mission.[6]

God of love, whose will it is that all should be saved, bless the Church Mission Society and all who have gone in its fellowship to preach, to teach and to heal. Guard, guide and use them; raise up more people in your world-wide Church to pray and to work, to care and to understand, to give to you and to go for you, that your Church may grow, your will be done, your kingdom come and your glory be revealed, through Jesus Christ our Lord. Amen.

The CMS family prayer

Almighty God, whose kingdom is for the poor in spirit, and whose best provision for your chosen people is a tent and a pilgrim staff; grant that we look not for permanence in the work of human hands, nor seek safety other than in the company of that Wayfarer who had nowhere to lay his head, even your Son Jesus Christ our Lord. Amen.

Lord, what is the cost of one person's freedom?
Lord, what is the cost of safety for a child?
Lord, what does it cost to give a young man a future?
Lord, what does it cost to preserve a woman's dignity?
Lord, why did you pay so much for the words you spoke?
Lord, why were your actions for justice so expensive?
Lord, why did you pay so dearly for your dreams?
Lord, did you pay all that for me?
Lord, how much must I pay to follow you?
Amen.

Jim Cotter (1942–)

Jim Cotter was involved in training candidates for the ordained ministry before setting up a centre of prayer in Sheffield, from which he publishes books of prayer which have been widely influential.

Dear God, thank you for all that is good, for our creation and our humanity, for the stewardship you have given us of this planet earth, for the gifts of life and of one another, for your Love which is unbounded and eternal. Amen.[7]

We repent the wrongs we have done:
our blindness to human need and suffering;
our indifference to injustice and cruelty;
our false judgements, petty thoughts, and contempt;
our waste and pollution of the earth and oceans;
our lack of concern for those who come after us;
our complicity in the making of weapons of mass destruction,
and our threatening of their use.[8]

Be present, living Christ, within us, your dwelling place and home, that this house may be one where all darkness is penetrated by your light, all troubles calmed by your peace, all evil redeemed by your love, all pain transformed in your suffering, and all dying glorified by your risen life. Amen.[9]

God bless this city
and move our hearts with pity
lest we grow hard.
God bless this place
with silence, solitude and space
that we may pray.
God bless these days
of rough and narrow ways
lest we despair.
God bless the night
and calm the people's fright
that we may love.
God bless this land
and guide us with your hand
lest we be unjust.
God bless this earth
through pangs of death and birth
and make us whole. Amen.[10]

Michael John Radford Counsell (1935–)

The following prayers are the editor's contribution to this anthology.

Baby of Bethlehem,
born among humble men,
cared for and shared with them;
you help me see
this is God's sympathy,
shown unreservedly
for all in poverty –
even for me.

Jesus of Nazareth,
lowly you came to birth,
lived as a child on earth
by Mary's knee.
This you have done for us,
lovingly come to us,
just like each one of us,
and just like me.

Christ in Gethsemane,
dreading your destiny,
wishing from agony
you could be free;
tempted to run away
and fight another day;
but all the world can say,
'tempted like me'.

Jesus on Calvary,
divine vitality
killed by brutality,
hanged on a tree.
God's love that never ends
down to death's depths descends,
dying for all your friends –
dying for me!

Risen in Galilee,
Jesus in majesty,

living eternally
for all to see!
Bring us before God's face,
in heaven prepare a place
for all the human race –
even for me![11]

God, you have put down the mighty from their seat and exalted the humble and meek; we ask you in our day also to show strength with your arm and to scatter the proud in the imagination of their hearts. Guide those in authority, and show your people when to support them in all things lawful and honest with the obedience of Mary, and when to sing a revolutionary Magnificat in the name of Jesus Christ her Son our Lord. Amen.

Lord God, who by the leading of a star brought wise men to the Babe in a manger; may those to whom, in their search for truth, you have revealed the glory of your creation, be led to behold the fulfilment of that glory in the humility which sacrifices itself in the service of others; for the sake of him who gave himself to be the Way, the Truth and the Life, the same Jesus Christ our Lord. Amen.

Almighty God, dwelling in the beauty of holiness, from whom all skills of mind, hand and tongue do come; may those who give their lives to the creation of beauty be surprised by the joy of discovering your presence in your world, and give others the hope of beholding your glory unveiled in heaven, where you are alive and reign, Creator, Redeemer and Sanctifier, one God for ever and ever. Amen.

God, who wrestled with chaos to create matter, and overcame death to bring us to eternal life, give to writers, musicians and artists a share in the work and joy of creation, that, like you, they may draw forth beauty out of nothingness, and reveal to us some glimpses of your eternity, where you are enthroned, Life-giver, Pain-bearer, Love-maker, alive for ever and ever. Amen.

Risen Christ, you came to your disciples in the evening on the first day of the week. Forgive us when, like Thomas, we hug our doubts and worries to ourselves. Grant us such a hunger for the fellowship of those who believe in you, that no excuses may prevent us from meeting together in the evening stillness. Then may we find you standing among us, to strengthen us and send us out in your service; for you are alive and reign, with the Father and the Holy Spirit, one God now and for ever. Amen.

L ord Jesus, you were ever ready to listen to those who cried out to you. You gave us ears to hear: help us to hear. May we listen to all we meet, and to those who come to us in trouble. Remind us daily that there is a time for silence and a time for speaking, and show us when to speak and when to hold our peace. Never let us miss a cry for help, because we are too busy talking about ourselves. Make us ready to listen to others, because we listen each day in silence to you, O Jesus Christ our Lord. Amen.

Magnificat

M y spirit magnifies the Lord, my soul is filled with love,
for God has sent an only Son to earth from heaven above;
to earth from heaven above; so sing the birth of such a boy:
My spirit magnifies the Lord, my soul is filled with joy.

My spirit magnifies the Lord, my soul is filled with peace,
for God has sent an only Son the prisoners to release;
the prisoners to release; and all the tyrants to destroy:
My spirit magnifies the Lord, my soul is filled with joy.

My spirit magnifies the Lord, my soul is filled with faith,
for God has sent an only Son to break the power of death;
to break the power of death; and cleanse us all from sin's alloy:
My spirit magnifies the Lord, my soul is filled with joy.

My spirit magnifies the Lord, my soul is filled with grace,
for God has sent an only Son the wealthy to displace;
the wealthy to displace and fill the hungry they annoy:
My spirit magnifies the Lord, my soul is filled with joy.

My spirit magnifies the Lord, my soul is filled with song,
for God has sent an only Son to right all earthly wrong;
to right all earthly wrong that sinful people can deploy:
My spirit magnifies the Lord, my soul is filled with joy.

Luke 1:46–55[12]

Nunc Dimittis

M aster, who repeated
promise of release:
all my tasks completed,
let me leave in peace.

That we've seen salvation
could not be denied:
light for every nation
and your people's pride.

Glory to the Father,
glory to the Son,
glory, Holy Spirit.
Heaven has begun! Amen.

Luke 2:29–32[13]

F or the racism which denies dignity to those who are different,
Lord, forgive us;
Lord, have mercy.
For the racism which recognizes prejudice in others
and never in ourselves, Christ, forgive us:
Christ, have mercy.
For the racism which will not recognize the work of your Spirit
in other cultures, Lord, forgive us:
Lord, have mercy.

Mutual Absolution

I ask your forgiveness for what my people and I have done to you and
yours, and I forgive you for what your ancestors did to my ancestors.
Will you do the same for me?
We ask your forgiveness for what our people and we have done to you
and yours, and we forgive you for what your ancestors did to our
ancestors.
Now God has forgiven our sins, and torn the heavy veil of guilt, suspicion
and bitterness which divided us. We are all children of God; we are sisters
and brothers in God's family of love. **Amen.**

God the Father of all, your Church is not catholic because we do not seek to comprehend all the ways in which you are understood within one family. Forgive us and make us truly catholic. Lord, have mercy:
Lord, have mercy.
God the Son who died for all, your Church is not evangelical because the gospel of your universal love is concealed by our narrowness and prejudice. Forgive us and make us truly evangelical. Christ, have mercy:
Christ, have mercy.
God the Spirit, you work through all and are in all. Your Church is not charismatic because we have pretended that our gifts are better than other people's, and have not made them subservient to the best gift of love. Forgive us and make us truly charismatic. Lord, have mercy:
Lord, have mercy.
God through his forgiveness draws you closer to him, and in him closer to one another. **Amen.**

Christ the Way, every day,
we will walk with you.
No more fear, you are near,
loving us anew.
Friend of all, when we call,
bring us, as we roam,
all our days filled with praise,
nightly nearer home.

Those we love, now above,
live in rapture there;
happy they, night and day
in your love they share.
When they leave, while we grieve,
they are free from cares;
we rejoice in your choice
that your home is theirs.

All we do is for you,
Jesus, Lord most high;
so must we, therefore, be
unafraid to die.
Till that day, come what may,
when no more we roam,

let each breath sing till death
'We are going home!'

Then on high, when we die,
we shall be at home . . .
in our Father's home.[14]

L ord, you call us to confess our sins,
  but I don't often tell you what a fool I've been.
It would be a relief to tell someone.
So many things I could have done for you,
but I failed, by making senseless decisions.
I tried to speak your word, but it was misunderstood,
because I expressed it foolishly.
I have harmed other people, when I was too stupid
        to foresee the effects of what I had done;
and broken fellowship with them, through not knowing
        how silly my speech would sound.
Lord, how can you love such a fool?
And yet, foolish as it may seem, I really believe you do love me.
Do you? You do! Thank God. Amen.

Albert Kenneth Cragg (1913–)

*Kenneth Cragg has been warden of St Augustine's College, Canterbury
and Assistant Bishop in Jerusalem, as well as in three English dioceses.
His writings have helped Christians to understand Islam, and he is a gifted
poet, as is perhaps necessary in order to appreciate the Qur'an.*

T he story, Lord, is as old as history, as remorseless as man:
  Man the raider, the plunderer, the terrorist, the conqueror,
Defiling the light of dawn with
The conspiracies of night,
Perverting to evil the fine instruments of nature,
Dealing fear among the tents and the homesteads
Of the unsuspecting or the weak,
Confiscating, purloining, devastating.
The passions are more subtle in our time –
The fire-power of bombs for the dust-clouds of cavalry,

Napalm and incendiary and machines in the skies,
Devices for war decrying the stars,
New skills with the same curse of destruction,
The sanctity of mankind in the jeopardy of techniques,
Gracelessness against the majesty on high.
By the truth of the eternal exposure,
By the reckoning of the eternal justice,
By compassion upon kin and kind,
By the awe of thy sovereignty,
Turn our deeds, O good Lord,
Repair our ravages,
Forgive our perversities.
O God, give peace, grateful peace.[15]

Every history of ours, O Lord, is the history of all. For no church is an island, entire to itself. For the fire of thy servants in far centuries, thy name be praised, O Lord; for ancient stones and liturgies, for ripened learning and long disciplines of prayer and peace, thy name be blessed, O Lord, and every saint, O Lord, preserve, renew and multiply, in the eternal Christ.[16]

Hassan Dehqani-Tafti (1920–)

Bishop Dehqani-Tafti was the first locally born Anglican Bishop in Iran, and a distinguished poet in his own language. At the time of the rise of Muslim fundamentalism his son, Bahram, was murdered. Since then he has been in exile in England.

O God we remember not only our son but also his murderers; not because they killed him in the prime of his youth and made our hearts bleed and our tears flow, not because with this savage act they have brought further disgrace on the name of our country among the civilized nations of the world; but because through their crime we now follow thy footsteps more closely in the way of sacrifice. The terrible fire of this calamity burns up all selfishness and possessiveness in us; its flame reveals the depth of depravity and meanness and suspicion, the dimension of hatred and the measure of sinfulness in human nature; it makes obvious as never before our need to trust in God's love as shown in the cross of Jesus and his resurrection; love which makes us free from hate towards our persecutors; love which brings patience, forbearance, courage, loyalty, humility, generosity, greatness of heart; love which more than ever deepens our trust in God's final victory and his eternal designs for the Church and for the world; love which teaches us how to prepare ourselves to face our own day of death. O God, our son's blood has multiplied the fruit of the Spirit in the soil of our souls; so when his murderers stand before thee on the day of judgement remember the fruit of the Spirit by which they have enriched our lives. And forgive.[17]

Richard Foster (1942–)

Richard Foster's Celebration of Discipline *surprised many readers by making a plea for a disciplined approach to Christian discipleship, using many of the practices more associated in their minds with Roman Catholicism, yet coming from an American background in the Society of Friends. He has followed up the section on the discipline of prayer with another book called simply* Prayer.

D ear God, I am so grateful for your invitation to enter your heart of love. As best I can I come in. Thank you for receiving me. Amen.[18]

Billy Graham (1918–)

William Franklin Graham is a minister of the Southern Baptist Church who by his crusades in every continent has won millions of souls for Christ. Often criticised for over-emotionalism, his preaching is in fact a model of low-key, simple, biblical presentation of the love of God for the individual. It is a very moving thing to realize that God loves you, but all Billy Graham asks people to do when they 'get up out of your seats and come forward' is to make a simple prayer, accepting God's love and committing themselves to him:

L ord Jesus, I know I am a sinner. I believe you died for my sins. Right now, I turn from my sins and open the door of my heart and life. I receive you as my personal Lord and Saviour. Thank you for saving me now. Amen.[19]

David Head (1922–)

Just as Jesus used humour in the parables to show us how ridiculous we are, so a handful of books are able to portray the sort of prayers that we would all like to pray if we dared. He Sent Leanness: a book of prayers for the natural man, *is one such.*[20]

The Prayer of the Author

Grant, I beseech thee, that all who read this book may be conscious of the deep spiritual insight of the writer; that the sale of this book may result in a nice little nest-egg, even after income tax has been deducted; that copies of this book, nicely bound, may make an impressive sight in the study, in the bookshelf which is level with the eye; that amid all the congratulatory applause, the writer may remain conspicuously humble.

A General Confession

Benevolent and easy-going Father, we have occasionally been guilty of errors of judgement. We have lived under the deprivations of heredity and the disadvantages of environment. We have sometimes failed to act in accordance with common sense. We have done the best we could in the circumstances; And have been careful not to ignore the common standards of decency. And we are glad to think that we are fairly normal. Do thou, O Lord, deal lightly with our infrequent lapses. Be thy own sweet Self with those who admit they are not perfect; According to the unlimited tolerance which we have a right to expect from thee. And grant as an indulgent Parent that we may hereafter continue to live a harmless and happy life and keep our self-respect.

Prayers of pious intention

O Lord, so long as the weather is reasonably fine,
so long as I have no visitors,
so long as nobody asks me to do any work,
so long as I can sit in the back pew but one on the left,
so long as it isn't a local preacher planned,
so long as they don't choose hymns I don't know,
so long as my Joe is asked to recite at the Anniversary,
so long as I can get home in time for the play,

I will honour Thee with my presence at Church
whenever I feel like it.

Andrew Linzey (1952–)

*Professor Andrew Linzey is an Anglican priest who holds the world's first
post in theology and animal welfare at Mansfield College in Oxford.*

Heavenly Father, your Holy Spirit gives breath to all living things;
renew us by this same Spirit, that we may learn to respect what you
have given and care for what you have made, through Jesus Christ your
Son, our Lord. Amen.[21]

Almighty God, you have given us temporary Lordship of your
beautiful creation.
But we have misused our power,
turned away from responsibility,
and marred your image in us.
Forgive us, true Lord,
especially for our callousness and cruelty to animals.
Help us to follow the way of your Son, Jesus Christ,
who expressed power in humility
and lordship in loving service.
Enable us, by your Spirit, to walk in newness of life,
healing injury, avoiding wrong
and making peace with all your creatures.[22]

Michael John Saward (1932–)

*Michael Saward, Canon of St Paul's Cathedral, London, has written books
about evangelism, as well as many hymns, including 'Christ triumphant,
ever reigning'.*

Lord of the Church, enable your people to be the Church: a redeemed
people, a holy people, a united people, a missionary people: and in
all things a people gladly submissive to the truth as it is found in Jesus,
in whose name we pray. Amen.[23]

Massey Hamilton Shepherd, Jr (1913–90)

Massey Shepherd was an Episcopal priest and a professor at Berkeley, California.

Almighty God, we thank you that in your great love you have fed us with the spiritual food and drink of the Body and Blood of your Son Jesus Christ, and have given us a foretaste of your heavenly banquet. Grant that this Sacrament may be to us a comfort in affliction, and a pledge of our inheritance in that kingdom where there is no death, neither sorrow nor crying, but the fulness of joy with all your saints; through Jesus Christ our Saviour. Amen.[24]

Remember this night, O Lord, in your goodness: those who stand guard for us while we rest; those who work to serve our needs on the morrow; those who comfort the suffering and the bereaved; those who minister to and wait upon the dying. Grant that as we know their watching, so we may share their loving care; through Jesus Christ our Lord. Amen.[25]

David Silk (1936–)

David Silk was Archdeacon of Leicester and a leading Anglo-Catholic member of the Church of England Liturgical Commission, before being appointed Bishop of Ballarat in Australia.

Almighty God, by your gift the tree of life was set at the heart of the earthly paradise, and the bread of life was set at the heart of your Church. Let this divine nourishment bring us, not to judgement, but to life eternal; through Jesus Christ our Lord. Amen.[26]

Almighty God, you have shed upon us the new light of your incarnate Word, giving us gladness in our sorrow, your presence in our isolation. Fill our lives with your light until they overflow with gladness and praise; through Christ our Lord. Amen.[27]

Grant to us, Lord God, to trust you not for ourselves alone, but for those also whom we love and who are hidden from us by the shadow of death; that, as we believe your power to have raised our Lord Jesus Christ from the dead, so we may trust your love to give eternal life to all who believe in him; through Jesus Christ our Lord. Amen.[28]

O God, who in the work of creation commanded the light to shine out of darkness; we pray that the light of the glorious gospel of Christ may shine into the hearts of all your people, dispelling the darkness of ignorance and unbelief, and revealing to them the knowledge of your glory in the face of Jesus Christ our Lord. Amen.[29]

O Lord, you have given us your word for a light to shine upon our path. Grant us so to meditate on that word, and to follow its teaching, that we may find in it the light that shines more and more until the perfect day; through Jesus Christ our Lord. Amen.[30]

My God, for love of you
I desire to hate and forsake all sins
by which I have ever displeased you;
and I resolve, by the help of your grace,
to commit them no more;
and to avoid all opportunities of sin.
Help me to do this,
through Jesus Christ our Lord. Amen.[31]

The Society of Ordained Scientists

The days when science and religion were regarded as enemies are hopefully long past: Christians listen to scientists to discover how the world comes to be as it is, and scientists turn to Scripture to answer the question 'Why?' Scientific method and coming to faith are similar processes, requiring the sifting of evidence, an inspired hypothesis, and testing this by experiment. Many Christian believers are involved in scientific work, and some have written prayers about it.

Almighty God, Creator and Redeemer of all that is, source and foundation of time and space, matter and energy, life and consciousness: Grant us and all who study the mysteries of your creation, grace to be true witnesses to your glory and faithful stewards of your gifts; through Jesus Christ our Lord. Amen.[32]

Aleksandr Solzhenitzyn (1918–)

He served with distinction in the Red Army during the Second World War, but was imprisoned from 1945 to 1953 for criticising Stalin. The Gulag Archipelago, *exposing conditions in the prison camps, was published in the West between 1973 and 1975, by which time he had been awarded the Nobel Prize for Literature.*

How easy, Lord, it is for me to live with you.
How easy it is for me to believe in you.
When my understanding is perplexed by doubts
    or on the point of giving up,
when the most intelligent men see no further
    than the coming evening,
and know not what they shall do tomorrow,
you send me a clear assurance that you are there
and that you will ensure that not all the roads of goodness
    are barred.
From the heights of earthly fame I look back in wonder
at the road that led through hopelessness to this place
whence I can send mankind a reflection of your radiance.
And whatever I in this life may yet reflect,
that you will give me;
And whatever I shall not attain,
that, plainly, you have purposed for others.[33]

John Robert Walmsley Stott (1921–)

John Stott was Rector of All Souls, Langham Place in London from 1950–75. Since then he has continued to be attached to the church as Rector Emeritus. He was also Founder-Director of the London Institute of Contemporary Christianity, and has been deeply involved in the Lausanne movement. He has been responsible, with others, for broadening the evangelical understanding of mission as including both evangelism and social action.

We ask you, Lord Jesus, as your apostles did, to teach us to pray. For our spirit is willing, even though our flesh is weak. Yet we thank you for permitting us to call your Father our Father. Help us to come to him with the simplicity of a child, to be concerned for his glory and to share with him our needs, for your name's sake.[34]

Heavenly Father, you have blessed our weekday work both by your own work of creation and by your Son's labour at a carpenter's bench: give the nation's leaders the wisdom to solve the problem of unemployment. Enable those of us with work to do, not only to find fulfilment in it ourselves, but also to enjoy the privilege of cooperating with you in the service of the community, through Jesus Christ our Lord.[35]

O Lord Jesus Christ, who at the carpenter's bench didst manifest the dignity of honest labour, and dost give to each of us our tasks to perform, help us to do our weekday work with readiness of mind and singleness of heart, not with eye-service as men-pleasers, but as thy servants, labouring heartily as unto thee and not unto men, so that whatever we do, great or small, may be to the glory of thy holy name.[36]

R. S. Thomas (1913–)

Born in Cardiff, educated at Bangor and Llandaff, and ordained in the Anglican Church in Wales, R. S. Thomas is one of the greatest poets writing in English today.

The Prayer

Moments of great calm
Kneeling before an altar
Of wood in a stone church
In summer, waiting for God
To speak; the air a staircase
For silence; the sun's light
Ringing me, as though I acted
A great role. And the audience
Still; all that close throng

Of spirits waiting, as I,
For the message.
Prompt me, God
But not yet. When I speak
Though it be you who speak
Through me, something is lost.
The meaning is in the waiting.[37]

From 'Kneeling'

D eliver us from the long drought of the mind;
Let leaves from the deciduous cross fall on us
Washing us clean,
Turning our autumn to gold
by the affluence of their fountain.[38]

The United Society for the Propagation of the Gospel

When the Society for the Propagation of the Gospel in Foreign Parts was founded by Thomas Bray, vicar of Sheldon, in 1701, ministry to British settlers overseas often took priority over the second aim of evangelizing the heathen. The SPCK, which he founded in 1698, was the Society for Promoting Christian Knowledge, to provide Christian books for settlers who were without them. Through a long history of heroic service the SPG became a pioneering missionary organization, always by providing personnel and finance for the local bishop to use in support of the local church. The Universities Mission to Central Africa was founded as a result of David Livingstone's call in the Cambridge Senate House. Its first head, Bishop C. F. Mackenzie, trekked up the Zambezi river with crozier in one hand and rifle in the other, to defend himself against the Arab slave traders who dominated the area. When UMCA and SPG amalgamated they became the USPG. These are a few examples of the imaginative and challenging prayer literature which they produce.

I am weary of the dark voices crying doom;
I am weary of the fearful voices crying only for their nation;
I am weary of the disinherited voices crying in hopelessness;
let my voice sing the laughter of God;
let my voice sing good news to the poor;
let my voice sing restitution of the oppressed;

let my voice sing healing of the violated;
let my voice sing the return of the banned;
let my voice be the laughter of God. Amen.[39]

God, you are doing a new thing in our world, leading us along new paths of mutual discovery, joint learning, exchange and encounter, calling us to cross barriers of prejudice, fear, anxiety. Lead us on into your new world as the new people of God, with Jesus Christ, our partner and pioneer. Amen.[40]

We confess that in our lives we do not always choose
      the way of peace.
We spread gossip which fans the flames of hatred.
We are ready to make any sacrifice when the world demands,
but few when God invites.
We worship the false God of security.
We hold out one hand in friendship,
but keep a weapon in the other behind our back.
We have divided your body of people
into those we trust and those we do not.
Huge problems challenge us in the world,
but our greed, fear and selfishness
      prevent us from uniting to solve them.
Lord, we need your help and forgiveness, your reconciling power.[41]

Michael Walker (1932–89)

Michael Walker was a Baptist minister who contributed a number of prayers to the hymn-book of his denomination.

Thanksgiving after a death

Father, we thank you for the life of N:
      for the life we lived together,
for the love we shared,
for the truths that shaped our lives,
for the memories that remain.
Father, we thank you for Christ our Lord:

for the death he died,
for the grave in which he was laid,
for the victory he won,
for his resurrection on the third day.
Father, we thank you for what you have promised:
for the eternal life you give us,
for the heaven you have opened to N,
for the day we shall see each other,
for holding us together until then.
In Jesus' name.
Amen.

Baptist Praise and Worship 520

S. J. Wallace (1929–)

Another prayer, based on the gifts of the Magi to the infant Jesus, in Baptist Praise and Worship.

King Jesus, we bring you our gold:
talents your Father gave us,
skills we have acquired,
a little money, a little power,
a little success perhaps,
and plenty of ambition.
These we offer to you,
so that you may make them really worth something
in your kingdom.
Jesus, great High Priest, we bring you our frankincense:
deep needs and longings,
which are sometimes easier to admit in church:
the need for forgiveness and peace,
the need for friendship and love,
the wish to do good
and the knowledge that we must have help
if we are to do it.
Lord, help us,
pray for us.
Jesus, crucified Saviour, we bring you our myrrh:
shadows on our path,

weakness, illness, limitations,
grief for ourselves and others,
our knowledge of parting and pain.
These we offer to you
so that what we bear
may be touched with the holiness
of what you bore for us;
and so that, by your grace,
we may have part
in the world's redemption.

Baptist Praise and Worship 194[42]

Harry Abbott Williams (1919–)

Dean of Trinity College, Cambridge, where he gained a reputation for political radicalism, then a monk at the Community of the Resurrection at Mirfield in Yorkshire, Harry Williams' writings, such as The True Wilderness *and* Some Day I'll Find You, *have always shown a painful honesty before God.*

Hello, it is me, your old friend and your old enemy, your loving friend who often neglects you, your complicated friend, your utterly perplexed and decidedly resentful friend, partly loving, partly hating, partly not caring. It is me.[43]

O God, I am hellishly angry; I think so-and-so is a swine; I am tortured by worry about this or that; I am pretty certain that I have missed my chances in life; this or that has left me feeling terribly depressed. But nonetheless here I am like this, feeling both bloody and bloody-minded, and I am going to stay here for ten minutes. You are most unlikely to give me anything. I know that. But I am going to stay for the ten minutes nonetheless.[44]

Anonymous Prayers

Infinite Lord and eternal God,
Rouse your Church in this land,
Restore your people's sense of mission,
And revive your work in holiness and strength.
By your Spirit, teach us to give our energy,
Our time, our money, our service and our prayer,
That your kingdom may be advanced
Here and in all the world;
In the name of Jesus Christ our Lord.

The Church in Wales

Lord of light – shine on us;
Lord of peace – dwell in us;
Lord of might – succour us;
Lord of love – enfold us;
Lord of wisdom – enlighten us.
Then, Lord, let us go out as your witnesses,
in obedience to your command;
to share the good news of your mighty love for us
in the gift of your Son, our Saviour, Jesus Christ.

The Church in Wales

Lord Jesus Christ, who prayed that all your children might be one in you: we pray for the restoration of visible unity to your Church. Forgive the pride and the lack of love which have driven us apart. Take away our narrow-mindedness, our bitterness, our prejudice. May we never consider as normal the disunity which is a scandal to the world and an offence to your love. Teach us to recognise the gifts of your grace in all those who call upon you through Jesus Christ our Lord. Amen.

The French Reformed Church Liturgy

How fine a thing it is when brothers
can dwell in love and unity!
Their mutual love and love for others,
O Holy Spirit, comes from thee,
and claiming one Church as their mother,
sweet songs they sing in harmony.

'In all the world's remotest places
thy Church is one in thee,' they say,
and by thy manifold sweet graces
their souls are gladdened day by day;
the light of joy shines on the faces
of the redeemed whene'er they pray.

May all our souls with joy be ringing,
our sacrifice of praise outpoured,
our hymns from happy hearts now springing
rise up to heaven with one accord,
and, with triumphant spirits singing,
proclaim the glory of the Lord!

From The French Reformed Hymnal[85]

When my soul sheds its tears,
When my heart languishes in longing,
When my whole being shivers in fatigue,
Come, O Jesus, I beg you to come.

A prayer written by Lithuanian prisoners

Gather us or scatter us, O Lord, according to your will. Build us into
one church: a church with open doors and large windows, a church
which takes the world seriously, ready to work and to suffer, and even to
bleed for it. Amen.

Hungarian, source unknown

O Lord, our Lord, you have decided that all people, whatever their
colour or race, are equal before you: break down the hatred between
us, especially hatred due to national differences. We ask you to help those
in whose hands are the various governments of the world. Reconcile them

to one another, so that each may respect the rights of the other. We ask
all this in the name of our Saviour, Jesus Christ.

The Student Christian Movement in Zambia

W e offer our thanks to you
for sending your only Son to die for us all
In a world divided by colour bars,
how sweet a thing it is to know
that in you we all belong to one family.
There are times when we
unprivileged people,
weep tears that are not loud but deep,
when we think of the suffering we experience.
We come to you, our only hope and refuge.
Help us, O God, to refuse to be embittered
against those who handle us with harshness.
We are grateful to you
for the gift of laughter at all times.
Save us from hatred of those who oppress us.
May we follow the spirit of thy Son Jesus Christ.

By a Bantu pastor

F ather, my Father, enlarge my heart that it may be big enough to receive
the greatness of your love. Stretch my heart that it may take into it
all those who with me around the world believe in Jesus Christ. Stretch it
that it may take into it all those who do not know him, but who are my
responsibility because I know him. And stretch it that it may take in all
those who are not lovely in my eyes, and whose hands I do not want to
touch; through Jesus Christ my Saviour. Amen.

From Morning, Noon and Night[46]

P ray not for Arab or Jew, for Palestinian or Israeli, but pray rather for
yourselves, that you may not divide them in your prayers but keep
them both together in your hearts.

By a Palestinian Christian

A lmighty God, we thank you for having renewed your Church, at various
times and in various ways, by rekindling the fire of love for you
through the work of your Holy Spirit. Rekindle your love in our hearts

and renew us to fulfil the Great Commission which your Son committed to us; so that, individually and collectively, as members of your Church we may help many to know Jesus Christ as their Lord and Saviour. Empower us by your Spirit to share, with our neighbours and friends, our human stories in the context of your divine story; through Jesus Christ our Lord.

Anglican Church of West Malaysia

Gracious God, let your will for us all be known. Let all be partners in shaping the future with a faith that quarrels with the present for the sake of what yet might be. Amen.

Taiwan, source unknown

Let not our souls be busy inns that have no room for you and yours, but quiet homes of prayer and praise where you may find fit company; where the needful cares of life are wisely ordered and put away; and wide sweet spaces kept for you, where holy thoughts pass up and down, and fervent longings watch and wait your coming. Amen.

Lucknow Diocese[47]

O Jesus
Be the canoe that holds me in the sea of life.
Be the steer that keeps me straight.
Be the outrigger that supports me in times of great temptation.
Let your spirit be my sail that carries me through each day.
Keep my body strong,
so that I can paddle steadfastly on,
in the long voyage of life.

A New Hebridean prayer

Lord, today you made us known to friends we did not know,
And you have given us seats in homes which are not our own.
You have brought the distant near,
And made a brother of a stranger,
Forgive us Lord . . .
We did not introduce you.

Prayer from Polynesia

Lord, if this day you have to correct us, put us right not out of anger, but with a mother and father's love. So may we, your children, be kept free from falseness and foolishness. Amen.

Mexican, source unknown

Look graciously upon us, O Holy Spirit, and give us for our hallowing thoughts which pass into prayer, prayers which pass into love, and love which passes into life with thee for ever.

Grant, O God, that our Church may be as a city set upon a hill, a witness to your love, a powerhouse of prayer, and a joy and help to all who worship within its walls. Here may the tempted find strength and the sorrowful comfort. Here may the aged find consolation and the young be inspired. Shew your mercy upon us, and grant us your salvation through Christ our Lord. Amen.

We thank you, O Lord, for all who have chosen poverty or solitude for your sake, for people of prayer, for saints in common life who have borne suffering for noble ends, and for those who have endured pain with patience and purity of life, in the strength of him who for the joy that was set before him endured the cross, even Jesus Christ our Lord. Amen.

May the seed of your kingdom, O God, in its greatness and marvel, grow in our hearts, in our homes, and in all the councils of the world; through Jesus Christ our Lord. Amen.

Lord, what we know not, teach us; what we have not, give us; and what we are not, make us; through Jesus Christ our Lord. Amen.

Eyes of Jesus look upon them. Lips of Jesus speak to them. Hands of Jesus bless them. Arms of Jesus enfold them. Feet of Jesus come to them. Heart of Jesus pour your love upon them. Amen.

We thank you, O God, for the saints of all ages; for those who in times of darkness kept the lamp of faith burning; for the great souls who saw visions of larger truth and dared to declare it; for the multitude of quiet and gracious souls whose presence has purified and sanctified the world; and for those known and loved by us, who have passed from this earthly fellowship into the fuller light of life with you, where you live and reign, Father, Son and Holy Spirit, for ever and ever. Amen.

May the Lord forgive what you have been, sanctify what you are, and direct what you will be; and the blessing of God almighty, the Father, the Son and the Holy Spirit, be upon you and those whom you love, now and always. Amen.

Lord, in your pierced hands we lay our heart; Lord, at your pierced feet we choose our part; Lord, in your wounded side let us abide. Amen.

O God, you turn the hearts of the parents to the children, and have granted to youth to see visions and to old age to dream dreams: draw together the old and the young, that in fellowship with you, they may understand and help one another, and in your service find their perfect freedom; through Jesus Christ our Lord. Amen.

Source unknown, quoted by Frederick Macnutt

O God, Father, moment by moment you hold us in being; on you we depend. O God, eternal Son, friend and brother beside us, in you we trust. O God, Holy Spirit, life and love within us, from you we live. O God beyond us, God beside us, God within us; Father, Son and Holy Spirit, three persons in one God, you are ever to be worshipped and adored. Amen.

Heavenly Father, pour down your Spirit upon your whole Church. Grant us a new vision of your glory, a new experience of your power, a new faithfulness to your word, a new consecration to your service, that through our renewed witness your holy name may be glorified and your kingdom advanced, through Jesus Christ our Lord. Amen.

Come, Holy Spirit of truth, and teach us all truth. O may there come the sound of a rushing mighty wind from heaven, and strike us and all the world, and stir us up from our indifference and despair. Come, O fire and flame of divine love, and burn away our sins. Speak to us, that we may speak to others. Cleanse us, that we may cleanse others. Enlighten us, that we may enlighten others, and set us on fire with love for you and for all people; through Jesus Christ our Lord. Amen.

May the blessing of God almighty, the Father, the Son and the Holy Spirit, rest upon you and upon all your work and worship done in his name. May he give you light to guide you, courage to support you, and love to unite you, now and evermore. Amen.[48]

Prayers for a New Millennium

Lord Jesus Christ,
Lord of time and eternity,
prepare our minds to celebrate with faith
the Jubilee of the year 2000.
Fill our hearts with joy and wonder
as we recall the precious moment
when you were conceived in the womb of the Virgin Mary,
that moment when you became our brother.
Praise and glory to you, O Christ,
today and forever.

Lord Jesus, bring us with you and your Mother
on your journey to Bethlehem
the place where you were born.
May we travel with you,
firm in the faith,
loyal to the truth,
obedient to the will of our Father
along the one true path that leads to life.
Praise and glory to you, O Christ,
today and forever.

Jesus, at your birth the angels sang:
Glory to God in the highest
and peace to his people on earth.
Two thousand years later
we need to hear that song again.
We need to pray for peace
in our hearts,
in our families,
in our country,
in our sad and wonderful world

Praise and glory to you, O Christ,
today and forever.

With the shepherds from Bethlehem
and the wise men from the east
we kneel before your manger, Lord Jesus.
We commit ourselves once again
to the great missionary work of bringing you
to those who have never heard your name.
And we reach out the hand of fellowship
to those who are worshipping you
in different churches
and searching for Christian unity.
Praise and glory to you, O Christ,
today and forever.

Lord, your Mother Mary kept all these things
and treasured them in her heart.
Open our hearts to the richness of our faith.
Open our minds to its meaning.
We adore you and bless you as our Lord and Saviour,
Son of God and son of women,
the way, the truth and the life,
the only mediator between us and God.
Praise and glory to you, O Christ,
today and forever.

Vatican Millennium Committee[49]

God of all ages, Lord of all time,
you are the Alpha and the Omega,
the origin and goal of everything that lives,
yet you are ever close to those who call on you in faith.

We look with expectant joy
to the Jubilee of your Son's coming among us,
two thousand years ago.
We thank you for the years of favour
with which you have blessed your people.

Teach us to share justly the good things
which come from your loving hand;

to bring peace and reconciliation
where strife and disorder reign;
to speak out as advocates
for those who have no voice;
and to rejoice in a bond of prayer and praise
with our sisters and brothers throughout the world.

When Christ comes again in glory
may he find us alive and active in faith,
and so call us to that Kingdom
where, with you and the Holy Spirit,
he is God, to be praised, worshipped and glorified,
both now and for ages to come.
Amen.

Catholic Fund for Overseas Development (CAFOD)

Lord God, we thank you for calling us into the company of those who trust in Christ Jesus and seek to follow him. Through your Holy Spirit, lead us to journey deeper into the mystery of your love, to be stronger in the bond of unity, and to be bolder in the ways of witness to the world. Give us the courage to invite many others to join us in pilgrimage, for the glory of your holy name. Amen.

The Diocese of Rochester

The Millennium Resolution

Let there be
respect for the earth
peace for its people
love in our lives
delight in the good
forgiveness for past wrongs
and from now on a new start

Churches Together in England[50]

Notes and Acknowledgements

The Background

1. Scripture quotations are from the New Revised Standard Version of the Bible, copyright 1989 by the Division of Christian Education of the National Council of the Churches of Christ in the USA. Used by permission. All rights reserved.

The First Four Christian Centuries

1. Translated by Walter Mitchell in *Early Christian Prayers*, edited by A. Hamman OFM (Longman Green, London, and Henry Regnery, Chicago, 1961). Out of copyright.
2. Translation from *The Divine Office*, © 1974 the hierarchies of Australia, England and Wales, and Ireland. Used by permission of A. P. Watt Ltd, London.
3. Translated by Walter Mitchell, op. cit.
4. The English Translation of excerpts from *The Eucharistic Prayer of Hippolytus*, © 1983, International Commission on English in the Liturgy (ICEL). All rights reserved.
5. Translated by Walter Mitchell, op. cit.
6. Ibid.
7. Translation © 1994 by Michael Counsell.
8. Translated by Walter Mitchell, op. cit.
9. Ibid.
10. *On Prayer*, translated in *The Divine Office*, © 1974 the hierarchies of Australia, England and Wales, and Ireland. Used by permission of A. P. Watt Ltd, London.
11. Translated by Walter Mitchell, op. cit.
12. Ibid.
13. Ibid.
14. Ibid.
15. Translated by Benedicta Ward SLG in *The Sayings of the Desert Fathers* (1975). Reproduced by permission of Cassell/Mowbrays.

16. Ibid.

17. Translated in *Western Asceticism, Library of Christian Classics XII*, edited by Owen Chadwick (SCM Press, London, 1958 and Westminster John Knox Press, KY 40202–1396, USA). Used by permission.

18. Translation taken from *Patrologia Latina* in *The Desert of the Heart*, by Benedicta Ward SLG, published and © 1988 Darton, Longman & Todd, London, and as *Daily Readings with the Desert Fathers* by Templegate Publishers (www.templegate.com), Springfield, Illinois 62710, USA. Used by permission of the publishers.

19. Translated by Benedicta Ward SLG in *The Sayings of the Desert Fathers*, op. cit.

20. Translated in *The Desert of the Heart*, © 1988 Benedicta Ward SLG, op. cit.

21. Translation by Florestine Audette RJM of *Fathers of the Desert* by Marcel Droit, © 1992 St Pauls (formerly St Paul Publications), UK. Original title: *Les Pères du Désert*, © 1991 Editions Médiaspaul, Paris.

22. Ibid.

23. Translated in *Saint Athanasius on the Incarnation* (1944, Centenary Press, London, and the Macmillan Company, USA), by a Religious of CSMV (Sister Penelope). © Community of St Mary the Virgin and used with permission.

24. Adapted from *Bishop Serapion's Prayerbook*, edited by Bishop Wordsworth (SPCK, 2nd edn, 1910).

25. Translated by Walter Mitchell, op. cit.

26. Approximately 157 words from *The History of the Church by Eusebius*, translated by G. A. Williamson, all rights reserved (Penguin Books, 1965, revised edition, 1989). © G. A. Williamson, 1965. Reproduced by permission of Penguin Books Ltd.

27. Translation © 1996 Robert Van de Weyer, all rights reserved by Arthur James Ltd.

The Early Western Church

1. Translated by Walter Mitchell in *Early Christian Prayers*, edited by A. Hamman OFM (Longman Green, London, and Henry Regnery, Chicago, 1961).

2. Translated by the compilers of the 1904 edition of *Hymns Ancient and Modern*. Out of copyright.

3. Translated by J. Ellerton and F. J. A. Hort.

4. Translation in *The Book of Common Prayer* (1549), based on the pre-Reformation Primers.

5. Translation © 1998 by Michael Counsell.

The Eastern Church

1. Translation from *The SPCK Book of Christian Prayer*, © SPCK 1995. By permission of SPCK, London, and The Continuum Publishing Group, USA.

2. Translated in *The Fount Book of Prayer*, © 1993 Robert van de Weyer, (HarperCollins*Religious*, London). Used by permission of HarperCollins*Publishers*, London.

3. Translated by Walter Mitchell in *Early Christian Prayers*, edited by A. Hamman OFM (Longman Green, London, and Henry Regnery, Chicago, 1961).

4. Ibid.

5. Ibid.

6. Ibid.

7. Translation in *The Book of a Thousand Prayers*, © 1996 Angela Ashwin (HarperCollins*Religious*, London). Used by permission of HarperCollins*Publishers*, London.

8. Translation from *The Christian Testament since the Bible*, Part III, © 1985 Waterstone & Co. Ltd. First published in the USA as *The Living Testament* (Harper & Row, 1985). By permission of Waterstone for the UK and Commonwealth and HarperCollins*Publishers*, New York, for the USA, Canada and the Philippines.

9. Translated in *The Philokalia*, Vol. I, © 1981 The Eling Trust (Faber & Faber, London).

10. From *The Philokalia*, translated by R. M. French in *The Way of a Pilgrim*, © Winchester Diocesan Board of Finance. First published 1930; published by SPCK, 1942.

11. From *Hymns of Divine Love by St Symeon the New Theologian*, translated by George A. Maloney SJ, re-issued in a new edition in 1999 by Dimension Books Inc., P. O. Box 811, Denville, NJ 07834, USA).

12. Translated by Brother George Every SSM in the third edition (1969) of *Mysticism* by F. C. Happold (Penguin Books, Harmondsworth, 1962). Permission sought.

13. Translated by G. Moultrie (1929–1835).

14. Translated by C. W. Humphreys for *The English Hymnal*.

15. Translated in *The Book of Common Prayer* (1549).

16. Ibid., Prayer of the Third Antiphon.

17. From 'Confession and Thanksgiving to Christ, Son of God, the Saviour of the World', translated by Helen Iswolsky, in *A Treasury of Russian Spirituality*, edited by G. P. Fedotov (Sheed & Ward, London, 1950).

18. Ibid.

19. Translated by E. Kadloubovsky and E. M. Palmer in *The Art of Prayer*, compiled by Igumen Chariton of Valamo (Faber & Faber Ltd, 1965).

20. Translated by R. M. French in *The Way of a Pilgrim*, op. cit.

21. Approximately 228 words from *The Brothers Karamazov* by Fyodr Dostoevsky, translated by David Magarschack, (Penguin Classics, 1958) © 1958 David Magarschack. Reproduced by permission of Penguin Books Ltd.

22. From *My Life in Christ*, translated by Erast Evenievich Gulyaev. (Last known copyright: Cassell & Co., London, 1897.)

23. Ibid.
24. Translation © 1995 by Michael Counsell in *The Secret Name*. Suggested tune: 'Angels from the realms of glory'.
25. Translated by F. C. Burkitt in *The English Hymnal*, © SPCK, London.
26. Translated by Walter Mitchell, op. cit.
27. Deacon's prayer during Communion of the people.
28. Translated by Walter Mitchell, op. cit.
29. Ibid.
30. From Thursday Compline in *The Maronite Weekday Office*, published in Beirut, 1876.
31. Ibid.

Celtic Christianity

1. Now at St Paul, Carinthia. Translated by Robin Flower in *Records of Christianity*, Vol. II, edited by David Ayerst and A. S. T. Fisher, © 1977 Basil Blackwell. The verse is anonymous and in Gaelic, *bán* is the word for 'white'.
2. Early Middle Welsh. The 'three springs' in line 4 refer to the sun, moon and sea. Translation © 1995 by Oliver Davies in *Celtic Christian Spirituality* (SPCK, London, 1995). By permission of SPCK, London and The Continuum Publishing Group, USA.
3. Translated in *Celtic Fire*, © 1990 Robert Van de Weyer (Darton, Longman & Todd, London, and Doubleday, New York, USA – a division of Random House Inc.) Used by permission of the publishers.
4. Ibid.
5. Ibid. Also known as 'Be thou my vision'.
6. Translation © 1998 by Michael Counsell.
7. Translated by Robert Van de Weyer in *Celtic Fire*, op. cit.
8. Translation © 1995 by Oliver Davies in *Celtic Christian Spirituality*, op. cit.
9. A prayer to St Patrick, recited by Patrick O'Donnell.
10. Copied down in County Mayo.
11. These extracts are from the 1983 Scottish Academic Press reprint, by permission of the publishers.
12. Translated in *Western Liturgies*, edited by Ronald Cameron West (SPCK, London, 1938). Permission sought.
13. Ibid.
14. Ibid.

Anglo-Saxon Christianity

1. Bede placed this prayer at the end of his *History of the English Church and People*.
2. Translation © 1999 by Michael Counsell, based on *The Caedmon Poems* by Charles W. Kennedy.

3. Translated by Dom A. Kuypers in *The Prayerbook of Aedelwald the Bishop, commonly called the Book of Cerne* (Cambridge, 1902). Out of copyright.

The Medieval West

1. Translation from *The Divine Office*, © 1974 the hierarchies of Australia, England and Wales, and Ireland. Used by permission of A. P. Watt Ltd, London.
2. The first two verses were translated by Percy Dearmer, the next two by J. M. Neale. Reprinted from *The English Hymnal* by permission of Oxford University Press.
3. Translated in *The Book of Common Prayer* (1549), Trinity 12.
4. Translated in *The Book of Common Prayer* (1662), Morning and Evening Prayer.
5. Translated in *The Book of Common Prayer* (1549), Easter 3.
6. Ibid., Good Friday.
7. Ibid., The Communion.
8. Translated in *The Book of Common Prayer* of the Episcopal Church of the USA (1979).
9. Translated in *The Book of Common Prayer* (1549), Trinity 21.
10. Ibid., Trinity 15.
11. Ibid., Trinity 10. Set to music by Thomas Weelkes (1576?–1623) among others.
12. Ibid., Evening Prayer.
13. Ibid., Trinity 7.
14. Ibid., altered in 1662, Trinity 18.
15. Ibid., Trinity 20.
16. Ibid., modified in 1662, Easter 4.
17. Ibid., altered in 1662, Trinity 19.
18. Ibid., Evening Prayer.
19. Adapted from the translation by William Bright in *Ancient Collects* (1861).
20. A Gelasian antiphon on the Magnificat. The Collect of the Sunday after Ascension on page 196 is based on this anthem.
21. Translated in *The Book of Common Prayer* (1549), Trinity 1.
22. Translated in *The Book of Common Prayer* (1662), Trinity 8.
23. Translated in *The Book of Common Prayer* (1549), altered in 1662, Trinity 11.
24. Translated in the American *Book of Common Prayer* (1789).
25. Translated in *The Book of Common Prayer* (1549), Trinity 6.
26. Translated in the American *Book of Common Prayer* (1789).
27. Translated in *The Book of Common Prayer* (1549), Easter 5.
28. Ibid., Advent 4.
29. Ibid., Trinity 16.
30. Translated in *The Book of Common Prayer* of the Episcopal Church of the USA (1979), from Ambrosian Friday Vespers.

31. Translated in *The Book of Common Prayer* (1549), Epiphany 3.
32. Ibid., Epiphany 2.
33. Ibid., Lent 2.
34. Translated in *The Book of Common Prayer* of the Episcopal Church of the USA (1979), Palm Sunday.
35. Translated in *The Book of Common Prayer* (1549), Good Friday.
36. Ibid., Easter Day.
37. Ibid., Trinity Sunday
38. Ibid., modified in 1662, Whitsunday.
39. Translated in *The Book of Common Prayer* (1549), Ascension Day.
40. Ibid., Lent 4.
41. Ibid., Trinity 17.
42. Ibid., Trinity 22.
43. Ibid., Trinity 23.
44. Ibid., Trinity 4.
45. Ibid., Epiphany 4.
46. Translated in *The Litany* (1558) and placed among the Prayers and Thanksgivings in *The Book of Common Prayer* (1662).
47. Translated in *The Book of Common Prayer* (1549), Sexagesima.
48. Ibid., Epiphany 5.
49. Ibid., Trinity 3.
50. Ibid., Epiphany 1.
51. Ibid., Septuagesima.
52. Ibid., modified 1662, Trinity 2.
53. Translated in *The Book of Common Prayer* (1549), The Communion.
54. Ibid., Trinity 25. Because of this collect, the Sunday before Advent became known in England as 'stir up Sunday', when Christmas puddings should be made.
55. Ibid., Lent 3.
56. Ibid., Lent 5.
57. Ibid., Trinity 13.
58. Ibid., Ordering of Priests.
59. Translated in *The Prayer Book as proposed in 1928*, Christmas 2. By permission of the Central Board of Finance of the Church of England.
60. Translated in *The Book of Common Prayer* (1549), Trinity 14.
61. Ibid., Easter 3.
62. Translated in *The Alternative Service Book* (1980), Pentecost 16. By permission of the Central Board of Finance of the Church of England.
63. Compline, translated in *The Prayer Book as proposed in 1928*, op. cit.
64. Translated in *The Book of Common Prayer* (1549), Trinity 5.
65. Ibid., Trinity 9.
66. Ibid., Trinity 24.

67. Translated by J. Armitage Robinson (1858–1933).
68. From Alcuin's *Life and Letters*, edited by Stephen Allott (Sessions, York, 1974). Courtesy of Sessions of York.
69. Ibid.
70. Translated by Helen Waddell in *More Latin Lyrics*, edited by Dame Felicitas Corrigan OSB (Victor Gollancz, 1976). Used by permission.
71. In *Letters and Poems of Fulbert of Chartres*, translated by Frederick Behrends (Clarendon Press, Oxford, 1976). By permission of Oxford University Press.
72. Approximately 730 words from *The Prayers and Meditations of Saint Anselm*, translated by Benedicta Ward SLG, © 1973 Benedicta Ward, reprinted by permission of Penguin Books Ltd.
73. Ibid.
74. Translated by Helen Waddell in *Medieval Latin Lyrics* (Constable, 1929).
75. Translated by J. M. Neale (1818–66).

Monastic Spirituality

1. From *The Golden Epistle of William of Saint-Thierry*, translated by Walter Shewring (Sheed & Ward, London, 1930/1980).
2. 'On Contemplating God' 9, translated in *The Divine Office*, © 1974 the hierarchies of Australia, England and Wales, and Ireland. Used by permission of A. P. Watt Ltd, London.
3. From *Saint Bernard on the Christian Year*, translated by a Religious of CSMV (i.e. Sister Penelope). A. R. Mowbray & Co., London, 1954. © Community of St Mary the Virgin and used with permission.
4. Ibid.
5. Ibid.
6. From *For Crist luve: Prayers of St Aelred*, texts selected and introduced by Dom Anselm Hoste, translated by Sister Rose de Lima (St Pietersabdij, Steenbrugge; Martinus Nijhoff, Den Haag, 1965). Permission sought.
7. Ibid.
8. Ibid.
9. Ibid.
10. Ibid.
11. Ibid.
12. Translated in *The Fount Book of Prayer*, © 1993 Robert Van de Weyer (HarperCollins*Religious*).
13. Ibid.
14. Translated by D. S. Wrangham in *The Liturgical Poetry of Adam of Saint Victor* (Kegan, Paul & Co., London, 1881).
15. Ibid.
16. Ibid.
17. From *The Book of the Rewards of Life*, translated by Bruce W. Hozesci (Garland, New York and London, 1994).

18. Ibid.

19. Ibid.

20. From *The Revelations of Mechtild of Magdeburg, 1210–1297; or The Flowing Light of the Godhead*, translated by Lucy Menzies (Longman, Green & Co., London, 1953). Permission sought.

21. Ibid.

22. Ibid.

23. From *The Flowing Light of the Godhead* 1:4, translation © 1989 by Oliver Davies in *Beguine Spirituality: An Anthology*, edited by Fiona Bowie (SPCK, London, 1989). By permission of SPCK, London and the Crossroad Publishing Co. Inc., USA.

24. Ibid.

25. In *The Ladder of Monks by Guigo II*, translated by Edmund Colledge and James Walsh (Last known copyright: Mowbrays, London, 1978).

26. Ibid.

27. From 'The Life of Christ', translated in *The Divine Office*, © 1974 the hierarchies of Australia, England and Wales, and Ireland. Used by permission of A. P. Watt Ltd, London.

28. Translation © 1996 by Michael Counsell. May be sung to the tune of the Sans Day Carol.

29. Translated by John Henry Newman (1801–90).

30. Translated by Robert Bridges (1844–1930). Reprinted from *The Yattendon Hymnal*, by permission of Oxford University Press.

31. From *Hours of the Blessed Virgin Mary* (before the fourteenth century).

32. Pynson's *Horae* (1514).

33. Translated by Merton Jerome Hubert in *The Crusade of Richard Lionheart by Ambroise*, © 1941 Columbia University Press, New York.

34. Translated by William Caxton (c. 1422–c. 1491).

35. Anonymous, fifteenth century.

36. From *Montaillou* by Emmanuel Le Roy Ladurie, © 1978 Editions Gallimard. English translation by Barbara Bray, © 1978 Scolar Press, Aldershot, England. By permission of Ashgate Publishing, London.

37. From 'The Inquisition' in a MS in the University of Lyons.

The Mendicant Orders or Friars

1. Translated by Gerard Manley Hopkins (1844–89) from 'Adore te supplex, latens deitas', © Society of Jesus 1967, 1970. Reprinted from *The Poems of Gerard Manley Hopkins* (4th edition), edited by W. H. Gardner and N. H. MacKenzie, (1967), by permission of Oxford University Press.

2. Translated by Matthew Arnold (1822–88), modernized.

3. Anonymous hymn used for the Feast of the Holy Name. Translated by E. Caswall (1814–78).

4. From *The Tree of Life*, edited by Ewart Cousins in the *Classics of Western Christianity* series (SPCK, 1978). Permission sought.
5. Ibid.
6. Ibid.
7. Lauda LXXXVI from *Jacopone da Todi, Poet and Mystic, a spiritual biography*, by Evelyn Underhill, with a selection from the spiritual songs translated into English verse by Mrs Theodore Beck (J. M. Dent & Sons, London and Toronto, 1919; E. P. Dutton & Co., New York, 1919).
8. Ibid.
9. From *The Book of the Lover and the Beloved*, translated by E. Allison Peers (SPCKMDNM, London, 1923).
10. Translated by Donald Attwater in *An Anthology of Mysticism* (Burns & Oates, London, 1935, 1977). By permission of Burns & Oates.

Italian Spiritual Writers

1. Paraphrase © 1999 by Michael Counsell.
2. Translated by Serge Hughes in *Catherine of Genoa: Purgation and Purgatory, the Spiritual Dialogue* (Paulist Press, NJ 07430, USA). By permission of Serge Hughes.

Teutonic Mysticism

1. From *Wisdom's Watch upon the Hours*, by Blessed Henry Suso, Chapter 8 of Book 2, translated by Edmund Colledge OSA (The Catholic University of America Press, Washington, DC, 1994).
2. Translated by R. L. Pearsall (1795–1856). This type of carol is called a 'macaronic'. The original words in German and Latin are said by a fourteenth-century writer to have been sung by angels to Henry Suso, who was thus drawn into a dance with them.

English Christianity before the Reformation

1. By Leofric (d. 1072), last Bishop of Crediton, in the Sarum Missal, translated in *The Book of Common Prayer* (1549).
2. Translated by J. H. Newman in *The Dream of Gerontius*.
3. Office of the Dead in the Sarum rite.
4. Compline, adapted from the Sarum rite by Edward Willis in *The Cuddesdon Office Book*.
5. From the Sarum Manual.
6. Antiphons on Good Friday, from the Sarum Breviary, translated in *The Book of Common Prayer* (1549), Visitation of the Sick.
7. Modernized by Michael Counsell, © 1998.
8. Approximately 190 words (pp. 109–10) from *The Cloud of Unknowing and*

Other Works, translated by Clifton Wolters (Penguin Classics, 1968, revised edition, 1978). © Clifton Wolters 1961, 1978. Reproduced by permission of Penguin Books Ltd.

9. *Revelations of Divine Love*, Ch. 5, edited by Grace Warrack (Methuen, 1901).
10. Ibid., Ch. 41.
11. Ibid., Ch. 68.
12. Ibid., Ch. 86.
13. Translation © 1993 by Robert Van de Weyer in *The Fount Book of Prayer* op. cit.
14. Ibid.
15. Ibid.
16. Ibid.
17. Ibid.
18. Ibid.
19. Translated by Francesca Maria Steele (Burns & Oates, London, 1905). By permission of Burns & Oates.

The Humanists

1. Quoted from Erasmus in *Christian Prayers* (1578).
2. Composed for St Paul's School, probably at the request of Dean Colet. This version is slightly shortened.
3. Translated by Charles Simeon Coldwell in *Prayers of Erasmus* (London and Frome, 1872).
4. Quoted from Erasmus in *Christian Prayers* (1578).
5. From 'A Devout Prayer made by Sir Thomas More, Knight, after he was condemned to die and before he was put to death'.
6. After his final confession.
7. Quoted in *Christian Prayers* (1578).

The Protestant Reformation

1. Eric Milner-White in *After the Third Collect* (Mowbrays, 1959), based on a phrase of William Tyndale.
2. Part of Luther's hymn, '*Vom Himmel hoch*', translated by Catherine Winkworth.
3. Translated by George R. Potter in *Huldrych Zwingli* (Edward Arnold, London, 1978). By permission of Arnold, a member of the Hodder Headline Group.
4. From *The Theology of Anabaptism*, by Robert Friedmann, © 1973 by Herald Press, Scottdale, Pensylvania 15683, USA, p. 74.
5. From *The Complete Writings of Menno Simons*, translated from the Dutch by Leonard Verduin and edited by John Christian Wenger (Herald Press,

Scottdale). © 1956 by the Mennonite Publishing House, Scottdale, PA 15683, USA.

6. Ibid., 'Hymn of Discipleship' (c. 1540).
7. Translated by Peter Matheson in *The Collected Works of Thomas Münzer* (T. & T. Clark, Edinburgh, 1988).
8. Ibid.
9. Ibid.
10. Ibid.
11. Translated by John H. Leith (Harper & Row, San Francisco and London, c. 1984). By permission of HarperCollins*Publishers*, New York.
12. Ibid.
13. From Knox's *Book of Common Order*. See also below under 'Scots Protestants', p. 263.
14. From Hermann's *Consultation*, translated anonymously in 1547.
15. From *The Way to Christ*, translated by Peter C. Erb in *Pietists, Selected Writings* (SPCK, London, 1983). Permission sought.
16. Ibid.
17. Ibid.

The English Reformation

1. Based on the Sarum Collect in the Mass 'for tribulation of heart'. *The Book of Common Prayer* in all editions prior to 1662 is in the public domain.
2. An original contribution by Cranmer.

The Counter-Reformation

1. 'St Teresa's Bookmark', translation © 1997 by Michael Counsell.
2. Translated by Evelyn Underhill (1875–1941) in *Immanence, a book of verses* (J. M. Dent, London, 1913; E. P. Dutton, New York). Used by permission of the Orion Publishing Group, London.
3. Translation © 1998 by Michael Counsell.
4. Translation © 1998 by Michael Counsell.
5. Translated by Edgar Allison Peers in *The Complete Works of Saint Teresa of Jesus* (Sheed & Ward, London, 1946).
6. Ibid.
7. Ibid.
8. Ibid.
9. Translated from the Latin of St Thomas Aquinas by Queen Mary when aged eleven.
10. Translated by Edgar Allison Peers in *The Complete Works of Saint John of the Cross* (Burns, Oates & Washburn, London, 1934, revised 1953). By permission of Burns & Oates.

11. Ibid.
12. Translated by Roy Campbell in *Poems of St John of the Cross* (Harvill Press, 1951, and Fount Paperbacks, William Collins Sons & Co. Ltd, Glasgow, 1979). By permission of The Harvill Press, London.
13. Ibid.
14. Translation by Michael Day (Burns & Oates, London, 1959). By permission of Burns & Oates.
15. From Letter 2546, translated in *The Divine Office*, © 1974 the hierarchies of Australia, England and Wales, and Ireland. Used by permission of A. P. Watt Ltd, London.
16. From *Till God Will*, edited by Mary Emmanuel Orchard (Darton, Longman & Todd, London, 1985).
17. Ibid.
18. Ibid.

English Christianity after the Reformation

1. By kind permission of the Provost and Fellows of King's College, Cambridge.
2. From *The Literary Remains of Lady Jane Grey*, edited by Sir Nicholas Harris Nicolas G C M G, (London, 1825).
3. From A. Scoloker, *Daiphantus* (1604).
4. King Charles I copied out this prayer by Sir Philip Sidney for his own use.
5. The US *Book of Common Prayer* (1979), from Lancelot Andrewes.
6. From *After the Third Collect*, by Eric Milner-White (A. R. Mowbray & Co. Ltd., London, 1952), based on Lancelot Andrewes.
7. Ibid.
8. Ibid.
9. Ibid.
10. King Henry V after Agincourt. It is related that after the battle the English army, on their knees, sang the first verse of Psalm 115: 'Not unto us, O Lord, not unto us, but unto thy name give the praise.'
11. Soliloquy of Henry, Earl of Richmond (afterwards King Henry VII), before the Battle of Bosworth.
12. Donne is pronounced 'done' and this poem contains several puns on the poet's name.
13. In *The Story Books of Little Gidding* by Nicholas Ferrar.
14. From *Original Sources*, edited by Robert Van de Weyer and P. Saunders.
15. Ibid.
16. Ibid.
17. From *The Book of Common Prayer* (1662), Prayers and Thanksgivings, and Cosin's *A Collection of Private Devotions*. Extracts from *The Book of Common Prayer* (1662), the rights in which are vested in the Crown, are reproduced by permission of the Crown's Patentee, Cambridge University Press. Outside the UK they are in the public domain.

18. From Cosin's *A Collection of Private Devotions*.
19. Ibid.
20. Ibid.
21. From *The Book of Common Prayer* (1662), Epiphany 6.
22. Ibid., Advent 3.
23. Adapted from a letter which Cromwell wrote after the Battle of Dunbar, 1650.
24. From Carlyle's *Letters of Cromwell*.
25. Adapted in *Daily Prayer*, by Eric Milner-White and G. W. Briggs (Oxford University Press, 1941). By permission of Oxford University Press.

Pietism

1. From *Spiritual Songbook*, translated by Peter C. Erb in *Pietists, Selected Writings* (SPCK, London, 1983).
2. Translation © 1998 by Michael Counsell.
3. Translated by John Wesley (1703–91).

Scots Protestants

1. Psalm CXXXIII, from the Scottish Collects from *The Scottish Metrical Psalter* of 1595; Occasional Paper No. 5, Church of Scotland Committee on Public Worship and Aids to Devotion (Edinburgh, no date). By permission of the Church of Scotland Office for Worship and Doctrine.
2. Ibid., Psalm CXXXVII.
3. Ibid., Psalm CXLVI.
4. From the 'Letter to the Laird of Carleton', 10 May 1637, in *Letters of Samuel Rutherford*, edited by Andrew Bonar (Oliphants, 1863).
5. Adapted in *The Book of Common Prayer* (1662), Easter Eve.
6. Ibid., Prayers and Thanksgivings, in the Ember weeks.

The Seventeenth Century

1. From *A Walsingham Prayer Book* by Elizabeth Ruth Obbard (Canterbury Press Norwich, 1997). Used by permission of the Canterbury Press Norwich.
2. From *Mr Joseph Alleine's Directions for Covenanting with God* (London, printed for Nevil Simmons at the Prince's Arms in St Paul's Church-Yard, 1674).
3. Modernized. From *The Methodist Service Book,* © Trustees for Methodist Church Purposes. Used by permission of the Methodist Publishing House.
4. From *The Rule and Exercise of Holy Living*.
5. Ibid.
6. Jeremy Taylor's *Works*, Vol. IV, adapted by Eric Milner-White in *Memorials upon Several Occasions*.

7. From *The Rule and Exercise of Holy Living*.

8. Ibid.

9. Note: 'perspective' = a small telescope.

10. This account was written on a paper found sewn into his clothes.

11. From *Selected Writings from Blaise Pascal*, translated by Robert Van de Weyer (Hunt & Thorpe, 1991).

12. Ibid.

13. From *Centuries of Meditations* (Clarendon Press, Oxford, 1908). Out of copyright.

14. Ibid.

15. From *Memorials upon Several Occasions* by Eric Milner-White, based on Thomas Traherne.

16. From *A Manual of Prayers for the use of Scholars of Winchester College*.

17. In *The Spectator*, No. 453, 9 August 1712.

18. Translated by Kitty Muggeridge in *The Sacrament of the Present Moment* (William Collins & Co., Glasgow, 1981).

19. Translated by Algar Labouchere Thorold in *Self-Abandonment to the Divine Providence* (Burns, Oates & Co., 1933). By permission of Burns & Oates.

20. Ibid.

21. Ibid.

Methodism

1. The latter part of this hymn and the next make reference to Jacob's encounter with the angel (Genesis 32:24–30).

Early American Christianity

1. From Edward Taylor's *Treatise Concerning the Lord's Supper* (c. 1684), edited by Norman S. Grabo (Michigan State University Press, East Lansing, 1966).

2. Edited by J. E. Smith (Yale University Press, New Haven, 1959).

3. From Jonathan Edwards, *Memoirs of the Rev. David Brainerd, Missionary to the Indians, chiefly taken from his own diary* (New Haven, 1822).

The Eighteenth Century

1. Translated by John Wesley (1703–91).

2. Translated by Jane Laurie Borthwick (1813–97)

3. From *Hymns founded on Various Texts in the Holy Scriptures* (1755), Hymn 171.

4. It was Dr Johnson's custom to write a prayer in the early hours of New Year's Day. He did this every year from 1745 onwards.

5. Johnson's Diary, 25 April 1752.

6. Translated by D. M. Black in *Modern Poetry in Translation*, New Series, No. 13. Used by permission of the translator.

7. Quoted in *The Spirit of the Sacred Heart* (1891).

The Evangelical and Missionary Revival

1. 'Letter to Mr Thomas Atkinson' (16 June 1783), in *The Life and a selection from the Letters of the late Rev. Henry Venn*, edited by his grandson, the Rev. Henry Venn, (John Hatchard & Sons, London, 1834).
2. From William Wilberforce, *Family Prayers*, edited by his son, Robert Isaac Wilberforce, (John Hatchard & Sons, London, 1834).
3. Ibid.
4. From *The Book of Common Worship of the Church of South India* (1963), page 60, (Oxford University Press, 1963). Used by permission.

The Nineteenth Century

1. Translated in *Selected Readings*, edited by Robert Van de Weyer (Hunt & Thorpe, 1991).
2. Ibid.
3. From 'Forsaken once, and thrice denied'.
4. Modified in *After the Third Collect*.
5. Published by Bemrose & Sons, London & Derby, 1905; George Allen & Unwin, London, 1916.
6. From *Morning and Evening*.
7. Ibid.
8. From 'Amidst us our beloved stands'.
9. From *The Prayer at Eventide* (J. F. Shaw & Co., London, 1878).

The Anglo-Catholic Revival

1. In *Prayers for the Third, Sixth and Ninth Hours* by Keble, Pusey and Marriott (1845), modernized.
2. Based on phrases in Newman's sermon on 'Wisdom and Innocence' (1834).
3. Adapted from *Parochial and Plain Sermons*, Vol. IV, No. 13.
4. From ' The earth, O Lord, is one great field'.
5. From *A Pocket Manual of Prayers* (Farnham Hostel, 1860)
6. From *Sursum Corda* by Walter Frere and Mrs Illingworth (Mowbrays, 1898).

Nineteenth-Century Roman Catholicism

1. The poems 'Pied Beauty' and 'Thee, God, I come from' are out of copyright. 'Moonless darkness stands between' © 1967, 1970 The Society of Jesus. Reprinted from *The Poems of Gerard Manley Hopkins* op. cit., by permission of Oxford University Press.
2. From *The Spiritual Autobiography* of Charles de Foucauld (Dimension

Books, P. O. Box 811, Denville, NJ 07834, USA, 1972) , edited by Jean-François Six.

3. Ibid.

4. *Autobiography of a Saint*, © 1958 Office Central de Lisieux; translation © 1958 Executors of Ronald Knox (Fontana Books, William Collins, 1960). By permission of HarperCollins*Publishers*, London.

Nineteenth-Century Scots Protestants

1. From *A Book of Prayers* (Blackwell, Oxford, 1932).
2. Ibid.

American Christianity in the Nineteenth Century

1. Adapted from William Reed Huntingdon and William Bright.
2. From *A Book of Collects* (Morehouse, Milwaukee, 1919). Out of copyright.
3. Adapted in the American Episcopal *Book of Common Prayer* (1979).
4. Ibid., adapted.

The Early Twentieth Century

1. From *Rose from Brier* by Amy Carmichael, © 1933 The Dohnavur Fellowship. Used by permission of the Christian Literature Crusade, Fort Washington, PA 19034, USA.
2. From *Towards Jerusalem* by Amy Carmichael, © 1936 The Dohnavur Fellowship. Used by permission of the Christian Literature Crusade.
3. In the American Episcopal *Book of Common Prayer* (1979).
4. Ibid.
5. Used by permission of A. P. Watt Ltd, London, on behalf of the Royal Literary Fund.
6. Reprinted from *Daily Prayer*, compiled by Eric Milner-White and G. W. Briggs (Oxford University Press, 1941). Used by permission of Oxford University Press.
7. Ibid.
8. Ibid.
9. Ibid.
10. Ibid.
11. Ibid.
12. Ibid.
13. From *Memoirs of Childhood and Youth*, reprinted by kind permission of his daughter, Rhena Schweitzer Miller.
14. In *The Temple* (J. M. Dent & Sons, London and Toronto, 1913; E. P. Dutton, New York).
15. © Elinor F. Downs, copyright control.

16. There are two versions of this meditation. This one is from *Writings in Time of War*, translated by René Hague (New York: Harper & Row, 1968, and London: Collins, 1968). Originally published in French as *Ecrits du temps de la guerre* by Les Editions Bernard Grasset, Paris. © 1965 by Editions Bernard Grasset. Reprinted by permission of Georges Borchardt, Inc., New York, and Editions Grasset, Paris.
17. Reprinted from *Journal of a Soul*, translated by Dorothy White, published 1965, revised edition 1980, © 1980 by Geoffrey Chapman (a division of Cassell Ltd). Used by permission of Cassell plc and Doubleday, a division of Random House, Inc.
18. Ibid.
19. From *Readings in St John's Gospel* (Macmillan, London, 1939). Used by permission of Macmillan Publishers Ltd, London, and Morehouse Publishing in the USA.
20. From *Life and Liberty* (Macmillan, London, 1917). Used by permission of Macmillan Publishers Ltd.
21. Ibid.
22. From *A Book of School Worship*. Used by permission of Macmillan Publishers Ltd.
23. From *The Prophet*, first published in 1926 by William Heinemann Ltd. Permission sought from The National Committee for Gibran in New York.
24. From *Jesus: the Son of Man* (Oneworld, Oxford, 1993; originally published in 1928). Permission sought from The National Committee for Gibran in New York.
25. From *The Unutterable Beauty*, © 1927 G. A. Studdert Kennedy (Hodder & Stoughton, London). Reproduced by permission of Hodder and Stoughton Ltd.
26. Ibid.
27. From *After the Third Collect* (Last known copyright: A. R. Mowbray & Co., 7th edn, 1959). Previously published anonymously as *Memorials upon Several Occasions* (Mowbray, London and Oxford, 1933).
28. From *A Cambridge Bede Book* (Longmans, Green & Co., 1935). Used by permission of Longmans Group UK.
29. From *After the Third Collect*, op. cit.
30. Ibid.
31. From *A Procession of Passion Prayers* (SPCK, 1966). Used by kind permission of SPCK.
32. Ibid.
33. From *After the Third Collect*, op. cit. Used in York Minster.
34. From *After the Third Collect*, op. cit.
35. Ibid.
36. Ibid.

37. Ibid.
38. From *A Procession of Passion Prayers*, op. cit.
39. From *After the Third Collect*, op. cit.
40. From *A Procession of Passion Prayers*, op. cit.
41. From *After the Third Collect*, op. cit.
42. From *A Cambridge Bede Book*, op. cit.
43. Bidding Prayer at the Service of Nine Lessons and Carols, by kind permission of the Provost and Fellows of King's College, Cambridge.
44. From *Call of God*, translated by A. Mackay (SCM Press).
45. Ibid.
46. From *A Diary of Private Prayer* (1936). Used by kind permission of Oxford University Press.
47. Ibid.
48. From *Meditations on the Cross*, translated by Helen F. Topping and Marion R. Draper (SCM Press, London, 1936), page 135.
49. From the IX Chorus from 'The Rock' from *Collected Poems 1909–1962* by permission of Faber and Faber Ltd, London, and Harcourt Brace Trade Publications, San Diego, CA 92101, USA.
50. From *Scouts Own* (C. Arthur Pearson, 1933).
51. © Christopher Niebuhr, 140 Marble Street, Lee MA 01238, USA. Originally published in 1943 in *Justice and Mercy* (Harper & Row).
52. From *Hymns of Worship*, edited by Ursula Niebuhr (Association Press, New York, 1939). Used by permission of Christopher Niebuhr, Executor.
53. 'Ancient Prayer' quoted in *Psychology, Religion and Healing* (Hodder & Stoughton, 1951).
54. Edward England Books (UK) Ltd, by permission of Arthur James Ltd, Berkhamsted, UK.
55. From *Poems*, © the Executors of the Estate of C. S. Lewis (Geoffrey Bles, London, 1964). Used by permission of HarperCollins*Publishers*, UK, and Harcourt Brace Trade Publishers, San Diego, CA 92101, USA
56. From *Pilgrim's Regress* (Geoffrey Bles, London, 1943), revised by the author for inclusion in *Poems*, op. cit.
57. Reprinted from *Complete Poems 1904–1962* by E. E. Cummings, edited by George J. Firmage, by permission of W. W. Norton & Company. © 1991 by the Trustees for the E. E. Cummings Trust and George James Firmage.
58. From *The Shape of the Liturgy* (Dacre Press, Westminster, 1945). By permission of the Abbot of Elmore Abbey.
59. From *The Prayers of Peter Marshall*, edited by Catherine Marshall, used by permission of Random House, Inc., New York, USA. Permission also sought from Chosen Book Publications Ltd.
60. Ibid.
61. Ibid.

62. From *Instrument of thy Peace* (Fount Books, 2nd edn, 1983). Permission sought from Winston Press, the licensors, but address not traced.
63. Ibid.
64. Ibid.
65. In *Joyful Journey*, compiled by Bob Knight, © 1982 by Toc H. Used by courtesy of Toc H and Oliver Warner.
66. From *Markings*, © 1964, translated by W. H. Auden and Leif Sjöberg (Faber & Faber Ltd, London, and Random House Inc., New York). Reprinted by permission.
67. Ibid.
68. From *Letters and Papers from Prison*, The Enlarged Edition, (SCM Press, London, 1972), page 142. Used by permission of SCM Press, London, and Simon & Schuster, Prentice Hall, USA.
69. From *The Plain Man's Book of Prayers*, © 1959 William Barclay (Fontana Books, Collins, London and Glasgow). By permission of HarperCollins*Publishers*, London.
70. Ibid.
71. From *Epilogues and Prayers*, © 1963 William Barclay (SCM Press, London).
72. From *The Lord's Supper* © 1967 William Barclay (SCM Press, London).
73. From *The Little World of Don Camillo*, © 1950 Giovanni Guareschi, translated by Una Vincenzo Troubridge, (Victor Gollancz, London, 1951). By permission of his sons, Alberto and Carlotta Guareschi, Roncole Verdi, Italy. Visit their web page:
http://www.erols.com/welbourn/Camillo.htmcontents
74. © The Christian Conference of Asia.
75. From *The Boy's Prayer Book*, edited by Alexander Devine (Methuen & Co., London, 1913).
76. Translation © 1965/1997 Michael Counsell.
77. Translation © 1966 Michael Counsell.

Prayers from Two World Wars

1. 'Litany of Reconciliation', by permission of the Provost and Council of Coventry Cathedral.
2. Blessing at the consecration of Coventry Cathedral, 1962.

Black Worship

1. By Charles Albert Tindley. Out of copyright.
2. "Listen, Lord – A Prayer", from *God's Trombones* by James Weldon Johnson. © 1927 The Viking Press, Inc., renewed © by Grace Nail Johnson. Used by permission of Viking Penguin, a division of Penguin Putnam Inc., New York, USA.

3. Blessing spoken to his congregation in Montgomery as he left them to devote all his time to political action. Reprinted by permission of Writers House, Atlanta, Georgia, USA.

4. At the Lincoln Memorial, Washington DC, August 1963. Reprinted by permission of Writers House, Atlanta, Georgia, USA.

5. From the inauguration of Nelson Mandela as State President of South Africa, Pretoria, 1994.

6. By Andrae Crouch, © Bud John Songs/EMI Christian Music Publishing. Administered by Copycare, P. O. Box 77, Hailsham, BN27 3EF, UK. Used by permission.

7. By Andrae Crouch, © 1978 Bud John Songs/Crouch Music/EMI Christian Music Publishing. Administered by Copycare, P. O. Box 77, Hailsham, BN27 3EF, UK. Used by permission.

8. Words and music by William J. and Gloria Gaither and Richard Smallwood, © 1988 Gaither Music Company and Century Oak/Richwood Music/Kingsway's Thankyou Music, P. O. Box 75, Eastbourne, East Sussex, BN23 6NW, UK. All rights reserved. Used by permission of Gaither Copyright Management, P. O. Box 737, Alexandria, IN 46001, USA; BMG Music Publishing International, London; Copyright Management, Inc. USA and Kingsway's Thankyou Music.

The Pentecostal and Charismatic Movements and the Healing Ministry

1. From *Soul Friend*, © 1977 Kenneth Leech (Sheldon Press, London).

2. From 'The gift of tongues in the New Testament', *Expository Times* 84:5 (1973). T. & T. Clark, Edinburgh.

3. Ibid.

4. From *Prison to Praise* (Hodder & Stoughton, London, 1972). © 1970 by Logos International, Plainfield, New Jersey. Reproduced by permission of Hodder and Stoughton Ltd, and the author, Merlin Carothers.

5. © 1983 Kingsway's Thankyou Music, P. O. Box 75, Eastbourne, East Sussex, BN23 6NW, UK. All rights reserved. Used by permission.

6. © 1977 Kingsway's Thankyou Music, P. O. Box 75, Eastbourne, East Sussex, BN23 6NW, UK. All rights reserved. Used by permission.

7. Graham Kendrick, © 1987 Make Way Music, P. O. Box 263, Croydon, Surrey, CR9 5AP, UK. International copyright secured. All rights reserved. Used by permission.

8. From *Live a New Life*, © 1975 David Watson (Inter-Varsity Press, Leicester).

9. Ibid.

10. Quoted in *The Vision of Dorothy Kerin*, © 1991 Morris Maddocks, (Hodder & Stoughton, Sevenoaks), republished by Eagle (Guildford, 1999). Reproduced by permission of the Director of Dorothy Kerin Trust, Hodder and Stoughton Ltd, and the William Neill-Hall Agency.

11. © 1980 Mercy/Vineyard Publishing, administered by Music Services, Franklin, TN 37069, USA, and Copycare, P. O. Box 77, Hailsham, East Sussex, BN27 2EF, UK. All rights reserved. Used by permission.
12. Excerpted from *Healing* by Francis MacNutt. © 1974 by Ave Maria Press, P. O. Box 428, Notre Dame, IN 46556, USA. Used with permission of the publisher.
13. From *The Bible and Counselling*, © 1992 Roger Hurding (Hodder & Stoughton, Sevenoaks). Reproduced by permission of Hodder and Stoughton Ltd, and the William Neill-Hall Agency.

Twentieth-Century Liturgies

1. Extracts from *The Prayer Book as proposed in 1928* are © The Central Board of Finance of the Church of England and are reproduced with permission.
2. Copyright in The Scottish Episcopal *Book of Common Prayer* (1929) is not claimed by the Scottish Episcopal Church or the Cambridge University Press.
3. *A Book of Common Prayer, South Africa* © Provincial Trustees of the Church of the Province of Southern Africa.
4. *The Book of Common Prayer*, © 1960, The General Synod of the Church of Ireland, published by APCK/Oxford University Press. Reproduced with permission from the Church of Ireland.
5. *The Book of Common Worship Supplement*, page 33, no. 12, © Oxford University Press, 1967, used by permission.
6. Ibid., page 106.
7. *Modern Collects, the Church of the Province of Southern Africa* © Provincial Trustees of the Church of the Province of Southern Africa.
8. Adapted from the *Christarakana* in *The Book of Common Prayer* of the Church of India, Pakistan, Burma and Ceylon (ISPCK, Delhi, 1978). Used by permission of SPCK.
9. From the US *Book of Common Prayer* (1979), adapted from the proposed *Book of Common Prayer of the Protestant Episcopal Church in the United States of America* (1786). Prayers from *The Book of Common Prayer* of the American Episcopal Church (1979) are in the public domain.
10. From the US *Book of Common Prayer* (1979), from *The Book of Common Prayer of the Protestant Episcopal Church in the United States of America* (1928).
11. Chants from Taizé are all © Ateliers et Presses de Taizé, 71250 Taizé communauté, France.
12. Extracts from *The Alternative Service Book 1980* are © The Central Board of Finance of the Church of England, 1980, and The Archbishop's Council, 1999, and are used by permission.
13. Extracts from *Lent, Holy Week and Easter: Services and Prayers* (1984) are © The Central Board of Finance of the Church of England, 1984, 1996; The Archbishop's Council, 1999, and are used by permission.

Feminist Spirituality

3. Permission sought.

The Twentieth-Century Celtic Revival

1. From *The Whole Earth shall cry Glory*, by the Revd George F. MacLeod, © The Iona Community (Wild Goose Publications, Glasgow, 1985).
2. *A Wee Worship Book*, p. 32. © 1989 The Wild Goose Worship Group, The Iona Community, Pearce Institute, Govan, Glasgow G51 3UT, Scotland.
3. Ibid., p. 8.
4. From *Wind and Fire*, reprinted by permission of Dr Ian Fraser.
5. From *The Edge of Glory, Prayers in the Celtic Tradition*, © David Adam (Triangle, SPCK, 1985).
6. From *The Open Gate*, © David Adam (Triangle, SPCK, 1994).
7. Translated by Leonora A. Timm in *A Modern Breton Political Poet, Anjela Duval: A Biography and an Anthology*, 1990, Edwin Mellen Press, Box 450, Lewiston, NY 14092, USA. Used with permission.

Prayers by Indigenous Peoples

1. Reprinted from *Black Elk Speaks* by John G. Neihardt, by permission of the University of Nebraska Press; © 1932, 1959, 1972 by John G. Neihardt; © 1961 by the John G. Neihardt Trust.
2. Reprinted from 'Aboriginal Justice (Prayer by an Indigenous Australian)', © Anne Pattel-Gray, in *Seeing Christ in Others*, edited by Geoffrey Duncan, and published by the Canterbury Press, Norwich, 1997. Reprinted by permission of the author.

Twentieth-Century Roman Catholic Spirituality

1. Taken from *Into Your Hands, Lord*, by Dom Helder Camara, published in 1987 by Darton, Longman & Todd, London, and used with the publisher's permission.
2. Translated by Rose Marie Hancock in *Letters from the Desert* (originally published by La Scuola Editrice, Brescia, 1964; © 1972 Orbis Books, Maryknoll, New York). By permission of Orbis Books; Darton, Longman and Todd, London; and permission sought from St Paul Publications, Manila, Philippines.
3. The prayers are all from *The Splendor of the Rosary* by Maisie Ward (Sheed & Ward, 1945). The rights have reverted to the estate of Caryll Houselander; permission sought, but the assignee, Mr Henry John Taylor, has not been traced.
4. These prayers are all from *O God, Why?*, © 1993 Gerard W. Hughes (The Bible Reading Fellowship, Oxford).
5. From *Prayers for Peace, an anthology of readings and prayers*, selected by

Archbishop Robert Runcie and Cardinal Basil Hume, © 1987 Robert Runcie and Basil Hume (SPCK, London).

6. Prayer at the Shrine of Merciful Love, Collevalenza, 22.11.81, from *Prayers of Pope John Paul II*, edited by John F. McDonald, © 1982 St Paul Publications, Slough.

7. General Audience during the Week of Prayer for Christian Unity, 21.1.81, from *Prayers of Pope John Paul II*, op. cit.

8. From *Sadhana, a Way to God*, © 1978 Anthony de Mello SJ, Poona, India; St Louis (Mo) Institute of Jesuit Sources in cooperation with Gujarat Sahitya Prakash (Anand Press, 1980; first published 1978).

9. From *The Seven Storey Mountain*, published in 1975, by permission of Sheldon Press, SPCK, London, and Harcourt Brace and Co., Orlando, Florida, USA.

10. Ibid.

11. Taken from *The Road to Daybreak*, © 1988 by Henri J. M. Nouwen. Used by permission of Darton, Longman & Todd (UK) and of Doubleday, a division of Random House, Inc., USA. Used by permission of the publishers.

12. From *A Cry for Mercy*, © 1981 by Henri J. M. Nouwen. Used by permission of Doubleday, a division of Random House, Inc., USA. Included in *Seeds of Hope, a Henri Nouwen Reader*, edited by Robert Durback, © 1989 by Darton, Longman & Todd (UK) and used by permission of the publishers.

13. From *Your Word is Near* (Newman Press, Maryland, USA). Permission sought.

14. The poem 'Lord, I have time' from Michel Quoist's *Prayers of Life* is reproduced with the permission of the publishers, Gill & Macmillan, Dublin, and Theological Book Service, Franklin, WI 53132, USA.

15. From *Life from Within* by Brother Roger of Taizé (Geoffrey Chapman Mowbray; © Ateliers et Presses de Taizé).

16. From *A Heart that Trusts* by Brother Roger of Taizé (Mowbray; © Ateliers et Presses de Taizé).

17. From the Revised Standard Version of the Bible, copyright 1946, 1952, and 1971 by the Division of Christian Education of the National Council of the Churches of Christ in the USA. Used by permission. All rights reserved.

18. From *In the Silence of the Heart, Meditations by Mother Teresa*, compiled by Kathryn Spink (SPCK, London, 1983).

19. Ibid.

Ecumenical Spirituality Today

1. From *With All God's People* (World Council of Churches, 1989). Prayer from Latin America.

2. From the World Council of Churches Harare Assembly, 1998. By kind permission of the World Council of Churches Office of Communication. Based on Isaiah 42:3; Matthew 19:30, 10:39.

3. Ibid.
4. *The Lima Liturgy* is © the World Council of Churches. The Litany of Intercession is based on the liturgy of the Russian Orthodox Church. The second prayer is the Preface, paragraph 19, shortened.
5. *The Next Steps for Churches Together in Pilgrimage*, BCC/CTS, 1989, p.8.
6. Kate Compston for Christian Aid.
7. Janet Morley, from *Feast for Life*, 1994.
8. From *The Women's World Day of Prayer 1993 Service*, by permission.
9. From *The Daily Office (Revised)*, © 1978, The Joint Liturgical Group of Great Britain.
10. Ibid.
11. Ibid.
12. © 1987 Corrymeela Press, 8 Upper Crescent, Belfast BT7 1NT.
13. From *For the Sake of Justice*, the 1995 Service on Housing and Homelessness, written by Christine Allen and Barbara d'Arcy, produced by CHAS and the Churches National Housing Coalition.

More Contemporary Prayers

1. From *Mister God, this is Anna*, © 1974 Fynn, (William Collins & Sons, London). By permission of HarperCollins*Publishers*, London.
2. From *Living Prayer*, © 1966 Archbishop Anthony Bloom (first published 1966, new edition 1999, by Darton, Longman & Todd, London, and Templegate Publishers [www.templegate.com], Springfield, IL 62701, USA.
3. From *School for Prayer*, © 1970 Anthony Bloom (first published 1970, new edition 1999, by Darton, Longman & Todd, London. Published as *Beginning to Pray* by Paulist Press, Inc., USA.) Used by permission of the publishers.
4. © 1996 Angela Ashwin (Marshall Pickering, an imprint of HarperCollins*Religious*, London). By permission of HarperCollins*Publishers*, London.
5. From *A Silence and a Shouting*, p. 7 (The Leprosy Mission International, 80 Windmill Road, Brentford, Middlesex TW8 0QH, UK, 1982). ISBN 0 90273 121 1.
6. © The Church Mission Society.
7. From *Prayer at Night* by Jim Cotter (Cairns Publications, Sheffield, 4th edn 1991).
8. Ibid.
9. Ibid.
10. From *Prayer in the Morning* by Jim Cotter (Cairns Publications, Sheffield, 1989).
11. © 1992 by Michael Counsell. May be sung to 'Blow the wind southerly'.
12. Translated in *The Secret Name*, © 1995 by Michael Counsell. Suggested carol tune: 'The Seven Joys of Mary'.
13. Translated in *More Prayers for Sundays*, © 1997 by Michael Counsell. Suggested tune: 'Glenfinlas'.

14. © 1983 by Michael Counsell. May be sung to the slow movement from Dvorak's *Symphony from the New World*.

15. From *Common Prayer: A Muslim/Christian Spiritual Anthology*. (Oneworld Publications, Oxford, 1999). Previously published as *Alive to God* by Oxford University Press (1970). By permission of Kenneth Cragg.

16. Ibid.

17. From *The Hard Awakening* (Triangle, SPCK, London, 1981).

18. From *Prayer*, © 1992 Richard J. Foster (published in the UK by Hodder & Stoughton). Reproduced by permission of Hodder and Stoughton Ltd, and the William Neill-Hall Agency.

19. Not copyrighted. Used with thanks to the Billy Graham Evangelistic Agency, Minneapolis, USA.

20. From *He Sent Leanness*, © 1959 Epworth Press. Used by permission of the Methodist Publishing House.

21. From *Animal Rites: Liturgies of Animal Care*, © Andrew Linzey (SCM Press, London, 1999).

22. Ibid.

23. From *Task Unfinished*, © Michael Saward (Falcon Press and Patmos Press).

24. A prayer by Massey Shepherd used in the American Episcopal *Book of Common Prayer* (1979); Burial of the Dead, Rite Two, p.498. In the public domain.

25. From *A Companion of Prayer for Daily Living*, © 1978 by Morehouse Publishing. Reproduced by permission of Morehouse Publishing, P. O. Box 1321, Harrisburg, PA 17105, USA.

26. In *Prayers for Use at the Alternative Services*, © 1980 David Silk (Mowbray, London and Oxford). By permission of Cassell plc.

27. Ibid.

28. Ibid.

29. Ibid.

30. Ibid.

31. From *In Penitence and Faith, Texts for use with the Alternative Services*, © 1988 David Silk, compiler (Mowbray). By permission of Cassell plc.

32. Adapted from the Collect of the Society of Ordained Scientists, by permission of the Warden, the Revd Canon Dr Maureen Palmer.

33. World © Aleksandr Solzhenitzyn, translated by Alwyn and Dermot McKay. Permission sought.

34. From *The SPCK Book of Christian Prayers*, by permission of Dr John Stott.

35. From *Your Confirmation, a Christian handbook for adults* (illustrated edition, Hodder and Stoughton, London, 1991) by permission of Dr John Stott.

36. Ibid.

37. From *Selected poems 1946–1968* (William Collins). By permission of HarperCollins*Publishers*, London.

38. Ibid.
39. From *Go tell it on the mountain*, with prayers and meditations by Robin Green, © USPG, London, 1996, p. 18.
40. From *A Still Place of Light, A book of prayers for sharing in God's mission today*, edited by Robin Green, © USPG, London, 1990, p. 20.
41. By the Revd Pat Vowles in *Let All the World* . . . edited by Wendy S. Robins, © USPG, London, 1990, p. 27.
42. Adapted from *There's a Time and a Place*, (HarperCollins*Publishers*) reprinted by permission of the author.
43. From *True to Experience, an anthology of the words and teaching of Harry A. Williams*, edited by Eileen Mable (Mitchell Beazley, London, c. 1984). Reprinted by permission of Mitchell Beazley (a division of Octopus Publishing Group Limited).
44. Ibid.
45. Translation © 1973 Michael Counsell.
46. © The Church Mission Society.
47. © The Church Mission Society.
48. From *The Kingdom, the Power and the Glory* (1925), an American edition of *The Grey Book*. © renewed 1961 by Bradford Young (Oxford University Press, New York). By permission of Oxford University Press, London.
49. Permission sought.
50. © Churches Together in England.

Index of Authors and Sources

Index of Themes / First Lines